TURNER'S RIVERS OF EUROPE

The Rhine, Meuse and Mosel

CECILIA POWELL

TURNER'S RIVERS OF EUROPE

The Rhine, Meuse and Mosel

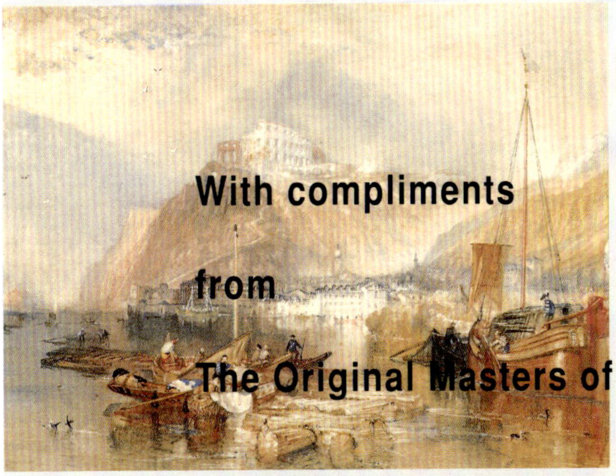

TATE GALLERY

EXHIBITION AND CATALOGUE SPONSORED BY VOLKSWAGEN

cover/jacket
'The Ruined Monastery at Wolf' *c.*1839
detail (cat.no.56)

ISBN 0 85142 079 0 paper
ISBN 0 85142 080 4 cloth

Published by order of the Trustees 1991
on the occasion of the exhibition at the Tate Gallery
11 September 1991 – 26 January 1992
Also shown at the Musée d'Ixelles, Brussels
February – April 1992
Designed by Caroline Johnston
Maps on pp.24, 38, 50 and 173 by John Flower
Published by Tate Gallery Publications, Millbank, London SW1P 4RG

Typeset in Monophoto Baskerville by Servis Filmsetting Limited, Manchester
Printed and bound in Great Britain by Balding + Mansell plc,
Wisbech, Cambridgeshire on 150gsm Parilux matt

Contents

Foreword

This publication presents the results of the research of Dr Cecilia Powell, the second of the Turner Scholars to be supported by Volkswagen with the aim of furthering research into chosen areas of Turner's work.

During her two years' research Cecilia Powell has been following Turner's travels in the Rhineland and the Ardennes. She has been able to identify thousands of pencil sketches in his sketchbooks made during his three main tours to these areas and has now redated two of the tours. An appendix in this catalogue identifies the subject matter of the sketches Turner made on the three tours studied.

Central to the exhibition is the series of small gouaches on blue paper of subjects connected with the rivers Meuse and Mosel which Cecilia Powell has now identified and dated for the first time. This achievement constitutes an important contribution to Turner scholarship. To do it full justice, this volume provides a catalogue raisonné of these drawings, not all of which are exhibited (works included are given exhibition numbers while those not displayed are listed without numbers at the appropriate places in the topographical sequences).

Although most of the works studied are to be found in the Turner Bequest, others have come to light during Cecilia Powell's researches; and the magnificent finished watercolours from Turner's first tour along the Rhine in 1817, once in Walter Fawkes's collection, are now widely dispersed. It is thanks to the generosity of several private collectors and museums that we are able to include a number of important loans and we are most grateful to them.

I should also like to thank Cecilia Powell herself for her endless energy and enthusiasm. Her excitement over her discoveries has infected all those colleagues who have worked alongside her.

Finally I want to express deep gratitude to Volkswagen and in particular to John Meszaros, formerly their Marketing Manager. They have continued to support these research projects with genuine interest and have recently undertaken to award further scholarships. It is this imaginative and generous support that is making new Turner research possible.

Nicholas Serota
Director

Sponsor's Foreword

Turner's Rivers of Europe: The Rhine, Meuse and Mosel is the second exhibition and catalogue in the Turner Scholarship series, which Volkswagen is once again proud to support. The Turner Scholarships are offered by the Tate Gallery in association with Volkswagen for important new research related to the works in the Turner Bequest. They are open to students in the United Kingdom proposing original topics in the areas covered by the Bequest, much of which has never been properly catalogued.

The subject of this exhibition is almost irresistible to our company. We believe that Dr Cecilia Powell's research into Turner's tours along the great rivers of Northern Europe is important. Her exhibition makes it possible for us to know Turner that much better: it gives us the rare opportunity to see some of the work he did during these tours and Cecilia Powell's insight and commentary add much to our enjoyment and appreciation. If, as a result of this exhibition, the viewer's quality of life has been improved, in no matter how small a measure, our support of this scholarship will have been fully justified.

My thanks and that of my company goes to Cecilia Powell for her imagination, expertise and hard work. Thanks also to all involved at the Tate Gallery – and a very special thank you to Nicholas Serota.

There will be many more Turner Scholars in future years, and our hope is that they can all maintain the standard set so far.

Michael Cornish
V.A.G. (United Kingdom) Ltd
Head of Marketing

The Turner Scholarships – Sponsored by Volkswagen

The Turner Scholarships were established by the Tate Gallery in 1988, with the support of Volkswagen, to fund original research by visiting scholars into the works contained in the Turner Bequest at the Tate Gallery. The Scholarships provide an opportunity for scholars to work as 'guest curators', and to prepare an exhibition and publication based on their researches.

Awards are made biennially to one or more candidates and in 1988 two Scholars were appointed: Peter Bower and Dr Cecilia Powell. The results of Peter Bower's researches were seen in the successful exhibition *Turner's Papers* which opened at the Tate Gallery in October 1990. Mr Bower, a paper historian, examined Turner's use of paper during the first half of his working life and charted the developing relationship between Turner's materials and his vision of each individual drawing. He is continuing his research into the later years of Turner's life. Dr Cecilia Powell's researches have culminated in the present exhibition *Turner's Rivers of Europe: The Rhine, Meuse and Mosel.*

Two further Turner Scholars were appointed in November 1990; Mr Maurice Davies and Dr Jan Piggott.

Maurice Davies is investigating material in the Turner Bequest connected with the Perspective Lectures given by Turner at the Royal Academy between 1811 and 1828. He is also examining Turner's use of perspective in a wider context, and will work towards an exhibition with accompanying catalogue for the autumn of 1992.

Dr Jan Piggott is studying the vignettes engraved after Turner and prepared by him to illustrate works of literature. Turner made numerous drawings and watercolours for engravers and publishers during the period 1825–39 and many in the Bequest have yet to be identified. Dr Piggott is investigating these in detail, exploring their commission and publication history, and discussing their relationship to the texts of poets and authors from Milton to Byron. His work will lead to an exhibition and publication in autumn 1993.

Acknowledgments

Research is always exciting but in Britain today it is notoriously underfunded and it can be a very solitary occupation. Over the last two years I have been immensely grateful to Volkswagen and the Tate Gallery for providing the finance and the context to enable me to concentrate on what I knew to be an important area of research in the Turner Bequest and which I could not possibly have tackled without their support. My chief thanks must therefore go to Nicholas Serota, John Meszaros and Andrew Wilton for inaugurating the Turner Scholarship at the Tate Gallery and for giving me the opportunity to carry out this work which has in every way lived up to my expectations.

I have received much practical help during 1989–91 from friends, colleagues and experts in various fields and I should like to take this opportunity of thanking all the following very warmly: A.G.H. Bachrach, Marian Barker, Hildegard Fritz-Denneville, John Gage, Paul Goldman, Craig Hartley, Luke Herrmann, Evelyn Joll, Pieter van der Merwe, Virginia Murray, Kathy Newstead, Bruno H. Pauwels, Betty Rennie, William Ruddick, Ursula Seibold, Edmund Swinglehurst, Rosalind Turner, Helen Valentine, Henry Wemyss and Edward Yardley. I have particularly benefited from the advice, encouragement and knowledge of all the curators in the Clore Gallery and of my fellow Turner Scholar Peter Bower and it has been a great pleasure to work among them.

In the preparation of this catalogue and the organisation of the exhibition I have been constantly helped by the permanent staff of the Tate Gallery in the Conservation, Exhibitions, Photographic, Publications and Registrar's Departments and I am indebted to them all for their patience and expertise.

I am enormously grateful to all the museums and private owners who have so kindly agreed to lend works to the exhibition, particularly those whose homes are thus deprived of a treasured oil or watercolour for a period of several months at a stretch. Their exceptional generosity will be appreciated by all who visit the exhibition.

My deepest debt is, as always, to my husband Nick who has been such a constant support to me both at home and in our explorations of Turner's Europe, a kindly critic and an intrepid driver.

Cecilia Powell

Turner's Rhine, Meuse and Mosel

Turner was an insatiable traveller. Throughout his long and immensely productive working life, he made dozens of tours of both Britain and the Continent in search of material and inspiration. Almost every summer he would be 'on the Wing', as he put it, in late July or August, not returning to London until six or seven weeks later.[1] After this he would spend the winter months working alone in his studio, transforming the mass of sketches and memoranda in his notebooks into the highly wrought watercolours and often complex oil paintings which he sold to private patrons and exhibited at the Royal Academy. Each of the tours commemorated in this exhibition has its own special importance in Turner's career, but they also form part of this larger cycle of summer touring and winter painting which extended from the sixteen-year-old boy's first sketching tour around Bath and Bristol in 1791 to his final visit to northern France in 1845 at the age of seventy. Those were comparatively modest affairs, but the tours of his middle years were almost invariably characterised by being long and complicated and both physically and mentally demanding; the three tours of this exhibition were no exception.

Turner's interest in rivers and river scenery, too, should be viewed in a much broader context than that of his own trips to this particular part of northern Europe. For centuries, rivers had been of paramount importance in the social, political, economic and cultural life of the West. They frequently provided the quickest, safest and cheapest form both of travelling and of transporting goods from one part of England to another and across much of Europe. Over 800 miles long, the Rhine had been 'the great highway of Europe' from the Alps to the North Sea since time immemorial and the scene of countless battles as one tribe or state, petty prince or nation sought to gain control of it. The Rhine had formed the north-eastern frontier of the Roman province of Gaul and many of the familiar names of the Rhineland date from the Roman occupation and its large-scale building of forts and colonies for veteran soldiers in the first centuries BC and AD: Colonia Agrippina (Cologne), Confluentes (Coblenz, at the confluence of the Rhine and the Mosel), Augusta Trevirorum (Trier) and Castellum Mattiacorum (Mainz together with Kastel on the opposite shore). Of the innumerable power struggles during the centuries that followed, that which left its most devastating mark on the countryside was the attempt of Louis XIV to claim the Palatinate and thus extend his kingdom eastwards. Only a few of the dozens of medieval strongholds and toll castles perched high above the banks of the Rhine and the Mosel escaped the savagery of his troops in the 1680s and 1690s, as can be seen all too clearly even today.

Although the territorial importance of the Rhineland went back far into antiquity, as Turner was well aware,[2] its appeal to popular aesthetic taste was scarcely older than the artist himself. Before this, many generations of educated Britons had travelled down the Rhine with barely a glance at the superb scenery through which they were carried. Although it was standard practice for eighteenth-century Grand Tourists to return from Italy and Switzerland to England by this route, since it so conveniently linked Basel to Holland, they paid scant attention to their new surroundings. Most of the towns in Germany and the Low Countries were considered little more than passing curiosities, fine from afar but on closer inspection backward, dirty and depressing. However, the final three decades of the eighteenth century witnessed an important change in taste. Mountains and rocks, cliffs and crags ceased to be objects of terror and inconvenient barriers to travel, and in the new cult of the Sublime and the Picturesque they became attractions to be sought out and enjoyed, explored and recorded. These years saw the gradual discovery of the English Lake District by writers, artists and tourists; a new fascination with the Alps, including the first ascent of Mont Blanc in 1786; and the discovery of the Middle Rhine, that magnificent winding stretch of about 120 miles between Mainz and Cologne, gouged out by the Alpine floods of countless millennia, its towering hills so frequently crowned by the shattered ruins of castles, the last silent witnesses of centuries of war. The three areas appealed to the same public, so it is less surprising than appears at first sight that one of the most influential descriptions of the Rhineland of this period – that by Mrs Ann Radcliffe, the author of such 'Gothick' novels as *The Mysteries of Udolpho* (1794) – formed part of a composite work, *A Journey made in the Summer of 1794 through Holland and the Western Frontier of Germany, with a Return down the Rhine: to which are added Observations during a Tour to the Lakes of Lancashire, Westmoreland, and Cumberland* (1795). A few years later another traveller on the Rhine, who was well steeped in the writings on the Picturesque of the Revd William Gilpin, was interested to find that 'The River winds incessantly & presents all those varieties of Turning of Vista of Angle which Gilpin so well describes'; while a little later still, another visitor to the Rhine was reminded of that quintessentially Sublime artist, the seventeenth-century painter Salvator Rosa, declaring that Rosa would have hailed the stretch between St Goar and Oberwesel as 'a fit subject for his bold and savage delineations' and it only needed a stray brigand here and there to be indistinguishable from a Calabrian defile.[3] At the most famous cliff of the Middle Rhine, the Lorelei, as on Lake Windermere, horns were blown and pistols were fired into the air to entertain the early tourists, the echoes rebounding evocatively from rock to rock and hill to hill.[4]

Turner himself was undoubtedly influenced by the Picturesque aesthetic in his youth. He explored the Lake District in the late 1790s and the Alps in 1802, so it was in many ways inevitable that he should turn his attention to the Rhineland once circumstances allowed. His continuing interest in the area was sparked off by a variety of individual catalysts which will shortly be identified, but it also moved in a line parallel to that of popular taste. The prototype of the Baedeker guidebooks, so essential to generations of travellers, was the handbook to the Rhine from Mainz to Cologne published in German in 1828; John Murray's guidebook to the Rhine and other parts of northern Europe followed in 1836; in 1855 the first Continental tour organised by Thomas Cook incorporated a passage up the Rhine between Cologne and Mainz. By this date a visit to the Rhine had become such a commonplace experience that it was the subject of popular satire, most notably in Thomas Hood's *Up the Rhine* of 1840, a parody of eighteenth-century epistolary novels following the travel experiences of a middle-class British family and their Cockney maidservant. During the years covered by this exhibition thousands of Britons were sharing the same travel experiences as Turner himself; and it should also be remembered that these same people composed his future audience at the Royal Academy, his potential patrons and the purchasers of the books he was to illustrate.

The three rivers which Turner was to come to know so well have much in common but provide very different experiences for the traveller and did so too in Turner's day. By far the largest, grandest and most complex is the majestic Rhine which has inspired artists, writers and composers of many nationalities. One poet with whose evocation of the Rhine Turner was undoubtedly well acquainted was Byron, who in the third canto of *Childe Harold's Pilgrimage* (1816) spent several verses describing the emotions of his melancholic hero as he viewed the river, longing for his distant beloved and recalling the heroism of ancient and recent wars. However, Byron's lines on the Rhine are surprisingly dull, apart from one memorable phrase, 'The castled crag of Drachenfels' (the 'Dragon's Rock', in the centre of fig.1, where the legendary hero Siegfried had vanquished the serpent).[5] They certainly do not rival Victor Hugo's all-embracing stream of tribute of 1842: 'as swift as the Rhône, broad as the Loire, enclosed as the Meuse, winding as the Seine, limpid and green as the Somme, historic as the Tiber, royal as the Danube, mysterious as the Nile, sparkling with gold as a river of America, clothed in fables and phantoms as a river of Asia'.[6] Many are the writers who have attempted to describe the beauties of the

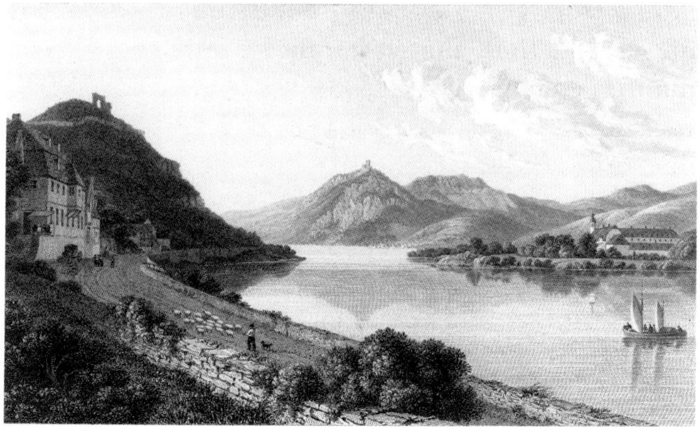

fig.1 Robert Wallis after Robert Batty, 'Drachenfels and Roland's Eck'. Line engraving from *Scenery of the Rhine, Belgium and Holland, from Drawings by Captⁿ. Batty, of the Grenadier Guards, F.R.S.*, 1826

Rhine, but no words can evoke it as lyrically as the music of Schumann's Third Symphony of 1850, the 'Rhenish', or as sublimely as that of Wagner's epic music-drama *Der Ring des Nibelungen* of 1848–74, from the rippling underwater prelude to *Das Rheingold* through to the apocalyptic finale of *Götterdämmerung*.[7] Over the last two hundred years both French and Germans have felt passionately about the Rhine in a way that has rarely been possible for foreigners coming to the Rhineland as tourists or artists in search of pictorial inspiration, so it is unfair to measure Turner's Rhine against that of Wagner or Schumann. Nevertheless, the breadth of his interest in the river and the intensity of his feelings must both be clear to all who view his works, making him supreme among the foreign artists who have portrayed it.

The Middle Rhine's chief tributary the Mosel derives its name from the Latin 'Mosella', or 'Little Meuse', which distinguished it from the Meuse itself close by and almost twice as long. The Mosel rises in the Vosges and is, for the last part of its course, in many ways a miniature version of the Rhine, taking 120 miles to travel 60 miles as the crow flies. The river itself is narrower, the hills lining it somewhat lower, its bends more tortuous. Its villages and castles spring to the eye even more frequently than those of the Rhine and, although the river itself is busy and its precipitous vineyards a hive of activity from spring to autumn, it is far more peaceful than the Rhine (fig.2). Several of Turner's contemporaries were charmed by the Mosel between Trier and Coblenz, priding themselves on having discovered an unspoilt and unhackneyed corner of Europe, and then proceeded – in the thoughtless manner all too familiar today – to popularise it through words and images and thus, inadvertently, to reduce the very qualities which had rendered it so agreeable.[8] While the Rhine has inspired some of Europe's most sublime music, the Mosel had – very much earlier – inspired one of the earliest known long poems devoted entirely to a single river and its scenery, the *Mosella* written in the fourth century AD by a tutor at the imperial court of Trier. As the Romans strove to protect their frontier against the Germanic tribesmen, Ausonius responded to the delights of the Mosel – its shadows and reflections, its fish and pebbles, its vine-clad banks and sandy shores – with a sensitivity and a Romantic feeling for natural beauty that looked forward directly to Turner and his contemporaries.[9]

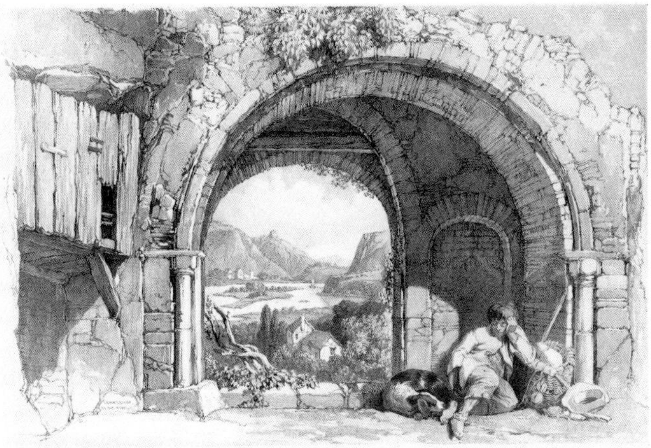

fig.2 Thomas Shotter Boys after Clarkson Stanfield, 'Lehmenhof on the Moselle'. Lithograph from *Sketches on the Moselle, the Rhine, & the Meuse. By Clarkson Stanfield, Esq. R.A.*, 1838

While the Rhine and the Mosel both rose dramatically in the popular estimation during the years of Turner's lifetime, the reputation of the Meuse pursued a more sober course. Some parts of it were already very well known to Britons long before Turner's day, chiefly perhaps because in 1695 British and Dutch troops under William of Orange had succeeded in regaining the city of Namur after it had fallen to Louis XIV – or, more precisely, to his great military engineer Vauban – three years earlier; it was during this latter siege that Laurence Sterne's incomparable character Uncle Toby in *Tristram Shandy* (1759–67) had received the mysterious wound in his groin.[10] The famous wooded hills of the Ardennes, which stretch south and east of Namur, had long ago helped to inspire Shakespeare's Forest of Arden in *As You Like It* and were much admired by the Poet Laureate Robert Southey on his visit to Belgium in 1815, as was the Meuse itself. By this date Liège was already a thriving industrial city, with many British firms playing prominent roles, but Southey found the road from Namur to Huy 'one of the most beautiful' that he had ever travelled, on a par with that from Ambleside to Keswick.[11] The Meuse became steadily more popular in the 1820s and 1830s, thanks in part to publications such as George Arnald's *Picturesque Scenery on the River Meuse* (1828, 2nd edition 1835) which made up for its somewhat schematic illustrations by a full and highly appreciative text.[12] The Meuse is dotted not with the ruins of wrecked medieval castles but with picturesque small towns (fig.3), a variety of eye-catching mansions and abbeys, and – most famous of all – colossal cliffs of white or red oolitic limestone which rear their heads in a multiplicity of bizarre forms both above and below Namur itself (fig.4). In Turner's day the river was also particularly noted for its trees, which far outshone those of the Rhine and the Mosel, where the hillsides between the villages were so frequently shared by vineyards and uncultivable rocks. When Wordsworth and his wife and sister crossed Belgium on their tour of the Continent in 1820 they were all three enchanted by the meadows and groves lining the Meuse and the glimpses of cottages amidst gardens and orchards.[13] Dorothy Wordsworth wrote to a friend that the trees of the Meuse were superior to any they had seen elsewhere in Europe, closely resembling those in the north of England and far superior to those of the Rhine. Wordsworth himself stated that the scenery of the Meuse pleased him more 'upon the whole, than that of the Rhine, though the river itself is much inferior in grandeur' and his appreciation of the Meuse was encapsulated in his poem 'Scenery between Namur and Liège':

What lovelier home could gentle Fancy choose?
Is this the stream, whose cities, heights, and plains,
War's favourite playground, are with crimson
stains
Familiar, as the Morn with pearly dews?
The Morn, that now, along the silver MEUSE,
Spreading her peaceful ensigns, calls the swains
To tend their silent boats and ringing wains,
Or strip the bough whose mellow fruit bestrews
The ripening corn beneath it. As mine eyes
Turn from the fortified and threatening hill,
How sweet the prospect of yon watery glade,
With its grey rocks clustering in pensive shade –
That, shaped like old monastic turrets, rise
From the smooth meadow-ground, serene and still!

This sonnet forms part of a sequence of nearly forty, Wordsworth's *Memorials of a Tour on the Continent* (1822) which also includes the delightfully named 'In a Carriage, upon the Banks of the Rhine' where the poet laments the rapidity with which he is rushing past so many historic sites. Such a sentiment was wholly understandable: it was only two years since he had published his thirty-four *Duddon Sonnets* which follow the twelve-mile course of another river, his beloved Duddon in the Lake District, in immense detail, with reflections on numerous themes, past and present, earthly and metaphysical. All these poems of Wordsworth's merit a mention here since they serve as a reminder that Turner's interest in the Rhine, Meuse and Mosel and his lifelong fascination with rivers in general have contemporary parallels too numerous to be itemised. In the days before photography, the cinema, television and videos, not

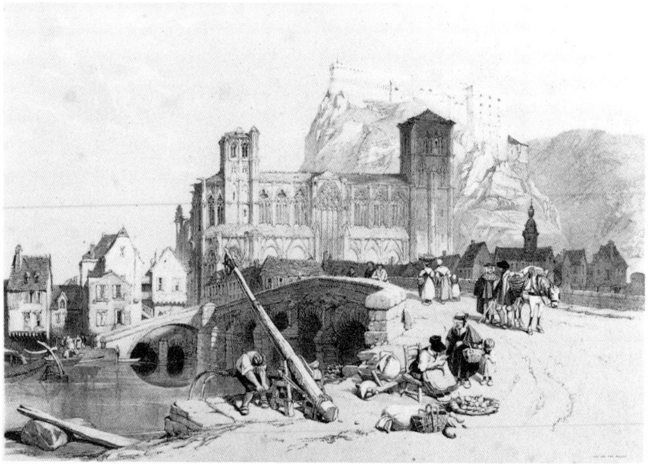

fig.3 Thomas Shotter Boys after Clarkson Stanfield, 'Bridge, Cathedral and Citadel; Huy on the Meuse'. Lithograph from *Sketches on the Moselle, the Rhine, & the Meuse . . .*, 1838

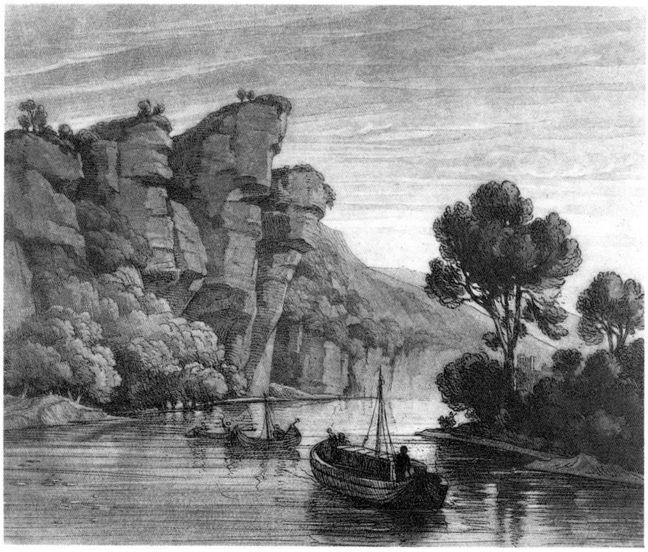

fig.4 S.W. Reynolds after George Arnald, 'Near Namur. Left Bank of the Meuse'. Mezzotint from *Picturesque Scenery on the River Meuse, from the City of Liège to that of Mézières*, 1835

to mention steamers, trains and aeroplanes, the public had an almost insatiable demand for written descriptions and images of natural scenery, near or far. A very high proportion of these were river-oriented, catering for popular taste at a variety of levels. Turner himself contributed watercolours to be engraved in *The Rivers of England* in the 1820s and *The Rivers of France* in the 1830s, but there were innumerable other publications illustrated with steel engravings, lithographs and aquatints after the work of many other artists, commemorating rivers not only in Europe but also as far afield as Egypt and India. Their illustrators included many of Turner's colleagues at the Royal Academy such as William Daniell, Clarkson Stanfield and David Roberts; noted watercolourists such as Samuel Prout (fig.5) and William Havell; highly competent amateur artists such as Robert Batty; younger artists influenced by Turner such as W.L. Leitch. Their engravers and publishers were frequently the very same men that Turner was working with on other publications at precisely the same time: W.B. and George Cooke, Edward and William Finden, John Murray and Charles Heath.

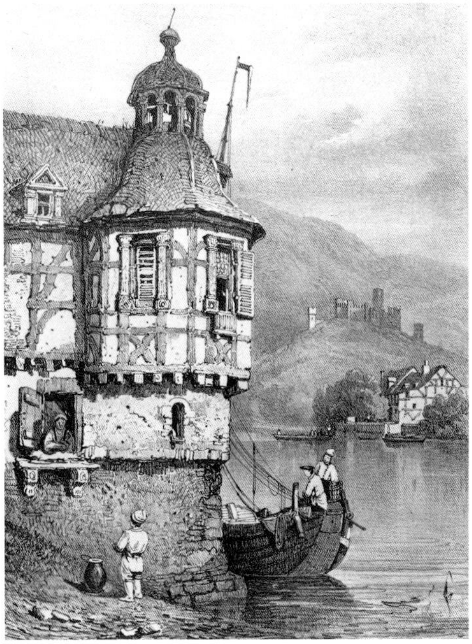

fig.5 Samuel Prout, 'Nieder Lahnstein'. Lithograph from *Illustrations of the Rhine*, 1826

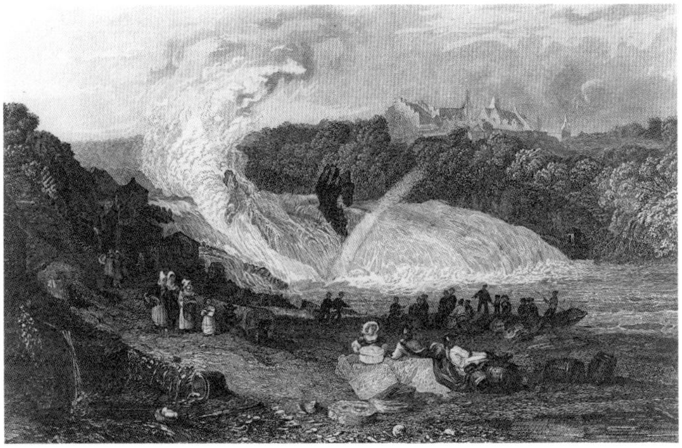

fig.6 Léonce Lhuillier after J.M.W. Turner, 'Vue de la Chûte du Rhin'. Line engraving from a nineteenth-century guidebook

Turner first saw the Rhine in 1802 but along a stretch very different from that described in this exhibition: the High Rhine between Lake Constance (the Bodensee) and Basel. All visitors to this area made a point of admiring the Rhine falls at Schaffhausen, one of the finest cascades in all Europe, where the river surges across a limestone ledge little more than twenty yards high but around 130 yards in width and with irregular mountainous peaks of rock emerging from the foam (fig.6). The churning falls, fed by the melting Alpine snows, provided Turner with a memorable experience which he was later to embody in both oil and watercolour, and he continued to revisit the falls and draw inspiration from them until his very last years.[14]

Turner's visit to the Alps in the summer of 1802 had been snatched during the very brief respite from the Napoleonic and Revolutionary Wars afforded by the Peace of Amiens signed in March of that year. Within fourteen months Europe was at war once more and it was not until after the final defeat of Napoleon by the allied forces of Britain and Prussia at the Battle of Waterloo on 18 June 1815 that British citizens could again travel safely on the Continent. It is worth pausing to consider the Europe which Turner experienced on his first visit there after the war, since although – as will appear in due course – he was influenced by certain pre-war publications on the Rhineland, it is scarcely to be believed that he approached it with the naive and blinkered vision of Mrs Radcliffe and her disciples. These, from the comfort of a carriage or an armchair, could enjoy a delicious thrill at the thought of a rowing boat about to be wrecked on the rocks by a whirlpool or a castle so precariously perched on a cliff that it might tumble to the ground, and she herself – clearly no historian – had remarked that the number of fortresses along the Rhine appeared unnecessary, since the river itself seemed a natural fortification.[15] From the early 1790s onwards French armies had simply poured into the Netherlands and the Palatinate. Within ten years Napoleon had annexed all the territory west of the Rhine from Basel down to Holland; by 1807 he dominated all the German states as far as 300 miles beyond it, under the umbrella of his newly created 'Confederation of the Rhine'. The Holy Roman Empire was abolished and for some twenty years the areas governed since the Middle Ages by the Archbishop-Electors of Cologne, Mainz and Trier and other secular rulers and princes were no more than departments of France, ruled directly – and absolutely – from Paris. The very few medieval castles and fortresses along the Rhine which had escaped destruction at the hands of Louis XIV were now systematically blown up and rendered ineffective (see cat.no.3). Convents and monasteries were abolished (see cat.no.4). Cathedrals and churches were desecrated and destroyed. Liège cathedral, for instance, began to be demolished by troops on the very day of its patronal festival, adding insult to injury, while those of Mainz and Cologne – at this date still unfinished (fig.7) – were used as magazines and barracks and to store hay for the horses of the cavalry. Small wonder, then, that in 1817 Turner did not sketch their interiors. At the time of Turner's first visit to Belgium and Germany, things were by no means back to normal. There was conspicuous desolation, poverty and squalor both in towns and in the countryside, much of it probably endemic but undoubtedly aggravated by the recent turmoils of war.[16] There was a large military presence at garrison towns such as Mainz, chiefly composed of Austrians and Prussians,[17] since under the territorial reorganisation following Napoleon's downfall and the Congress of Vienna the lands bordering on the Middle Rhine became part of Prussia itself, far away to the east, on the Baltic. Most of the recently burnt-out castles and fortresses were still a very desolate sight, their blackened shells stark against the sky, but a mammoth programme of reconstruction of forts and citadels was soon under way. By far the largest was that of Ehrenbreitstein, opposite Coblenz and guarding the confluence of the Rhine and the Mosel, but spectacular new forts were

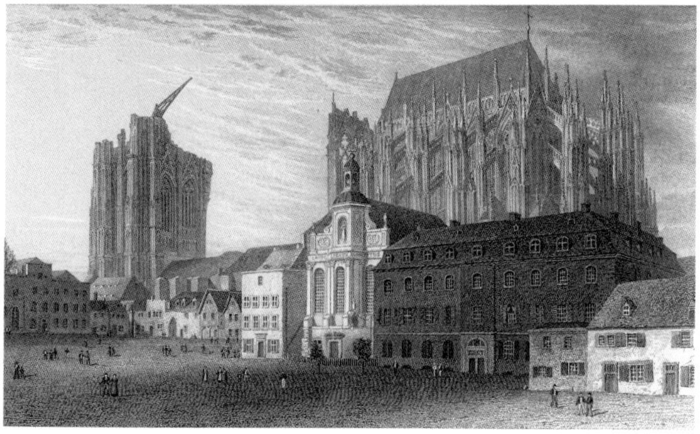

fig.7 J. Redaway after Robert Batty, 'Cathedral at Cologne'. Line engraving from *Scenery of the Rhine . . .*, 1826

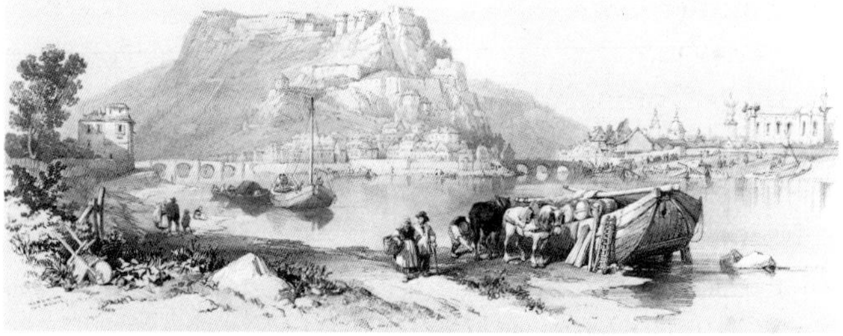

fig.8 Louis Haghe after Clarkson Stanfield, 'Namur; Junction of the Meuse and Sambre'. Lithograph from *Sketches on the Moselle, the Rhine & the Meuse . . .*, 1838

also built at the confluence of the Meuse and the Sambre at Namur (fig.8) and above the Meuse towns of Huy and Dinant. Like all who had suffered in the recent wars, Prussia and the Netherlands were determined never to fall victim again to a French aggressor.

The new fortress of Ehrenbreitstein was partly built from stone quarried from the wreck of Burg Rheinfels above St Goar until this process was halted by Prince Friedrich Wilhelm Ludwig of Prussia, the future Kaiser Wilhelm I, in the 1840s (see cat.nos.3 and 7). The prince, his cousin and his brothers did much to save the wrecked medieval castles lining the Middle Rhine, transforming the Bautsburg, Burg Sooneck and Schloss Stolzenfels (see cat.nos.10 and

17) into medieval-style summer retreats or hunting castles: the Rhine became once more studded with magnificently crenellated castles, while their interiors were rich in antique furniture and frescoes, 'old armor, colored glass, quaint carvings, narrow turrets and dark chambers' – in short, all the paraphernalia of medievalism that went hand-in-hand with the emergence of the German Nazarenes and the English Pre-Raphaelites.[18] In these intricately adorned and highly evocative interiors they gave banquets in historical costume and musical entertainments (in 1845, for instance, Queen Victoria and Prince Albert stayed at Schloss Stolzenfels and heard the famous soprano Jenny Lind). Turner, of course, experienced none of this, though the newly reconstructed castles of the 1820s and 1830s feature in several of his sketches, looking very different from their battered predecessors recorded in 1817.[19] He did, however, make two attempts to curry favour with royalty by painting notable German buildings, neither of them as it happens in the Rhineland, and on neither occasion with any success. Following Queen Victoria's marriage to Prince Albert of Saxe-Coburg-Gotha in February 1840, Turner visited Coburg itself on his way back from Venice in the September of that year and in 1841 he exhibited an oil painting of Schloss Rosenau, Prince Albert's birthplace, at the Royal Academy (B & J 392; Sudley Art Gallery, Liverpool). However, far from buying the painting at the Academy, the Queen never even noticed it. Turner's other oil painting of this period with German subject matter made an even worse impression on those it was intended to please. This was 'The Opening of the Wallhalla' (B & J 401; Clore Gallery), a very large work commemorating the completion of a 'Temple of Fame', resembling the Parthenon in Athens, near Regensburg on the Danube in 1842. The painting was well enough received in England at the Royal Academy of 1843 but when Turner sent it to be exhibited at the Congress of European Art in Munich in 1845 as a tribute to King Ludwig I of Bavaria, the guiding spirit behind the temple, it was seen as an insulting daub, scarcely recognisable as the work of a man who was renowned for his beautiful effects of light and colour.

The historicism implicit in the restoration of the Rhine castles and the building of the Walhalla, with its marble frieze and array of busts depicting the great Germans of history, can also be seen in the nineteenth-century obsession with stories and legends relating to the Rhineland. Many of these are undoubtedly both medieval and Rhenish in origin and some, like the horrific story in Robert Southey's 'God's Judgment on a Bishop' of 1799, centring on the Mäuseturm near Bingen, had been known in England for centuries.[20] However, many others were actually invented in the early nineteenth century or were grafted on to Rhineland sites from elsewhere in Germany. For instance, the romantic story attached to Rolandseck and Nonnenwerth and recast for a British audience by Thomas Campbell in 1820 (see cat.no.29) derived from an old German ballad and only became associated with the Rhine in 1811. The siren who lured sailors to their deaths at the Lorelei (see cat.no.8) was invented in 1802 by Clemens von Brentano. It is hard to know how far Turner was aware of these stories, which were absorbed instantly into popular culture through both verse and prose, or was influenced by them. Some he would have known through reading Campbell and perhaps Southey, some he may have heard at inns and taverns on his wanderings; but it was not until the 1830s and 1840s that the corpus of stories became at all well known in England, thanks to its publication there in two forms: interwoven with the sentimental narrative of Bulwer-Lytton's poetical story *Pilgrims of the Rhine* (1834, with topographical illustrations after Turner's friend David Roberts), and, more straightforwardly, in an illustrated compendium, the two volumes of Joseph Snowe's *The Rhine, Legends, Traditions, History, from Cologne to Mainz* (1839).

These were the very years when Turner was illustrating the works of Byron, Scott and Campbell with topographical scenes including ones depicting both Belgium and the Rhineland (cat.nos.25–9). More often than not, these are based on the pencil drawings in Turner's sketchbooks of 1817, though one, 'The Castellated Rhine', which served as the title-page vignette to the very last volume of Byron's collected works in 1833, is a visionary amalgamation of many different ruins and towers, brilliantly encapsulating the whole of the Middle Rhine in less than three by four inches (fig.9). This was Turner's Rhine: a river not of myths and legends but of breathtaking scenery and evocative architecture. It is probably without parallel in the work of other artists, but is completely characteristic of Turner's illustrations to poetry at about this time: his vig-

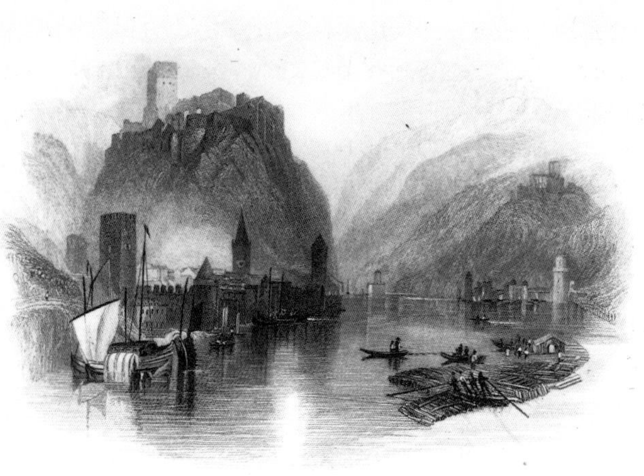

fig.9 Edward Finden after J.M.W. Turner, 'The Castellated Rhine'. Line engraving from *The Works of Lord Byron*, vol. XVII, 1833

nettes to Samuel Rogers's *Italy* (1830) present as complete and as ravishing a vision of that country in an equally tiny compass.[21]

Wordsworth's memorable phrase 'War's favourite playground' sums up what Turner and his contemporaries must have felt at almost every town and village as they travelled through these regions. Turner's depictions of many of the castles and forts along the Rhine, Meuse and Mosel are so stunning and so familiar (e.g. cat.nos.93–9, 128–36) that it is easy to forget the historical and military nature of what they depict: while some are picturesque ruins, others are functioning, much-needed and recently constructed strongholds. It is also easy for the casual observer to assume that the fortress of Ehrenbreitstein depicted by Turner is the same edifice throughout his many works in pencil, watercolour and oil. This is not the case. Ehrenbreitstein at last succumbed to the French in 1799 after five years of repeated sieges and was blown up and rendered harmless. When it became Prussian property after 1815, it was reconstructed on an even vaster scale than hitherto, an enterprise taking over fifteen years at a cost which has been estimated as equivalent, in today's terms, to around DM 600 million. By around 1840, when Turner showed it as a visionary cliff or mountain swathed in a multitude of colours (cat.nos. 128–34), it had 400 pieces of heavy ordnance on its ramparts. Some accounts described its cisterns as holding enough fresh water for a three-year siege, its stores sufficient provisions to feed 8,000 men for ten years; in other accounts it was estimated as capable of housing an army of 100,000.[22]

Another – more conspicuous – difference between Turner's various depictions of Ehrenbreitstein concerns the bridge across the Rhine. In the early nineteenth century there were stone bridges across the Meuse at all the main towns studied by Turner; on the Mosel there were just two – both dating back to antiquity – at Trier and at Coblenz (fig.10). But the Rhine was too broad and too powerful, and the passageway down it too important, for it to be bridged in stone.[23] At the time of Turner's first visit in 1817, Mainz had a bridge of some forty boats, fixed together with crossbeams, which was strong enough to bear carriages and horses – indeed, entire armies – but could easily be adjusted to allow the passage of boats, barges and rafts. Cologne and Coblenz, on the other hand, still had the flying bridges used at many smaller towns and villages on both the Rhine (see cat.no.5) and Mosel (cat.no.57). That at Coblenz was neatly described by one traveller in 1818 as 'a spacious round platform, railed in, and placed upon a couple of stout barges. It is attached by a long chain to a boat moored higher up in the middle of the river, so that it swings in the stream at this chain's length. When filled with passengers, it is shoved off from the Quay, and its own impulse carries it to the other side, its streamers flying from long posts striped with the loyal Prussian blue and white. In this way it keeps up its monotonous swing, like the pendulum of a clock.'[24] The crossing at Coblenz is recorded as taking around three minutes; that at Cologne operated from dawn till late at night, a bell being rung at each departure, and was capable of carrying up to 500 people in comfort, 1,500 if necessary, at the cost of a penny a head.[25] The flying bridge at Coblenz was replaced by one of wooden pontoons like that at Mainz in 1819 (all but the soldiers having to pay a farthing to cross it), that at Cologne in 1822.[26] All these bridges appear again and again in Turner's sketches and drawings (see cat.nos.24, 81–2, 129–36).

Even more numerous are Turner's representations of the various craft that plied up and down the Rhine, the Meuse and the Mosel: the colossal rafts which floated all the way from Switzerland down to Holland, housing hundreds of men on board for weeks at a time as they took both the timber itself

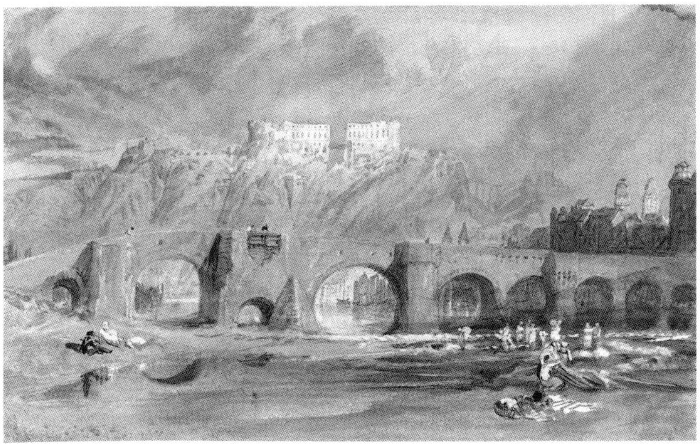

fig.10 'The Mosel Bridge at Coblenz' (w 659). Gouache and watercolour on white paper prepared with a grey wash, 1817. On loan to the Art Gallery of Ontario, Toronto

and other cargoes to the North Sea ports for shipbuilding and export (cat.no.133); the moored salmon-fishing boats with high curved levers for manoevring their nets (cat.no.8); the barges and boats towed upstream not only by horses and oxen but also – to the indignation of some British travellers[27] – by men, women and children (cat.no.4); the huge sailing vessels of the wealthy or the military (cat.no.24); the covered passenger-boats (cat.no.25); and the innumerable ferry-boats.

In many respects river travel in the early nineteenth century remained largely as it had been for centuries past, but there were two ways in which it became much improved: by Napoleon's strategic road-building and by the introduction of steam vessels. Napoleon's occupation of the Rhineland resulted in one tangible benefit, a really first-class road, constructed by his troops all along the west bank from Cologne to Mainz. Turner himself used this road in 1817 and – like thousands of other travellers – must have found it of inestimable value. It was widely acclaimed as the finest in Europe, facilitating travel and – since at many points it was separated from the river only by a fence of posts – providing magnificent views. Turner's interest in scientific discoveries and inventions in his later years is well known and it is perhaps not surprising that some of his gouaches from the late 1830s depict factories and feats of civil engineering (cat.nos.49, 50, 85). It is thus all the more fascinating that one of the celebrated series of works inspired by his 1817 Rhine visit, 'Hirzenach, below St Goar', shows a totally insignificant stretch of the river which had recently been transformed by the *route Napoléon* (fig.11). It had always been a good mountain road, though 'liable, as all such roads . . . to be cut up by the torrents. But the French military engineers, by blasting the basaltic rocks, levelling down the inequalities, and forming arched sewers for the swollen torrents to pass under the road instead of sweeping across, as heretofore, when they swept also at the same time a portion of it into the Rhine, have now made it a most perfect, level, macadamized road, on which neither hole nor rut is to be seen.'[28]

One of the earliest voyages of a steam-powered vessel on the Rhine took place in the same year as Turner's first visit there, when James Watt the younger, son of the inventor of the steam engine, crossed the Channel to Holland in the *Caledonia* – the first steamship to leave an English port – and sailed right up to Coblenz. However, it was not until 1827 that a regular service was opened between Mainz and Cologne, with several boats a week travelling both upstream and downstream.[29] On the Mosel the first experiments were made at the very end of 1839 and in 1840, a proper service being introduced in the summer of 1841.[30] In 1815 Southey was so upset by the hardships endured by the men and horses towing barges up the Meuse that he 'hoped for mercy's sake that steamboats will soon be introduced here', but nearly twenty years later the journey between Liège and Namur was still being made in dirty and uncomfortable little packet-boats.[31] Steam pas-

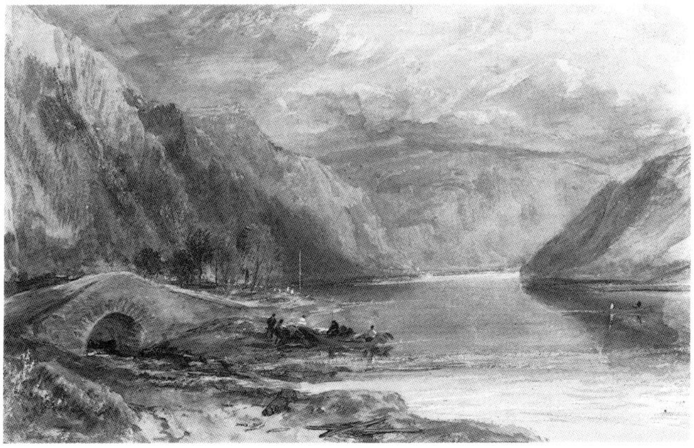

fig.11 'Hirzenach, below St Goar' (w 681). Gouache and watercolour, with scratching out, on white paper prepared with a grey wash, 1817. British Museum

senger-boats were clearly a godsend to the new tourist industry of the mid-nineteenth century, but their speed positively discouraged the close study of the countryside through which they passed. It is impossible to be sure precisely what use Turner made of these services on the Continent, but there can be little doubt that he used the Rhine steamers on his last trips to Switzerland in the early 1840s. He was getting older; he was not short of money but had a limited number of weeks available for his complex tours; the steamer service itself would have been a new and exciting way of experiencing the river scenery he already knew so well.

On Turner's first visit to the Rhine, he stuck closely to the river itself and to the *route Napoléon*, so that nearly all the watercolours commemorating this visit have low viewpoints with solemn hills, swirling skies and the vast grey stream dominating any tiny figures that may be included (cat.nos.4–11). In his late watercolour 'Oberwesel' (cat.no.30) both viewpoint and vision are entirely different. Turner himself is standing high on the hillside so that the entire stretch of the Rhine from Oberwesel up to Kaub and Burg.Gutenfels can be seen, gleaming with light and embosomed like a lake in far-extending hills of miraculous beauty. Men, women and children fill a foreground characterised by a calm and fertility as visionary and idealised as the landscape itself. In the far distance a tiny trail of smoke can be traced to the dark smudge of a steamer passing the island-castle of the Pfalz. This work is a masterpiece among Turner's late watercolours and it enshrines his most recent experiences in the Rhineland. It is, in short, the final consummation of his long love of the Rhine and is his greatest painting of the greatest river of Europe.

Waterloo and the Rhineland, 1817

Turner's visit to the Low Countries and the Rhineland in 1817 was prompted by several interrelated desires. As a painter to whom European travel had been denied by the long years of war he would naturally have been keen to study parts of the Continent which had stimulated earlier generations of artists. The Field of Waterloo had been attracting hundreds of visitors – writers, artists, relations of the combatants, and the merely curious – from the summer of 1815 onwards and the battle itself had already inspired paintings, poetry and large quantities of prose. November 1816 saw the publication of canto III of *Childe Harold's Pilgrimage* in which Byron's hero stood upon 'this place of skulls, / The grave of France' before contemplating the mingled sweetness and sublimity of the Rhineland. Turner's desire to explore both these destinations in 1817 is far less surprising than his two-year delay before doing so. He is sometimes represented as a cautious man, watching and waiting to see how the land lay before himself making a move, and sometimes even as being essentially 'provincial' and without the all-embracing vision necessary in a truly great artist.[1] In this view of Turner, the two summers of 1815 and 1816 which were spent with his friend and patron Walter Fawkes at Farnley Hall in Yorkshire rather than in exploration of the newly accessible riches of Europe would be prime examples of his provincialism. But whatever the reasons for his delay, in 1817 he hesitated no longer. He set off alone for the Continent on what was to be the first of at least twenty such tours which embraced many different parts of Europe. Timidity and provincialism – if these had indeed ever existed – instantly became things of the past, and for the rest of his many working summers he explored the Continent with vigour, enthusiasm and originality, responding to its rivers and mountains, cities and villages in paintings and drawings with an unparalleled breadth of vision.

Turner prepared for his 1817 tour with all the care

he had brought to his earlier British tours, seeking out useful publications and arming himself with essential information (such preparations had not been necessary for his 1802 tour of France and Switzerland with a companion and servant, as I have already suggested elsewhere[2]). He bought three leather-bound sketchbooks of different sizes, the two larger ones containing the high quality paper of J. Whatman which he preferred to any other (TB CLIX, CLX, CLXI; cat.nos.1–3); the most up-to-date English guidebook available, *The Traveller's Complete Guide through Belgium and Holland . . . with a Sketch of a Tour in Germany* (2nd edition, 1817) by Charles Campbell; and another brand-new but more discursive book on some of the areas he was about to explore, *A Picturesque Tour through France, Switzerland, on the Banks of the Rhine, and through Part of the Netherlands* (1817) by J. Mawman. Into the smallest of his sketchbooks (TB CLIX, *Itinerary Rhine Tour*; cat.no.1) he wrote a large quantity of notes covering famous sights, distances, inns, currencies, useful foreign phrases and transport in all the regions he was about to visit. Some of these derive from Campbell's book itself (and may thus date from a period before Turner had actually decided to buy it) but most are copied from two large illustrated volumes which he could certainly have neither afforded nor carried with him: *Sketches in Flanders and Holland; with some Account of a Tour through Parts of those Countries, shortly after the Battle of Waterloo; in a Series of Letters to a Friend* (1816) by the printseller Robert Hills and *Views taken on and near The River Rhine, at Aix la Chapelle, and on the River Maese* by the Revd John Gardnor, first published between 1788 and 1791 and then reissued in a smaller format in 1792 (fig.12). The greater part of Turner's notes from Hills's book relate to the towns and cities of Holland rather than those of Belgium, so that for the present study the most interesting ones are those taken from the 'Hints of Occurrences in the Tour' accompanying Gardnor's Rhine scenes. These notes themselves are extremely scrappy and condensed – indeed virtually meaningless without reference to their source – but they are highly significant in revealing Gardnor as a dominant force in Turner's attitude to the Rhineland.[3]

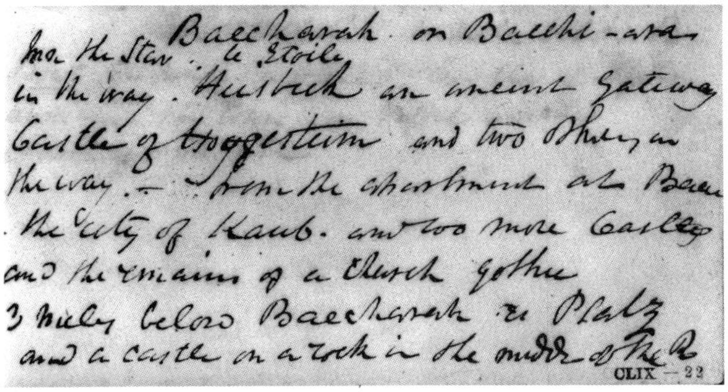

fig.12 Turner's notes on Bacharach, Kaub and the Pfalz, copied from John Gardnor's *Views taken on and near The River Rhine* (TB CLIX 22r). Pen and ink, 1817

The Revd John Gardnor (1729–1808) was not, as might be supposed, that typical eighteenth-century figure, a country clergyman with a taste for the Picturesque. He was a Londoner who began his career as an artist and art teacher and only took holy orders after he had achieved considerable success in the field of art, exhibiting at the Free Society of Artists, winning a prize from the Society of Arts and being the principal of an Academy in Kensington Square. In 1778 he became vicar of St Mary's parish church, Battersea, where he conducted the marriage service of William Blake and Catherine Boucher in August 1782, and he remained the incumbent there until his death thirty years later. During his years in Battersea, Gardnor was a frequent exhibitor at the Royal Academy, his last scenes appearing in 1796. His subjects – always landscapes – were dictated by the taste of the time, and included many that also attracted the young Turner: views in North and South Wales, Cumberland and Westmorland, Surrey and the Isle of Wight. However, he made one important foreign tour, travelling to the Rhine in the summer of 1787, and this had a dramatic effect on his artistic output. From 1788 to 1791 his exhibits at the Academy consisted almost exclusively of large watercolours of Rhine subjects and during the identical period these same views were published as large, folio-size aquatints in Parts I–VIII of the *Views on the Rhine* mentioned above which ultimately contained thirty-two scenes. Gardnor's influence upon Turner can thus be seen as twofold, beginning around 1790 and returning in 1817. The young Turner was avidly studying the work of established artists around 1790 – the year in which the Royal Academy first accepted one of his works, the watercolour 'The Archbishop's Palace, Lambeth' (W 10). If he had overlooked Gardnor's two Rhine exhibits in 1788 and those of 1789, he could hardly have failed to notice Gardnor's six large Rhine watercolours in 1790, especially in view of their proximity to his own watercolour in the Academy's printed catalogue: there can be no aspiring fifteen-year-old boy who does not gloat over the first appearance of his name in print.[4] But, in any case, Gardnor's 'Bacharach', exhibited in 1790, was exactly the sort of work to which he would naturally have been drawn (fig.13).

At this date Turner could only have admired the aquatint versions of Gardnor's scenes in printshop windows, but by the middle or late 1790s he could have handled the lavishly produced book for himself in the libraries of his new-found friends and patrons. Joseph Farington RA, for instance, whose advice Turner constantly sought when he was seeking advancement within the Academy, was one of the subscribers to the sets of prints.[5] Turner's interest in Gardnor's work in the 1790s would probably have centred on its technical and formal qualities and he may well have noted that Gardnor had been responsible for aquatinting many of his own scenes rather than delegating them to the hand of a professional engraver (Turner was soon to act in a similar fashion himself, etching and engraving many of his own *Liber Studiorum* plates from 1807 onwards). A visit to the Continent was at this date out of the question so Turner would probably not have bothered to glance at the text accompanying the aquatints. In 1817, however, this text was of paramount importance, since it not only described the highlights to be sought but also suggested the best viewing spots for sketching them. As the narrative of Turner's 1817 tour will show, he often took heed of Gardnor's recommendations and followed closely in his footsteps. And it is also perhaps worth mentioning here that Gardnor's publication would, in addition, have introduced Turner to many other places, not on the Rhine itself but nearby, that he was later to study carefully: Aachen (Aix-la-Chapelle) and the Meuse towns of Liège, Huy and Namur.

It was, however, Charles Campbell's recently published guide to Belgium and Holland that exerted the greatest influence on Turner's itinerary in 1817, since there can be no doubt that he deliberately adopted the route it described from Margate to Brussels and the Field of Waterloo, across Belgium to Cologne, along the Middle Rhine, and finally through Holland. In his first edition (1815), Campbell's tour had begun in Holland but he rearranged his material radically in the second edition to accommodate and give prominence to its most important new feature, the chapter on the Field of Waterloo. It was from this edition that Turner made his brief notes in the *Itinerary Rhine Tour* sketchbook in amongst those from Hills's book.[6] They cannot have been made long before the tour itself and it seems very likely that the appearance of these two books in 1816 and 1817 – inspiring, instructive and informative – was in itself a factor that precipitated Turner's departure.

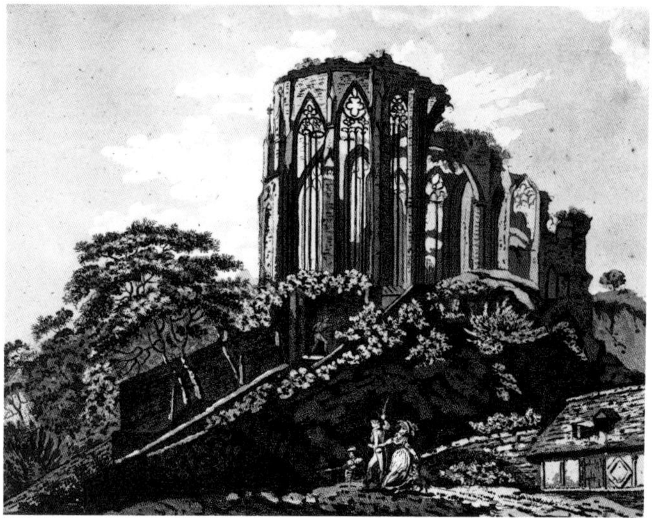

fig.13 John Gardnor and Richard Gardnor junior after John Gardnor, 'The Ruins of a Church at Baccharah'. Aquatint from the second edition of *Views taken on and near The River Rhine* (1792)

The 1817 tour is one of the best documented of Turner's entire career. He himself recorded his movements – an extremely rare occurrence – in the *Itinerary Rhine Tour* sketchbook, listing dates and places from his departure from London on Sunday 10 August through to his arrival in The Hague nearly four weeks later, on Saturday 6 September (fig.14). These entries were all clearly written in full, but those following – for 7–15 September – were written in pencil and the place names appear in an abbreviated form, so that Turner's movements in Holland in 1817 are far less easily traced than those in Belgium and Germany. From these notes the following timetable emerges: Sunday 10 August: left London; Monday 11: off Margate; Tuesday 12: Ostend–Bruges; Wednesday 13: Ghent; Thursday

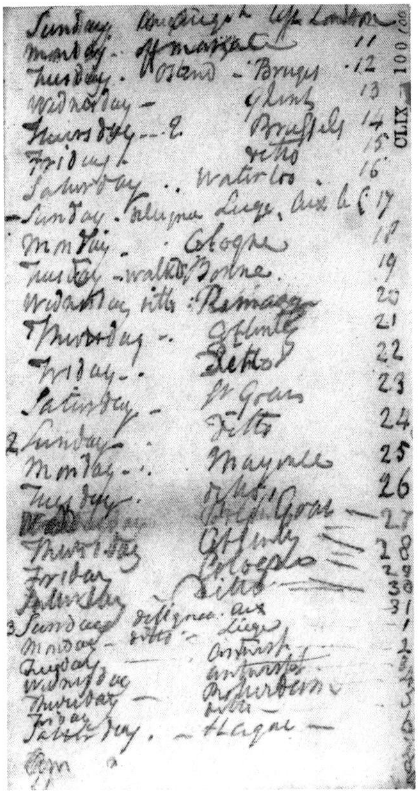

fig.14 Turner's timetable of his 1817 tour to the Low Countries and the Rhineland (TB CLIX 100r). Pen and ink followed by pencil, 1817

14: Brussels; Friday 15: Brussels; Saturday 16: Waterloo; Sunday 17: Liège, Aachen (Aix-la-Chapelle); Monday 18: Cologne; Tuesday 19: Bonn; Wednesday 20: Remagen; Thursday 21: Coblenz; Friday 22: Coblenz; Saturday 23: St Goar; Sunday 24: St Goar; Monday 25: Mainz; Tuesday 26: Mainz; Wednesday 27: St Goar; Thursday 28: Coblenz; Friday 29: Cologne; Saturday 30: Cologne; Sunday 31: Aachen; Monday 1 September: Liège; Tuesday 2: Antwerp; Wednesday 3: Antwerp; Thursday 4: Rotterdam; Friday 5: Rotterdam; Saturday 6: The Hague.

Since Turner left London for Ostend on a Sunday, he may well have travelled on one of the three 'fast-sailing Packets' which were advertised in *The Times* in August 1817. These were the 80-ton *Albion*, the 80-ton *Marquis of Anglesea* and the 100-ton *Duke of Wellington* which sailed alternately on Thursdays and Sundays from Botolph-wharf near London Bridge.[7] In his timetable only one place name is usually entered for each date, so it is probably a record of where he spent each night. On the occasions for which he lists two places for one date, these may be explained as brief memoranda of the different stages of his journey, i.e. where he changed from boat to carriage or from one carriage to another. Thus on 12 August he crossed to Ostend and then journeyed on to Bruges, while on 17 August he probably used one vehicle from Brussels to Liège and another from Liège to Aachen.

The first sketches Turner drew on this tour are those starting at the opposite end of the *Itinerary Rhine Tour* sketchbook from his manuscript notes, and showing marine views, shipping and distant harbours, closely followed by studies of peasants with notes on their vehicles, clothing, implements and utensils.[8] He evidently kept this small notebook ready at hand throughout most of his tour and it was as natural that he should start using it from the untouched end as it was that he should record the picturesque peasants of Flanders and their life style in vignettes similar to those published by Robert Hills. He continued using it, on and off, for the rest of his time in the Rhineland (cat.no.1) and for some weeks afterwards, chiefly for the briefest of memoranda but sometimes to plan pictorial compositions.[9]

His more composed sketches, showing the architecture of Brussels, Bruges and Ghent, were made on the following days in a medium-sized sketchbook (*Waterloo and Rhine*; TB CLX; cat.no.2). Turner clearly found these cities extremely interesting though his timetable appears to have allowed him little leisure for sketching; Bruges was the subject of half a dozen drawings, Ghent and the centre of Brussels only one each (fig.15). He did, however, draw several quick sketches of the outskirts of Brussels, which he later used as the basis of a watercolour for engraving (cat.no.26).[10] However, his main interest on this first visit to Belgium lay in the Field of Waterloo of which he drew seventeen pages of sketches, some schematic, others detailed, and many annotated with data about the battle: which country's forces were stationed at which spot, the numbers of casualties on each side, the places where individual commanders fell.[11] It is clear from these pages that Turner toured the battlefield in the conventional sequence, as described in Campbell's guidebook, but it is equally clear that he was accompanied by one of the guides who attached themselves to all visitors for a gratuity. The details and statistics

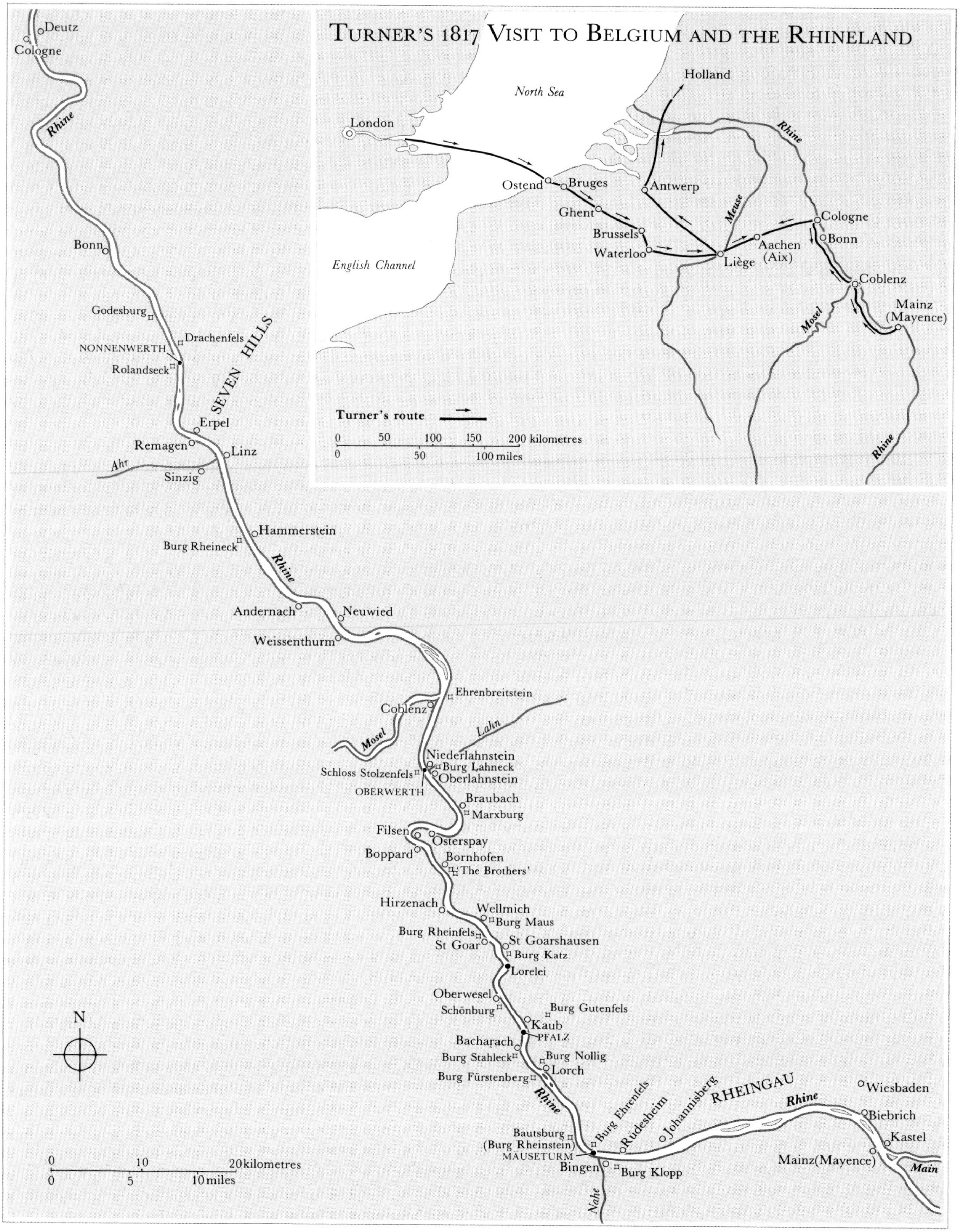

TURNER'S 1817 VISIT TO BELGIUM AND THE RHINELAND
North Sea
Holland
London
Ostend
Bruges
Ghent
Brussels
Waterloo
Antwerp
Liège
Aachen (Aix)
Cologne
Bonn
Coblenz
Mainz (Mayence)
Rhine
Meuse
Mosel
English Channel
Turner's route
0 50 100 150 200 kilometres
0 50 100 miles
Deutz
Cologne
Rhine
Bonn
Godesburg
Drachenfels
NONNENWERTH
Rolandseck
SEVEN HILLS
Erpel
Remagen
Linz
Ahr
Sinzig
Hammerstein
Burg Rheineck
Rhine
Andernach
Neuwied
Weissenthurm
Ehrenbreitstein
Coblenz
Mosel
Lahn
Niederlahnstein
Burg Lahneck
Schloss Stolzenfels
Oberlahnstein
OBERWERTH
Braubach
Marxburg
Filsen
Osterspay
Boppard
Bornhofen
'The Brothers'
Hirzenach
Wellmich
Burg Maus
Burg Rheinfels
St Goar
St Goarshausen
Burg Katz
Lorelei
Oberwesel
Schönburg
Burg Gutenfels
Kaub
PFALZ
Bacharach
Burg Stahleck
Burg Nollig
Lorch
Burg Fürstenberg
Rhine
Burg Ehrenfels
Rüdesheim
Johannisberg
RHEINGAU
Rhine
Wiesbaden
Biebrich
Kastel
Mainz(Mayence)
Main
Bautsburg (Burg Rheinstein)
MÄUSETURM
Bingen
Burg Klopp
Nahe
N
0 10 20 kilometres
0 5 10 miles

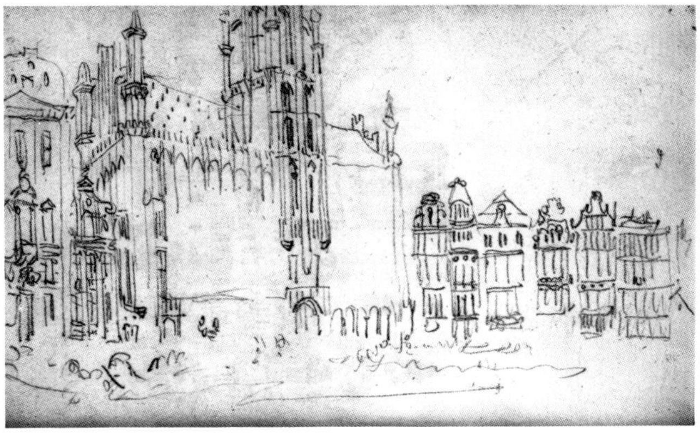

fig.15 The town hall at Brussels from the Grand' Place (TB CLX 9V). Pencil, 1817

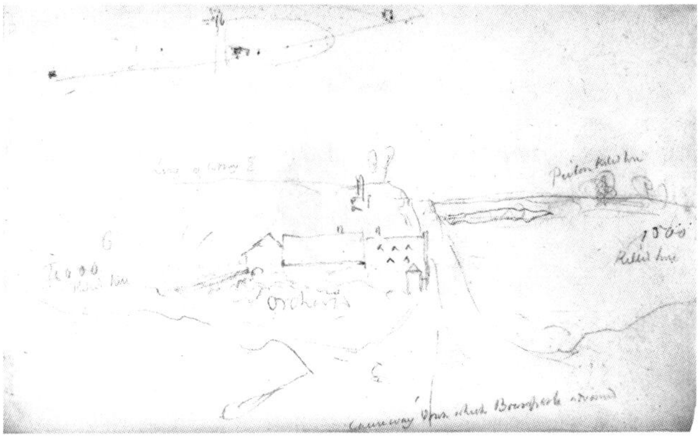

fig.16 The farm of La Haye Sainte and the Field of Waterloo (TB CLX 21V). Pencil, 1817

in Turner's sketchbook have no counterparts in Campbell and must have come from a verbal source on the spot.

Arriving from the north he first sketched the village of Waterloo with its domed royal chapel, as seen from the inn that had served the Duke of Wellington as his rear headquarters. He then walked south, making many sketches from Mont St-Jean, the high ground where the British forces and their allies had been stationed. Periodically he drew diagrams of the causeways used by the troops, important crossroads and the positions of the various units of allied infantry and cavalry. As he proceeded southwards on his clockwise tour he looked closely in turn at each of the three buildings at the heart of the battlefield – the farms of La Haye Sainte and La Belle Alliance and the fortified farm of Hougoumont, which lie about half a mile apart, forming the angles of an equilateral triangle (fig.16). The allied forces protecting their front lines from the cover afforded by La Haye Sainte and Hougoumont had been attacked ceaselessly by the French throughout the day of the battle, with Hougoumont resisting right to the end; while La Belle Alliance, as the centre of the Napoleonic front line, had been the meeting-place of the allied leaders on the evening after the battle. These three buildings – the sites of so many passions, fears and hopes – formed the core of Turner's tour of Waterloo, as they did for all his contemporaries.

Turner's most profound reaction to the site and to the accounts of the battle itself and its aftermath which he heard and read between 1815 and 1817 is embodied in the great oil painting he exhibited at the Royal Academy in 1818, 'The Field of Waterloo' (cat.no.12) but he also returned to the subject in several illustrative watercolours (including cat.no.27). Looking at all these scenes, their conflagrations and corpses, it is hard to believe that Turner himself saw no more than a vast plain, a handful of trees and a few burnt and battered buildings, but such indeed was the case. And modern observers may well find that the sheer emptiness of many of Turner's pencil sketches of Waterloo in 1817 is in itself extraordinarily moving, the sight of such a wasteland bringing a far greater chill to the spirit than depictions of cannon-fire.

After visiting Waterloo Turner probably returned to Brussels for the night and on Sunday 17 August he travelled by public transport – the 'diligence' – to Liège and Aachen. From here it was an easy day's journey to Cologne which he reached on Monday 18 August. From then until 31 August when he returned by diligence from Cologne to Aachen, he devoted himself to an intensive study of the Middle Rhine, tirelessly sketching its towns and villages, its hills and ruined castles, and accumulating thousands of images both in his sketchbooks and in his mind. His exploration of the Rhineland was largely carried out on foot. He himself wrote 'walked' for his entry for 19 August and 'ditto' for 20 August; and 'ditto' should also be understood for all the entries for the ensuing week of his progress upstream. He travelled light, his luggage consisting of a 'wallet', the nineteenth-century pedestrian's equivalent of a backpack, which was defined by one contemporary writer as 'a kind of long bag closed at each end but with a slit in the centre for the insertion of things'.[12] Such a bag would normally have been of modest size and capacity (it was in a wallet that Little Nell and her grandfather carried their meagre belongings when they were obliged to take to the road in *The Old Curiosity Shop*), and it would customarily have been slung over the shoulder.[13] At some stage of his travels Turner managed to lose his wallet and thus came to record its contents on a page of a sketchbook. The most irritating items to have lost must have been the guidebooks and drawing materials which included his interleaved copy of Campbell's *Guide through Belgium and Holland*, half a dozen pencils and a box of colours; but it must also have been somewhat inconvenient to have lost his razor, nightshirt, spare umbrella ferrule, stockings, cravats, waistcoat and supply of clean shirts.[14]

But even without Turner's own record that he walked up the Rhine and the evidence of his pedestrian's luggage, there would be no doubt that this was how he studied the river banks between Cologne and Mainz. In sketch after sketch as he proceeded upstream his viewpoint and his foreground are annotated in pencil with the word 'Road'. Clearly they were drawn as he stopped at frequent intervals by the side of the recently constructed *route Napoléon* along the west bank of the Rhine and it is still possible for a late twentieth-century traveller to identify most of the stopping-places. His tour was not an unusually energetic one by nineteenth-century standards for an active healthy man in his early forties. There were few days on which he would need to have walked more than about thirty-five miles (and Southey, in his sixties, thought little of walking twenty-five miles over high ground in the English Lake District). Moreover, the road was excellent, the days long, and by stopping to sketch he broke his walk at frequent intervals. Furthermore, he did not attempt to walk long distances each and every day. Having spent a whole day walking to reach Coblenz, he spent the next exploring the town and its environs; the same pattern was followed over the next few days both at St Goar and at Mainz. The last part of his journey upstream was made by boat as was the greater part of his journey downstream, when he was content to travel more quickly past the now familiar landmarks.

Turner's walk from Cologne to Bonn on 19 August was the shortest of his days along the Rhine in terms of mileage (only around twenty miles) and would have eased him gently into his intended routine. Most of his sketches of Cologne were drawn later, on 30 August, when he spent an entire day there, but the careful depiction of the church of Great St Martin and the Rhine Gate which occurs early in the *Waterloo and Rhine* sketchbook certainly belongs to 18–19 August.[15] It thus acquires an almost symbolic significance, as though Turner stood gazing upstream along the river he already knew was to be of such importance to him, drew just the one sketch and then set forth on his journey. Shortly afterwards he made a handful of quick sketches of Bonn and the famous range of the Siebengebirge or Seven Hills in the distance across the Rhine,[16] but, if his first day along the Rhine did not provide him with many picturesque sights worth noting (the flatness of this stretch was a frequent disappointment to contemporary tourists who had expected the river to be consistently spectacular throughout its course), his second day was more than adequate compensation. On 20 August he saw his first Rhine castle, the Godesburg, and – immediately across the river – a truly awe-inspiring view of the Seven Hills, dominated by the mighty Drachenfels, itself crowned by a jagged and menacing ruined castle.

Today the Godesburg and the resort of Bad Godesberg – neither of them situated directly on the Rhine – have been virtually swallowed up in the spreading suburbs of the federal capital, but in Turner's day it was possible to leave Bonn behind and walk peacefully through several miles of cornfields providing excellent views of both the Godesburg and the Seven Hills. He drew seven sketches of these subjects, together with an ornate medieval roadside cross nearby, the Hochkreuz, and some of the houses of Bad Godesberg.[17] This series gives the impression that Turner stopped every hundred yards or so to draw yet another sketch, understandable enough in the case of an artist's first sight of a much noted landscape. But he was probably also glad to pause under the trees or next to the streams which occupy so many of his foregrounds: it was August and he may well have been as hot and tired as the harvesting peasants whom he depicted. Having reached the Godesburg, he turned and made for

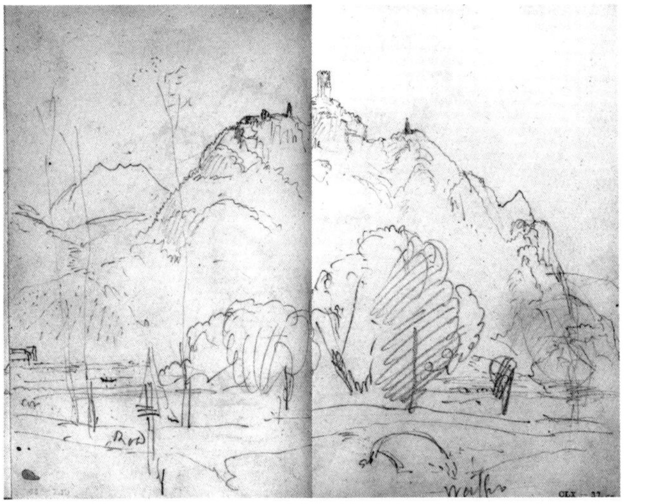

fig.17 The Drachenfels from across the Rhine (TB CLX 36v–37r). Pencil, 1817

the Rhine itself, and gazed across at the massive Drachenfels, recorded in three sketches which show it looming over the river like a vast monster (fig.17).[18]

Almost all the Rhine sketches mentioned so far occur in the *Waterloo and Rhine* sketchbook (TB CLX) and they are notable in practically always using the full double-page spread of about 6 × 7½ inches for single views. Turner now seems to have realised that he was not making sensible and economical use of the sketchbooks he was carrying with him. Slightly upstream of the Drachenfels, he took the as yet unused large *Rhine* sketchbook (TB CLXI; cat.no.3) from his wallet and made two full-page sketches[19] and from this point onwards he generally – though not invariably – used the pages of that book, measuring about 8 × 10 inches, for his larger views. Meanwhile he started the practice of dividing the pages of the *Waterloo and Rhine* sketchbook into smaller rectangles of different proportions according to the subject he wished to record. Sometimes a page is merely divided into two compartments, sometimes into as many as six tiny strips, but the quality of the sketches remained as high as ever, thanks to Turner's unrivalled draughtsmanship, the sharpness and hardness of his pencils and the fine surface of his chosen paper. In the later stages of his time on the Rhine, he became increasingly concerned to get as much as possible into this sketchbook. Minute sketches were tucked into corners, and gaps on pages were sometimes filled a day – or several days – later. Finally – when he reached Holland – he bought himself a new sketchbook.[20] Unfortunately, the order of the pages in both the *Rhine* and the *Waterloo and Rhine* sketchbooks has been disturbed since Turner's death, sometimes with confusing results. However, there can be no doubt at all that he used these books simultaneously during the period 20–30 August, taking out now one, now the other as he explored the Rhineland.

As Turner walked upstream close to the Rhine, a huge variety of changing prospects opened before him. One very characteristic sight was that of towns facing each other across the river, their watersides crowded with towers and the nearby slopes dotted with castles or churches. Shortly before reaching Remagen, his stopping-place for 20 August, he drew a sketch showing just such a view which extends over four pages of the *Waterloo and Rhine* sketchbook. The first spread shows Erpel on the far shore, beneath the abrupt cliff of the Erpeler Lei, Linz beyond it in the distance and Remagen itself on the right; St Martin's chapel perched on the Apollinarisberg just downstream of Remagen provided a satisfying conclusion for the right-hand side of the composition.[21] At this point the Rhine flows gently through a wide valley edged by low hills, but on the following day a much more impressive scene greeted Turner's eyes as he looked south towards the evocatively named Hammerstein cliff and castle looming precipitously over the opposite bank. These he sketched again and again as he approached them. At first his views were dominated by the steep hill on his own side of the Rhine with Burg Rheineck at its top and – at its foot – some of the first vines recorded on this tour. But soon afterwards Hammerstein became more and more prominent, its nearly perpendicular drop contrasting markedly with the forty-five degree angle of the hills on the west bank and dwarfing the town of Andernach now visible in the distance.[22]

Andernach is one of the most ancient and striking towns on the Rhine and the most important between Bonn and Coblenz. Turner had noted its Roman origins and its ancient castle and walls before his departure from London[23] and when he got there he found that its notable architectural features included not only the extensive town walls and ruins of the castle of the Archbishops of Cologne, but also an

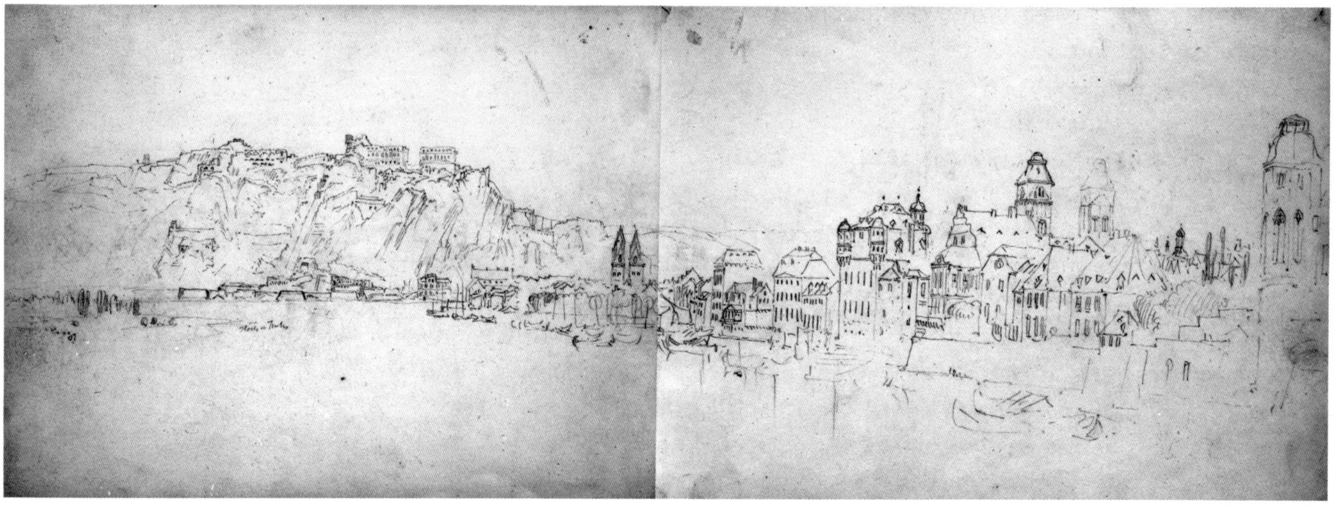

fig.18 View from the Mosel bridge at Coblenz (TB CLXI 7v–8r). Pencil, 1817

imposing sixteenth-century watchtower culminating in a gabled octagonal attic storey, several churches including the parish church with its four stately Romanesque towers, and – on the Rhine front itself – a colossal sixteenth-century crane. All these features appear many times in Turner's sketches, the details of the watchtower being especially carefully delineated, and the ruins of the castle complex being shown in all their magnificence from two different viewpoints.[24]

Turner spent two nights at Coblenz – 21 and 22 August – and thus had an entire day to study the town itself, the confluence of the Rhine and the Mosel dominated by the fortress of Ehrenbreitstein, and its environs. By far and away the greater part of his sketches depict the fortress, studied from many different viewpoints. Some of these were on the east side of the Rhine: in the village of Ehrenbreitstein at the base of the great rock; behind the fortress in the valley; and on the road southwards to Pfaffendorf, this last viewpoint having been particularly recommended by the Revd John Gardnor.[25] For all these sketches Turner used single pages in his *Waterloo and Rhine* sketchbook, reserving the large spreads of the *Rhine* sketchbook for his most ambitious sketches of all, those depicting both Ehrenbreitstein itself and Coblenz's other glory, the Mosel bridge and waterfront.[26] In one of these his viewpoint was upstream of the bridge, so that Ehrenbreitstein towers over its northern arches while the St Florinskirche and the Liebfrauenkirche appear perched over its southern ones. In the second his viewpoint must have been the bridge itself. In this the vast rocky cliff of Ehrenbreitstein is now fully revealed, as are all the multifarious medieval buildings fringing the Mosel with their spires and towers, picturesque turrets and steeply pitched roofs. Unfortunately the page with the right-hand half of this sketch is currently misplaced in the sketchbook, so it is only in a photographic reproduction that one can appreciate the full splendour of Turner's depiction of Coblenz (fig.18). For the third sketch Turner was even closer to the fortress and shows it in yet greater detail – still from across the water – together with the buildings lining the Rhine front beneath. He also made several other, smaller, sketches of the buildings in Coblenz that are visible from the Mosel front but he seems to have totally ignored the interior of the town and only to have drawn two small sketches of its Rhine front.[27] However, there is perhaps nothing odd about this, since the view of Coblenz and the confluence from the Mosel offered much greater visual interest than that from the Rhine.

As Turner walked upstream from Coblenz along the west bank on the morning of Saturday 23 August, he stopped three times to look back and gaze at the city and fortress he had left behind.[28] These sketches – previously identified as 'Ruins of a castle' and 'A bend of the river' – show an unusual aspect of the site that was to acquire a peculiar fascination for

Turner over the next twenty-five years. The ruined but still formidable fortress was clearly a compelling sight to record in detail both from Coblenz and from its southern and eastern flanks, but in these three large sketches from some miles away to the south-west, Turner recorded a very different Ehrenbreitstein in which fortress and rock are virtually one, the work of nature, not of military engineers.

The area immediately south of Coblenz and Ehrenbreitstein affords numerous splendid views: on the west bank lies the castle of Stolzenfels high above the village of Kapellen, and just at this point the Lahn flows into the Rhine from the east between Niederlahnstein and Oberlahnstein, the last-named being situated right under the shadow of Burg Lahneck. Turner drew many pencil sketches of all these subjects, some on a large scale, others within quite a small compass.[29] The 'proud rock' of Stolzenfels was the subject of his first large castle 'portrait' on the Rhine – a slightly stilted production, typical of an earlier generation of topographical artists. By contrast, his depiction of Burg Lahneck, with the landing-stage at the junction of the Lahn and the Rhine in the foreground, affords a much more dynamic composition and a more revealing glimpse of river life. Beneath the ancient ruined castle, men and horses take to the ferry, with the produce of the land, as they must have done at this very spot since time immemorial.

Both these sketches were drawn from the east bank of the Rhine to which Turner evidently crossed by ferry in order to achieve better views. He then walked a short way southwards to Braubach and the Marxburg, the third castle in this neighbourhood that he drew and the only one on the entire Middle Rhine never to have been captured and wrecked. His three fine large sketches show the Marxburg from very different viewpoints: from the fields as the traveller enters Braubach from the Lahnsteins; from among the old houses that fringe the shore at the Braubach landing-place; and from back across the river on the west bank.[30] It was the first of these views that appealed most to Turner's imagination – partly perhaps because it enshrined his first sight of this highly evocative castle, but also perhaps because it corresponded closely to that which the Revd John Gardnor had used, described and extolled (fig.19). As well as his large detailed sketch of the Marxburg from this viewpoint, Turner also made several tiny composition studies of his view, adjusting it until he felt it was totally satisfactory. He was later to return to this composition, using it as the basis for finished watercolours (see fig.23).[31]

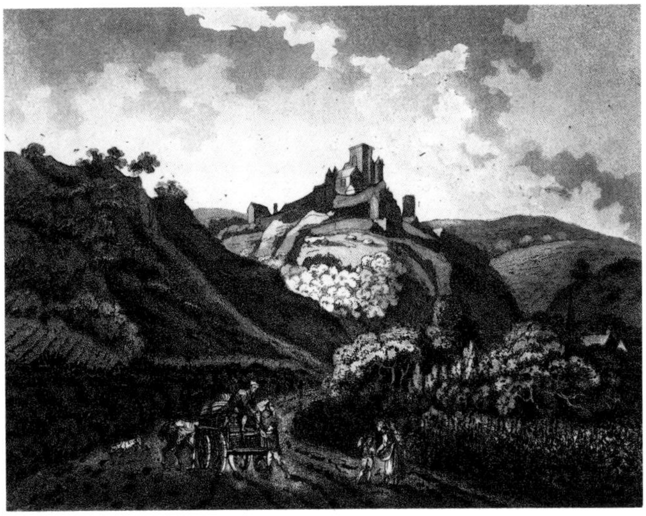

fig.19 John Gardnor and Richard Gardnor junior after John Gardnor, 'The Second View of Marxburg Castle'. Aquatint from the second edition of *Views taken on and near The River Rhine* (1792)

Above the Marxburg the Rhine winds lazily in a huge bend fringed with vineyards, with the town of Boppard on its outer curve. Turner drew several sketches of this pleasant small town and of the pilgrimage church at Bornhofen, just upstream on the opposite bank beneath the two castles traditionally believed to be those of two hostile brothers, Burg Sterrenberg and Burg Liebenstein.[32] By now he had almost reached his destination for 23 August, St Goar, and his final sketches grew increasingly rough and ready as he reached the last lap of his journey. Burg Thurnberg (almost invariably known by its nickname, 'Maus') is one of the most beautiful of the castles of the Middle Rhine, with its circular tower soaring above the compact square building below and it is situated in the most delightful spot conceivable – on a hill of its own above the Gothic church of Wellmich, commanding both upstream and downstream views. But Turner could only summon the energy to make one small sketch that recorded the ensemble at all clearly; the remaining tiny sketches show his sketching technique at its swiftest and most cursory and one can almost sense the fatigue that he must have been feeling.[33]

By the next morning he was completely back on form again. He spent the whole of Sunday 24 August exploring St Goar and its environs, crossing the Rhine to St Goarshausen opposite and making numerous fine large sketches across the double-page spreads of the *Rhine* sketchbook, showing the river, the towns and their superb castles, Burg Rheinfels and Burg Neukatzenelnbogen ('Katz'). It would be theoretically possible to assign all the sketches of these subjects to this day, but they occur in two distinct clumps in the sketchbook, making it probable that the first group belongs to 24 August, while those in the second (using viewpoints in another, quite distinct, area) date from Turner's downstream journey three days later. Turner began his sketching at St Goar by going to the waterfront and recording first the view downstream to Wellmich and Burg Maus (cat.no.3) and then that upstream to St Goarshausen and Burg Katz.[34] It was one of the features of St Goar that Turner's mentor the Revd John Gardnor had emphasised, that he could enjoy both these choice prospects from the window of his room at the inn, the Bois Vert.[35] There is no evidence that Turner himself stayed at this inn, though he could possibly have done so since it was still in existence, but in any case the two sketches just referred to were both drawn from ground level on the very edge of the river and not from inside a building. Moreover, they have two quite different viewpoints: each uses as a framing device the castle above St Goar itself, the huge and complex fortress of Burg Rheinfels which appears to frown across at the hills and castles of the opposite bank. Turner showed a third and even larger face of Burg Rheinfels by walking a little way up the side valley at its base, the Grundbachtal, from where it can be seen spread-eagled across the hills like a second Ehrenbreitstein, the only Rhine fortress to exceed it in size. He then walked along the river front at St Goar, recording views along the road and across the river with evident delight and fascination.[36]

The latter part of 24 August was spent across the Rhine near St Goarshausen from where Turner could look upstream and catch his first sight of the Lorelei, the most famous – or, from the point of view of river craft, most notorious – rocky cliff on the Middle Rhine.[37] He climbed up the hillside to get as close to Burg Katz as possible and drew several sketches looking out across to St Goar, Burg Rheinfels and the hills beyond them.[38] From here the tourist sees a new and unexpected face of the mighty Rhine, and the relationship between the gorge and the plateau is suddenly apparent. The river is seen to thread its way peacefully in a narrow channel, while high above it extend mile after mile of rolling countryside and fertile fields as far as the eye can see. For an artist of Turner's generation, trained to be sensitive to the sublime, the beautiful and the picturesque, the contrasting ingredients in the scene must have been especially captivating. He evidently lingered up on the hillside for as long as he dared, since one of his sketches shows the evening sun descending in a trail of vaporous cloud towards the hills beyond Burg Rheinfels.

On the following day Turner travelled all the way from St Goar to Mainz, around thirty-five miles, but he walked only about half this distance, as far as Bingen, where he took to a boat, almost certainly the regular passenger boat. On the first stage of this journey, the Rhine continues to be highly picturesque with many a winding curve and with brooding rocks alternating with fertile vineyards. Here, too, one village, cliff or castle succeeds another with extraordinary speed, and Turner responded to the changing scene with a multiplicity of sketches. As soon as he had recorded the diverse faces of the Lorelei, he caught his first sight of the Schönburg and many-towered Oberwesel.[39] From here he could already see Kaub, perched on the waterside between a hillside castle, Burg Gutenfels, and an island one, the Pfalz, and thus his walk continued, past castles and landing-stages, cows drinking and peasants gathering wood. At one moment, he would be sketching a castle or the buildings of a town in great detail. At the next, he would be making expansive sketches of the riverscape in which numerous villages and castles could all be glimpsed together.[40] By now he was reaching Bingen and the upper end of the Rhine gorge where the river assumes an entirely different character, tranquil, rural and peaceful. Its width is two or three times greater than below Bingen and it is bordered by low-lying land which rises above the eastern shore to the gently sloping famous vineyards of the Rheingau. Its banks are dotted with villages and the broad river itself contains numerous islands. Turner's sketches of this part of the Middle Rhine as seen from a boat are entirely different from those drawn from the riverside road further north: he swiftly divided the pages of the *Waterloo and Rhine* sketchbook into minuscule boxes and strips, often less than an inch high but sometimes as much as seven inches wide. In each he drew a low distant shore with a backdrop of hills, more or less identical but characterised by one or two carefully drawn towers or spires or a hastily scribbled name.[41] Only a very few pages were used in this fashion, but the sights they recorded were pure magic – Mainz caught between sky and water like a Venice of the North, tall churches and colourful castles sparkling across the wide glassy surface of the river. These made as deep an impression on Turner as anything else he saw on the Rhine.

At Mainz, as at Coblenz, all Turner's 1817 sketches were drawn from a quay or bridge (he was to explore both towns more thoroughly on subsequent visits, as will appear later in this catalogue). In these Mainz has an exotic, almost fairy-tale, appearance with ornate medieval and baroque buildings crowding its waterfront, and in one sketch Turner's gaze embraced not only Mainz itself but also the view downstream to the bridge of forty boats across the vast expanse of water to Kastel on the opposite bank, and beyond this to the hills of the Rheingau.[42] In 1787 the Revd John Gardnor had been informed that this bridge afforded a view of Mainz 'more beautiful than any other'. He visited it and confirmed this fact to his readers; Turner duly included a mention of the bridge in his notes from Gardnor in the *Itinerary Rhine Tour* sketchbook and later in that same sketchbook he drew his own three-page sketch of Mainz as seen from the bridge of boats. Here, as at St Goar, he followed closely in Gardnor's footsteps.[43]

After his two nights at Mainz (25 and 26 August), Turner travelled downstream back to Cologne, stopping overnight, as on his upstream journey, only at St Goar and Coblenz. He was now able to see all the previously studied sights from new angles and viewpoints, so he continued to sketch avidly, though it was frequently impossible to linger over his sketches or to choose his viewpoints since a large part of the journey was made by boat. On 27 August he made only a few sketches in the large *Rhine* sketchbook, all showing places near Bingen where he may well have waited to change boats.[44] In the *Waterloo and Rhine* sketchbook he recorded several superb views that can only be experienced from a boat in mid-stream. One shows the entrance to the Rhine gorge at Bingen, his composition bounded by Burg Klopp to the west and Burg Ehrenfels to the east, with the Mäuseturm on its island in the centre of the river and the Rhine, girdled by hills, appearing like a vast lake (see cat.no.2); another depicts the stately group of the Pfalz, Kaub and Burg Gutenfels, with a detailed separate sketch of the Pfalz, floating like a galleon, drawn as he passed between its island and the eastern bank (see under cat.no.9); others show the Lorelei, after which the downstream traveller is suddenly confronted with Burg Katz and the large square watchtower at the southern edge of St Goarshausen.[45] On the following day, Turner began by repairing an omission from his previous visit to St Goar and thoroughly explored the ruins of Burg Rheinfels. He drew many fine large sketches of the castle which reveal its enormous size before its early nineteenth-century demolition was far advanced and on his way back down to St Goar he captured a final view of the town.[46] These sketches in the *Rhine* sketchbook are followed by several others drawn from the road along the west bank, showing that for this one day of his downstream journey – 28 August – Turner was again travelling on foot, and it is not surprising that he chose to do so once more in such a dramatic area as that between St Goar and Coblenz.[47] His onward journey by boat on the following day continued to present him with familiar sights seen afresh from new viewpoints but there were few prospects that were wholly different from those already seen. However, as he approached the Drachenfels and Rolandseck, with the convent island of Nonnenwerth below, he saw a very much finer scene than the road on the west bank had afforded him earlier, for the hills appear considerably higher and the island is clearly distinguishable as such.[48] It was this sight that was to linger in his mind and haunt his imagination (see cat.no.4).

Turner's final day travelling down the Rhine was a long one, covering the 80 or so miles from Coblenz to Cologne, but his two nights at Cologne, 29 and 30 August, enabled him to make many good sketches of that city in the *Rhine* sketchbook. Most are taken from the waterfront but he also drew three outstandingly fine sketches of the cathedral and town hall (fig.20).[49] These bear witness to his early training as a copyist of architectural drawings, their accuracy in rendering complicated details appearing effortless

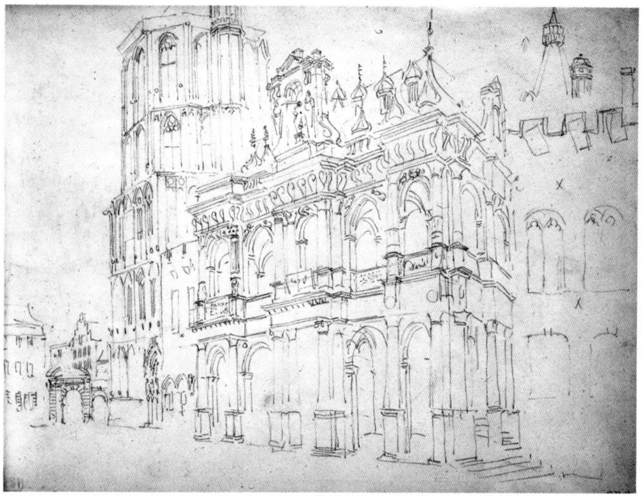

fig.20 The town hall at Cologne (TB CLXI 57r). Pencil, 1817

and never mechanical. If Turner had neglected the riches of Cologne when he first passed through the city on 18–19 August, he amply made up for this now, and when he left the Rhineland on the last day of the month, on the first stage of his journey to Holland, he took with him an abundant record not only of its enthralling landscape but also of some of its finest buildings.

Turner's first tour of the Rhineland inspired a large group of works that are one of the glories of his entire career, a series of fifty-one coloured drawings representing virtually all the celebrated sights on the river between Mainz and Cologne. These drawings were bought by Walter Fawkes – for about £500 – almost as soon as they were completed, so that the series is not represented at all in the Turner Bequest, and their dispersal in museums and private collections throughout the world makes it impossible to show more than a selection in this exhibition (cat. nos.4–11). However, the series is one of the most important and beautiful that Turner ever painted and clearly deserves close attention here.[50]

These drawings have been much misunderstood in the past, largely due to the fact that both Ruskin and Turner's first biographer, Walter Thornbury, believed them to be sketches from nature, drawn in the course of the Rhine tour itself. In 1851 Ruskin declared that Turner 'made a series of sketches on the Rhine . . . Every one of those sketches is the almost instantaneous record of an *effect* of colour or atmosphere, taken strictly from nature, the drawing and the details of every subject being comparatively subordinate'.[51] A decade later Thornbury informed his readers that on Turner's arrival in England in the autumn of 1817, he went straight to Farnley Hall where, 'Before he had even taken off his great-coat he produced these drawings rolled up slovenly and anyhow, from his breast-pocket'.[52] These statements have not only been widely regarded as accurate, but they have also led to further implausible suggestions, namely that the drawings recorded the effects Turner saw from the windows of his lodgings and that they came from one or more 'roll' sketchbooks, i.e. sketchbooks in soft covers that could be rolled up and easily carried in an artist's coat pocket.[53] All these picaresque stories must be discarded, in the face of incontrovertible evidence against them.

First, the paper on which Turner's scenes are drawn is not the kind which would have been made up into a roll sketchbook. In most cases it is a very lightweight, heavily sized writing paper which Turner would have bought in a quire of twenty-four foolscap sheets, each measuring $17 \times 13\frac{1}{2}$ inches. This he would have folded and cut with a knife to create forty-eight sheets measuring $8\frac{1}{2} \times 13\frac{1}{2}$ inches.[54] The Rhine drawings are not uniform in size or proportions, but all must have been cut to approximately their present sizes by Turner himself soon after this initial preparation. Clearly he may have used these sheets during his tour, but there is no need to postulate that he did so simply because the drawings were completed by the time he arrived at Farnley Hall. Contrary to what Thornbury stated, nearly two months elapsed between Turner's arrival in England and his visit to Farnley, providing him with ample time and opportunity to work on his drawings. Most of this time was spent at Raby Castle in County Durham where there is every reason to suppose them to have been painted.[55]

Turner's scenes were very swiftly executed, using both watercolour and gouache over pencil outlines, with broad sweeps of paint overlaid with dabs and flurries, expressive scribbles and fingerprints, while the more finished areas are characterised by delicacy rather than precision. All these practices contribute to their sketch-like appearance, as also does the fact that they were executed on paper prepared by the artist with a wash of grey. Turner used such paper for sketches for much of his working life (see, for

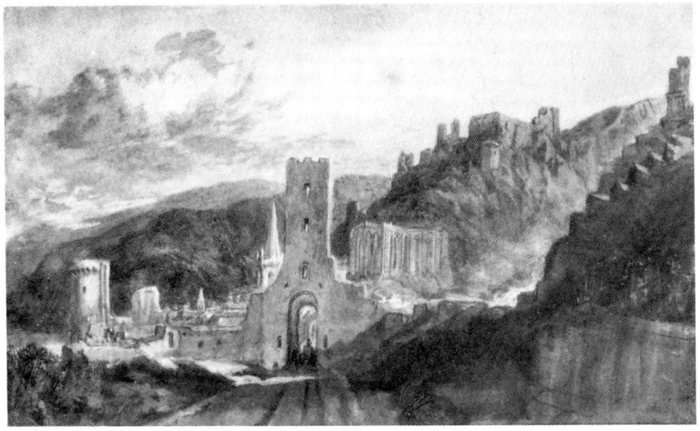

fig.21 'Bacharach and Burg Stahleck' (w 642). Gouache and watercolour on white paper prepared with a grey wash, 1817. Present whereabouts unknown

example, cat.nos.39 and 40) but he did not use it for his more formal works, the watercolours he sold and sent to exhibitions. Another aspect of the drawings that might suggest that they are sketches from nature rather than a premeditated artistic series is Turner's unashamed and repeated use of a road as his viewpoint (fig.21); yet another is the idiosyncratic, almost haphazard, nature of the subjects painted. Some very famous places, such as Bonn and Burg Maus were omitted entirely, while others (Burg Lahneck, Schloss Stolzenfels) appear only in the distance. Meanwhile there are no less than seven depictions of the Lorelei, two more or less identical views of St Goarshausen and Burg Katz, and others of scenery so undistinguished that their true subject matter long remained unidentified.[56] Nevertheless, the Rhine drawings were not painted from nature; they are based on the pencil sketches made in 1817. The topographical 'details of every subject' – which Ruskin regarded as 'comparatively subordinate' – were carefully recorded on the spot, while the effects of colour and atmosphere – which Ruskin believed to be direct transcriptions from nature – were superimposed upon these predetermined compositions out of the rich storehouse of Turner's memory.

The relationship between Turner's pencil sketches of the Rhine and his coloured scenes has hitherto received little attention,[57] but a number of important points are worth stressing. First, most of his coloured drawings are based on the pencil sketches in his *Waterloo and Rhine* sketchbook rather than those of the much larger *Rhine* sketchbook. The careful sketches of the complicated architecture of Coblenz and Ehrenbreitstein in the latter were used as a basis for two of his four drawings of those places and some of his other architectural sketches in that book contributed to his two Cologne views; but in only four other cases out of the fifty-one scenes did the sketches in the *Rhine* sketchbook play any part at all, cat.nos.6 and 7 being two of them.[58] This may seem extraordinary, given the excellence of many of the sketches in that book, but Turner evidently preferred to base his scenes on the swift and wonderfully vivid little records in the *Waterloo and Rhine* book.[59] Often a cluster of sketches there led to a similar cluster of coloured drawings, as if he had opened his sketchbook to consult it and simply carried on transforming one pencilled scene after another into the new medium of watercolour and gouache. For example, his depictions of Hammerstein and Andernach are based on sketches on the very same page, while a sequence of eighteen page-openings used between Mainz and Coblenz and crammed with sketches of many different shapes and sizes led to an identical number of coloured drawings, one of these openings alone (fig.22) leading to no less than four watercolours. It is hardly surprising that some of Turner's yellow paint got splashed onto a page in the process. Sometimes he transferred commonly observed motifs such as rafts, barges or salmon fishing boats from one part of the river to

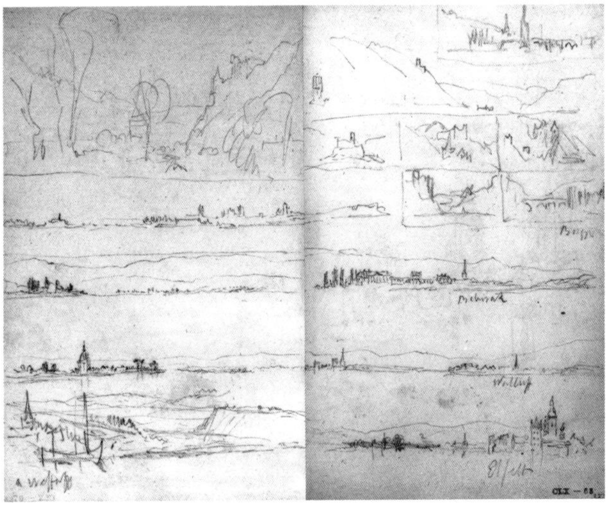

fig.22 Sketches of the Rhine between the Bautsburg and Mainz (TB CLX 67v–68r). Pencil, 1817

another, but in a conspicuously large number of instances the coloured drawings develop features which Turner had observed and quickly recorded at the very same spot: linen drying in the sun, a cow by the riverside, boats landing, a shower and a rainbow, the sun sinking behind a castle. It is easy to imagine Turner, in a quiet room at Raby Castle, working on several scenes at once: referring to his sketchbooks, washing in backgrounds, developing similar areas of sky, river or foreground simultaneously, copying or adapting motifs as the fancy took him on different days of his stay. It is hard to imagine all this taking place during the course of a tour when he was almost constantly on the move and – moreover – is known to have lost his 'Box of Colors', but it is not impossible that the initial pencil outlines were drawn while he was still abroad.

The highly variable sizes and shapes of Turner's coloured scenes were directly related not only to the scenery depicted but to the sketches on which they were based. In order to sketch the lumpy mass of the Drachenfels Turner used a double-page spread of his *Waterloo and Rhine* sketchbook which gave him a nearly square composition suitable to the subject; for his distant view of Mainz, where the Rhine reaches a width of several hundred yards, he used very different proportions, with the width of the sketch being ten times its height. The drawings based on these sketches not only follow their details but also reflect their proportions in the way in which they are composed and the same is consistently true throughout the series. The emphasis on width over height occurs not only in the two distant drawings of Mainz but also in the three of the Rheingau. All these were based on the tiny strip-like drawings in the *Waterloo and Rhine* sketchbook, which themselves were perfectly gauged to suit the river scenery Turner was recording (see cat.no.2).

If the shapes and sizes of Turner's Rhine drawings are deliberately varied, so too – and more importantly – are their moods. Poetic sublimity is the keynote at the Lorelei (cat.no.8); the picturesqueness of everyday life that at Boppard (see under cat.no.14). Calm and storm, morning, noon and evening are all evoked in incomparable fashion. In their variety, as in their execution, the scenes strike the viewer with all the acuteness and directness of sketches – hence the misinterpretations noted above – and this must have been Turner's calculated aim. It is as though he were saying to the viewer, 'This is what I actually experienced.' And were it not for the evidence of so many identical preliminary on-the-spot sketches in the *Waterloo and Rhine* and *Rhine* sketchbooks (of which both Ruskin and Thornbury were, surprisingly, unaware), every viewer would readily believe him.

Very soon after Turner's drawings had passed into the hands of Walter Fawkes, he repeated several of the scenes in that series, some with spectacular success for private purchasers, others as a commercial venture which, sadly, had to be abandoned, probably within months of its inception. Within the first of these categories are 'Biebrich Palace' and 'The Marxburg' (fig.23) which were both made for the Swinburne family, northern friends and neighbours of the Fawkes family, living at Capheaton, Northumberland.[60] These were intended simply as finished watercolours of exhibition quality (they are executed with far more precision and detail than their 1817 equivalents, on a much grander scale, and in watercolour alone on white paper), and they were commissioned either by the 6th Baronet, Sir John Swinburne, or his son Edward after they had seen and admired the drawings owned by Fawkes. Turner was already on very friendly terms with the Swinburne family whom he had known for some time. He had taught painting to Lady Swinburne's sister Julia in the 1790s and remained in touch with her and, later on, her husband Sir James Willoughby Gordon, for the next thirty years, painting three oil paintings specifically for the couple, while Sir John Swinburne himself had bought an oil painting from Turner in 1813.[61] The early history of another detailed enlargement, 'Burg Sooneck with Bacharach in the Distance' (cat.no.17), is not yet known, but 'Cologne from the River' was painted for Turner's close friend, James Rivington Wheeler (1758–1834).[62] He bought this some time between 1818 and 1820 for thirty guineas, which may well be an indication of the prices paid by the Swinburnes for their works, by the owner of 'Burg Sooneck' and perhaps also by the equally unknown first owner of another superb large watercolour of this period 'Kaub and the Castle of Gutenfels' (cat.no.20). This last work, however, has no counterpart in the Fawkes Rhine series which makes the circumstances of its commission all the more intriguing and it may well be that Turner would have charged a higher fee

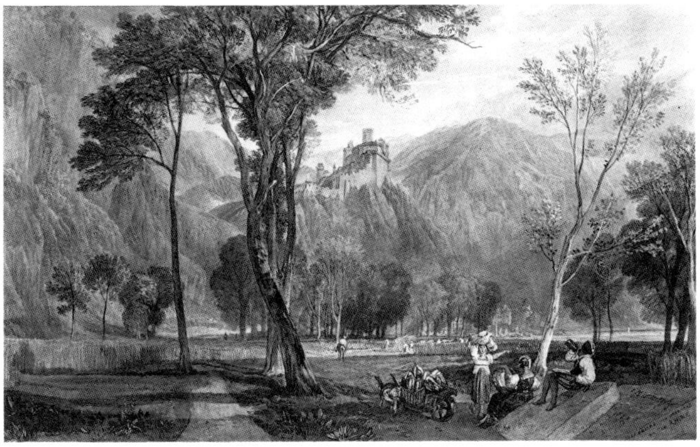

fig.23 'The Marxburg' (w 692). Watercolour, 1820. British Museum

for producing it. Much thought went into its planning, as can be seen from the related colour studies in the Turner Bequest (cat.nos.18 and 19), a production stage absent from the Fawkes drawings but part of Turner's regular working practice when it came to important watercolour commissions.

The years around 1819–20 saw not only the production of these magnificent watercolours but also the sad failure of a publishing venture whereby Turner was to have produced a series of thirty-six Rhine views for engraving in a book to be published by the firm of John Murray in conjunction with W.B. Cooke, the printseller with whom Turner so often collaborated. The manuscript contract for this once belonged to Ruskin who took particular pride in owning it, since it had been signed by Turner on the very day after that on which Ruskin himself had been born. Although the project came to nothing, its detailed programme is nevertheless worth recording:[63]

> Agreement between J.M.W. Turner, Esq., W.B. Cooke, and J.C. Allen, February the Ninth, One Thousand Eight Hundred and Nineteen.
>
> Mr. Turner agrees to make Thirty Six Drawings on the Rhine, between Cologne and Mayence, at the Price of Seventeen Guineas each Drawing. – The first Two Drawings to be made in advance, which are to be paid out of the Profits of the Work. – The Second Two Drawings to be paid by W.B. Cooke in June 1819, and the rest to be paid on delivery.
>
> It is agreed that none of the Drawings shall be sold for less than Thirty-four Guineas each under the Penalty of One Hundred Guineas. Mr. Turner to be paid Two Pounds on the Sale of every Five Hundred Numbers. The Plates to be estimated at Fifty Guineas each – they are to be the Size of Eleven Inches and a half by Eight Inches and a Quarter.
>
> The Work to be divided as follows, – Mr. Turner to hold one Eighth Share, W.B. Cooke to hold Five Eighths of the Work, J.C. Allen to hold Two Eighths. The Work to pay its Expenses by its returns before any Dividend is made between the Parties.
>
> Mr. Turner to have a best copy of the Work, with Etchings.
>
> A Settlement for all Numbers and Copies sold, to be made at regular half Yearly periods within a Week after Mr. Murray settles his half Yearly Accounts on the Work.
>
> When Seven Drawings are made for the Work, Mr. Turner to have one of them by casting lots. When the second Seven are made, a like casting of Lots to take Place for one of them. The Third Seven the same. The fourth Seven the same, and Mr. Turner to have the casting of lots for one out of the remaining Eight.
>
> No other Engraver to be employed in the Work than W.B. Cooke, and J.C. Allen, without the Consent of Mr. Turner. It is agreed that three Numbers containing Two Plates each shall be published in a Year, and that the Proofs shall be printed in Imperial Folio. The Prints in Quarto Grand Eagle French Paper. The first Number, which is to contain Two Plates, to be published during the Year 1819.
>
> JOS. MALLORD W. TURNER.
> W.B. COOKE.
> J.C. ALLEN

The failure of this endeavour was undoubtedly due to the appearance of another series of engraved Rhine views in 1819–20, the English version of a book that had already appeared in Germany in 1818 by Baron Johann von Gerning. *A Picturesque Tour along the Rhine, from Mentz to Cologne*, with von Gerning's text translated by John Black and illustrated with twenty-four engravings, chiefly by Thomas Sutherland after drawings by C.G. Schütz, appeared in six regular monthly parts from October 1819 to March 1820, over the imprint of Rudolph Ackermann's publishing house in the Strand. On hearing news of this – or perhaps seeing the first advertisements in the press in August 1819[64] – W.B. Cooke and Turner met in order to discuss how Ackermann could be bought off and prevented from going ahead with von Gerning's book.[65] This manoeuvre clearly failed to work, if indeed their plan was ever finalised and discussed with Ackermann. The rival monthly parts duly appeared and received much critical acclaim. Von Gerning was, after all, a person of some consequence both at home and abroad, being intimate not only with all the leading German intellectuals and writers of his age but also many of its ruling princes. When the six parts of his work were issued as a single volume in 1820, it was fulsomely dedicated to George IV with a reminder of their personal acquaintanceship and the many royal and political connections between their two countries.[66]

Meanwhile Turner's publishing project came to nothing. He abandoned at least one work (cat.no.14) and the few he had completed began to be dispersed. W.B. Cooke's accounts show that he bought three of Turner's Rhine views in 1822 for twenty-seven guineas each.[67] These three must certainly have included 'Osterspey and Feltzen' and 'Neuwied and Weissenthurm' (W 688, W 689), which he exhibited at his Soho Square gallery in 1823, by which time they were owned by James Slegg.[68] The third must have been the similarly sized 'Ehrenbreitstein' (W 687) which was the only Turner Rhine scene which J.C. Allen would come to engrave, albeit not until 1824 (R 202). All these views closely resemble Turner's depictions of the same scenes in the Fawkes series, but they are executed with far greater precision and care, and with additional foreground incidents (see under cat.no.5), so that the full extent of the loss to posterity of Turner's engraved Rhine series is felt all the more acutely. As for Turner's own feelings, if he ever discovered that Fawkes himself had actually subscribed to von Gerning's rival publication, these are best left to the imagination.[69]

The 1820s and the First Meuse–Mosel Tour

It was several years before Turner paid any further visits to the Low Countries and the Rhineland but these visits – and the paintings in which they resulted – are among the most fascinating of his achievements. It is only now, in this exhibition and catalogue, that the correct order and chronology of the north European tours of the 1820s and 1830s is being established and, although it is too soon to claim that Turner's study of the Meuse and the Mosel is understood in its entirety, much has become clear. Both of his principal tours of these rivers have been wrongly dated in the past (the first to 1826 instead of 1824, the second to 1834 instead of 1839), so that a much longer period separated the two tours than has previously been thought. Although their itineraries were nearly identical, Turner organised his two tours in very different ways. His other visits to these same rivers took place in the years between his two major tours rather than following the second. Finally, the series of about a hundred brilliant gouaches on blue paper of Belgium, Germany, France and Luxembourg were all inspired by Turner's second tour of the Mosel valley and the Ardennes, not by the first, as was once believed. These superb works can now be appreciated for what they really are: the triumphant culmination of a long-standing relationship between Turner and the landscape he studied which had begun during an intensive summer of sketching no less than fifteen years earlier.

Turner's first Meuse–Mosel tour – which also took him back to part of the Middle Rhine – is recorded in four sketchbooks, each of which has its own special characteristics (cat.nos.37–40). By far

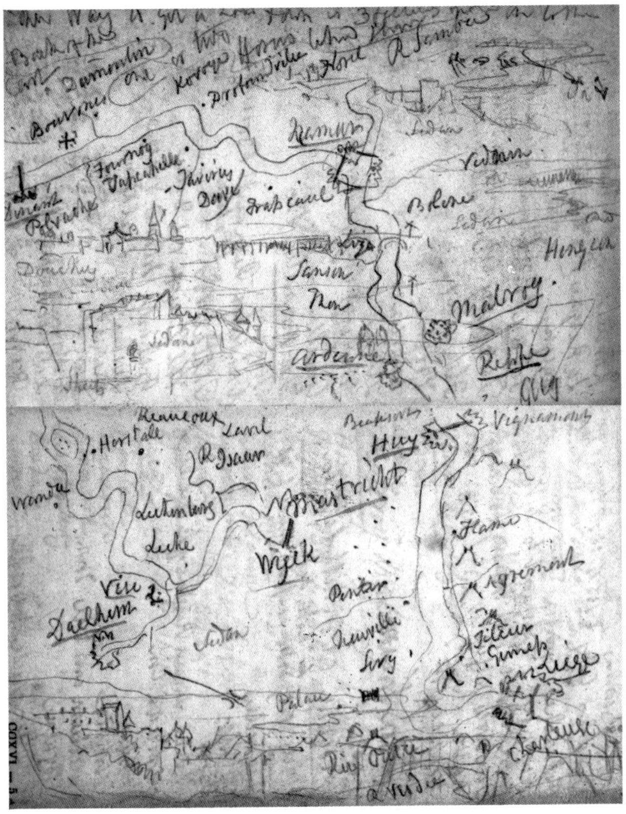

fig.24 Sketch maps of the Meuse between Maastricht and Dinant (TB CCXVI 4v–5r). Pencil with red and blue pencil underlining and symbols, 1824

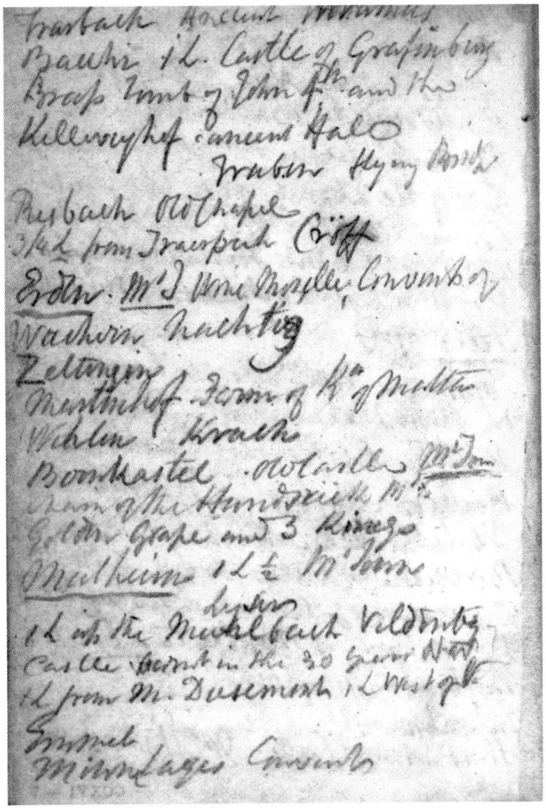

fig.25 Notes on the Mosel between Trarbach and Minheim, copied from A. Schreiber, *The Traveller's Guide down the Rhine* (TB CCXVI 7v). Pencil with red pencil underlining, 1824

the most important for the understanding of the tour as a whole is that with the smallest pages, the *Rivers Meuse and Moselle* sketchbook (TB CCXVI; cat.no.37), an upright book scarcely bigger than a pocket diary but containing 270 pages and stoutly bound in leather. Into this book (as with the *Itinerary Rhine Tour* sketchbook of 1817; cat.no.1) Turner wrote several pages of useful notes before he set off on his travels, providing himself with data concerning mileages, inns and sights worth seeing. Here, too, he drew himself tiny sketch maps of the Meuse and the Mosel, complete with the names of numerous villages (fig.24). The source for Turner's notes on the Mosel between Trier and Coblenz and his maps of the same stretch of the river was the 'Third Excursion' in Alois Schreiber's guidebook, *The Traveller's Guide down the Rhine*, of which he himself owned a copy of the first English edition of 1818 (cat.no.36).[1] This book had not yet been available in English at the time of his 1817 visit to the Rhineland and, although he was certainly aware of its existence in both French and German,[2] his ignorance of these languages would have prevented him from actually making use of it.[3] From 1815 onwards English travellers on the Continent gradually became very much better provided for than they had been in the previous two decades and now, thanks to Schreiber's book and his own notes, Turner would have been able to travel down the Mosel in full awareness of all the sights it had to offer (fig.25).

The *Rivers Meuse and Moselle* sketchbook opens with Turner's preparatory notes and closes with the timetable of his tour, probably written once it was all completed rather than in instalments as he went along (fig.26). Through this it can be seen that he left for his tour on 10 August, reached the Meuse at Liège on the 13th and then travelled up river as far as Verdun where he was on the 23rd. From here he

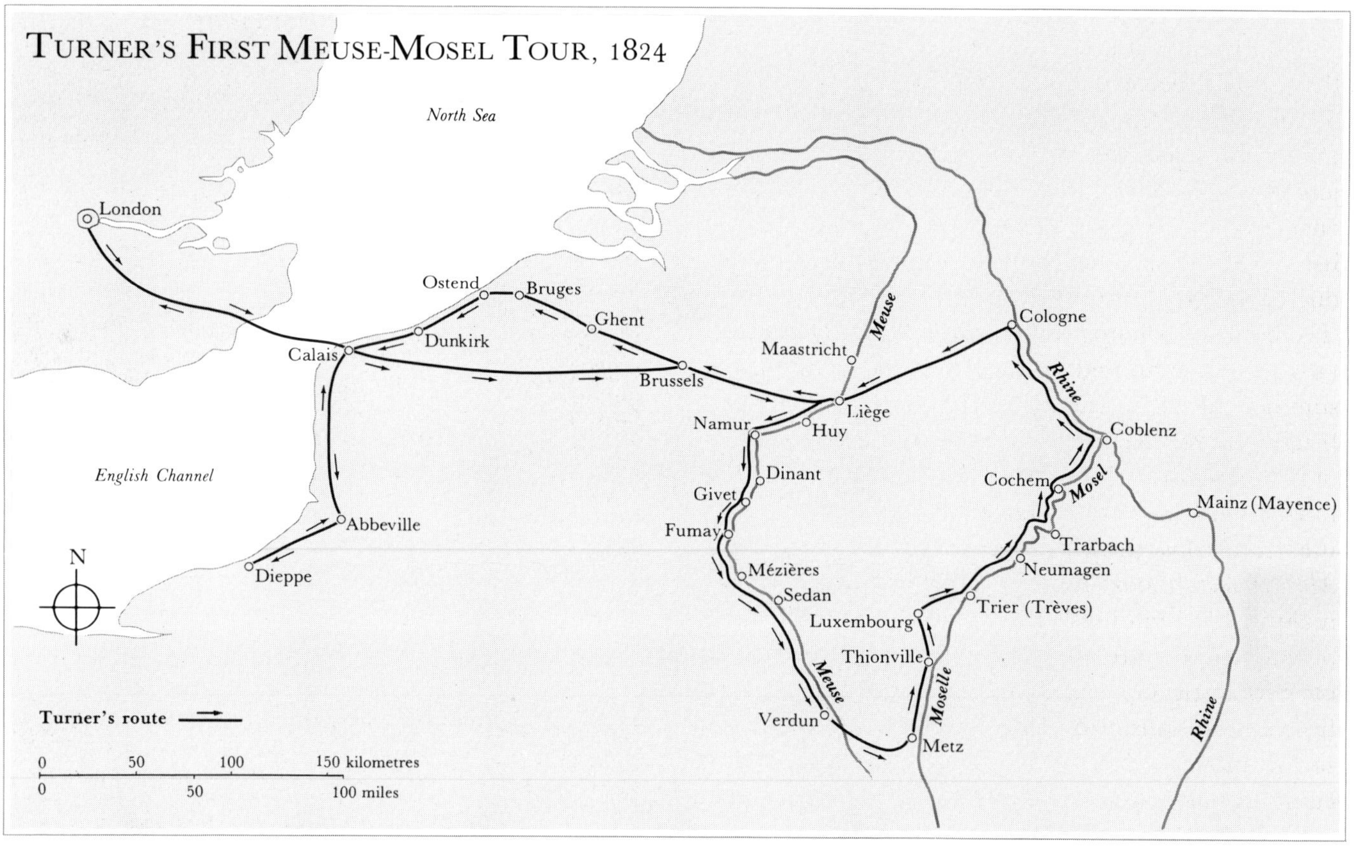

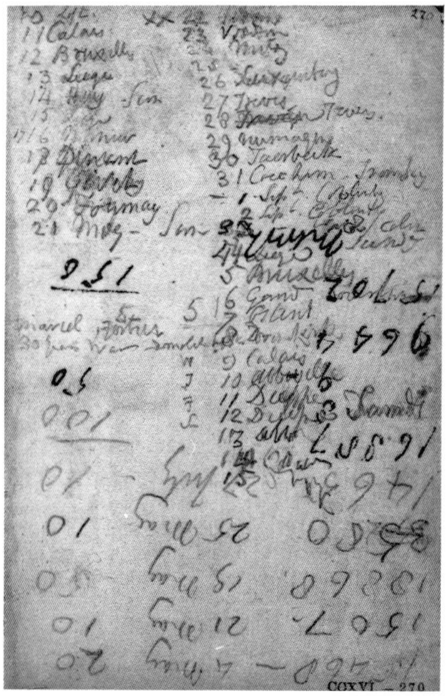

fig.26 Turner's timetable of his first Meuse–Mosel tour (TB CCXVI 270r). Pencil, 1824

went eastwards to the Mosel south of Metz, then north to Luxembourg, and he reached Trier on 27 August. He then travelled down the Mosel, arriving at Coblenz on 1 September, down the Rhine to Cologne and back across Belgium to northern France where he spent several days before sailing home. The form of the very last entries, '14 Calais 15' followed by a blank space, makes it virtually certain that on 15 September Turner reached home or, at any rate, England.

Turner's apparently straightforward list is complicated by the fact that at several points he added the names (or initial letters of the names) of the days of the week, now in French, now in English, and often in a self-contradictory manner. Turner's tour has traditionally been dated to 1826, following the suggestion of A.J. Finberg in 1909, who read two of the annotations in the centre of Turner's list as 'Sun(day)' and regarded them as applying to the dates on their right.[4] They must definitely, however, be related to the words and dates on their left (to which they are linked by Turner's own dashes) and they should be read not as 'Sun' but as 'Sam' (i.e. Samedi or Saturday). This would be correct for 1824. However, the strongest proof that Turner's journey took place in 1824 is provided by the presence – in the *Rivers Meuse and Moselle* sketchbook itself – of the sketches Turner used as the basis for one of the greatest oil paintings of his middle years, 'Harbour of Dieppe (Changement de Domicile)' (B & J 231), exhibited at the Royal Academy in the summer of 1825 (fig.27). Although Turner had briefly visited Dieppe in 1821, that visit resulted in only the slightest of sketches.[5] His oil painting cannot have been based on these but clearly derives from the numerous drawings in the *Rivers Meuse and Moselle* sketchbook: here the harbour at Dieppe, its magnificent buildings, its massed boats and its colourful local life are all recorded in meticulous detail over some twenty pages, accompanied by a host of little annotations, providing Turner with exactly the sort of material from which to work up a large and complex painting over the ensuing winter (fig.28).[6]

Once it is clear that Turner's first Meuse–Mosel tour was made in 1824, certain features about the sketchbooks he used there fall easily into place. His timetable shares a page with financial calculations relating to 1823–4. The last entry is for 26 July 1824, just a fortnight before the start of his tour, and it seems entirely natural both that Turner should have chosen this particular moment to take stock of his financial position, and that he should have done so in the same notebook that he was currently using for all his other memoranda. Meanwhile two of the other sketchbooks used on the Mosel (cat.nos.39 and 40) contain paper manufactured in 1823 and 1824. These soft-bound books which could be rolled up and stowed away in a coat pocket were the first sketchbooks of this particular type used by Turner on a foreign tour; clearly they were bought immediately before the tour and expressly for it.

Another significant event in Turner's career also becomes clearer once the first Meuse–Mosel tour is correctly assigned to 1824. During the 1820s and 1830s he was also making tours studying other Continental rivers, most notably the Loire and the Seine, which he depicted in three famous series of gouaches in 1830–4. His only known visit to the Loire must have taken place in 1826, since he could not have

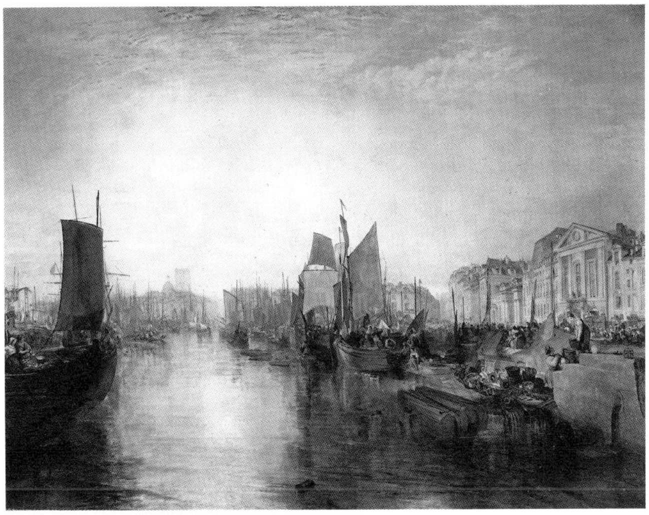

fig.27 'Harbour of Dieppe (Changement de Domicile)' (B & J 231). Oil on canvas, RA 1825. The Frick Collection, New York

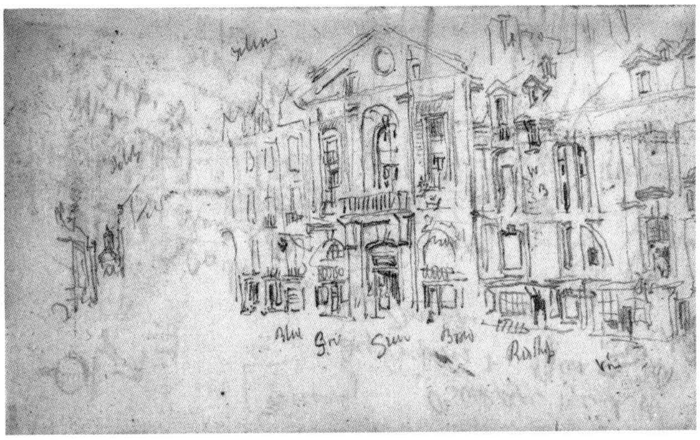

fig.28 The harbour at Dieppe (TB CCXVI 223v). Pencil, 1824

gone there at any other time in the 1820s and in 1829 he exhibited the oil painting entitled 'The Banks of the Loire' (B & J 329, now untraced) at the Royal Academy. It used to be postulated that this visit was squeezed into the later part of September and early October 1826, after the Meuse–Mosel tour was over, though it has never been satisfactorily explained precisely how Turner reached the Loire from Calais, nor why such an important and disparate French tour should have been tacked on to the other one with almost indecent haste. It now seems certain that Turner toured the Loire in the summer of 1826 at an ordinary and more leisurely pace, during the months of August and September.[7]

There were numerous reasons why Turner should have been interested in revisiting the Rhine and exploring further afield in Germany and Belgium in the early 1820s. In 1822 Wordsworth published his *Memorials of a Tour on the Continent, 1820* which included not only the ethereal evocation of the Meuse between Liège and Namur (see above, p.14) but also recollections of Bruges, Aachen and Cologne. The early months of 1823 brought not only the death of Mrs Ann Radcliffe and obituaries recalling her dynamic writings about the Rhine in the 1790s but also the publication of Sir Walter Scott's celebrated novel *Quentin Durward* of which the most thrilling passages are set in Liège and in the countryside of the Ardennes.[8] By then Samuel Prout's lithographs of Rhine subjects were also beginning to appear and, most important of all, May 1824 saw the first of the twelve parts making up Captain Robert Batty's *Scenery of the Rhine, Belgium and Holland* which was greeted with much acclaim by the reviewers. Of the sixty fine steel engravings that appeared in this work between 1824 and 1826, half depicted Germany, half the Low Countries. Turner could hardly fail to have taken note of this publication since it was only a very short time since its companion volume, *Batty's Italian Scenery* (the work of Robert's sister Elizabeth), and his own very similar work for James Hakewill's *Picturesque Tour of Italy* (1818–20) had run a neck-and-neck race in competing for the public's attention.[9] Furthermore, in 1824 Turner himself was thoroughly involved in the production of watercolours for engraving in yet another part-work, *The Rivers of England*, published in seven instalments by W.B. Cooke between 1823 and a somewhat abrupt termination in 1827. By August 1824, six of Turner's scenes had been published, all engraved in mezzotint, three by Charles Turner, three by Thomas Lupton, and the project still seemed set fair to succeed. At this stage it might well have occurred to Cooke that Turner's depictions of English rivers could profitably be followed by others of Continental rivers; and, despite the failure of the Cooke Rhine project of 1819, Turner may well have set off for the Meuse and the Mosel with such an idea – alas, never to be realised – foremost in his mind.

The earliest stages of Turner's tour – which took him via Calais and Brussels to Liège on 10–13 August – are recorded in a mere dozen or so pages of small and hastily drawn pencil sketches in the *Rivers Meuse and Moselle* sketchbook and, were it not for his manuscript timetable, his precise route would probably remain unknown. At Liège, however, he started using another, somewhat larger, sketchbook of horizontal format (*Huy and Dinant*; TB CCXVII; cat.no.38) alongside the tiny one and continued to use the two simultaneously for the ensuing week, during which he explored the Belgian part of the Meuse up as far as Dinant. His method of doing so was not straightforward: having reached Liège and spent the night of 13 August there, he immediately travelled up river to Huy, staying there for the night of the 14th. He then went back to Liège for another night, after which he headed up river again, on past Huy to Namur.[10] After two nights there, 16 and 17 August, he carried on southwards to Dinant. This stretch of the river presented Turner with innumerable impressive sights and much beautiful scenery which many of his contemporaries rated even more highly than that of the Rhine. He sketched incessantly, often drawing several scenes on the same small page as he had done along the Rhine in 1817, but using the slightly larger sketchbook for his more careful pencil drawings in the towns where he stayed overnight.

From the small sketches recording every sight along the Meuse as it came into view it is clear that Turner travelled upstream in a boat or barge towed by horses. His viewpoints are sometimes in mid-river, sometimes close to the shore but not actually on it; he shows other boats immediately adjacent and on the same level as himself; and annotations such as 'Horses obliged to swim' or 'Horses again across the River' are undoubtedly memoranda of his own travel experiences.[11] At various places between Liège and Namur it was necessary for the horses to pull the boats and barges not from a towpath but from the middle of the river, a dangerous task for both horse and rider since the river bed was full of holes, and a spare horse was always on board the passenger-barge in case of accidents.[12] Clearly the vicissitudes of travel up the Meuse were not on a par with the shock of being tumbled into the snow whilst crossing the Alps, but Turner's Belgian notes are nevertheless a characteristic response from one to whom the incidents of travel had a perennial appeal. Towards the end of this same tour, on 6 September,

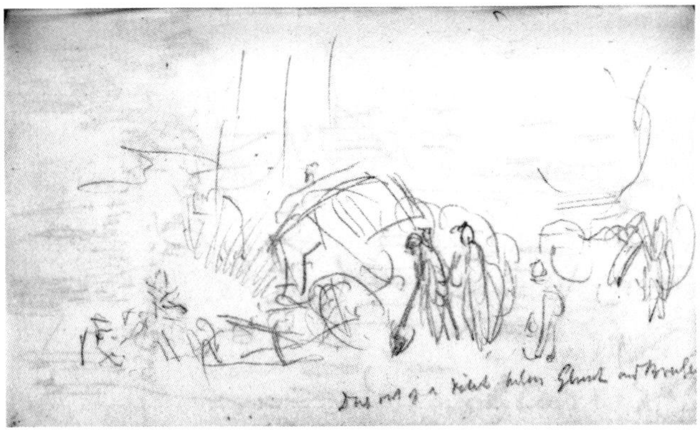

fig.29 The overturned diligence (TB CCXVI 154v). Pencil, 1824

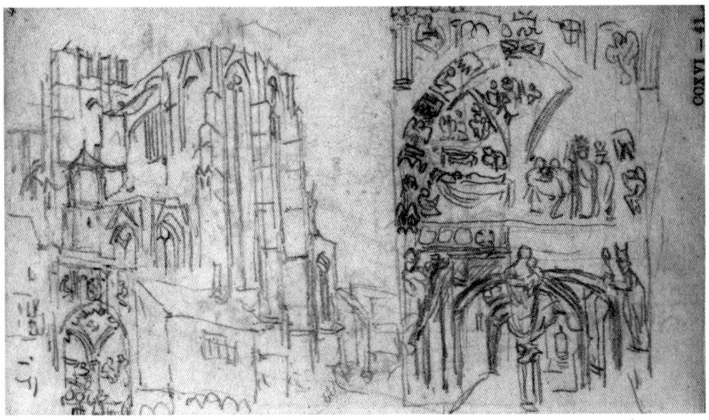

fig.30 The Bethlehem portal at Huy (TB CCXVI 41r). Pencil, 1824

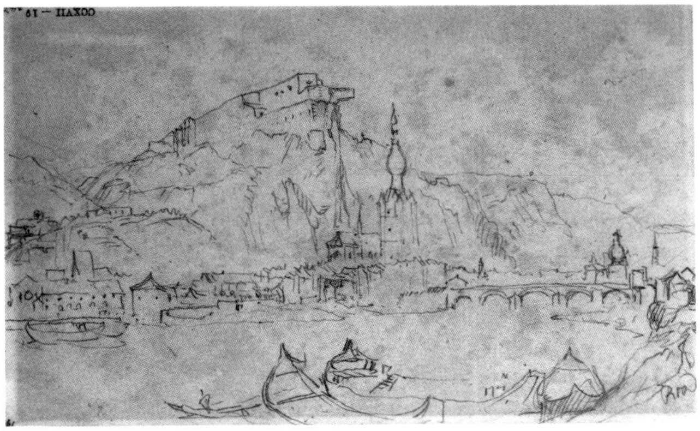

fig.31 The citadel and church at Dinant (TB CCXVII 19r). Pencil, 1824

he was to record a more serious occurrence, this time on land, when his overturned diligence had to be 'Dug out of a ditch between Ghent and Brussels' (fig.29).[13] This drawing uncannily prefigures his well-known watercolour of 1829, '*Messieurs les Voyageurs* on their return from Italy (*par la diligence*) in a snow drift upon Mount Tarrar' (W 405), so it is likely that this work brings together the Belgian accident and that in the Alps, and possibly other comparable incidents in which Turner had been involved. His most powerful works usually sprang from just such a process of synthesis, of which further prime examples will appear at the end of this section.

Travelling along the Meuse in 1824 his eye was caught by a variety of different sights: its lofty rocks, fine old buildings such as the castle of Chokier (cat.no.37), the abbey of Flône and the mansion at Neuville-sous-Huy but chiefly by its towns.[14] At Huy he drew several detailed sketches of the stone bridge, the medieval church and the recently completed fort (cat.no.38), recording not only the church as a whole but also its celebrated Bethlehem portal with fourteenth-century reliefs of the nativity (fig.30).[15] At Liège he concentrated on the Pont des Arches, depicting it in both upstream and downstream views.[16] At Namur his entire attention was, naturally, taken by the confluence of the Meuse and the Sambre beneath its massive citadel.[17] At Dinant he was plainly captivated by the picturesqueness of its church, bridge and fort, the ancient church with its bulbous spire contrasting so strongly with the hard straight lines of the newly built fort perched high above it.[18] Nearly all Turner's best sketches of Dinant show it from the west bank looking downstream, which is indeed the finest spot from which to enjoy its eye-catching charm, but from a historical point of view his upstream views are the most interesting since they record in precise detail the Dinant of the early 1820s (fig.31). Although the fort had been finished in 1821, in 1824 it still retained the hoist used in its building, which brought the stone from the barges of the Meuse up to their final destination over 100 yards above (fig.32). By the time Turner next visited Dinant in the 1830s this had been removed (see cat.nos.42, 96–9).

Although Turner certainly travelled along many parts of the Meuse by boat, he also explored other stretches on foot and just south of Dinant he left the river and walked from Anseremme to Givet along

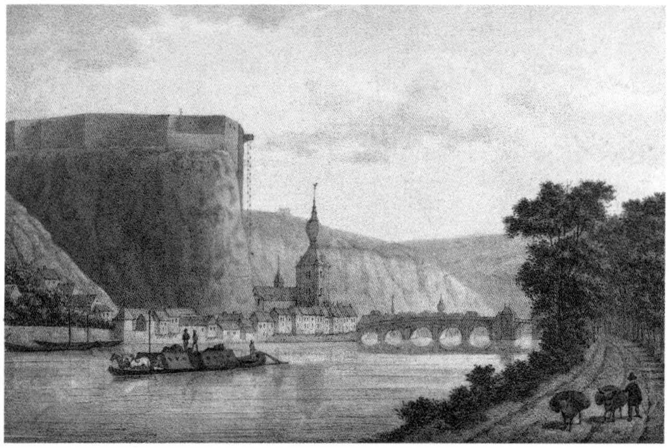

fig.32 Unknown artist, 'Vue de la Ville, et de la Citadelle de Dinant'. Mixed media, early nineteenth century. Private Collection

the road, thus taking a much shorter route and achieving numerous good views of the distant town and Fort Charlemont from the higher ground.[19] By now he was on French soil where he remained for almost a week, staying successively in Givet (19 August), Fumay (20th), Mézières (21st), Sedan (22nd), Verdun (23rd) and Metz (24th and 25th). After Givet he stopped using the *Huy and Dinant* sketchbook and for several days drew only in the small *Rivers Meuse and Moselle* book; none of the other fortified towns along the French part of the Meuse received anything like the detailed attention which had been accorded to the Belgian ones on his overnight stops the week before.[20] It is not entirely clear why this should have happened, but the distances between some of the French Meuse towns are much greater than between the Belgian ones. A number of Turner's sketches suggest that he was by now sometimes travelling by the diligence and it is quite possible that the rigorous timetable this imposed, with departures at dawn and arrivals at dusk, would have given him little opportunity for sketching.

At Verdun, or shortly afterwards, Turner left the Meuse and travelled across country to the Moselle south of Metz, drawing on his way a dozen or so small sketches of the remaining arches of the fine Roman aqueduct spanning the Moselle at Ancy and Jouy-aux-Arches.[21] From Metz his journey by diligence took him northwards through Thionville to Luxembourg of which he really only enjoyed the briefest of glimpses and recorded at breakneck speed.[22] From Luxembourg he sped on again, reaching German territory, where the Moselle becomes the Mosel, just above Trier.[23] By now it was 27 August, he was exactly halfway through his tour and he had come to the second river he wished to study. He spent two nights here, obviously revelling in the city and its situation. His pencil sketches in the *Rivers Meuse and Moselle* book ceased being scribbles and jottings and became once more tiny miracles of subtlety and precision. He brought out an as yet unused large sketchbook (*Trèves and Rhine*; TB CCXVIII; cat.no.39) and started to work in it in watercolours; the sketches in this book – on pages already tinted with a grey wash – are Turner's only coloured drawings of the Meuse or the Mosel dating from this tour, all the gouaches on blue paper previously associated with it (cat.nos.47–127) having now been recognised as being inspired by his second. In short, in Turner's work at Trier there is a sense not only of arrival and fulfilment but also of great enjoyment.[24]

The same pleasure in his surroundings is evident in the sketches made over the following four days during which he travelled by boat down the Mosel, stopping overnight at Neumagen (29 August), Trarbach (30th) and Cochem (31st). He reached the confluence with the Rhine at Coblenz on 1 September. Sailing, drifting or being rowed down the Mosel with its current over a period of three or four days was the standard means of seeing the river at this period, for the land route was tediously long, the roads poor and it was to be seventeen years before a steamer service could take passengers from Trier to Coblenz in a matter of hours. In the 1820s and 1830s travellers would either take the regular public passage boat or hire a boat and boatmen to convey them down the river. A Mosel voyage very comparable to Turner's was enjoyed by Mary Shelley, widow of the poet, in June 1840 and she later described both its delights and its drawbacks: the ravishing scenery and the miserable inns; the golden evenings with their sense of peace and the 'chill, white, and dank' misty mornings when they passed many barges being 'towed up the stream by horses up to their middles in the cold foggy river'.[25] She and her companions hired a boat with an awning, directed by a queer-looking old man who steered and two youths at the oars and, by dint of early rising, they travelled all the way from Trier to Coblenz with only two overnight stops on land. Turner's journey took a whole day longer, giving him more opportunities for sketching and study.

As Mary Shelley remarked, 'The finest scenery of the Moselle occurs after leaving Trarbach',[26] so Turner's third day on the Mosel would undoubtedly have been its high point. Along the stretch he saw on the first day, between Trier and Neumagen, the Mosel winds its way placidly in huge curves through low vine-clad hills dotted with villages, each with its own small church and huddle of houses. Turner recorded everything he could, dividing up the small pages of the *Rivers Meuse and Moselle* sketchbook into eight or nine tiny rectangles – even smaller than those he had created for his 1817 Rhine sketches.[27] He turned his head constantly in order to catch the views both up- and downstream before they changed and disappeared, and sometimes he not only numbered his sketches but also took compass bearings so that he himself at a later date would be able to recall in complete detail his experiences of the river (fig.33). This meticulous practice, however, was largely abandoned after the first day. From then on, as the course of the Mosel became more tortuous, its hills and villages more spectacular, Turner was far too occupied in recording castles and churches, ferries and flying bridges to keep an eye on the compass. Simply naming the villages on his sketches was both easier and potentially more useful.

Travelling as he did, Turner had very little opportunity for exploring the villages of the Mosel valley or for climbing the hills that line it in order to gain a different perspective on the landscape (both these deficiencies were, it will be seen, to be remedied on his second major Meuse–Mosel tour, making his return to this territory a very different experience). However, his overnight stop at Trarbach gave him the chance to make a few full-page sketches not only of its river front but also of gabled medieval houses at a street corner in the town and of a butcher's shop where he recorded 'Dogs and Cats' prowling around beneath the carcasses.[28] At his next overnight stop, at Cochem, he also made careful full-page sketches, this time only of views along its river front, which was and remains the most densely and most picturesquely built up of any town on this stretch of the river.[29] Meanwhile he had also started using his fourth sketchbook of the tour (*Moselle or Rhine*; TB CCXIX; cat.no.40) where he made about thirty pencil drawings on pages which he had previously

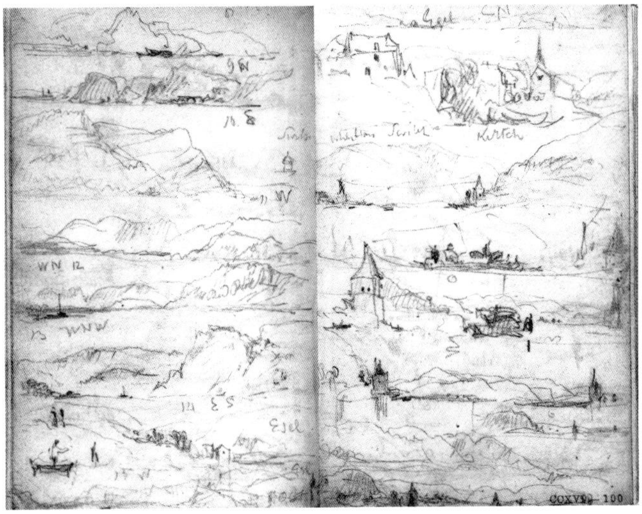

fig.33 Sketches of the Mosel between Ehrang and Kirsch, marked with compass bearings (TB CCXVI 99v–100r). Pencil, 1824

prepared with a grey-tinted wash. These swift but beautiful sketches, in many of which the pencil work is now barely discernible against its grey background, cannot have taken Turner long to draw. They record a number of places he passed on the second and third days of his journey down the Mosel and were presumably drawn when the boatmen periodically moored up against the river bank.

When Turner reached Coblenz on 1 September he had a fortnight still to go before crossing the Channel back to England, but only a small part of that time was devoted to the Rhine and the Meuse. During his two-night stay at Coblenz he returned to some of his favourite subjects of 1817, sketching the fortress of Ehrenbreitstein and making a short detour, probably on foot, up the east bank of the Rhine as far as its junction with the Lahn.[30] Travelling down the Rhine to Cologne he sketched Andernach and Hammerstein, the Seven Hills and Cologne itself, but only very cursorily.[31] The road journey by diligence to Liège (4 September), Brussels (5th) and Ghent (6th) led only to pages of disjointed scribbles and illegible notes dashed off at top speed and the same is true of his journey by canal boat from Ghent through Bruges to Ostend.[32] After reaching Ostend on 7 September he headed south into France and proceeded to spend six days in Calais, Abbeville and Dieppe before catching the boat home from Calais.[33]

Turner's first visit to the Meuse and the Mosel was undoubtedly a productive one in terms of pencil sketches (in the smallest sketchbook alone, there must be well over a thousand) but it did not lead directly to finished watercolours or oils encapsulating his experiences on these rivers. The most important product of his 1824 tour was, as was mentioned earlier, his 1825 oil painting 'Harbour of Dieppe (Changement de Domicile)', the fruit of his two days of intensive study there on 11 and 12 September. 'Dieppe' had been commissioned by a Mr John Broadhurst before Turner's departure from London, which accounts for the last lap of this tour having taken place at all. However, it may be suggested that he would not have responded so sensitively to the harbour of Dieppe, and later depicted it with such magical intensity, if he himself had not spent the preceding five weeks travelling up and down rivers on a variety of craft, observing sunshine and reflections on water, tying up endlessly at one landing stage after another, watching cargoes being loaded and unloaded each day and sleeping in a different town or village nearly every night. By grafting his experiences of the Meuse and the Mosel on to those of Dieppe itself, he produced a masterpiece.

Mr John Broadhurst also commissioned a companion to 'Dieppe'. This was Turner's first oil painting of a Rhine subject, 'Cologne, The Arrival of a Packet Boat, Evening' (B&J 232), which was exhibited exactly a year later, at the Royal Academy of 1826 (fig.34). In the summer of 1825 Turner made a comprehensive tour of Holland after which he journeyed up the Rhine as far as Cologne, across country westwards to Aachen and Liège and then briefly down the Meuse to Maastricht before he travelled on once more to Ostend. This tour lies outside the scope of the present exhibition,[34] but a few points about it should nevertheless be made, since the redating of Turner's first Meuse–Mosel tour to 1824 makes the tour of 1825 his third visit to Germany and the Low Countries, not the second as previously thought.

Turner had evidently found his method of data collection in 1824 highly convenient and in 1825 he repeated it almost exactly. He simultaneously used a small fat upright sketchbook for quick records, sometimes in minuscule compartments, and a slightly larger book of horizontal format for more expansive sketches, usually stretching over two pages at once.[35]

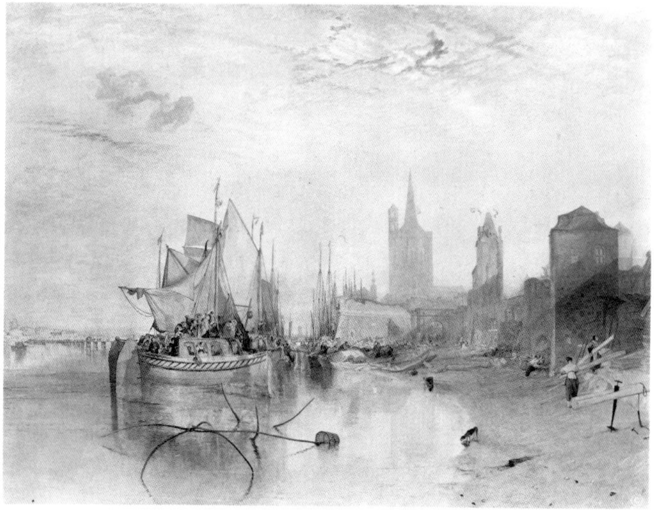

fig.34 'Cologne, The Arrival of a Packet Boat, Evening' (B&J 232). Oil on canvas, RA 1826. The Frick Collection, New York

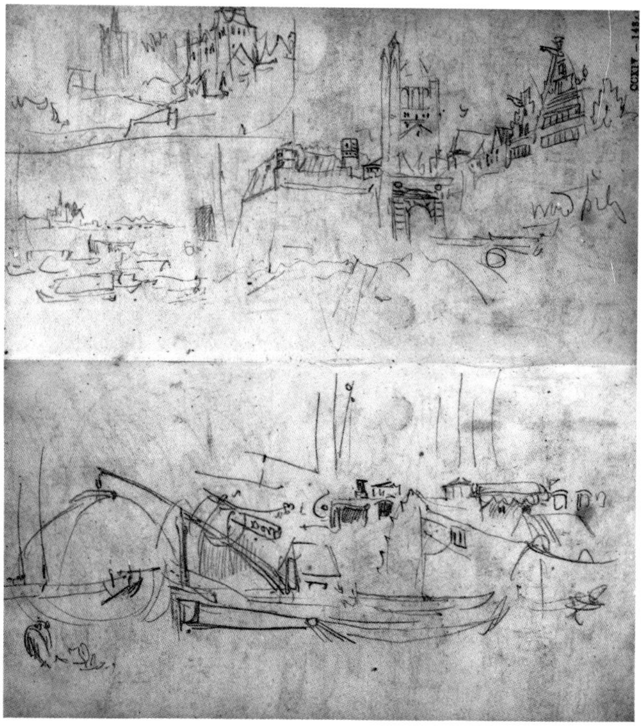

fig.35 The Rhine gate, Cologne (TB CCXIV 142v–143r). Pencil, 1825

He does not, however, appear to have used any larger sketchbooks as in 1824. By 1825 he was studying Cologne, Aachen and Liège for the third time and his sketches in both his sketchbooks suggest that he deliberately paid careful attention to all these sights, as though compensating for having neglected them in 1824 (see cat.no.32).[36] Turner's 1825 tour cannot have lasted very long, since he apparently left London only on 28 August and he would not have stayed abroad far into October. Whatever its length, however, its primary purpose was to study Holland, but – as in 1824 – he ended up by producing a painting of something entirely different, a subject seen in the very last days of his tour, almost incidentally in the course of travelling. It is not known whether Mr Broadhurst had specified the subject for his picture; and Turner may well have gone to Holland in order to find a suitable one.[37] But in any event, no painting of Holland itself was executed. Instead he painted 'Cologne' and – as in the case of 'Dieppe' – it drew on all his recent experiences. 'Cologne' is based – both in its general plan and in some of its specific details – upon Turner's most recent sketches of that city, those in the *Holland* sketchbook (fig.35).[38] It does not show Cologne's most famous building, the cathedral, but a landing-stage that could be on practically any sizeable river in northern Europe; and the chief force behind it is not the picturesque Middle Rhine but the sights Turner had been enjoying earlier on his tour: the skies and water and boats of Holland so magical in themselves, so dear to the seventeenth-century Dutch painters whom he admired, and which he had already celebrated in his 'Dort or Dordrecht' of 1818 (B&J 137), painted soon after his visit to the Low Countries in 1817. Had Turner painted an oil painting of Cologne at any other moment than straight after an extensive tour of Holland, he would surely have portrayed it in a very different manner. This is not to play down the significance he attached to the Rhine, but merely to emphasise the unity of his works, the cross-currents which underlie them and the ways in which his imagination transformed the thousands of tiny pencil sketches and the hours of patient, prosaic recording into masterpieces that are both unique and unpredictable.

The 1830s and the Second Meuse–Mosel Tour

The third tour covered by this exhibition was easily the longest, the most complex and the most ambitious of all Turner's tours of the Rhine, Meuse and Mosel. On this tour, unlike the previous two, he studied all three rivers in detail, and again and again examined their contours, towns and villages from vantage points well away from the rivers themselves, high up on neighbouring hills. He made detours to places not previously visited (and apparently not visited again), such as Louvain, Spa and Franchimont in Belgium and Mayen in Germany; he made his only known intensive study of Luxembourg; and he also made many sketches of towns that he had already explored, such as Huy and Dinant, Trier and Mainz. However, the chief importance of this tour resides in the fact that it inspired him to paint a large and breathtaking series of small gouaches on blue paper (cat.nos.47–127).

The majority of these gouaches depict the Meuse and the Mosel and they are, in many cases, Turner's only known coloured drawings of the towns and villages which they show. They are approximately half the size of his Rhine drawings of 1817, they are executed on paper with a positive colour of its own rather than on paper which he himself had prepared with a cold grey wash, and they are almost invariably simpler in design and more brilliant in colouring than their predecessors depicting the larger and grander river. Nevertheless, a strong sense of continuity may be felt between the two groups, whether the subject matter compared be the lofty riverside cliffs of the Lorelei and the Roche à Bayard (cat. nos.8 and 100) or the ruined buildings rearing their heads high above the Binger Loch and the Gockelsberg (cat.nos.11 and 56). Like the Rhine drawings, those of the Meuse and the Mosel were based on a multiplicity of pencil sketches, some quite tiny, accumulated in the course of his travels. However, their palette and their technique are attributable to highly significant developments in his career since 1817. He had paid two long visits to Italy – in 1819 and 1828 – both of which had led to his colours becoming lighter, brighter and more various. He had also worked extensively in gouache on blue paper with brilliant colours in two other large series: those of the late 1820s depicting Petworth House in Sussex and the equally famous scenes painted in the early 1830s for engraving in the volumes which have become known as *The Rivers of France*.[1] These French scenes were published by the firm of Longmans as *Turner's Annual Tour* in three successive volumes of uniform format which appeared in the autumns of 1832, 1833 and 1834 as 'annuals', i.e. Christmas and New Year gift books for the following year: *Wanderings by the Loire* (for 1833) and *Wanderings by the Seine* (in two parts, for 1834 and 1835).[2] Advertisements for these works led readers to believe that they were parts of a projected series of huge scope, variously referred to as 'Great Rivers of Europe' and 'River Scenery of Europe'.[3] However, no further volumes of *Turner's Annual Tour* were issued, probably because by the later 1830s the market for such publications was reaching saturation point.[4] It is not yet clear whether the painting of the Meuse and Mosel scenes sprang from a determination on the part of Turner or his publisher that the series should now be resuscitated; or whether perhaps the works were executed simply for pleasure, as with the Petworth gouaches. What is certain is that they constitute a superb corpus of work which, to this day, remains largely unknown. Those with easily recognised subjects have traditionally been regarded as the products of his first Meuse–Mosel tour, an idea which has only recently been called into question.[5] However, it can now be conclusively established that they are all the fruit of his later tour, and that tour itself is now redated. The gouaches can at last take their rightful place in Turner's oeuvre: as the dazzling culmination of his study of this part of northern Europe – and probably, too, as the grand finale to his works on blue paper.

In the past Turner's second Meuse–Mosel tour has been universally dated to the summer of 1834,[6] purely on the basis of three pieces of evidence so flimsy that they cannot really count as evidence at all: (a) one tiny sketchbook (TB CCLXXXVI) contains manuscript material relating to Oxford (in a hand other than Turner's[7]) which is inscribed 'July 2 1834' and one or two minuscule sketches that seem to show Bruges; (b) a second sketchbook (TB CCLXXXIX), which contains numerous sketches of both Oxford and the Mosel, is composed of paper watermarked 1834; and (c) Turner exhibited an oil painting of Ehrenbreitstein (B&J 361; cat.no.41) at the Royal Academy in 1835. It must be immediately apparent that the first of the two sketchbooks is barely germane to the question of the dating of Turner's second Meuse–Mosel tour, since the Oxford and Bruges material need not necessarily date from the same summer and, in any case, the artist could have passed through Ostend and thence to Bruges on his way to a very large number of different European destinations. Second, the watermarked paper of TB CCLXXXIX merely provides a *terminus ante quem* its sketches of the Mosel cannot have been drawn. Finally, it is as inappropriate to postulate an 1834 visit to the Rhine and Mosel to account for the painting of 'The Bright Stone of Honour (Ehrenbreitstein)' in 1835 as it would be to insist that a tour of central Italy must have immediately preceded the painting and exhibition of 'Childe Harold's Pilgrimage – Italy' (B&J 342) in 1832. 'The Bright Stone of Honour' belongs to a group of large oil paintings of the 1830s – which also includes 'Caligula's Palace and Bridge' (B&J 337; 1831), 'The Golden Bough' (B&J 355; 1834) and 'Juliet and her Nurse' (B&J 365; 1836) – in which, through one English winter after another, Turner drew on his existing knowledge of far-off regions, countries and cities to create fairytale scenes which owe as much to the artist's imagination as they do to his experiences.

Meanwhile Turner's own letters and sketches reveal the correct dating for his second major tour of the Meuse and Mosel. On 9 August 1834 he was definitely at home in London, writing a letter about one of his recently completed paintings, and on 15 September he arrived in Edinburgh for a sketching

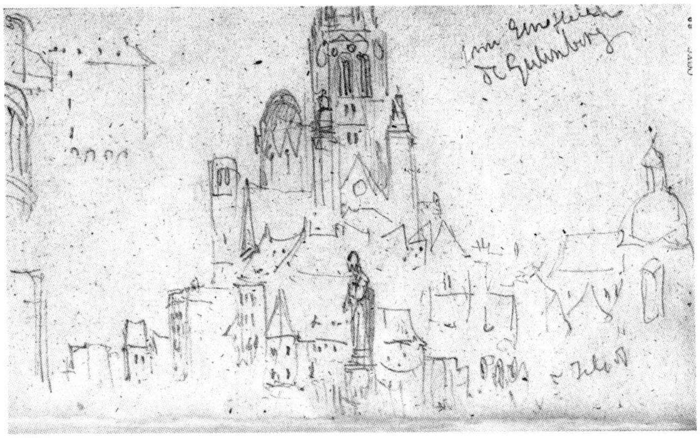

fig.36 Mainz cathedral and Thorvaldsen's statue of Johannes Gensfleisch Gutenberg (TB CCXC 69r). Pencil, 1839

tour financed by Sir Walter Scott's publisher Robert Cadell.[8] Clearly he could not have completed a mammoth Continental tour between these two dates. Furthermore, a full-page sketch in one of the group of five sketchbooks undoubtedly used on that tour (TB CCXC; *Trèves to Cochem and Coblenz to Mayence*) places it well beyond the year 1834. This sketch shows the statue honouring the inventor of printing, Johannes Gutenberg (*c.*1397–1468), erected in Mainz in 1837 (fig.36). The history of this important monument is exceptionally well documented, for its unveiling constituted not only the realisation of a long-cherished dream on the part of Mainz itself but also the culmination of an endeavour shared by many different countries throughout Europe. Turner could hardly have been unaware of the circumstances leading up to its inauguration, since these were reported in a number of British newspapers and journals between 1835 and 1837, while his annotation on his sketch, 'Fete de', is a clear indication that he also heard on-the-spot reports of the great celebratory day itself. Some of these events merit a brief mention here, reflecting, as they do, the new Europe through which Turner was now so frequently travelling. At the end of 1831 Mainz had set up a committee to organise a monument to its most famous son and in 1832 an appeal was launched for financial contributions from all over the educated world. In Rome the young Mainz painter Heuss persuaded the greatest European sculptor of the day, the Dane Bertel Thorvaldsen, to prepare designs for the statue, which he agreed to do at no charge (a gesture for which Mainz gratefully created him an honorary citizen). These designs were ready by July 1834 and the bronze statue itself was cast by Crozatier in Paris in April 1835; its foundation stone was laid in the Gutenbergplatz to the north-west of Mainz cathedral on 8 July 1837 and the statue finally unveiled on 14 August, the central event among three days of public festivities on a colossal scale. These involved not only speeches and presentations and the reception of countless deputations but also the performance in the square itself of a specially written *Te Deum* by 1,500 musicians and a choir of 1,300, and, on 15 August, a regatta on the Rhine of innumerable richly decorated boats watched by an estimated crowd of some 30,000 spectators. Although it had ultimately been Mainz itself which provided the largest financial contribution (nearly 11,000 out of over 18,500 florins), many other European towns and countries – including France and London – had also made donations and were accordingly represented at the festivities.[9]

The presence of Thorvaldsen's statue in Turner's pencil sketch places the latter's tour definitively in the closing years of the 1830s. It thus becomes possible to associate it with two of his letters – neither of them previously connected with the tour – which can be shown to be firmly anchored to the summer of 1839. The first was written from his home in Queen Anne Street either late on Friday 2 August or in the very early hours of Saturday 3 August, to the portrait painter H.W. Pickersgill, declining an invitation on the grounds that 'I am on the Wing for the continent (Belge) this morning'.[10] This departure date is confirmed by Turner's absence from a meeting, held on that very day, of the General Assembly of the Royal Academy of which he was usually an assiduous attender.[11] He was back in London by the end of September when another meeting of the General Assembly was called, to announce the vacancy in the office of Professor of Architecture caused by the death on 31 August of William Wilkins, designer of many neo-classical buildings including the newly completed National Gallery in Trafalgar Square.[12] Turner attended this meeting, on Monday 30 September, taking with him a map of the Mosel which he planned to give to another member, Clarkson Stanfield. However, finding Stanfield absent, he sat down and wrote to him then and there, from the Royal Academy, explaining that the old map of the Mosel which Stanfield had lent him had been '*worn out* in the Campaign' and he was therefore providing him with a new one.[13] One has only to study the contents of the *Trèves to Cochem and Coblenz to Mayence* sketchbook (TB CCXC) and the *Cochem to Coblenz – Home* sketchbook (TB CCXCI), with their evidence of rigorous, indefatigable legwork, to realise that 'Campaign' was the *mot juste* for Turner's recent tour and that no nineteenth-century map – unprotected by plastic – could possibly have withstood it.

Turner's second tour of the Meuse and the Mosel becomes far more comprehensible on a variety of levels once it has been correctly dated to 1839. His interest in the ornate medieval architecture of Louvain, for instance, has parallels in the illustrative work of other artists in the late 1830s such as Thomas Allom, Thomas Shotter Boys and W.H. Bartlett.[14] One of his Dinant gouaches (cat.no.99), a strangely beautiful moonlight scene, is almost certainly a deliberate echo of one of the lithographs in Stanfield's *Sketches on the Moselle, the Rhine, & the Meuse* of 1838 (fig.37). Indeed, this fine book of thirty magnificent plates must have acted as a catalyst for the entire tour. It drew Turner back to all three rivers of its title in the same spirit of amicable competition that had led him to exhibit his first oil painting of Venice at the Royal Academy in 1833 after hearing that Stanfield was employed on the same theme and was a characteristic feature of so many of his friendships.[15]

It must, however, be stated plainly that the redating of this tour leaves several matters unanswered. One is the question of where Turner went in August of 1834, for he undoubtedly did leave London for a while.[16] Second, a number of drawings which have in the past been loosely associated with 'the 1834 tour' – notably those depicting Burg Eltz (W 1333–5) – now need to be reassessed, since there is no evidence at all that Turner made a detour from the Mosel to visit Burg Eltz in 1839.[17] Most importantly, the redating serves as a somewhat uncomfortable reminder of just how much work still remains to be done on Turner's Continental tours of the 1830s. His movements in that decade are far less well documented than those of the 1820s or the 1840s, and there are many sketchbooks and loose sheets in the Turner Bequest which were almost certainly used in the 1830s but have yet to be identified as belonging

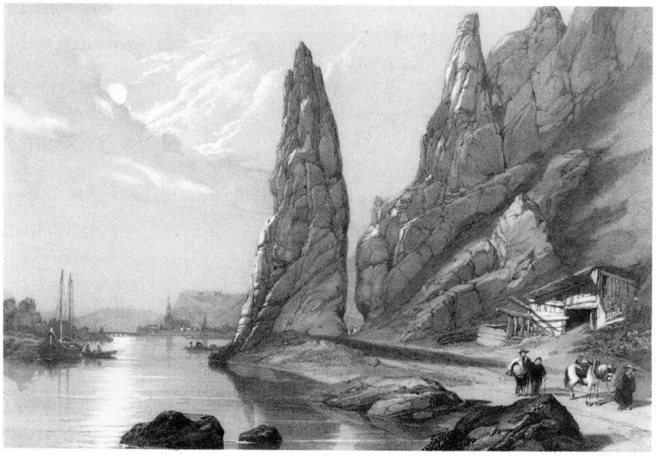

fig.37 Thomas Shotter Boys after Clarkson Stanfield, 'Roche Bayard by Moonlight on the Meuse'. Lithograph from *Sketches on the Moselle . . .*, 1838

to particular tours.[18] Some of these contain depictions of places on the Rhine, Meuse and Mosel (e.g. cat.nos.33, 34) but for the moment they can only be tentatively dated, unlike some of the Rhine material from the 1840s where the watermarked paper provides conclusive evidence as to when Turner must have used it (cat.no.35).

If the 1830s witnessed a broadening of British artists' interests in northern Europe, the same decade saw vital changes in Belgium itself. The enforced union of that country with Holland under the post-Waterloo settlement had been irksome to it right from the beginning, but it was not until 1831 – as the result of the successful uprising in Brussels in August 1830 – that it became an independent kingdom under Leopold of Saxe-Coburg, uncle to the future Queen Victoria. The Dutch resisted this secession strongly, even to the point of taking up arms, but in 1839 they finally accepted the independence of Belgium which was agreed under the terms of the Treaty of London signed in April of that year.[19] Turner can hardly have been ignorant of all these events which must surely have played their part in leading him to revisit Belgium in 1839.

His 1839 tour is revealed in all its complexity in a group of five sketchbooks. He himself listed all five together, as a group, on a paper label affixed to the cover of one of them but, even without this label, there could be no doubt that the four small upright books of near-identical dimensions (TB CCLXXXVII, CCLXXXVIII, CCXC and CCXCI; cat.nos.42, 43, 45,

46) were all used on the same tour. All four are of Continental manufacture and are bound neither in leather nor in drab-coloured boards but in boards covered with marbled paper, a form of binding widely used on the Continent throughout the nineteenth century both for books of blank paper and for a wide variety of printed books. The first two contain sketches of the Meuse from Liège up to Dinant and from Dinant up river into France respectively; the second two share the Mosel in a similar fashion, one depicting the river from Trier down to Cochem, the other from Cochem on to Coblenz. Across the four books Turner's habits as both artist and traveller are remarkably consistent: full-page sketches in landscape format predominate; at practically every town or village of note he ascended a hill to study the ensemble from afar and above; and he made several excursions (not always entirely explicable) away from his main route. The fifth sketchbook (TB CCLXXXIX; cat.no.44), already referred to above as having been used in Oxford as well as on the Mosel, displays none of these characteristics and, were it not for Turner's own association of it with the other four, might well have been excluded from consideration here. However, the evidence of Turner's paper label should not be lightly disregarded, since his descriptions are both detailed and accurate. It will be seen later in this section that when Turner's sketches of the Mosel in the *First Mossel and Oxford* sketchbook are taken in conjunction with those of the river in the two smaller sketchbooks, his exploration appears as an even more complex and time-consuming activity than it would have been without them; but this in itself is entirely comprehensible, since a close and detailed study of the Mosel was one of his prime objectives.

Turner set off for Belgium on Saturday 3 August and made directly for the Meuse at Liège. All his pencil sketches of Belgium are contained in the *Spa, Dinant and Namur* sketchbook (TB CCLXXXVII; cat.no.42) which was evidently bought in Brussels since it bears the printed label of a stationer and printer in the Rue de la Madeleine. This purchase and Turner's known departure date make it very tempting to believe that he travelled by the General Steam Navigation Company's steam yacht, the *Earl of Liverpool* which left London for Brussels via Ostend at 2 a.m. on that very Saturday.[20] By then the railway from Ostend to Brussels had been opened

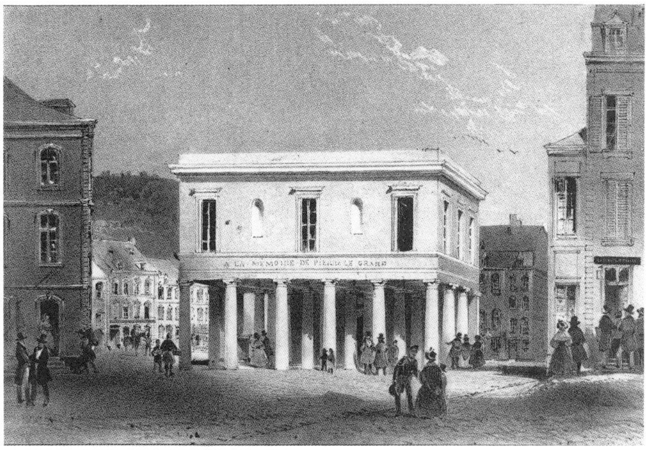

fig.38 Théodore Fourmois, 'Vue de la Fontaine du Pouhon, à Spa'. Lithograph from *Les Délices de Spa et de ses Environs*, Brussels, 1839

and passengers on the *Earl of Liverpool* proceeded directly onto the train so that the entire journey from London to Brussels could be made in only twenty hours. After visiting the Brussels stationer, Turner immediately began to use his new sketchbook which he himself called 'Brussels up to Givet': a very early sketch in the book, showing a square close to the town hall, was almost certainly drawn as he waited for the diligence that was to take him to Louvain.[21] This sketch and two of his numerous ones of Louvain,[22] in common with around a hundred others drawn on this tour, formed the basis of the gouaches on blue paper referred to earlier (cat.nos.47–127). However, it seems highly improbable that he painted these scenes while he was actually at the places they depict. As will be shown at the end of this section, there are common stylistic traits within the group as a whole which suggest that they were produced in batches of up to perhaps ten or so at a time, not necessarily of the same topographical area. This work must have taken place months later, once he was back in England.

Although Turner had come to Belgium with the express intention of studying the Meuse upstream of Liège, the first thing he did on reaching that city was to make a detour to Spa some twenty miles to the south-east. He may well have stayed a night at Liège, in order to break his journey, which enabled him to perambulate around the city making a handful of sketches of some of its principal sights such as the Pont des Arches.[23] However, he did not linger

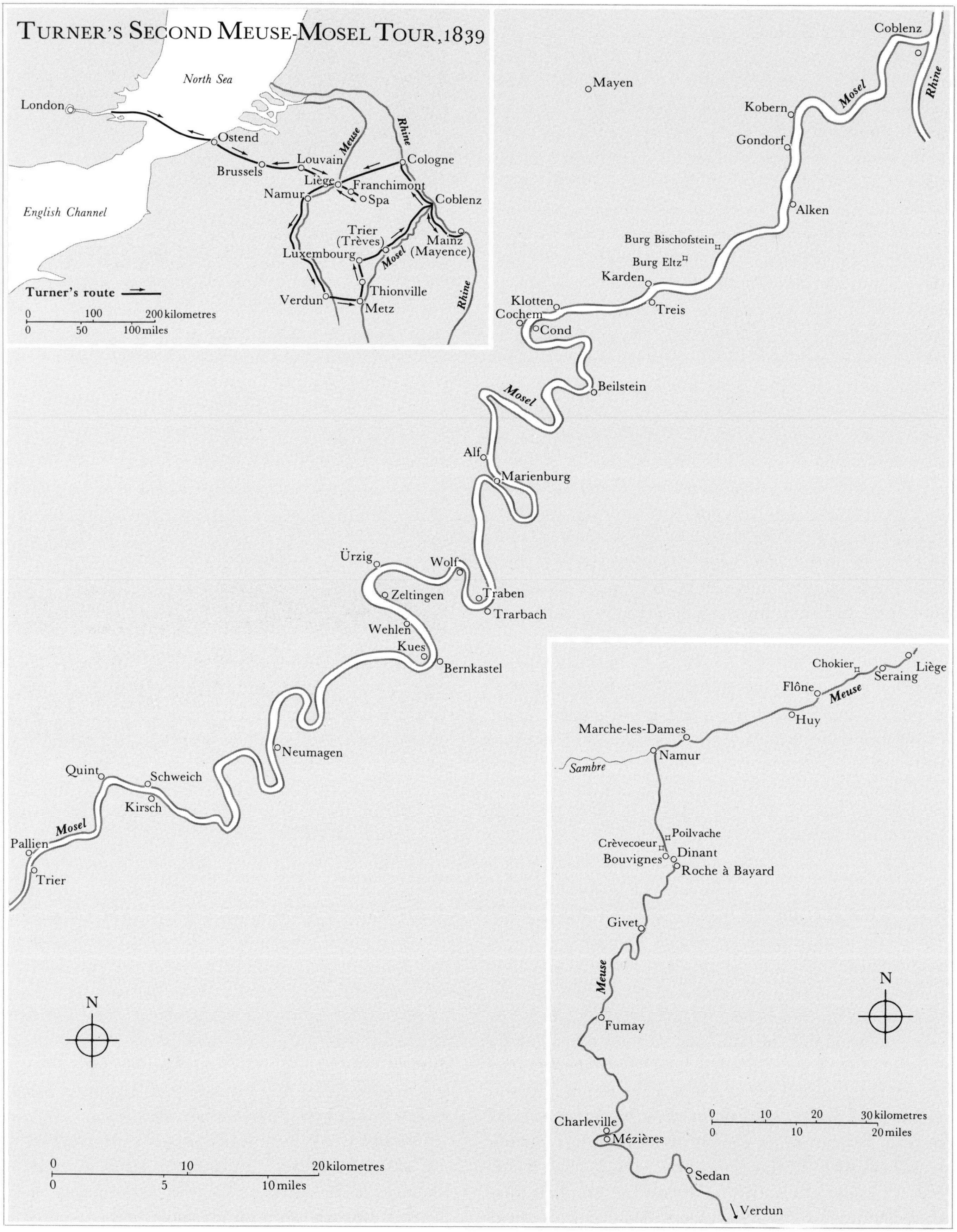
TURNER'S SECOND MEUSE-MOSEL TOUR, 1839
North Sea
London
Ostend
Brussels
Louvain
Meuse
Rhine
Cologne
Liège
Franchimont
Namur
Spa
Coblenz
English Channel
Trier
(Trèves)
Mainz
(Mayence)
Luxembourg
Mosel
Thionville
Verdun
Metz
Turner's route
0 100 200 kilometres
0 50 100 miles
Coblenz
Mayen
Kobern
Gondorf
Alken
Burg Bischofstein
Burg Eltz
Karden
Treis
Klotten
Cochem
Cond
Beilstein
Alf
Marienburg
Ürzig
Wolf
Zeltingen
Traben
Trarbach
Wehlen
Kues
Bernkastel
Neumagen
Quint
Schweich
Kirsch
Pallien
Trier
N
0 10 20 kilometres
0 5 10 miles
Chokier
Liège
Seraing
Flône
Huy
Marche-les-Dames
Namur
Sambre
Poilvache
Crèvecoeur
Dinant
Bouvignes
Roche à Bayard
Givet
Fumay
Charleville
Mézières
Sedan
Verdun
0 10 20 30 kilometres
0 10 20 miles

long over these, since his interest on this visit lay further afield. By this time Spa – after which all spa towns are, of course, named – had been a popular resort for well over a hundred years, with foreign travellers frequently seeking it out both to drink its health-giving mineral waters and to enjoy its agreeable setting and society. Turner clearly enjoyed his time here. He visited and sketched all the main springs both in the town and in the nearby woods – the Pouhon built to celebrate the centenary of the visit of Peter the Great (fig.38); the Géronstère; and the Groesbeck and Sauvenière (see cat.nos.115–17). He made sketch after sketch of the town nestling in its hollow among the hills, of its leafy promenades (fig.39) and of its mixture of grand and unpretentious dwellings. And – as a comparison between figures 38–40 and cat.nos.115, 118 and 119 makes abundantly clear – he placed himself smartly in all the most popular viewpoints of the time. The *Spa, Dinant and Namur* sketchbook was justifiably so named by its later cataloguer, for no fewer than twenty-six of its pages carry recognisable depictions of Spa and its environs, while others – such as that showing a bevy of delightful ladies with elaborate hairstyles and revealing corsages (f.17v) – may well have been drawn there also.[24]

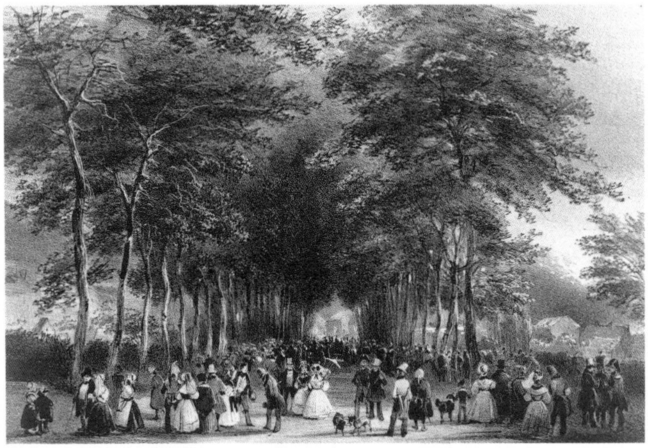

fig.39 Théodore Fourmois and Paulus Lauters, 'Promenade de Sept Heures, à Spa'. Lithograph from *Les Délices de Spa et de ses Environs*, Brussels, 1839

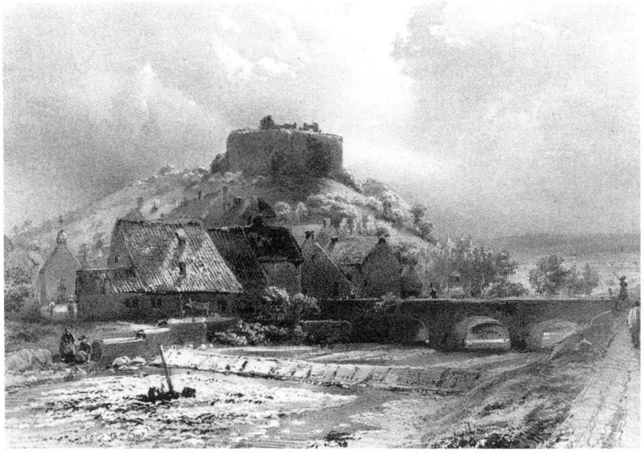

fig.40 Théodore Fourmois, 'Vue des Ruines du Château de Franchimont. Une Lieu de Spa'. Lithograph from *Les Délices de Spa et de ses Environs*, Brussels, 1839

Turner's visit to Spa meant that he passed close under the ruins of the medieval castle of Franchimont, of which the road from Liège afforded – and still affords – excellent views (fig.40). This had been the stronghold of the 'Wild Boar of the Ardennes', William de la Marck, whom Scott had portrayed in so terrifying a manner in *Quentin Durward*. There was also a mysterious legend attached to the castle about an ancient treasure guarded by the devil; this Turner could have read in one of the volumes of Scott's poetry which he had so recently illustrated.[25] He drew about a dozen pencil sketches of the castle in his sketchbook, from the moment it first came into sight until it disappeared from view (see under cat. nos.109–13). Furthermore, from the village of Marché de Theux, he climbed right up to the castle's very portal and recorded, when he reached it, the three heraldic shields carved in stone above the portal that still greet the visitor to Franchimont today.[26] Such energetic exploration of sites – regardless of whether or not they lay on the Meuse or the Mosel – and such careful recording of their distinguishing characteristics were both to be typical features of the weeks that followed. Whereas in 1824 Turner had travelled largely by river, rarely going off the beaten track, fifteen years later he behaved with all the independence and inquisitiveness of a youthful adventurer. All accounts of Turner – including especially that of Ruskin – which depict him in the late 1830s as flagging in mind, body or spirit must be firmly cast aside in the face of such overwhelming evidence to the contrary.

Turner is only known to have visited Franchimont on this one occasion, so that the handful of pencil sketches of the castle on loose sheets of paper in the Turner Bequest must surely have been executed at the same time as the very similar ones in the *Spa, Dinant and Namur* sketchbook.[27] During the 1830s he seems to have used the same type of blue paper, torn into pocket-sized pieces measuring about $5\frac{1}{2}$ by $7\frac{1}{2}$ inches, both for gouaches and for on-the-spot pencil sketches in many different parts of Europe. The majority of these – over 150 – have yet to be dated and identified, but those showing Franchimont and at least eight places on the Meuse and the Mosel should be regarded as products of the 1839 tour.[28] It is not surprising to find Turner sketching the same views simultaneously in a sketchbook and on loose sheets of paper, since this is not very different from using two sketchbooks in partnership as he had done on so many earlier tours including those of 1817 and 1824. The interest of these extra sketches lies in the paper used, since such drawings could themselves be overpainted and become gouache scenes. It will be apparent from the relevant catalogue entries for these works (cat.nos.47–127) that some are precisely based on pencil sketches in sketchbooks whereas others are slightly different but nevertheless very closely related. In some of these latter cases it may be postulated that Turner's on-the-spot sketches actually lie beneath the gouaches – a fact which would in itself account for the remarkably small number of Meuse–Mosel pencil sketches on blue paper still extant.

Turner undoubtedly travelled up the Meuse from Liège to Huy on the north bank and by road, almost certainly by public transport. His sketches of the castle of Chokier and the abbey of Flône have the uncontrolled and jagged lines of sketches made from a moving vehicle, while those of Huy in the distance can only have been made from the Liège road.[29] But not all the sketches he made on this part of his journey were of ancient towns and buildings; one group of sketches shows the view back downstream towards Liège from its south-western outskirts, with a group of factories – probably near Seraing – shown prominently in the foreground (see cat.no.85). In this scene – as in so much of the area around Liège in the early nineteenth century – industry and rural beauty confront each other above the roofs of the city; and one cannot help being reminded of the similar contrast portrayed by Turner himself earlier that very year between the modern tug and the obsolete sailing ship in 'The Fighting Téméraire' (B&J 377; RA 1839; National Gallery, London).

He also made sketches of many of the dramatic rock formations along the Belgian part of the Meuse which had caught his attention – and indeed that of numerous travellers – in the 1820s.[30] Sometimes his sketches of these can be precisely identified, sometimes not, since the quarrying of the last century and a half and two world wars have left many parts of the banks of the Meuse very different from the landscape seen by Turner. At Marche-les-Dames, for example, the picturesqueness which delighted Turner and his contemporaries (see cat.no.91) is now transformed by the presence of an army camp while many of the gaunt cliffs nearby have been hewn away, leaving vast chasms behind.

During the weeks that followed, Turner revisited many of the places he had studied in 1824. He travelled up the Meuse, making many sketches of the Belgian towns of Huy, Namur and Dinant and the French ones of Givet, Mézières, Sedan, Verdun, Metz and Thionville before heading north for Luxembourg and Trier.[31] His sketches of all these places were consistently larger and more detailed than those of 1824 and there are very few sketches of the river and countryside between the towns, so he may be presumed to have travelled by road in a public carriage, stopping at each important centre as he came to it. He clearly made a determined effort to study those towns which he had been unable to sketch sufficiently in 1824, such as Mézières, Thionville and Metz but most especially Luxembourg. This was universally regarded in Turner's day as the grandest fortress town in northern Europe – 'the Gibraltar of the north' – and he responded enthusiastically to its breathtaking natural grandeur and complex system of fortifications in nearly thirty pages of fine pencil sketches. Subsequently he depicted Luxembourg in the greatest number of gouaches devoted to a single town, probably painting over twenty. If the emergence of Belgium as an independent kingdom in 1839 inspired Turner both to visit that country and to paint it, a similar influence may well have directed his attention towards Luxembourg. It was the Treaty of London that transformed the frontiers of the Grand-Duchy (to the positions they occupy today). After a lifetime of supplying whatever topographical views were dictated by current fashion, Turner would not have neglected the opportunity of studying places that were in the news, were likely to be increasingly

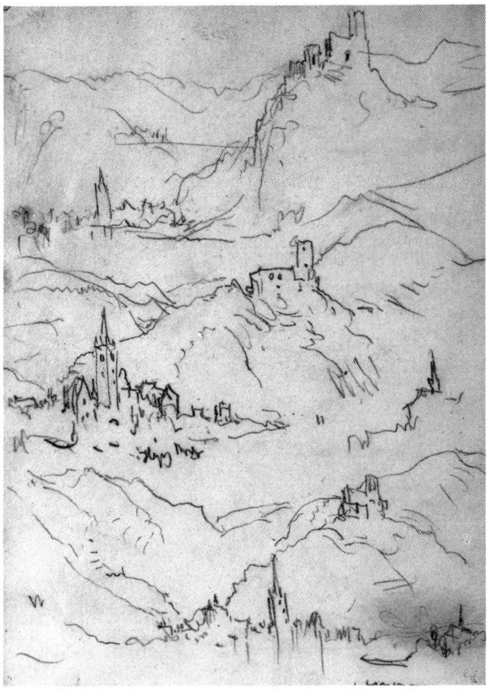

fig.41 Three views of Bernkastel and the Landshut from a boat moving downstream (TB CCLXXXIX I IV). Pencil, 1839

visited and could profitably be depicted in the future.

At Trier, Turner spent most of his time surveying and sketching the city from across the Mosel, just as he had done in 1824 (see cat.nos.39 and 47), and then descended the river by boat as he had also done previously. This journey is recorded in the sketchbook Turner himself called *First Mossel and Oxford* (cat.no.44), as a reminder that it contained his first Mosel sketches of this tour as distinct from those made shortly afterwards during his detailed exploration of the river and its banks in his two other sketchbooks (cat.nos.45 and 46). In *First Mossel and Oxford* Turner's sketches are flung helter-skelter into the nooks and crannies left by the earlier Oxford sketches, their lines are often jerky and uncontrolled, their viewpoints are consistently low and in mid-river, and sequences of sketches show recognisable towns coming closer and closer as Turner was carried downstream towards them (fig.41).

After this voyage down to Coblenz Turner doubled back up the Mosel to study it from the land and sketch its scenery at leisure from a multiplicity of viewpoints of his own choosing in the *Trèves to Cochem and Coblenz to Mayence* and *Cochem to Coblenz – Home* sketchbooks (cat.nos.45 and 46). Unfortunately, the first of these was dismembered in the nineteenth century and its pages subsequently reassembled in what is clearly the wrong order, so one cannot be absolutely certain about Turner's movements on the Mosel. However, it seems very probable that he based himself at Cochem, where he had stayed in 1824. From here he travelled slowly back up to Trier, sketching everything very carefully.[32] He would then have returned to Cochem by boat to stay a night, after which he turned his attention to the lower half of the river, recording it in a similarly detailed fashion.[33]

These two sketchbooks contain dozens of sketches of the Mosel that were to be developed into gouaches (cat.nos.47–79) and also – in the case of the first – pencil sketches of the southern part of the Middle Rhine. Besides the sequence of pages devoted to Mainz, which has led to the redating of this tour, this sketchbook also contains many sketches of Oberwesel as seen from the hillside downstream of the town and on the ascent up to the Schönburg.[34] This was a particularly enchanting area, as other visitors before Turner, such as Robert Batty, had already discovered (fig.42); but it seems to have been only in this one year that Turner explored it. Along the Rhine, as along the Meuse and the Mosel in 1839, Turner avidly sought out high viewpoints that would give him far more sweeping and wide-ranging views than he had enjoyed on previous visits; and, although no single sketch provides an exact parallel to what must be regarded as the crowning achievement in watercolour of Turner's study of the Rhine,

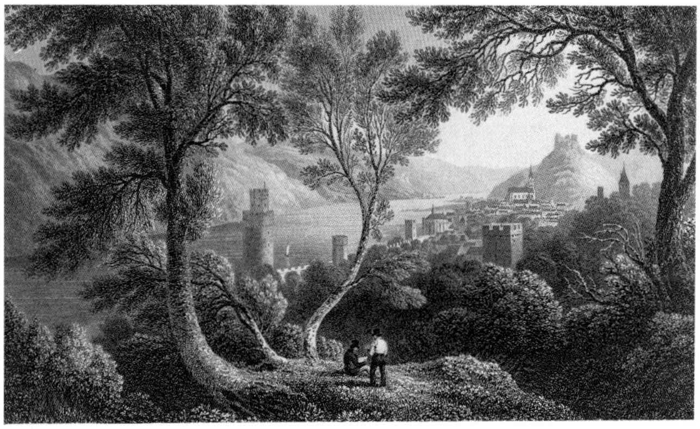

fig.42 Robert Wallis after Robert Batty, 'Ober Wessel'. Line engraving from *Scenery of the Rhine . . .*, 1826

the 'Oberwesel' of 1840 (cat.no.30), there can be no doubt whatever that it was inspired by his experiences high on this hillside in the summer of 1839.

Turner's gouaches of the Meuse and the Mosel form an enchanting series, as delightful as those of Petworth, as richly varied as those of the Seine, as subtle as those of the Loire. The Mosel scenes tend on the whole to be executed with a lighter, more feathery touch while the Belgian ones have a more restricted palette and contain more work in pen and ink but this is not invariably the case: for example, one view of Huy (cat.no.89) is particularly vaporous, one of Dinant (cat.no.96) is among the most colourful of all the scenes, and two of the Mosel views contain dynamic areas of pen drawing (cat.nos.54, 61). Sometimes a closely knit topographical group shares a common colour scheme, as in the case of the Louvain pair and the Spa group (cat.nos.107–8 and 114–19). At other times the same or a similar colour combination is found in scenes with unrelated subject matter: Trier is painted with the same twilight radiance as Namur (cat.nos.47 and 93); a Luxembourg view is dominated by the same warm brown as the view of Sedan (cat.nos.123 and 104). In some of the architectural views Turner preferred to use just two or three colours and rely on thin grey washes and a liberal amount of white to achieve his chiaroscuro (cat.nos.105, 106). Here Turner's colours may be regarded as naturalistic but tinged with poetry. Elsewhere he goes far beyond naturalism, as when yellow and lavender are used in architectural views to signify light and dark or light and shade (cat. nos.48, 107). In the river views he goes even further in imposing his own colours on to what he saw: a sunlit hillside may be almost any bright hue that he fancied, while shadows are frequently patches of dense and brilliant colour – a dark green set against orange, deep blue against pink, purple against green, orange against yellow (cat.nos.77, 56, 96).

Although the gouaches are executed in such a dazzling variety of colours and media, they are bound together as a group by their relationships to the pencil sketches in the four small sketchbooks used in 1839. They must have been produced in several different batches over the autumn and winter following his tour, in an inspired outpouring of experimentation and a determination to realise in colour as many as possible of his recent experiences while the visions were still fresh in his mind. On 11 December Turner declined an invitation to spend Christmas with an old friend, J.H. Maw, in Hastings with the excuse that 'I have been so idle all the summer'.[35] This was hardly true as far as travelling around Europe was concerned, but such white lies are the familiar and perennial fallback of creative artists engrossed in their own work – and always have been. One may feel slightly sorry for J.H. Maw, in that he was deprived of Turner's company, but one can only rejoice that Turner stayed at home and painted such a glorious series of gouaches.

Turner's Rhine in the 1840s

During the last ten years of his life much of Turner's energy and attention was focused on Switzerland which he visited in four successive years from 1841 to 1844. On all of these tours he travelled along parts of the Rhine which therefore figures large in a number of late sketchbooks (e.g. cat.no.35) and in many sketches on loose sheets of paper both in the Turner Bequest and scattered in collections around the world.[1] Some of these were probably once pages of 'roll' sketchbooks, others are on large sheets of paper folded – and usually, but not always, cut – into sixteen small sheets equivalent in size to the pages of a pocket-sized sketchbook. One of the most striking features about these late images is their tendency to replicate sketches and drawings Turner himself had produced a quarter of a century earlier. This charac-

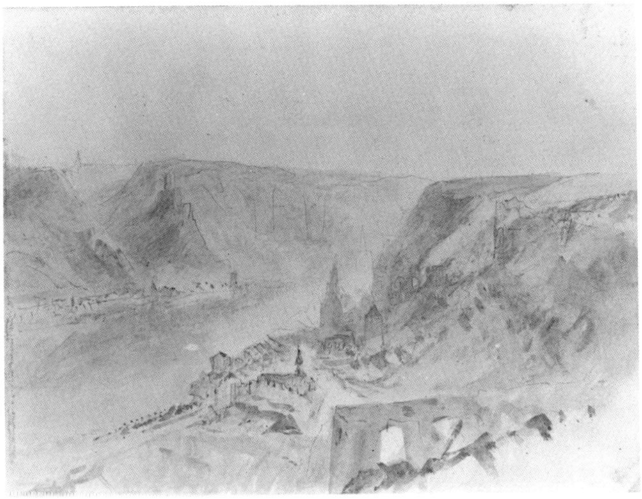

fig.43 'On the Rhine: looking over St Goar to Burg Katz from Burg Rheinfels' (w 1329). Watercolour over pencil, ?1844. Ashmolean Museum, Oxford

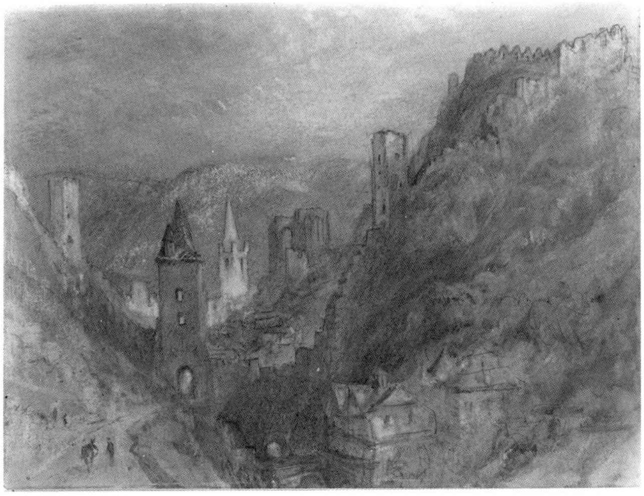

fig.44 'Bacharach' (w 1324). Gouache and watercolour over pencil, ?c.1840. Fitzwilliam Museum, Cambridge

teristic extends over a wide range of European subject matter and is not special to the Rhineland, but it is none the less fascinating to find Turner, in the 1840s, climbing up to Burg Rheinfels to catch the same view of the Rhine gorge that he had drawn in 1817 (cat.no.7) and recording it in the same soft colours (fig.43). His sketch of Bacharach, while taken from a different viewpoint from the 1817 drawing (fig.21) is self-evidently close to that work in its enjoyment of the town's dramatic skyline and picturesque situation at the mouth of the Steegertal (fig.44); it, too, has a counterpart among Turner's pencil sketches of 1817.[2]

Another important feature of Turner's late travels through the Rhineland is that he was not content to stick to the valley itself but continued to explore its tributaries right through to his very last visit. Two of the large subdivided sheets in the Turner Bequest bear a total of twenty sketches of the Ahr valley which he explored in detail all the way from Sinzig up to its source at Blankenheim, some 55 miles away in the Eifel.[3] These sketches cannot as yet be dated, but the numerous ones of Burg Reichenberg in the *Rhine and Rhine Castles* sketchbook (cat.no.35) were definitely drawn on Turner's last Swiss tour. Burg Reichenberg is situated a few miles away from the Rhine, up the Hasenbachtal close to St Goarshausen, so it did not lie on Turner's direct route and he does not appear to have studied it on any earlier tour. Thanks to its secluded position it has escaped the centuries of destruction and demolition and is still one of the most complex and impressive castle-fortresses in the Rhineland. Turner clearly found it of very great interest since he drew ten large pencil sketches, a fitting culmination to all the thousands he had already drawn in this area in the course of so many tours.[4]

Many of Turner's other late depictions of the Rhine are less clearly attributable to particular tours. However, his colour studies of Ehrenbreitstein (cat.nos.128–34) can probably be associated with the 1841 tour. Their technique and palette appear similar to those used in many Swiss sketches of that year. Moreover, their underlying concern – the representation of a land mass seen across water, assuming various hues under different atmospheric conditions – is precisely the same as that of his studies of the Rigi across Lake Lucerne which originated in 1841. At this time, too, Turner was also working on a study of the Mosel bridge at Coblenz (cat.nos.135–6), but he did not return to the Meuse after 1839.

During the 1840s Turner's vision of the Rhine reached a wide audience. This was achieved partly through the publication of new engravings – 'Oberwesel' (cat.no.31) and 'Ehrenbreitstein' (see under cat.no.41) – and partly through the continued dissemination of those which served as book illustrations (cat.nos.25–9).[5] Shortly after Turner's death two further large engravings were published, both of which – like the vignettes to poetry – had their roots in Turner's very first Rhine tour of all: 'Neuwied and Weissenthurm' (see under cat.no.5) and 'Osterspey and Feltzen' (fig.45). Both of these subjects should have appeared in W.B. Cooke's intended publication of Turner's Rhine views in 1819 and, if the artist saw the proofs of these plates in the autumn of 1851, it must surely have given him pleasure to think that they would, after all, be reaching the public for which they had been destined.[6] The intense drama of the storm in 'Osterspey and Feltzen' provides a counterbalance not only to the tranquillity of 'Neuwied and Weissenthurm' but also to that in 'Oberwesel' and many of his other, smaller, Rhine views, but it also does far more than that, for it is one of Turner's most powerful statements about the Rhine. In 1817 he experienced a storm, with a rainbow, on this very stretch of the Rhine just above the Marxburg.[7] He developed this motif into a drawing for his friend Walter Fawkes. He then chose to repeat it as a suitable subject for a book of Rhine views, notwithstanding the fact that this river view has no historical or topographical interest whatever. His subject here was no town or castle, village or ruin but the storm itself which can be seen as symbolising or embodying the turbulent history of the Rhineland.

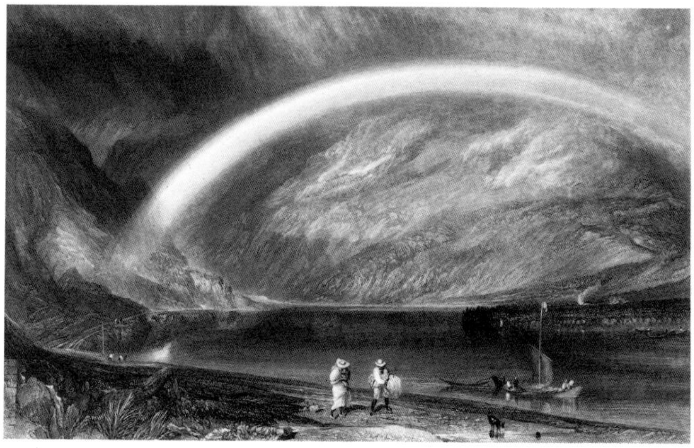

fig.45 William Miller after J.M.W. Turner, 'Osterspey and Feltzen' (R 669). Line engraving, 1852. British Museum

Again and again, throughout his life, Turner used landscape painting not simply as a descriptive medium but to speak of the human condition. His art, his writings and his publications all proclaim this intention, manifested most famously perhaps in his oil painting of 1812, 'Snow Storm: Hannibal and his Army Crossing the Alps' (B & J 126; Clore Gallery). In 'Osterspey and Feltzen' Turner's theme was far less grandiloquent but he says more about the Rhineland in this scene than a score of history books or a dozen siege paintings. His viewpoint is compassionate, humane, optimistic – as wide as the vast river itself and as full of light as his own rainbow.

NOTES

TURNER'S RHINE, MEUSE AND MOSEL

1 Gage (1980), no.227.

2 See, for instance, his notes from Schreiber's guidebook to the Rhine (cat.no.36) on TB CCXVI f.8r; his sketches and drawings of the Porta Nigra at Trier (cat.no.48); and his curious misapprehension about Mayen (cat.no.83). Wyttenbach's history of Trier, mentioned on TB CCXVI 8r, was later published in an illustrated English version (1839), edited by Turner's friend Dawson Turner.

3 *Crabb Robinson in Germany 1800–1805. Extracts from his Correspondence*, ed. E.J. Morley, 1929, p.43; W. Beattie, *Journal of a Residence in Germany . . .*, 1831, vol.1, p.186.

4 C.E. Dodd, *An Autumn near the Rhine*, 1818, p.434; *Heath's Picturesque Annual for 1833*, pp.135–6.

5 Byron, *Childe Harold's Pilgrimage* canto III, verses xlvi–lxi. His verses are also extremely vague, with only three places (the Drachenfels, Coblenz and Ehrenbreitstein) being mentioned by name.

6 Victor Hugo, *Le Rhin*, 1842, letter XIV; translation by the present writer.

7 Although Wagner wrote the first words of the *Ring* – actually part of what was to become the second drama, *Siegfried* – in Turner's lifetime, the poem was not published until 1853, nor was any of the music publicly performed before the first production of *Das Rheingold* in 1869. Schumann's 'Rhenish' Symphony was first performed in February 1851, just ten months before Turner's death.

8 E.g. Mrs Shelley (1844) and Quin (1843). Quin (vol.1, pp.298–9) claimed that the Mosel was known only to himself, J.D. Harding, Clarkson Stanfield and the editor of Murray's *Handbook*. Thanks to Schreiber's earlier guidebook (cat.no.36), Turner discovered it in the early 1820s but characteristically kept the discovery to himself until the moment was ripe for him to capitalise on his knowledge.

9 See Ausonius, *The Mosella*, trans. E.H. Blakeney, 1933.

10 Sterne's works were much read, enjoyed and discussed by Turner's friends and contemporaries (see e.g. Farington's *Diary* for 6 December 1802). Foremost among the artists inspired by Sterne was C.R. Leslie whose once-celebrated oil painting 'Uncle Toby and the Widow Wadman' (Tate Gallery) was painted in 1831, during a period when he was particularly intimate with Turner, thanks to their shared association with Petworth.

11 Southey (1903), p.118. Such comparisons occur frequently throughout Southey's journal of his tour, with Belgian scenery being consistently praised and likened to familiar British beauty spots on famous rivers, such as Monmouthshire, the Thames at Richmond, and Durham.

12 The Meuse and the Ardennes also received the highest praise in two books by the traveller and writer Henry Inglis which were very well received: *Tales of the Ardennes* (1825), pp.137–9, 161; *Solitary Walks through Many Lands* (1828), vol.2, pp.142–50.

13 The best account of this tour, combining extracts from the writings of all the participants (who also included Henry Crabb Robinson), is found in *The Poetical Works of William Wordsworth*, ed. W. Knight, vol.V, 1896. See also *Letters of Dorothy Wordsworth*, ed. A.G. Hill, 1981, pp.156–60, and *Journals of Dorothy Wordsworth*, ed. E. de Selincourt, vol.2, 1941.

14 B & J 61; W 406 (engraved as R 329; see under cat.no.24); W 1460–9 and 1540 (some of which show the town). The engraving illustrated here (not recorded in Rawlinson) is a Continental plagiarisation of R 329, in which the engraver has cheekily placed his own signature on the rock in the foreground which had previously held Turner's.

15 A. Radcliffe, *A Journey made in the Summer of 1794 . . .*, p.306.

16 See e.g. Dodd, op. cit., pp.2–4, 471; *A Family Tour through South Holland; up the Rhine; and across the Netherlands, to Ostend*, 1831, p.197; *Heath's Picturesque Annual for 1833*, pp.160–2; Mrs Shelley (1844), pp.16–17. These four accounts, relating to visits made in four successive decades, show Byron's depiction of life in the Rhineland, gay with smiling peasants, to be utterly fanciful; and Turner's own 'Oberwesel' (cat.no.30) for the visionary ideal that it is.

17 George Meredith, *A Tour to the Rhine*, 1825, p.57.

18 M. Griffin, *Impressions of Germany by an American Lady*, 1866, p.57. Her description refers to Burg Rheinstein, the earliest castle to be restored (1825, for Prince Friedrich Ludwig, cousin of the future Kaiser).

19 For example, the new Burg Rheinstein appears on TB CCXC 72v and TB CCXCVI 71r; the restored Burg Sooneck in W 1344.

20 Southey's own headnote to this ballad gave his principal source as *Coryats Crudities* (1611), the travel narrative of Thomas Coryate (?1577–1617). According to popular belief, Archbishop Hatto of Mainz lured his starving peasantry into his well-stocked barn with promises of corn and then burned them alive. He was immediately beset by a plague of rats and fled to his island tower on the Rhine whither the rats duly pursued him.

21 The phrase 'the castellated Rhine' comes from the brief appearance of that river in *Don Juan* canto X, verses lxi–lxii, which was actually printed at the very end of vol. XVI of the 17-volume edition, not in that adorned by Turner's vignette. For the Rogers illustrations, see C. Powell, 'Turner's vignettes and the making of Rogers' *Italy*', *Turner Studies*, vol.3, no.1, 1983, pp.2–13.

22 Wright (1841–2), vol.2, p.20; J. Aiton, *Eight Weeks in Germany*, 1842, p.113. The most reliable account of Ehrenbreitstein is probably that in J.H. Humfrey, *An Essay on the Modern System of Fortification adopted for the Defence of the Rhine Frontier . . . exemplified in a Copious Memoir on the Fortress of Coblenz*, 1838. This was dedicated to one of Turner's patrons, Sir James Willoughby Gordon, Quarter-Master General of HM Forces.

23 It may be noted in passing that the Romans had constructed three bridges on the Middle Rhine: Julius Caesar's timber trestle bridge on piles, probably between Coblenz and Andernach (55 BC); a bridge on piles at Mainz (AD 90); and Constantine's stone bridge at Cologne (AD 308). These had all disappeared well before Turner's visits.

24 Dodd, op. cit., p.443.

25 W.E. Frye, *After Waterloo. Reminiscences of European Travel 1815–1819*, ed. S. Reinach, 1908, p.46; J. Mitchell, *A Tour through Belgium, Holland, along the Rhine . . . in the Summer of 1816*, 1816, pp.281–3; Campbell (1817), pp.148–9 describes the wooden frame above the platform as 'like a gallows'.

26 *Journals of Dorothy Wordsworth*, ed. cit., p.48; Beattie, op. cit., vol.2, p.149.

27 *Heath's Picturesque Annual for 1833*, pp.160–1, an extended passage of social criticism curiously inappropriate to a 'picturesque annual'.

28 *A Family Tour . . .*, p.195.

29 The earliest attempts to use steam on the Rhine centred on Rotterdam and were largely due to the initiative of the Dutch government (Mitchell, 1816, pp.136–7 reports on one experimental voyage of that year in which the Dutch king participated). By 1825 a regular service existed between Rotterdam and Cologne with several vessels of different types in operation; and in that year the Dutch Steamship Company and

the Cologne Chamber of Commerce agreed to operate separately on the stretches of river below and above Cologne. After the success of several experimental voyages on the Middle Rhine, the Prussian Rhine Steamship Line (Preussisch-Rheinische Dampfschiffahrts-Gesellschaft), the forerunner of today's KD company, was founded and a regular service between Mainz and Cologne was inaugurated in 1827.

30 R. Pilkington, *Small Boat on the Moselle*, 1968, p.31; Mrs Shelley (1844), vol.1, p.18; Quin (1843), vol.1, pp.300–3; vol.2, p.37.

31 Southey (1903), p.119; Mrs Trollope (1834), vol.1, p.96. The first attempts at steam navigation on the Meuse were not made until 1838 and were fraught with considerable difficulty because of the low level of the water during the summer. See *Guide du Voyageur sur la Meuse*, Brussels, 1844.

WATERLOO AND THE RHINELAND, 1817

1 T. Hilton, *Times Literary Supplement*, 28 December 1990–3 January 1991, p.1402.

2 Powell (1990), pp.12–15.

3 Notes from Campbell: TB CLIX 13v; from Hills: TB CLIX 1r–15r; from Gardnor: TB CLIX 16r–30r (both interspersed with later notes and sketches). These notes are transcribed in the Appendix which also provides a detailed analysis of the contents of all books used on this tour. I am grateful to Professor A.G.H. Bachrach for sharing with me his identification of the notes from Hills, to be discussed in his forthcoming book on Turner and the Netherlands and in an article in *Turner Studies*.

4 In the RA catalogue for 1790, Turner's watercolour was no.644, Gardnor's Rhine scenes nos.419, 530, 540, 582, 652, 653.

5 See the 1791 edition of Gardnor, p.71 (subscribers' list).

6 Certain words among Turner's notes on TB CLIX 13v are precisely those of the 1817 edition where it differs from the 1815 edition, e.g. 'Haerlem' is described as 'ten' miles from Amsterdam (as in the 1817 edition, p.249) whereas in the 1815 edition (p.69) 'Harlem' had been given as 'seven' miles from it.

7 See *The Times*, 9 August 1817, p.1.

8 TB CLIX 101v–88v, interspersed with other, later, material.

9 Carrying on through the sketchbook pages in the opposite direction to that in which they carry their *Inventory* numbers, Turner's sketches record his progress via Aachen to the Rhine and up it as far as Bacharach (87r–75v). The pattern thereafter becomes more complicated, with some pages being used in England immediately after Turner's return home (see note 55 below). The most famous composition study in the sketchbook must be the Dutch scene on f.50r, looking forward to 'Dort, or Dordrecht, the Dort Packet-Boat from Rotterdam becalmed' (B&J 137; RA 1818); but there are also other, smaller, ones relating to the Rhineland.

10 TB CLX 2v–15r. Turner's only other recorded watercolour of Brussels, a vignette showing the town hall (W 1146, *c.*1833, present whereabouts unknown), must have been based on TB CLX 9v. For his newly discovered gouache of Brussels, see cat.no.106.

11 TB CLX 16v, 17v–26r.

12 R. Jefferies, *Round about a Great Estate*, 1880, p.141.

13 Dickens, *The Old Curiosity Shop*, 1840, chapter 12.

14 The lost items are recorded on TB CLIX 101r. The form of wording used, 'A Book with Leaves', 'ditto Cambells Belgium', suggests that Turner's copy of Campbell was interleaved with blank pages for sketching, after the fashion of a similar guidebook-cum-sketchbook, *The British Itinerary*, which he had used in the West Country in 1811 (TB CXXIII, *Devonshire Coast No.1* sketchbook). The 'Book with Leaves' must have been another volume of a similar nature, since it seems unlikely that Turner would have referred thus to a sketchbook.

15 TB CLX 27v.

16 TB CLIX 86r–84v.

17 TB CLX 28v–35r.

18 TB CLX 35v–36r, 36v–37r, 37v–38r.

19 TB CLXI 2r, 3r.

20 The *Dort* sketchbook, TB CLXII. This sketchbook is not discussed in the present study since Turner used it exclusively in Holland.

21 TB CLX 39v–40r, 40v–41r.

22 TB CLX 48r, 48v, 92v.

23 TB CLIX 28r.

24 TB CLX 49v, 50r, 50v–51r.

25 See Gardnor (1792), pp.99–100, repeated by Turner in his notes on TB CLIX 26r. Turner's spelling of Pfaffendorf as 'Haverdorf' follows that used by Gardnor.

26 TB CLX 53r, 53v, 54v, 56r; TB CLXI 6v–7r, 7v–8r, 8v–9r.

27 TB CLX 41v–42r; 42v, 55r.

28 TB CLXI 10r, 10v–11r, 11v–12r.

29 TB CLIX 81v, 79r; TB CLX 57r, 57v, 93r; TB CLXI 16r; 16v–17r.

30 TB CLXI 17v–18r, 18v–19r, 19v–20r.

31 See Gardnor, pls. XIV and XV and his remarks (1792, p.76).

32 TB CLX 58v, 93v; TB CLXI 20v–21r.

33 TB CLX 60r, 60v.

34 TB CLXI 21v–22r, 22v–23r.

35 See Gardnor, pls. IX and XI and his remarks (1792, p.55). Turner's transcription of these last (TB CLIX 24r) gave Mary Tussey (York, 1980, p.66) the idea that Turner himself had sketched and painted from the windows of his rooms overlooking the Rhine. This is clearly an attractive idea but there seems to be no evidence to support it.

36 TB CLXI 23v–24r. At this point it is again clear that the pages of TB CLXI are no longer in their original order. The two pages f.24v and f.26b undoubtedly once formed a double-page spread across which Turner depicted the view along the main street at St Goar which passes between the crane on the waterfront (f.24v) and the parish church behind (f.26b). Another pair of pages now separated (ff.27v and 25r) must also have faced each other when Turner used them at St Goar, as can be seen from the extension of some of the lines across from one page to the next. These pages do not contain one single sketch but two sketches drawn in very quick succession from nearly identical viewpoints. One of the ways in which Turner's sketching style can vary most from day to day within a single sketchbook is in the size and degree of attention given to its human staffage; another is the size, legibility and angle of his handwriting and what he chose to mention on any given occasion. In both these respects f.27v and f.25r are in perfect accord and have no other counterparts in the whole of the *Rhine* sketchbook.

37 TB CLX 59v; TB CLXI 25v–26r.

38 TB CLXI 26v, 28r, 28v, 29r, 29v–30r.

39 TB CLX 1v–2r, 90v, 91r.

40 TB CLX 62r; 64r; 62v–63r, 63v, 64v (Bacharach); 65r, 65v (the Bautsburg); TB CLXI 30v–31r, 33v–34r.

41 TB CLX 67v–68r, 70v–71r, 71v–72r.

42 TB CLX 68v–69r, 69v–70r.

43 Gardnor (1792), p.25; TB CLIX 18r; 59r, 59v, 60r.

44 TB CLXI 32v–33r, 33v–34r, 34v–35r, 35v–36r.

45 TB CLX 71v–72r; 73v–74r; 74v–75r, 75v.

46 TB CLXI 37v–38r, 38v–39r, 39v–40r, 41r, 42r.

47 TB CLXI 43r–52r.

48 Compare TB CLXI 3r and TB CLX 81v, 82v–83r.

49 TB CLXI 53v–54r, 55r, 57v–58r, 58v; 53r, 56r, 57r.

50 W 636–86. This list, however, includes two accidental duplications (W 640 is the same work as W 683 (see cat.no.10) and W 647 the same as W 686) and it omits two depictions of the Lorelei (for details, see cat.no.8). The drawings were listed while they were all still in the hands of the Fawkes family (see Thornbury (1862), vol.2, pp.394–5) and they were all lent by Ayscough Fawkes to the Royal Academy Winter Exhibition of 1889, *Works by the Old Masters, and by Deceased Masters of the British School*. The

catalogue to this carried detailed descriptions of all fifty-one scenes.

51 Ruskin (1903–12), vol. XII, pp.376–7.

52 Thornbury (1862), vol.2, p.86.

53 York (1980), p.65. Regrettably these misapprehensions have now been repeated in the publications of some of the museums holding examples from the series, e.g. the Whitworth Art Gallery, Manchester, and the British Museum.

54 Peter Bower, *Turner's Papers 1787–1820: A Study of the Manufacture, Selection and Use of his Drawing Papers*, 1990, pp.102–3. Some of the series exceed these sizes slightly in one dimension or another, but could have been painted on paper cut from whole sheets rather than half-sheets of the same or similar paper or on half-sheets of Large Post writing paper (approximately $21\frac{1}{2} \times 16\frac{1}{4}$ inches).

55 Finberg (1961), pp.249–50. At Raby Castle Turner would certainly have discussed his recent trip with its owner, Lord Darlington, and his neighbour, Turner's own travelling companion of 1802, Newbey Lowson, since they had both made a Continental tour embracing many of the same places in the summer of 1816 (see Powell, 1990). Turner continued to use his *Itinerary Rhine Tour* sketchbook at Raby, recording not only the castle itself but also the deer in the park and the hounds and horsemen of the Raby Hunt in a series of delightful vignettes (which at least two German writers (Cologne, 1980, p.33 and Stader, 1981, p.13) have assumed to have been made in the Rhineland!).

56 The closeness of the two Burg Katz views (W 645, 676) suggests that one was a trial run for the other. While 'Hirzenach' (W 681) records the *route Napoléon* (see above, p.19), the 'Abbey near Coblenz' (W 672) shows the island of Oberwerth, south of Coblenz, with the ruins of the nunnery suppressed in 1788. Schloss Stolzenfels can just be distinguished on the hillside in the distance in the coloured drawing, the Martinsburg at Oberlahnstein in its preparatory sketch (TB CLX 56v, inscribed with a word that has in the past been read as 'Abernath(?)' but can easily be read as 'Oberwerth').

57 The chief exception to this is Stader (1981) which contains many useful pages on this subject (pp.17–27). This publication was the first to elucidate the subject matter of W 640/683 (cat.no.10) and W 672 (pp.25, 31). Nine of the series were exhibited at York in the summer of 1980 but the relevant entries in that catalogue (pp.64–70) are consistently unreliable not only regarding Turner's tour and works but even over the topography of the Rhineland itself. For example, the Rhine flows from Mainz to Cologne, not vice versa; the Bausenberg and the Brohltal are nowhere near the Binger Loch and, in any case, are not what is shown in W 640/683; W 669, 'The Rhine Gate, Cologne', is not based on TB CLX 85v (which shows Bonn, not Cologne); the superb 'castled crag' on the left of W 666 is not Drachenfels but Rolandseck. As mentioned above, this exhibition also promulgated the mistaken belief that W 636–86 were painted, or at any rate begun, during the course of Turner's tour, on the pages of a 'roll' sketchbook.

Nineteen of the series were exhibited in Cologne in the autumn of 1980. The short catalogue for that exhibition (by Agnes von der Borch) ranged over the whole subject of Turner and the Rhineland and could therefore only dwell briefly on the 1817 tour and works. Although frequently good on historical background and descriptive detail, this catalogue left unresolved many problems relating to Turner's work after 1817. It is hoped that some of these are clarified in the present exhibition.

58 'Coblenz: The Quay' (W 658, at present untraced but probably similar to W 687): TB CLXI 8v; 'The Mosel Bridge at Coblenz' (W 659): TB CLXI 6v–7r; 'The Rhine Gate, Cologne' (W 669): TB CLXI 53v–54r, augmented by architectural detail from TB CLX 27v; 'Cologne' (W 670, at present untraced but probably similar to W 689a, 690): TB CLX 87v, 88r and TB CLXI 57v–58r in equal measure. Of the other scenes, 'Burg Rheinfels' (W 650) is derived from TB CLXI 22v–23r but brings the two castles much closer together; 'Katz Castle and Rheinfels' (W 649) is chiefly based on TB CLX 41v but includes the evening sun and Burg Rheinfels from TB CLXI 29r.

59 Taking the remaining drawings in topographical order from Mainz to Cologne, they are based on the sketches in TB CLX as follows: 'Mainz' (W 636): 68v–69r; 'Mainz and Kastel' (W 678): 67v (second sketch); 'The Palace at Biebrich' (W 638): 67v–68r (centre), augmented by a raft such as that sketched on TB CLIX 58r; 'The Johannisberg' (W 673): 70v–71r (first sketch); 'Rüdesheim' (W 639): 70v–71r (last sketch, for the landscape) and 71v–72r (first sketches, for Rüdesheim itself); 'The Binger Loch and Mäuseturm' (W 679): 71v–72r (centre); 'Bingen from the Nahe' (W 682): 66v–67r (centre); 'The Abbey at Bingen' (W 680): 68r; 'The Bautsburg' (W 640/683): 67v (first sketch); 'Burg Sooneck with Bacharach in the Distance' (W 671): 62r; 'Burg Fürstenberg' (W 641): 64r; 'Bacharach and Burg Stahleck' (W 642): 61v; 'The Pfalz on the Rhine' (W 643): 73v–74r with 62r for Burg Gutenfels; 'Oberwesel and the Schönburg' (W 644): 2r, 90v, 91r; 'The Lorelei' (W 646): 1v (last sketch); 'The Lorelei with Burg Katz and St Goarshausen' (W 684): 1v (first sketch); 'Hirzenach below St Goar' (W 681): 60r; 'Brüderburgen' (W 651): 90v–91r, 93v; 'Boppard' (W 652): 93v; 'Osterspey and Feltzen' (W 674): 73v–74r; 'The Marxburg' (W 653): 52r; 'Oberlahnstein' (W 654): 93r; 'Abbey near Coblenz' (W 672): 56v; 'Ehrenbreitstein from the Zathel' (a strange title, almost certainly due to an early misreading of 'Thal' Ehrenbreitstein, the village below the fort) (W 656): 53v; 'Neuwied and Weissenthurm' (W 661): 78v–79r (third sketch); 'Weissenthurm and the Hoche Monument' (W 660): 77v–78r; 'Andernach' (W 662): 50v–51r; 'The Watch Tower at Andernach' (W 663): 92v (second sketch); 'Hammerstein, below Andernach' (W 664): 92v (first sketch); 'Remagen and Linz' (W 665): 39v–40r and 40v–41r; 'Rolandswerth, Nunnery and Drachenfels' (W 666): 83r (last sketch); 'Rolandseck and Drachenfels' (W 667): 38v–39r; 'Drachenfels' (W 675): 36v–37r; 'The Hochkreuz and the Godesburg' (W 668): 31v–32r and 32v–33r.

60 W 691, W 692 (signed and dated 1820). British Museum, Lloyd Bequest (1958–7–12–420 and 1958–7–12–422), not available for loan owing to the terms of that bequest.

61 B & J 234, 269, 328a; 114.

62 W 689a, documented in two sketchbooks, *Hints River* (TB CXLI 35v) and *Liber Notes (2)* (TB CLIV(a) 58r). See E.H. Yardley, 'The Turner Collector: "That Munificent Gentleman" – James Rivington Wheeler', *Turner Studies*, vol.6, no.2, 1986, pp.51–60.

63 Ruskin (1903–12), vol. XXXV, pp.595–6.

64 See e.g. *Literary Gazette*, 16 August 1819, repeated on 21 and 28 August, 4 and 11 September.

65 A memorandum of the meeting and the points discussed occupies three pages of the *Aesacus and Hesperie* sketchbook (datable by other evidence to 1819), TB CLXIX 7r, 7v, 8r of which only the last two pages are in Turner's handwriting, the first in W.B. Cooke's, a hand with a number of characteristics quite different from Turner's and known from other documents:

> (7r) to pay Mr Akerman in the Work of the Rhine to the value of 40£ – Mr Akerman promising to suppress his publication of the Rhine and becomes responsible for the Drawings made for him shall not be sold to any one for the purpose of publishing until 3 or 4 Numbers of
> (7v) our Work are out if Mr Skeutz should produce a work from the above drawings which Mr A agrees to stop the publishing of then nothing to be paid of the forty pounds. If Mr Ackerman can have an additional 5 per cent from Mr Murray's arrangements or the same as Murray he will urge the work. Mr A to be paid by Numbers of the work when published.
> (8r) Mr Gerning to have an equivalent for his notes for the 24 drawings to the

value of 30L: Drg. Mr A agreed to give him 10 Numbers at about 3L per Number the Map now on the road £6

On f.35r of the same sketchbook Turner made a list of Rhine subjects for his own book, including Oberwesel, Burg Lahneck, Johannisberg, Remagen, Mainz, the Brothers, Bacharach, the Mouse Tower, Burg Katz and St Goarshausen.

66 See the biographical notice of von Gerning in the *Literary Gazette* no.70, 23 May 1818, pp.321–2; review in ibid., no.146, 6 November 1819, pp.705–6.

67 Cooke's accounts relating to Turner for 1818–22 are reproduced in Thornbury (1862), vol.2, pp.423–5, where £85 1s appears four times in 1822 against 'Three Drawings of the Rhine'. Prior to this (see p.423) he had spent £1 4s on a copy of Gardnor's *Views on the Rhine*, presumably bought as a pattern-book for the project or perhaps to clarify Turner's more elusive details.

68 These two works (and the watercolour on which cat.no.21 was based) were almost certainly the only Rhine views by Turner to be seen by the public at this date, the others remaining in private houses. There is nothing to suggest that the exhibition held by Fawkes in his London house in 1819 included any of Turner's Rhine views – indeed all the evidence points to the contrary – so it is useless to speculate, as several recent German publications have done, on the influence of these works in the early nineteenth century. The Rhine was simply not connected in the public mind with Turner at this date and there were – in any case – numerous other reasons (already suggested in the first section of this introduction) for the widespread production of Rhine views.

69 According to its subscription list (p.vii), two copies of von Gerning's book were ordered by Messrs Robinson & Co. of Leeds, one copy being specifically destined for 'Walter Fawkes Esq of Otley'.

THE 1820S AND THE FIRST MEUSE – MOSEL TOUR

1 TB CCXVI 1r–9v. Twelve pages relating to the Meuse (ff.1r–6r) are followed by seven on the Mosel (ff.6v–9v). Apart from a few accidental errors, Turner's use of red pencil underlining, a circle and a jagged circle on his maps of the Mosel (ff.8v, 9r, 9v) corresponds exactly to the usage in Schreiber's map of bold type for important places, a circle for 'Walled or open towns' and a similar jagged circle for 'Fortified towns'.

2 A note on TB CLIX 98r gives its French title; another note on CLX 90v gives its German one.

3 From 1817 onwards Turner frequently noted down useful foreign words or sentences in his sketchbooks and during the 1830s he acquired two phrase books to help him in his travels through Germany: F. Ahn, *Handbuch der englischen Umgangssprache* (Cologne, 1834) and Madame de Genlis, *Manuel du Voyageur, or, The Traveller's Pocket Companion, in English and German* (1829). In both these books Turner has added a selection of further phrases in various languages.

4 See Finberg (1909), vol.2, p.681. This dating seems never to have been questioned until, in 1977, Clifford attempted to place the tour in 1825; his mistake was repeated in Wilton (1979), p.409 and Wilton (1982), p.29 but has been corrected in more recent books such as Wilton (1987) and Gage (1987) which returned to the conventional date of 1826.

5 *Paris, Seine, Dieppe* sketchbook (TB CCXI), 21r; *Dieppe, Rouen, Paris* sketchbook (TB CCLVIII), 16r.

6 TB CCXVI 205r–236r. The sketch on f.211r shows the scene of the painting as a whole, with practically no detail. Other pages (ff.221r, 223v) provided all the data needed for the precise depiction of the Collège Communal and Hôtel d'Anvers on the right of the painting. None of these sketches was recognised by Finberg as relating to Turner's oil painting – and indeed only one of them was listed as showing 'Probably Dieppe' – so it did not occur to him to use them as evidence in dating Turner's tour.

7 The *Loire, Tours, Orleans, and Paris* sketchbook contains a memorandum of 23 August 1826 about an order for a set of Turner's *Liber Studiorum* (TB CCXLIX, inside cover). This is not in itself sufficient evidence to date that tour, but can certainly be taken as confirmation of the book's use in 1826. Two other sketchbooks (TB CCXLVII and TB CCXLVIII) were also used during this French tour.

8 The extent to which novels as well as travel books influenced nineteenth-century British visitors to the Continent can be gauged from some of the references of Mrs Trollope on her tour of Belgium and Germany in 1833: 'a most Udolpho-like-looking castle' near Namur (1834, vol.1, p.94); her imagined recognition of many parts of Liège from *Quentin Durward* (pp.103–4); her recollection of one of that novel's minor characters at Coblenz (p.209).

9 Turner's library was to include part III of Robert Batty's *Hanoverian and Saxon Scenery* (proofs and etchings) of 1827. In 1820 Thomas Campbell (see cat.no.29) had travelled from Vienna to Regensburg in Batty's company, describing him as 'brother of the lady who sketched the Italian scenes'.

10 The sequence Liège–Huy–Liège is shown both by Turner's timetable and by the sketches in TB CCXVI and TB CCXVII.

11 TB CCXVI 28v, 29v.

12 Southey (1903), p.119.

13 TB CCXVI 154v.

14 TB CCXVI 30r–36v; TB CCXVII 1v–2r. Turner also sketched the famous rock formations of the Meuse elsewhere in TB CCXVI, as he came across them.

15 TB CCXVI 37r–41r; TB CCXVII 2v–6v.

16 TB CCXVI 43r–44r; TB CCXVII 8v–12r.

17 TB CCXVI 49r–50r; TB CCXVII 12v–15r.

18 TB CCXVI 53r–55v; TB CCXVII 16r–19r.

19 TB CCXVI 57v–60r; TB CCXVII 19v–20r.

20 TB CCXVI 62r–75r.

21 TB CCXVI 75v–80r.

22 TB CCXVI 80v–86r.

23 TB CCXVI 86v–90r.

24 TB CCXVI 90v–97v.

25 Mrs Shelley (1844), vol.1, pp.20–6. See also her description quoted under cat.no.40.

26 Ibid., p.23.

27 TB CCXVI 98r–102r. The sketches on ff.102v–111r must have been drawn on Turner's second day on the Mosel; those on ff.111v–121r on the third; and those on ff.121v–137r on the fourth. Clearly, however, one cannot tell which sketches at Turner's overnight stops belong to the evening, which to the morning. Other sketches were later inserted by Turner on pages used on the Mosel; plainly these are not covered by the break-down above.

28 TB CCXVI 110v–111r.

29 TB CCXVI 121r–123r.

30 TB CCXVI 136r–142r.

31 TB CCXVI 143r–147r.

32 TB CCXVI 147v–180r.

33 It was close to Abbeville that Turner drew the last two sketches in the *Huy and Dinant* sketchbook (TB CCXVII 22r, 23r), which show the same ingredients as those on TB CCXVI 193r, 194r, 194v, 195r. Finberg (1909) identified the windmill in these sketches as that of Crécy-en-Ponthieu (i.e. that at the spot whence Edward III watched the Battle of Crécy), but this is clearly wrong, Turner's viewing station being merely on the outskirts of Abbeville

rather than a dozen miles away.

34 For this tour see Bachrach (1974) and the same author's forthcoming book on Turner and the Netherlands; Cologne (1980), pp.68–9.

35 I.e. *Holland* (TB CCXIV) is used in a very similar way to *Rivers Meuse and Moselle* (TB CCXVI), while *Holland, Meuse, and Cologne* (TB CCXV) follows the precedent set by *Huy and Dinant* (TB CCXVII). Finberg (1909) allocated TB CCXIV to 1825 but was less certain about TB CCXV having been used that year; Wilton (1987), p.166 assigned TB CCXV to the first Meuse–Mosel tour but this does not seem possible since it contains sketches only of the lowest part of the Meuse.

36 TB CCXIV contains three pages of close-up sketches of the imperial chapel at Aachen (ff.152v, 153v, 154r); also a careful record of the Maison Curtius at Liège, with each of the numerous small reliefs of men, birds and animals on its façade being drawn separately and named (ff.155v, 156r). Both TB CCXIV and TB CCXV contain sketches of Düsseldorf (TB CCXIV 140r, 140v; TB CCXV 35v–36r, 36v–37r).

37 Indeed, little is known of Mr John Broadhurst at all. On 16 July 1828 he sold all three of the Turner oils he owned at Phillips's auction house in New Bond Street. That same summer he failed to buy one that Turner had just painted expressly for him ('Dido Directing the Equipment of the Fleet', B & J 241, RA 1828). By May 1854 he lived at Campden Hill, Kensington (see the entries for B & J 91, 231, 232; *The Times* 14 July and 15 July 1828, p.4; *Willis's Current Notes*, May 1854, p.44). At the time of the Phillips sale Turner's 'Dieppe' and 'Guardship at the Great Nore' were both sketched by Captain Robert Batty, along with fifteen other paintings also being sold there, but Batty's collection of sketches does not include Turner's 'Cologne' (pen and ink sketches, private collection).

38 The sketches in the *Holland* sketchbook (TB CCXIV, especially ff.142v–143r and 164v) show both the general scene and individual motifs; they do not, however, include such a detailed depiction of the buildings on the far right as one of Turner's large sketches of 1817 (TB CLXI 54r) which he must surely have consulted.

THE 1830S AND THE SECOND MEUSE–MOSEL TOUR

1 For Turner's visits to Italy, see C. Powell, *Turner in the South*, 1987. For his Petworth gouaches, see M. Butlin, M. Luther and I. Warrell, *Turner at Petworth*, 1989, which reproduces all these scenes and dates all except two (in a rather different style) to 1827. In view of the wide disparity of styles amongst those discussed here, it may be felt that even those two may perhaps be dated to 1827. For the French gouaches, see the essays by N. Alfrey in *Turner en France*, Paris, 1981, pp.187–98 and 327.

2 W 930–90, engraved as R 432–92. Many other gouaches of French river scenery, which were not engraved, are among the sheets catalogued as TB CCLIX.

3 See e.g. the advertisements in the *Athenaeum*, 25 May 1833, p.336 and *Gentleman's Magazine*, May 1833, p.448.

4 The three volumes of *Turner's Annual Tour* were produced 'under the superintendence of' Charles Heath, although they were published by Longmans, and the text accompanying the plates was written by Leitch Ritchie. Meanwhile, *Heath's Picturesque Annual for 1833* (also published by Longmans) had consisted of 'Travelling Sketches on the Rhine, and in Belgium and Holland' by Leitch Ritchie, accompanying 26 engravings after Clarkson Stanfield. It would have been very difficult to market a *Turner's Annual Tour* devoted to the Rhine immediately after this – even if Charles Heath's financial situation had been healthy enough for him to envisage it; especially since the year 1832 had also seen the appearance of another very similar publication, *Tombleson's Views of the Rhine* edited by W.G. Fearnside.

Since the Longmans–Heath–Ritchie collaboration extended beyond the confines of the *Turner's Annual Tour* project, there must be some doubt as to whether the umbrella title 'Great Rivers of Europe' attached to their advertisement really does indicate that all the rivers were to be illustrated solely by Turner – a point which all Turner scholars have hitherto taken for granted.

5 See Finberg (1909), pp.685–92. However, when Finberg came to catalogue the contents of the sketchbooks of the second tour he realised that close parallels existed with these drawings, a matter pursued by Wilkinson (1975) and other recent writers. Finberg was probably misled by 'received opinion' on dating at the time he was writing, presumably deriving from Ruskin.

6 Following the date given by Finberg (1909), pp.916–30 and apparently never subsequently questioned.

7 This hand has now been identified by the present writer and the manuscript material and its author will form the subject of a forthcoming article.

8 Gage (1980), no.187 (to Henry McConnell about 'Venice', RA 1834, B & J 356). G. Finley, *Landscapes of Memory*, 1980, chapter 9, especially pp.176–83. This well-documented Scottish tour of Turner's has, curiously, been omitted from several more recent books on the artist containing chronologies.

9 See A.M. Reitzel, *Die Renaissance Gutenbergs*, Mainz, 1968; A. von Stolterfoth, *Malerische Beschreibung von Mainz und der Umgegend* (Mainz, 1840), facsimile reprint, Mainz, 1987; *The Times*, 6 October 1835, p.6; 26 August 1837, p.3; *Literary Gazette*, 2 September 1837, p.565; *Athenaeum*, 9 September 1837, p.662; E. Plon, *Thorvaldsen. His Life and Works*, 1874, pp.116, 242.

10 Gage (1980), no.227. This is apparently dated 'Saturday Augt 2', an understandable slip of the pen if Turner was writing very late at night.

11 Royal Academy, General Assembly Minutes Book, vol.IV (1826–41), 3 August 1839.

12 Ibid., 30 September 1839.

13 J. Gage, 'Further Correspondence of J.M.W. Turner', *Turner Studies*, vol.6, no.1, 1986, no.201a where the letter, which Turner himself merely dated '30 September', is associated with the year 1836 when Stanfield visited the Meuse and the Mosel. This is, however, an impossible connection, given the dates of Stanfield's tour: see *The Spectacular Career of Clarkson Stanfield 1793–1867*, exhibition catalogue by Pieter van der Merwe (1979), pp.124–8, 181.

14 For Allom's views, see Roscoe (1841). Allom's depictions of Dinant and Louvain (pls.13, 14, 16) are very close to Turner's (cat.nos.96, 97, 107). Engravings after Bartlett's views of the Rhine appeared in Wright (1841–2).

15 See the entry for 'Bridge of Sighs, Ducal Palace and Custom-House, Venice: Canaletti Painting' (B & J 349).

16 Gage (1980), no.186, dated 1 or 7 August, includes the phrase 'I am about leaving Town for some time'.

17 The Burg Eltz drawings were dated to 1844 by Wilton (1979) but these have subsequently been associated with a number of loose sheets in the Turner Bequest with drawings of recognisable German subjects (Cologne, Andernach, Bingen) and redated to *c.*1834 (Cologne, 1980). The firm dating of all these must, however, await further research into both TB CCXCII and TB CCCXLI.

18 For instance, one summer tour on the Continent about which nothing is yet known is that of 1837. Turner was absent

from home from late July until 5 September when he belatedly acknowledged the book sent to him on 28 July by Dawson Turner (see Gage, 1980, no.211 (last paragraph) and no.210, where '28 July' was unfortunately misprinted as '28 August').

19 It was the Treaty of London, signed by Austria, Great Britain, France, Prussia and Russia and guaranteeing the independence and neutrality of Belgium, that was violated in 1914 when it was so notoriously referred to as 'a scrap of paper'.

20 See the advertisement in *The Times*, 31 July 1839, p.1.

21 TB CCLXXXVII 1v–2r (see under cat.no.106).

22 TB CCLXXXVII 2v–5r, 10r–12r. The sketches on f.8r almost certainly show the series of square supports built to carry railway lines across valleys at this date (compare those of the Val-Benoît railway bridge in *Vues de Liège* (1849), pl.21).

23 TB CCLXXXVII 13r, 14r.

24 TB CCLXXXVII 18v–26r, 34v–39v.

25 Scott's description of the grotesque physical appearance which led to de la Marck's nickname and his foul murder of the Bishop of Liège are both to be found in chapter XXII of *Quentin Durward*; his unseen but threatening presence hangs over much of the novel. The superstitious legend relating to the treasure was known to Scott through Richard Heber. His account and Scott's retelling of the story both form part of the Introduction to the sixth canto of *Marmion* (see cat.no.111). This was printed in vol. VII of Scott's *Poetical Works* (pp.301–3), to which Turner had contributed two illustrations (R 505–6).

26 TB CCLXXXVII 27r, 28r, 28v–33r.

27 TB CCXXIV 21, 22, 23, 25, 87.

28 TB CCXXIV 18 (Klotten); 19 (Namur); 20 (Huy); 33 (Klotten); 34 (Namur); 54 (?Klotten); 91 (Kobern); 100 (Kobern); 108 (Alken and Burg Thurandt); 110 (Cochem); 111 (Cochem); 138 (Gondorf); 209 (Dinant). In every case Turner's viewpoints are consistent with those used in the 1839 sketchbooks. The many drawings catalogued together as TB CCXXIV have traditionally been associated with Turner's first Meuse–Mosel tour and dated to *c*.1826.

29 TB CCLXXXVII 57r; 49v.

30 TB CCLXXXVII 46v–47r.

31 For details of these sketches in TB CCLXXXVII and CCLXXXVIII, see the Appendix.

32 TB CCXC 5r–40v. Finberg assumed that Turner travelled downstream (hence the name of the sketchbook) but this is clearly wrong. Turner obviously returned from Coblenz to the Mosel on one of the roads through the Eifel described in Murray's *Handbook for Travellers* of 1836; this accounts both for his sketches of Mayen on the misplaced pages ff.42v–43r (see cat.no.83) and also for the distant views of Cochem from the hills on ff.4r–4v. A sketch on f.42r, inscribed 'Wiellin', may well show Welling, which Turner would have seen as he approached Mayen from Coblenz along the Nette valley.

33 TB CCXCI 2r–34v.

34 TB CCXC 55r–60r, 61v.

35 Gage (1980), no.228.

TURNER'S RHINE IN THE 1840S

1 Many of the traditional titles given to W 1318–48 are wrong, but the Middle Rhine is certainly well represented in this group. On one tour Turner also went up the Mosel from Coblenz, but probably not as far as has been previously supposed. It has not been possible to study photographs of every work in this group, but the following re-identifications (and de-identifications) should be noted:

W 1319 does not show Andernach
W 1322 does not show Ehrenbreitstein and Coblenz
W 1325 is unlikely to show the Mosel near Traben-Trarbach
W 1327: Burg Rheinfels on the Rhine
W 1328: Bacharach on the Rhine
W 1330: The Leyen Burg at Gondorf on the Mosel
W 1336 does not show Beilstein
W 1337 does not show Cochem
W 1339 does not show 'A bridge over the Mosel' since the scene is clearly neither Trier nor Coblenz
W 1340 does not show Burg Sooneck
W 1343: Wellmich and Burg Maus on the Rhine
W 1345: Burg Rheinfels
W 1346: The Leyen Burg at Gondorf
W 1347: Oberwesel

Within the confines of this catalogue it is not possible to do more than touch on the many late representations of the Rhine in the Turner Bequest, but the author hopes to present this material elsewhere on a future occasion.

2 TB CLX 63r.

3 Turner's sketches of the Ahr valley are among the loose sheets catalogued as TB CCCXLIV. Sixteen images are on different parts of a folded and separated imperial sheet watermarked T EDMONDS 1825/NOT BLEACHED and can be identified as follows:

f.39r The Saffenburg
f.39v Ahrweiler
f.43r Ahrweiler
f.43v The Saffenburg
f.44v Ahrweiler
f.45r The Saffenburg
f.46r The Saffenburg
f.46v Ahrweiler
f.99 Ahrweiler
f.100 Guckley and Altenahr
f.101 A church on the Ahr
f.102 Ahrweiler
f.103 Rech
f.104 Two views of the 'Bunte Kuh' rock on the Ahr
f.105 Blankenheim
f.106 Buildings on the Ahr

The remaining images on this sheet show the Godesburg (ff.23, 34, 35, 36, 37), Bonn (f.44r), Nonnenwerth and Rolandseck (f.339r), the Drachenfels (f.339v) and the view down the Rhine from Linz (f.340v).

Four more sketches of Ahrweiler appear on different parts of a folded and separated imperial sheet watermarked J WHATMAN/TURKEY MILL/1834/N (ff.97r, 97v, 98r, 98v). Other identified sketches on this sheet also include ten of the Godesburg (ff.24–33) which is a strong indication that both these groups of sketches were drawn on the same tour.

Turner's Ahr sketches were first noted by Stader (1981). The above correlation between images and sheets was made possible through Peter Bower's analysis of Turner's papers.

4 TB CCCLI 10r, 14r, 15r, 16r, 17r, 19r, 20r, 21r, 22r, 24r. See also Turner's own comments of December 1844 on this tour (Gage (1980), no.275); this reference to marching up 'some of the small valleys of the Rhine' and finding them 'more interesting than I expected' seems from its context, however, to apply to the High Rhine rather than the Middle Rhine.

5 All of Turner's illustrations to Byron (including cat.no.25 and fig.9) were also published, alongside the works of other artists, in *Finden's Landscape and Portrait Illustrations to the Life and Works of Lord Byron*, with a text by William Brockedon, in 1833–4.

6 L. Herrmann, *Turner Prints*, 1990, p.240.

7 TB CLX 73v–74r (see under cat.no.9), developed into W 674 and W 688.

Select Bibliography

All books published in London unless otherwise stated.

TURNER

Armstrong, W. (1902), *Turner*

Bachrach, A.G.H. (1974), *Turner and Rotterdam. 1817, 1825, 1841*

Clifford, T. (1977), *Vues pittoresques de Luxembourg. Dessins et aquarelles de J.M. William Turner (1775–1851)*, Luxembourg

[Cook, E.T.] (1905), *Hidden Treasures at the National Gallery*

Cormack, M. (1975), *J.M.W. Turner, R.A., 1775–1851 A Catalogue of Drawings and Watercolours in the Fitzwilliam Museum, Cambridge*, Cambridge

Herrmann, L. (1968), *Ruskin and Turner*

Herrmann, L. (1970), 'Ruskin and Turner: A Riddle Resolved', *Burlington Magazine*, no.811, October, pp.696–9

Finberg, A.J. (1909), *A Complete Inventory of the Drawings of the Turner Bequest*, 2 vols.

Finberg, A.J. (1961), *The Life of J.M.W. Turner, R.A.*, 2nd ed., Oxford

Gage, J. (1980), *Collected Correspondence of J.M.W. Turner*, Oxford

Gage, J. (1987), *J.M.W. Turner: 'A Wonderful Range of Mind'*

Holme, C. (ed.) (1903), *The Genius of J.M.W. Turner, R.A.*

Powell, C. (1990), 'Turner's Travelling Companion of 1802; A Mystery Resolved?', *Turner Society News*, no.54, pp.12–15

Ruskin, J. (1903–12), *The Works of John Ruskin*, ed. E.T. Cook and A. Wedderburn, 39 vols.

Stader, K.H. (1981), *William Turner und der Rhein*, Bonn

Thornbury, W. (1862), *The Life of J.M.W. Turner, R.A.*, 2 vols.

Thornbury, W.G. (1877), *The Life of J.M.W. Turner, R.A.*, 2nd ed.

Wilkinson, G. (1975), *Turner's Colour Sketches 1820–34*

Wilton, A. (1979), *The Life and Work of J.M.W. Turner*

Wilton, A. (1982), *Turner Abroad*

Wilton, A. (1987), *Turner in his Time*

Yardley, E.H. (1988), 'The Turner Collector: the Birket Foster Collection of Turner Watercolours', *Turner Studies*, vol.8, no.1, pp.41–5

EXHIBITION CATALOGUES

Athens (1981), *J.M.W. Turner (1775–1851)* (National Pinakothiki and Alexander Soutzos Museum)

Brussels (1971), *Turner Watercolours lent by the British Museum* (Musée Provisoire d'Art Moderne)

Cologne (1980), *J.M. William Turner: Köln und der Rhein* (Wallraf-Richartz-Museum)

International Exhibitions Foundation (1977–8), *Turner Watercolours from the British Museum* (Cleveland, Detroit and Philadelphia)

London (1974), *Turner 1775–1851* (Royal Academy)

London (1975), *Turner in the British Museum: Drawings and Watercolours* (British Museum)

Luxembourg (1984), *J.M.W. Turner in Luxembourg and its Neighbourhood* (Musée de l'Etat)

Madrid (1983), *J.M.W. Turner: dibujos y acuarelas del Museo Británico* (Museo de Prado)

Paris (1981), *Turner en France* (Centre Culturel du Marais)

Paris (1983), *J.M.W. Turner* (Grand Palais)

Texas (1982), *J.M.W. Turner* (Museum of Fine Arts, Houston)

York (1980), *Turner in Yorkshire* (City Art Gallery)

THE RHINE, MEUSE AND MOSEL

Campbell, C. (1817), *The Traveller's Complete Guide through Belgium and Holland . . . with a Sketch of a Tour in Germany*, 2nd ed.

Gardnor, J. (1792), *Views taken on and near The River Rhine, at Aix la Chapelle, and on the River Maese*, 2nd ed.

Hills, R. (1816), *Sketches in Flanders and Holland; with Some Account of a Tour through Parts of those Countries, shortly after the Battle of Waterloo; in a Series of Letters to a Friend*

Quin, M.J. (1843), *Steam Voyages on the Seine, the Moselle, and the Rhine . . .*, 2 vols.

Roscoe, T. (1841), *Belgium Picturesque & Romantic*

Schreiber, A.W. (1818), *The Traveller's Guide down the Rhine*

Shelley, Mrs (1844), *Rambles in Germany and Italy, in 1840, 1842, and 1843*, 2 vols.

Southey, R. (1903), *Journal of a Tour in the Netherlands in the Autumn of 1815*, ed. W. Robertson Nicoll

Tower, C. (1913), *The Moselle*

Trollope, Mrs (1834), *Belgium and Western Germany in 1833*, 2 vols.

Wright, G.N. (1841–2), *The Rhine, Italy, and Greece*, 2 vols.

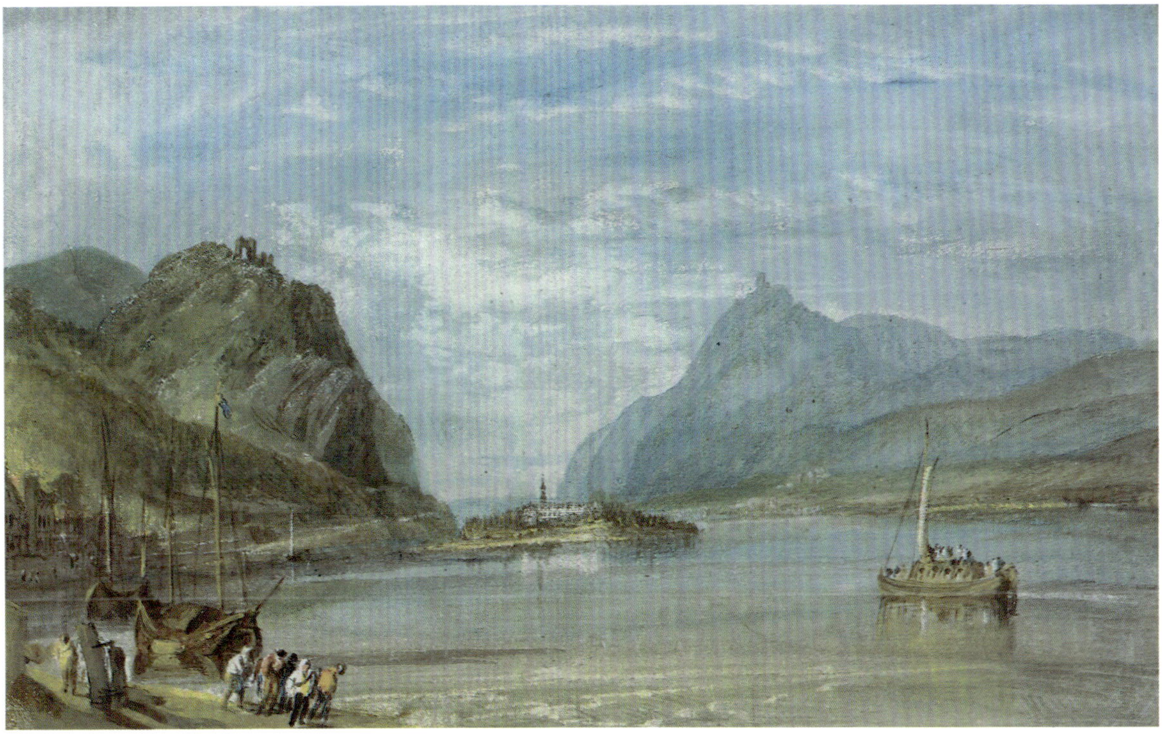

4 **Rolandswerth, Nunnery and Drachenfels** 1817

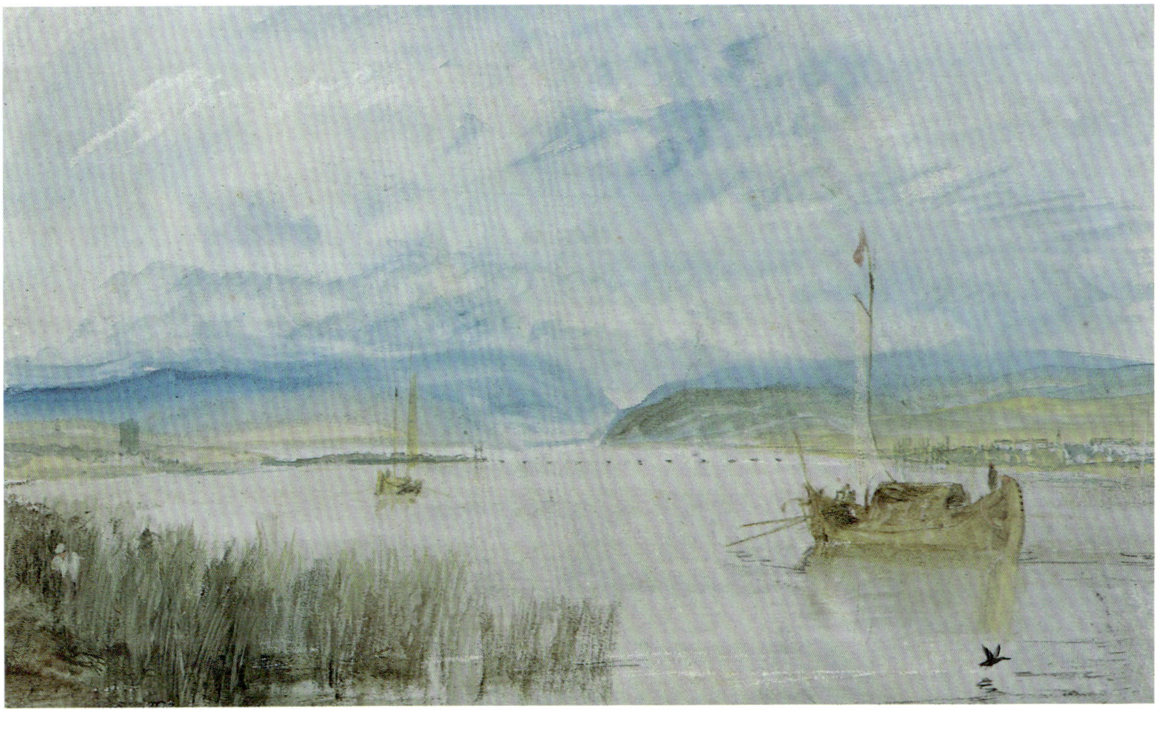

5 **Neuwied and Weissenthurm** 1817

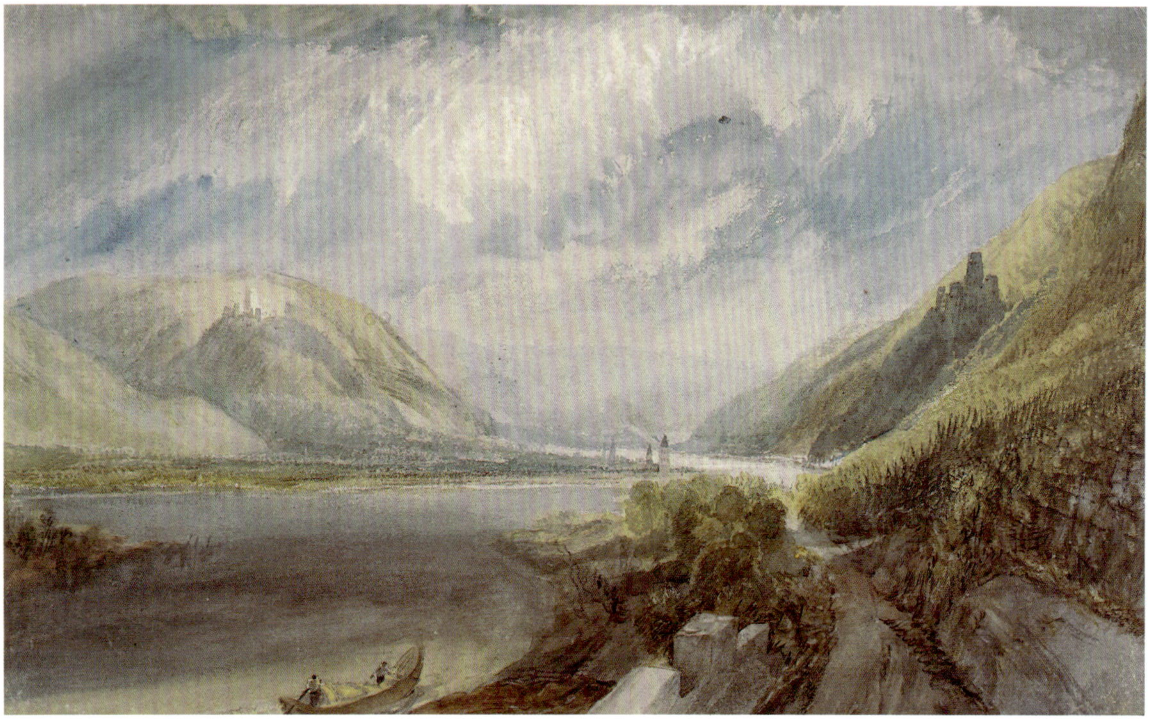

6 **Junction of the Lahn** 1817

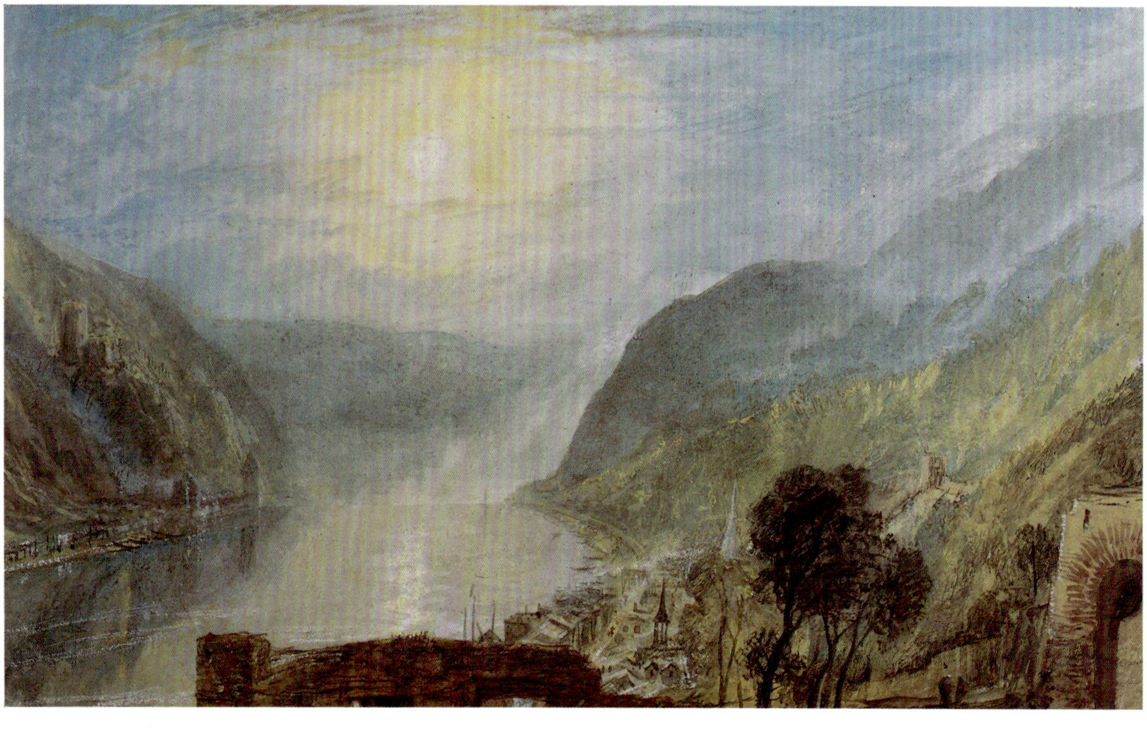

7 **From Rheinfels, Looking over St Goar to Burg Katz** 1817

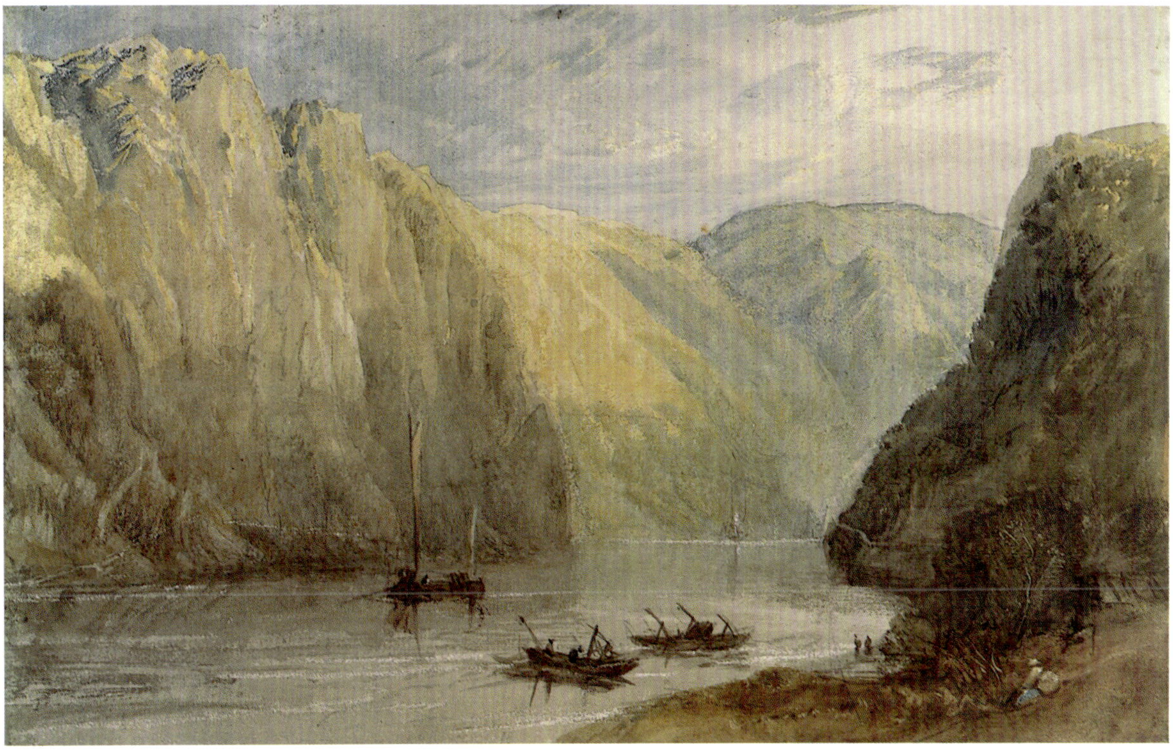

8 **The Lorelei** 1817

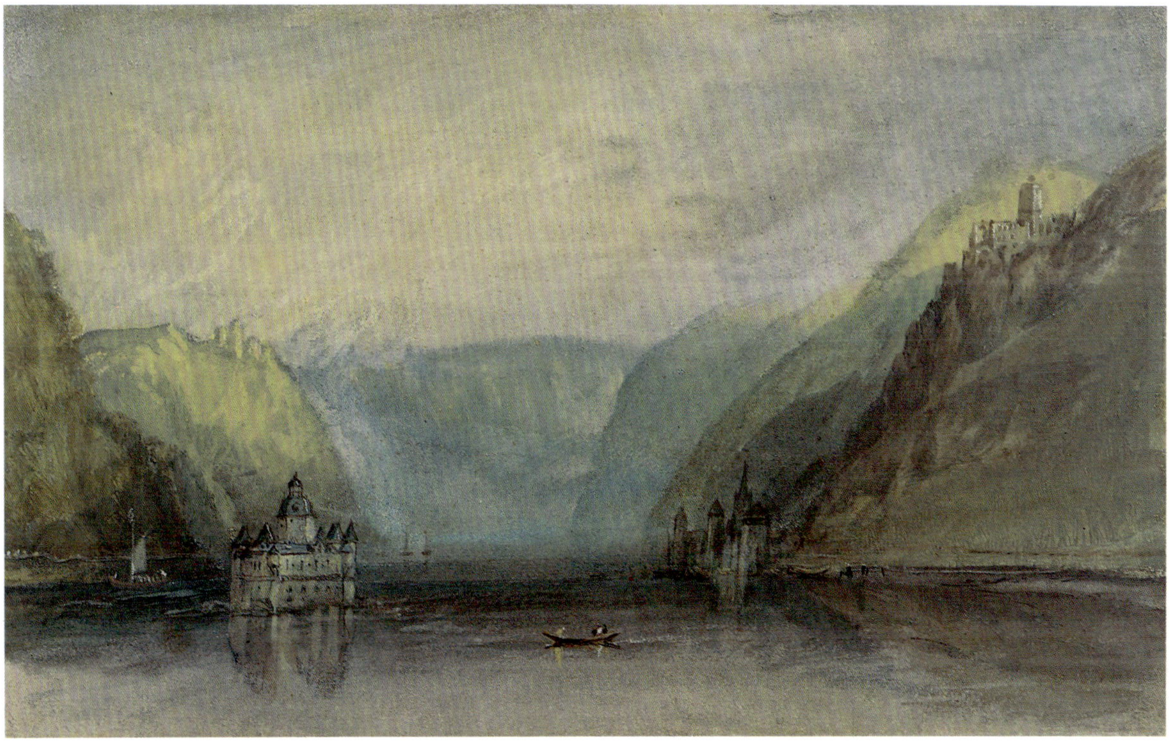

9 **The Pfalz on the Rhine** 1817

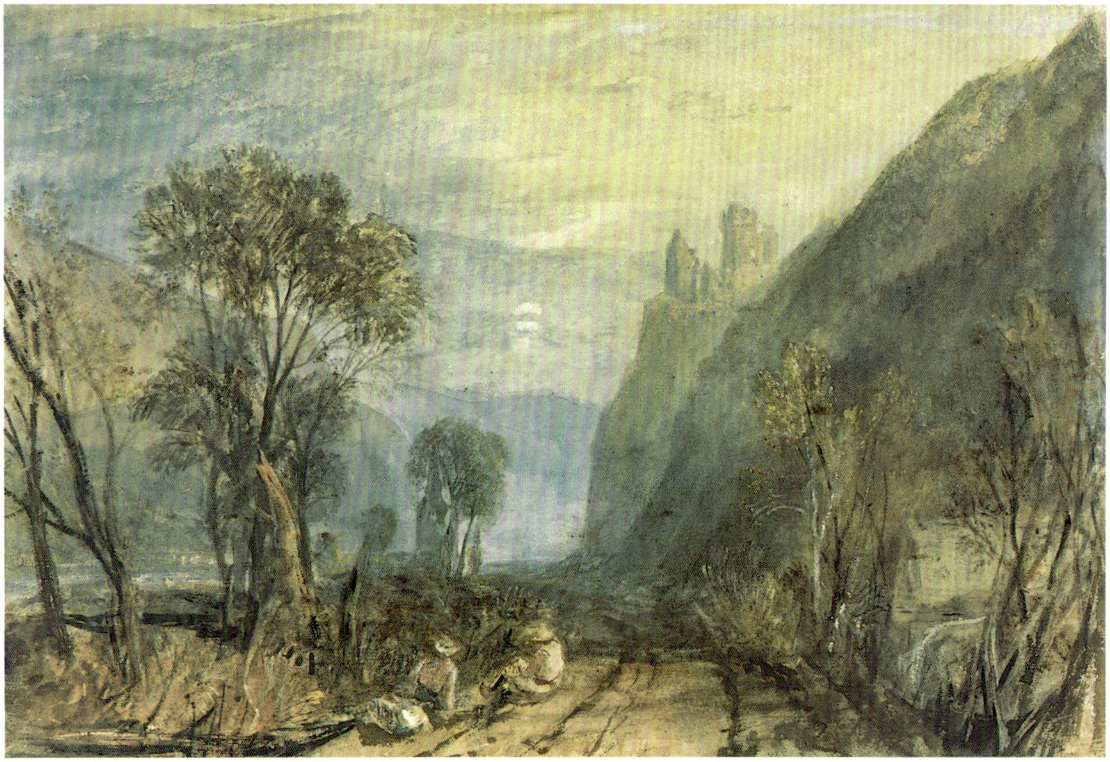

10 **The Bautsburg** 1817

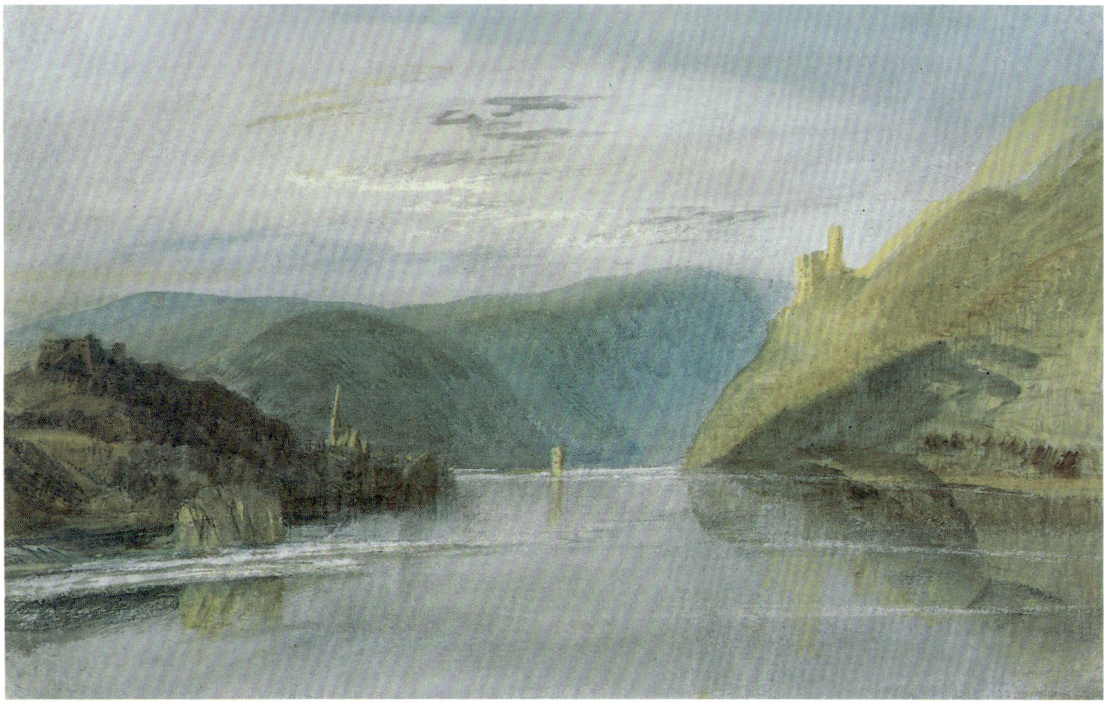

11 **The Binger Loch and Mäuseturm** 1817

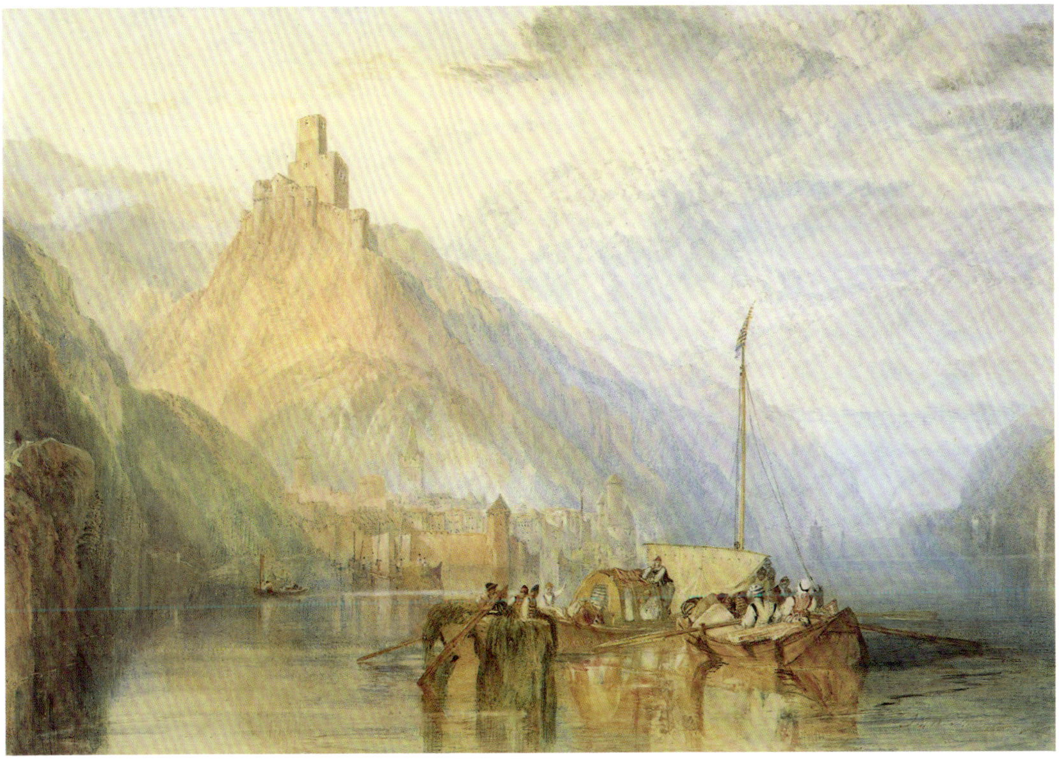

20 **Kaub and the Castle of Gutenfels** *c.*1820

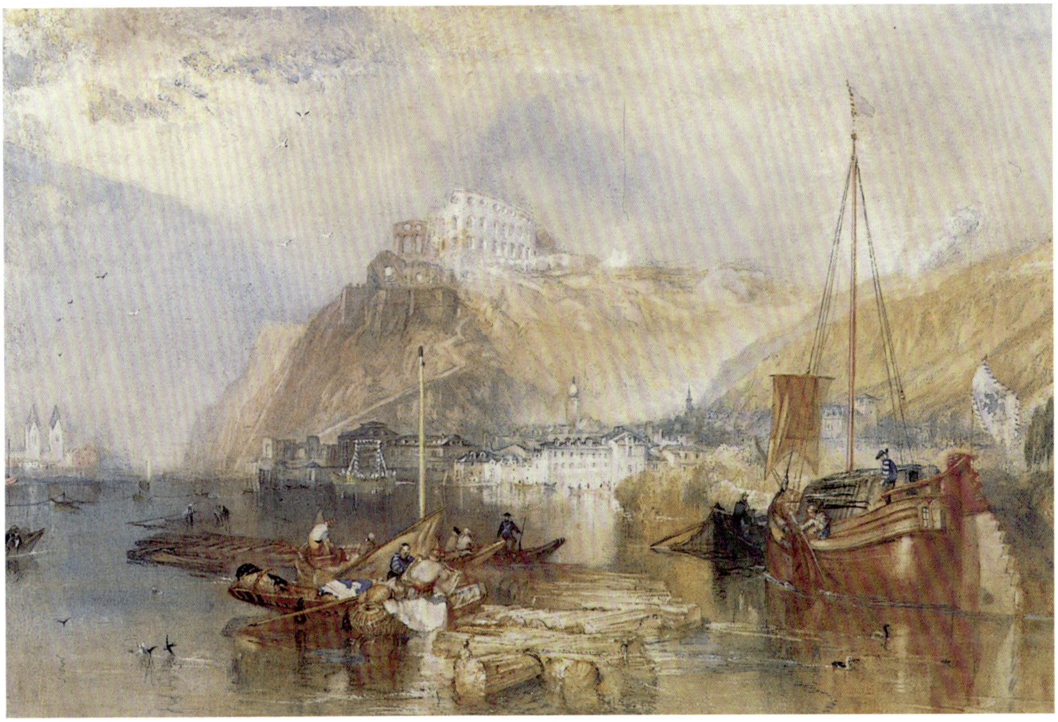

24 **Ehrenbreitstein** *c.*1832

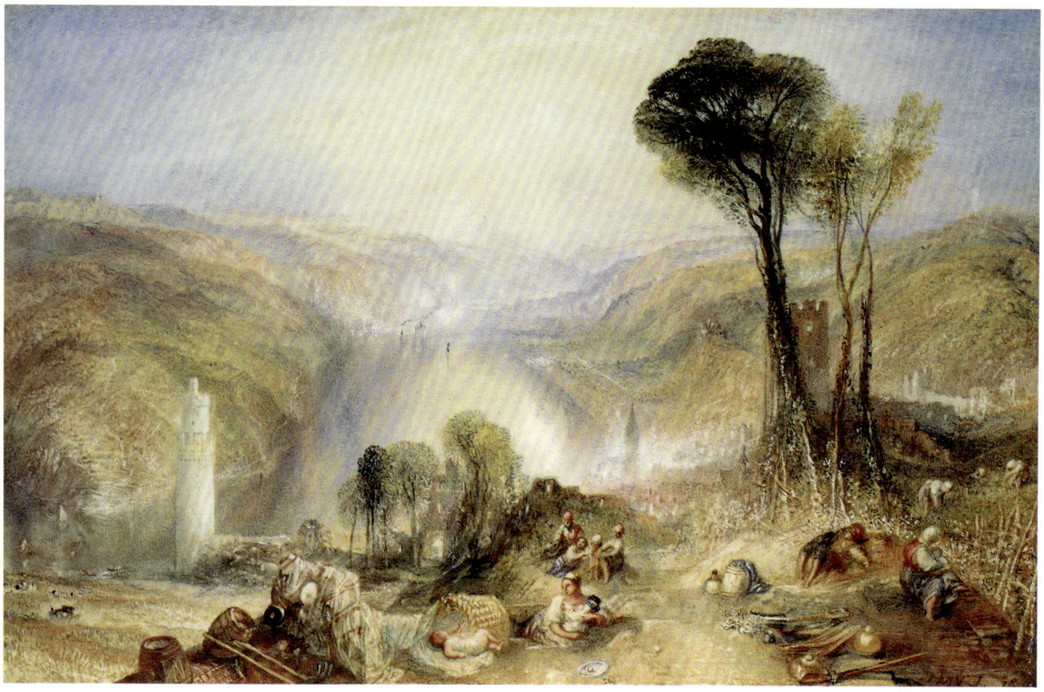

30 **Oberwesel** 1840

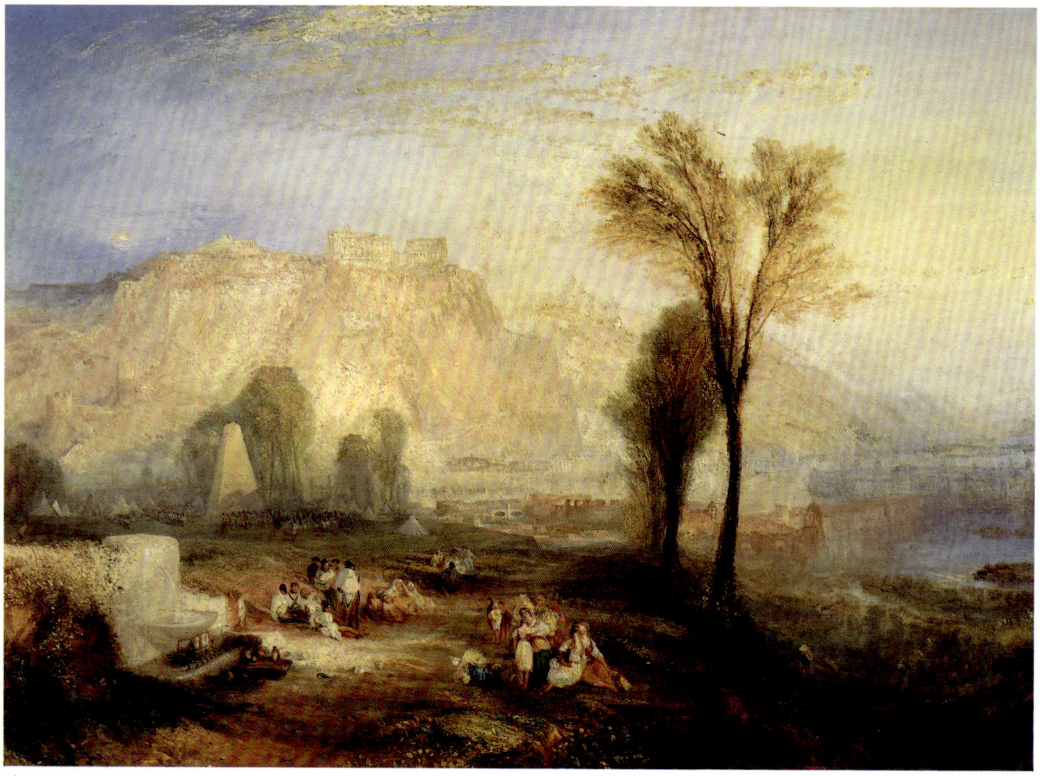

41 **The Bright Stone of Honour (Ehrenbreitstein), and Tomb of Marceau, from Byron's 'Childe Harold'** 1835

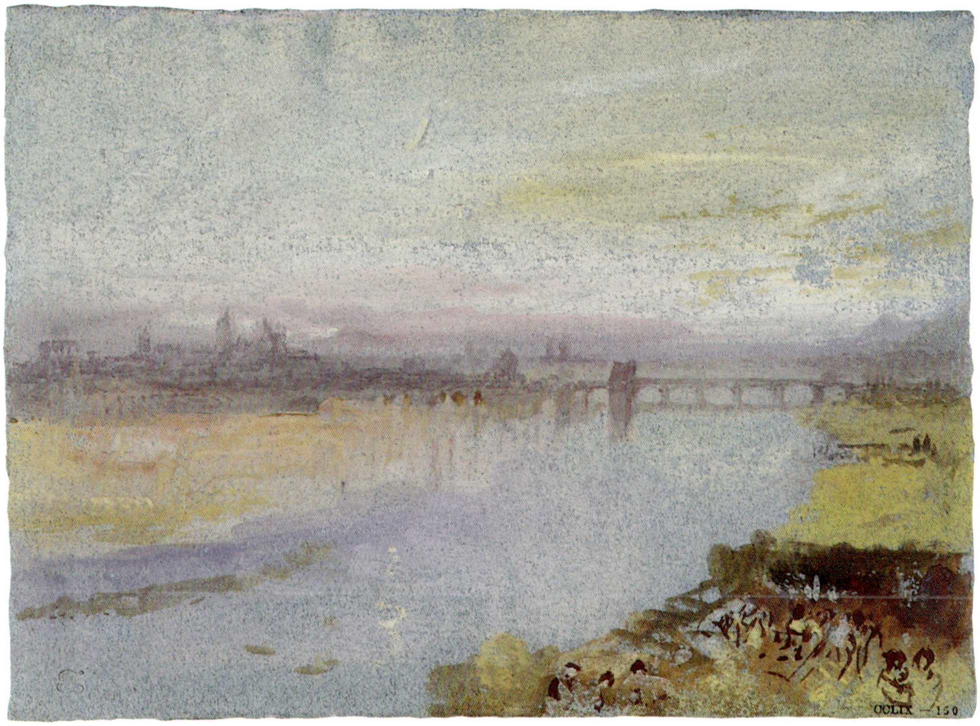

47 **Trier from the West** *c.*1839

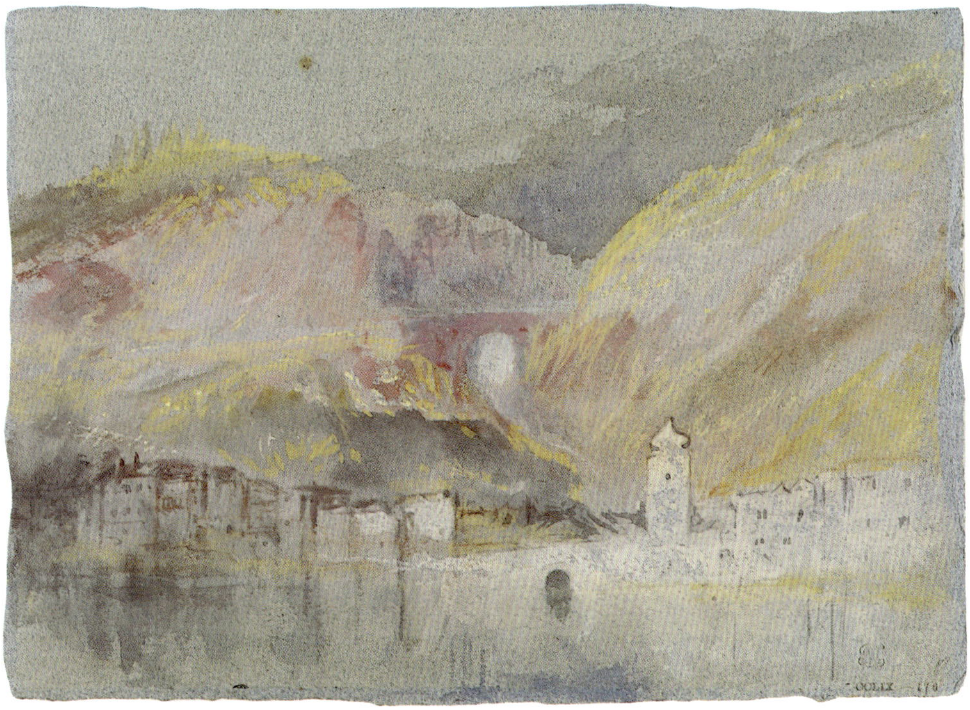

49 **Pallien and the Napoleonsbrücke** *c.*1839

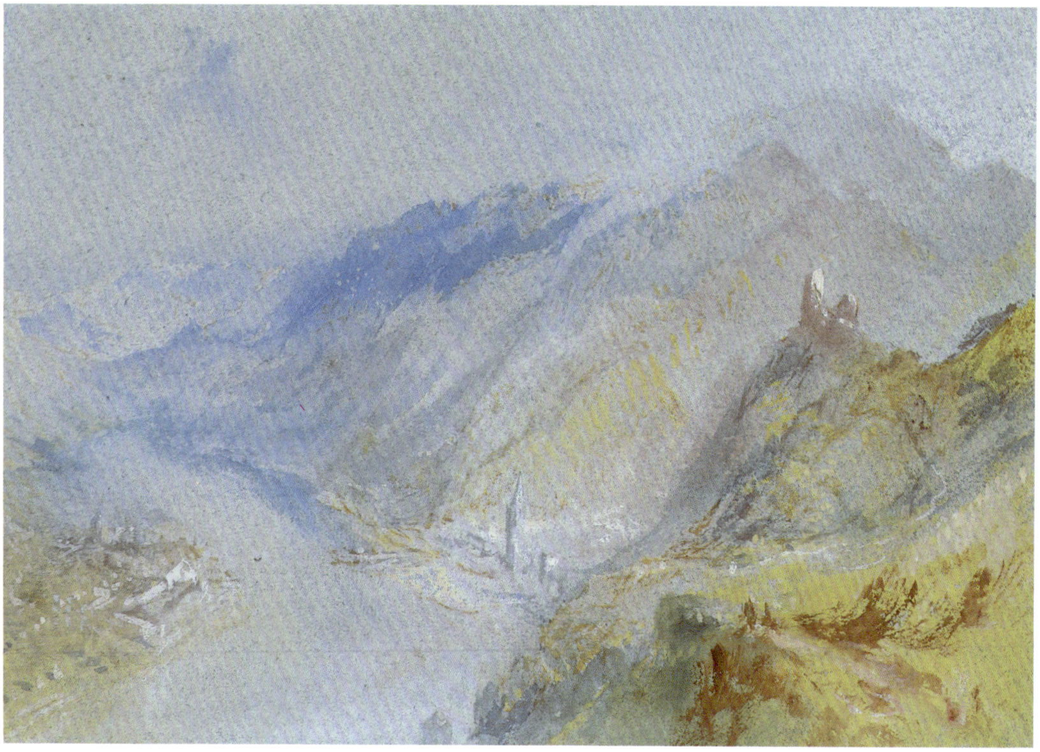

52 **Bernkastel and the Landshut** *c.*1839

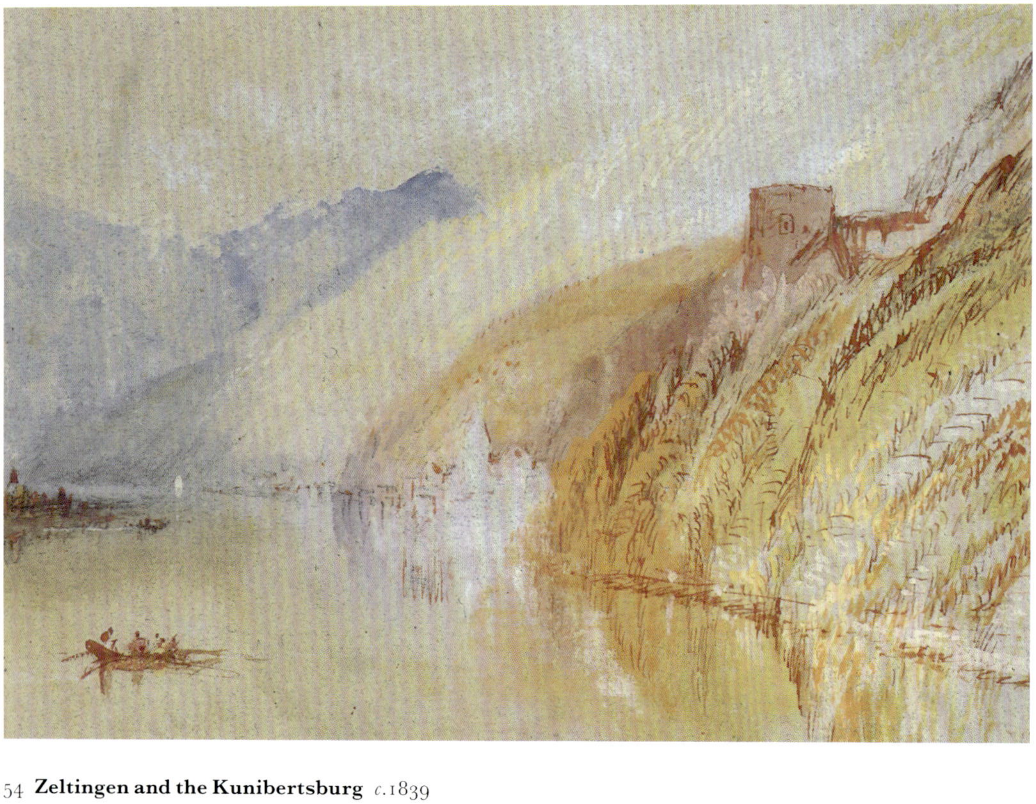

54 **Zeltingen and the Kunibertsburg** *c.*1839

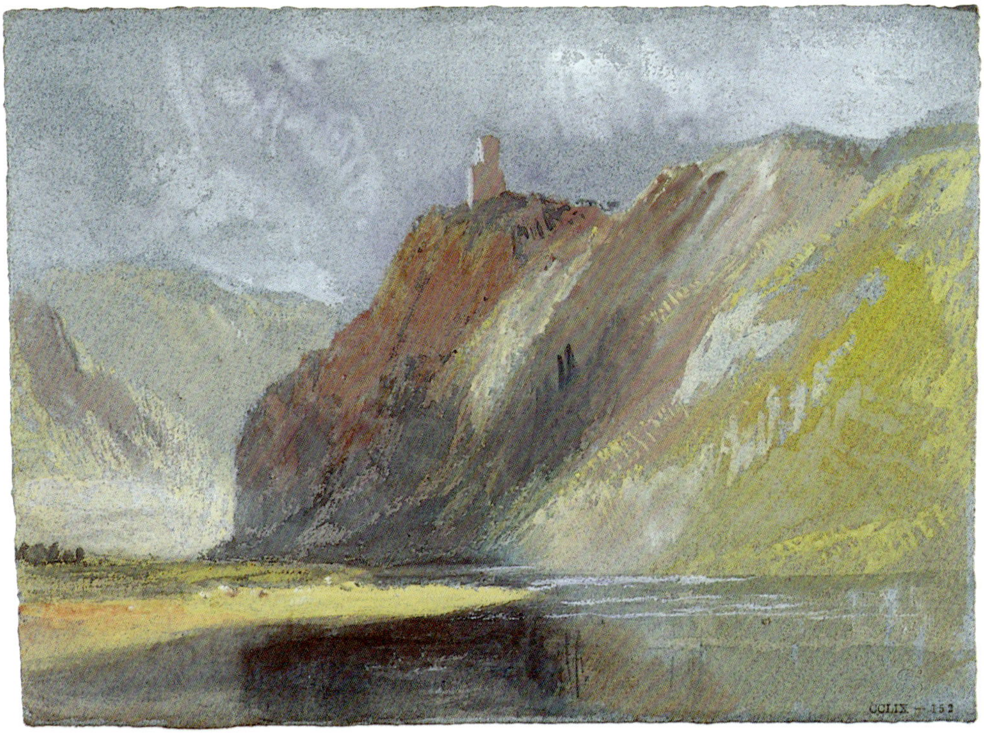

56 **The Ruined Monastery at Wolf** *c.*1839

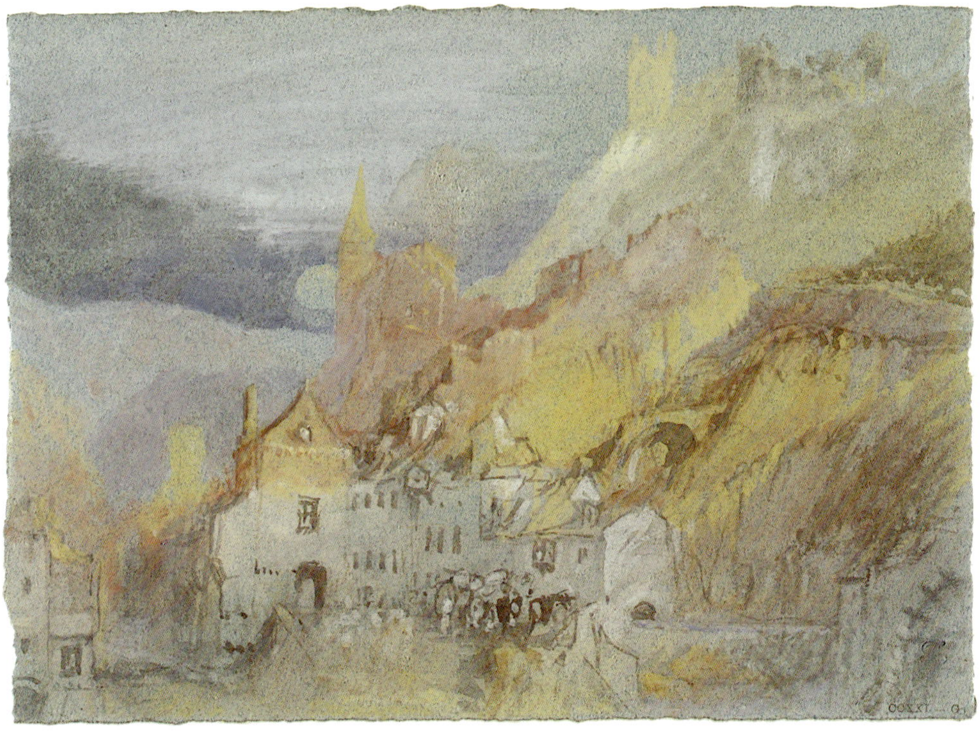

58 **The Entrance to Trarbach from Bernkastel** *c.*1839

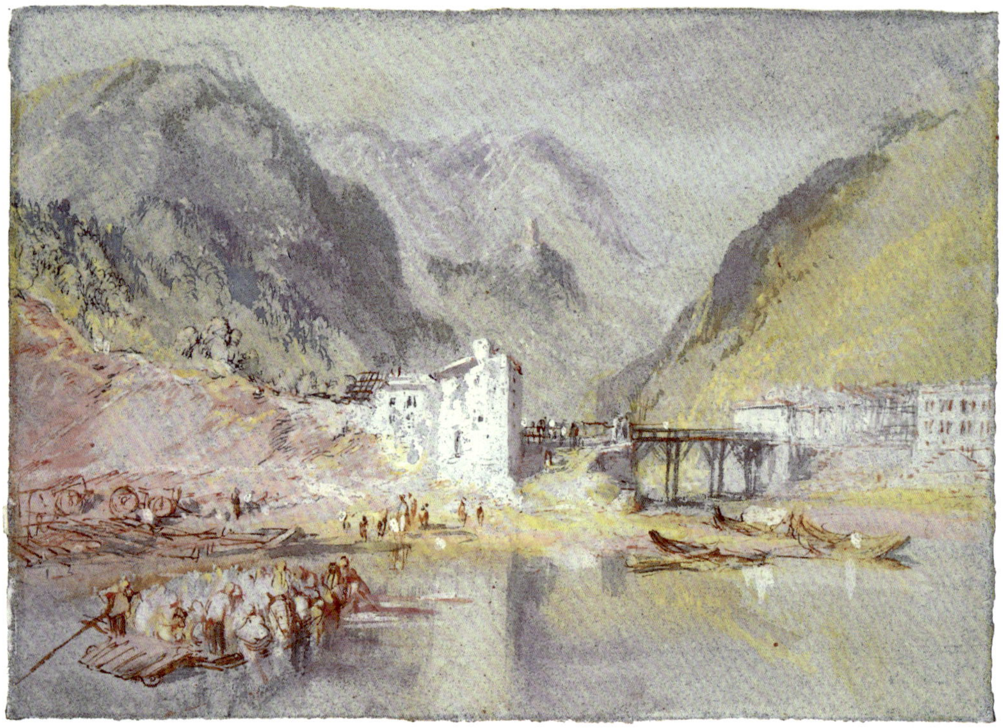

61 **Alf and Burg Arras** *c.*1839

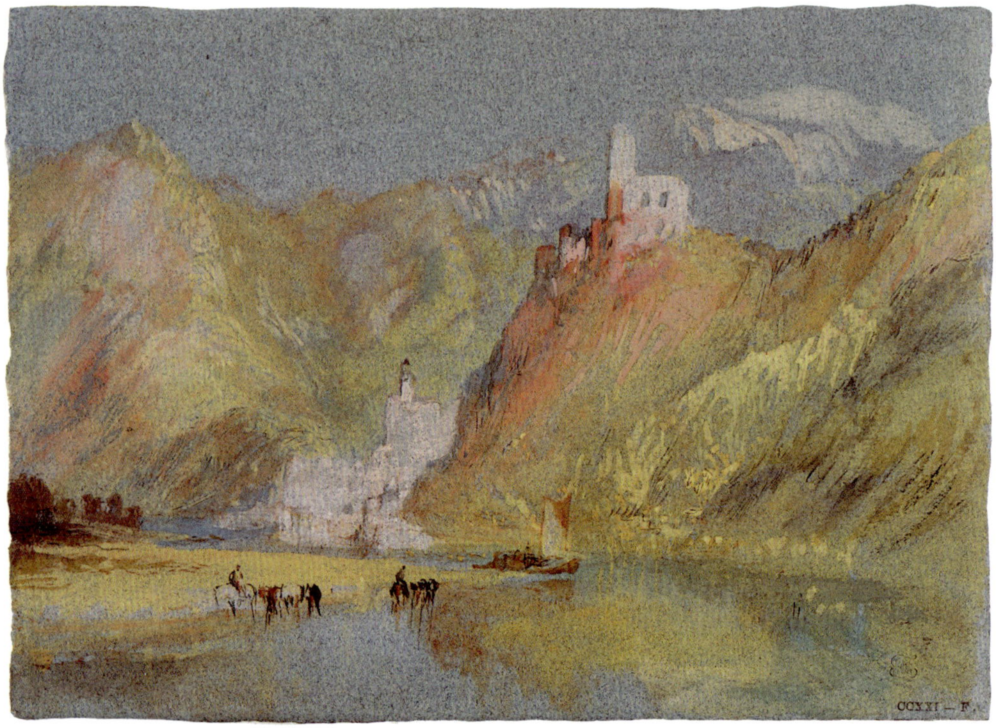

62 **Beilstein and Burg Metternich** *c.*1839

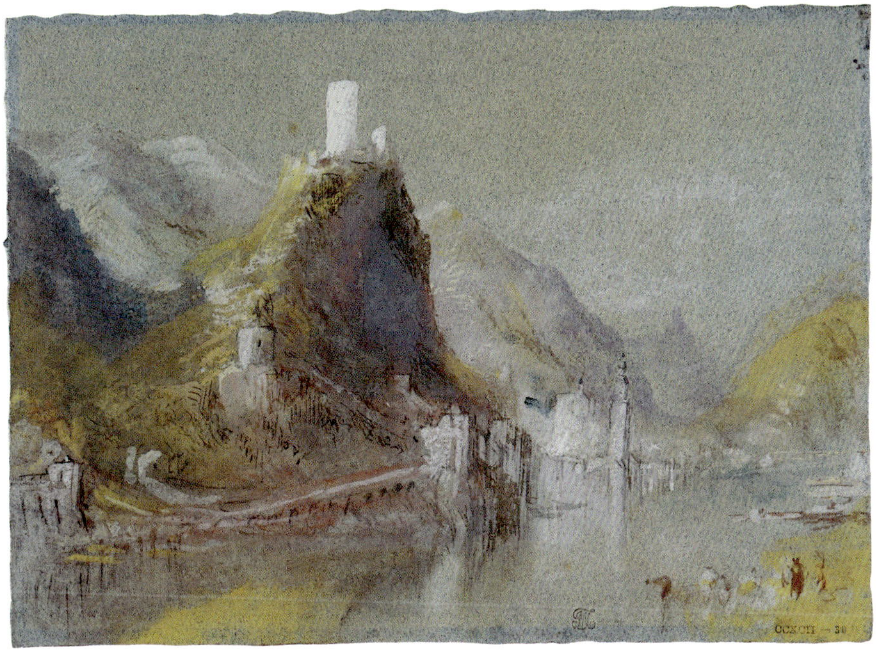

63 **Cochem from the South** *c.*1839

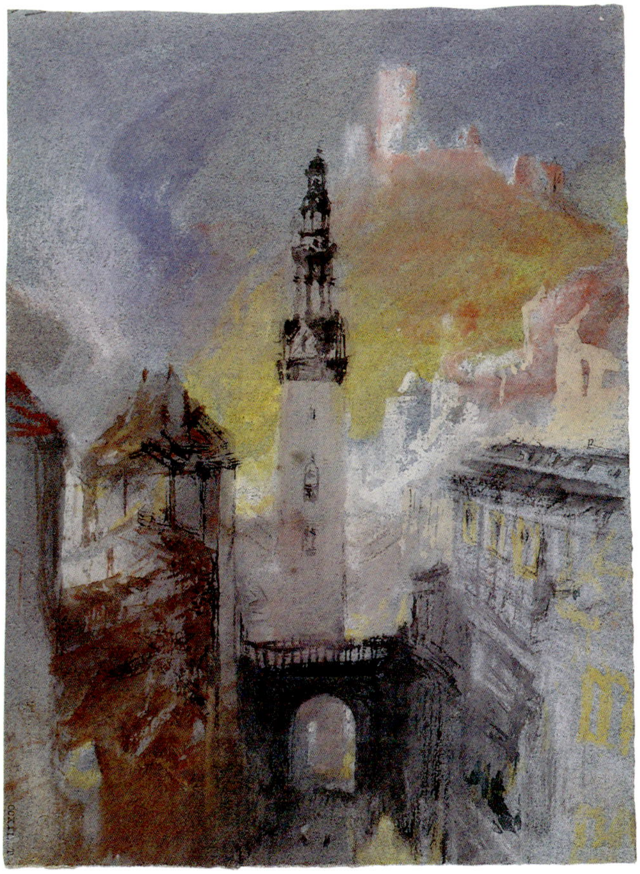

64 **St Martin's Church, Cochem** *c.*1839

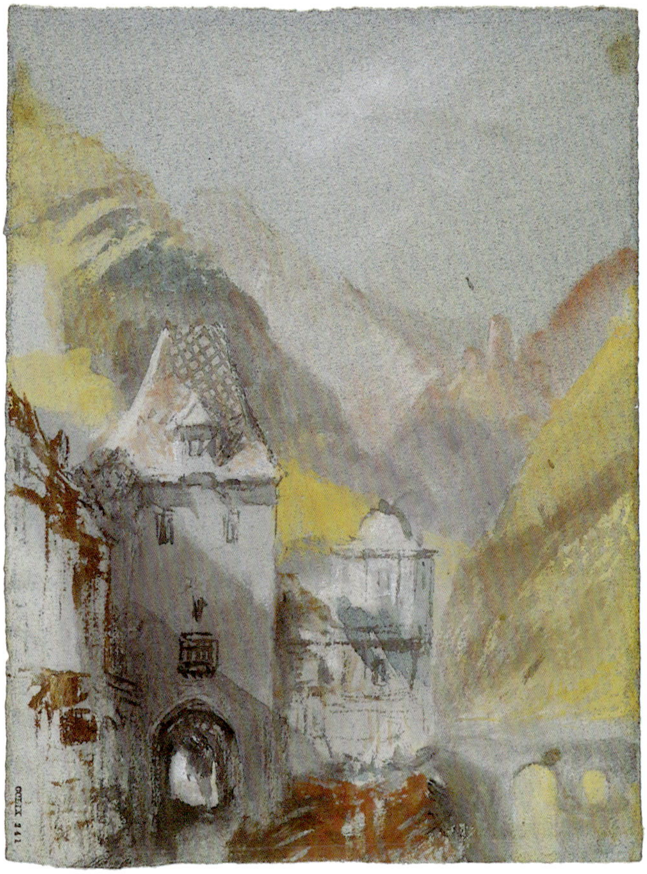

65 **The Enderttor and Alte Thorschenke, Cochem** *c.*1839

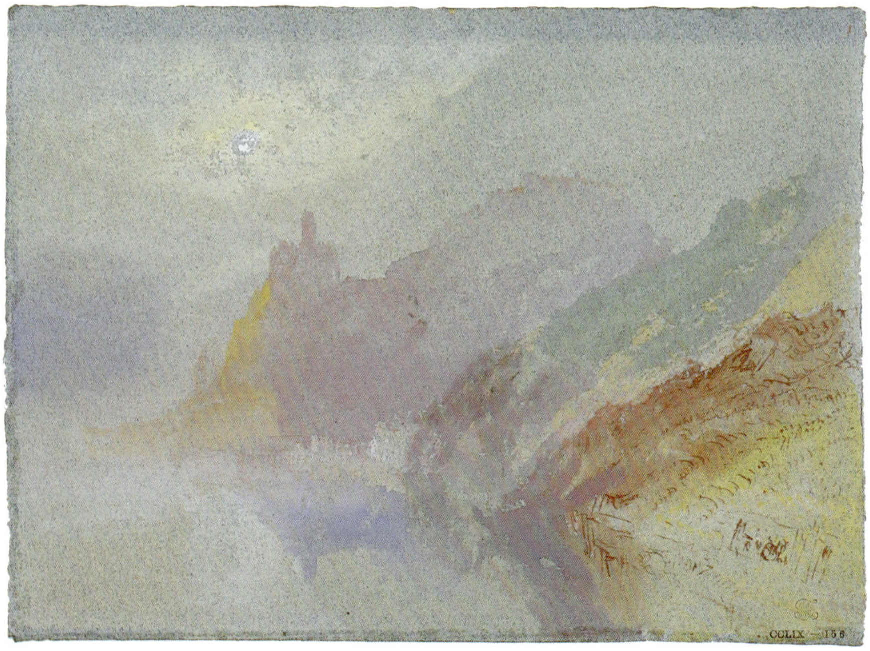

68 **Distant View of Cochem** *c.*1839

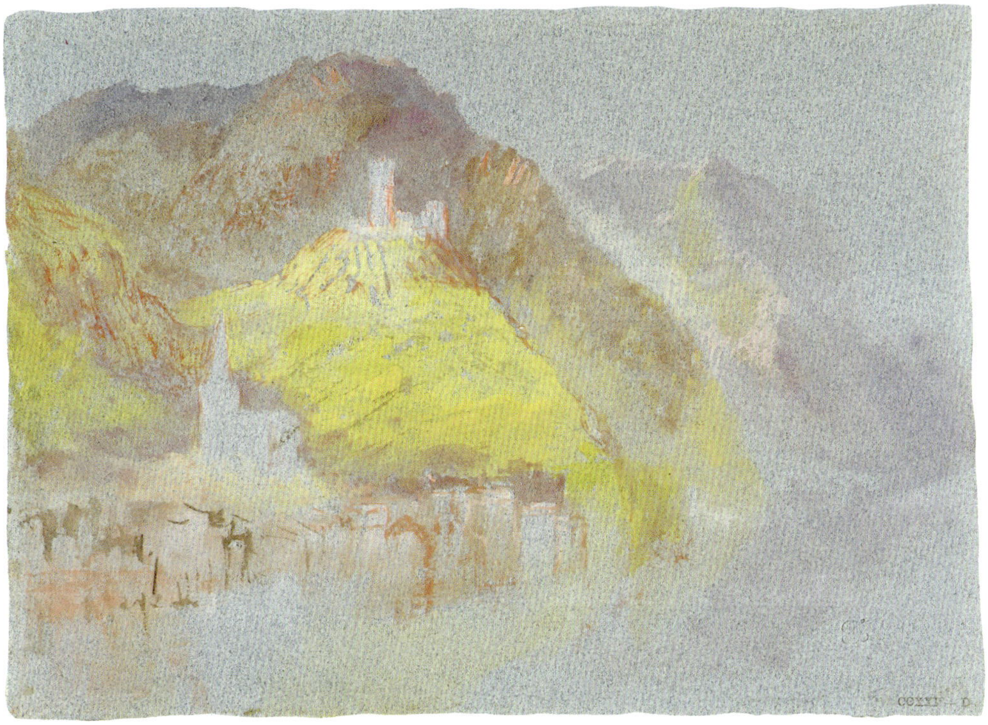

69 **Klotten and Burg Coraidelstein from the West** *c.*1839

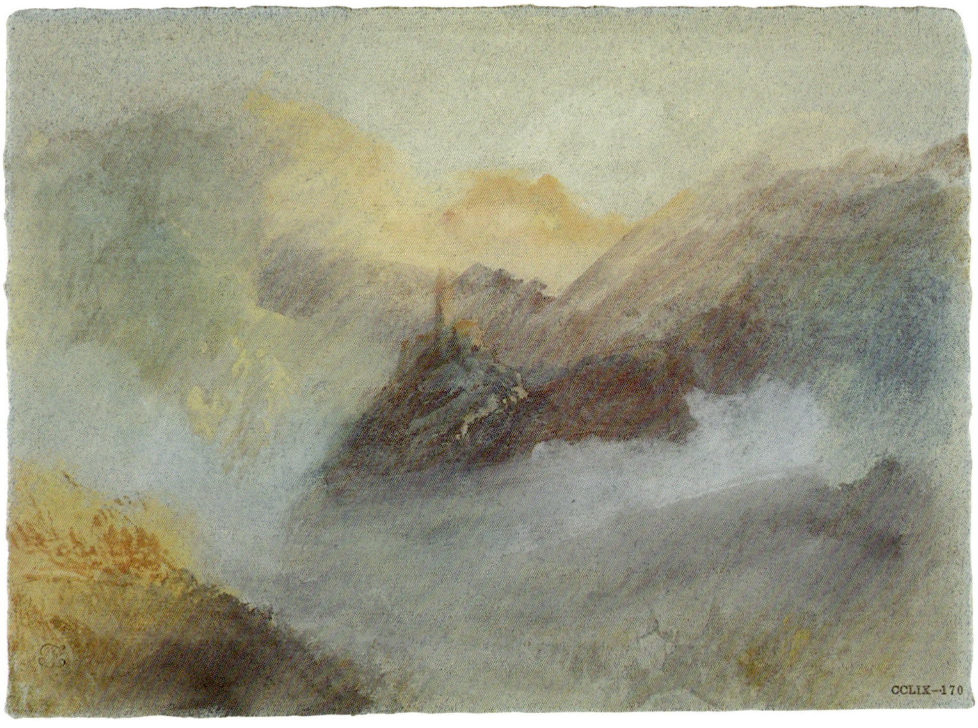

71 **Burg Treis** *c.*1839

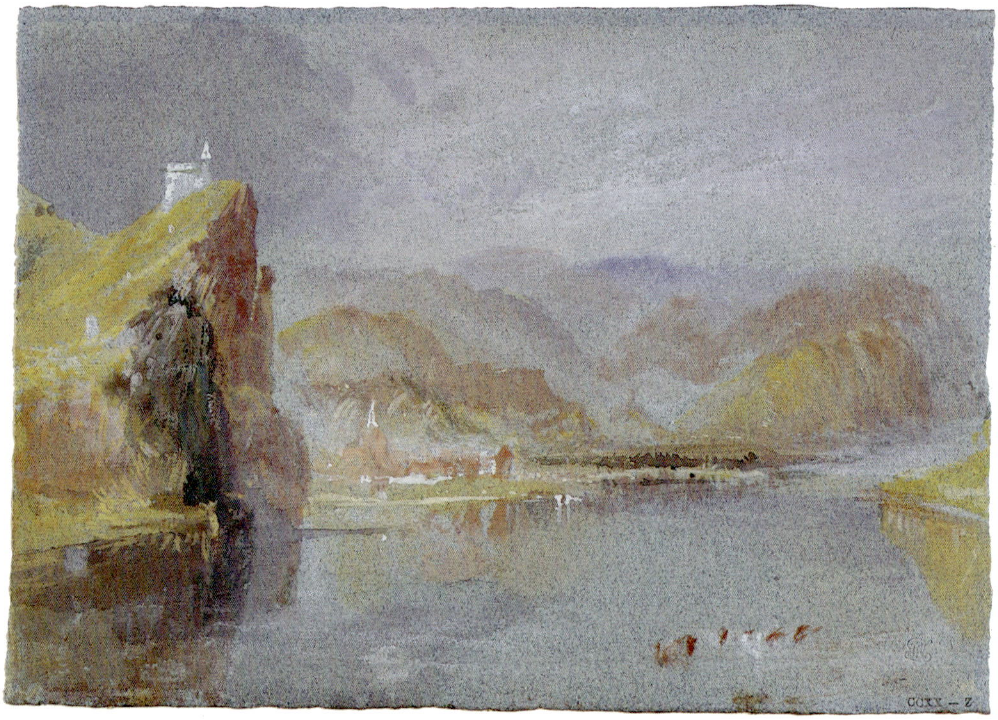

72 **Treis from the North** *c.*1839

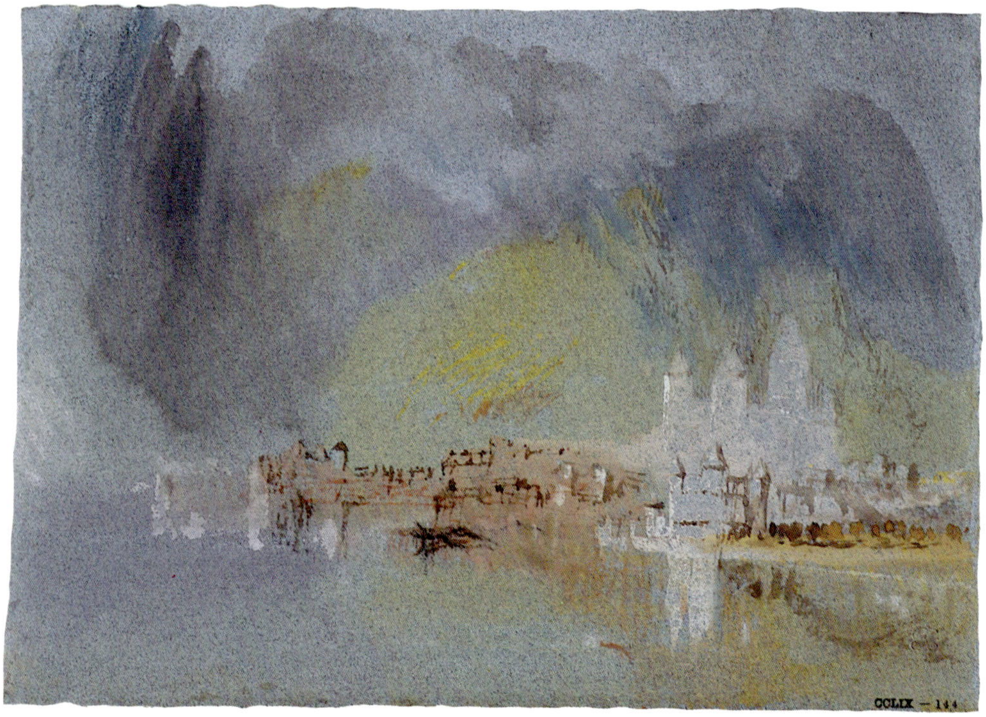

73 **Karden from the North** *c.*1839

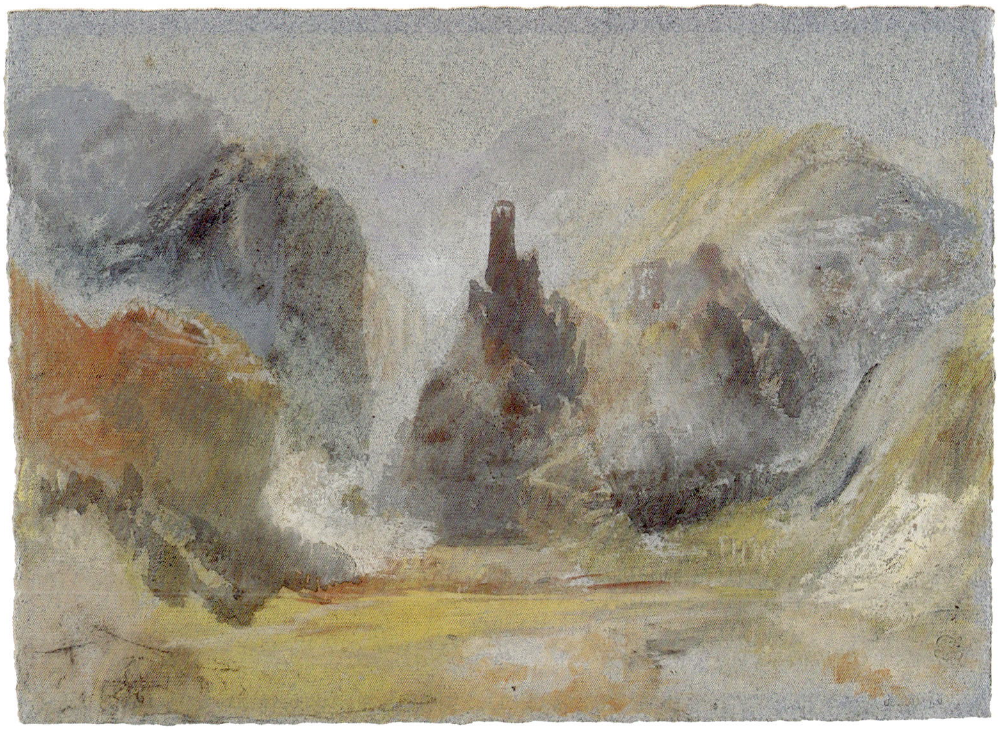

74 **Burg Bischofstein** *c.*1839

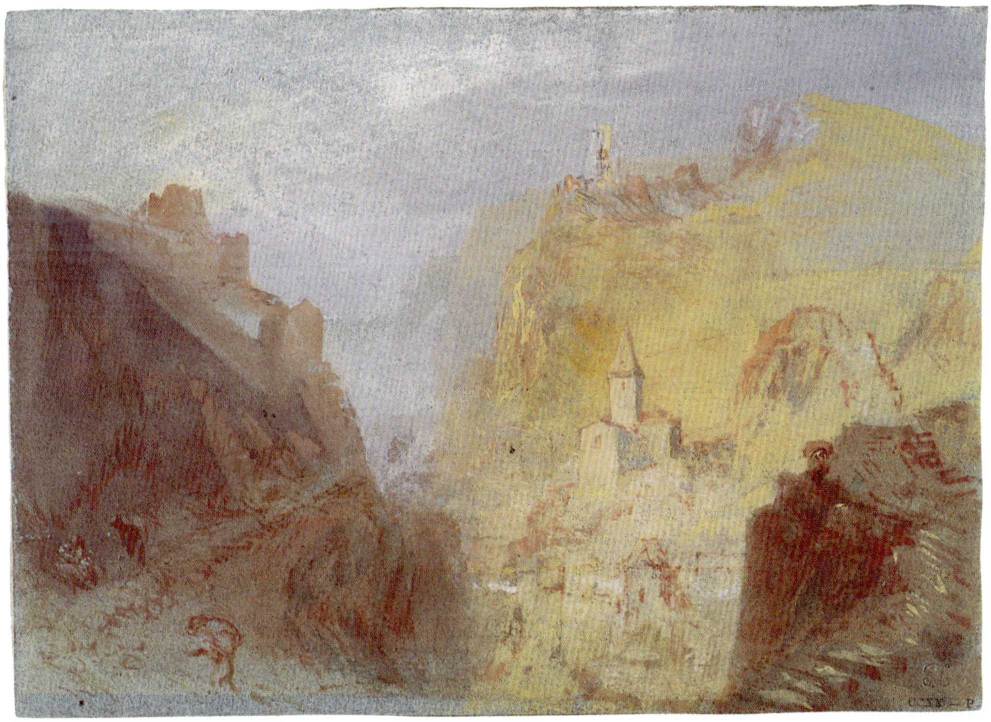

76 **Alken and Burg Thurandt from the North** *c.*1839

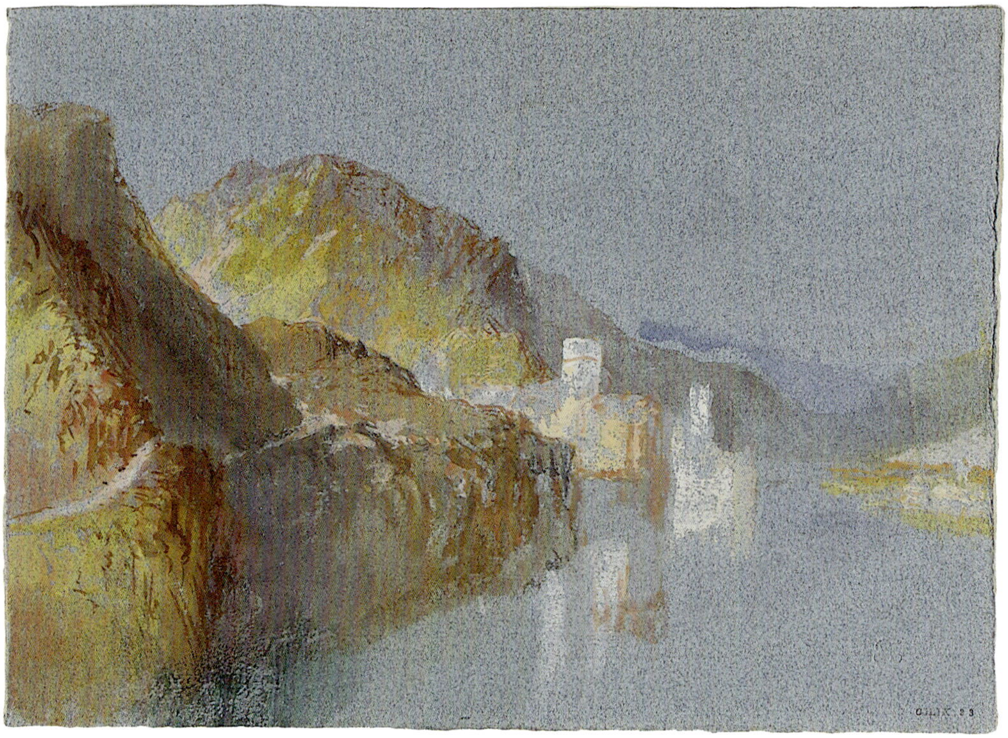

77 **The Leyen Burg at Gondorf** *c.*1839

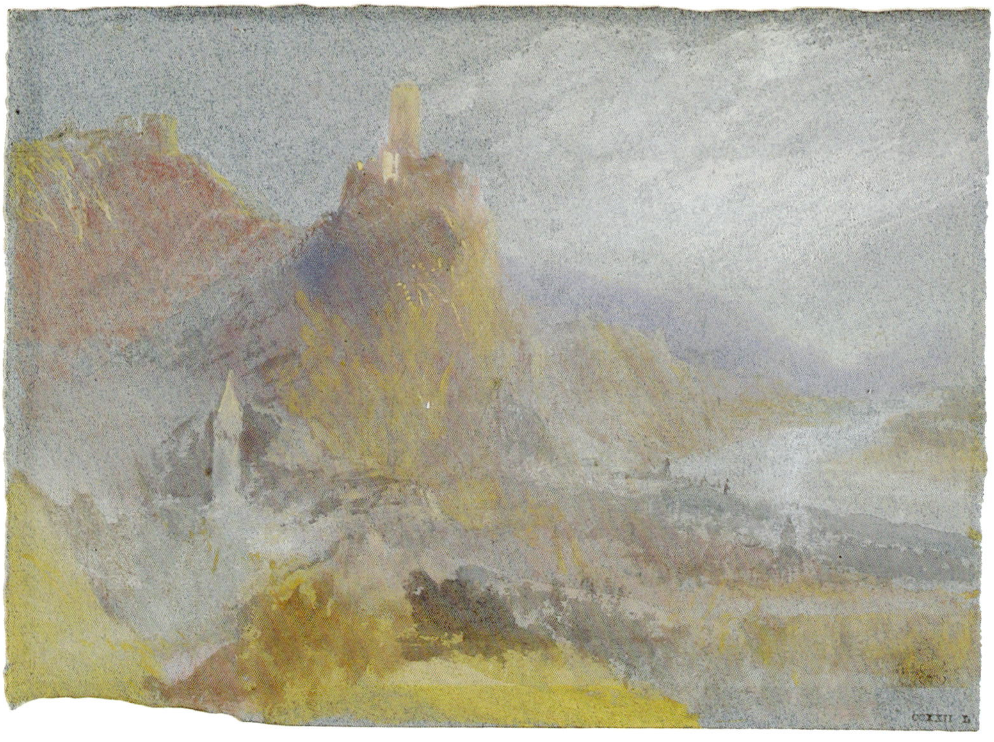

78 **Kobern from the South** *c.*1839

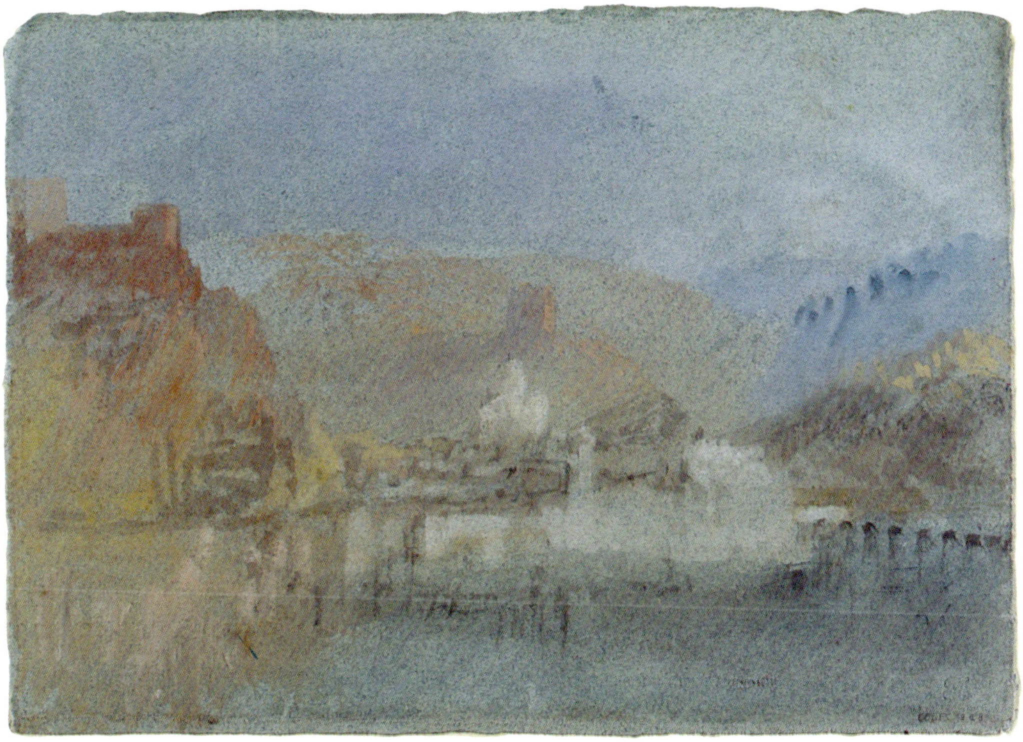

81 **Ehrenbreitstein from Coblenz** *c.*1839

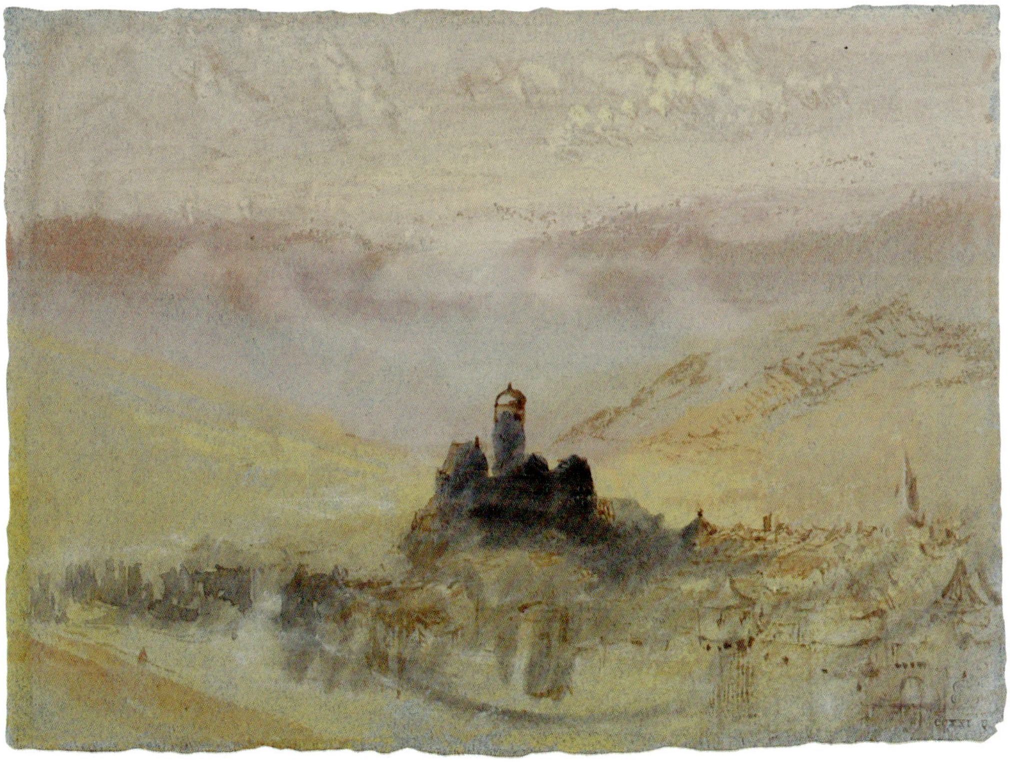

83 **Mayen in the Eifel** *c.*1839

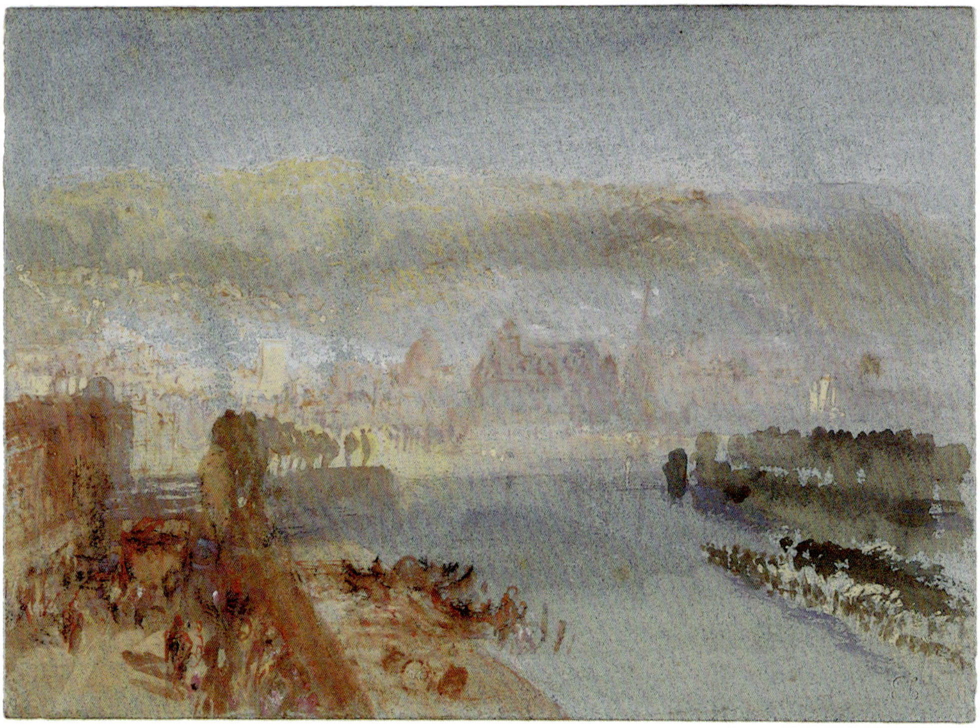

84 **Liège from the Pont des Arches** *c.*1839

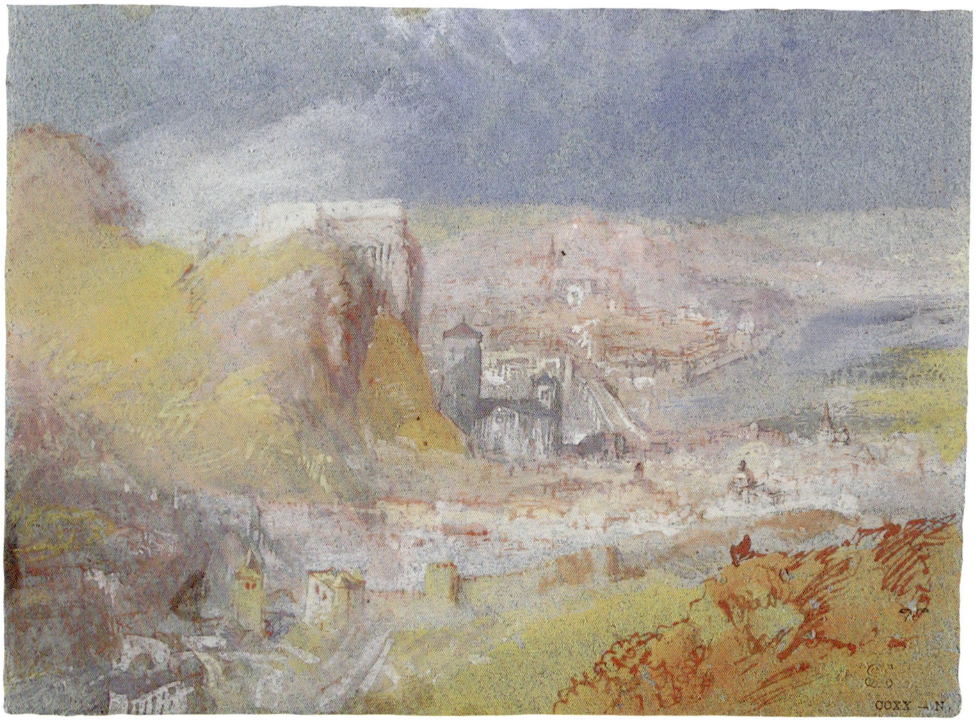

87 **Huy from the South-east** *c.*1839

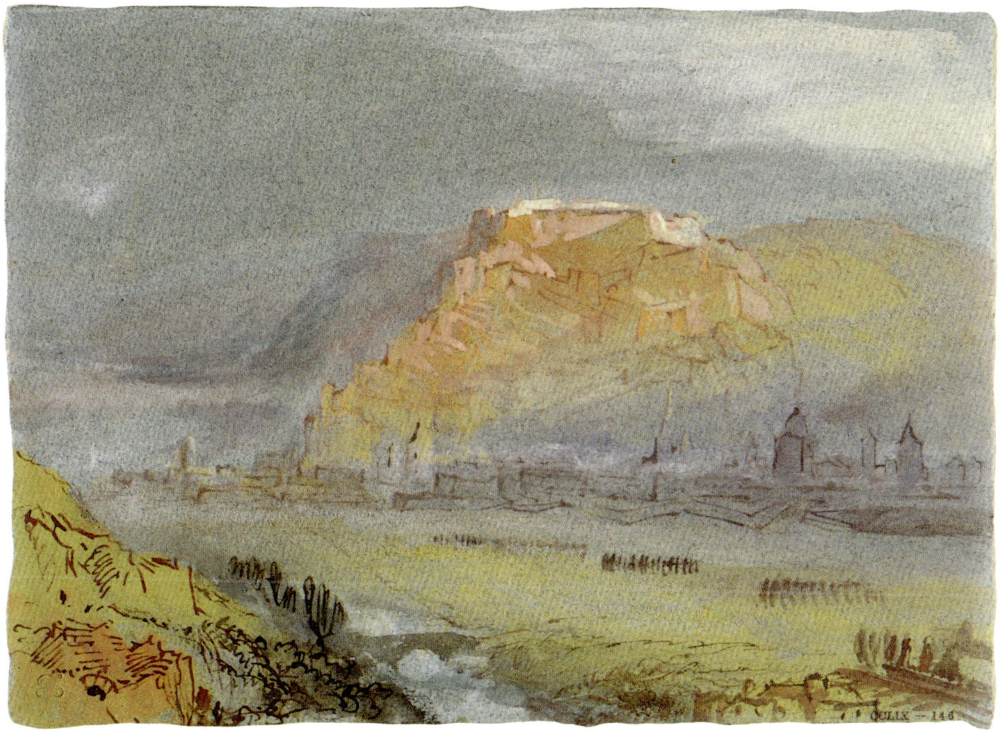

93 **Namur from the Fields** *c.*1839

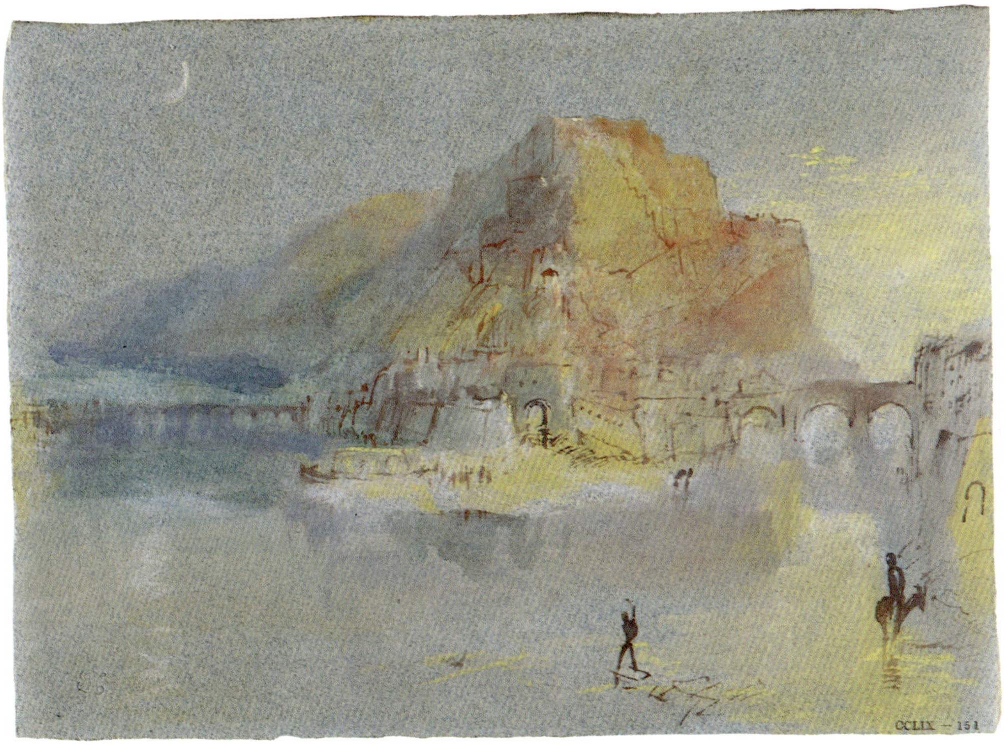

94 **The Confluence at Namur: Moonlight** *c.*1839

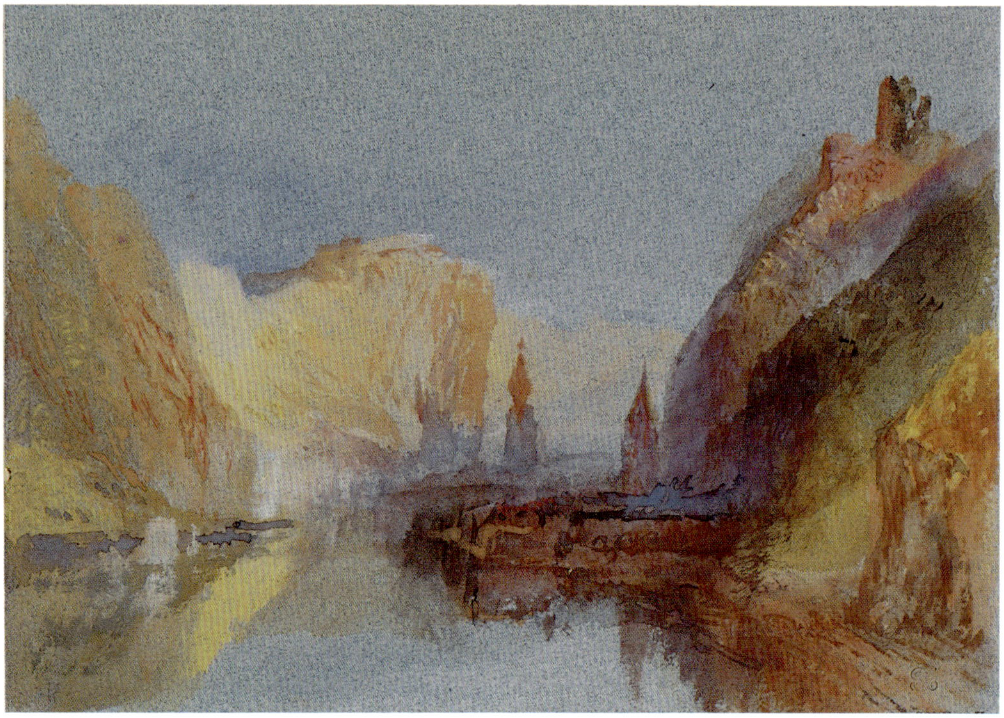

96 **Dinant, Bouvignes and Crèvecoeur: Sunset** *c.*1839

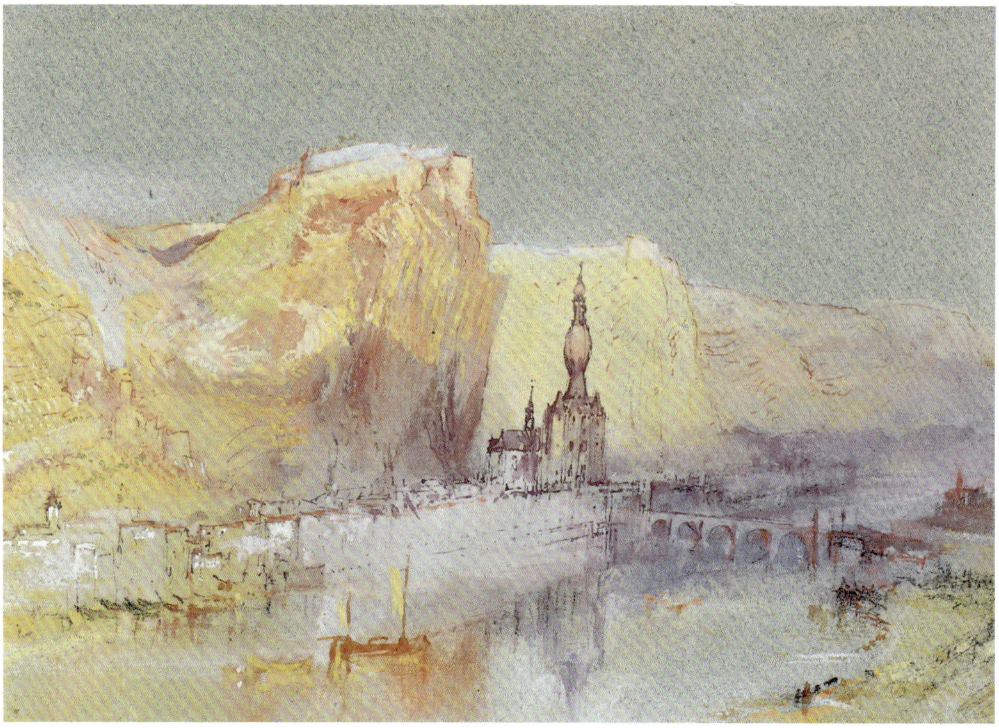

97 **Dinant from the North-west** *c.*1839

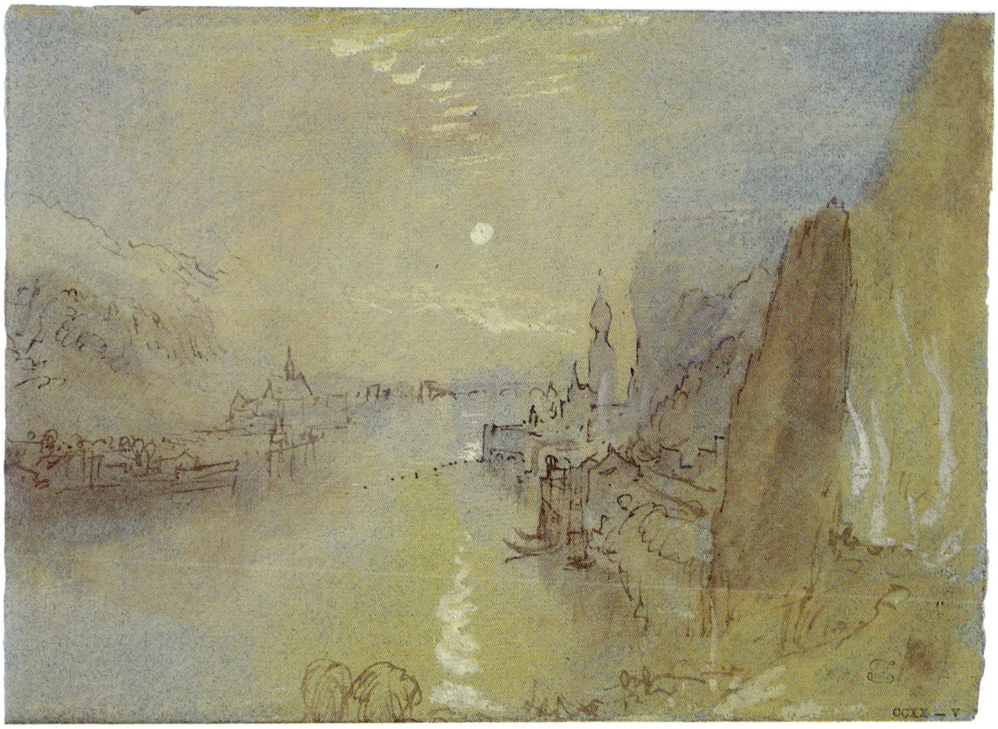

99 **Dinant from the Roche à Bayard: Moonlight** *c.*1839

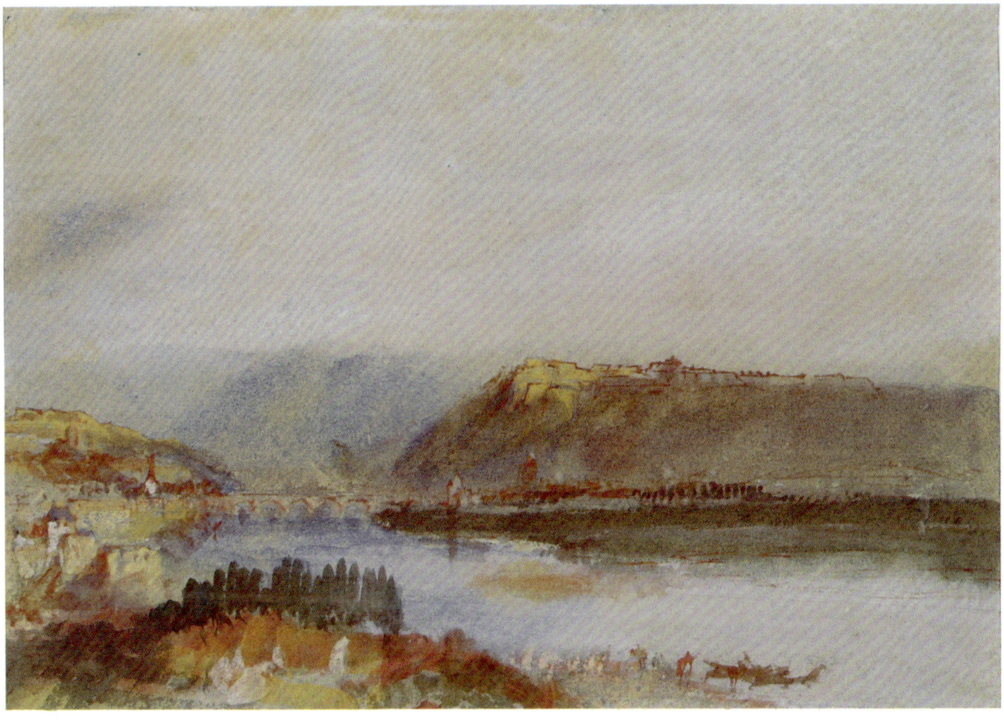

102 **Givet from the North** *c.*1839

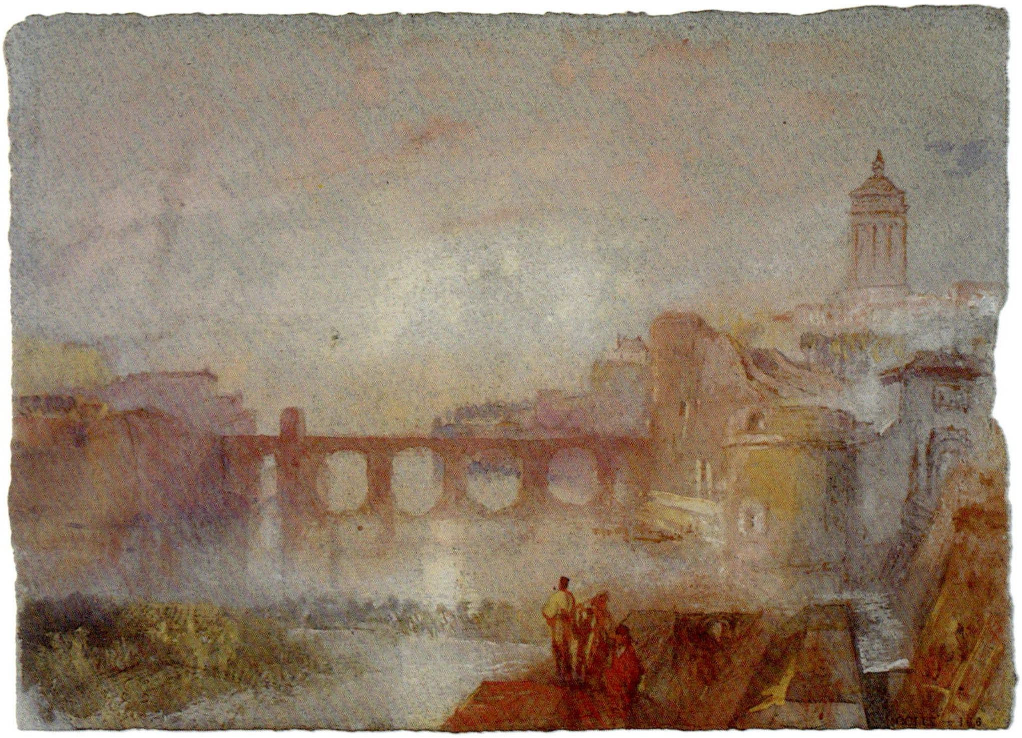

103 **Mézières, with the Pont de Pierre and Church of Notre-Dame** *c.*1839

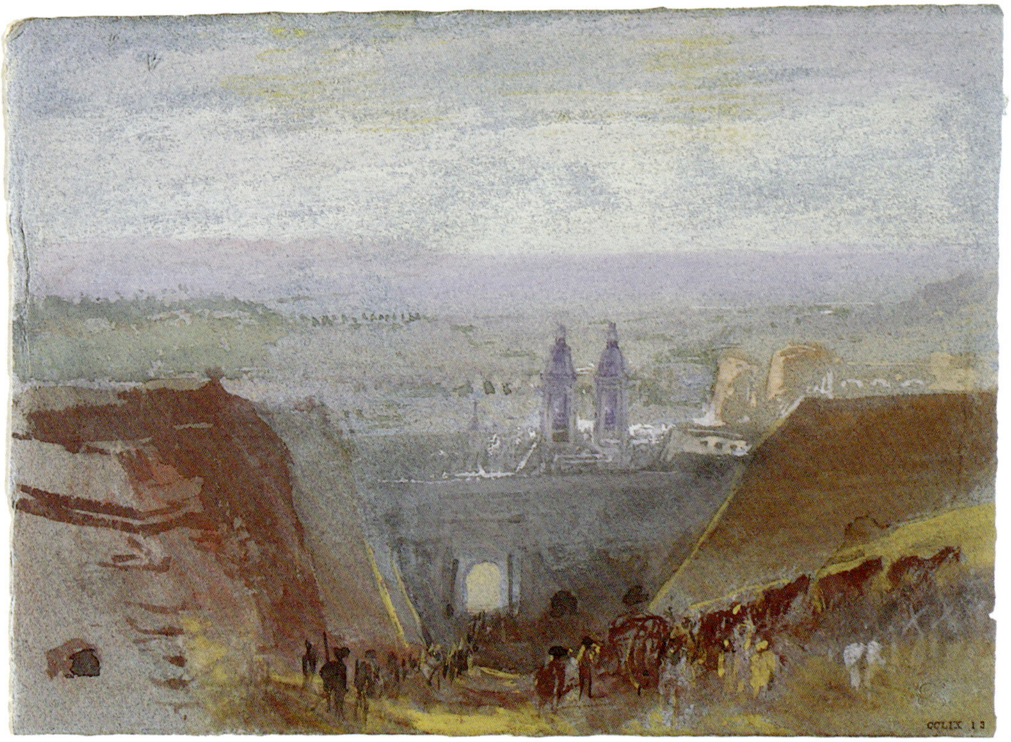

104 **Sedan from the South-east** *c.*1839

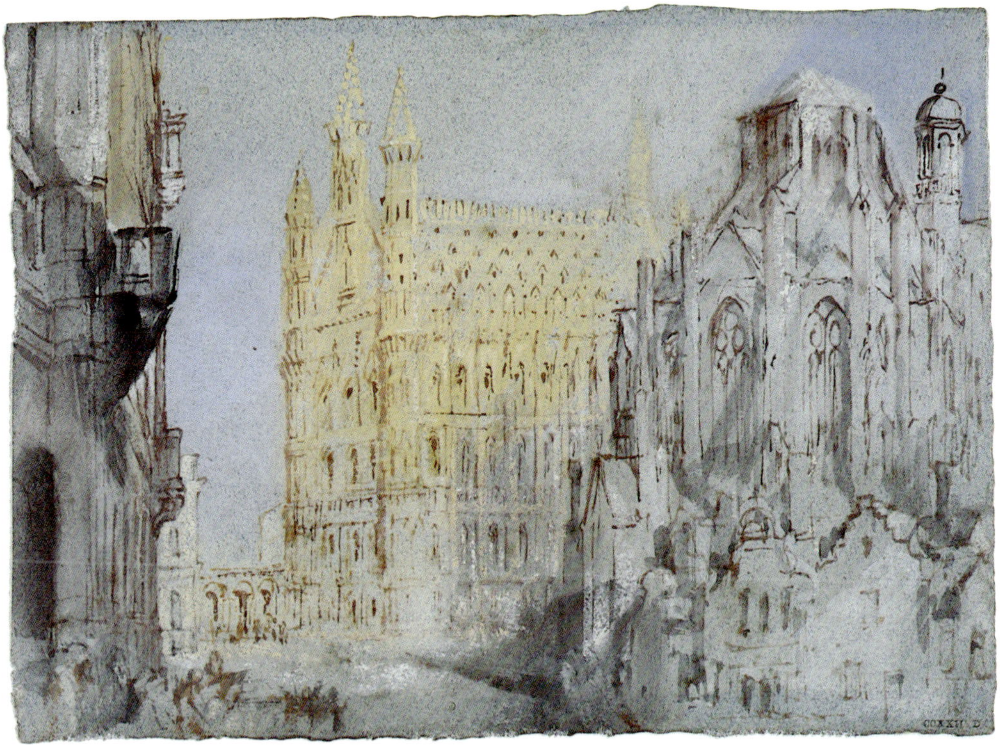

107 **The Town Hall, Louvain, and the Choir of St Peter's Church** *c.*1839

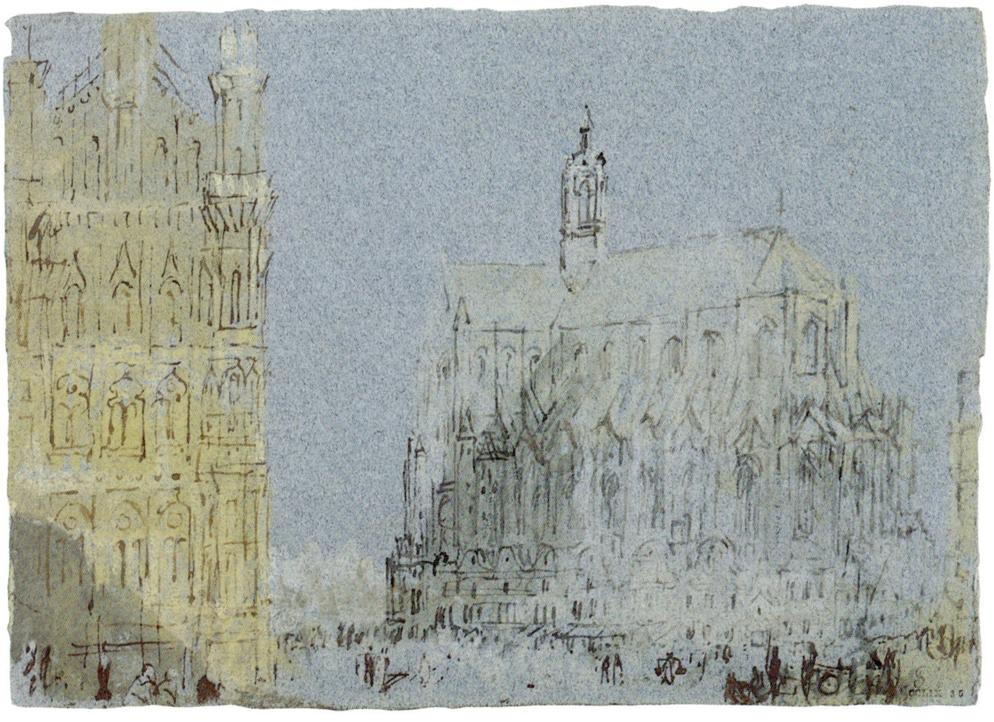

108 **St Peter's Church, Louvain, from the East Side of the Town Hall** *c.*1839

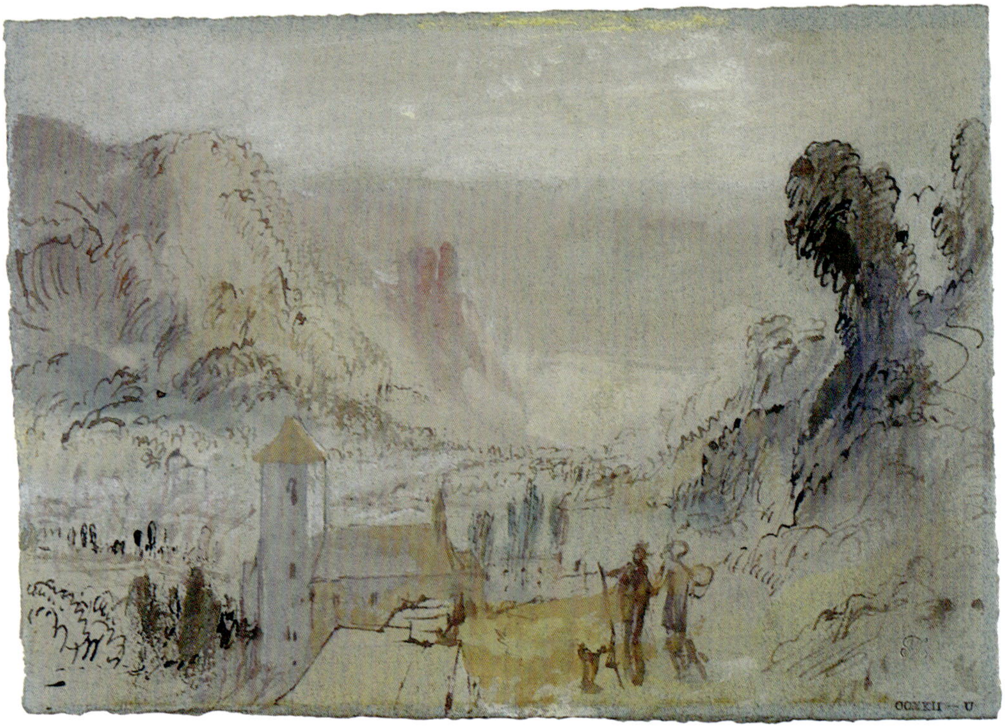

109 **Franchimont with the Church of SS. Hermes and Alexander, Theux** *c.*1839

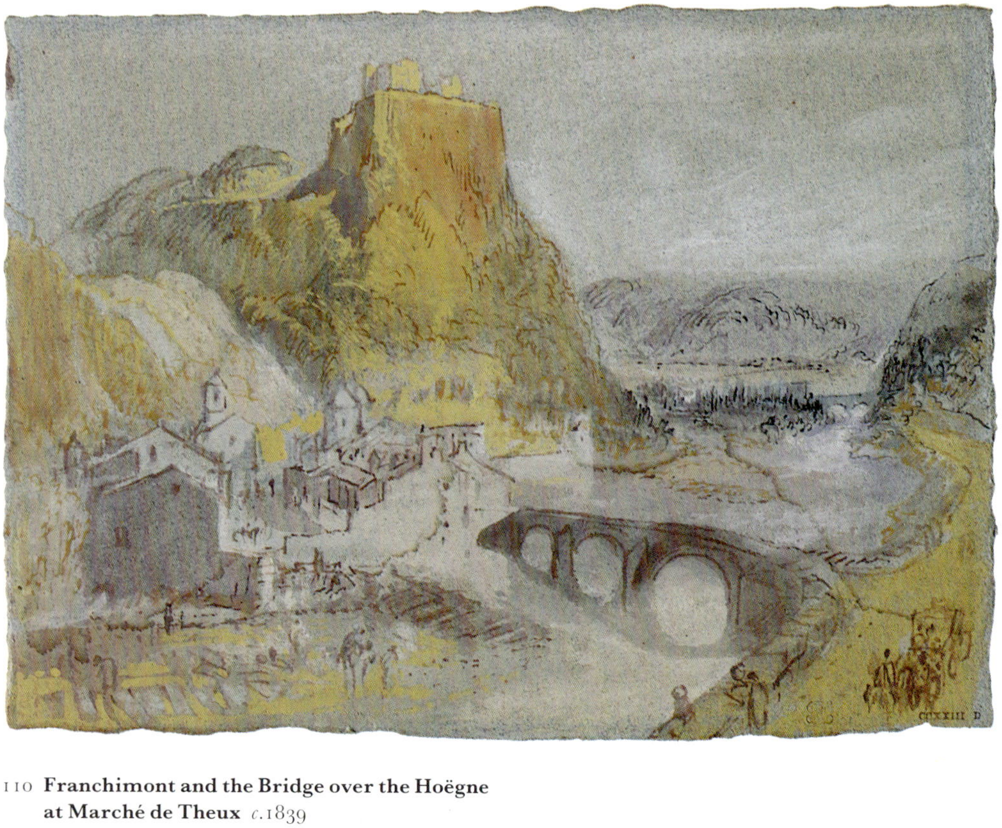

110 **Franchimont and the Bridge over the Hoëgne at Marché de Theux** *c.*1839

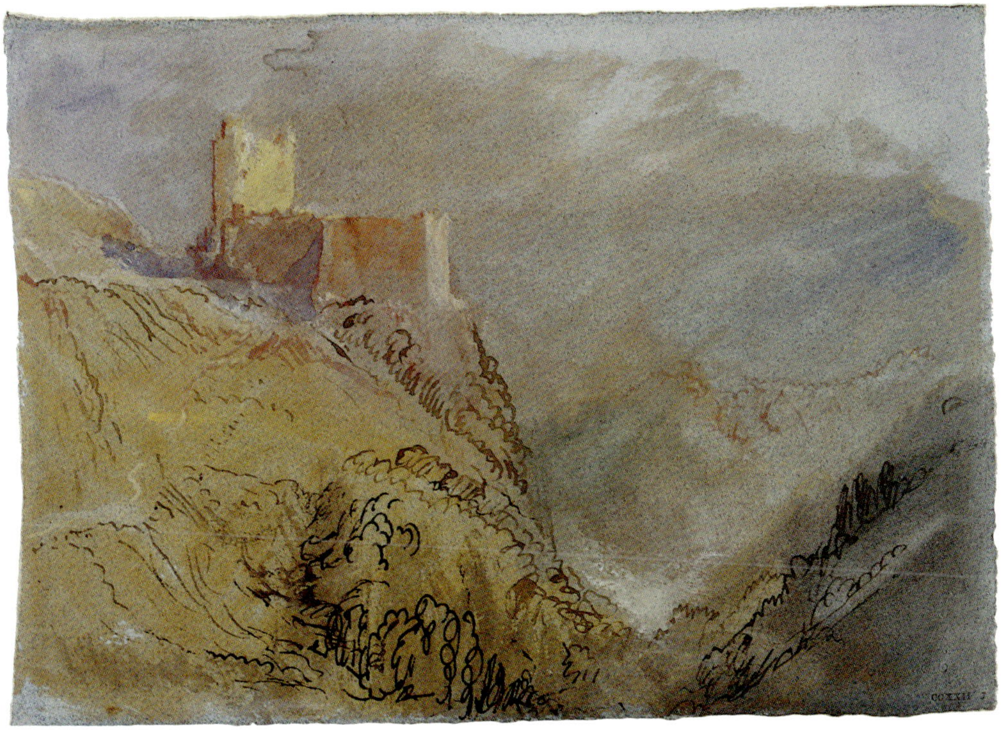

111 **Franchimont and the Valley of the Hoëgne** *c.*1839

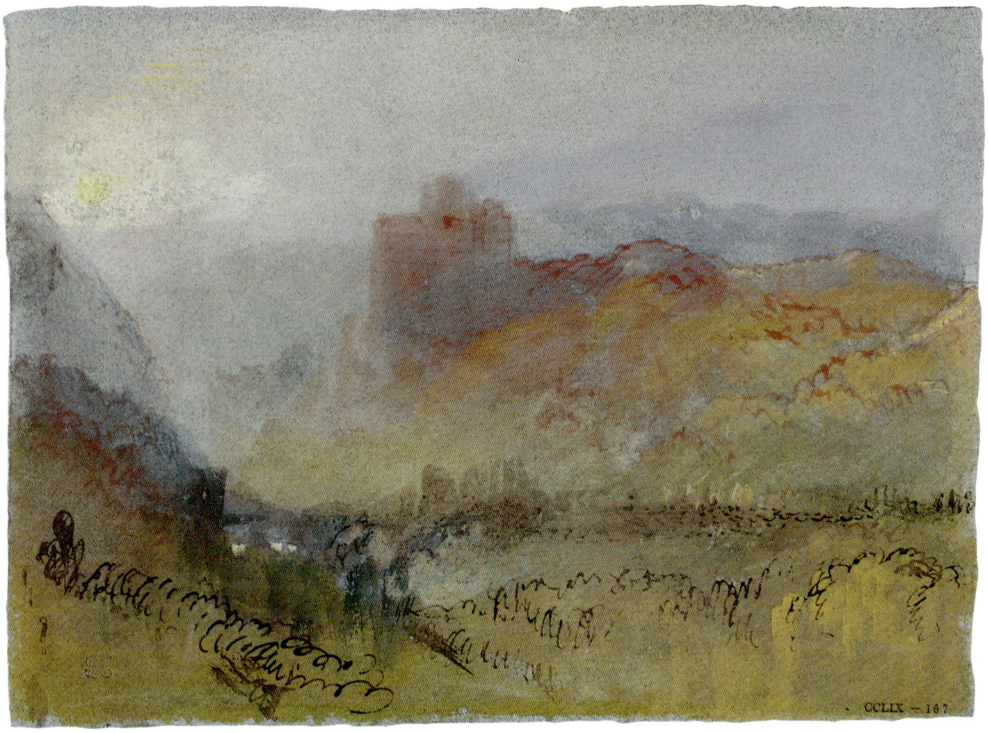

112 **Franchimont from the South** *c.*1839

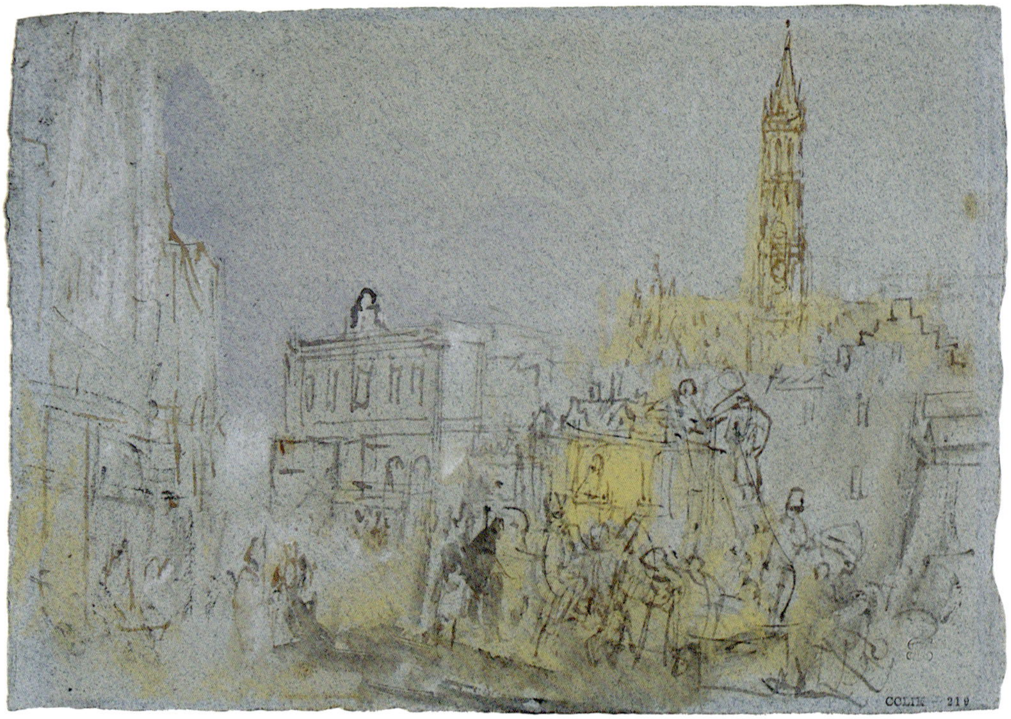

106 **Brussels: the Diligence** *c.*1839

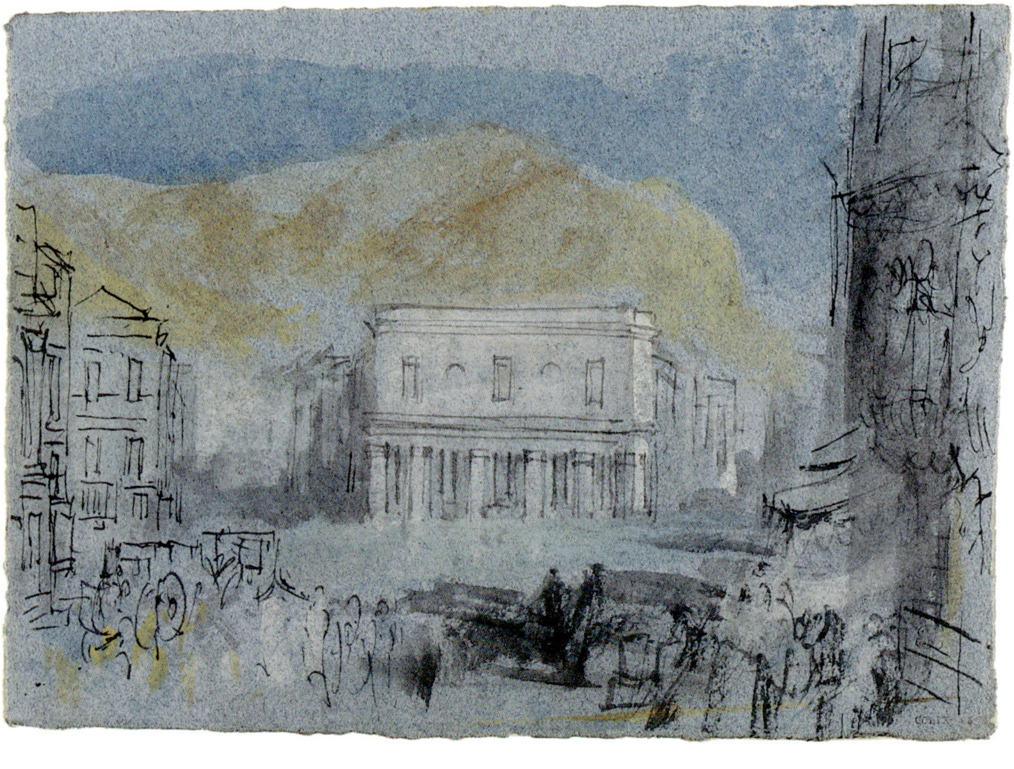

115 **The 'Pouhon Pierre Le Grand' at Spa** *c.*1839

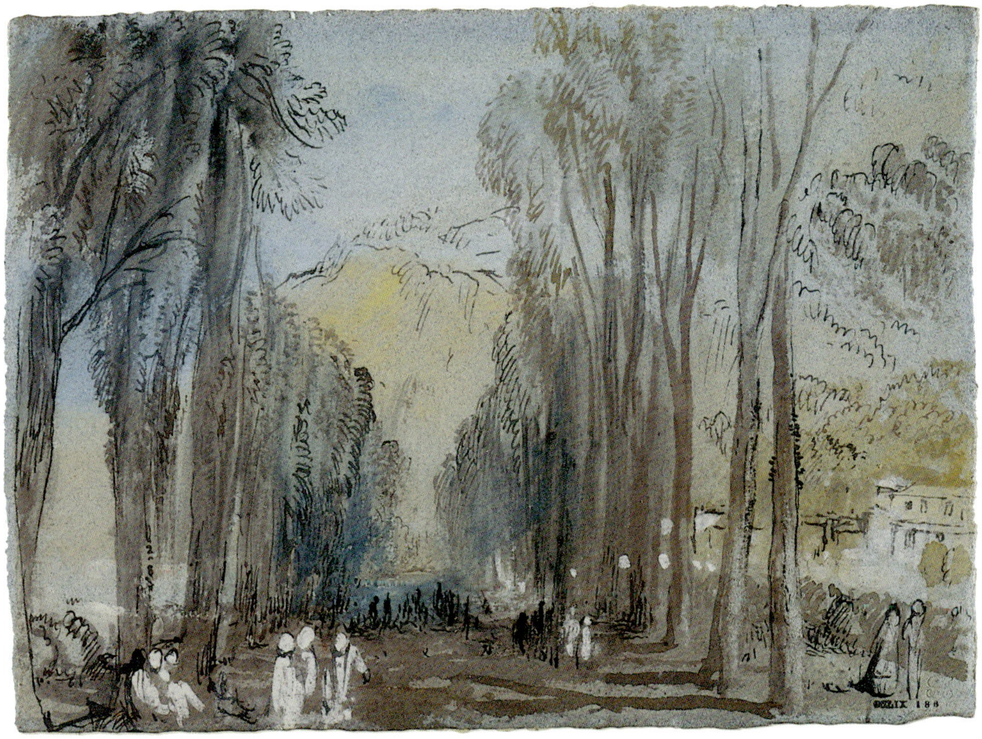

118 **The 'Promenade de Sept-Heures' at Spa** *c.*1839

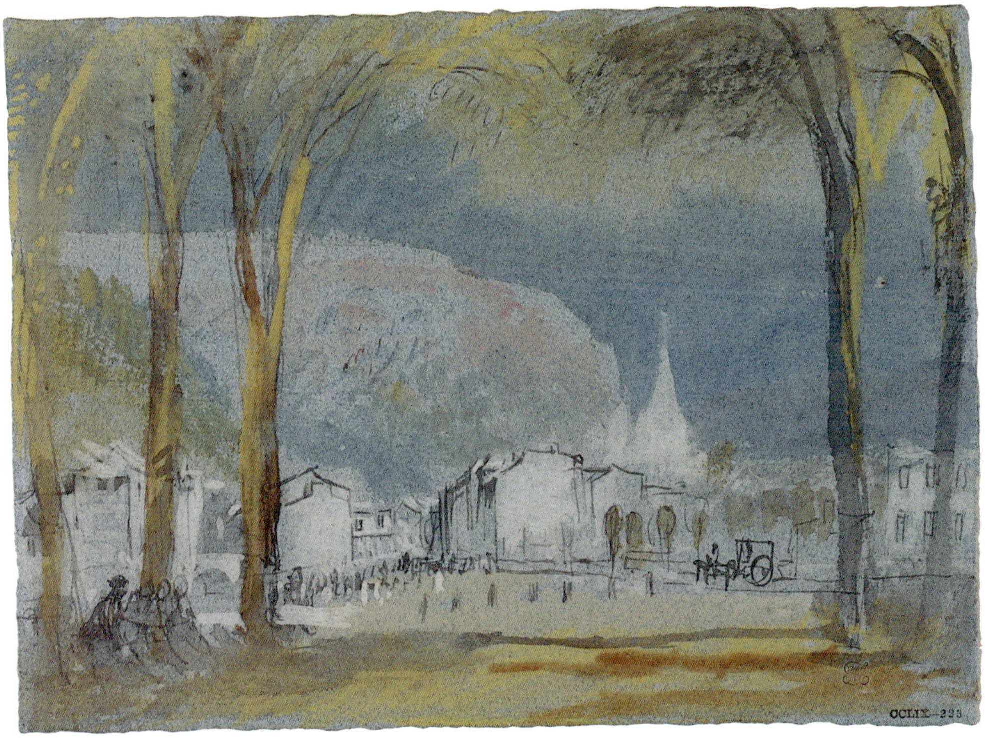

119 **The Place Royale, Spa, from the Entrance to the 'Promenade de Sept-Heures'** *c.*1839

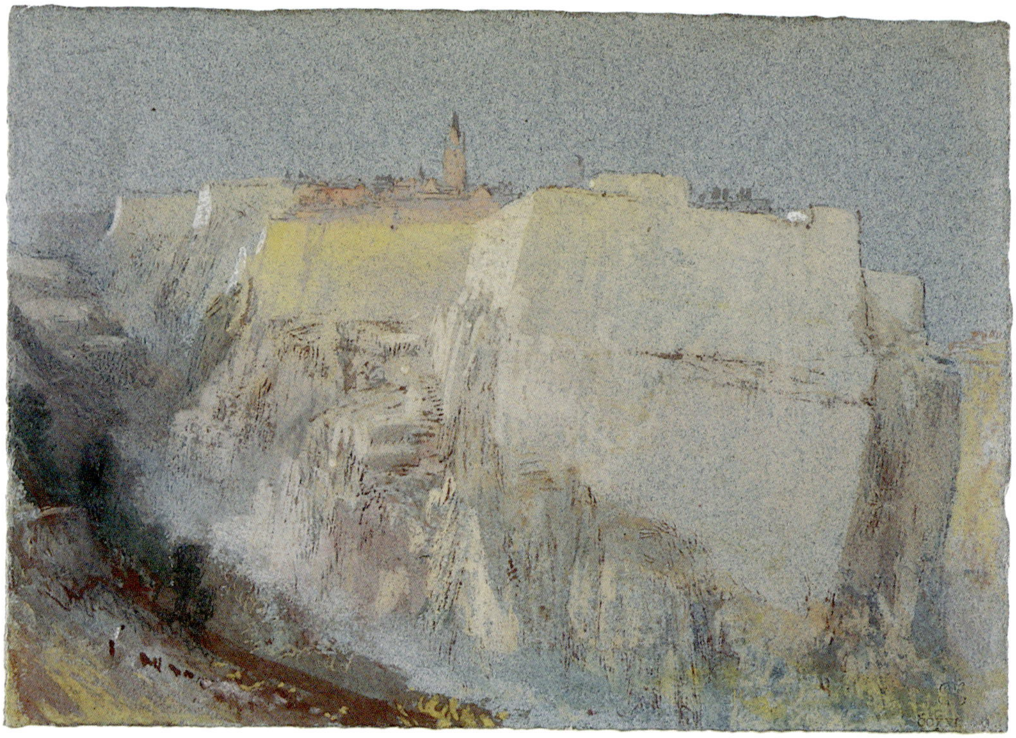

121 **The Citadel of St-Esprit, Luxembourg** *c.*1839

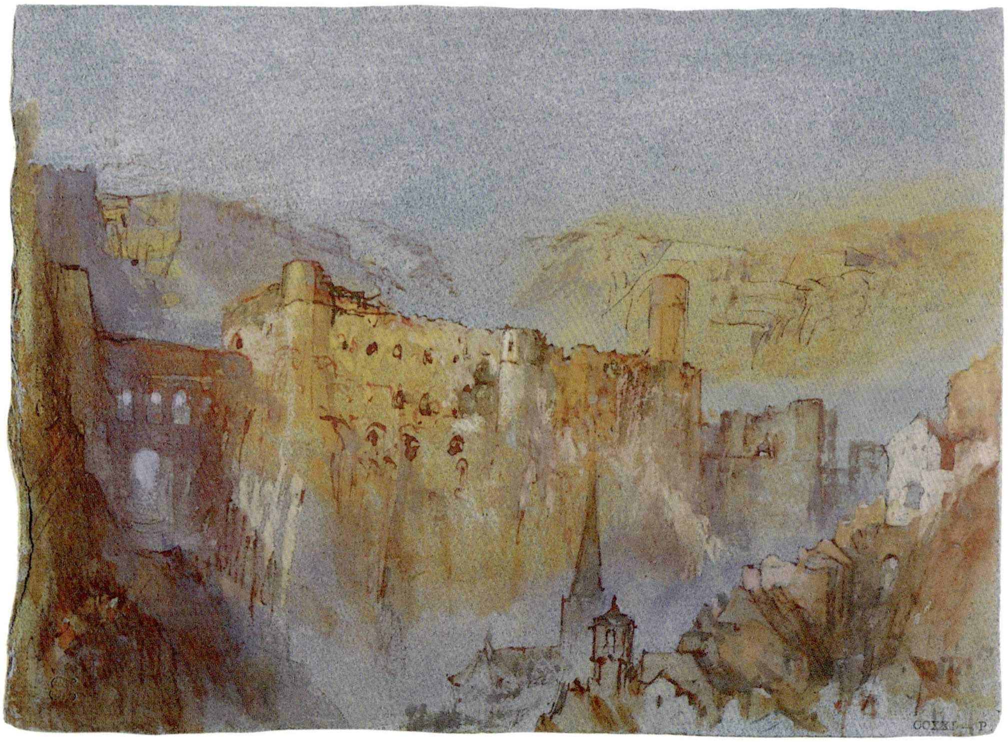

124 **The Pont du Château and the Bock, Luxembourg** *c.*1839

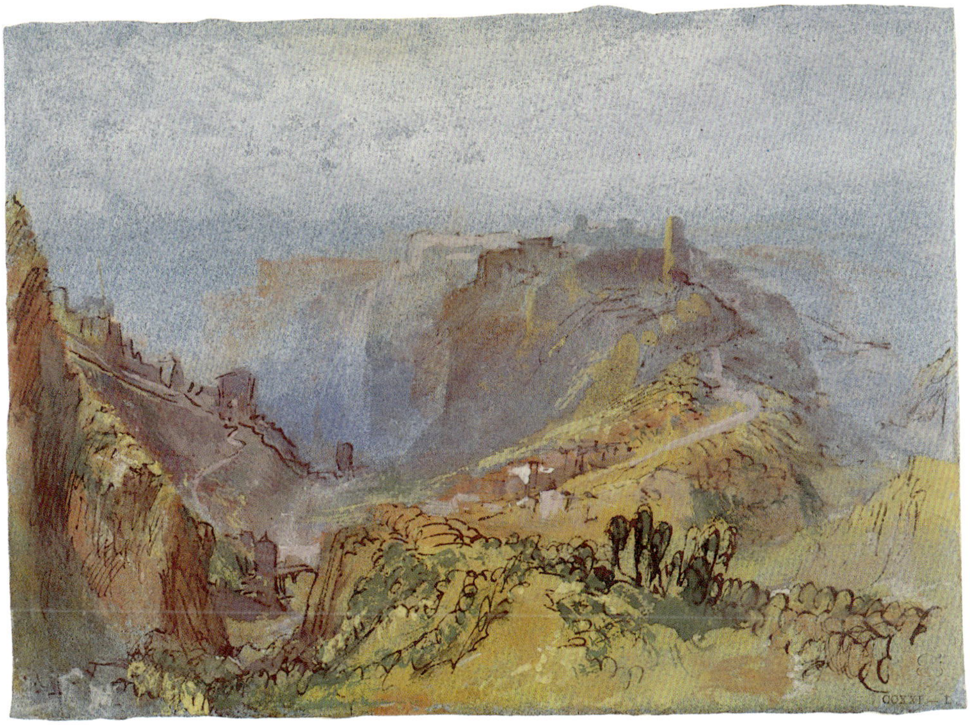

126 **The Rham Plateau and the Bock, Luxembourg from the North-east** *c.*1839

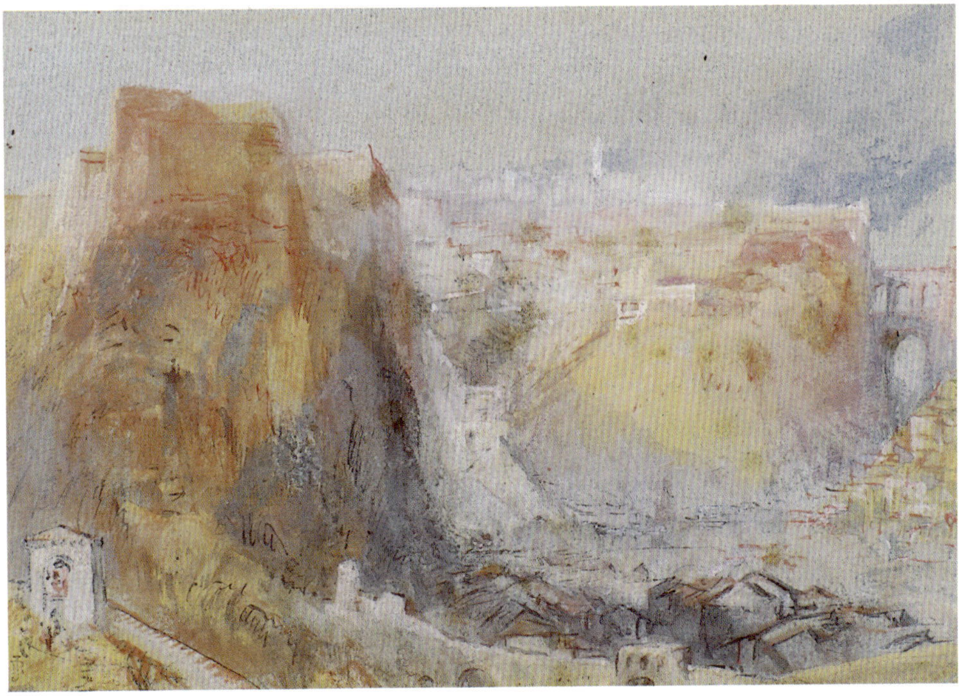

122 **Luxembourg from the South** *c.*1839

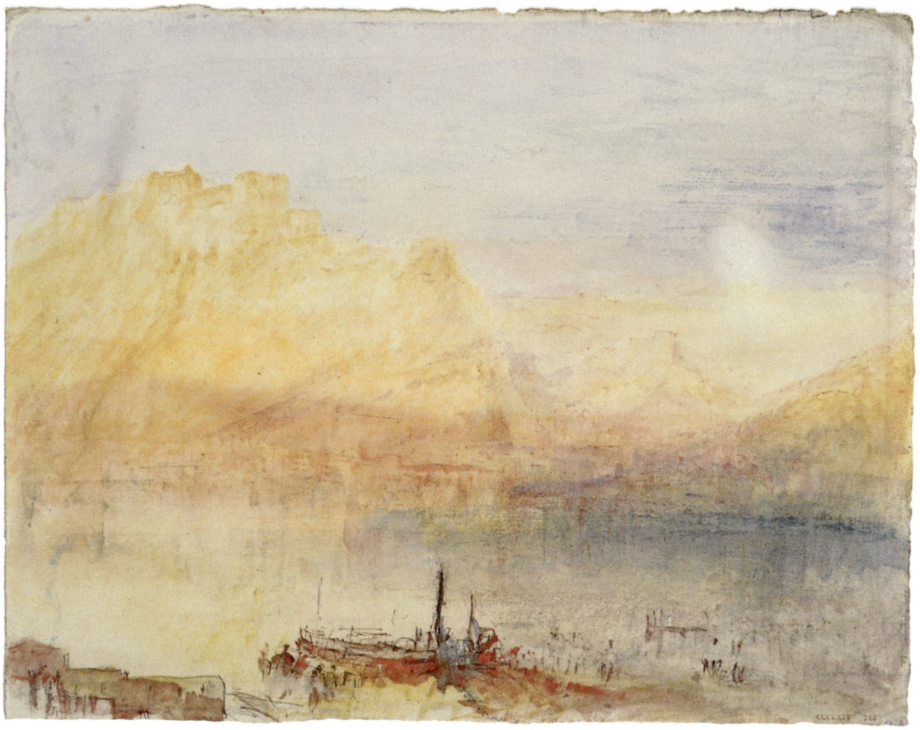

128 **Ehrenbreitstein** 1841

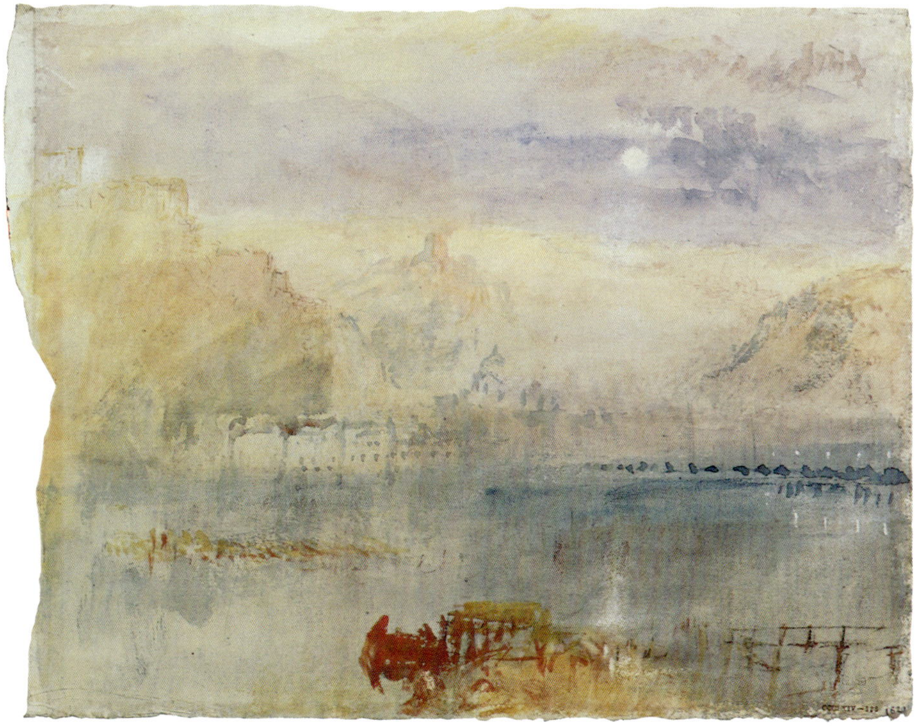

129 **Ehrenbreitstein** 1841

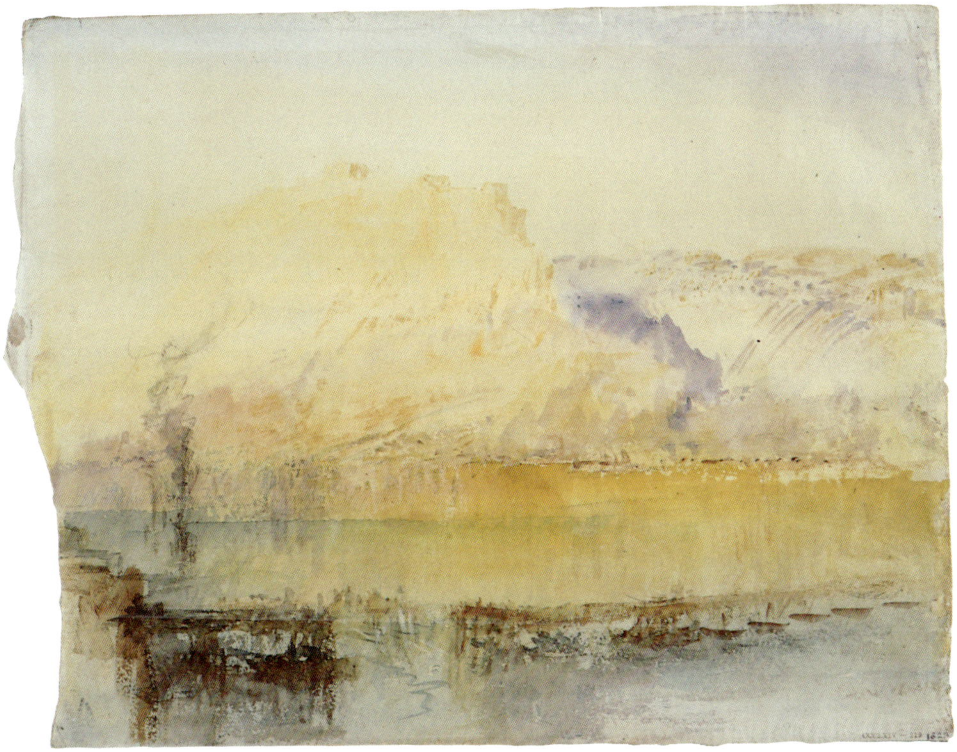

132 **Ehrenbreitstein** 1841

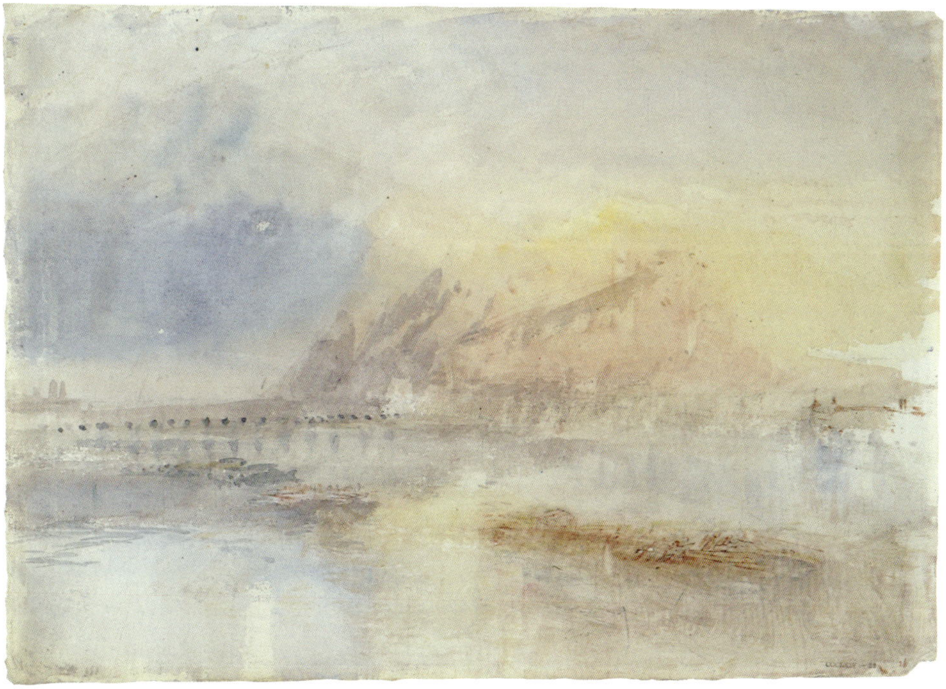

134 **Ehrenbreitstein** 1841

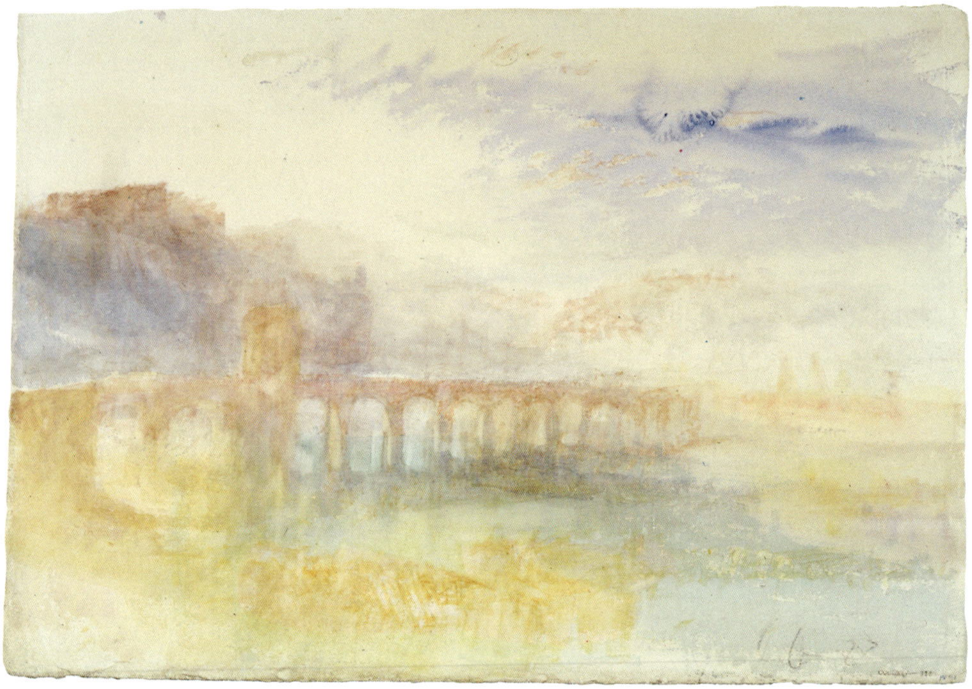

135 **The Mosel Bridge at Coblenz: Colour Study** *c.*1841–2

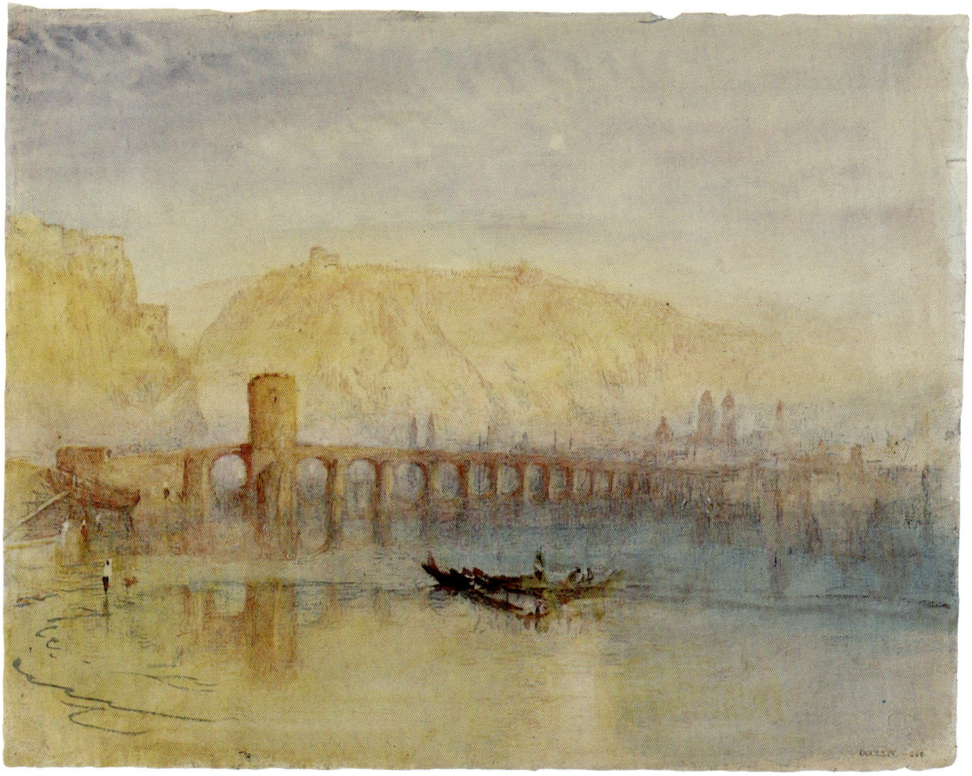

136 **The Mosel Bridge at Coblenz: Sample Study** *c.*1841–2

Catalogue

Unless otherwise stated, all works are by J.M.W. Turner. All measurements are given in millimetres followed by inches in brackets, height before width. Place names are given according to current national usage rather than that of Turner's day (e.g. Aachen, not Aix-la-Chapelle; Mainz, not Mayence; Trier, not Trèves) except where common English usage demands otherwise (e.g. Cologne). The use of French forms of names has, however, been retained in the familiar titles of Turner's own sketchbooks and works.

The watermarks recorded in the blue wove paper of cat.nos.47–127 were read by Peter Bower using a fibre-optic light source and are not visible under normal lighting conditions. Unnumbered works in the gouaches series are not included in the exhibition.

Items illustrated in colour are marked with an asterisk.

Abbreviations

B & J Martin Butlin and Evelyn Joll, *The Paintings of J.M.W. Turner*, 2 vols., revised ed. 1984

R W.G. Rawlinson, *The Engraved Work of J.M.W. Turner, R.A.*, 2 vols., 1908 and 1913

TB A.J. Finberg, *A Complete Inventory of the Drawings of the Turner Bequest*, 2 vols., 1909

W Andrew Wilton, *The Life and Work of J.M.W. Turner*, 1979 (catalogue of watercolours)

RA Exhibited at the Royal Academy

For other published material which is abbreviated in the text, see Bibliography.

Belgium and the Rhineland, 1817–44

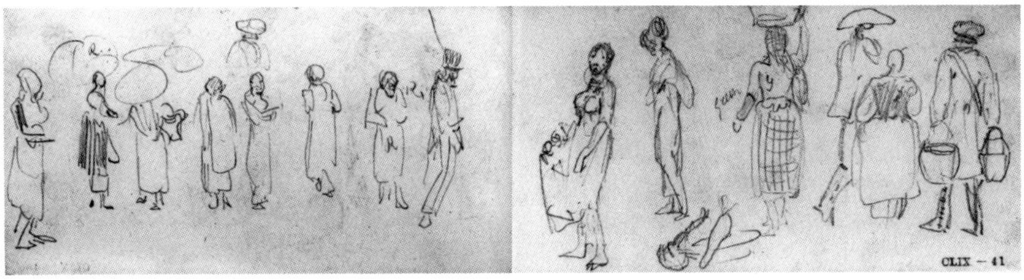

Itinerary Rhine Tour sketchbook 1817

1 Country Folk near Sinzig

Pencil
Page size: 56 × 106 ($2\frac{3}{16} \times 4\frac{3}{16}$)
White wove paper
Watermarked: RUSE & TURNERS/1817
Inscribed: 'R'; 'R'; 'R' (f.40v); 'Green'; 'Y' (f.41r)
TB CLIX ff.40 verso, 41
D12587, D12588

The *Itinerary Rhine Tour* sketchbook acquired its name when the Turner Bequest was first catalogued, because it contains Turner's own record of his movements during his 1817 tour (ff.100r–99v). Before he left England, he had already written notes in this book from several authoritative works on the areas he was about to visit, thus providing himself with an extremely convenient pocket guidebook at no personal expense. This was in fact to prove so successful an idea that he adopted the identical practice two years later before his next important foreign tour, his first visit to Italy in 1819 (in the *Italian Guide Book* sketchbook, TB CLXXII).

Turner used this sketchbook at many places during his tour of the Middle Rhine, alongside his two other, larger, sketchbooks (cat.nos.2 and 3). All three are filled with innumerable sketches of the Rhine and its towns and castles, but it is only in this sketchbook that Turner made any sustained effort to record the appearance and life of the people he saw around him. The present sketches fall within a group of five pages of studies which were all made near Sinzig, about halfway between Bonn and Coblenz (ff.39r–41r). Some show the soldiers who were still very much in evidence in the whole region in 1817; others show country folk with the huge variety of jugs, bottles, barrels and pitchers which were in daily use for the storage and transport of the wine for which the Rhine has long been famous. The drawings are often accompanied by brief notes on the costumes Turner observed, though his memoranda sometimes amount to no more than the initial letters of colour names, e.g. 'R' for red, 'Y' for yellow.

While the people sketched on f.40v are little more than the ciphers so commonly found in Turner's sketches, f.41r shows his figure drawing at its best. Men and women alike are completely credible individuals carrying out their daily tasks, and the village maiden on the left must surely be one of the most delightful that Turner ever sketched.

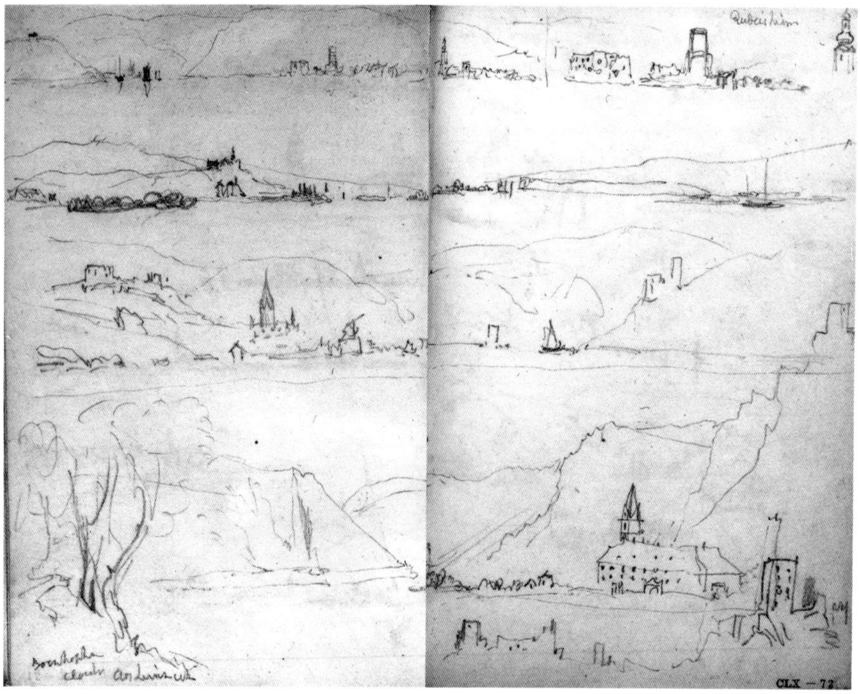

Waterloo and Rhine sketchbook 1817

2 Bingen, Rüdesheim and Bornhofen

Pencil
Page size: 150 × 94 ($5\frac{7}{8} \times 3\frac{11}{16}$)
White wove paper
Watermarked: J WHATMAN/1816
Inscribed: 'Rudesheim' (f.72r); 'Bornhophen Church'; 'Burg Liebeneck' (f.71v)
TB CLX ff.71 verso, 72
D12840, D12841

Turner used this sketchbook intensively for the first two and a half weeks of his 1817 tour and, as its name implies, it contains not only many of his sketches of the Rhine, but also those of the Field of Waterloo. These Rhine sketches take a variety of forms ranging from large, detailed drawings occupying an entire double-page opening to tiny memoranda tucked into a corner, as is the case here with that of Rüdesheim at top right.

All the sketches on ff.71v–72r belong to Turner's return journey down the Rhine from Mainz to Cologne in late August and show clearly how he adapted his sketching mode to suit the objects of his study. The long, strip-like sketches extending across the upper part of the two pages were made in an area where the Rhine runs a fairly straight course, is broad and calm and fringed by low hills (the famous vineyards of the Rheingau lie on the right). These drawings were made from a boat which was bearing Turner steadily downstream towards the Bingen gorge where the river becomes very much narrower, more tortuous and enclosed by steep hills. For that type of scenery – which continues from Bingen down to Coblenz – Turner consistently used a different format altogether with much larger, sturdier images, partly for the simple reason that he himself was physically much closer to what he was sketching. The last sketch on these pages was drawn from the west bank of the Rhine and shows the pilgrimage church at Bornhofen beneath the rocky ridge occupied by the two castles of Burg Liebenstein and Burg Sterrenberg. These are popularly known as 'The Brothers' and are the subject of many romantic legends.

This sketchbook was to provide Turner with innumerable images for watercolours of the Rhine right up to the mid-1830s (see cat.nos.4–28). The first to be painted were those in the series bought by Walter Fawkes in 1817 of which 'The Binger Loch and Mäuseturm' (cat.no.11) was directly based on the central sketch running across ff.71v–72r.

Rhine sketchbook 1817

3 Burg Rheinfels and Burg Maus from St Goar

Pencil
Page size: 202 × 265 ($7\frac{15}{16} \times 10\frac{7}{16}$)
Contains two different white wove papers
Watermarked: J WHATMAN/1816 and J WHATMAN/1817
Inscribed: 'Wood, Timber and Trees'
TB CLXI ff.21 verso, 22
D12918, D12919

Turner used the *Rhine* sketchbook between 20 and 30 August 1817 for bigger and better pencil sketches of the Middle Rhine than those he was drawing on the same days in his much smaller sketchbooks TB CLIX and CLX (cat. nos.1, 2). The most outstanding sketches in the book are those drawn at towns at which he stayed overnight – Cologne, Coblenz and St Goar. In each of these three places he chose his viewpoints with great care and, with leisure to record all their notable buildings in detail, produced a series of prospects and vistas as fine as any in his career. The drawings are, however, if anything, too fine and too carefully balanced for the type of rugged scenery depicted and, when Turner came to paint his deliberately sketch-like coloured Rhine scenes in the weeks that followed his tour (see cat.nos.4–11), he based only about six of the fifty-one on the sketches in this book, preferring to use the much smaller but far livelier sketches in the *Waterloo and Rhine* sketchbook as his starting points for all the others.

Like many other travellers at this date, Turner made St Goar his only overnight stopping-place between Coblenz and Mainz, staying two nights there on his way upriver and one on his way downstream. The attractions of the spot lay in its very close grouping of towns and ruined castles at a point where the Rhine gorge itself was at its most picturesque. The sketch on ff.21v–22r was drawn from the waterside on the northern edge of St Goar looking downstream to Burg Rheinfels, perched high on its rock. This castle fortress – the largest on the Middle Rhine apart from Ehrenbreitstein and one of the most formidable in Germany – was built by the Counts of Katzenelnbogen in the thirteenth century as a toll castle. With the building a century later of the Neukatzenelnbogen castle – 'Burg Katz' –

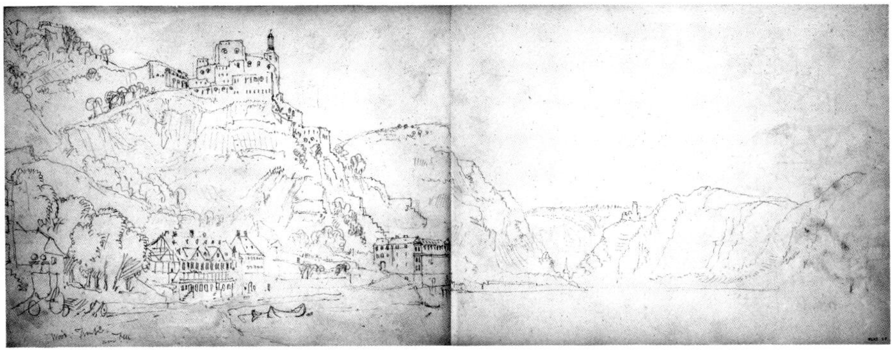

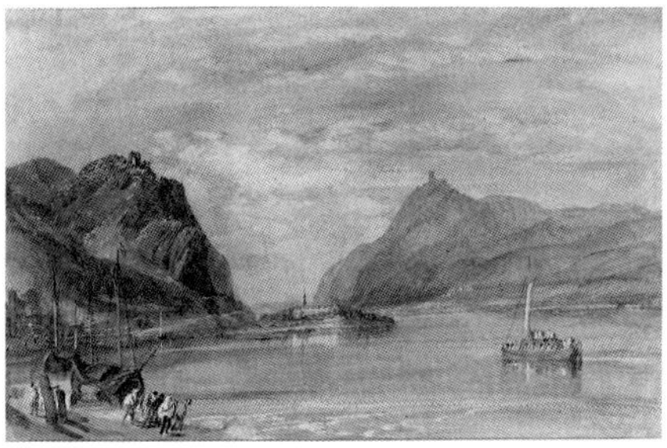

4 Rolandswerth, Nunnery and Drachenfels* 1817

Gouache and watercolour on white paper prepared with a grey wash
195 × 303 ($7\frac{11}{16} \times 11\frac{15}{16}$)
Private Collection
w 666

slightly upstream, above St Goarshausen on the opposite bank, the family achieved complete control of the Rhine valley (see cat.no.7). After the Katzenelnbogen family died out in 1479 both castles passed to the Landgraves of Hesse who enlarged Burg Rheinfels into a sumptuous Renaissance castle as well as a military stronghold. It was successfully defended against the troops of Louis XIV in 1692 but in 1794 it surrendered to those of the French Revolutionary Army which blew it up in 1796–7.

Turner's view also shows the third ruined castle to be seen from St Goar, Burg Thurnberg, which was built by the Archbishop of Trier, Kuno von Falkenstein, in the fourteenth century above the village of Wellmich, the church of which is just visible in this drawing. It was immediately nicknamed 'Burg Maus' by the predatory owners of Burg Katz, but it was not despoiled until it fell into the clutches of an even more ambitious enemy: in 1806 Napoleon had it blown up as part of his systematic destruction of all the extant fortresses along the Rhine.

The contrast between the crisp and detailed handling of the nearer hillside and buildings and the schematic, softer treatment accorded to the distance is typical of Turner's double-page sketches in this book. The drawing also shows two other characteristic features: Turner's interest in local life and occupations (woodcutting was evidently taking place nearby) and his use of time-saving devices while sketching (the numerous bays of the house near the centre are left bare but are annotated '16').

As soon as Turner reached England in September 1817 he painted fifty-one Rhine scenes based on the pencil sketches in the sketchbooks used on his summer tour. He sold all of these that very autumn to his friend Walter Fawkes and they are now widely scattered throughout the world in public and private collections, but cat.nos.4–11 here are able to stand as a representative sample. The stretch of the Rhine south of Bonn shown in cat.no.4 provides the traveller's first glimpse of the magnificence of the gorge further upstream, hemmed in by towering precipices studded with ruined castles. It inspired Byron's famous description of 1816 which was to form part of the intellectual baggage of all subsequent nineteenth-century visitors to the Rhine:

The castled crag of Drachenfels
Frowns o'er the wide and winding Rhine
Whose breast of waters broadly swells
Between the banks which bear the vine
(*Childe Harold's Pilgrimage* III, LV, 1)

Paradoxically, however, the lofty hills above the convent island are only seen to good effect when looking downstream from a distance, as in Turner's view here: thus the Drachenfels is the smaller and far less threatening hill on the right, while the ruin on the left is Roland's Arch, all that remained of a once mighty castle.

In Turner's day this scene was particularly evocative because of the historical and legendary events connected with it. One of the reasons why Childe Harold longed so passionately for his absent love at this spot was that a highly romantic legend of separated lovers had recently become attached to the convent and Roland's castle (see cat.no.29). On a more prosaic level, when the French annexed the Rhineland and the convent was sequestrated, Josephine interceded with Napoleon on behalf of its occupants who were allowed to remain there for their lifetimes. After the last of the nuns died, the building was sold. In the 1820s and 1830s it was variously described as a public house and a commodious hotel. For two or three summers in the early 1840s, when Turner often passed it on his way to and from Switzerland, the composer Franz Liszt rented it for himself, his companion Countess Marie d'Agoult and their children – which may perhaps be regarded as a suitably Byronic conclusion to its early nineteenth-century history.

Turner's scene combines strength with delicacy in a way that is characteristic of the group to which it belongs. Its palette is comparatively restricted, with earth colours predominating, but these are variously blended together with tiny strokes into clearly demarcated areas, each with its own special characteristics and truth to nature. His composition is essentially based on the lowest pencil sketch on TB CLX 83r, a drawing taken from a boat on the water which provides easily the best viewpoint (note how even the convent spire is seen against the sky). However, he did not follow this absolutely, but added a passenger boat on the river and a section of road at lower left, complete with houses, boats and local people. These additions provided not only essential asymmetrical touches but also – and equally important – the sense that the Rhineland is rich in people, not merely in rocks and ruins.

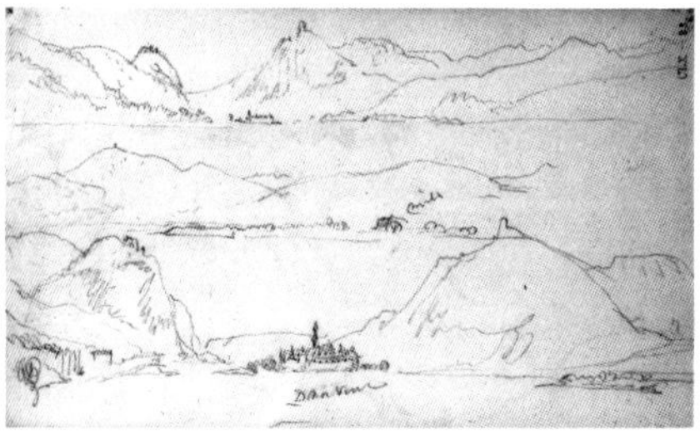

Rolandswerth, Nonnenwerth and Drachenfels (TB CLX 83r)

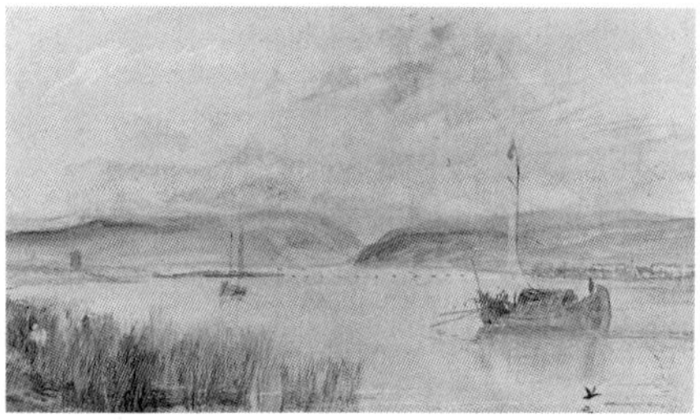

5 Neuwied and Weissenthurm* 1817

Gouache and watercolour, with scratching out, on white paper prepared with a grey wash
190 × 305 ($7\frac{1}{2}$ × 12)
The Warden and Scholars of Winchester College
W 661

'Neuwied and Weissenthurm' is one of the least elaborate of Turner's 1817 Rhine series and, looking at such a wonderfully free drawing as this, it is easy to see how the belief arose that they were executed, in part at least, on the spot. It is, however, based exactly on a tiny pencil sketch (the third of the five on TB CLX 78v–79r) which recorded all the key topographical elements in the central band of the drawing: the town of Weissenthurm, named after its massive white tower (which Turner here depicts in shadow so as not to give it undue prominence), the flying bridge across the Rhine to the eighteenth-century town of Neuwied, and the long rounded contours of the hills closing in behind them as the river bears down towards Andernach. The horizontal band containing these features occupies less than a quarter of the drawing, but the sky and foreground are so lightly brushed in that it completely dominates the work as a whole, forcing the viewer's attention over the glassy expanse of water and on towards the distant hills.

A few years later Turner painted a second version of this scene, slightly smaller but far more elaborate, which was exhibited by the engraver and publisher W.B. Cooke in 1823 and is now in the National Gallery of Scotland (W 689). This was to have been engraved in a book of Rhine views to be supervised by Cooke himself but the project never came to fruition and Turner appears to have painted only three of the thirty-six drawings specified in the 1819 contract (see above, pp.35–6).

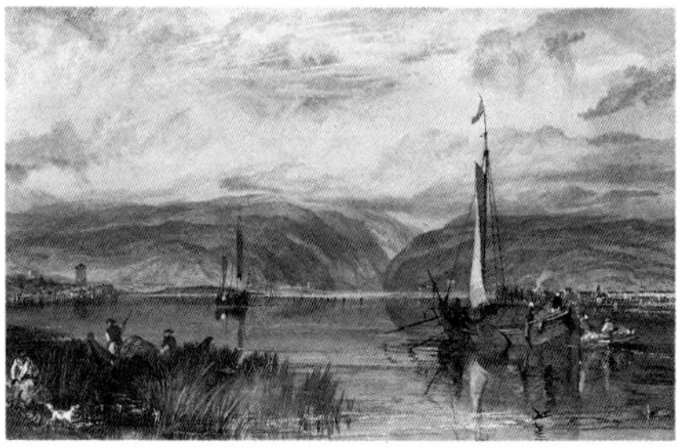

'Neuwied and Weissenthurm' (W 689)

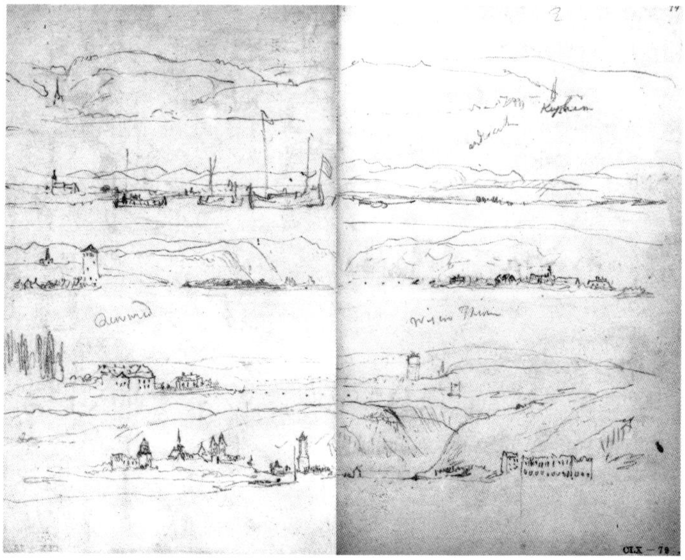

Weissenthurm, Neuwied and Andernach (TB CLX 78v–79r)

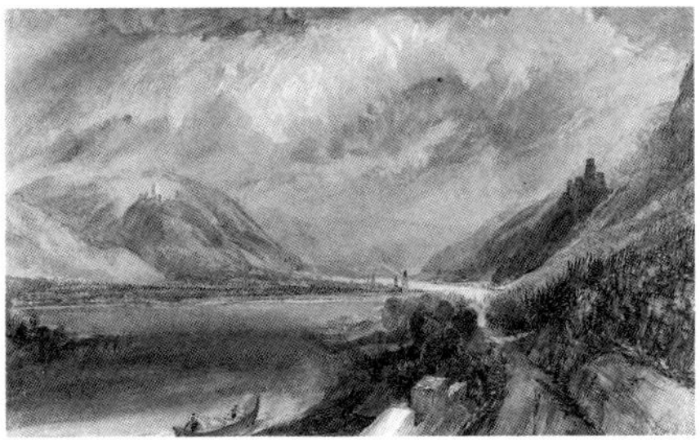

6 Junction of the Lahn* 1817

Gouache and watercolour on white paper prepared with a grey wash
196 × 314 ($7\frac{3}{4} \times 12\frac{3}{8}$)
Private Collection
w 655

Many tributaries join the Rhine between Mainz and Cologne, some dramatically, some almost invisibly, but in 1817 Turner paid attention only to three of these: the Mosel at Coblenz, the Nahe at Bingen (see under cat.no.11) and the Lahn, a few miles south of Ehrenbreitstein. In the present drawing, the Lahn is, strictly speaking, out of sight since its junction with the Rhine occurs just beyond the church at the centre (St John's, Niederlahnstein); its mouth is guarded by the pale castle on the left, Burg Lahneck, situated high above Oberlahnstein on its other bank. However, Turner made many pencil sketches in this area in 1817, including a fine one showing the Lahn itself quite clearly, together with horse-drawn carts waiting for the ferry and its ancient domed toll-house (TB CLXI 17r).

Cat.no.6 is one of only a handful of Turner's 1817 series to be based on a sketch in the largest sketchbook used on this tour – TB CLXI 12v–13r, drawn as he walked upstream along the west bank towards the castle of Stolzenfels. Though quite large, his sketch is not as detailed as many in that book (its lines were swiftly drawn and in the foreground he merely scribbled 'Boat Coming in' rather than stopping to record it). From this starting point he created an even more dramatically asymmetrical composition with the right-hand side now plunged into shadow, the left caught by fitful light; he added the threat of an imminent storm, and he heightened the tension throughout by his vigorous handling of paint, often applied in rapid scratch-like strokes and here and there smudged into place with his fingertips.

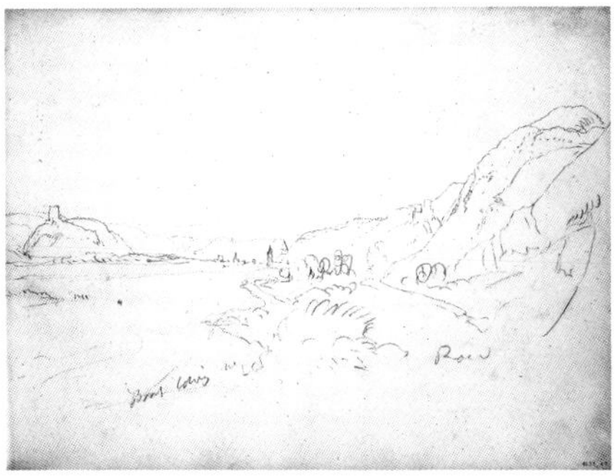

The junction of the Lahn (TB CLXI 13r)

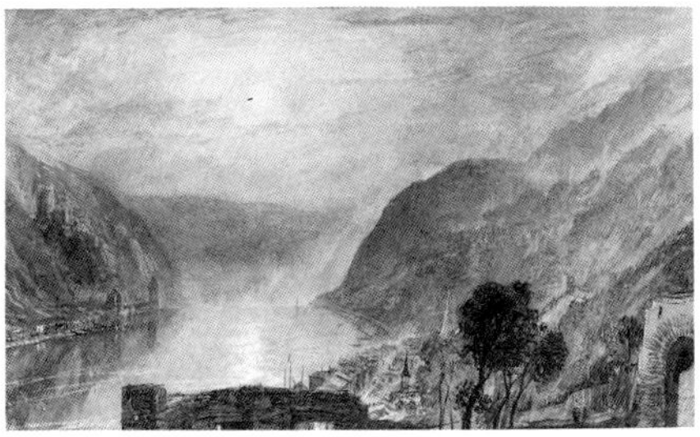

7 From Rheinfels, Looking over St Goar to Burg Katz* 1817

Gouache and watercolour, with scratching out, on white paper prepared with a grey wash
195 × 313 ($7\frac{11}{16} \times 12\frac{5}{16}$)
Private Collection
w 677
[Exhibited in London only]

Turner's overnight stops at St Goar on 23, 24 and 27 August 1817 enabled him to climb the hillsides both behind and facing the town so as to get an entirely new perspective of the Rhine from that afforded by the lower ground. It is easy to see from this drawing not only how the builders of Burg Rheinfels and Burg Katz had been able to dominate the Middle Rhine but also why Turner spent so much time sketching in this area (see also cat.no.3). In 1817 St Goar and St Goarshausen, seen here on the left, were the only places on the Rhine where Turner sought out a broader view in this way, but such excursions were to be a characteristic feature of his study of the Rhine, Meuse and Mosel in 1839. Cat.no.7 therefore looks forward prophetically both to the late watercolour of Oberwesel (cat.no.30) and to his many gouaches of the Meuse and Mosel from hillside viewpoints (cat.nos.47–104).

At the time of Turner's 1817 visit, the vast ruins of Burg Rheinfels, which had been devastated by the French in the 1790s, were in private ownership and were just beginning to be used as a stone quarry for the rebuilding of Ehrenbreitstein. Access was therefore easy and Turner made numerous large pencil sketches both behind and inside the ruins. Its demolition was finally halted only by the intervention of the future Kaiser Wilhelm I who bought the castle in 1843 and thus ensured its preservation. The part of Burg Rheinfels shown here can be seen again at the top of the left-hand page of cat.no.3. This provides a good idea of Turner's lofty viewpoint itself and the other prospect afforded by St Goar, looking downstream to an equally fine scene as that depicted here.

Cat.no.7, like cat.no.6, is one of the very few coloured drawings in the 1817 series to derive from Turner's pencil sketches in the large *Rhine* sketchbook (cat.no.3). This sketch (f.42r) contains numerous details found in the watercolour such as the church towers and the riverside crane, but in the final work Turner has slightly modified his viewpoint, made the contours of his shoreline and hillside far bolder and more rounded, inserted parts of the ravaged brickwork of Burg Rheinfels into his foreground and introduced magical atmospheric effects. Even if Turner did not claim on his deathbed that 'The sun is god', as is popularly believed, he knew from very early on in his career exactly how to demonstrate that colour is a function of light.

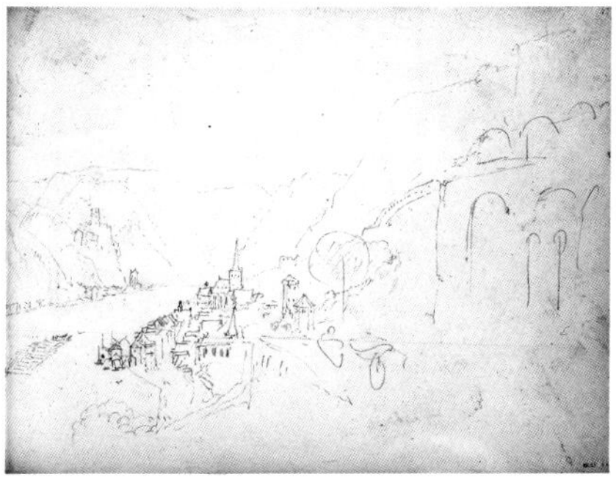

View upstream from Burg Rheinfels (TB CLXI 42r)

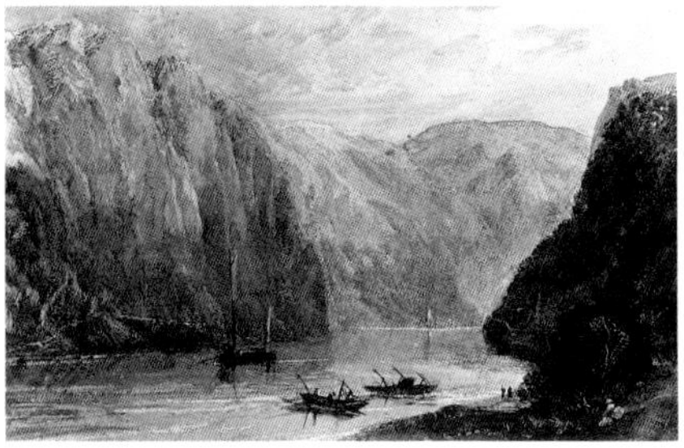

8 The Lorelei* 1817

Gouache and watercolour, with scratching out, on white paper prepared with a grey wash
197 × 305 ($7\frac{3}{4}$ × 12)
Whitworth Art Gallery, University of Manchester (D.57.1925)
W 646

The massive rock known as the Lorelei rises very steeply from the east bank of the Rhine half way between Coblenz and Bingen and thus lies at the very heart of the most celebrated stretch of the river. Here the gorge is particularly narrow with several dangerous bends, that around the Lorelei being especially perilous on account of its hidden rocks, currents and whirlpools. Turner was evidently greatly impressed by its grandeur and sublimity, for he depicted it in no less than seven watercolours in his 1817 series, a far larger number than he devoted to any other sight. It is almost certainly a mistake, however, to assume that he was captivated by the romantic legends of a siren luring sailors to their deaths, which became so popular later in the nineteenth century (as was suggested when this work was exhibited at York in 1980). The evidence of his watercolours suggests that it was the sheer scale and severity of the scenery that held his attention. In the present instance, the soft evening light serves only to highlight the terrible grandeur of the rock, so vast that it can scarcely be contained within the picture space, and neither here nor in the other views of the Lorelei is there anything that could remotely be regarded as anecdotal.

While cat.no.8 and two other drawings (W 648, W 647/686) show the view from just below the Lorelei, looking upstream, with the rock on the left, another two record the reverse view, i.e. looking downstream from just above the rock (W 685, W 684). (In this last, the gap between the opposing rocks is sufficiently wide to allow a glimpse of Burg Katz perched above St Goarshausen, the subject of another two scenes, slightly further downstream, which just manage to exclude the Lorelei on their right, W 645, W 676.) The last two Lorelei scenes from the series are now untraced and have not featured in any recent literature on Turner but both received detailed descriptions in the Royal Academy catalogue when the complete series was exhibited there in 1889. The second of these (no.46 below) was sold at Agnew's in 1915 and is known from the old photograph reproduced here.

45 Early morning; the air full of mist; high cliff on the l., lit up by the sun; on the river is a raft, and to the l., a sailing vessel; on the bank to r., a group of trees, and a footpath with figures on it; fleecy clouds in the sky, lit up by the rising sun. Size $7\frac{1}{2}$ by $11\frac{7}{8}$ in.

46 A steep bluff on the far side of the river, which flows swiftly below it, occupies the centre of the picture; in the shadow of the cliff, the upper part of which is lit up by the sun, is a vessel sailing; the river and near bank are in shadow; a ferry-boat is in mid-stream; another is near the bank on the r., where some figures are waiting to cross; overcast sky. Size $7\frac{1}{2}$ by $11\frac{7}{8}$ in.

All these scenes are based on some of the smallest and hastiest of Turner's pencil sketches of 1817, the last of the four on TB CLX IV being especially comparable to cat.no.8.

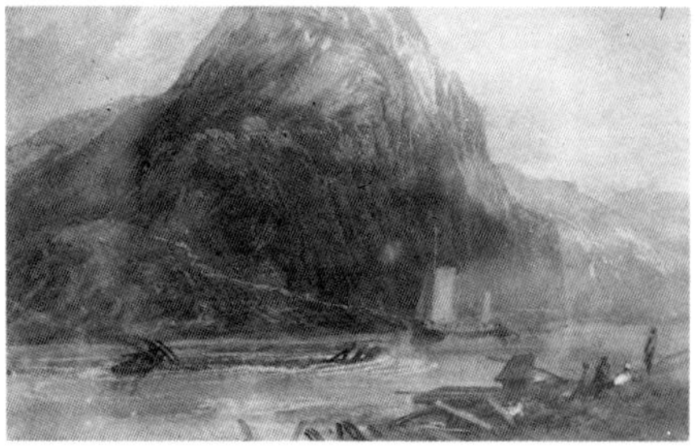

'The Lorelei'. Present whereabouts unknown

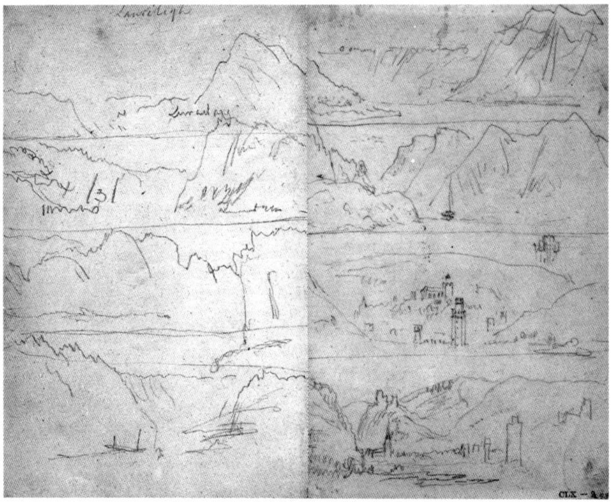

The Lorelei and Oberwesel (TB CLX IV–2r)

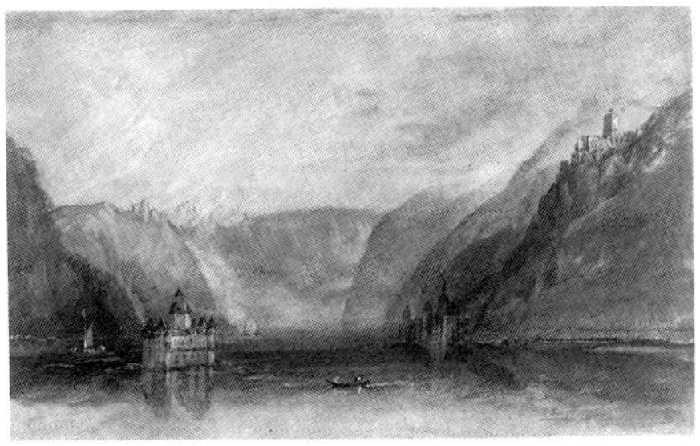

9 The Pfalz on the Rhine* 1817

Gouache and watercolour on white paper prepared with a grey wash
190 × 305 ($7\frac{1}{2} \times 12$)
Private Collection
W 643

This is one of the most serene of Turner's 1817 Rhine series, with the river itself appearing more like a tranquil lake, its ancient buildings having a fairy-tale character and its present-day inhabitants sailing and rowing their boats under a calm sky. Turner's view is downstream past the Pfalz on its island to the many towers of Kaub beneath the cube-like structure of Burg Gutenfels which gave that town its name. High on the opposite bank can be seen the Schönburg, but the town below it, Oberwesel, is obscured by the hills. There were several points on the Middle Rhine where many historic buildings could be seen together, as here, providing instant inspiration to any artist. However, Turner has not simply painted what he saw, but has brought together information from several sketches drawn on the Rhine: two views looking downstream from a boat towards this overall view, a detailed sketch of the Pfalz itself drawn as his boat passed between the island and the eastern shore, and a detailed sketch of Burg Gutenfels drawn two days earlier on his journey upstream on foot along the west bank (TB CLX 73v–74r, 62r). These have all been blended perfectly together, so that the crisply depicted buildings with their delicate glowing highlights are seen against the more summary handling of river, sky and hills like jewels on a crown.

One of the reasons for the multiplicity of ancient buildings along the Middle Rhine was that Germany had for centuries been fragmented into hundreds of separate cities, states and territories. The most powerful rulers in the Middle Rhineland were the Elector Palatine and the Archbishops of Cologne, Mainz and Trier. These not only controlled vast lands but also, together with three other Electors from territories much further afield, determined the choice of the Holy Roman Emperor from 1356 until Napoleon abolished the Empire itself in 1806. According to tradition, the Palatine Countesses always retired to the seclusion of the Pfalz to give birth to their children (see cat.no.20). However, at the time of Turner's visit, and for long afterwards, Kaub was far more famous as the place from which Marshal Blücher and the newly invigorated Prussian army had crossed the Rhine on a pontoon bridge on New Year's Night 1813/14 and begun driving out the French invaders, a process which reached its triumphant conclusion on the Field of Waterloo.

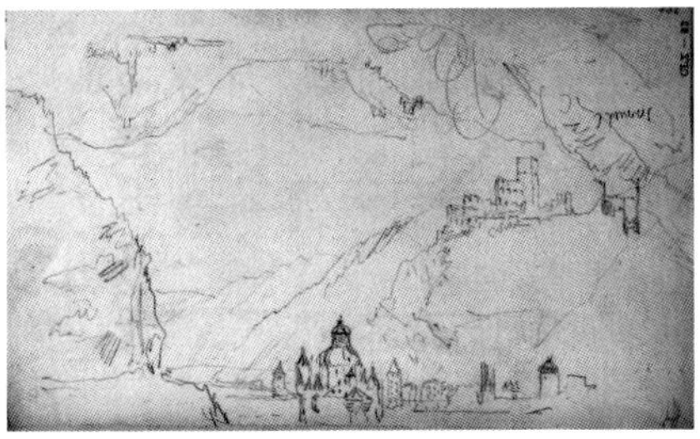

Kaub, the Pfalz and Burg Gutenfels; Burg Sooneck (TB CLX 62r)

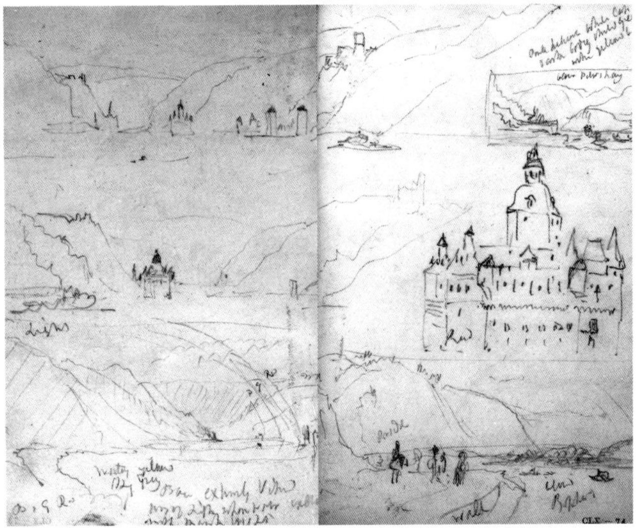

Kaub, the Pfalz and Burg Gutenfels; Osterspay and Feltzen (TB CLX 73v–74r)

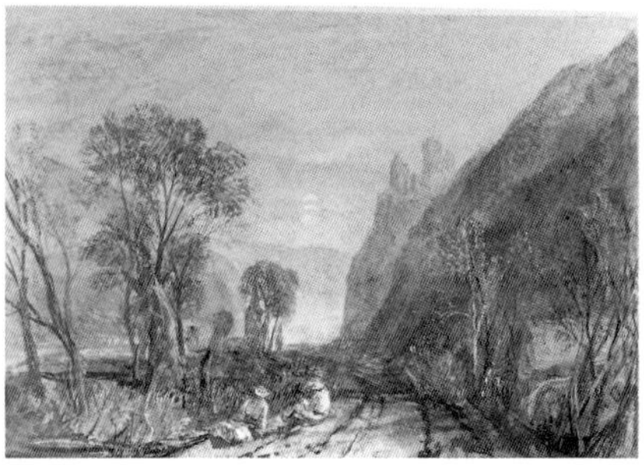

10 The Bautsburg* 1817

Gouache and watercolour, with scratching out, on white paper prepared with a grey wash
225 × 316 ($8\frac{7}{8} \times 12\frac{7}{16}$)
Board of Trustees of the Victoria and Albert Museum, London
w 640/w 683

Like a substantial number of the 1817 Rhine drawings (including cat.nos.5 and 6), this scene is emphatically sketch-like and strongly suggests to the viewer that Turner has executed it in the open air, sitting alongside the woodcutters resting on the edge of the road. It is, however, based on a swift pencil outline drawn on his walk up the Rhine (TB CLX 67v) and its extremely naturalistic effects are the product of artistic skill, memory and knowledge rather than simply records made on the spot.

Although this work has never been lost to view since Turner painted it, it has for some time been deprived of its proper title. In the earliest known nineteenth-century listing of the Rhine drawings – that in the first biography of Turner by Walter Thornbury (1862, vol.2, p.394) – it is given as 'Bautsburg'; by 1889 when it was exhibited at the Royal Academy it had become 'Bausenberg'; and for many years it led a dual life, as 'Bausenberg in the Brohltal' (w 640) and 'A View on the Rhine' (w 683). There is, however, no connection between this drawing and the volcanic area of the Brohltal. It is a Rhine-side view looking upstream towards two buildings that formed an ensemble depicted by many early nineteenth-century artists: the Clemenskapelle, glimpsed through the grove of trees near the centre, and the Bautsburg, a medieval toll castle which had been slowly crumbling into ruin since the sixteenth century. Its name is variously explained as a corruption of 'Fatzberg' or 'Vogtsburg', referring respectively to St Boniface and the office of castle steward. The guidebook used by Turner in 1817 called it 'Bauzberg' (Campbell, 1817, p.186). In both Thornbury's list and the RA catalogue of 1889, this drawing is listed in its correct topographical place, i.e. between 'The Binger Loch and Mäuseturm' and 'Burg Sooneck'.

One of the charms of this scene is the way in which the delicately concave spire of the chapel and the rugged ruins of the castle are both shown against the light. Soon after Turner enjoyed this view, the castle was rebuilt for Prince Wilhelm Ludwig of Prussia in a highly wrought medieval style, thus becoming the first castle on the Middle Rhine to receive a new lease of life (1825–9). The same spirit of romantic medievalism also led to its acquiring a new name, 'Burg Rheinstein', by which it is still known today.

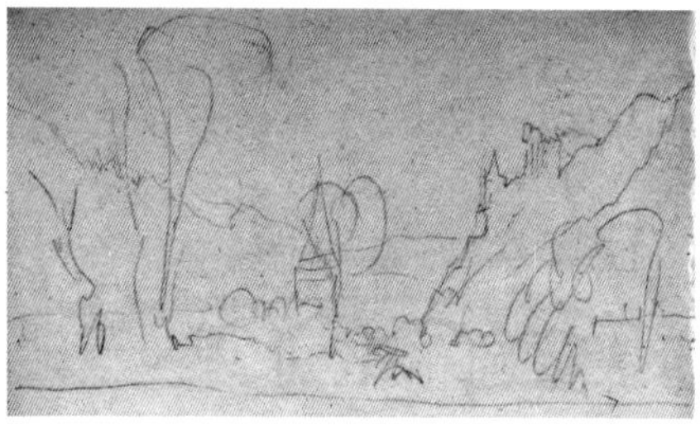

The Bautsburg (TB CLX 67v)

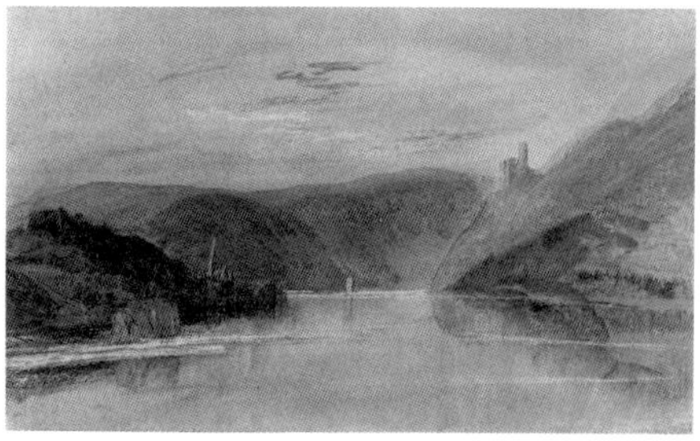

11 The Binger Loch and Mäuseturm* 1817

Gouache and watercolour, with scratching out, on white paper prepared with a grey wash
194 × 311 ($7\frac{5}{8} \times 12\frac{1}{4}$)
Private Collection
w 679

Turner here shows the view down the Rhine to the Bingen gorge with the ruins of Burg Klopp and Bingen itself on the left, the Mäuseturm on its island in the centre and Burg Ehrenfels on the right. For centuries this was a particularly dangerous stretch of the Rhine, since vessels coming downstream from the broad and peaceful reach below Mainz had now to keep carefully within a very narrow channel – the 'Binger Loch' – between the Mäuseturm and Burg Ehrenfels, where hidden rocks and currents claimed the lives and cargoes of numerous travellers. Turner's drawing – itself based on a sketch made in a boat (see cat.no.2) – magnificently conveys this sense of imminent danger through a variety of devices which are both true to nature and overlaid with meaning: the foreground is light and serene in contrast to the brooding hills beyond; rocks above the shoreline are surrounded by swirling foam and are prominently reflected in the water; Burg Ehrenfels appears in a halo of light as though acting as a lighthouse to guide travellers to safety.

This part of the Rhine has always been rich in history and associations. Popular thought has long linked the Mäuseturm with the legend of Bishop Hatto, devoured by rats in the tenth century as a punishment for his loathsome behaviour towards his subjects whom he regarded simply as troublesome vermin. However, the probability is that the tower, which actually dates from considerably later than the bishop, was merely a toll-post, like scores of other castles and towers on the river.

Turner painted two other scenes of the Rhine at Bingen in the same series as cat.no.11. In one of these (W 680) he shows the view up the Nahe, the tributary which joins the Rhine from the valley just beyond Burg Klopp in cat.no.11. In the other (W 682) he shows the reverse view, looking down the Nahe to its ancient stone bridge and beyond this to Burg Ehrenfels, Bingen church and Burg Klopp. The topography of both these two scenes has been completely misunderstood in the past, leading them to acquire meaningless titles which obscure the fact that they both show the same river. The three Bingen scenes are greatly enhanced by being considered together, since the peaceful view up the Nahe and away from the Rhine and the storm-ridden view down the Nahe towards the Binger Loch develop yet further the contrasts and tensions present in cat.no.11 itself.

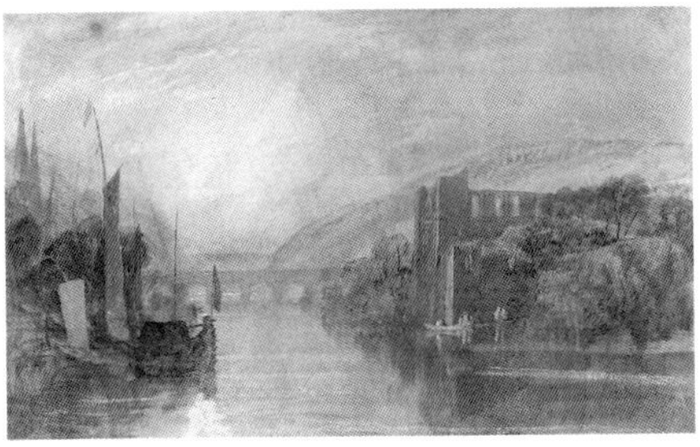

'The Abbey at Bingen' (W 680)

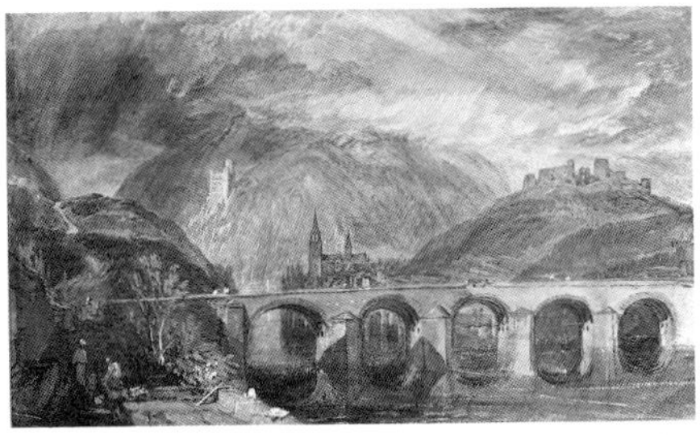

'Bingen from the Nahe' (W 682)

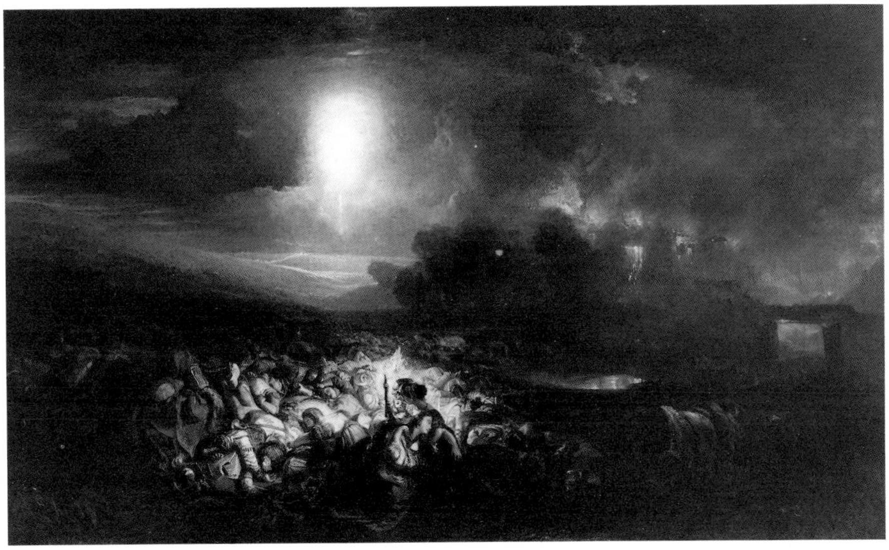

12 The Field of Waterloo RA 1818

Oil on canvas
1473 × 2388 (58 × 94)
Turner Bequest; B&J 138
N00500
[Exhibited in London only]

Turner's desire to visit the Field of Waterloo was one of the chief reasons for his visit to the Low Countries and the Rhineland in 1817. He visited the battlefield on 16 August and drew seventeen pages of pencil sketches of the huge plain and the now-derelict buildings where the allies under the Duke of Wellington and Marshal Blücher had scored their final, decisive victory over Napoleon on 18 June 1815. He learned much about the course of the battle itself from his guidebook to Belgium and Holland by Charles Campbell, but even more about its details from the guide who escorted him around the site. Like any professional reporter, Turner noted the facts down without comment – '4000 killed here', '1500 killed here', 'Hollow where the great Carnage took place' – but he was profoundly moved by what he heard, seeing all too clearly in his mind's eye the reality behind the guide's cold statistics. Once back in England, he produced this sombre painting, showing the night after the victory and what a battle really means in human terms: corpses, bereavement and chaos.

As all the spectators at the 1818 Royal Academy would have been well aware, the allied victory on 18 June had been preceded by an unusual train of events. On 15 June the British army was stationed at Brussels and, believing Napoleon to be far away, Wellington and his officers had spent the night of 15–16 June at a magnificent ball given there by the Duchess of Richmond. Suddenly news came that Napoleon had crossed the Sambre, had taken Charleroi and was only a few miles off. Within minutes the dancing had ceased, within hours the entire army had left Brussels. They then engaged with the French at Quatre Bras and took up their positions on Mont St Jean south of the village of Waterloo. The lines which Turner quoted in the RA catalogue from Byron's *Childe Harold's Pilgrimage* (canto III, verse xxviii) were no poetical fancy but a reminder of real events. England's élite had literally gone from the ballroom to the battlefield, many of them to their death.

Throughout his life Turner himself was obsessed by the fickleness of fortune, a theme which he expounded in some of his most famous history paintings including two with unmistakable relevance to the events of his own age: 'Dido building Carthage' (RA 1815, B&J 131, National Gallery, London) and its sequel 'The Decline of the Carthaginian Empire' (RA 1817, B&J 135, Clore Gallery). The events of 15–18 June 1815 provided a real-life example of just such a rise and fall cycle, and Turner used all his skills as a painter of spectacular, theatrical and historical subjects to produce a painting not of the battle itself but of its aftermath described by Byron:

Last noon beheld them full of lusty life
Last eve in Beauty's circle proudly gay,
The midnight brought the signal-sound of strife,
The morn the marshalling in arms, – the day
Battle's magnificently stern array!
The thunder-clouds close o'er it, which when rent
The earth is cover'd thick with other clay,
Which her own clay shall cover, heap'd and pent,
Rider and horse, – friend, foe, – in one r
burial blent!

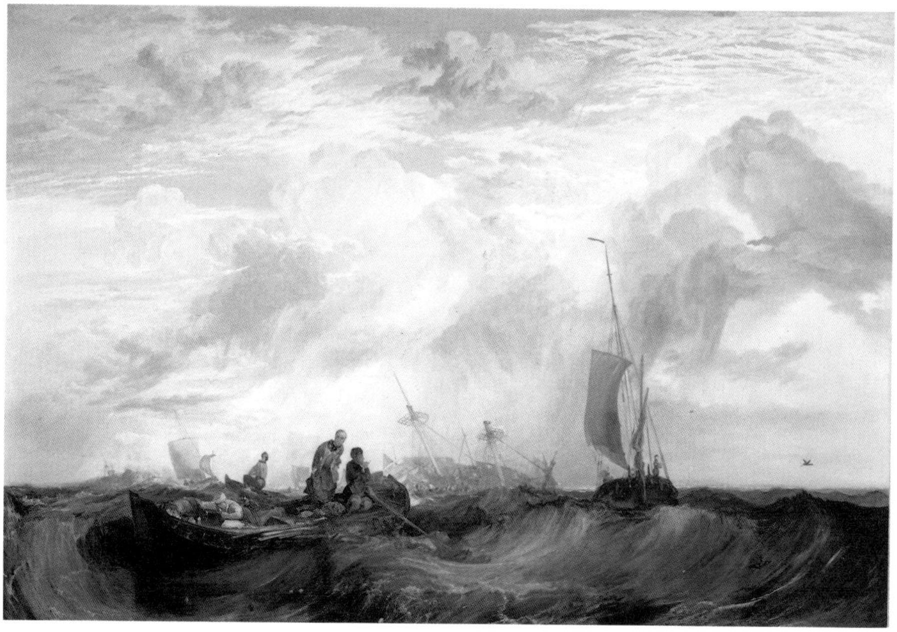

13 Entrance of the Meuse: Orange Merchant on the Bar, Going to Pieces; Brill Church Bearing S.E. by S., Masensluys E. by S. RA 1819

Oil on canvas
1753 × 2464 (69 × 97)
Turner Bequest; B&J 139
N00501
[Exhibited in London only]

The foreground of this painting shows the North Sea close to the Hook of Holland, with the artist looking (as he says in his title) eastwards to Maassluis (on the left) and south-eastwards to Brielle on the island of Voorne (right). At the centre, a Dutch merchant ship has gone aground in blustery weather, and has keeled over, scattering its cargo into the waves. Turner could never resist making a pun if the opportunity arose, and here he would have the viewer believe that the unfortunate vessel not only belonged to the country ruled by the House of Orange but had also been carrying a cargo of oranges.

Turner visited many parts of Holland including this area on his 1817 tour and in his preparatory notes from his guidebook to Belgium and Holland he made mention of Maassluis and noted that one could travel the twelve miles up the Meuse (or, to use its Dutch name, the Maas) from Brielle to Rotterdam for two ducats or four francs (TB CLIX 13v). 'Entrance of the Meuse' commemorates the marine dimension of Turner's 1817 tour in much the same invigorating manner as 'Calais Pier' of 1803 (B&J 48; National Gallery, London) had celebrated his first crossing of the Channel in 1802, but its debt to Dutch painting is, understandably, even greater.

It was not until five years after painting this work that Turner visited the most picturesque stretches of the Meuse, which rises on the Plateau de Langres in the Haute-Marne and pursues a tortuous course through the hilly Ardennes regions of France and Belgium before reaching the lower land north of Maastricht in Holland. Thereafter it follows a complex and meandering path which has altered over the centuries, sometimes close to, and sometimes merging with, that of the Waal branch of the Rhine. In the 1950s the mouth of the Maas was dammed and the two rivers were thus forever united in their final passage to the sea.

Twenty years after this huge and – it has to be admitted – occasionally ponderous painting, the Meuse inspired Turner to paint some of the most dazzling of his tiny gouaches on blue paper (cat.nos.84–104). The liberation of his colour and the emergence of his own artistic personality are immediately apparent in these works which provide the greatest possible contrast to cat.no.13. 'Entrance of the Meuse' was not engraved in Turner's lifetime but in 1859 a print of it, engraved by Robert Wallis (which will replace cat.no.13 in the exhibition in Brussels (Trustees of the British Museum, London)), was published as part of the large series known as *The Turner Gallery* (R 711).

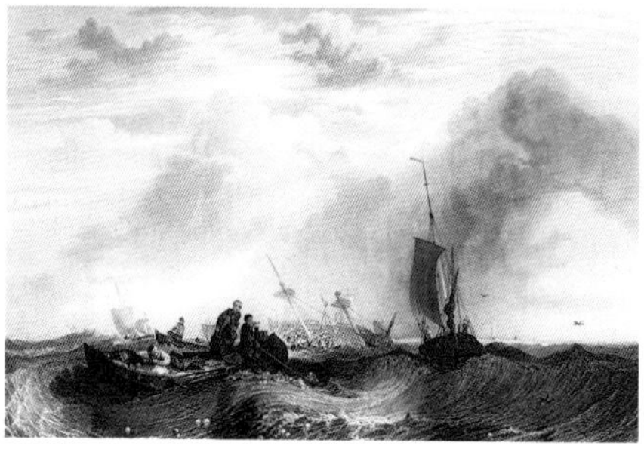

Robert Wallis after J.M.W. Turner, 'Entrance of the Meuse' (R 711)

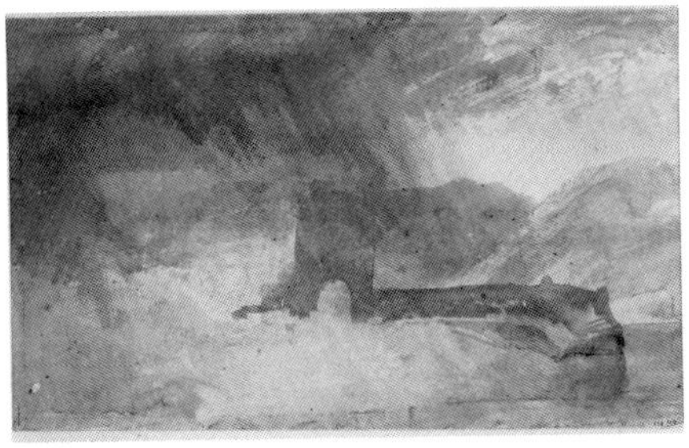

14 **Boppard: Colour Study** *c.*1819

Pencil and watercolour on white wove paper
186 × 295 ($7\frac{5}{16} \times 11\frac{5}{8}$)
TB CCLXIII 259
D25382

The view of Boppard which Turner sold to Walter Fawkes in the autumn of 1817 (W 652) is not only one of the liveliest of the series to which it belongs but also historically one of the most interesting since the view depicted is no longer extant. The scene was closely based on one of the quick pencil sketches in the *Waterloo and Rhine* sketchbook (TB CLX 93v) and shows the view downstream from outside the town walls. The twin-spired parish church, the turreted former Franciscan church and the ornate Ritter-Schwalbach-Haus of 1450 still exist much as Turner saw them, though from this viewpoint they are now largely obscured by trees and by more recent buildings. Of the massive gateway, the Sandtor, however, only the lower part remains, while the adjacent mole, which formerly protected the town from the heavy winter floods of the Rhine, was swept away in a severe winter storm some thirty years after Turner first sketched it.

During the years immediately following his Rhine tour, Turner executed, on demand, eight repetitions of the Fawkes scenes as finished watercolours (W 687–93, 689a). These were all painted on white paper and they are executed with a much higher degree of finish (see cat.no.17). The present sheet is evidently a preparatory study for a repetition of the 1817 view of Boppard, just as cat.nos.15 and 16 were for cat.no.17. Its colour scheme of blues, yellows and soft greens is very close to that of cat.no.16, as too must have been its original size (its clean edges point to its having been cut down at some stage, probably from a sheet similar to that of which cat.no.16 still forms part). A finished version of 'Boppard' is not recorded and was presumably never executed. It must have been intended as one of the thirty-six subjects destined for engraving in the book of Rhine views planned by Turner, W.B. Cooke, John Murray and J.C. Allen in 1819 which was, however, abandoned at a very early stage (see above, pp.35–6). The pencil lines squaring up the composition – an incongruity in such a free and fluid study – are unlikely to be Turner's work. They were probably added by Ruskin in connection with an early display of the drawing.

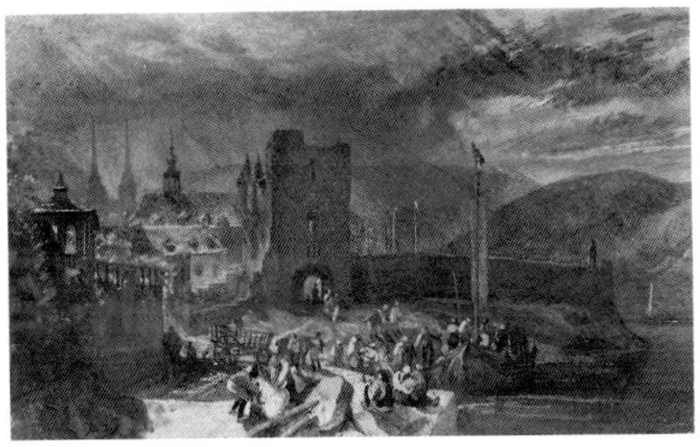

'Boppard' (W 652)

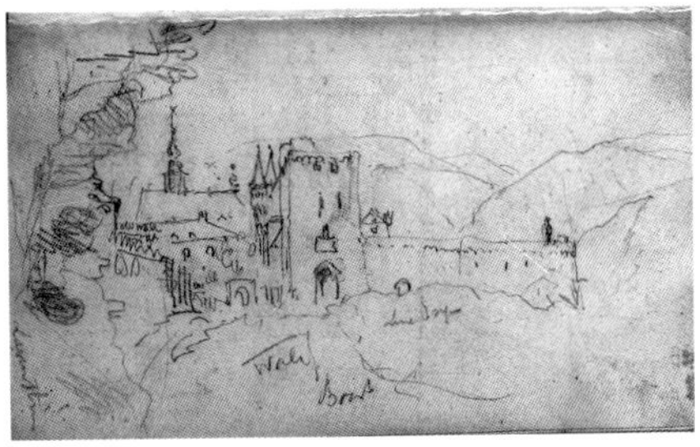

Boppard and The Brothers (TB CLX 93v)

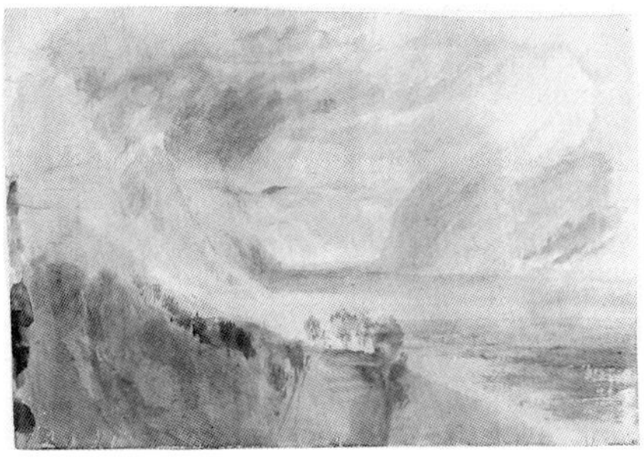

15 **Burg Sooneck with Bacharach in the Distance: Large Colour Study** *c.*1819–20

Watercolour on white wove paper
403 × 567 ($15\frac{7}{8} \times 22\frac{5}{16}$)
TB CCLXIII 182
D25304

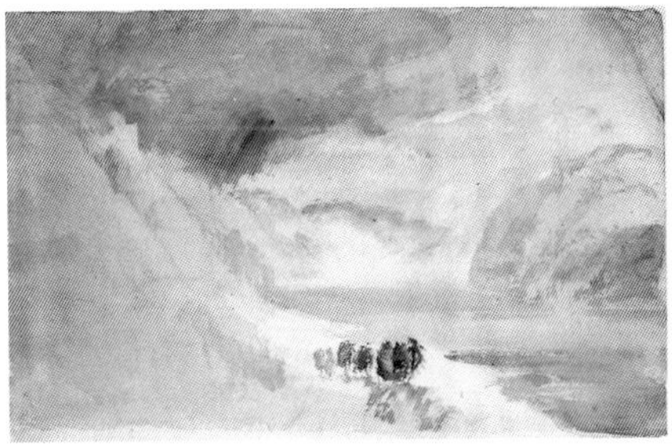

16 **Burg Sooneck with Bacharach in the Distance: Small Colour Study** *c.*1819–20

Watercolour on white wove paper
Sheet size: 494 × 386 ($19\frac{7}{16} \times 15\frac{3}{16}$)
Watermarked: J WHATMAN/TURKEY MILLS/1819
TB CCLXIII 120
D25242

It was not unusual for Turner to use the same sheet of paper for two different colour studies. In cat.no.16 the upper study can easily be related to the finished drawing of Burg Sooneck (cat.no.17) but the lower one shows only the bands of coloured washes which were Turner's habitual starting point. The contrast in size between cat.nos.15 and 16, which were presumably drawn at about the same time, is rather intriguing and one may perhaps postulate that he began by thinking that he needed to plan on a generous scale and subsequently decided that his scene would benefit from rather tighter planning. In the event, his finished watercolour is slightly marred by the exaggerated contours on its left which are unusual for Turner but typical of a large number of depictions of the Rhine by minor artists at this period.

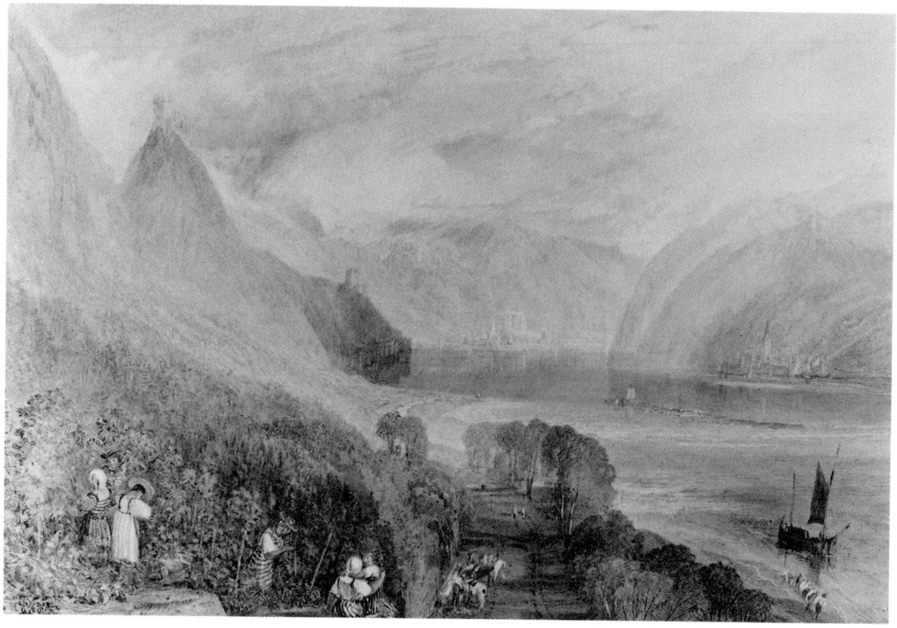

17 Burg Sooneck with Bacharach in the Distance *c.*1820

Watercolour
286 × 413 (11¼ × 16¼)
Aberdeen City Arts Department, Art Gallery & Museums (00 36 95)
W 693

This work is typical of the large-scale Rhine watercolours which Turner executed around 1820, in which he repeated and elaborated the compositions he had sold to Walter Fawkes in the autumn of 1817. The scene here is the same as that found in W 671, but the later work is not based on the earlier, nor is either of them absolutely faithful to the stretch of river depicted, since both are based on a fairly schematic small sketch (TB CLX 62r; see under cat.no.9), amplified from Turner's store of memories. He had enjoyed this prospect as he walked upstream in 1817 along the west bank of the Rhine and, turning to look backwards, saw such a superb configuration of hills, towns and castles as few other rivers can boast: on the left Burg Sooneck, the Heimburg above Niederheimbach and Burg Stahleck above Bacharach; on the opposite bank Burg Nollig above Lorch. W 671 is one of the very largest of the 1817 series, so that the extent to which Turner needed to enlarge his scene when he came to repeat it was far less for cat.no.17 than for his other repetitions. However, two sheets in the Turner Bequest (cat.nos.15 and 16) reveal the very careful planning that led up to its execution.

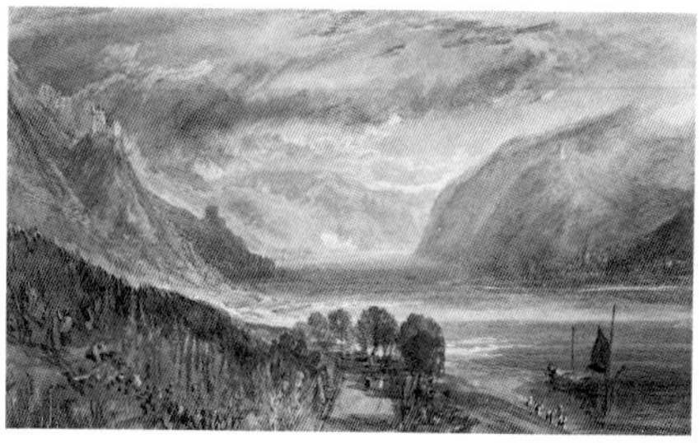

'Burg Sooneck with Bacharach in the Distance' (W 671)

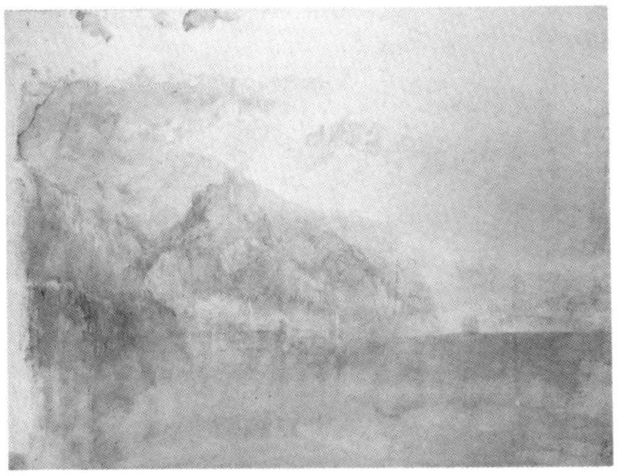

18 Kaub and the Castle of Gutenfels: Colour Study *c.*1820

Watercolour and pencil on white wove paper
396 × 507 (15 9/16 × 20)
Watermarked: J WHATMAN/TURKEY MILLS/1819
TB CCLXIII 387
D25511

19 Kaub and the Castle of Gutenfels: Colour Study *c.*1820

Watercolour on white wove paper
392 × 503 (15 7/16 × 19 13/16)
Watermarked: J WHATMAN/TURKEY MILLS/1819
TB CCLXIII 388
D25512

Cat.nos.18 and 19 are both colour studies for the same watercolour commission (cat.no.20). Turner has used the identical size and type of paper for each study and has positioned his images in exactly the same way on the two sheets. However he has experimented with different colour schemes, cat.no.18 being much lighter and brighter, with a greater emphasis on primary colours.

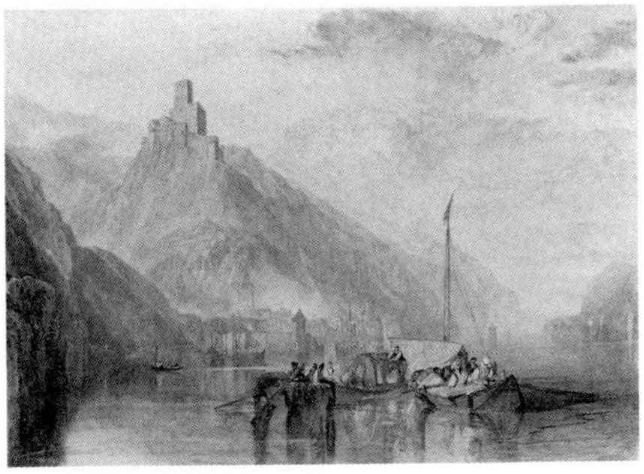

20 Kaub and the Castle of Gutenfels* *c.*1820

Watercolour
305 × 417 (12 × 16 7/16)
Inscribed, at lower right, 'J M W Turner R A'
Private Collection
W 1378

In the past this watercolour has been regarded as a work of the 1830s or even *c.*1840 but it now seems more likely that it was executed much earlier, during the period when Turner was painting other large watercolours of the Rhine for friends and patrons (W 689a, 690–2 and cat.no. 17). Unlike those watercolours, however, cat.no.20 has no earlier counterpart in the series sold to Walter Fawkes (cat. nos.4–11): in that group Turner's only depiction of Kaub, Burg Gutenfels and the Pfalz (cat.no.9) shows the ensemble from the opposite direction.

Turner's mature watercolour style is here seen at its very best, with a multitude of colours blended together in a seemingly infinite number of microscopic touches. Sky and water, hillsides and reflections are miraculously true to nature and at the same time infused with the grandeur and poetry that only he could produce. The many subtle transitions from warm areas to cooler ones, which had been so thoughtfully studied in cat.nos.18 and 19, are particularly noteworthy, since these provide the sense of shifting light and changing weather over the entire scene which make the picture so beautiful.

Little is known about the early history of this work which first appeared in the salerooms in 1927 after the death of its owner James Broughton Dugdale (born 1855) of Wroxall Abbey in Warwickshire. However, it is clearly based on a tiny pencil sketch in the *Itinerary Rhine Tour* sketchbook (cat.no.1) which Turner is known to have taken with him to the north of England in the autumn of 1817 (f.77v). He used the sketchbook at Raby Castle, County Durham, and must have had it with him also when he visited Hylton Castle and Gibside, both properties of the Earl of Strathmore. Since he was almost certainly engaged in converting many other pencil sketches into coloured Rhine views during his time at Raby Castle, he may well have received a commission there to develop this particular sketch into a watercolour. In the covered boat in the foreground Turner appears to show a bride in a white veil accompanied by an entourage. This entire group is so very different in character from the staffage of peasantry or soldiers found elsewhere in his Rhine scenes that it is tempting to speculate that Turner was given this commission to mark his unknown patron's marriage. This may, of course, be wishful thinking, but it is worth recalling the popular tradition of Turner's day that the Pfalz had been, for centuries, the place of *accouchement* for the wife of the Elector Palatine. This particular view would thus have been a very appropriate choice for an aristocratic patron looking eagerly forward to the prospect of a son and heir.

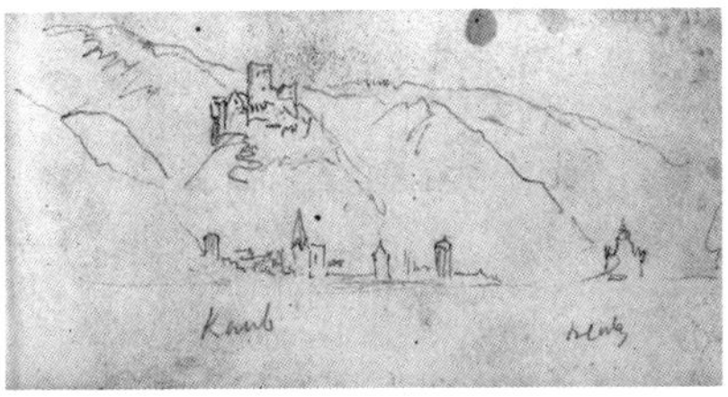

Kaub, Burg Gutenfels and the Pfalz
(TB CLIX 77V)

EDWARD GOODALL AFTER
J.M.W. TURNER

21 **Cologne** 1824

Line engraving on copper, first published state
337 × 470 ($13\frac{1}{4} \times 18\frac{1}{2}$)
Trustees of the British Museum, London
(1866–12–8–1)
R 203

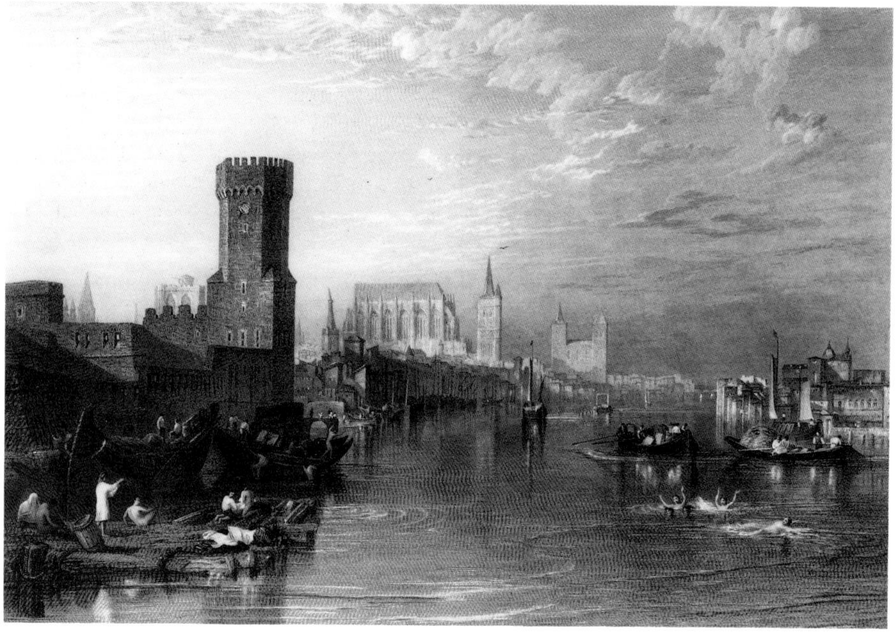

This fine large engraving is based on a watercolour painted by Turner in 1820 (W 690; Seattle Art Museum, Washington). This was bought by his friend and patron Thomas Tomkinson who lent it for exhibition at the Soho Square gallery of W.B. Cooke in 1822 (no.20, 'View of Cologne on the Rhine'). By that date Turner had, in fact, completed no less than three versions of this scene, for Tomkinson's watercolour had been preceded by an almost identical work sold to another close friend, James Rivington Wheeler (W 689a; private collection, Tokyo); and the 1817 series bought by Walter Fawkes had included a smaller version on grey-prepared paper (W 670; untraced).

Turner made many studies of Cologne during his life, from 1817 through to 1844, rarely missing an opportunity to make a sketch or two as he passed through the city (see cat.no.35). He experimented with a variety of views – looking upstream, downstream, across the water and even inventing views he thought ought to exist (cat.no.22). For the bravura performance in cat.no.21, however, the publication of a large single engraving – not in a book of prints or illustrating a text but simply standing alone to attract purchasers for its own sake – he chose the archetypal view of Cologne which he had drawn several times in 1817 (e.g. TB CLX 87v, 88r). In this all the city's chief buildings are shown to their best advantage while Turner himself was enabled, in one and the same work, to give a dazzling demonstration as both architectural draughtsman and river painter. His delineations of the Bayenturm and cathedral, Great St Martin's church and that of St Cunibert are all highly impressive achievements, while the vignettes of Rhineside life in the foreground have evidently been sharply observed and painted with great understanding and enjoyment.

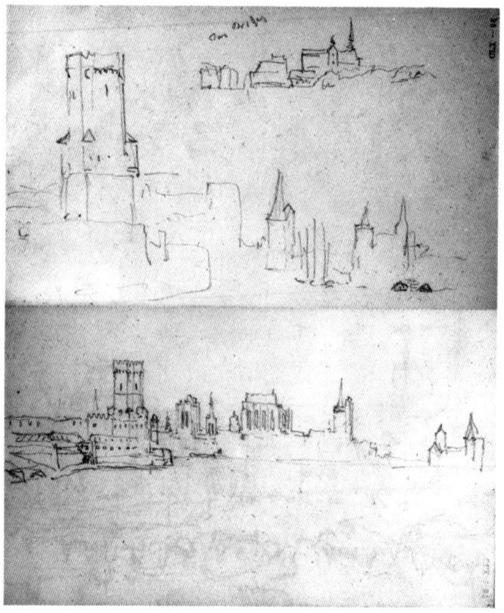

Cologne (TB CLX 87v–88r)

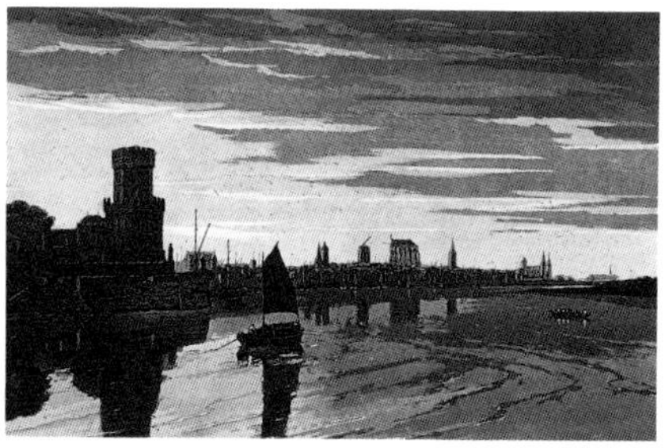

William Daniell junior after Sir John Carr, 'Cologne', aquatint

Turner did not discover this view for himself. It was already very popular with the British public, having been rendered with great sensitivity by William Daniell junior as one of his illustrations to Sir John Carr's *Views on the Rhine* (1807).[1] Turner and Daniell both thought very highly of each other's work: Turner voted for Daniell as an Associate member of the Royal Academy in 1807 and on one occasion around that date he tartly informed an engraver that parts of a plate were 'very bad . . . I should like to have them engraved like Mr. Daniell's.'[2] Goodall's large plate after Turner shows just how sophisticated line engraving had become in England by the mid-1820s, but even he could not improve upon the poetry of Daniell's image.

1 Daniell's name did not appear beneath these plates, since they were based on Carr's images. However, he is acknowledged as their engraver in Carr's note 'To the Reader'; see also Daniell's own account of the commission recorded in Farington's *Diary* for 1 June 1807.
2 Finberg (1961), p.140.

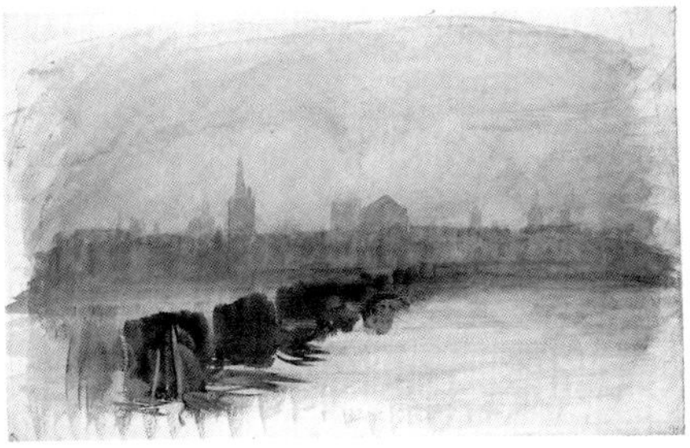

22 Cologne: Colour Study *c.*1824–32

Watercolour on white wove paper
268 × 408 ($10\frac{9}{16} \times 16\frac{1}{16}$)
Watermarked: J WHATMAN/1814
TB CCLXIII 190
D25312

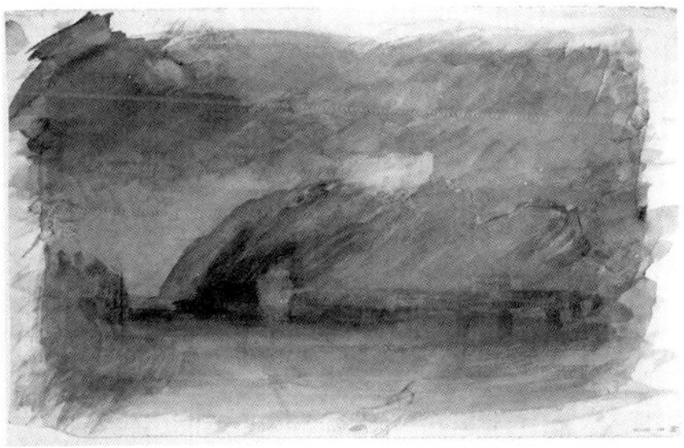

23 Coblenz and Ehrenbreitstein: Colour Study *c.*1824–32

Watercolour on white wove paper
264 × 410 ($10\frac{3}{8} \times 16\frac{1}{8}$)
Watermarked: J WHATMAN/1814
TB CCLXIII 185
D25307

At first sight these two drawings appear simply to be colour studies of familiar views on the Rhine. The fact that they are executed in a similarly limited colour range and on sheets of paper from the same manufacturer and of nearly identical size is a very strong indication that they are contemporary with one another.

They are both imaginative works, rather than strictly topographical ones, but in very different ways. Cat.no.23 is true to Coblenz and Ehrenbreitstein as Turner himself knew them but it is clearly related to his watercolours depicting a historical scene he had not witnessed, namely the demolition of the fortress (W 687, engraved in 1824, and cat.no.24, engraved in 1832). Meanwhile, cat.no.22 is imaginative in a completely different sense. The bridge of boats at Cologne was not opened until 1822 and Turner's first sight of it took place in 1824. He paid it extremely scant attention then – so much so that in this impressionistic study the pontoons are totally unlike those actually used and they are positioned a long way downstream of their true location. The painter in Turner postulated that an imposing bridge should lead to the cathedral, the traveller in him conveniently forgot the rather dull bridge well upstream of Great St Martin's church which he had not even bothered to sketch very carefully.

Turner's reason for producing these works is not known, though they may possibly relate to an unfulfilled illustrative project of which nothing else has yet come to light. They are painted on half-sheets of Large Post writing paper similar to that which he had used for his Rhine views of 1817 (see cat.nos.4–11). At a certain stage in their development those scenes probably looked not dissimilar to these, with coloured washes being gradually superimposed upon grey ones, but it seems unlikely that cat.nos.22–3 have any close connection with that group.

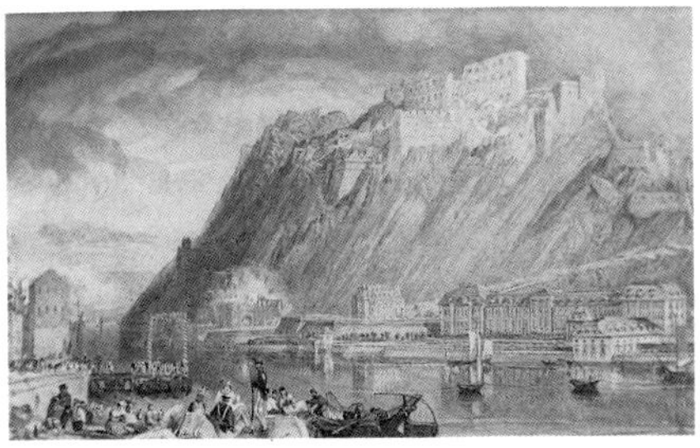

'Ehrenbreitstein during the Demolition of the Fortress' (W 687)

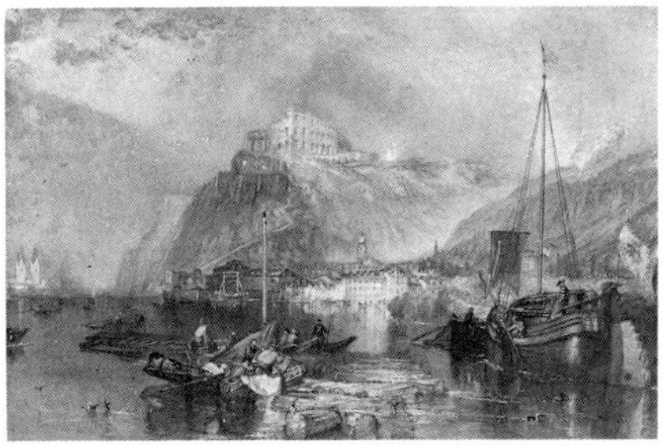

24 Ehrenbreitstein* *c.*1832

Watercolour
305 × 431 ($12 \times 17\frac{1}{8}$)
Bury Art Gallery and Museum (115)
W 1051

The first recorded owner of this work was the steel pen manufacturer and Turner collector Joseph Gillott who bought it for £300 on 5 April 1860 from the dealer Rought. Of its earlier history nothing is known, save that it was engraved in 1832 by Robert Wallis for one of the annuals, the *Keepsake for 1833* (R 328). In this volume it accompanied 'Recollections of Ehrenbreitstein, a Tale' by Ralph Bernal, the Whig MP for Rochester who was also a notable collector and a regular contributor to the annuals. The *Keepsake for 1833* contained several items relating to the Rhine – perhaps in deliberate rivalry with *Heath's Picturesque Annual for 1833* which took that river as its sole topic. Besides 'Ehrenbreitstein', the *Keepsake* also included J.B. Allen's engraving after Turner's 'Falls of the Rhine at Schaffhausen' (R 329; for another engraved version of this scene, see fig.6 on p.15), accompanied by an unsigned short story; and a poem 'To the Rhine' by Lord Mahon in which a bereaved lover mourns his former travelling companion and makes the inevitable comparison between the brief life of man and the eternal one of the river.

In the *Keepsake* and the other annuals it was quite usual for there to be little connection between the stories and the illustrations, the two having been commissioned or acquired separately by the editor. Readers would not have been surprised therefore to find that Turner's depiction of Schaffhausen in broad daylight was juxtaposed with an account of a visit to those celebrated falls by moonlight. A more curious and interesting discrepancy occurred, however, in the case of cat.no.24, since Bernal's story was very firmly set in the present while Turner's scene related equally clearly to a period some fifteen years earlier. In this the fortress is shown being blown up – not by French troops but by the Prussians themselves immediately prior to its rebuilding of 1815–32, since the scene is a peaceful one and the Prussian eagle is prominent on a flag in the right foreground. Turner also shows the old flying bridge between Coblenz and Ehrenbreitstein with its conspicuously striped pontoon. This was replaced in 1819 by a bridge of boats which lasted until 1945. In short, Turner's view – based on his own experiences of 1817 – depicted a scene that had already passed into history, the Ehrenbreitstein of the immediately post-Waterloo era, while Bernal's story – with its specific references to the bridge of boats and the near-impregnable fortress so recently completed – was set in the very year of its publication, 1832. Whether the contrast was deliberate or accidental must remain unclear, but it undoubtedly enriched both image and story, adding an unspoken extra dimension to each, exactly paralleling the contrast between night and day in the Schaffhausen tale and engraving.

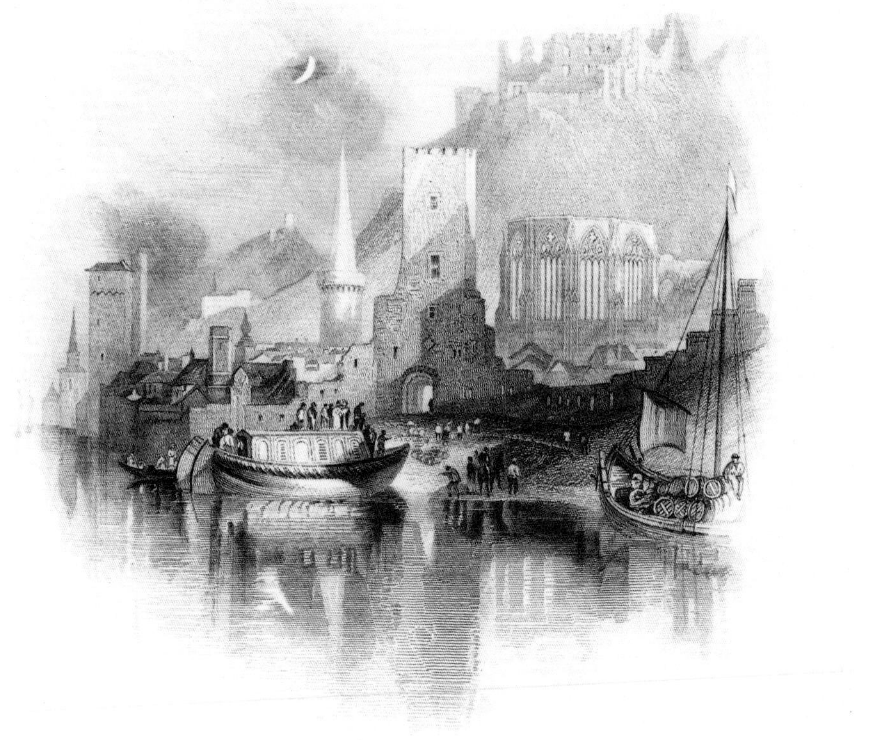

EDWARD FINDEN AFTER
J.M.W. TURNER

25 Bacharach. On the Rhine 1832

Line engraving on steel, engraver's proof
Vignette, 83 × 80 ($3\frac{1}{4} \times 3\frac{1}{8}$)
Trustees of the British Museum, London
(1868–8–22–4572)
R 418

This vignette appeared in 1832 as the frontispiece to Volume VIII of the *Works of Lord Byron*, a posthumous collected edition in seventeen volumes published by John Murray. That volume contained the whole of *Childe Harold's Pilgrimage* with its extensive passage on the Rhineland in canto III and its even better evocation of Italy in canto IV. Very appropriately, the only other illustration in the book was a title-page vignette, facing 'Bacharach' and also engraved by Edward Finden after Turner, 'The Castle of St Angelo' (R 419). The reader was thus presented with a *fait accompli*, namely that Turner and Byron shared a common vision of both Italy and the Rhineland; a view which was corroborated by Turner himself when he exhibited oil paintings at the Royal Academy accompanied by quotations from Byron such as 'Childe Harold's Pilgrimage – Italy' (B&J 342; Clore Gallery) in 1832 and cat.no.41 in 1835.

Byron nowhere specifically mentions Bacharach but it was – and remains – the archetype of all the historic small towns on the Middle Rhine. Its extensive walls and numerous towers, the rugged ruins of Burg Stahleck on the hills above and the Gothic chapel dedicated to the boy martyr St Werner, with its traceried windows, all make Bacharach exceptionally picturesque and Turner drew numerous pencil sketches there in 1817. The watercolour from which Finden produced this engraving (W 1222; Vassar College, USA) was essentially an amalgamation of two of Turner's pencil sketches of 1817 (the general view on TB CLX 61V and the close-up of St Werner's chapel on f.64V) which was then enriched by a vista of yet

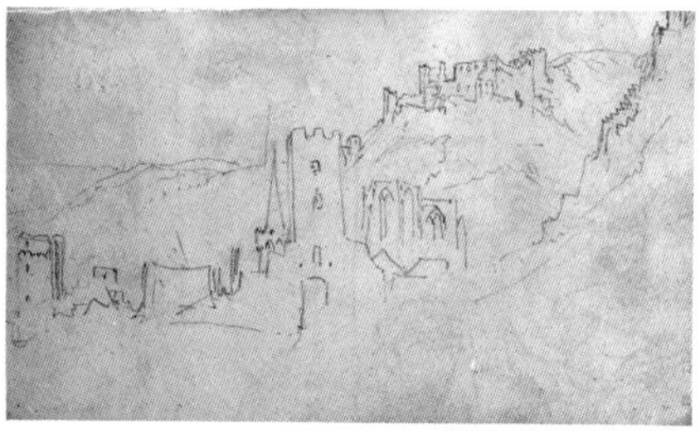

Bacharach (TB CLX 61V)

more hills and ancient buildings in the distance and important touches of local colour in the foreground. On the left is the crowded public passenger boat with its covered cabin and sturdy fender. On the right a sailing vessel is laden with barrels of the wine for which Bacharach has been famous since antiquity. The town derives its name from 'Bacchi ara' (the altar of Bacchus, god of wine), a huge rock in the middle of the Rhine which only becomes visible at times of prolonged drought. Here, it was said, the Romans sacrificed to their god for having granted them a hot dry summer and a fruitful vintage. However this may be, the wine of Bacharach has long been exported far and wide, and was even ordered for the Vatican cellars in the fifteenth century by Pius II.

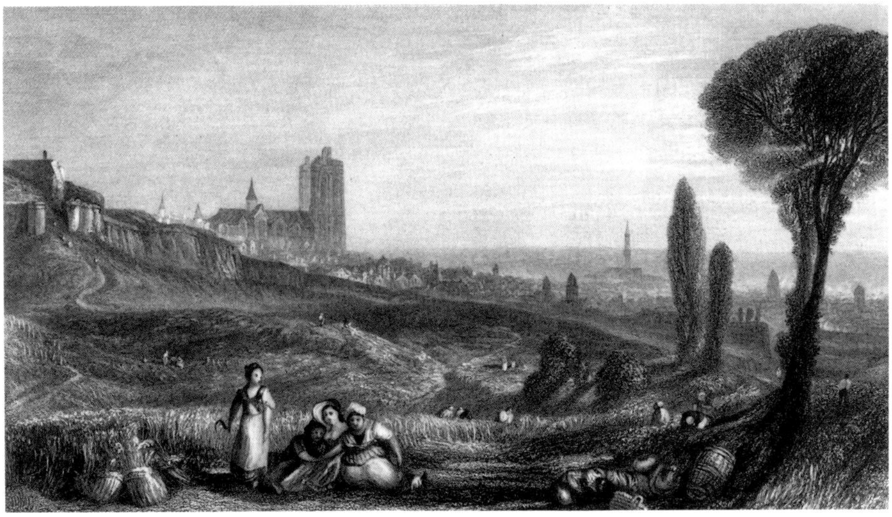

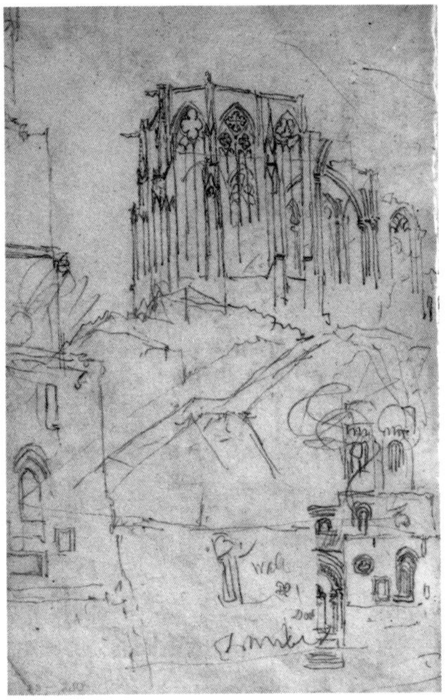

Bacharach (TB CLX 64v)

WILLIAM MILLER AFTER J.M.W. TURNER

26 Brussels – Distant View 1834

Line engraving on steel, engraver's proof
82 × 140 ($3\frac{1}{4} \times 5\frac{1}{2}$)
T04729
R 519

This scene served as the frontispiece to Volume V of *The Prose Works of Sir Walter Scott, Bart.*, published in Edinburgh and London in 1834. Both it and the title-page vignette (cat.no.27) were directly relevant to the contents of the volume, *Paul's Letters to his Kinsfolk*, which are essentially those written by Scott himself to his own family during his tour of the Continent in the summer of 1815. They were first published in January 1816.

The letters of 'Paul' to 'his Cousin Peter' and 'his Cousin the Major' range widely and in great detail over recent events in France and Flanders, most notably the Battle of Waterloo; while those addressed 'to his Sister Margaret' deal with more homely matters such as the cleanliness and costumes of Flemish cottage-women, romantic folk songs and the tourist attractions of Paris. A similar balance between male and female roles and preoccupations is also present in the two illustrations: man's work is war, women's place is in the fields.

Both Turner's illustrations originate in pencil sketches made in the very first days of his 1817 tour. William Miller based this engraving of Brussels on a watercolour which Turner had recently made specifically for this project (W 1096, untraced since 1877) but Turner himself based that scene on a sequence of seven pages of pencil sketches taken from the northern outskirts of Brussels in the *Waterloo and Rhine* sketchbook (TB CLX 10v–13v). The left-hand side with its wall-girdled hill and the cathedral of St Gudule are taken from ff.11v–12r, the distant prospect of the immensely tall town hall and the other, lesser towers of Brussels from ff.12v–13r. Meanwhile, two other sketches would have provided Turner with important reminders about this view. That on ff.10v–11r, showing the slope on the left, is inscribed 'Corn', while that on f.13v, which shows the entire scene but in a much more schematic way, includes a number of lofty trees articulating the right-hand half of the composition, much as in the final scene. As in the case of countless other watercolours painted throughout Turner's life, he skilfully wove all these ingredients together into an entirely convincing scene, adding an appropriate cast of characters and their utensils in the foreground from the storehouse of his memory.

Although Brussels was noted in Turner's day for its grand buildings, it was even more admired for its situation. In his copy of Charles Campbell's *Guide through Belgium and Holland* he would have read that, 'there are few cities where the surrounding country is so beautiful as that about Brussels' and 'The rising grounds, intersected by rills about the environs of this charming place, would almost persuade one that Brussels was placed here merely for the purpose of adding to the ornaments of Art the beauties of Nature' (1817, p.37). He may also have read other evocative descriptions of his route, such as, 'The road to Waterloo from Brussels lies through the little village of Ixelles, embosomed in woods, and close to the margin of a glassy lake. Immediately ascending from these, we enter the deep shades of the forest of Soignies, enlightened at intervals with neat whitewashed cottages and little villages' (p.71). Turner never wasted an experience. His 1817 sequence of sketches, culminating in a balanced composition study, must have been deliberately made so as to have a popular Brussels view almost at his fingertips when the need arose. The moment duly came – but not until the early 1830s.

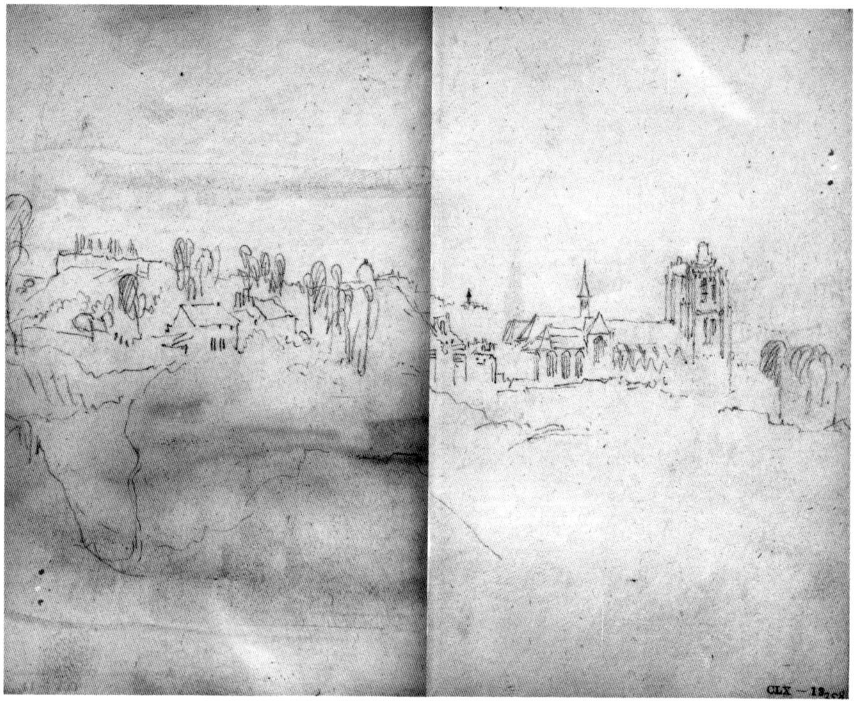

Brussels (TB CLX 11v–12r)

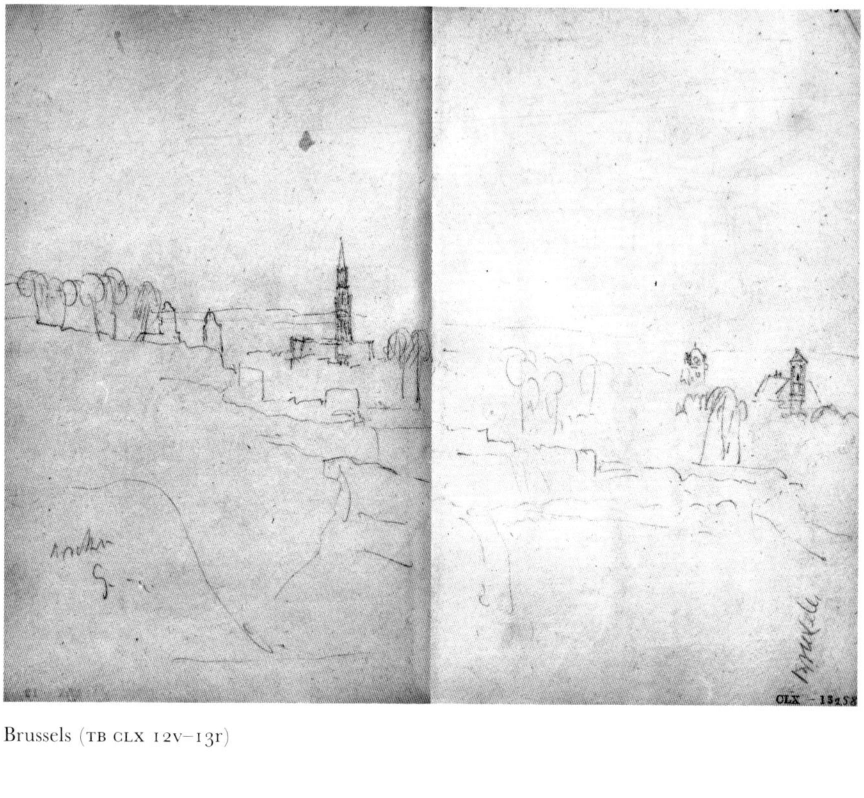

Brussels (TB CLX 12v–13r)

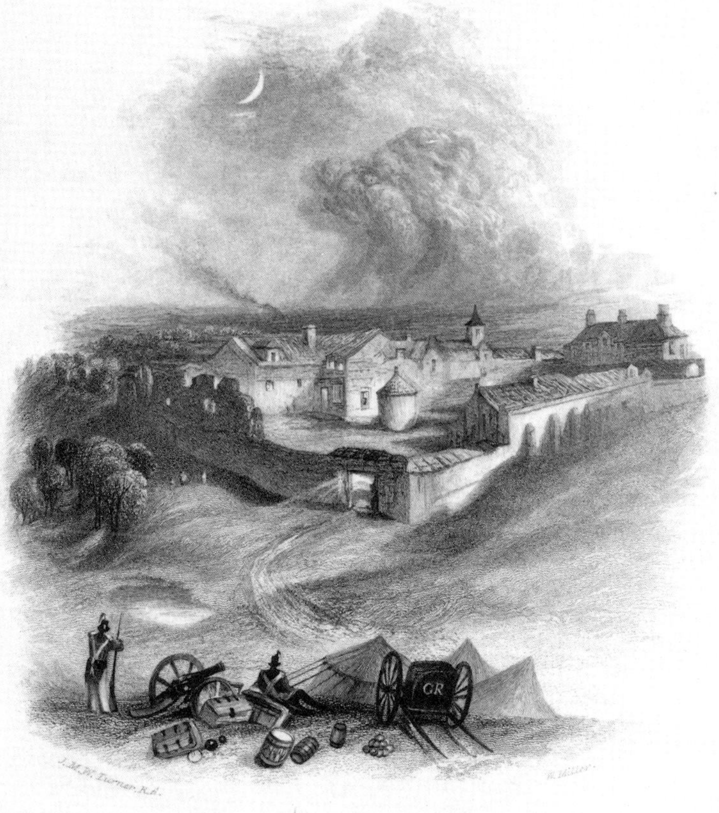

WILLIAM MILLER AFTER
J.M.W. TURNER

27 **Hougoumont** 1834

Line engraving on steel, first published state
Vignette, 100 × 88 ($3\frac{15}{16} \times 3\frac{7}{16}$)
T04730
R 520

Some of the fiercest fighting at Waterloo took place around the fortified farm complex of Hougoumont which was occupied by the allied forces protecting their front line further to the north. Hougoumont was repeatedly attacked by the French from 11.30 a.m. onwards but the allies succeeded in holding it right through till nightfall and the final victory. The ruined farmstead provided 'the most interesting point of all' for later visitors to the site of the battle: 'the battered walls, the dismantled and fire-stained chapel, which remained standing through all the wreck, . . . the traces of attack upon attack, still renewed and still resisted – all, together, bring the whole scene before one with a tremendous force' (Mrs Trollope, 1834, vol.1, p.89).

Turner's watercolour vignette of the early 1830s (W 1097; private collection) was based on his pencil sketch made on the spot in 1817 (TB CLX 26r, inscribed 'General View of Hugomont from the British Lines'). Other sketches and annotations on nearby pages show that he heard from his guide about all the events described by Scott in *Paul's Letters to his Kinsfolk* to which this vignette was to serve as the title-page illustration: how the entrance gate of Hougoumont was repeatedly attacked and how the Guards, together with the Black Brunswickers and the Nassau sharpshooters, inflicted enormous losses on the French. Turner illustrates none of the action, letting the ruined buildings and the British soldiers in the foreground speak for themselves. The billowing smoke is a deliberate reminder to the viewer of the final attempt of the French to gain Hougoumont. Shells were fired which set alight both the hay in the farmyard and the farmhouse itself. These blazed high in the air, spreading a vast cloud of thick black smoke. 'But', as Scott says (pp.123–4), 'the Guards continued to make good the garden and the courtyard, and the enemy's utmost efforts proved unable to dispossess them.'

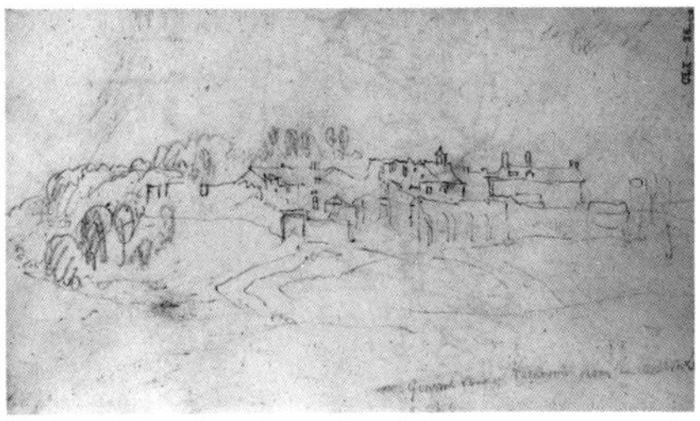

Hougoumont (TB CLX 26r)

WILLIAM MILLER AFTER
J.M.W. TURNER

28 Mayence 1834

Line engraving on steel, first published state
Vignette, 77 × 83 (3 × 3¼)
T04740
R 533

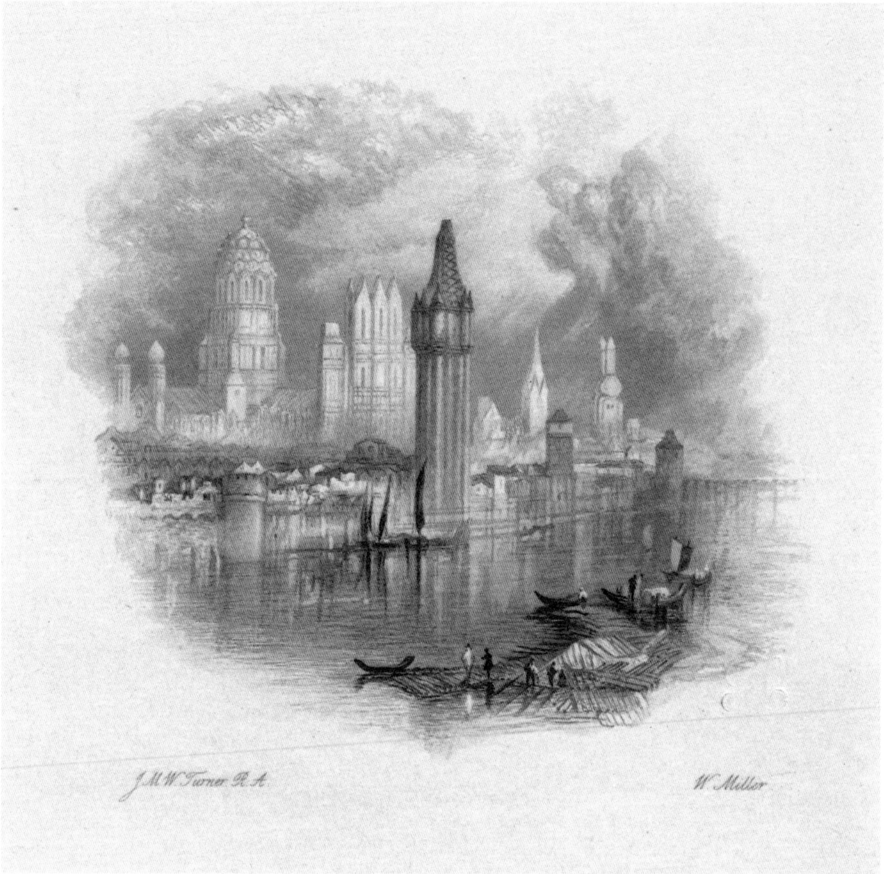

This vignette was published as the title-page illustration to Volume XII of Scott's *Prose Works* in 1835 and – like cat.nos.26 and 27 – it is included in Turner's own list of 1834 of eight of the forty subjects he contributed to this publication (TB CCLXXXVI 57r). Together with fifteen other scenes it relates to Scott's *Life of Napoleon* ('Nap' in Turner's list) which occupies Volumes VIII–XVI of the forty-volume project.

Mainz suffered particularly heavy damage during the French invasion of the Rhineland. In 1792 it was taken almost without a blow. The following year it was regained by Prussian forces after a siege which led to part of the cathedral being devastated by fire. However, it was soon afterwards retaken by the French, their repossession being accepted by the Prussians under the Peace of Basel (1795) and by the Austrians under the Peace of Campo Formio two years later. The French continued to hold Mainz until the defeat of Napoleon; it became 'Mayence', the capital of the Department of Mont Tonnerre, its archbishopric was abolished and its cathedral used as a magazine and barracks.

Although Turner's watercolour (W 1110, Blackburn Art Gallery, Lancashire) was painted in the early 1830s, it shows the buildings of Mainz as he himself had seen and sketched them in 1817 (TB CLX 69v–70r). The eastern end of the cathedral lacks a dome (this was eventually provided in 1828) and the pointed arches of its drum rise piercingly into the storm-ridden sky above empty window sockets.

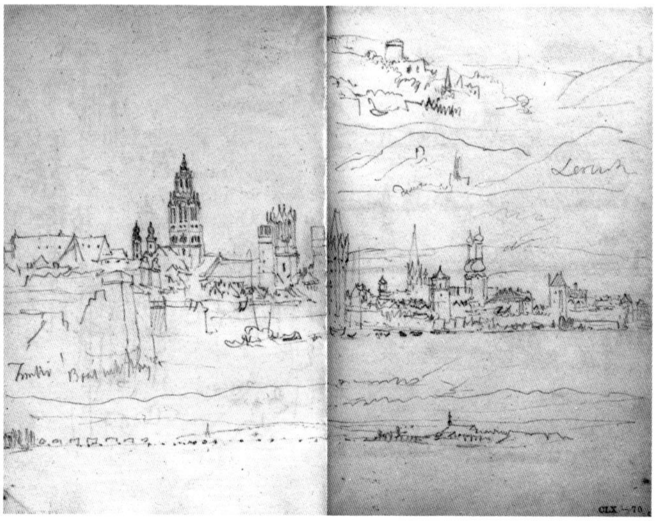

Mainz (TB CLX 69v–70r)

EDWARD GOODALL AFTER
J.M.W. TURNER

29 **Rolandseck** 1837

Line engraving on steel, engraver's proof
Vignette, 80 × 67 ($3\frac{1}{8} \times 2\frac{5}{8}$)
T04779
R 627

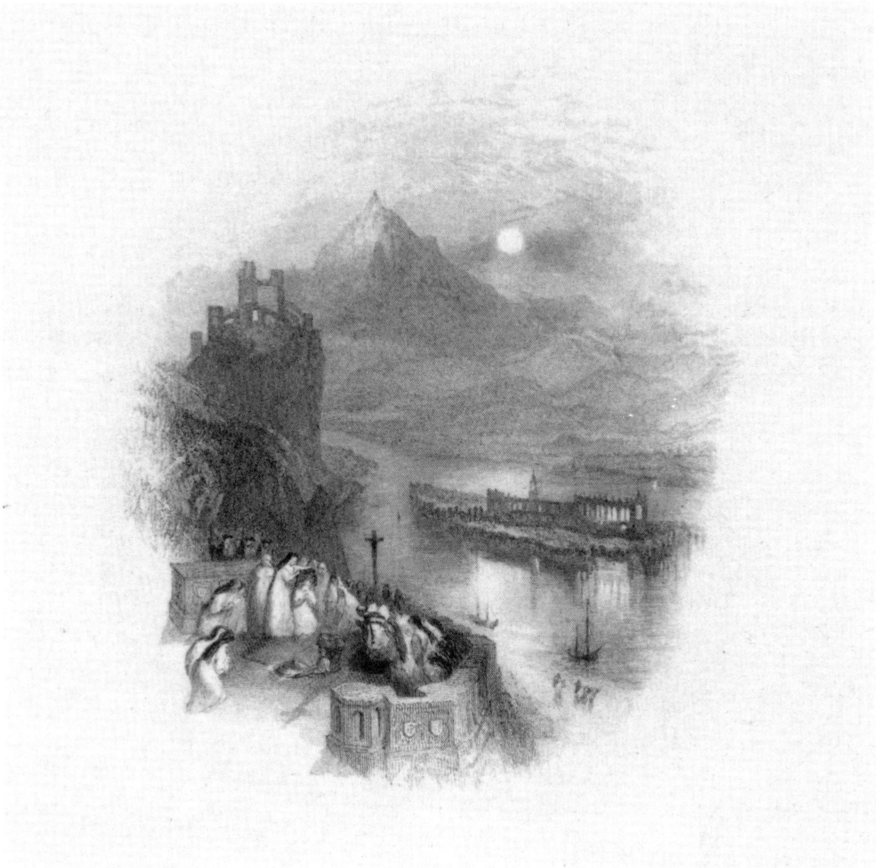

In 1837 Turner supplied twenty watercolour vignettes for engraving in a new edition of the poems of Thomas Campbell (W 1271–90). This Scottish-born poet (1774–1844), who spent most of his life in London, had very close associations with Germany, following the nine months he spent there in 1800–1. Like Wordsworth and Coleridge, he knew the poet Klopstock and he was a friend of the two Schlegel brothers, both noted for their contributions to Romantic literature. In 1820 Campbell paid a long visit to the Continent, with his wife and son, spending over a month in Bonn where he studied the German language and attended lectures. It was through his conversations with the professors at Bonn at this time that Campbell first conceived the idea of establishing a University of London, a scheme which was implemented very soon afterwards.

In June and July 1820 Campbell made many excursions with his German friends to nearby beauty spots and castles, such as the Seven Hills and the Godesburg, and listened to the numerous stories and legends associated with all the different sites. He was particularly enchanted by the Drachenfels and Rolandseck, which he pronounced the most beautiful scene he had ever beheld, and by the 'Paradisaical views of the Rhine' from the highest of the Seven Hills. On his last day he bade farewell to Rolandseck by repeating the ancient poem about Charlemagne's brave warrior, the 'Chanson de Roland', and composed his own version of the story which associates Roland with the Rhine:

THE BRAVE ROLAND

The brave Roland! – the brave Roland! –
False tidings reached the Rhenish strand
That he had fallen in flight;
And thy faithful bosom swooned with pain,
O loveliest maiden of Allemayne!
For the loss of thine own true knight.

But why so rash has she ta'en the veil,
In yon Nonnenwerder's cloisters pale?
For her vow had scarce been sworn,
And the fatal mantle o'er her flung,
When the Drachenfels to a trumpet rung –
'Twas her own dear warrior's horn!

Woe! woe! each heart shall bleed – shall break!
She would have hung upon his neck,
Had he come but yester-even;
And he had clasped those peerless charms
That shall never, never fill his arms,
Or meet him but in heaven.

Yet Roland the brave – Roland the true –
He could not bid that spot adieu;
It was dear still 'midst his woes;
For he loved to breathe the neighbouring air,
And to think she blessed him in her prayer,
When the Halleluiah rose.

There's yet one window of that pile,
Which he built above the Nun's green isle;
Thence sad and oft looked he
(When the chant and organ sounded slow)
On the mansion of his love below,
For herself he might not see.

She died! – He sought the battle-plain;
Her image filled his dying brain,
When he fell and wished to fall:
And her name was in his latest sigh,
When Roland, the flower of chivalry,
Expired at Roncevall.

Turner would surely have enjoyed painting his watercolour of this breathtaking scene with which he was already so familiar (W 1285; National Gallery of Scotland). A particularly striking feature of his vignette is its very high viewpoint. This does not derive from any of Turner's own experiences and must surely have been specifically requested by Campbell himself who had gazed down on Nonnenwerth and Rolandseck with such deep emotion in 1820.[1]

[1] See *Life and Letters of Thomas Campbell* ed. W. Beattie, 1849, vol. II, pp. 362–72, 386–7.

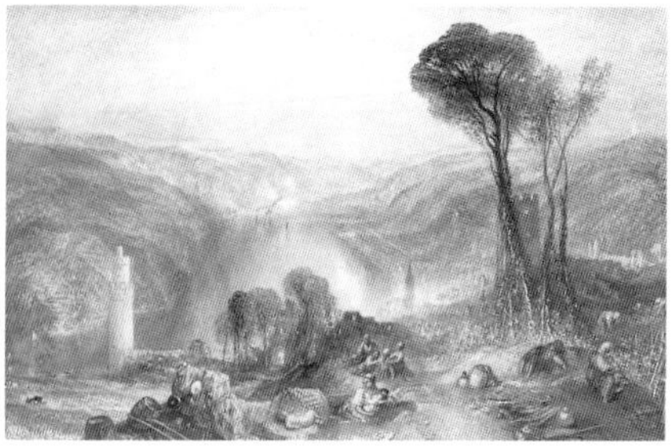

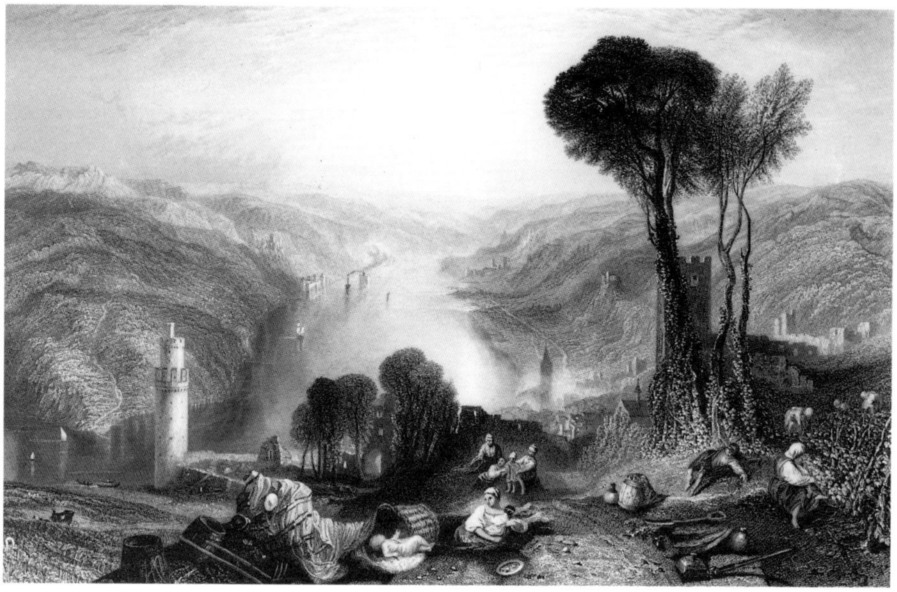

30 Oberwesel* 1840

Watercolour and gouache with scratching out
345 × 530 ($13\frac{15}{16} \times 20\frac{7}{8}$)
Inscribed, at lower right, 'JMWT.1840'
Private Collection, courtesy of the Leger Galleries
W 1380

This dazzling vision of the Rhine, based on his experiences in 1839, is not only the culmination of Turner's many visits to this part of Europe but also one of the most outstanding of all his late watercolours. Throughout his life his approach to landscape blended truth to nature with a much wider vision based on the study of earlier artists, the reading of poetry and a strong awareness of history. His late works convey this sense of the infinite splendour of the natural world through a technical skill which is in itself little short of miraculous.

The first owner of 'Oberwesel' was B.G. Windus, a retired coachbuilder and an avid collector of Turner's work who also owned its companion 'Lake Nemi' (W 1381; British Museum). In both works Turner transcends the minutiae of nature and imposes his own vision on his subjects: the German river and the Italian lake become vast pools of sparkling light, the ancient buildings of Oberwesel and those of Nemi and Genzano share a common antiquity, the modern-day inhabitants of each town pursue an age-old way of life which will be carried on into the future by the infants clasped in their arms. Turner's constant travels through Europe taught him much about the horrors of war and the fragility of peace, but his message in these two late works is one of faith and optimism. From Lake Nemi originated the classical story of the Golden Bough with its complex mythology of regeneration; and it is surely no accident that for its companion Turner chose the view looking straight up the Rhine to the very point where Marshal Blücher had crossed the river in 1813, at the head of the Prussian army which would help to drive out the French invaders and reclaim the Rhineland.

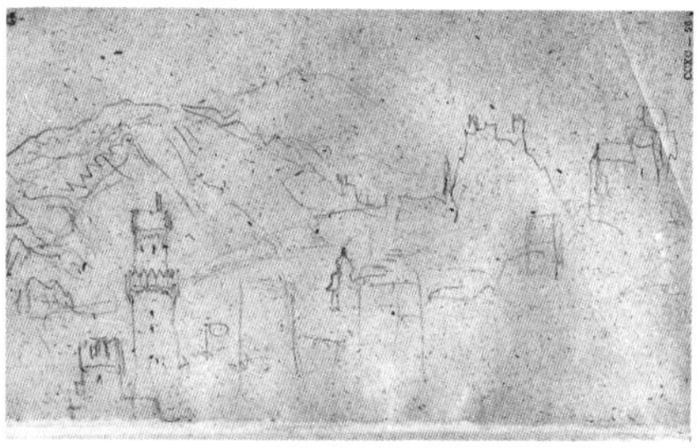

Oberwesel (TB CCXC 56r)

J.T. WILLMORE AFTER
J.M.W. TURNER

31 Oberwesel 1842

Line engraving on steel
222 × 343 ($8\frac{3}{4} \times 13\frac{1}{32}$)
Trustees of the British Museum, London
(1856-5-10-26)
R 660

This engraving and that of its companion 'Nemi' (R 659; see cat.no.30) were published in 1842, within a couple of months of each other, and both were dedicated to the owner of the watercolours, B.G. Windus of Tottenham Green in north London. By around this time Windus owned some 200 Turner watercolours and his celebrated collection was open to art lovers every Tuesday, so that these works became well known to writers and artists. However, the publication of thousands of copies of steel engravings brought Turner's art to an even wider public. His 'Oberwesel' was not only published in the *Royal Gallery of British Art* (1838–49) but was still available in the late 1870s. During these years the publisher John Sherer produced two mammoth compendiums for the new mass-tourist market, *Europe Illustrated* (1876) and *The Classic Lands of Europe* (1879). Both works consisted largely of texts and images plagiarised or reprinted from earlier publications and subscribers to *Europe Illustrated* who bought the entire work (at 2s 6d a part) were rewarded by 'Premium Plates – Gratis! . . . Two beautifully executed steel engravings, *Printed on Superfine Paper*, . . . entitled, respectively Oberwesel, on the Rhine, and Lake Nemi . . . engraved by James T. Willmore, A.R.A., and Robert Wallis.' 'Oberwesel' received a particularly full encomium, complete with quotations on the Rhineland by Byron. Just as the reader was left in no doubt that 'The original picture from which the above Engraving is taken, is, as already said, by the late TURNER, the *greatest* of England's many *great* Artists', so too – for this generation – his 'Oberwesel' became the quintessential and universal vision of the Rhineland.

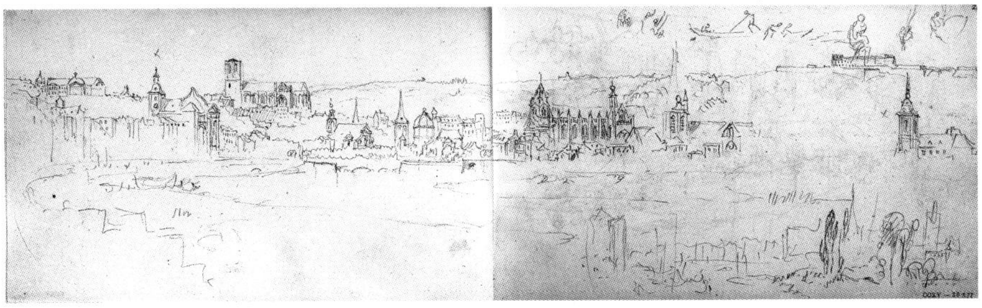

Holland, Meuse, and Cologne sketchbook
1825

32 The Churches of Liège

Pencil
Page size: 113 × 189 ($4\frac{7}{16} \times 7\frac{7}{16}$)
White wove writing paper
Watermarked: ALLEE/1819
TB CCXV ff.25 verso, 26
D19446, D19447

The *Holland, Meuse, and Cologne* sketchbook and the *Holland* sketchbook (TB CCXIV) were used simultaneously on Turner's visit to the Low Countries and the lower Meuse and Rhine in August–September 1825. Many of the same places, such as Liège, Cologne and Düsseldorf, feature in both sketchbooks and it is probable that Turner deliberately followed his practice of 1824 in taking with him a small upright book containing nearly 300 pages for note-taking and smaller sketches (TB CCXIV) and a larger horizontal one with far fewer pages for more extensive views and more detailed studies (cat.no.32).

Turner's 1825 tour was chiefly devoted to Holland, but he then travelled up the Rhine to Cologne, by road through Aachen to Liège and thence to Antwerp, Bruges and Ghent on his way to Ostend. He made a large number of sketches of Liège in both TB CCXIV and TB CCXV, all of those in TB CCXV being prospects of the city from nearby hills or along the Meuse. The sketch on ff.25v–26r shows Liège from the south, with a proud display of its many celebrated churches including the loftily situated St Martin's; the elegant slender spire and dome of St John the Evangelist; the strongly buttressed flank of St James's and (only partially realised) the tower of St Paul's church which became the cathedral of Liège in 1802, the earlier cathedral having been wrecked by Revolutionaries in 1794. Flanking these churches and framing Turner's view are the hills to the north of the city, crowned by the St Laurent barracks and the citadel respectively. Characteristically Turner later filled up the rest of the page with other, less careful, sketches, which probably also relate to Liège.

Besides its admirably precise depiction of buildings in many different architectural styles, Turner's drawing is also notable for his varied use of the pencil. Throughout the sketch innumerable touches – dark and light, sharp and blunt, firm and gentle – are constantly interwoven and tiny passages of hatching are also introduced, so that the viewer is aware not only of the volume of the buildings but also of the play of light and shade on their surfaces. While the majority of the sketches Turner drew on his foreign tours served chiefly as prosaic memoranda to be used for the production of future works of art, others – such as this one – can stand on their own as evidence of Turner's genius.

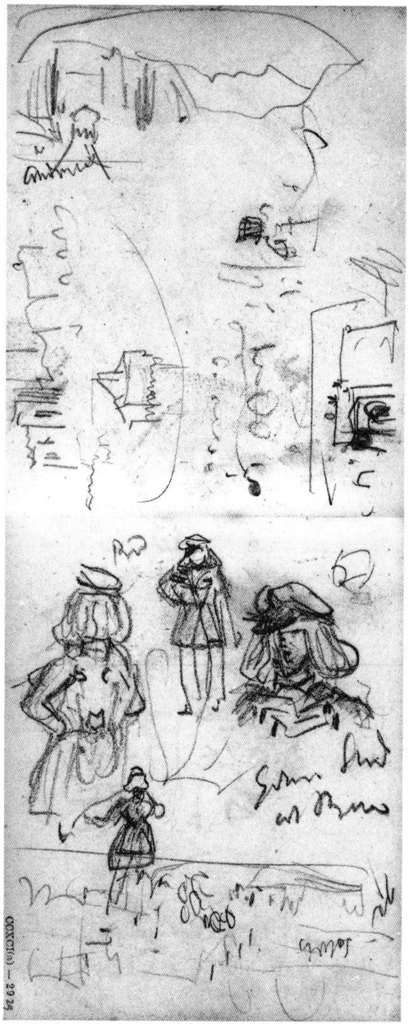

Rhine (between Cologne and Mayence), also Moselle and Aix-la-Chapelle sketchbook 1830s

33 German Students at Bonn

Pencil
Page size: 90 × 117 ($3\frac{9}{16} \times 4\frac{5}{8}$)
White wove writing paper
Watermarked: J WHATMAN/1832
Inscribed 'Andernach' (f.28v); 'Red'; 'German Stud[ents] at Bonn' (f.29r)
TB CCXCI(a) ff.28 verso, 29
D28710, D28711

This sketchbook is one of many in the Turner Bequest which it is not yet possible to date precisely, but it was probably used in 1834, 1837 or 1838. Turner's sketches here are not of the highest quality but many are of very great interest. Some show places on and near the Mosel, indicating that he visited that river on other occasions besides his intensive tours of 1824 and 1839 (e.g. Klotten appears on f.25v, Gondorf on f.65r). Among the others are studies of works of art, including a painting believed by Turner to be by De Hooch (f.2v), and two detailed anatomical drawings which Ruskin would certainly have torn out of the sketchbook had he been aware of them (ff.33v, 34v–35r). It is tempting to link these last either with Turner's stay at the resort of Bad Ems on the Lahn (see ff.15v–16r, 21v–22r, 57v) or that at Wiesbaden on the Rhine (see ff.23r, 54r), since German watering-places afforded many opportunities for relaxation and diversion.

Many British visitors to the Rhineland in the nineteenth century found the long hair and fancy costumes sported by the university students of Bonn highly picturesque and Turner's sketches exhibited here show that he was no exception.

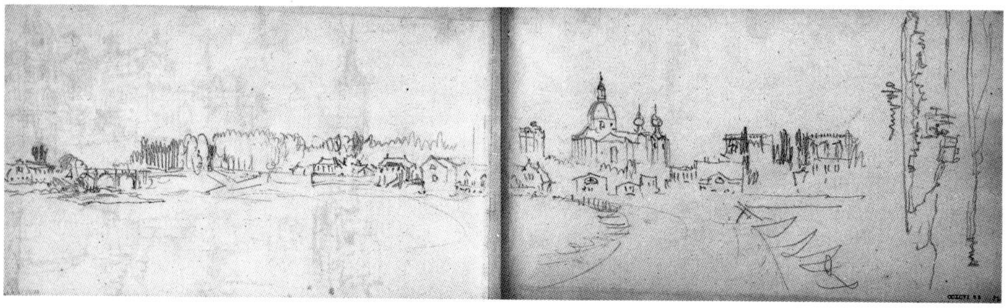

Brussels up to Mannheim sketchbook 1830s

34 Mannheim from the Bridge of Boats and Oppenheim from the Rhine

Pencil
Page size: 113 × 185 ($4\frac{7}{16} \times 7\frac{1}{4}$)
White wove writing paper
Watermarked: J JELLYMAN/1828
Inscribed, on f.82r, 'Openheim'
TB CCXCVI ff.81 verso, 82
D29755, D29756

This sketchbook contains numerous pencil sketches of the Meuse from Liège to Namur and the Rhine from Cologne to Mannheim. The principal sketch on ff.81v–82r shows an extensive view of Mannheim from the bridge of boats over the Rhine. On the far left is the little wooden bridge over the canal to the Neckar while the square building among trees on the right is the Electoral Palace. The sketch is dominated by the vast domed Jesuit church and it provides a good idea of a bridge of boats, securely overlaid by planking, such as Turner also saw and used on many of his visits to Mainz, Cologne and Coblenz.

Mannheim, which lies about forty-five miles up the Rhine from Mainz, was formerly the capital of the Elector Palatine. It was totally destroyed by the French in the Wars of the Palatinate Succession and the eighteenth century saw the creation of a completely new town, built on a grid plan and consisting of 136 square sections each identified by a letter and numeral. It was much admired by eighteenth-century British visitors for its regularity and for the classical grandeur of the buildings seen here, both of which features contrasted strongly with the medieval disorder found in most other German towns. A view very similar to this sketch was published in the Revd John Gardnor's *Views on the Rhine* of 1791 which Turner studied closely before his 1817 Rhine tour.

The tiny sketch on f.82r shows Oppenheim, conspicuously situated high above the west bank of the Rhine between Mainz and Mannheim. Many of the pages in this sketchbook were used in this fashion, with up to eight small sketches occupying a series of rectangles which invariably start at the outer edge of each page. It is easy to imagine the convenience of this method: Turner's left hand supported the half of the book which was being used, while the other half rested on his knees.

This sketchbook was evidently used in the 1830s but it is not yet known in which year, nor with which other sketchbooks it should be associated. Turner's exploration of the Neckar – which lies outside the scope of the present study – culminated in his oil painting 'Heidelberg' of *c.*1840–5 (B & J 440) and several watercolours of similar date (W 1326, 1376–7, 1554).

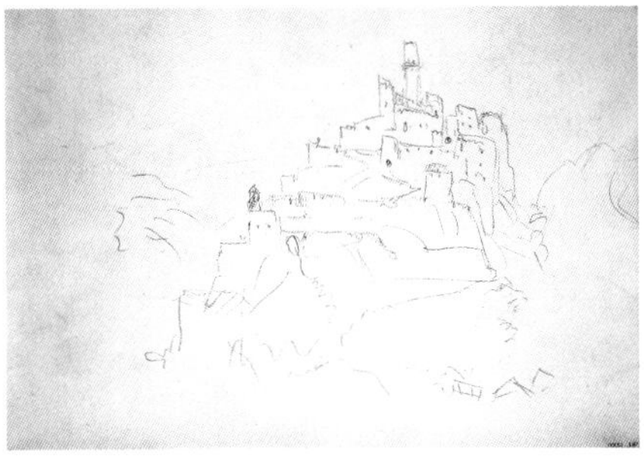

Burg Reichenberg: (TB CCCLI 10R)

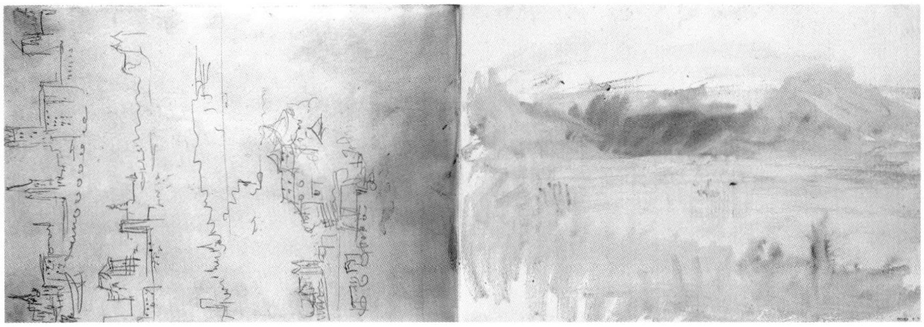

Rhine and Rhine Castles sketchbook 1844

35 **Cologne from the Rhine** and **Storm over the Rhine**

Pencil and watercolour
Page size: 229 × 327 (9 × 12⅞)
White wove drawing paper
Watermarked: J WHATMAN/1844
This sketchbook also contains one sheet (ff.3/22 and 9/16) of a cream wove drawing paper
Watermarked: J WHATMAN/TURKEY MILL/1839
TB CCCLI ff.6 verso, 7
D35181, D35182

This 'roll' sketchbook with its grey paper covers is typical of those used by Turner on foreign tours towards the end of his life and, thanks to its watermarked pages, it can be firmly linked with his last major European tour which took him to Switzerland between August and October 1844. The book is largely devoted to whole-page pencil studies of Rhine castles, which are very swiftly executed with many jagged lines and may have been drawn from a moving vehicle. Many show views at St Goar and St Goarshausen, with Burg Rheinfels and Burg Katz. Others record a detour to the magnificent Burg Reichenberg, situated above a secluded valley behind Burg Katz.

The pencil sketches on f.6v show the waterfront at Cologne in several instalments, with the town hall, Great St Martin's Church, the two parts of the cathedral, and the bridge of boats all clearly distinguishable. By this date Turner had already depicted Cologne from many different viewpoints on the water in numerous sketches and drawings (see e.g. cat.nos.21 and 22) but, characteristically, he was unable to see it again without producing yet another set of sketches. He must have used this sketchbook on his journey home down the Rhine, by the time he reached Cologne nearly all of its pages had already been used, and this fine but familiar view had to be squeezed into the space available. It is impossible to identify the precise stretch of the Middle Rhine depicted either on f.7 or in the four other watercolour sketches in this book, but they leave the viewer in no doubt that Turner was just as much excited by its sublimity and grandeur on his last visit there as he had been on his first, over a quarter of century earlier.

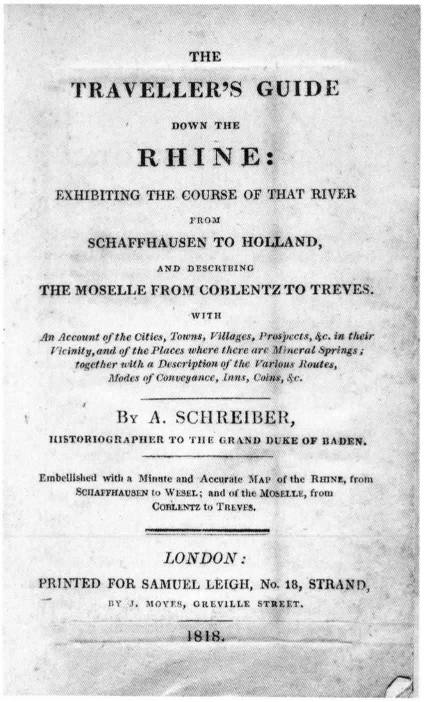
THE

TRAVELLER'S GUIDE

DOWN THE

RHINE:

EXHIBITING THE COURSE OF THAT RIVER

FROM

SCHAFFHAUSEN TO HOLLAND,

AND DESCRIBING

THE MOSELLE FROM COBLENTZ TO TREVES.

WITH

An Account of the Cities, Towns, Villages, Prospects, &c. in their Vicinity, and of the Places where there are Mineral Springs; together with a Description of the Various Routes, Modes of Conveyance, Inns, Coins, &c.

BY A. SCHREIBER,

HISTORIOGRAPHER TO THE GRAND DUKE OF BADEN.

Embellished with a Minute and Accurate MAP of the RHINE, from SCHAFFHAUSEN to WESEL; and of the MOSELLE, from COBLENTZ to TREVES.

LONDON:

PRINTED FOR SAMUEL LEIGH, No. 18, STRAND,

BY J. MOYES, GREVILLE STREET.

1818.

36 Turner's copy of Alois Schreiber, *The Traveller's Guide down the Rhine*, Samuel Leigh, London, 1818
140 × 88 ($5\frac{1}{2} \times 3\frac{1}{2}$)
Inscribed in pencil inside the front cover, 'J M W Turner'
Private Collection

Alois Wilhelm Schreiber's guide to the Rhine was originally published in German and shortly afterwards translated into French. It was easily the most detailed guidebook to the Rhineland at the time of Turner's first visit there and was recommended to him more than once by acquaintances in the course of his tour. He probably bought his copy of the first English edition soon after its publication in 1818. Around this time its publisher Samuel Leigh also issued several other, similar guidebooks in an identical format, including H.A.O. Reichard's *Itinerary of Italy* (1818) which Turner bought and took with him on his first tour of Italy in 1819 (this copy, sprinkled with notes and sketches, is TB CCCLXVII).

The *Rivers Meuse and Moselle* sketchbook (cat.no.37) contains four densely written pages of manuscript notes on the Mosel between Coblenz and Trier which Turner extracted from the 'Third Excursion' in Schreiber's book (ff.6v–8r, taken from pp.173–95). These consist chiefly of the names of towns and information on the distances between them, together with references to castles, inns, picture collections, flying bridges or notable antiquities as appropriate. It is not clear whether Turner also took the book itself with him on his 1824 tour or made any other subsequent use of it. It is in very good condition, the 'Minute and Accurate' maps facing the title-page seemingly never consulted again after Turner had copied that of the Mosel on to three pages of the *Rivers Meuse and Moselle* sketchbook (ff.8v, 9r, 9v).

Rivers Meuse and Moselle sketchbook 1824

37 The Château de Chokier near Liège

Pencil
Page size: 118 × 78 ($4\frac{5}{8} \times 3\frac{1}{16}$)
Lightweight white wove writing paper
Watermarked: SMITH & ALLNUTT/1822
Inscribed: 'Corn'; 'Only Light'; 'Boats'; 'Chateaux Chok'; 'Chock'
TB CCXVI ff.30 verso, 31
D19611, D19612

The *Rivers Meuse and Moselle* sketchbook provides an enormous amount of valuable evidence relating to Turner's 1824 tour, including his timetable and itinerary (f.270r), an unbelievable number of tiny sketches of everywhere he visited, and – most importantly – the evidence which establishes conclusively that his first Meuse–Mosel tour must have taken place in 1824 and not, as previously supposed by historians, in 1826 (see above, pp.38–9).

Most of the pages in this fat but diminutive book contain numerous sketches of the same or adjacent subjects, with continuations or extra details being crowded into the corners. Those on ff.30v and 31r all show the Meuse at and near the castle of Chokier, on the north bank between Liège and Huy. This imposing eighteenth-century castle with its one remaining medieval tower and its massive walls stands on one of the precipitous rocks for which the Meuse is famous and it was a conspicuously picturesque sight greatly admired by travellers in the early nineteenth century. The following pages contain many other sketches showing the castle from even closer viewpoints and also from the reverse direction once Turner had passed it (ff.31v–33v).

From these and other sketches in the same book it is clear that Turner travelled up the Meuse partly on foot and partly by a boat drawn by horses. Progress along the river must have been very slow, as can be seen from the fact that it took him ten days to travel the 200-odd miles up the Meuse from Liège to Verdun. The journey must have had a very different character from the four days occupied by his voyage gliding smoothly down the Mosel with its current, which followed shortly afterwards (see cat.no.40).

The castle of Chokier also features rather delightfully in Turner's correspondence of a much later date. When he reached Liège on 1 August 1842 on his way to Lucerne, he found waiting for him a letter intended for Emma Wells, daughter of his great friend W.F. Wells of Knockholt in Kent. This was from her brother-in-law Thomas Wheeler who was 'with friends wishing to get onward to the

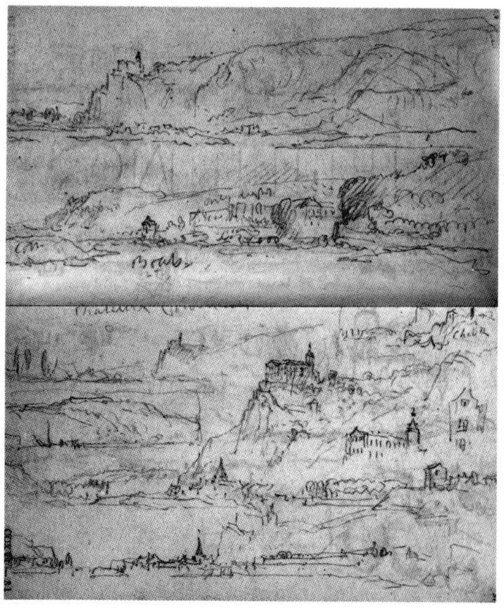

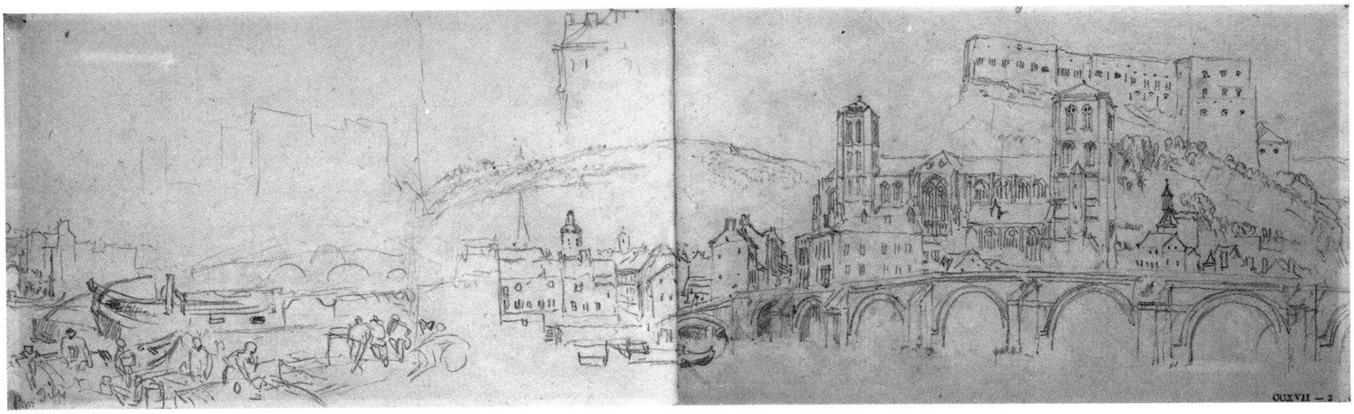

Rhine with all possible speed'. Turner duly forwarded it to her at 'Captain Chaplins, Chateau de Chokear, Pres de Liege, Belgique', commenting that 'had it been within distance I would have had the pleasure of being Poste – moi meme' (Gage, 1980, pp.188–9).

Huy and Dinant sketchbook 1824

38 Huy on the Meuse

Pencil
Page size: 99 × 162 ($3\frac{7}{8} \times 6\frac{3}{8}$)
Contains two different white wove papers
Watermarked: (a) . . . (E)LLS/. . .21
(b) 1821
Inscribed 'Pan Tiles'
TB CCXVII ff.2 verso, 3
D20087, D20088

Turner used this sketchbook for little more than a week of his five-week tour of the Meuse and Mosel in 1824, chiefly employing it for more detailed and careful sketches of the Meuse than those he was simultaneously making in the small *Rivers Meuse and Moselle* sketchbook (TB CCXVI; cat.no.37). According to his own timetable on f.270r of that book, his movements in August were as follows: 13: Liège; 14: Huy; 15: Liège; 16–17: Namur; 18: Dinant; 19: Givet. Sketches of all these places occur in the *Huy and Dinant* sketchbook, so-named by A.J. Finberg who identified only three of the sketches of other towns. For his more ambitious sketches of the Mosel and Rhine from late August onwards, Turner used the two larger sketchbooks TB CCXVIII and CCXIX (cat.nos.39 and 40) instead of continuing to use TB CCXVII, nearly half of which remained untouched. However, he brought it out again briefly at Trier (see ff.5r, 17v, 21r) and – very much later – at Abbeville in northern France (see ff.22r, 23r). During the latter part of the nineteenth century the leaves in this sketchbook were 'distributed and numbered' (Finberg, 1909, p.682). Most of the best drawings have been exhibited on successive occasions and have now become yellow through exposure to light.

On ff.2v–3r Turner drew two separate sketches of Huy, placing the emphasis on entirely different ingredients in each scene. On f.2v he depicted the bridge and fortress in the most sparing of outlines, his interest clearly being held by the barges and their cargo of 'Pan Tiles' at the quayside and the bargemen working and resting there. For the larger sketch, which extends from f.2v onto f.3r, he moved to the opposite side of the river, from the Quai Dautrebande to the Quai des Recollets, but he was still downstream of the bridge. Here he rendered all the town's buildings with the utmost precision, giving an admirably composed portrait of the fine Gothic collegiate church of Notre-Dame, the eighteenth-century stone bridge and the brand new fort. This last had been built in terraces on a rocky spur above the town – and partly into the rock itself – by the Dutch government between 1818 and 1824. In this drawing Turner shows its northern face measuring some 320 feet; its western face, looking upstream towards France, which had inflicted so much damage on the town in the past, is much longer, around 450 feet, and even more formidable. Just to the left of the bridge, and at right angles to it, can be seen the small single-arched Pont St-Nicolas. Through this flows one of the Meuse's many tributaries, the Houyoux, from which Huy takes its name.

These sketches and all the others in this book showing Huy from both river banks (ff. 3v–4r, 5r, 6r, 6v) must have been drawn on 14–15 August when Turner stayed the night here. The *Rivers Meuse and Moselle* sketchbook (cat.no.37) contains numerous tiny drawings of the town from the very first moment it came into sight as Turner journeyed up the Meuse towards it.

Trèves and Rhine sketchbook 1824

39 Trier from Pallien

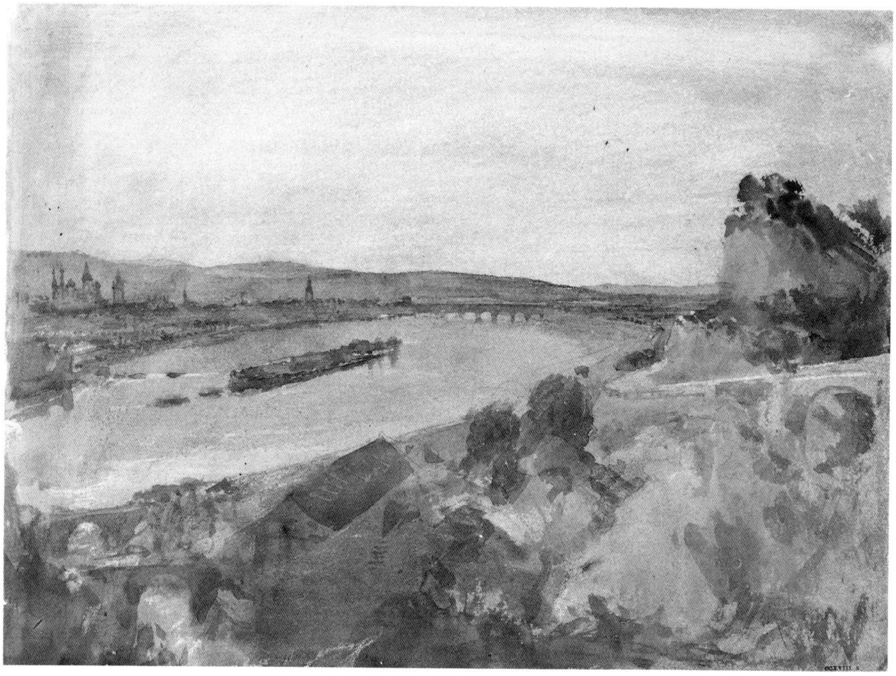

Pencil, watercolour and chalk
Page size: 220 × 291 ($8\frac{11}{16}$ × $11\frac{7}{16}$)
White wove drawing paper prepared with a grey wash
Watermarked: ghost watermarks present on some pages: J WHATMAN / TURKEY MILLS/1823
TB CCXVIII f.8
D20146

This sketchbook and TB CCXIX – *Moselle (or Rhine)* (cat.no.40) – were the first sketchbooks with soft covers that Turner took with him on a foreign tour. One sketchbook with paper covers and containing paper watermarked 1797 seems to have been used in England during the 1800–10 decade (TB LXXXVI; *Harvest Home*) but on his foreign tours of both 1817 and 1819 he continued his practice of 1802 of using large sketchbooks with hard (and heavy) covers despite their obvious inconvenience. Although cat. nos.39 and 40 contain the same type of paper, manufactured by J. Whatman, their page sizes and bindings are different, the larger cat.no.39 being bound in brown paper covers while cat.no.40 is bound in very soft red leather. It is as though Turner, experimenting for the first time with using a 'roll' sketchbook on a foreign tour, wished to test alternative bindings for their convenience and usefulness; and it may be noted here that most of the 'roll' sketchbooks used on later tours – notably in Switzerland in the early 1840s – have paper rather than leather covers (see cat.no.35).

One side of each page is prepared with a grey wash using a wide range of tones. This has sometimes marked the facing page. Four sketches (ff.1r, 2r, 8r, 10r) are extensively worked in watercolour and another shows traces of it (f.9r). The same limited range of colours – blues, greens, browns and yellows – occurs in each. White chalk and scratching out are used both in some of these and in some of the pencil drawings. There seems no reason to doubt that the colouring was done during Turner's tour (especially given the limited palette noted above), though it is impossible to know whether it was done immediately after or at a later time than the pencil drawing beneath. What is certain is that Turner closed the book, or at least turned the page, immediately after colouring all four scenes mentioned above. Both the green and the blue used on f.8r have left their mark on the edge of f.7v, and the pages facing the other coloured scenes are similarly marked. The order of the pages in the book appears undisturbed, with Trier and its environs dominating the first half and the stretch of the Rhine between the Mosel and the Lahn dominating the second.

Turner's drawing on f.8r shows the view looking up the Mosel at Trier, with the cathedral seen on the left and the Roman bridge in the distance. His viewpoint, on the heights above the village of Pallien (now occupied by part of the university) was one recommended to tourists in numerous guidebooks in the nineteenth century, for the splendid prospect of the city it afforded, especially towards evening when the last rays of the sun caught its many towers. Contrasting with the ancient buildings in the middle distance Turner shows on the right of his drawing an extremely recent piece of engineering: the Napoleonsbrücke. Between 1801 and 1815 Trier (then known as Trèves) was the capital of the French Department of the Saar and one of the legacies left here by the Napoleonic regime was this massive road bridge across a gorge, facilitating the passage through Germany of the emperor's armies. At this point in the drawing Turner also faithfully portrays the vivid redness of the abrupt cliffs which are a feature of the Mosel both at Trier itself and at many other places nearby. Unlike the storm-tossed rendering of a very similar view on f.10r (I. Warrell, *Turner: The Fourth Decade*, 1991, cat.no.44), f.8r portrays both sky and river with the utmost placidity, while its colours, too, suggest the deep calm of very early morning or twilight, precisely the times when Turner would have explored the environs of Trier on his overnight stops of 27–8 and 28–9 August. He was to depict the same scene again, bathed in an even greater tranquillity, after his second visit to Trier fifteen years later (see cat.no.47) and these same rocky cliffs and bridge from an entirely different viewpoint (cat.no.49).

Moselle (or Rhine) sketchbook 1824

40 Traben, Trarbach and the Grevenburg

Pencil, chalk and scratching out
Page size: 160 × 235 ($6\frac{5}{16} \times 9\frac{1}{4}$)
White wove drawing paper prepared with a grey wash
Watermarked: J WHATMAN/TURKEY MILLS/1823 and J WHATMAN/TURKEY MILLS/1824
TB CCXIX f.30
D20191

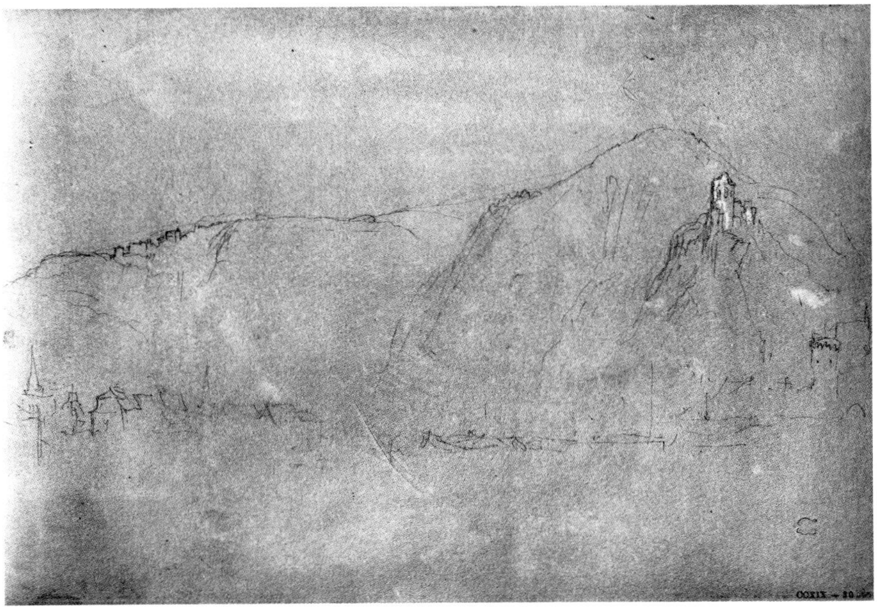

As in the case of the other 'roll' sketchbook used in 1824 (cat.no.39), one side of each page in this sketchbook is prepared with a grey wash which has marked the facing page, indicating that the paper was tinted by Turner himself after his purchase of the book rather than by the stationer before the paper was folded, cut and made up into a book. All the drawings in the book are on these grey pages, where Turner has used pencil with the frequent addition of chalk, scratching out and blotting out to achieve highlights. Some pages are quite light in tone, others so dark that Turner's pencil work is now scarcely visible.

Only the last two sections of the book (ff.32r–45r, all unused) remain undisturbed in their original positions. According to A.J. Finberg's note (1909, p.684), the remaining pages 'were found (unnumbered and in confusion) in a parcel, endorsed by Mr. Ruskin – "31. Pencil on gray with chalk. (On Rhine.) . . . Fine, though slight . . . ."' These pages were numbered by Finberg and listed by him in numerical order; they were then bound into the front of the book in apparently random order, though sketches of the same subject are sometimes placed together. Despite the disorder of its pages, this sketchbook is clearly a middle Mosel counterpart to cat.no.39 with Turner focusing chiefly on the stretch from Bernkastel down to Beilstein.

Most of the sketches in this book concentrate on the Mosel itself and its smooth and winding course through steep hills clothed in vines and bushes rather than on its picturesque towns and villages, so it is not always possible to identify the subject depicted. On f.30r Turner shows the view downstream towards Traben on the left bank and Trarbach on the right (today large and flourishing towns, united by a busy road bridge), both protected by the massive ruins of the Grevenburg high above Trarbach. Through its mixture of hatched pencil work, chalk and the scratching out of the grey wash to reveal the white paper beneath, Turner has evocatively captured the variety and charm of the hills surrounding the Mosel, while the complete lack of highlights on the river itself serves to emphasise its tranquil serenity. The experience of floating gently down the Mosel in a small passenger boat was one enjoyed by a number of Turner's contemporaries, including Mary Shelley, who thus recalled the first afternoon of her voyage in June 1840:

> We . . . dropped down the swift stream between verdant banks that rose into hills – not striking in their outline but agreeable to the eye, while frequent villages, each with its church and pointed spire, either nestled in the foldings of the hills, or graced some promontory that formed a bend in this much winding river. Peace seemed to brood over and lull us – a deeper peace, as at evening the green shadows of the mountains gathered on the quiet river; and now and then a ruined castle crowned a height, and with that peculiar impression of stately tranquillity which a time-honoured ruin imparts, added the touch of romantic dignity, which otherwise had been wanting, to the scene.
>
> (1844, vol.1, p.20).

41 The Bright Stone of Honour (Ehrenbreitstein), and Tomb of Marceau, from Byron's 'Childe Harold'* RA 1835

Oil on canvas
930 × 1230 ($36\frac{5}{8} \times 48\frac{7}{16}$)
Private Collection
B & J 361
[Exhibited in London only]

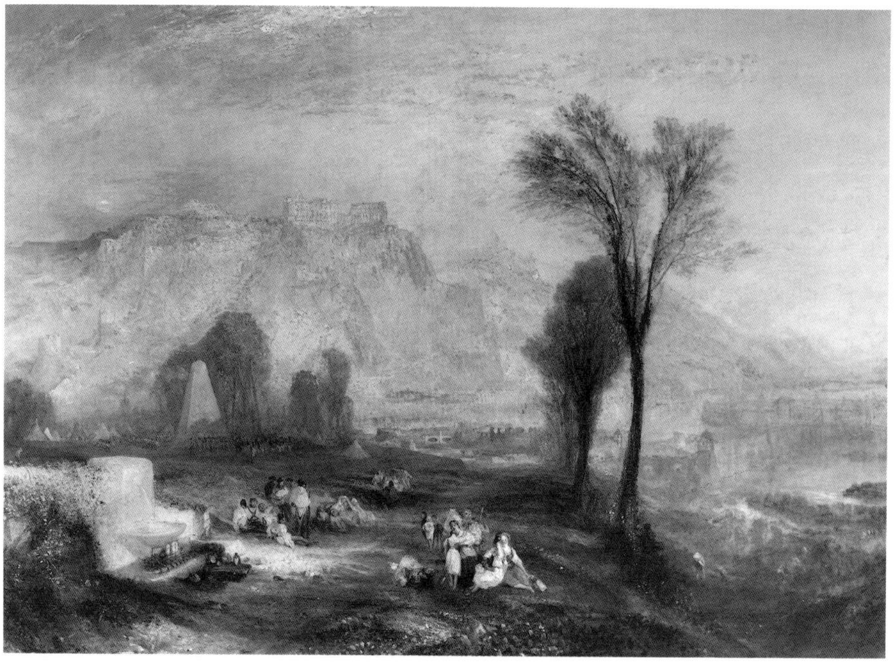

This painting is executed in the rich style typical of Turner's oils in the 1830s, such as 'Childe Harold's Pilgrimage – Italy' of 1832 and 'The Golden Bough' of 1834 (both in the Clore Gallery). Like those paintings, too, it is rich in references and allusions, for there are undoubtedly two bright stones of honour in the scene: the distant fortress of Ehrenbreitstein (a word which should really be translated as 'broad stone of honour') and the golden pyramid in the middle distance, the tomb of Marceau referred to in the title.

Marceau had been an outstanding French soldier during the Revolution and in the campaigns that followed, noted equally for his humanity and reckless bravery. As a twenty-year-old sergeant on leave in Paris he had participated in the storming of the Bastille under Jacob Elie; by twenty-four he was a general. In 1795 and 1796 he took part in the unsuccessful attempts on Ehrenbreitstein. Soon afterwards he was given charge of the 1st Division of the Sambre-et-Meuse army and it was while protecting their retreat at the battle of Altenkirchen in September 1796 that he was caught by the bullet of an Austrian huntsman behind a tree. The Austrian commander, Archduke Charles, requested that he might be acquainted with the moment of his interment, so that the Austrians could take part in performing the last military honours. Marceau's body was escorted back to the Rhine at Neuwied by a convoy of some 2,000 soldiers led by their generals, and thence to the headquarters of the Sambre-et-Meuse army north of the confluence at Coblenz. Here he was buried under the discharge of the artillery of both armies and a stone pyramid, still to be admired today (though at a different spot), was built over his tomb.

Marceau's early death and the many stories concerning his bravery gave him a widespread appeal as a Romantic hero, not least to Byron whose lines were adapted by Turner for inclusion in the Royal Academy catalogue:

By Coblentz, on a rise of gentle ground,
There is a small and simple pyramid,
Crowning the summit of the verdant
  mound;
Beneath its base are heroes' ashes hid,
Our enemy's – but let that not forbid
Honour to Marceau ————
———— He was freedom's champion!
Here Ehrenbreitstein, with her shattered
  wall,
Yet shows of what she was . . .

Although cat.no.41 is extraordinarily powerful as a painting, with brilliant colouring and breathtaking gradations of aerial perspective, it would appear to have been produced primarily with the publication of an engraving in mind. Its engraver John Pye took an unconscionable time over fulfilling this task, with Turner constantly fretting at the extended absence of his picture, but the very fine large engraving (which will replace cat.no.41 in the exhibition in Brussels (Trustees of the British Museum, London)) was at last completed; it was published in 1846, nearly eleven years after the completion of the picture itself (R 662).

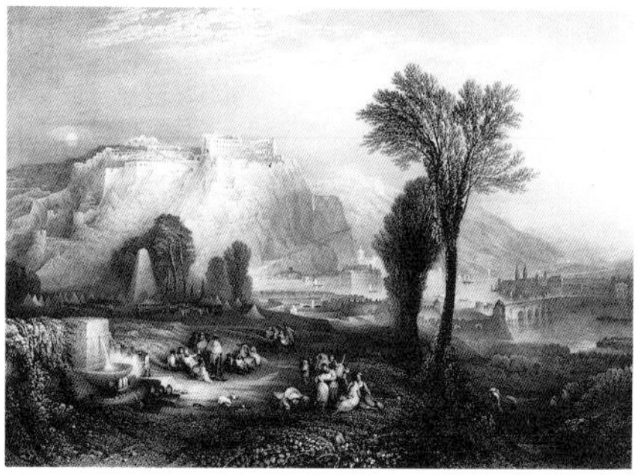

John Pye after J.M.W. Turner, 'Ehrenbreitstein' (R 662)

The Second Meuse–Mosel Tour, 1839

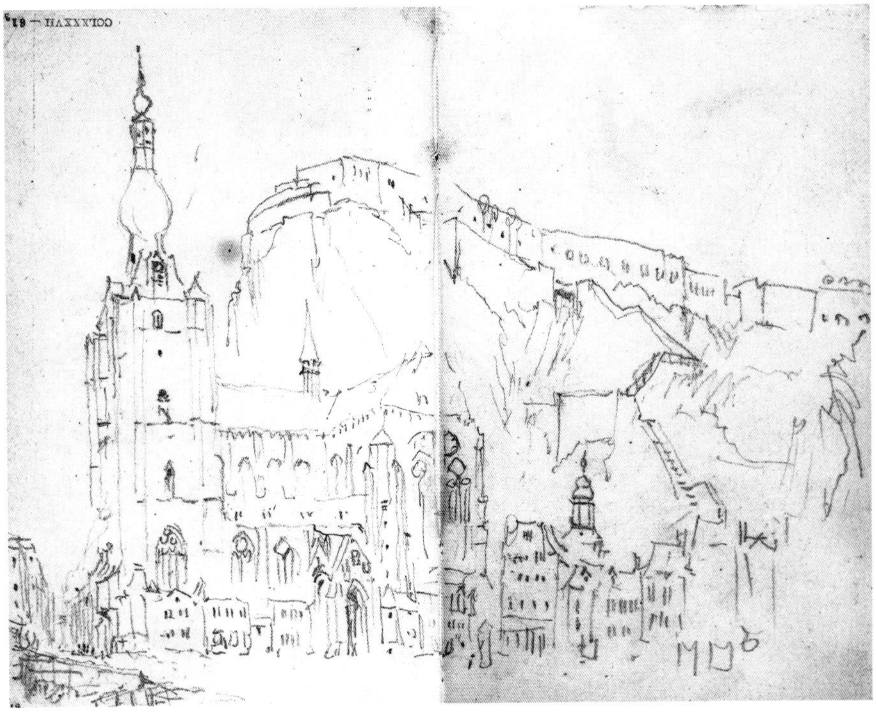

Spa, Dinant and Namur sketchbook 1839

42 The Grand' Place, Dinant

Pencil
Page size: 154 × 94 ($6\frac{1}{16} \times 3\frac{3}{4}$)
White wove writing paper
Watermarked: JOHN FELLOWS/1810/R
TB CCLXXXVII ff.60 verso, 61
D28155, D28156

This sketchbook contains British-made paper (from Eynsford Mill in Kent) which was presumably made up into a sketchbook by the stationer whose label it bears, P.J. Heyvaert Pauwels of 445 Rue de la Madeleine, Brussels. Turner must have bought it there at the start of his tour and it is undoubtedly that which he called 'No. 1 Brussels up to Givet' in the list of five sketchbooks glued to the front cover of TB CCXC (cat.no.45). It provides a very clear record of Turner's progress from Brussels almost as far as Givet, as he travelled across Belgium and up the Meuse, staying successively in Louvain, Liège, Huy, Namur and Dinant, with a detour from Liège to Spa early on in his tour.

Turner's 1839 sketches of the Meuse and the Mosel are very different from those of 1824. Full-page sketches abound in all the four small sketchbooks of upright format (TB CCLXXXVII, CCLXXXVIII, CCXC, CCXCI; cat.nos.42, 43, 45, 46) and in each sketchbook there are comparatively few occasions where he chose to squeeze several small drawings onto the same page. Turner's sketch on ff.60v–61r is unusual in using two pages for a single drawing but he obviously felt that a square format was essential to do justice to this magnificent view of Dinant with the church of Notre-Dame shown against the backdrop of its massive cliffs and citadel. The tiny houses fringing the square serve to emphasise the vast bulk of the church and the even greater size of the citadel. On the right he has clearly shown the steps up to the fort, sharply ascending in a vertiginous series of zigzags.

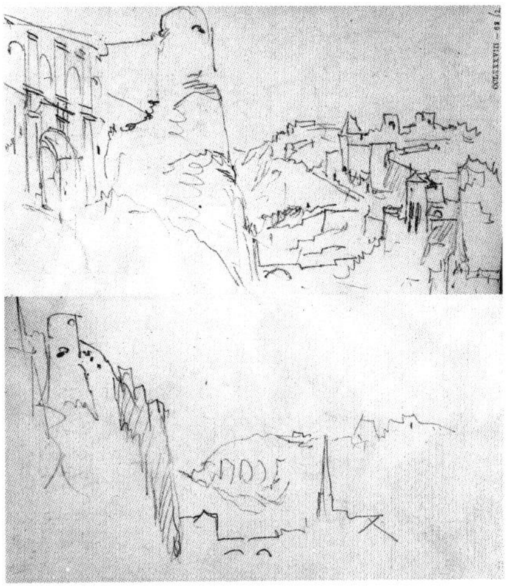

Givet, Mézières, Verdun, Metz, Luxemburg and Trèves sketchbook 1839

43 The Pont du Château, Bock and Rham, Luxembourg

Pencil
Page size: 168 × 101 ($6\frac{5}{8} \times 3\frac{15}{16}$)
Cream laid writing paper, possibly of Dutch make
Watermarked: *Pro Patria* + G
TB CCLXXXVIII ff.61 verso, 62
D28276, D28277

This sketchbook well deserves the name written on it in ink by Ruskin, 'great Fortress', since it is exclusively concerned with the fortified towns of the upper Meuse and adjacent areas: Givet, Mézières, Sedan, Verdun, Metz, Luxembourg and Trier. Turner made numerous sketches of each of these towns and cities, showing their vast and complicated fortifications, often situated on rocky cliffs (as at Givet and Luxembourg) or constructed between the whiplash meanders of much-winding rivers (as at Mézières on the Meuse and Metz on the Moselle). Many of the fortifications studied by Turner were dismantled in the second half of the nineteenth century, while Sedan and Verdun suffered severe damage during the Franco–Prussian war and the First World War. Notwithstanding these changes, it is still possible to identify nearly all the sketches in this book.

Luxembourg was the largest fortified town of those recorded in this sketchbook and it was also the town with the most complex sequence of citadels, fortifications and river valleys (see under cat. nos.120–7). It is not surprising that it was the one town on this tour for which Turner himself needed to draw a small sketch map in order to grasp its topography (ff.65v–66r). His viewpoint for both the two sketches on ff.61v–62r was the Alzette valley immediately beneath the eighteenth-century Pont du Château, looking eastwards towards the cliff-like Rocher du Bock and, further away, the four great fortified towers on the Rham. In the foreground can be seen the tiny bridge which crosses the Alzette at this point, leading to the church of St John in the suburb of the Grund with its slender spire. This view inspired the superb gouache now in the National Gallery of Ireland in Dublin (W 1010), where Turner placed all his emphasis on a dazzling vision of the Pont du Château and the towering Bock, ruthlessly simplifying or eliminating as many other features as possible. The result is one of the most brilliant of all his gouaches (see p.177 below).

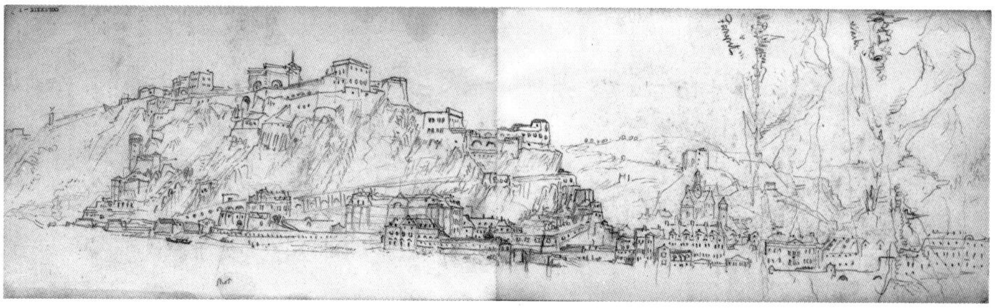

First Mossel and Oxford sketchbook
1839

44 Ehrenbreitstein

Pencil
Page size: 140 × 235 ($5\frac{1}{2} \times 9\frac{1}{4}$)
White wove drawing paper
Watermarked: J WHATMAN/ TURKEY MILL/1834
Inscribed, 'Shot' (f.7r); 'Washing', 'Fangel' (f.6v)
TB CCLXXXIX ff.6 verso, 7
D28302, D28303

'First Mossel and Oxford' was Turner's own name for this sketchbook. This title appears in the list affixed to TB CCXC (cat.no.45), for the third sketchbook among the five itemised, and there can be no doubt that it refers to TB CCLXXXIX which contains two distinct groups of sketches: careful full-page and double-page depictions of Oxford from its surrounding fields which were synthesised into the watercolour 'Oxford from North Hinksey' of 1840 (W 889), engraved by E. Goodall and published in 1841 (R 651); and small and hasty sketches of the Mosel which were subsequently fitted into the remaining spaces. The horizontal format of the book was highly suitable for expansive landscape studies around Oxford, but it was far less convenient for recording the changing scenery of the Mosel, so Turner adopted his customary expedient of using the pages as though they were of vertical format (compare cat.nos.34, 35) and dividing them up into small rectangular segments. The Mosel sketches were obviously drawn at some speed and on many occasions a single page contains numerous rough drawings facing in two or three different directions.

The only careful and detailed German sketch in TB CCLXXXIX is that of the fortress of Ehrenbreitstein, which extends across ff.6v–7r. This is the largest single sketch that Turner drew in any sketchbook on his 1839 tour and it provides the greatest possible contrast to the remainder of the German sketches in this sketchbook. It did not form the basis of any finished composition but is clear evidence of Turner's fascination with the great fortress on this visit to Coblenz as on so many others.

TB CCLXXXIX was not highly regarded by Ruskin who endorsed it 'Book of careless sketches on Rhine. One or two good at Oxford.' Despite this disparaging comment (and misidentification of the river depicted), the contents of TB CCLXXXIX are of very great interest since they reveal much about Turner's German tour. His sketches depict many different sights along the Mosel, ranging from the villages on the loops closest to Trier (e.g. Trittenheim and Neumagen on f.19r and Schweich on f.28v) to the confluence of the Mosel with the Rhine at Coblenz. All the villages and castles are sketched from low viewpoints in mid-river. Sequences of sketches on the same or adjacent pages consistently present the scenery of the Mosel from viewpoints that proceed steadily downstream (as with the sketches of Beilstein seen here on f.6v). Furthermore, Turner's lines are often very jerky and uncontrolled and his annotations more than usually indecipherable. It is clear from all these facts that TB CCLXXXIX records a downstream voyage by boat, raft or barge; that the journey took Turner all the way from Trier to Coblenz; and that it did not include stops at any villages. Turner registered the sketchbook as 'First Mossel' because it recorded his first reconnaissance of the river on this particular tour; shortly afterwards he explored the same part of the Mosel valley and its villages at a more leisurely and independent pace, recording its scenery more precisely and from a greater variety of viewpoints in the two smaller sketchbooks TB CCXC and CCXCI (cat.nos.45 and 46).

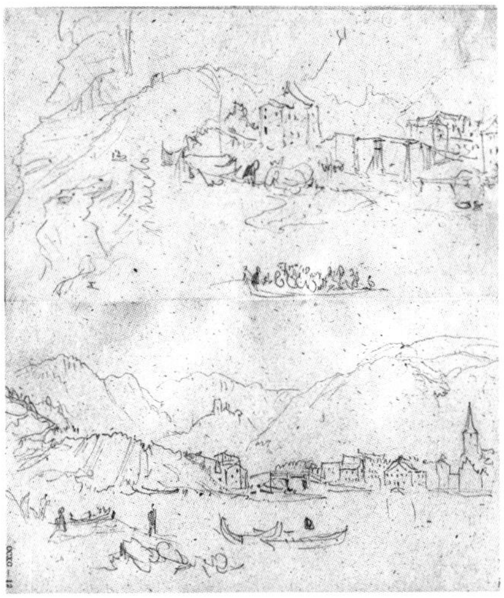

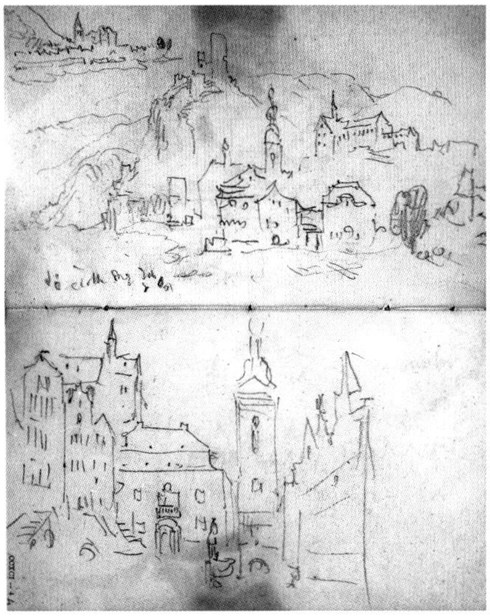

Trèves to Cochem and Coblenz to Mayence sketchbook 1839

45 Alf and Burg Arras

Pencil
Page size: 163 × 100 ($6\frac{7}{16} \times 3\frac{15}{16}$)
Lightweight flecked grey wove paper
Watermarked: traces of an unidentified mark present on two leaves
TB CCXC ff.11 verso, 12
D28372, D28373

The sketches in this book vary considerably in character and quality, those of the Mosel being far more careful and detailed than those of the Rhine. The first group forms a meticulous record of the scenery along the Mosel from Cochem up to Trier (not the reverse, as has previously been assumed). However, the Rhine sketches are executed in a much broader and more expressive style consistent with the fact that Turner was already well acquainted with the places depicted. A sketch in the second group, made towards the end of Turner's tour, has led to the tour itself being redated. This page (f.69r) shows Thorvaldsen's statue commemorating Gutenberg, the inventor of printing, which was not erected in his home town of Mainz until 1837.

The two sketches on ff.11v–12r and Turner's use of them are both typical of his studies of the Mosel on this tour. The two pages show slightly different versions of the same scene: the village of Alf at the mouth of the Mosel's principal tributary and, on a hill over the Alf valley, the ruins of the strategically placed Burg Arras. In the gouache based on these sketches (cat.no.61) Turner decided to exclude the church on the right, he modified not only the architecture of the houses but also the construction of the wooden bridge, and he considerably developed the theme of the villagers at their riverside tasks. Nevertheless, the essential character of Alf remains constant and recognisable and it could never be mistaken for any other village. German views of Alf very similar to Turner's were produced not only as nineteenth-century engravings but also as early twentieth-century postcards.

Cochem to Coblenz – Home sketchbook 1839

46 Two Views of Cochem

Pencil
Page size: 156 × 100 ($6\frac{1}{8} \times 3\frac{15}{16}$)
White laid writing paper
Watermarked: *French Imperial Eagle* + N
Countermarked: V D MEULEN / & COMP
Inscribed '[. . .] Cloth [. . .]'
TB CCXCI ff.3 verso, 4
D28543, D28544

This was the last of the five sketchbooks used by Turner on his tour of 1839. It is inscribed '5 Cockem to Cob' on a paper label cut in the shape of a butterfly affixed to the back cover and is also listed on the cover of TB CCXC as '5 Cockum to Cob. Home'. The first forty pages document Turner's journey down the Mosel from Cochem to Coblenz in considerable detail, with each page usually containing only a single sketch. Thereafter his return down the Rhine from Coblenz to Bonn is shown much less carefully and that back to the coast via Aachen in a very summary fashion.

In 1839 Turner drew more pencil sketches of Cochem than of any other town or village on the Mosel – ten in this sketchbook and a dozen in TB CCXC (cat.no.45) – and it inspired no less than seven gouaches of which six are exhibited here (cat.nos.63–8). The sketch on f.3v shows the view upstream towards the ruined medieval castle on its hill, a view largely dominated by St Martin's parish church and a former Capuchin monastery above it on the hillside. Characteristically, Turner left insufficient space to show the village on the opposite bank, Cond, and therefore had to squeeze this into a corner. The sketch on the facing page shows the monastery and church steeple again, but from an entirely different viewpoint. Turner was by now standing at a corner of the market square, looking in the opposite direction, towards the baroque town hall and the statue of St Martin and the beggar. Following the post Second World War rebuilding of the steeple and other renovation work, the square remains highly picturesque today and, indeed, picture postcards are sold there corresponding closely to Turner's view. However, it is rarely free from tourists and it is hard to believe that Turner himself could have seen it as deserted as this sketch suggests unless he had stayed the night here (as he did in 1824) and taken a solitary walk soon after daybreak.

Turner's Gouaches of Northern Europe, 1839

Unlike the famous gouache series of the Loire and the Seine, painted in the early 1830s, Turner's depictions of Belgium, Germany, north-eastern France and Luxembourg were never engraved and published. Only a very few left his possession, so that virtually all of these superb scenes have remained unresearched among the mass of material in the Turner Bequest ever since his death. The present exhibition is the first occasion on which practically all Turner's gouaches of the Meuse and Mosel and their neighbourhoods have been exhibited together as a coherent and datable project in his career, one which can now be seen as sharing both the charm and the brilliance of the earlier French scenes. It has unfortunately not been possible to include every known scene in this exhibition. For example, Ruskin specifically forbade the loan of the Turners which he gave to the University of Cambridge in 1861, which include two of the finest Meuse scenes (W 1024, 1025) and, since a large group of the popular Luxembourg gouaches was exhibited in that city as recently as 1984, only a representative selection is now being shown, to allow more space for a wider range of completely unknown German, French and Belgian scenes. The exhibition provides an opportunity, however, to publish a catalogue raisonné of the whole series, in so far as it is currently known. A number of scenes in the Turner Bequest previously associated with the Meuse–Mosel tours (e.g. TB CCXXI J) cannot yet be satisfactorily identified and are therefore not included here, but the author's continuing researches may, in due course, lead to the expansion of the present list. Unnumbered works are not included in the exhibition.

With the exception of cat.no.57, all the gouaches in the Turner Bequest are on blue wove paper. The watermarks (see e.g. cat.nos.48–9, 73–4) are the two halves of the same mark, that of Bally, Ellen and Steart.

For maps showing all the places depicted, see p.50.

The Mosel from Trier down to Coblenz

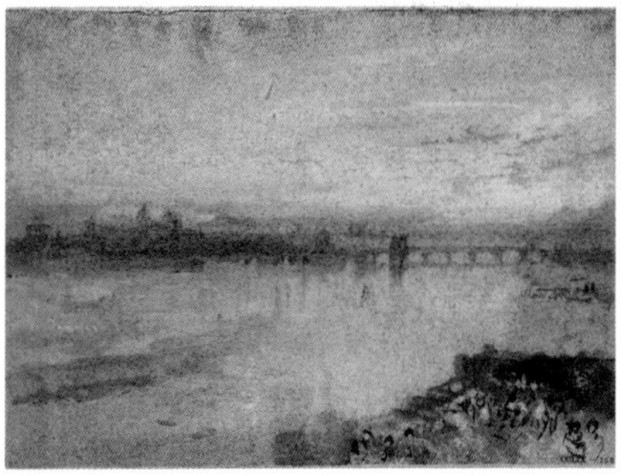

47 Trier from the West* *c.*1839

Gouache and watercolour on blue paper
141 × 188 ($5\frac{9}{16} \times 7\frac{7}{16}$)
TB CCLIX 150
D24715
EXH & LIT: National Gallery Exhibited Drawings no. 388; Finberg (1909), p.797 (as 'Avignon', *c.*1826–33); Wilton (1982), no.43 (as 'Avignon', *c.*1828)

Founded by the Emperor Augustus in 16 BC, Trier is Germany's oldest city with many notable antiquities. On his first visit to the Mosel in 1824, Turner depicted Trier many times from the hills above the west bank of the river, a viewpoint particularly recommended to tourists for their evening walks in guidebooks of all periods (see cat.no.39). In 1839 he sketched the same view several times in pencil in TB CCLXXXVIII; indeed, this theme dominates the Trier section of that sketchbook, ff.43v–55r, and it is on these sketches, especially those on ff.51r–52r, that this gouache is based. Its subtle colours leave no doubt as to its being a twilight scene, with a thin purple mist starting to veil the distance and late light gleaming on the river. From Turner's viewpoint, the village of Pallien, the spectator looks up the Mosel past a long island to the Roman bridge protected by its gate tower. The most conspicuous building in Trier is the many-towered complex of the cathedral and the Liebfrauenkirche; to the left of this appears the square block of the Porta Nigra guarding the city's northern entrance, an important building also depicted by Turner in a separate gouache of its own, TB CCXX W (cat.no.48).

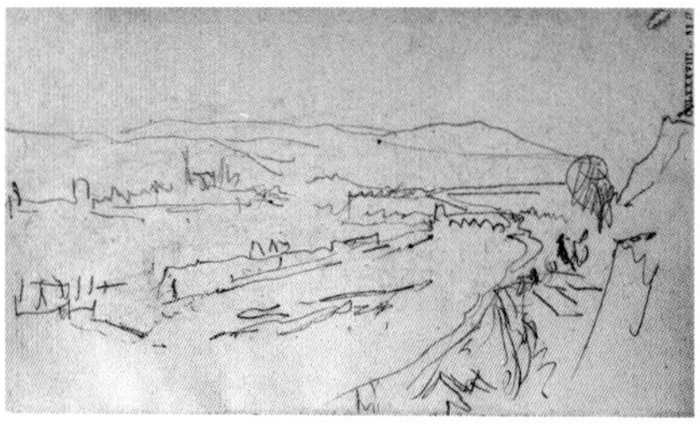

Trier (TB CCLXXXVIII 51r)

48 The Porta Nigra, Trier *c.*1839

Gouache and watercolour on blue paper
138 × 190 ($5\frac{7}{16} \times 7\frac{1}{2}$)
Watermarked: B, E . . ./18 . . .
TB CCXX W
D20230
EXH & LIT: National Gallery Exhibited Drawings no.628a; Finberg (1909), p.687 (as *c.*1826); Luxembourg (1984), no.38 (as *c.*1834)

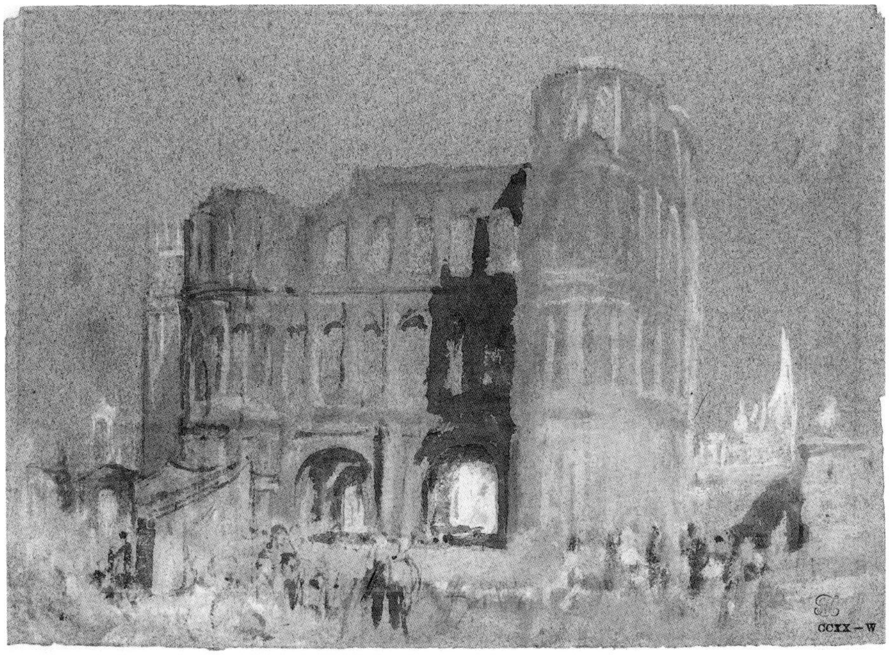

The Porta Nigra, built in the second century AD as the north gate of the Roman city of Augusta Trevirorum, is the largest extant Roman gateway. Though its sandstone has discoloured (hence its name), the iron clamps and molten lead which bind the masonry blocks together have rendered it virtually impregnable. From the eleventh century onwards it accommodated two churches, acquiring numerous accretions and embellishments, but by the time of Turner's visits these had all been stripped away, a process begun under the Napoleonic regime. There then remained simply the original magnificent Roman building, used once again as the city's gate from 1822 onwards. Turner's gouache (based on the pencil sketch on TB CCXC 41r) shows the outer face of the gate, a stark and stern defence against the barbarian hordes. However, it is noteworthy that he has not simply depicted it in the grey washes with black pen work used for sturdy buildings in the gouaches of Louvain (cat.nos.107–8) but in a softer manner and gentler colouring characteristic of the Mosel series as a whole.

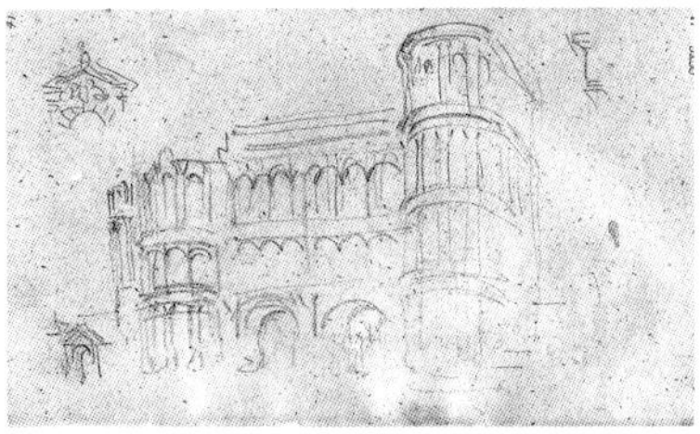

The Porta Nigra, Trier (TB CCXC 41r)

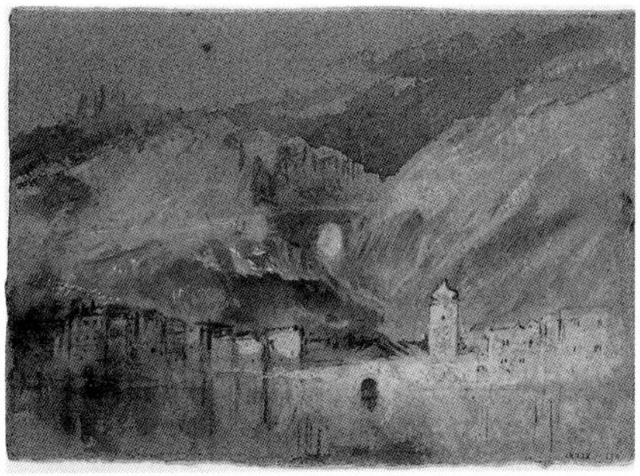

49 Pallien and the Napoleonsbrücke* *c.*1839

Gouache and watercolour on blue paper
139 × 192 ($5\frac{1}{2} \times 7\frac{9}{16}$)
Watermarked: . . . & S/. . . 8
TB CCLIX 176
D24741
EXH & LIT: National Gallery Exhibited Drawings no.432b; Finberg (1909), p.799 (as 'Bridge on mountain pass', *c.*1826–33)

In both 1824 and 1839 Turner made numerous studies of Trier from across the Mosel at Pallien (see cat.nos.39 and 47), but in this gouache (similar to his pencil sketch on TB CCXC 40v) he shows the reverse view which was in itself highly picturesque. At this point the west bank of the Mosel is lined with superb cliffs of brilliant red sandstone and a small river joins the Mosel after a steep descent noted in Turner's day for its waterfalls and watermills which were splendidly depicted in Clarkson Stanfield's *Sketches on the Moselle . . .* of 1838. During the French occupation of the Rhineland, Napoleon needed to link Trier to Aachen by a good road. He therefore constructed a massive bridge across the ravine of the Sirzenicherbach, the Napoleonsbrücke, which is the central feature of Turner's gouache and is also visible in the foreground of some of his 1824 sketches (including cat.no.39). The bridge is still in use today. The old parish church of Pallien, dedicated to SS. Simon and Jude and built in 1768, is also still in use, but its prettily curved spire has now been replaced by a small and narrow one.

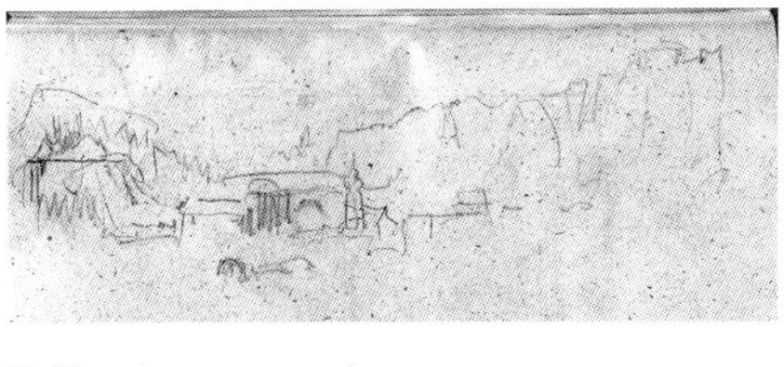

Pallien (TB CCXC 40v)

View down the Mosel from the Hillside above Pallien *c.*1839

Gouache on blue paper
140 × 187 ($5\frac{1}{2} \times 7\frac{3}{8}$)
PROV: . . .; W.G. Rawlinson; Agnew; R.A. Tatton, August 1917; T.A. Tatton sale, Christie's, 14 December 1928 (21); Agnew; Sir John Reid; private collection
Not in Wilton
EXH & LIT: Armstrong (1902), ill. on p.79, p.267 (as 'On the Moselle', no.2, 1830–5, the property of W.G. Rawlinson, and described as 'Blue river winding through green plain. Small bridge in left F[oreground]'); C. Lewis Hind, *Turner's Golden Visions*, 1925, col. pl. opposite p.132

This gouache shows the same church and bridge as TB CCLIX 176 (cat.no.49), namely SS. Simon and Jude, Pallien, and the Napoleonsbrücke, but Turner's viewpoint is now high on the hillside on the same bank of the river as the village and looking down on to the bridge. From here he could see much of Trier, including the Porta Nigra, and – moving his gaze further to the right – the whole of the city as in TB CCLIX 150 (cat.no.47). Turner drew many pencil sketches of all the prospects afforded by this hillside (TB CCLXXXVIII 43v, 49v, 50r, 50v, 51r, 51v, 52r) of which that on f.50v (inscribed 'Pallien' in the foreground) is very close to the present work.

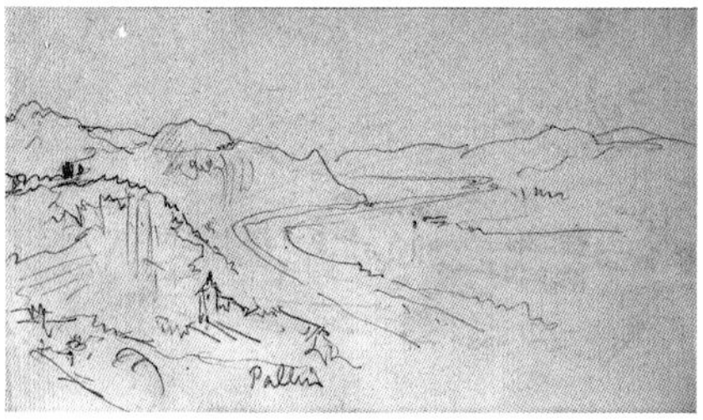

The Mosel from Pallien (TB CCLXXXVIII 50v)

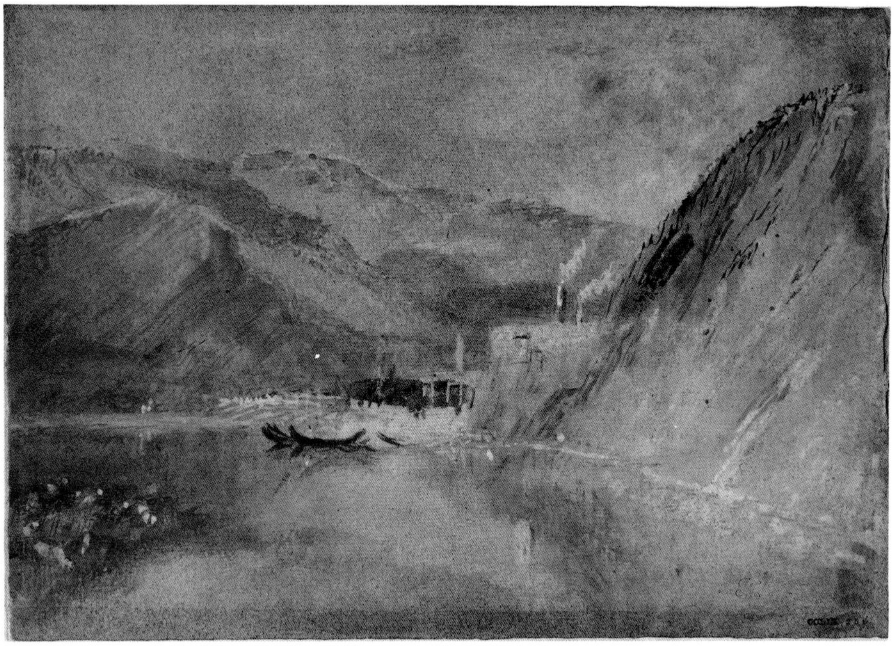

50 The Iron Forges of Quint *c.*1839

Gouache, pen and ink, and watercolour on blue paper
139 × 191 ($5\frac{1}{2} \times 7\frac{1}{2}$)
TB CCLIX 258
D24823
EXH & LIT: National Gallery 4th Loan Collection, 1891–1931, no.22; Finberg (1909), p.805 (as 'River scene, with factory works in distance', *c.*1826–33)

The pencil sketch which relates to this dramatic and colourful scene (TB CCXC 35r) bears no inscription and does not include any clearly defined buildings but there can be no doubt that it shows the valley of the Quint which meets that of the Mosel at the village of the same name situated at the fifth milestone on the Roman road from Trier to Andernach. By the time of Turner's drawing it was the site of a flourishing industry 'whose lofty chimneys indicate its extensive forges and works for the smelting of the iron ore which abounds in the neighbouring mountains. The iron of Quint enjoys a high reputation, and is much sought after' (Quin, 1843, vol.I, p.302).

Turner's technique and colouring here are similar to those used in his view of Zeltingen (cat.no.54) and this scene incorporates the same contrast between dynamic and tranquil passages as is found in that work.

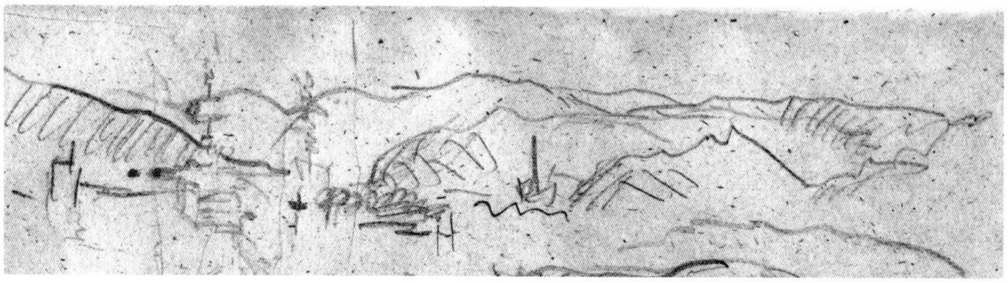

Quint (TB CCXC 35r)

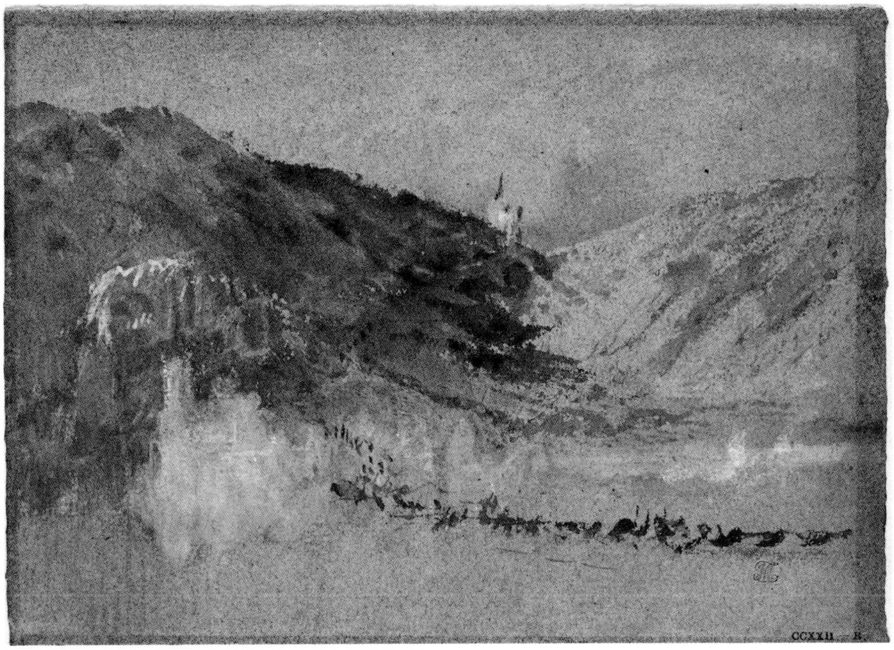

51 'Napoleon passed here' *c.*1839

Gouache and watercolour on blue paper
138 × 188 ($5\frac{7}{16} \times 7\frac{3}{8}$)
TB CCXXII R
D20277
EXH & LIT: National Gallery 6th Loan Collection, 1896–1931, no.38; Finberg (1909), p.691 (as 'Lake scene, with town and church', *c.*1826)

This delicately coloured and ethereal work corresponds to a pencil sketch with the most down-to-earth annotation possible: 'Napoleon passed here' (TB CCXC 36r). Turner's inscription enables his scene to be linked with Napoleon's journey to the Rhineland in September and October 1804, on a tour which took him from Cologne to Coblenz by boat, from Coblenz to Mainz on the new *route Napoléon,* and then on to Mannheim and further afield. The earliest stage of his tour had included visits to Brussels and Aachen (ostensibly as a pilgrimage to Charlemagne's tomb, but really as a prelude to his own coronation as Emperor at the end of 1804). On its final lap he returned home through Trier and Luxembourg. It has not yet been established precisely where he crossed the Mosel, but from the position of Turner's on-the-spot sketch in relation to others in this sketchbook it would seem to have been a few miles downstream from Trier, probably between Schweich and Kirsch. Turner would not, of course, have seen the temporary bridge of pontoons used by Napoleon: those shown in his 1839 sketch existed only in his imagination.

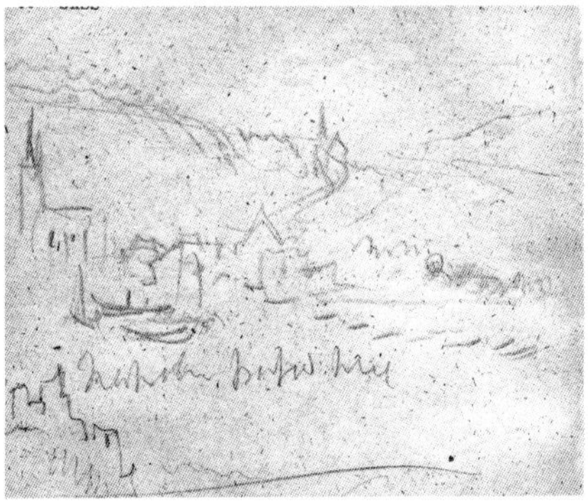

'Napoleon passed here' (TB CCXC 36r)

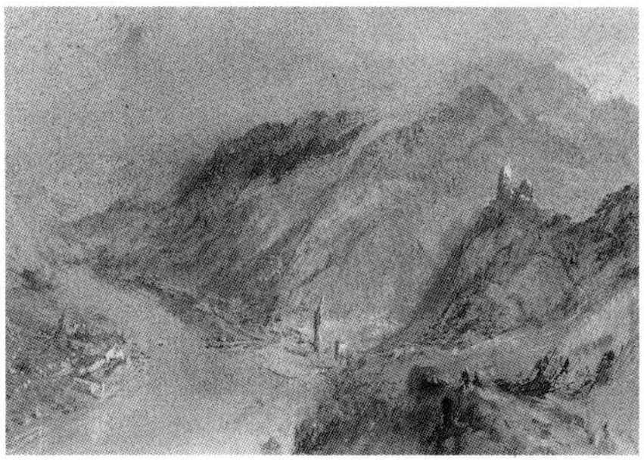

52 Bernkastel and the Landshut* *c.*1839

Gouache and watercolour on blue paper
133 × 184 ($5\frac{1}{4} \times 7\frac{1}{2}$)
PROV: . . .; Myles Birket Foster; his sale, Christie's, 28 April 1894 (40) (as 'In the Rhône Valley'); McLean; G.N. Stevens; his sale, Christie's, 14 June 1912 (70); Wallis; Margaret S. Davies; her sale, Sotheby's, 24 February 1960 (89); Agnew; Mrs Cecil Keith; Agnew 1984
Private Collection
W 1030
EXH & LIT: Album of Photographs of the Birket Foster Collection of Turner Watercolours, no.59; Armstrong (1902), p.255 (as 'St Goar', 1830–5); Otto Gerson Gallery, New York, 9 November–10 December 1960; Cologne (1980), no.51 (as 1834); Agnew, London, 1–25 May 1984, *The Watercolour Collection formed by Mrs Cecil Keith*, no.92; Yardley (1988), p.42 and ill.3 (as *c.*1834)

It is clear from Turner's pencil sketches in TB CCXC (ff.29r–31v) that he ranged extensively on foot over the hills above Bernkastel rather than simply viewing it from the Mosel. This gouache is based on one of his pencil sketches on TB CCXC 31v, drawn looking down the Mosel to-

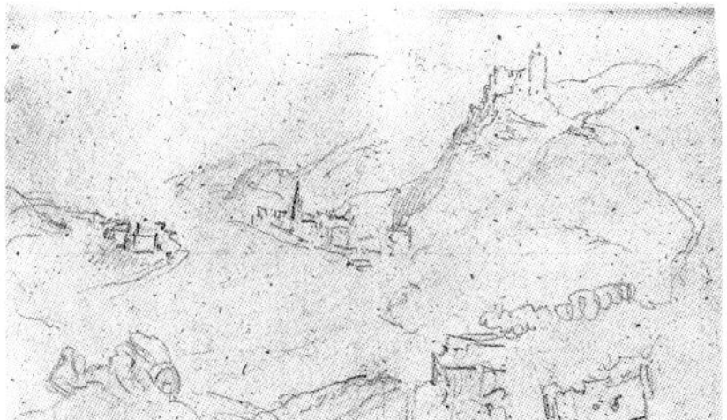

Bernkastel (TB CCXC 31v)

wards Bernkastel and the ruins of the Landshut from the hill immediately to the south. On the river bank opposite Bernkastel can be seen the village of Kues, birthplace of the Renaissance Cardinal Nicolaus Cusanus who founded its famous hospital, used as almshouses. The gouache is notable for the wonderful delicacy of its execution, typical of the Mosel series, and also for its golden and violet colouring set against a warm pinkish brown. Turner used a variety of yellows and mauves as keynotes in many of his gouaches of both Belgium and Germany, frequently juxtaposing them, as he does here, simply as a shorthand equivalent to light and shade (compare cat.nos.48 and 78).

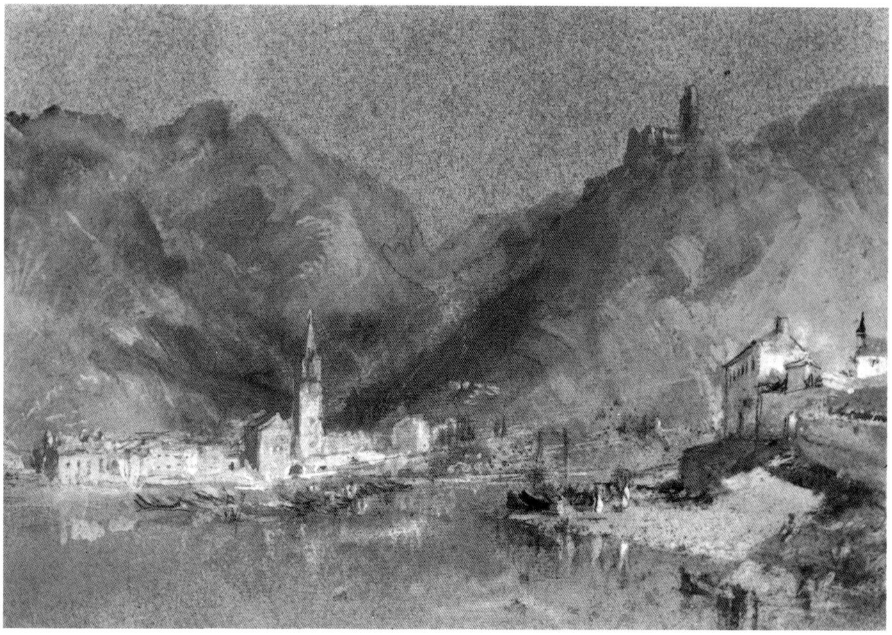

'Bernkastel, Kues and the Landshut' (W 1029)

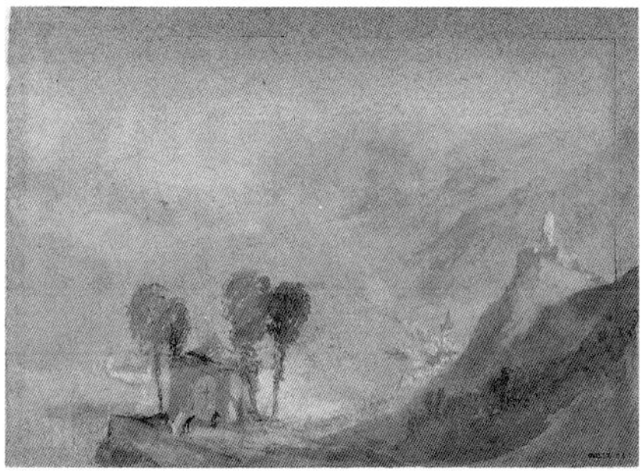

53 Bernkastel and the Landshut, with a Hillside Shrine *c.*1839

Gouache, pen and ink, and watercolour on blue paper
140 × 190 ($5\frac{1}{2} \times 7\frac{1}{2}$)
TB CCLIX 217
D24782
EXH & LIT: National Gallery Exhibited Drawings no.713; Finberg (1909), p.802 (as 'Lillebonne', *c.*1826–33)

This gouache is so similar in design to W 1030 (cat.no.52) that it is very likely to be an alternative or preliminary version of it. The Gothic church of St Michael at Bernkastel is notable for its very conspicuous spire, surrounded by turrets, which is clearly delineated in this drawing, while the features of the landscape echo both those in W 1030 and those drawn in Turner's pencil sketches in TB CCXC 29r–31v.

Bernkastel, Kues and the Landshut *c.*1839

Gouache, pen and ink, and watercolour on blue paper
137 × 184 ($5\frac{3}{8} \times 7\frac{1}{4}$)
PROV: John Ruskin; by whom given to J. Bunney; Mrs J.W. Bunney; Agnew; private collection
W 1029
EXH & LIT: Armstrong (1902), p.267 (as 'On the Moselle', no.3, 1830–5, the property of Mrs J.W. Bunney); Wilton (1979), p.167, pl.182 (as 'On the Moselle', *c.*1825–34); Cologne (1980), no.52 (as 1834); Yardley (1988), p.42

Unlike Turner's other two gouaches of Bernkastel and Kues, this one (based on his pencil sketches on TB CCXC 29r and 30r) is taken from the Mosel itself, looking back at the two villages from further downstream. In Turner's day a flying bridge linked Bernkastel and Kues; this can be seen just right of centre in the gouache, above the beached boats. On the extreme right is the hospital at Kues which is glimpsed on the left of cat.no.52.

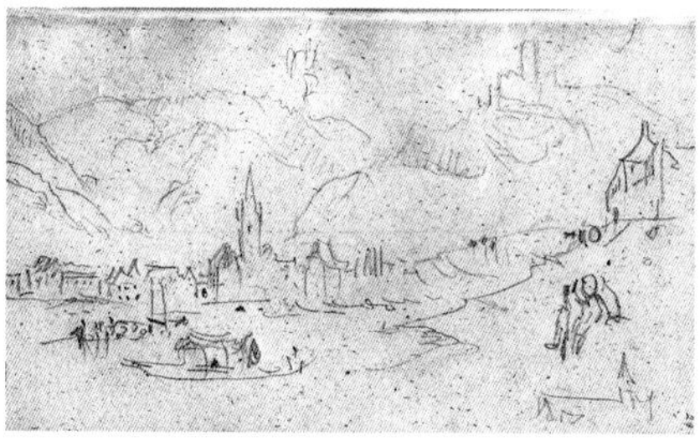

Bernkastel (TB CCXC 29r)

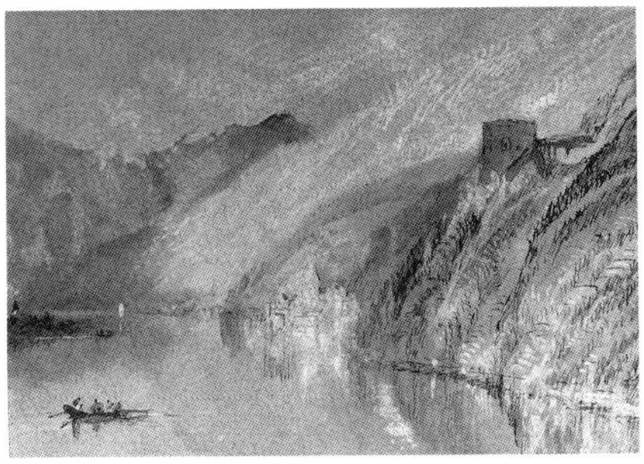

54 Zeltingen and the Kunibertsburg* *c.*1839

Gouache, pen and ink, and watercolour on blue paper
139 × 190 ($5\frac{1}{2} \times 7\frac{1}{2}$)
PROV: . . .; Christie's, London, 29 March 1983 (151, as 'On the Moselle')
Hildegard Fritz-Denneville Fine Arts Ltd, London
Not in Wilton
EXH & LIT: Westfälisches Landesmuseum, Münster, 13 September – 11 October 1987, no.45 (as 'Coblenz and Ehrenbreitstein', *c.*1834)

Immediately outside the village of Zeltingen the traveller's attention is caught by an enormous, dark, fort-like building built into the rock and perched on the hillside among the vines like a black cube. Turner recorded this forbidding structure, the remains of the Kunibertsburg, looming over Zeltingen and its slender Gothic-spired church, in two sketches showing the view in opposite directions (TB CCXC 28r, 28v). His gouache is very similar to the second of these, and it also shows part of the village of Wehlen upstream on the opposite bank, recorded in an adjacent sketch on f.28v. The hillside shown by Turner faces south-west, making it an especially sunny and fertile spot for the cultivation of vines, indeed one of the most famous vineyards on the Mosel, a fact admirably suggested by Turner's radiant colours.

A particular feature of this work – which is not uncommon in the 1839 gouaches (compare cat.no.102) – is the way in which the composition falls into two clearly demarcated halves with completely different characters. Many of Turner's contemporaries who travelled along the Mosel commented on the rapidity with which smiling vineyards alternated with gloomy grey rocks and it is clear that Turner too was struck by this phenomenon.

> One of the attractions, for an artist especially, in all these scenes, is the perpetual contrast which he discovers between the sunny animation of one side of the river, and the frowning, savage solitudes of the . . . other, upon whose rocky precipices and deep ravines no beam of light seems ever to have fallen. Quarries of dark slate . . . look across the smoothly flowing river upon meadows, corn-fields, vineyards, gentle eminences, hills, and valleys, endowed with every form of grace . . .
>
> Quin (1843), vol.II, p.21, on the Mosel slightly below Zeltingen

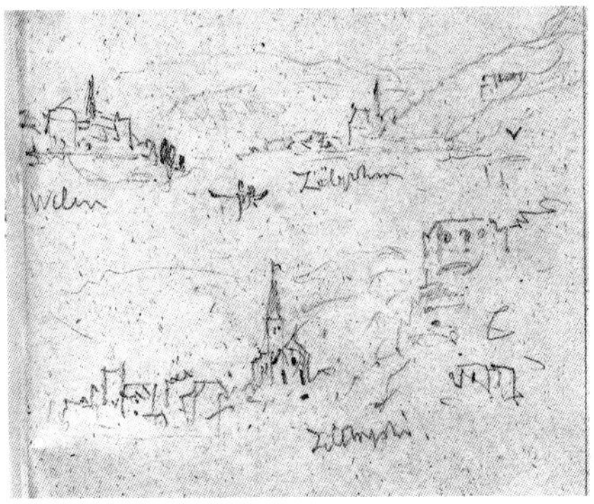

Zeltingen (TB CCXC 28v)

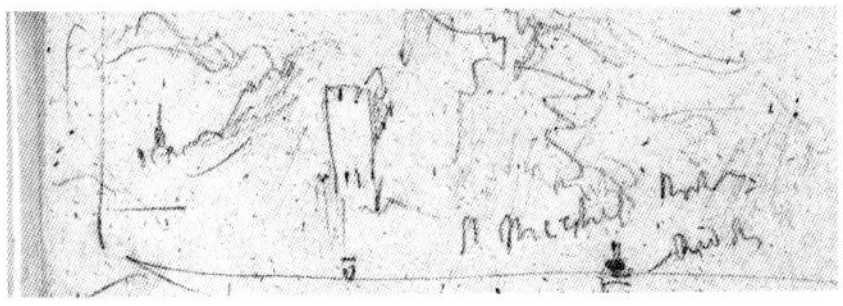

Ürzig (TB CCXC 27v)

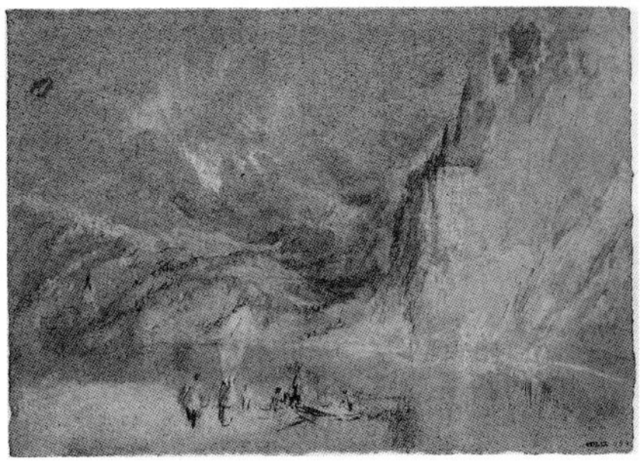

55 Ürzig and the Hermitage on the Michaelslei *c.*1839

Gouache and watercolour on blue paper
137 × 191 ($5\frac{3}{8} \times 7\frac{1}{2}$)
TB CCLIX 224
D24789
EXH & LIT: National Gallery Exhibited Drawings no.760; Finberg (1909), p.802 (as 'Tancarville', *c.*1826–33)

The most prominent feature in this view up the Mosel to the village of Ürzig is the large structure built into a rocky outcrop on the hillside to the right. This feature – which was recorded by Turner in two sketchbooks in 1839 (TB CCLXXXIX 11r and CCXC 27v) – was described in the early 1840s in terms which well account for its appeal to travellers: 'in the face of a high red cliff called Michaelsley, may be seen a castellated wall. This wall covers the mouth of a cavern, which was occupied in the olden time by a band of robbers, each of whom, however, claimed to be of some order of knighthood: it was in a later age the residence of a pious hermit. It can only be entered by means of ladders' (Quin, 1843, vol.II, p.8). Needless to say, over the centuries, a number of highly picturesque legends attached themselves to this site (see Tower, 1913, pp.126–9). The wall remains a very striking sight today, being embellished with a large sundial, and, on a bright day, the entire hillside with its red rocks and bright rows of vines frequently looks almost as glowing as Turner has portrayed it.

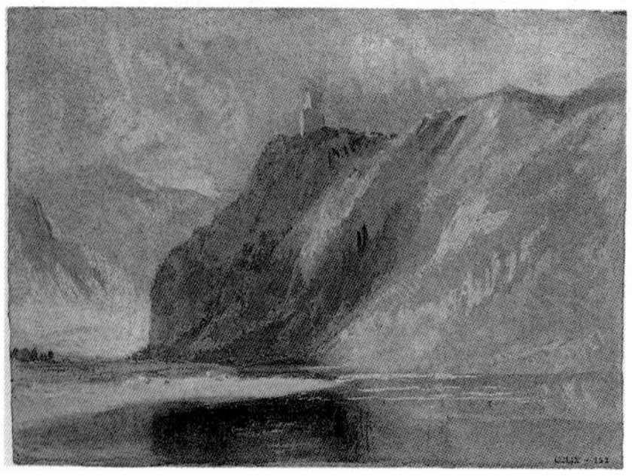

56 The Ruined Monastery at Wolf* *c.*1839

Gouache and watercolour on blue paper
141 × 190 ($5\frac{9}{16} \times 7\frac{1}{2}$)
TB CCLIX 152
D24717
EXH & LIT: National Gallery Exhibited Drawings no.390; Finberg (1909), p.798 (as 'On the Rhine(?)', *c.*1826–33); International Exhibitions Foundation (1977–8), no.44 (as 'Traben-Trarbach on the Moselle', *c.*1834); Paris (1983), no.176 (as 'Traben-Trarbach sur la Moselle', 1834?)

The solitary ruins of the monastery of Wolf, perched high on the Gockelsberg, form an impressive sight as the traveller approaches Traben-Trarbach down the Mosel, particularly at sunset. The river winds its way around the Gockelsberg in one of the loops for which it is so famous, leaving the village of Kröv to its west, so that travellers following its course see the ruins of Wolf from an ever-changing succession of viewpoints. Turner made several sketches of this subject on TB CCXC 27r. One of these corresponds very closely to the gouache and is inscribed 'Beaut[iful] Light' just at the very point where the gouache shows a dazzling spit of golden sand. Another of these tiny sketches is notable for the amount of hatching used to show contrasts of light and shade; this feature is recreated in the gouache by glorious colour juxtapositions including that of brilliant pink with dark velvety blue.

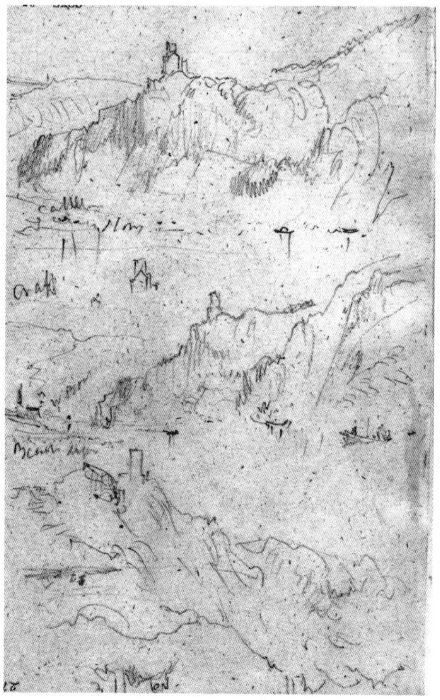

Wolf (TB CCXC 27r)

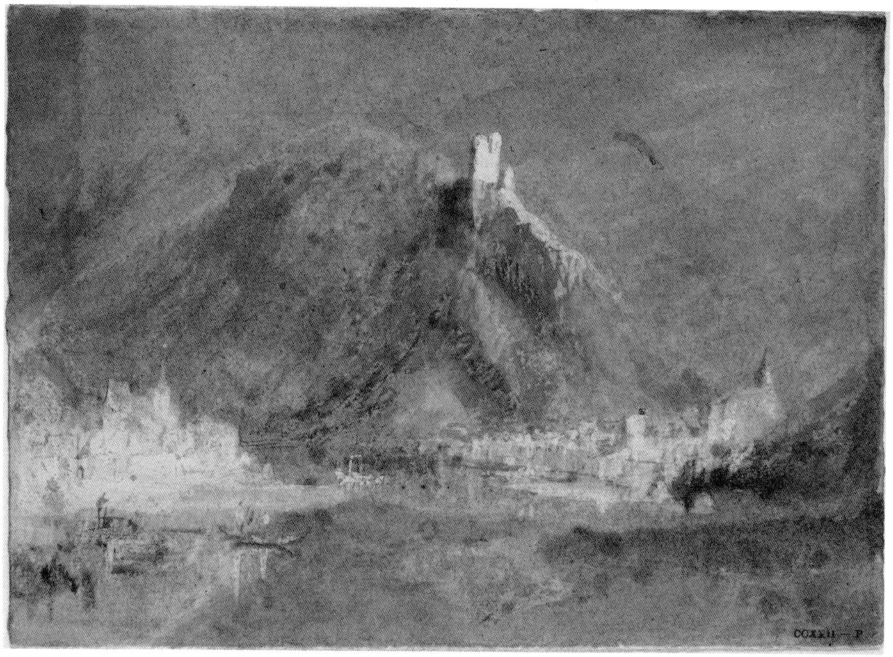

57 Traben, Trarbach and the Grevenburg *c.*1839

Gouache and watercolour on white wove paper prepared with a blue wash
138 × 187 ($5\frac{7}{16} \times 7\frac{3}{8}$)
TB CCXXII P
D20275
EXH & LIT: National Gallery 6th Loan Collection, 1896–1931, no.41 (as 'Italian Lake Scene &c'); Finberg (1909), p.691 (as 'River (or Lake) scene, with town and castle on hill', *c.*1826); Wilkinson (1975), p.85 (untitled)

As in W 1029, Turner here portrays the quintessential Mosel view of two villages on the river bank facing each other under a lofty ruined castle. His gouache is based on his pencil sketches on TB CCXC 20v and 21r, drawn as he approached the villages coming down the Mosel. From afar off, the majestic ruin of the Grevenburg is lost against the hillside on which it stands, but as the traveller comes close to Traben and Trarbach it rears its head suddenly against the sky, the hollow centre of its battlements giving it an especially dramatic presence. Traben and Trarbach, like Bernkastel and Kues, were linked in former times by a flying bridge; this is just visible on the left bank, at the end of the spit of sand below Traben.

This work has always been regarded as

a 'blue paper' drawing and it was not until it was removed from its old backing-sheet for the present exhibition that this assumption was proved wrong. There can be no doubt, however, that Turner regarded the drawing as part of his Mosel sequence and deliberately doctored the paper with a blue wash, either as an experiment or simply because he had run out of blue sheets. No other examples of this procedure are as yet known, though others may well exist, having successfully deceived generations of admirers!

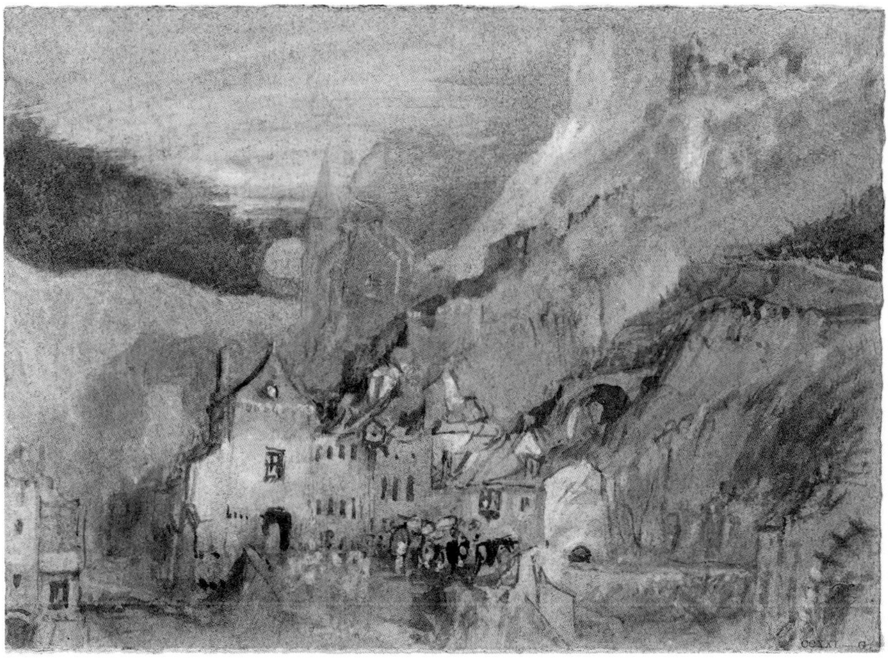

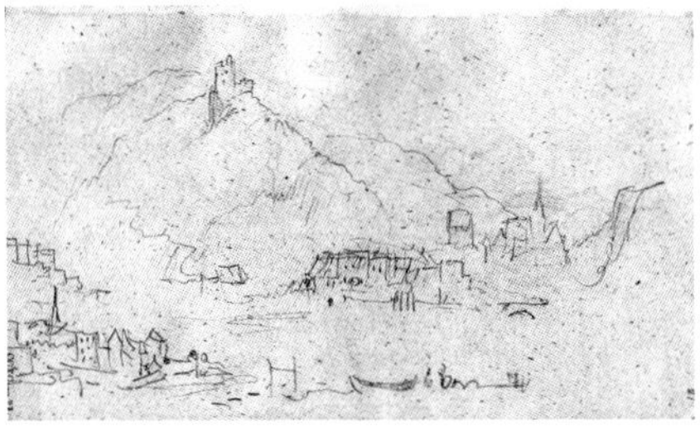

Traben and Trarbach (TB CCXC 21r)

58 The Entrance to Trarbach from Bernkastel* *c.*1839

Gouache and watercolour on blue paper
141 × 191 ($5\frac{9}{16} \times 7\frac{1}{2}$)
TB CCXXI G
D20240
EXH & LIT: National Gallery Exhibited Drawings no.180; Ruskin (1903–12), vol.XIII, p.386 ('Wonderful, but too wild'); Finberg (1909), p.688 (as 'Bacharach', *c.*1826); Wilkinson (1975), p.85 (as 'Bacharach'); Luxembourg (1984), no.39 (as *c.*1834)

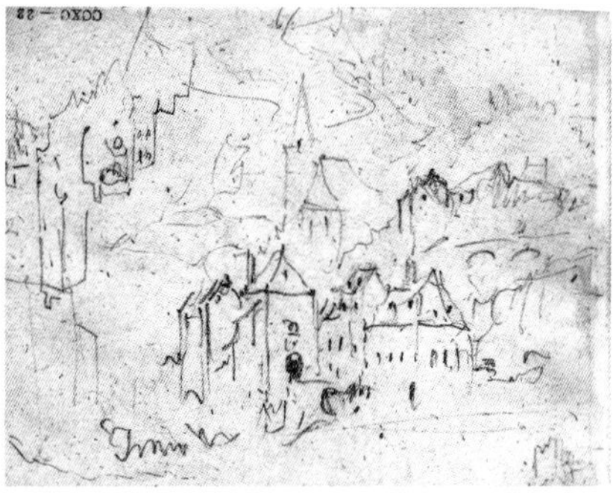

Trarbach (TB CCXC 22r)

The Mosel is absent from this gouache of Trarbach, since it depicts the village square reached from the path over the hills from Bernkastel (a route considerably shorter than that taken by the river). Turner's scene is based on his pencil sketches on TB CCXC 22r; it includes a full moon above the hills over Traben, St Nicholas's church, the Grevenburg and the town walls rising precipitously above a picturesque huddle of ancient houses. A very similar view to this, by David Roberts, was published as an illustration to Bulwer-Lytton's *Pilgrims of the Rhine* in 1834, a fact of which Turner would surely have been aware. However, it was a type of view that greatly appealed to him for its own sake, as can be seen from a comparison with two of his own depictions of Bacharach (figs.21 and 44 on pp.33 and 55).

59 Trarbach from the Grevenburg *c.*1839

Gouache and watercolour on blue paper
139 × 190 ($5\frac{1}{2} \times 7\frac{1}{2}$)
TB CCXXI Z
D20259
EXH & LIT: Oxford Loan Collection 136–208; Finberg (1909), p.689 (as 'Bacharach', *c.*1826); Cologne (1980), no.50 (as 'An der Mosel', 1834); Luxembourg (1984), no.40 (as 'Trarbach', *c.*1834)

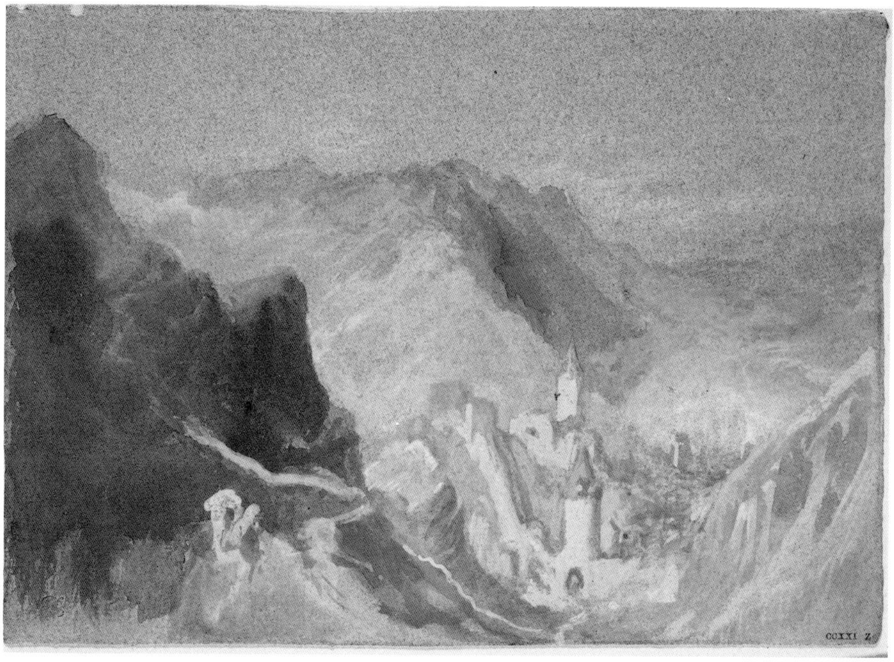

This work shows Trarbach as it appeared to Turner on his walk up to the Grevenburg and thus provides the opposite view to that given in cat.nos.57 and 58. When Turner sketched this appealing view (TB CCXC 25v), Trarbach (from the Roman 'Thronus Bacchi') was 'surrounded by a strong wall, still further strengthened by several towers. There are three gates, in good preservation, surmounted also by towers, which add much to the chivalrous aspect of the place' (Quin, 1843, vol.II, p.14). In 1857 the town was devastated by fire, an all-too-common occurrence in earlier centuries among these riverside villages of half-timbered houses closely packed together between the steep hillside and the water.

Although this work shares the same broad colour range as cat.no.58, it is executed in a far denser way with gouache predominating throughout. The richness of its medium makes the scene appear heavier than most others of this group, but its subject, viewpoint, colour and focus of attention all prove that it really does belong here.

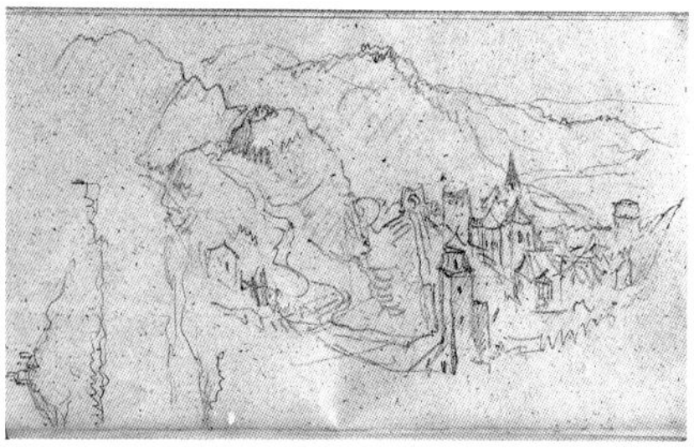

Trarbach (TB CCXC 25v)

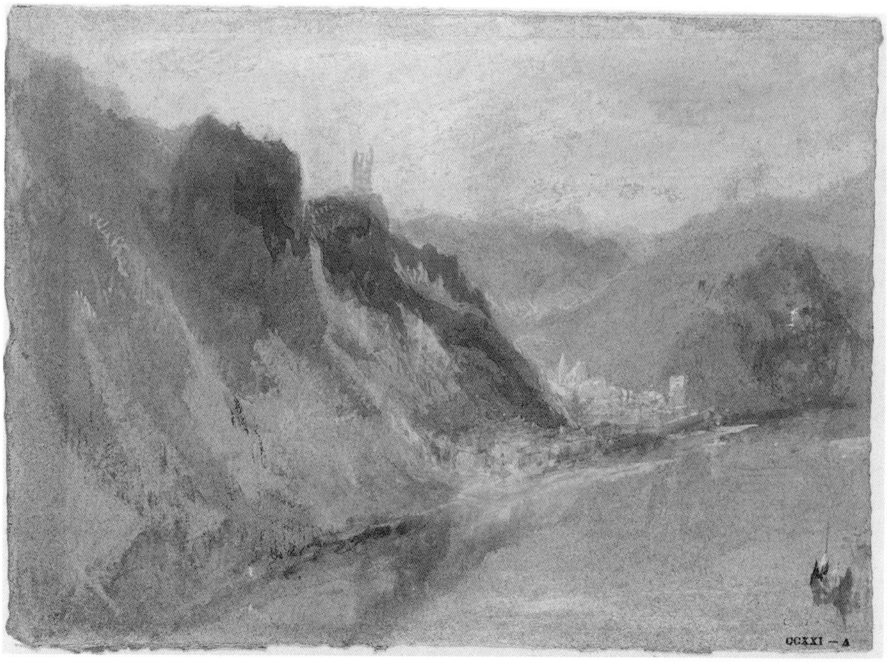

60 Trarbach and the Grevenburg *c.*1839

Gouache and watercolour on blue paper
140 × 189 ($5\frac{1}{2} \times 7\frac{7}{16}$)
TB CCXXI A
D20234
EXH & LIT: National Gallery Exhibited Drawings no.740; Finberg (1909), p.688 (as *c.*1826); Cologne (1980), no.48 (as 1834)

This gouache appears not to be based on any single pencil sketch in a sketchbook, so it may well have been painted over one on this very sheet. It undoubtedly shows the ruins of the Grevenburg and Trarbach, looking back upstream from the Mosel just before the river changes direction again and sweeps the traveller on to the north. Both its feathery touch and its mauve colouring are characteristic of many of Turner's Mosel gouaches.

A Bend on the Mosel *c.*1839

Gouache on blue paper
133 × 185 ($5\frac{1}{4} \times 7\frac{1}{4}$)
PROV: . . .; J.E. Taylor; his sale, Christie's, 5 July 1912 (81); Agnew; W.G. Rawlinson; Agnew; R.A. Tatton, August 1917; T.A. Tatton sale, Christie's, 14 December 1928 (20); Agnew; Sir John Reid; private collection
Not in Wilton
EXH & LIT: Burlington Fine Arts Club 1871; Armstrong (1902), p.267 (as 'On the Moselle', no.1, 1830–5, the property of J.E. Taylor, and described as 'Probably the "crook" of the river at Marienberg [*sic*]. Warm evening light')

The identification of this view with the Marienburg is almost certainly wrong, since the course of the Mosel beneath that ruin is far more tortuous than it here appears, with the neck of land north of the Marienburg being very much more slender. Had Turner ascended a nearby hill to observe this phenomenon (which there is no evidence to suggest that he did) he would surely have exaggerated the whiplash curve of the river rather than reduced it. There is a strong probability that this gouache does relate to Turner's exploration of the Mosel in 1839 but its exact subject remains unclear.

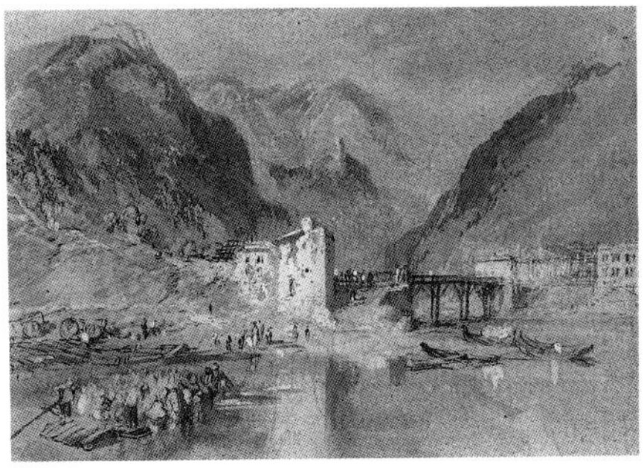

61 Alf and Burg Arras* *c.*1839

Gouache, pen and ink, and watercolour on blue paper
134 × 186 ($5\frac{1}{4} \times 7\frac{5}{16}$)
PROV: Thomas Griffith; Charles Stokes, May 1850: by descent to Hannah Cooper; from whom bought by John Ruskin, February 1858; by whom given to the University of Oxford, March 1861; transferred to the Ashmolean Museum, Oxford, 1938 (H 27)
Visitors of the Ashmolean Museum, Oxford
W 1023
EXH & LIT: Thornbury (1862), vol.2, p.396 and (1877), p.593 (as 'On the Meuse', the title used for this work in all subsequent references in this list); Armstrong (1902), p.266 (as 1830–5); Ruskin (1903–12), vol.XIII, pp.557 (no.80 or 81, 560 (no.25), 603; vol.XXXVI, pp.358–9; exhibited Whitechapel Art Gallery 1953; Herrmann (1968), pp.32–4; no.27, p.70 (as *c.*1826–30); Herrmann (1970), p.696; exhibited Ashmolean Museum 1989

Although this work left Turner's studio in his lifetime, passing through the hands of his agent Thomas Griffith, its subject matter was evidently forgotten at a very early stage. In March 1861, when Ruskin included it in his gift of Turner watercolours to the University of Oxford, he referred to it simply as 'On the Meuse' and it has been known by this title (or 'Scene on the Meuse') ever since. It is, however, a depiction not of the Meuse but of the Mosel: it shows the village of Alf, just north of the loop on which the Marienburg is situated, and it is closely based on Turner's small pencil sketches on TB CCXC IIV, 12r and 12v (see cat.no.45). At Alf the Mosel is joined by a tributary, also named Alf, which in Turner's day was spanned by a wooden bridge. In the background looms the ruined tower of Burg Arras, situated on a knoll commanding the valleys of the Alf and another stream, the Uess. However, Turner's chief concern – in both the sketches and the gouache – was with the riverside activities of the modern-day inhabitants of the village.

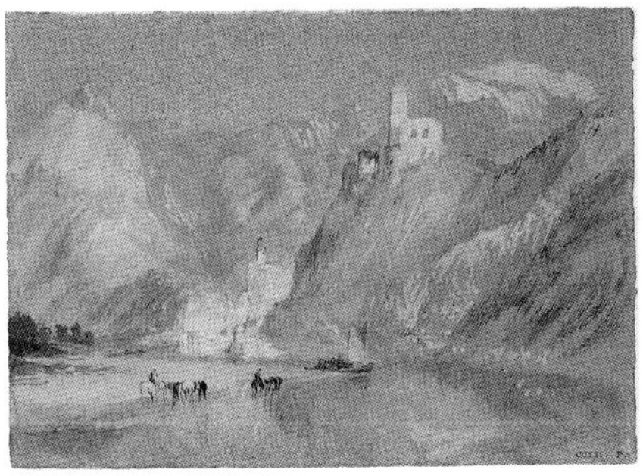

62 Beilstein and Burg Metternich* *c.*1839

Gouache and watercolour on blue paper
140 × 192 ($5\frac{1}{2} \times 7\frac{9}{16}$)
TB CCXXI F
D20239
EXH & LIT: National Gallery Exhibited Drawings no.179 (as 'Rhine(?) or Danube(?)'); Ruskin (1903–12), vol.XIII, p.386 ('very grand'); Finberg (1909), p.688 (as 'River scene, with castle on rock. Probably Moselle', *c.*1826); London (1975), no.112 (as 'A ruined castle on a rock above a town by a river', *c.*1827); Athens (1981), no.29 (as above, *c.*1827); Luxembourg (1984), no.41 (as *c.*1834)

Beilstein stands very picturesquely on one of the many bends of the Mosel, so that river travellers enjoy numerous changing views of the town nestling in its ravine and the gaunt ruins of Burg Metternich perched high above it. Turner's gouache, which captures this group in brilliant colours, emphasises with its tiny brush strokes the degree to which bare rock alternates with vines and bushes along the slopes of the Mosel, each slope catching the sunlight in a slightly different way. Turner shows Beilstein from the most dramatic viewpoint of all, slightly upstream. A very similar view had been depicted by Clarkson Stanfield in his

Sketches on the Moselle (1838) and Turner probably sought his viewpoint out deliberately. The architectural detail comes from his main pencil sketch on TB CCXC 9r but its setting also reflects other, smaller sketches taken from still further upstream (ff.9v and 10r).

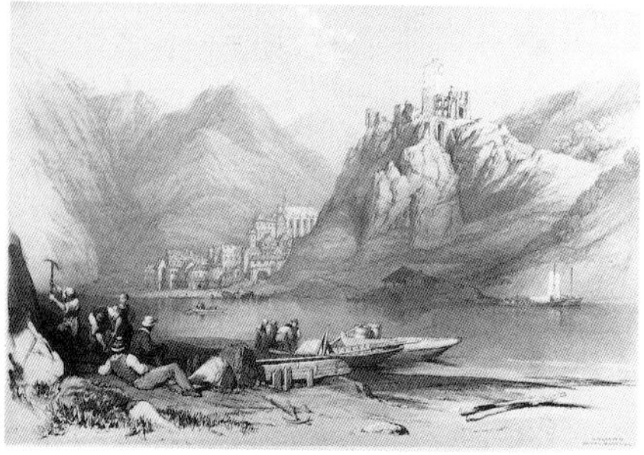

Louis Haghe after Clarkson Stanfield, 'Bielstein [sic] on the Moselle'

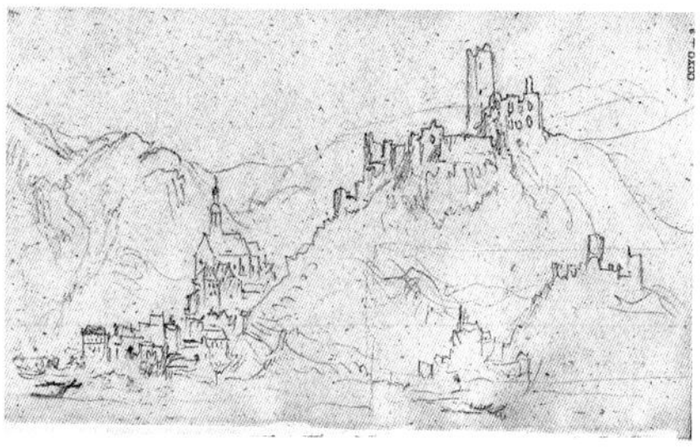

Beilstein (TB CCXC 9r)

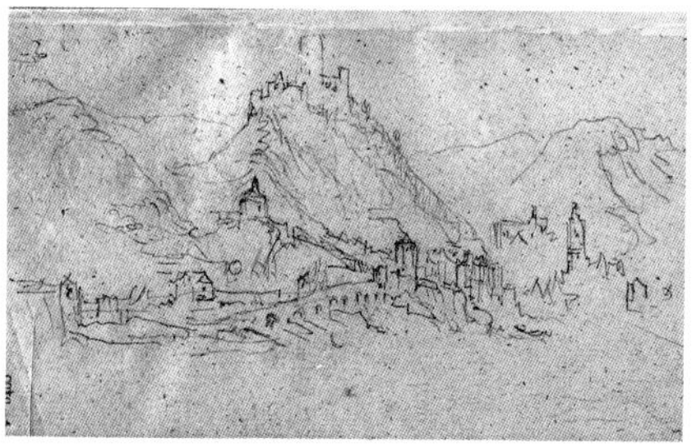

Cochem (TB CCXC 5r)

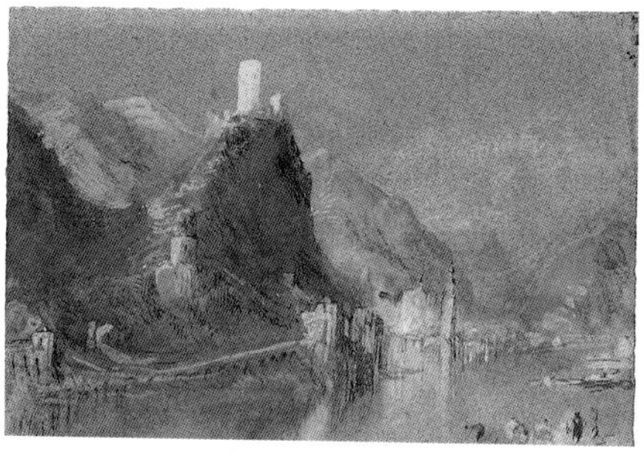

63 Cochem from the South* *c.*1839

Gouache and watercolour on blue paper
140 × 189 ($5\frac{1}{2} \times 7\frac{7}{16}$)
TB CCXCII 39
D28986
EXH & LIT: National Gallery 2nd Loan Collection, 1869–1931, no.107 (as 'River Scene'); Finberg (1909), p.940 (as 'Scene on Moselle, with ruined castles on rocks', *c.*1834); Luxembourg (1984), no.43 (as *c.*1834)

Cochem was – and remains – the largest town on the Mosel between Trier and Coblenz with two ruined castles, each on a conical hill, and numerous ancient buildings, towers and walls. In this downstream view (close to the pencil sketch on TB CCXC 5r) Turner shows clearly both the main castle, the Burg, above the little white plague chapel on the hillside on the left, and the distant Winneburg to the right of the parish church. Besides this, he also emphasises the setting that has led to the lasting popularity of Cochem, by making its surrounding hills appear far more awe-inspiring than they are in reality. The delight Turner took in Cochem can be gauged by the fact that he painted seven gouaches of it on blue paper in this series, far more than those of its nearest rivals, Bernkastel and Trarbach, and more than any other subject seen on his 1839 tour except Luxembourg.

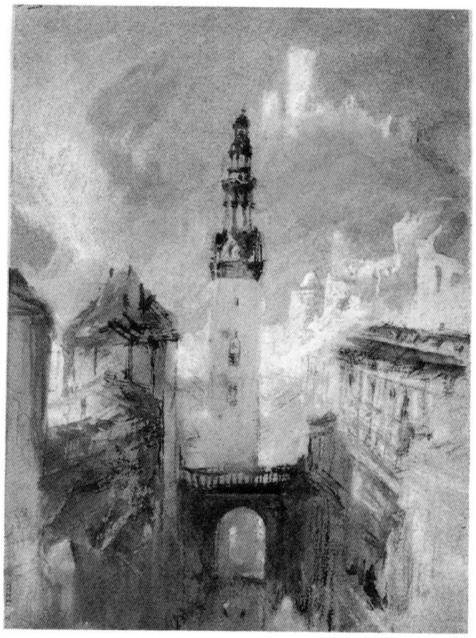

64 St Martin's Church, Cochem* *c.*1839

Gouache and watercolour on blue paper
190 × 139 ($7\frac{1}{2} \times 5\frac{1}{2}$)
TB CCXXI T
D20253
EXH & LIT: [Cook] (1905), p.13 (as 'An Italian Sketch'); Finberg (1909), p.689 (as 'Town on Moselle, with ruined castle on rock above. Possibly Trarbach', *c.*1826)

This gouache and those of the Enderttor (TB CCLIX 241 (cat.no.65) and W 1007) are the only Mosel scenes of the series with a vertical format. Turner was clearly working to produce a pair, since each shows the principal Burg (or Reichsburg) at Cochem not as its main subject but crowning the distance. In this striking scene (based on the pencil sketch on TB CCXCI 2r) the foreground is dominated by the early eighteenth-century steeple of St Martin's church; this was destroyed in 1945 but a nearly identical 1964 replacement has ensured that the picturesque character of the town – especially as seen from the river – has still been preserved.

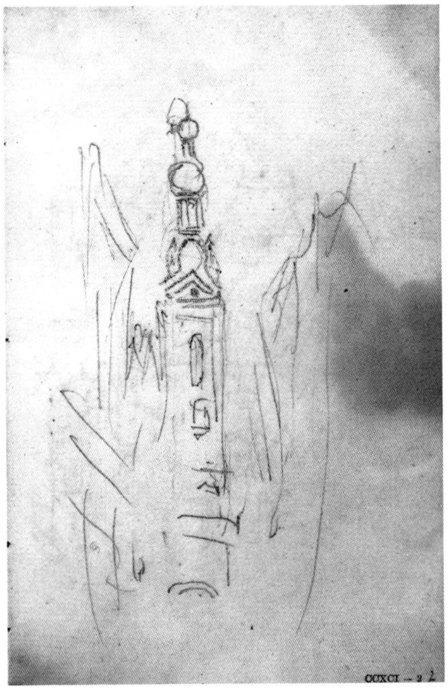

Cochem (TB CCXCI 2r)

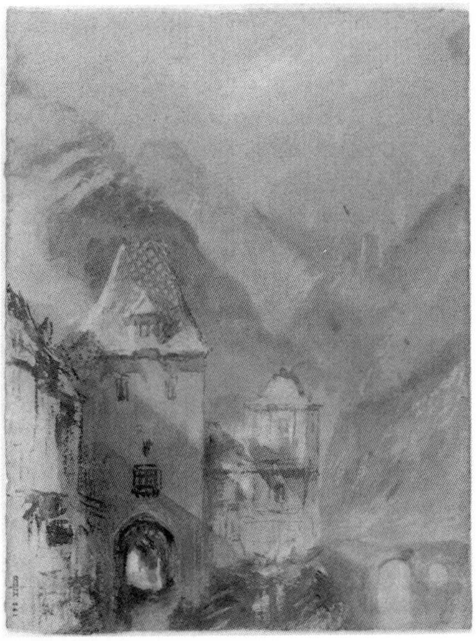

65 The Enderttor and Alte Thorschenke, Cochem* *c.*1839

Gouache and watercolour on blue paper
191 × 141 ($7\frac{1}{2} \times 5\frac{9}{16}$)
TB CCLIX 241
D24806
EXH & LIT: National Gallery 5th Loan Collection, 1896–1931, no.11; Finberg (1909), p.803 (as 'Tours, from the Loire', *c.*1826–33)

During Turner's visit to Cochem he drew two pencil sketches of one of the town's most delightful groups, the medieval Enderttor and the tavern built into the town walls next to the gate in 1625, the half-timbered Alte Thorschenke with its turreted roofline and gabled façade (TB CCXCI 2v, 3r). This gouache is based principally on the first of these sketches, but the distant rosy castle and the tiny bridge over the Endert have been taken from the second, drawn from the side of the gateway, opposite the façade of the tavern. The Enderttor appears in Turner's sketches, and indeed remains today, a formidably plain building. His anthropomorphic rendering of it as a grinning face may derive from his recollection of many happy hours spent in the Alte Thorschenke and other similar hostelries along the Mosel, but it is hard not to regard this work as a whole as a humorous riposte to the innumerable views produced by Samuel Prout using just such a vertical compositional formula for cities and villages in many parts of Europe including the Rhineland (see fig.5 on p.15).

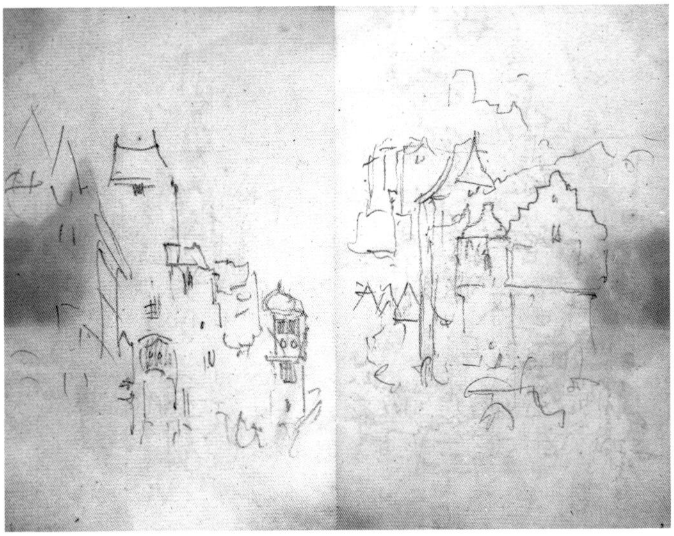

Cochem (TB CCXCI 2v–3r)

The Enderttor and Alte Thorschenke, Cochem *c.*1839

Gouache and watercolour on blue paper
180 × 130 ($7\frac{1}{16} \times 5\frac{1}{8}$)
PROV: John Ruskin; . . .; Christie's, 13 July 1971 (92, as 'The Bridge'); Kurt Pantzer; Indianapolis Museum of Art
W 1007
EXH & LIT: Paris (1983), no.190 (as 'Le pays natal de Claude Lorrain: Le pont de Buzet', *c.*1832)

This work has formerly been known as 'Claude Lorraine's Birthplace, the Pont de Buzet?' but it undoubtedly shows the same group of buildings as TB CCLIX 241 (cat.no.65) and is quite clearly related, like that drawing, to the pencil sketches on TB CCXCI 2v and 3r. Apart from the buildings in the foreground and the distant ruined Burg perched high on its conical hill which is such a prominent feature of Cochem, the drawing also includes the former Capuchin monastery halfway up the hillside beneath it (compare cat. nos.66 and 67).

Ruskin seems also to have owned a watercolour on buff-coloured paper inscribed 'Pont de Buset' (W 1008). However, as was pointed out in the Paris catalogue of 1983, the scene depicted there bears no resemblance to W 1007 and it is hard to understand how the latter came to acquire its previous misleading title.

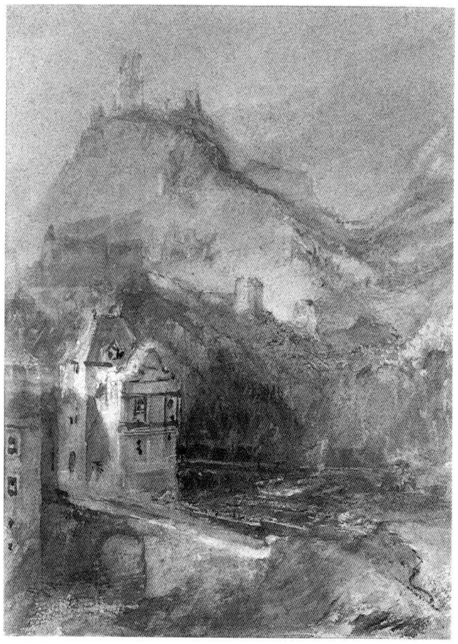

'The Enderttor and Alte Thorschenke, Cochem' (W 1007)

66 Cochem from Cond *c.*1839

Gouache and watercolour on blue paper
139 × 190 ($5\frac{1}{2} \times 7\frac{1}{2}$)
TB CCLIX 160
D24725
EXH & LIT: National Gallery Exhibited Drawings no.427d; Finberg (1909), p.798 (as 'Dinant', *c.*1826–33); Madrid (1983), no.64 (as 'Dinant?', *c.*1834?)

This complex scene can be related to two very detailed full-page pencil sketches, drawn on the river bank opposite Cochem at Cond (TB CCXC 5v, 6r). These show clearly the charm of Cochem with the jagged ruins of its vast castle and the softer outline of the baroque parish church soaring above the cluster of narrow-fronted gabled houses lining the river. In the sketch on f.5v two solitary tourists – like Turner himself – appear to be admiring the view just after sunset; these do not feature in the gouache but human interest is added here by the group of minute figures at lower right and the entire scene appears to be bathed in a warm twilight.

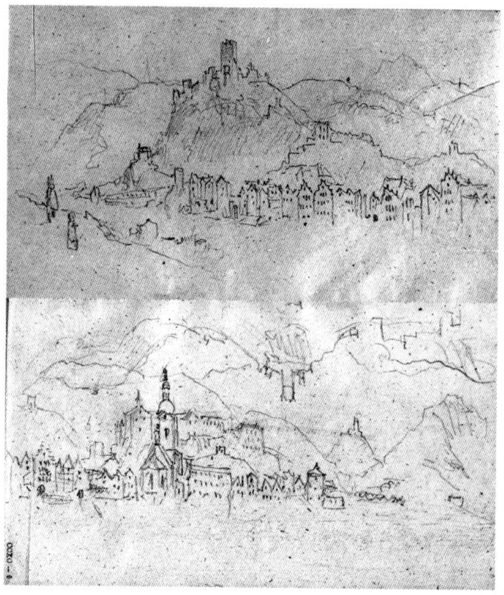

Cochem (TB CCXC 5v, 6r)

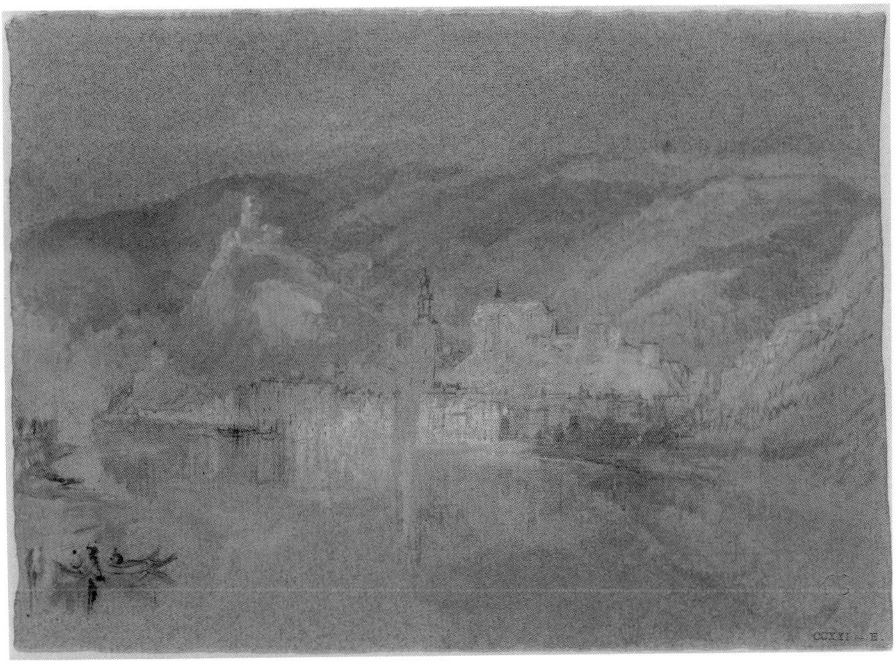

67 Cochem from the North *c.*1839

Gouache and watercolour on blue paper
140 × 190 ($5\frac{1}{2} \times 7\frac{1}{2}$)
TB CCXXI E
D20238
EXH & LIT: National Gallery Exhibited Drawings no.178 (as 'Rhine(?)'); Ruskin (1903–12), vol.XIII, p.386 ('Delicate, and very lovely'); Finberg (1909), p.688 (as 'Castle on rock. Probably on the Moselle', *c.*1826)

In this gouache (which can be related to two pencil sketches, TB CCXCI 6r, 6v) Turner shows Cochem from downstream with the break in the hills caused by the valley of the Endert visible on the right. Also given prominence in this view is the large building immediately next to St Martin's church, a seventeenth-century Capuchin church and monastery which was recorded in the 1840s as being a school (Quin, 1843, vol.II, p.49). Both the colouring and the execution of this gouache make it one of the most refined and jewel-like of the series.

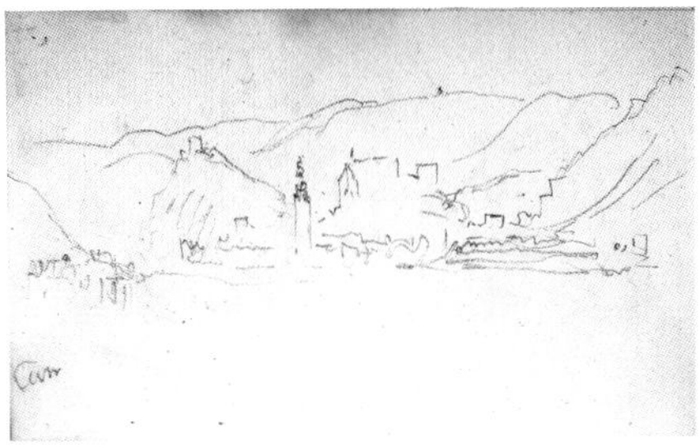

Cochem (TB CCXCI 6v)

68 Distant View of Cochem* *c.*1839

Gouache and watercolour on blue paper
141 × 190 ($5\frac{9}{16} \times 7\frac{1}{2}$)
TB CCLIX 158
D24723
EXH & LIT: National Gallery Exhibited Drawings no.427c; Finberg (1909), p.798 (as 'On the Meuse(?)', *c.*1826–33); Madrid (1983), no.61 (as 'On the Meuse', *c.*1834)

This final, ethereal view of Cochem, with its magical washes of colour, can hardly be regarded as based on a pencil sketch. However, the very spare one on TB CCXCI 7r would perhaps have served Turner as a reminder of his final view of the town bathed in light and glowing with brilliant colour.

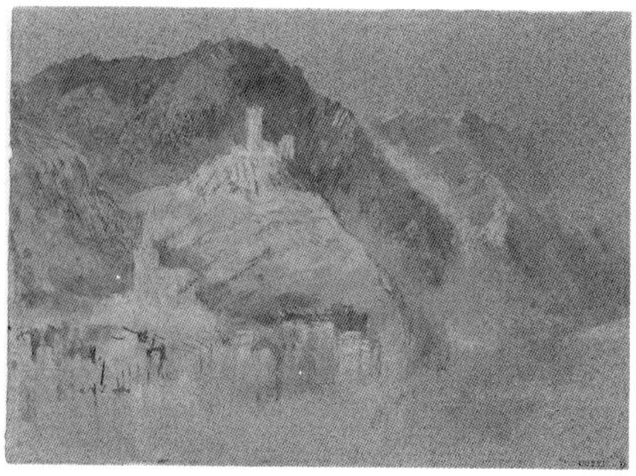

69 Klotten and Burg Coraidelstein from the West* *c.*1839

Gouache and watercolour on blue paper
140 × 189 ($5\frac{1}{2} \times 7\frac{7}{16}$)
TB CCXXI D
D20237
EXH & LIT: National Gallery Exhibited Drawings no.177 (as 'Rhine (?)'); Ruskin (1903–12), vol.XIII, p.386 ('Too red and yellow. Full of power in form'); Finberg (1909), p.688 (as 'Berncastel and the Landshut', *c.*1826); London (1975), no.110 (as 'Berncastel and the Landshut', *c.*1827); Athens (1981), no.28 (as 'Bernkastel and the Landshut', *c.*1827); Luxembourg (1984), no.44 (as *c.*1834)

In this gouache, based on Turner's pencil sketch on TB CCXCI 7v, the Gothic church of St Maximin at Klotten and the ruins of Burg Coraidelstein are seen from slightly upstream. From here Klotten appears the epitome of serenity, the Burg apparently rising from a gentle slope. The most dynamic area of the gouache is the hillside in the middle distance. In his pencil sketch Turner had captured the effects of brilliant sunlight on the rocks with bold but economical hatching; this is translated into pure colour in the gouache, creating a stunningly powerful effect.

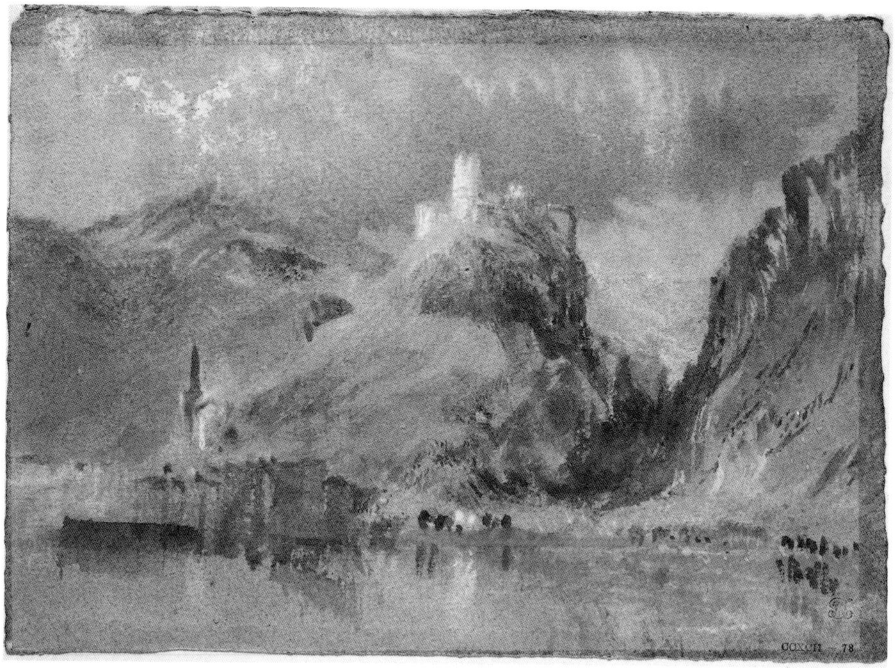

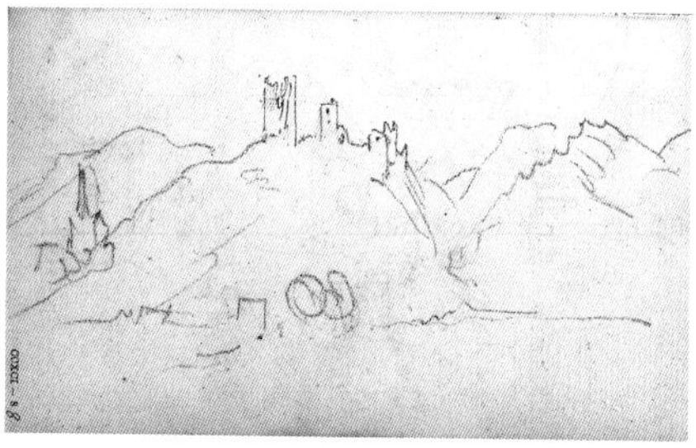

Klotten (TB CCXCI 8r)

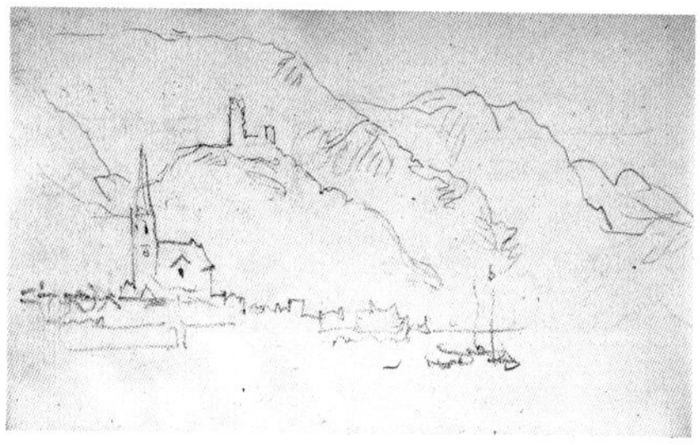

Klotten (TB CCXCI 7v)

70 Klotten and Burg Coraidelstein from the East *c.*1839

Gouache and watercolour on blue paper
143 × 191 ($5\frac{9}{16} \times 7\frac{1}{2}$)
TB CCXCII 78
D29029
EXH & LIT: National Gallery 3rd Loan Collection, 1869–1931, no.108; Finberg (1909), p.943 (as 'River scene', *c.*1834)

Shortly after drawing the pencil sketch on which cat.no.69 was based, Turner drew another little sketch (TB CCXCI 8r) from slightly further downstream, which shows a very different aspect of Klotten. Burg Coraidelstein now appears precipitously perched on the brink of a steep and dangerous-looking rocky gorge, a view found also in other contemporary depictions of the village, such as the lithograph which had formed the frontispiece to Clarkson Stanfield's *Sketches on the Moselle* of 1838.

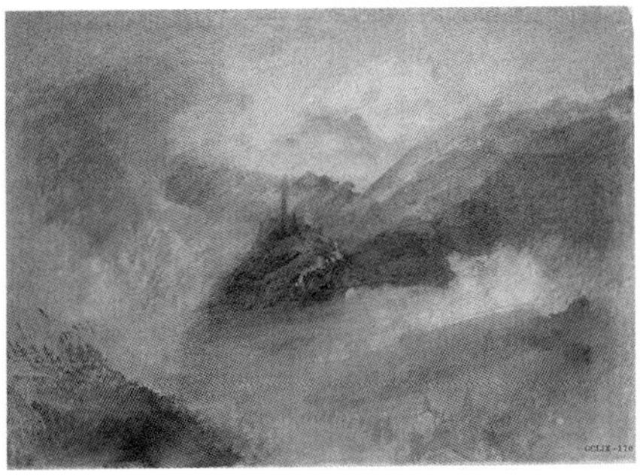

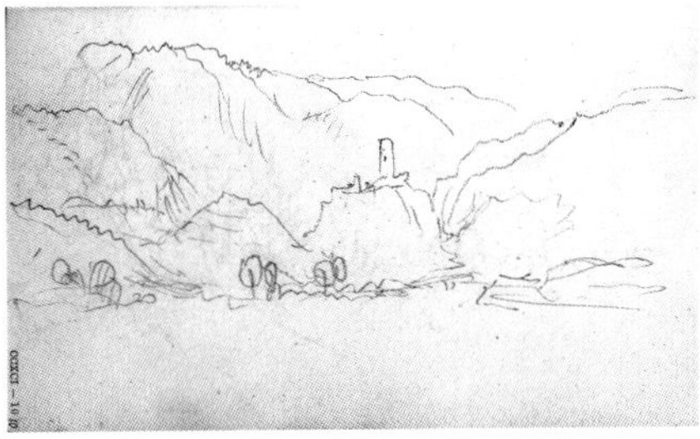

Burg Treis (TB CCXCI 10r)

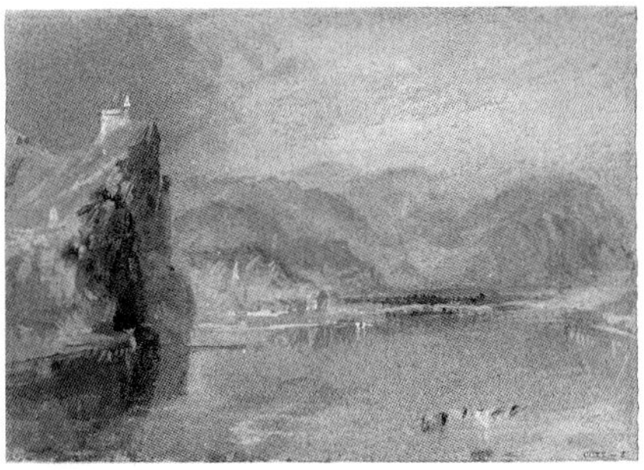

71 Burg Treis* *c.*1839

Gouache and watercolour on blue paper
140×190 ($5\frac{1}{2} \times 7\frac{1}{2}$)
TB CCLIX 170
D24735
EXH & LIT: National Gallery Exhibited Drawings no.430d; Finberg (1909), p.77 (as 'Tancarville(?)', *c.*1826–33)

Just upstream of Treis the traveller on the Mosel enjoys a very beautiful view of Burg Treis, situated on a conical hill at the entrance to the valleys of the Flaum and the Dunn or, as one writer has put it, 'in the midst of the hill-landscape opened like the petals of a rose to the eyes of him that can see' (Tower, 1913, p.304). Turner drew a minute sketch of this view in 1824 (TB CCXVI 124v), annotating it with the words 'Beaut. and light grey' and employing very delicate pencil hatching on the hills. He sketched it again in 1839 on a larger scale if somewhat less poetically (TB CCXCI 10r). His wonderfully subtle and mysterious gouache, probably painted directly over a pencil sketch, is an amalgam of these two visions, rendered more complex by the addition of buildings in the right foreground. On both occasions when Turner surveyed Treis his sketches of it were intermingled with those of Karden almost opposite (see cat.nos.72–3); these buildings may have been added as a reminder of Karden's proximity.

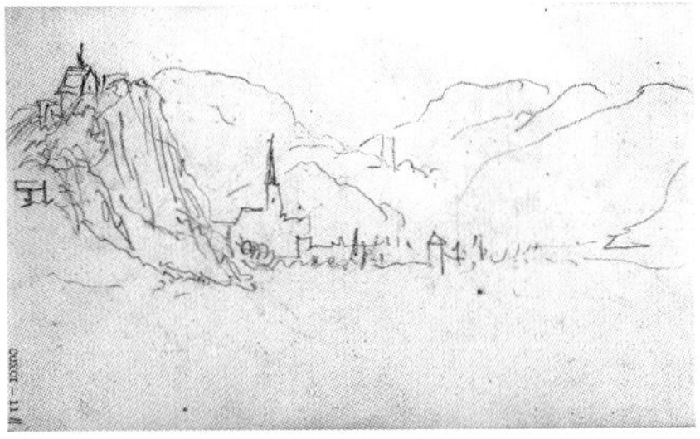

Treis (TB CCXCI 11r)

72 Treis from the North* *c.*1839

Gouache and watercolour on blue paper
136×190 ($5\frac{3}{8} \times 7\frac{1}{2}$)
TB CCXX Z
D20233
EXH & LIT: National Gallery Exhibited Drawings no.732; Finberg (1909), p.687 (as *c.*1826); Luxembourg (1984), no.45 (as *c.*1834)

Treis and Karden lie almost opposite to each other, so that Turner had to keep looking this way and that in order to sketch both of these towns as he travelled downstream (see TB CCXCI 9r–11v). His sketches led to two gouaches which record the very different ecclesiastical buildings in each town. Cat.no.72 is based on the pencil sketch on TB CCXCI 11r, drawn looking back at Treis as Turner travelled on past Karden. Prominent in it are the tiny and ancient Zilleskapelle, its precipitous and solitary hilltop situation somewhat exaggerated by Turner; the new church of St John the Baptist with its slender spire (designed by J.C. Lassaulx, consecrated in 1831, and described in 1843 (Quin, vol.II, p.51) as 'peculiarly elegant'); and the distant ruins of Burg Treis. The gouache is notable for its serene character and freshness of colouring, perhaps chosen to make a deliberate contrast with the somewhat stormy character of Turner's view of Karden.

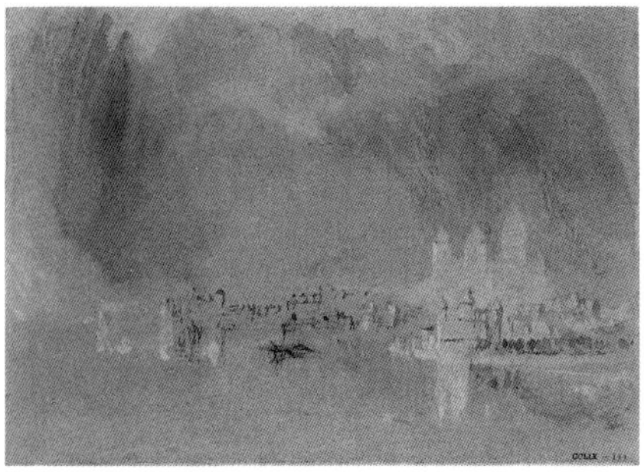

73 Karden from the North* *c.*1839

Gouache and watercolour on blue paper
139 × 193 ($5\frac{1}{2} \times 7\frac{9}{16}$)
Watermarked: B,E.../182...
TB CCLIX 144
D24709
EXH & LIT: National Gallery Exhibited Drawings no.382; Finberg (1909), p.797 (as 'On the Rhine(?)', *c.*1826–33); London (1975), no.111 (where it is dated '*c.*1827' and its resemblance to Karden is noted); Athens (1981), no.26 (as 'A town on the Moselle?', *c.*1827)

Karden abounds in fine old buildings and is dominated by the large Romanesque church of St Castor with its three lofty belfries. River travellers also enjoy views of an attractive and many-turreted sixteenth-century house (the 'Burghaus') right on the bank of the Mosel. Turner drew two pencil sketches of this ensemble in TB CCXCI: that on f.10v was drawn looking downstream as he approached the town, while that on f.11v (on which his gouache is based) was drawn looking back upstream just after he had passed the buildings. Almost immediately after this, the Mosel changes direction and both Treis and Karden are swiftly lost to view.

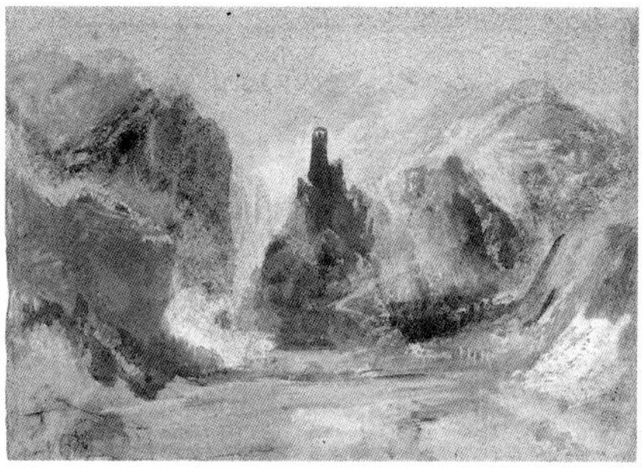

74 Burg Bischofstein* *c.*1839

Gouache and watercolour on blue paper
138 × 190 ($5\frac{7}{16} \times 7\frac{1}{2}$)
Watermarked: B,E.../182...
TB CCXCII 70
D29021
EXH & LIT: Finberg (1909), p.943 (as 'A mountain fortress', *c.*1834)

The tall cylindrical tower of Burg Bischofstein, which stands on a rugged ridge rising steeply from the river, is one of the most arresting sights on the entire Mosel and is visible for a considerable distance. Not surprisingly, Turner made many pencil sketches of it in both 1824 and 1839 (TB CCXVI 126r, 126v; TB CCXCI 13v–15v). Cat.no.74 is not based on any one pencil sketch in a sketchbook, though the left-hand part of that on TB CCXCI 14r might have provided Turner's starting-point. The softly rounded hills adjacent to Burg Bischofstein, and so very different from its own rocky perch, are shown on TB CCXCI 15v and also on TB CCXVI 126v. On this last page the very conspicuous darkness of the tower, more forbidding than any other on the Mosel, is rendered by fine hatching and the sketch also shows a lower, square ruin on the hillside behind the castle. This would not have been visible in the downstream view given in Turner's gouache but here, as in so many other scenes, he has enriched his composition by including as much about its subject as he possibly could.

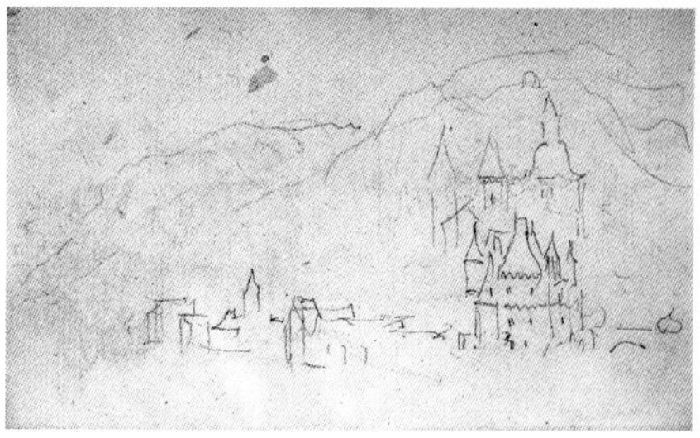

Karden (TB CCXCI 11V)

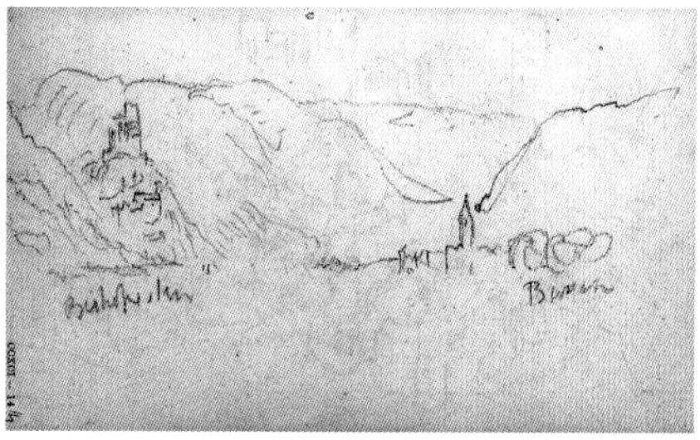

Burg Bischofstein (TB CCXCI 14r)

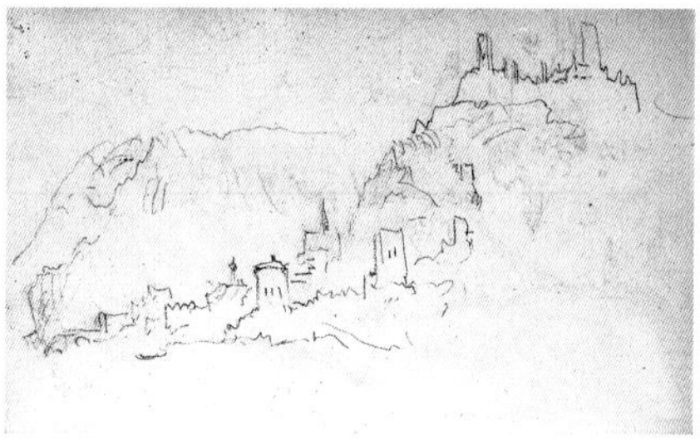

Alken (TB CCXCI 18v)

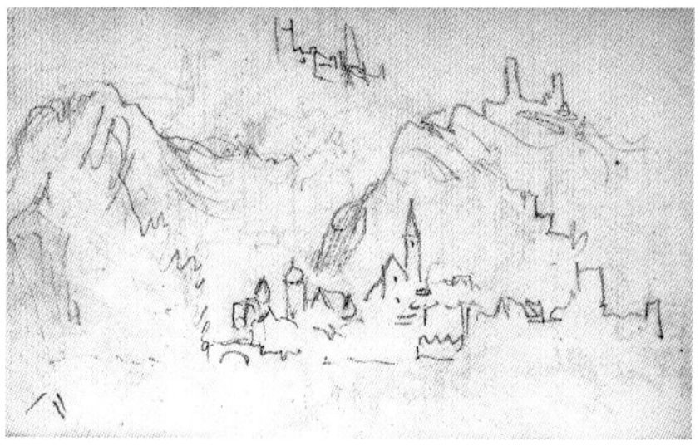

Alken (TB CCXCI 20V)

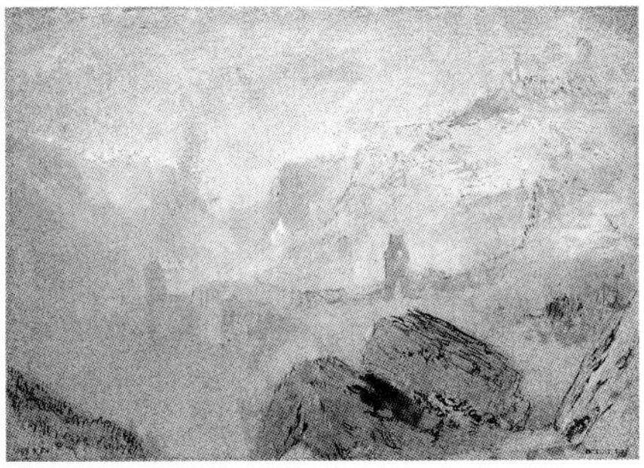

75 Alken and Burg Thurandt from the South *c.*1839

Gouache and watercolour on blue paper
139 × 190 ($5\frac{1}{2} \times 7\frac{1}{2}$)
TB CCXCII 72
D29023
EXH & LIT: Finberg (1909), p.943 (as 'Daybreak among the Mountains', *c.*1834); London (1974), no.382 (as 'Towers among Mountains: Daybreak', ?*c.*1828); International Exhibitions Foundation (1977–8), no.46 (as 'Daybreak among the Mountains', ?*c.*1834, and erroneously reproduced as cat.no.45); Luxembourg (1984), no.56 (as 'Bacharach?', *c.*1834)

This work has eluded identification in the past largely because of the indistinctness of its topography, barely visible through the layers of impasto. However, the ruined castle at top right with its twin towers can only be Burg Thurandt; while the rendering of the rocky terrain, ancient riverside gates and walls, and distant church spire all have parallels in Turner's pencil sketches of Alken (TB CCXCI 18r and especially 18v, drawn as the town first came into sight as he travelled downstream). The foreground rocks do not appear in these sketches but are typical of the neighbourhood; Turner added similar rocks to his other gouache of the same town (TB CCXX P; cat.no.76).

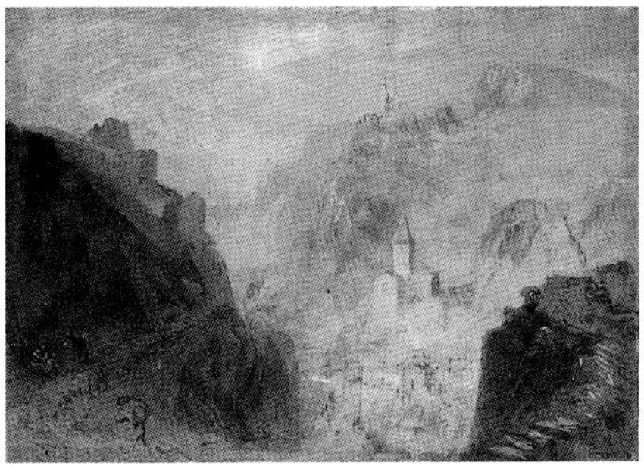

76 Alken and Burg Thurandt from the North* *c.*1839

Gouache and watercolour on blue paper
137 × 190 ($5\frac{3}{8} \times 7\frac{1}{2}$)
Watermarked: B, E . . ./182 . . .
TB CCXX P
D20223
EXH & LIT: National Gallery Exhibited Drawings no.444a; Finberg (1909), p.687 (as 'Sketch in colour, possibly on the Meuse', *c.*1826); Brussels (1971), no.30 (as 'Sur la Meuse', 1826 or 1834); Texas (1982), no.38; Wilkinson (1975), p.83 (untitled); Luxembourg (1984), no.55 (as 'Bacharach?', *c.*1834)

This gouache combines features from two of Turner's many pencil sketches of Alken and Burg Thurandt (TB CCXCI 20V, 21r) to which a dramatically large (and topographically confusing) rock has been added in the right foreground. Turner himself toiled up the steep hillside north of the town across the Alkenerbachtal in order to get a better view of its buildings (see TB CCXCI 19r, 19v); recollections of that climb probably lie behind his inclusion of the struggling walker with his burden seen in the left foreground. Rather curiously, Turner's depiction of Burg Thurandt shows only the taller of its two towers, but his rendering of the thirteenth-century parish church dedicated to St Michael and the similarity of the gouache to his pencil sketches leave no doubts as to its subject.

Burg Thurandt

Gouache and watercolour on blue paper
139 × 191 ($5\frac{1}{2} \times 7\frac{1}{2}$)
TB CCXXII H
D20267
EXH & LIT: National Gallery 5th Loan Collection, 1896–1931, no.26; Finberg (1909), p.690 (as 'Rocky crag, with torrent (?)', *c.*1826)

In its ingredients and technique this gouache is very similar to Turner's other depictions of Alken and Burg Thurandt (cat.nos.75, 76), so there can be little doubt as to its subject matter. It has not, however, progressed nearly so far as those works and is interesting chiefly in showing Turner's work in an uncompleted state.

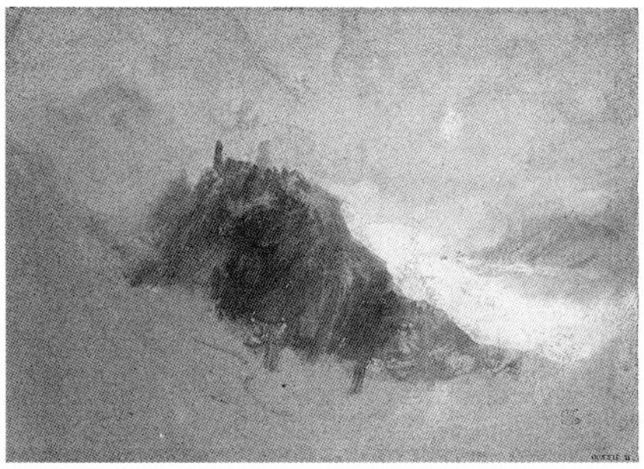

'Burg Thurandt' (TB CCXXII H)

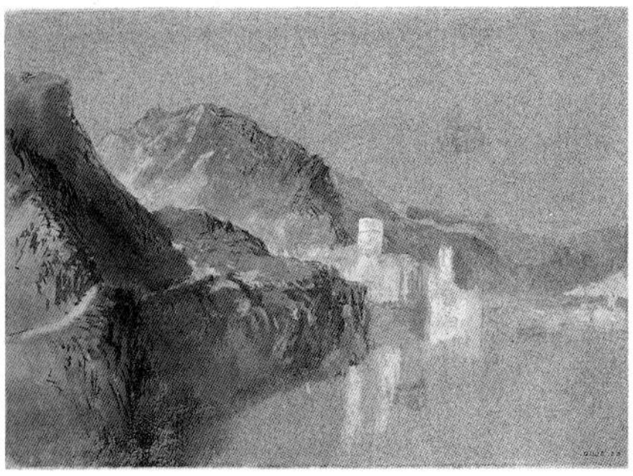

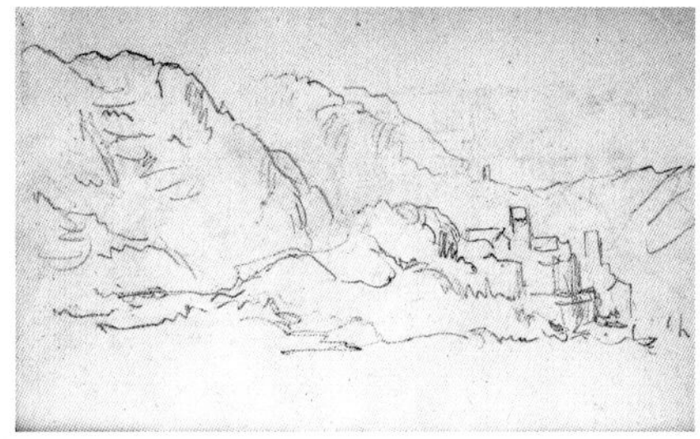

Gondorf (TB CCXCI 24v)

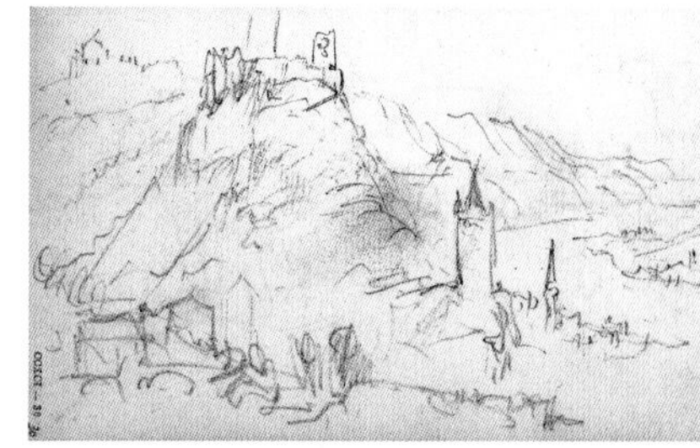

Kobern (TB CCXCI 30r)

77 **The Leyen Burg at Gondorf*** *c.*1839

Gouache and watercolour on blue paper
138 × 188 ($5\frac{7}{16} \times 7\frac{3}{8}$)
TB CCLIX 23
D24588
EXH & LIT: Finberg (1909), p.791 (as 'Mountains and castle beside river. Possibly on the Moselle', *c.*1826–33)

The Leyen Burg at Gondorf is the only castle on the Mosel that is situated immediately on the river bank and it presented a highly picturesque sight to river travellers before the castle complex was, quite literally, bisected by the Prussian engineers creating the Trier to Coblenz railway in 1876. Unlike most other castles on the Mosel, that at Gondorf was not a ruin but was maintained and occupied by the Counts of Leyen until the early nineteenth century. As Turner passed it, he made eight pencil sketches showing different aspects of its extensive Renaissance and neo-Gothic structures not only from the river but also from behind the castle (TB CCXCI 24v–27r; TB CCXXIV 91, 100). His gouache is based on the earliest of these, that on f.24v, and records the very strong impact it made on him as it first came into view. The sharp colouring of this gouache, its rock drawing and its rendering of light, shade and reflections through the juxtaposition of brilliant colours are all found again in one of the gouaches of Dinant on the Meuse (cat.no.96); this demonstrates not only the unity of the series but also the fact that Turner worked on the scenes in batches that cut across their topographical subject matter.

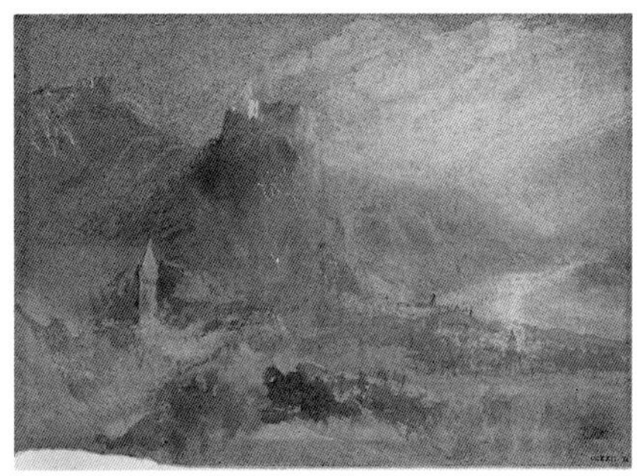

78 **Kobern from the South*** *c.*1839

Gouache and watercolour on blue paper
138 × 188 ($5\frac{7}{16} \times 7\frac{3}{8}$)
TB CCXXII L
D20271
EXH & LIT: National Gallery 5th Loan Collection, 1896–1931, no.44 (as 'View on Rhine, &c'); Finberg (1909), p.690 (as 'Ruined castle on lofty crag, with town below, beside river (?Moselle)', *c.*1826); Luxembourg (1984), no.50 (as *c.*1834)

Turner explored the towns of the Mosel far more thoroughly on his second tour than he had in 1824 when he stuck closely to the riverside. This gouache shows the solitary Romanesque bell-tower of Kobern and its two castles from a viewpoint significantly different from those of his three pencil sketches (TB CCXCI 28v, 30r; TB CCXXIV 138) and may perhaps be regarded as an artistic 'improvement' on them done from memory. Its colour scheme is utterly different from that of the gouache depicting Kobern's neighbour, Gondorf, but its pinks, mauves and greens are found in many others in the series, and it is particularly close to one view of Luxembourg (TB CCXXII Z).

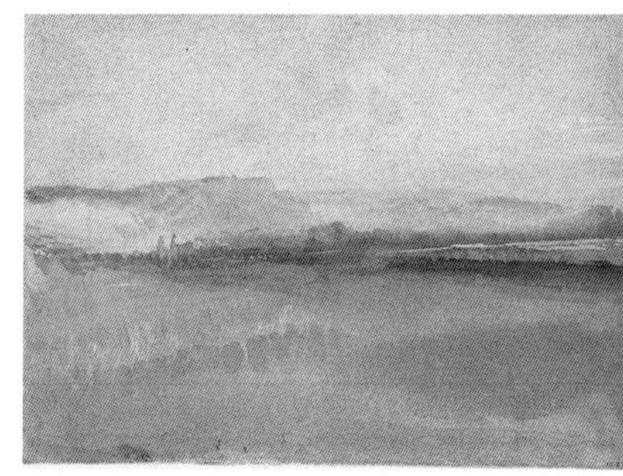

79 **Distant View of Coblenz and Ehrenbreitstein** *c.*1839

Gouache and watercolour on blue paper
Watermarked: B, E . . ./182 . . .
139 × 190 ($5\frac{1}{2} \times 7\frac{1}{2}$)
TB CCXXII B
D20261
EXH & LIT: Oxford Loan Collection no.132/215; Finberg (1909), p.690 (as *c.*1826); Clifford (1977) (unpag, as 'Moselle', 1834); Cologne (1980), no.46; Luxembourg (1984), no.51 (as *c.*1834)

The distant silhouette of Ehrenbreitstein, high above the confluence of the Rhine and the Mosel, was visible for miles to the traveller journeying down the Mosel. Turner recorded it several times in pencil sketches in TB CCXCI but his brilliantly coloured gouache does not correspond precisely to any of these and is, above all, a generalised and impressionistic recollection of his experiences.

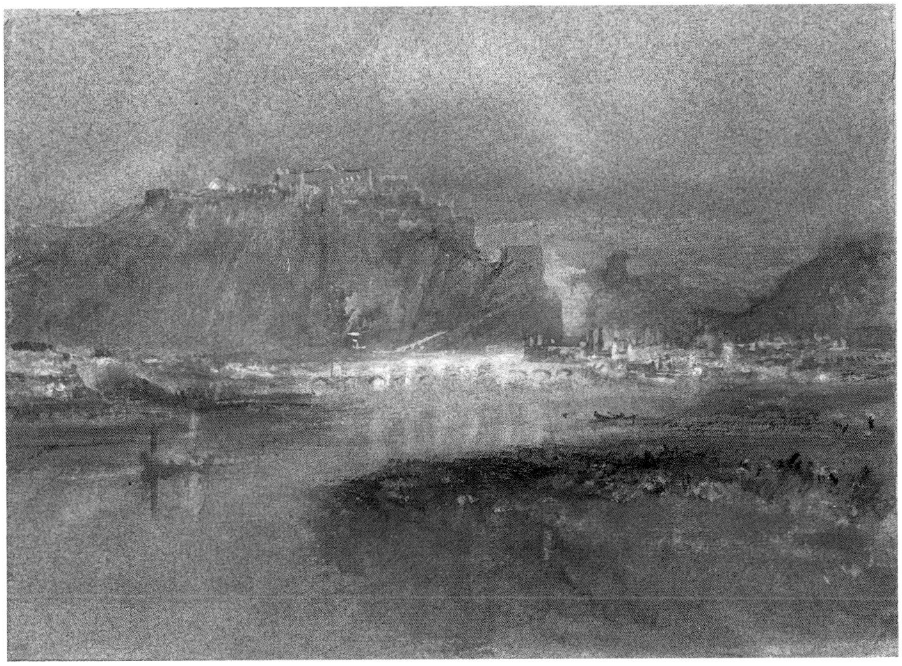

'Coblenz and Ehrenbreitstein from the Mosel' (W 1034)

Coblenz and Ehrenbreitstein from the Mosel *c.*1839

Gouache on blue paper
138 × 189 ($5\frac{7}{16} \times 7\frac{7}{16}$)
PROV: . . .; Henry Vaughan Bequest, National Galleries of Scotland, Edinburgh (D(NG)879)
W 1034
EXH & LIT: Armstrong (1902), p.252; National Gallery of Scotland (1980), pp.16–17

With this gouache Turner's Mosel series reaches a triumphant conclusion and, unlike TB CCXXII B (cat.no.79), it follows a pencil sketch in TB CCXCI, that at the top of f.34v. The Mosel is here seen placidly rounding the last of its many curves to flow beneath the arches of the ancient stone bridge – in Turner's day the only bridge over the river since that at Trier recorded in the first of his series, TB CCLIX 150 (cat.no.47) – and finally to merge its waters with those of the Rhine.

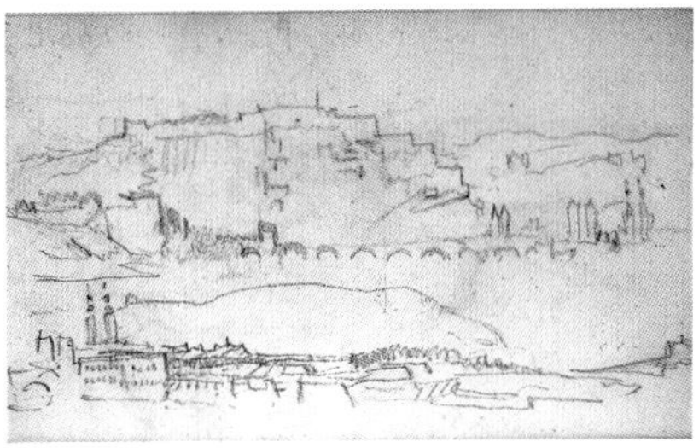

Coblenz and Ehrenbreitstein (TB CCXCI 34V)

Other German Subjects

Turner does not appear to have produced a complete series of gouaches depicting the Rhine at the same time that he painted those showing the Meuse and the Mosel. However, the Turner Bequest contains three of Ehrenbreitstein and one of the town of Mayen seen as Turner crossed the Eifel from Coblenz to Cochem, demonstrating that his interest in Germany in 1839 was not exclusively focused on the Mosel.

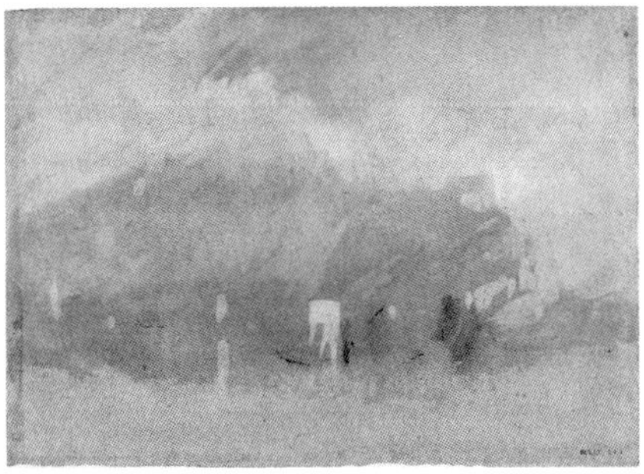

80 Ehrenbreitstein from Coblenz *c.*1839

Gouache and watercolour on blue paper
141 × 192 ($5\frac{9}{16} \times 7\frac{9}{16}$)
TB CCLIX 244
D24809
EXH & LIT: National Gallery 5th Loan Collection, 1896–1931, no.6 (as 'Riverside castle, Richmond, Yorks(?)'); Finberg (1909), p.804 (as 'Castle on cliff', *c.*1826–33)

81 Ehrenbreitstein from Coblenz* *c.*1839

Gouache and watercolour on blue paper
141 × 192 ($5\frac{9}{16} \times 7\frac{9}{16}$)
TB CCLIX 268
D24833
EXH & LIT: Finberg (1909), p.805 (as 'River scene, with ruined castles', *c.*1826–33)

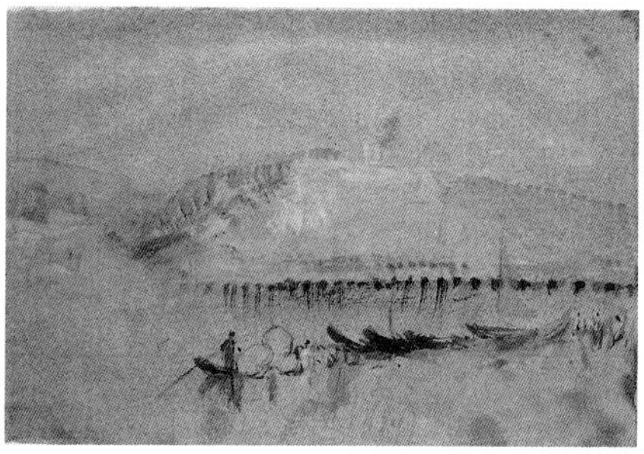

82 Ehrenbreitstein from Coblenz *c.*1839

Gouache and watercolour on blue paper
137 × 194 ($5\frac{3}{8} \times 7\frac{5}{8}$)
TB CCLIX 239
D24804
EXH & LIT: National Gallery 5th Loan Collection, 1896–1931, no.7; Finberg (1909), p.803 (as 'River scene, with boats', *c.*1826–33)

None of these three gouaches has previously been recognised for what it really is, but there can be no mistaking the fortress of Ehrenbreitstein, the large domed church of the Holy Cross and the bridge of boats – all so familiar from other sketches and drawings by Turner (see especially cat.nos.128–32). Taken together, the three gouaches show a wide-angled view from the same viewpoint – or very similar ones – in the extended horizontal format often found in topographical views of rivers. Turner would have been familiar with many different examples of this genre and he would undoubtedly have seen numerous Rhine views conforming to this pattern – especially those of Wenzel Hollar (1607–77) – in the print shops of Coblenz. Thus, despite their free handling and their expressive, forward-looking colours, the views are in fact deeply rooted in the artistic traditions of the past, as was the case with much of Turner's most avant-garde work in the late 1830s.

The three views appear to be Turner's only Rhine scenes in gouache on blue paper (others, such as W 1031, are topographically so indistinct that it remains unclear to which series they really belong). They are similar in their dynamic handling to sketches of similar segments of the same riverscape from the same viewpoint in the *First Mossel and Oxford* sketchbook (TB CCLXXXIX 4r, 6r). There can thus be no doubt that they are contemporary with the other gouaches in this exhibition relating to sketches of the Meuse and Mosel in the four other sketchbooks used on the same tour.

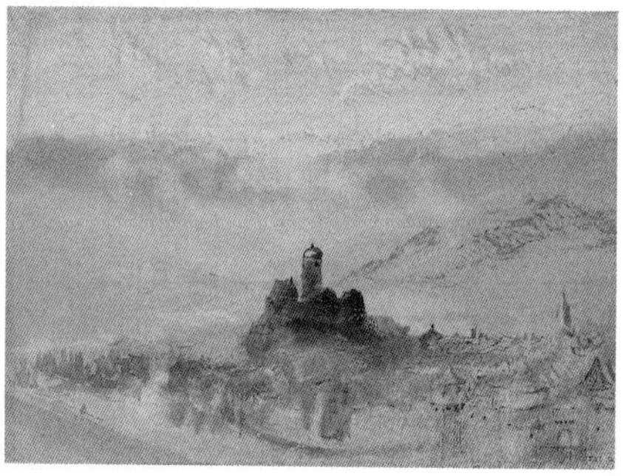

83 Mayen in the Eifel* *c.*1839

Gouache and watercolour on blue paper
141 × 188 ($5\frac{9}{16} \times 7\frac{3}{8}$)
TB CCXXI U
D20254
EXH & LIT: Finberg (1909), p.689 (as 'Town from river, with fortress on hill beyond', *c.*1826); Wilkinson (1975), p.83 (untitled)

The small town of Mayen was the subject of four pencil sketches in the *Trèves to Cochem and Coblenz to Mayence* sketchbook (TB CCXC 42v, 43r, 43v and 43v–44r) which provided Turner with all the necessary information to produce this stunning sunset scene, dominated by the vast black hulk of the Genovevaburg, a fortified castle built for one of the Archbishops of Trier between 1280 and 1311. Late nineteenth-century photographs of Mayen show both the town and the castle very much as Turner did, but the visitor there today finds it sadly altered: nearly 90 per cent of the town was destroyed in the Second World War and it has subsequently been reconstructed and expanded almost beyond recognition. In the foreground Turner shows the medieval town walls, with the Brückentor at lower right, above which can be seen St Clement's church with its twisted spire. Both these buildings have now been faithfully reconstructed.

Mayen is situated on neither the Mosel nor the Rhine but between the two, about halfway between Cochem and Sinzig. It lies in the Eifel, a bleak undulating plateau of volcanic origin, rich in castles and other historic buildings. Turner evidently felt the Eifel was worth exploring for its own sake for he wrote a page-long pencil memorandum on it in another sketchbook, probably used on an earlier tour (TB CCXCI(a) 68r). According to the note on TB CCXC 43r, Turner was under the impression that Mayen was 'built by Julius Caesar' – an opinion not mentioned in modern guidebooks but on a par with many other nineteenth-century beliefs about the Rhineland, e.g. that the Godesburg was built by the Emperor Julian; that Constantine's vision of the Cross occurred near Mainz – or alternatively near Neumagen; that Caligula was born at Moselweiss, and numerous other fictions.

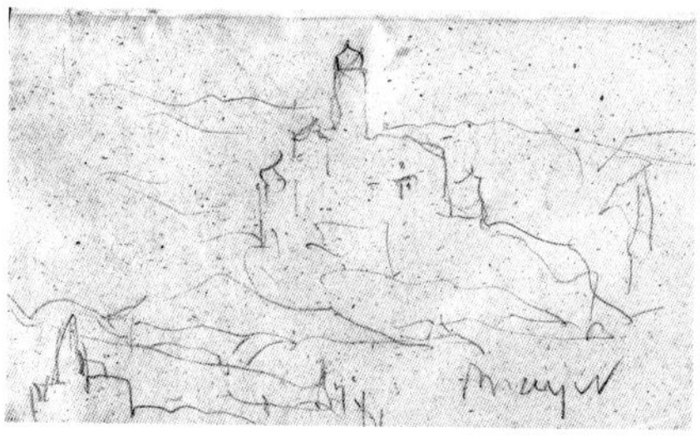

Mayen (TB CCXC 42v)

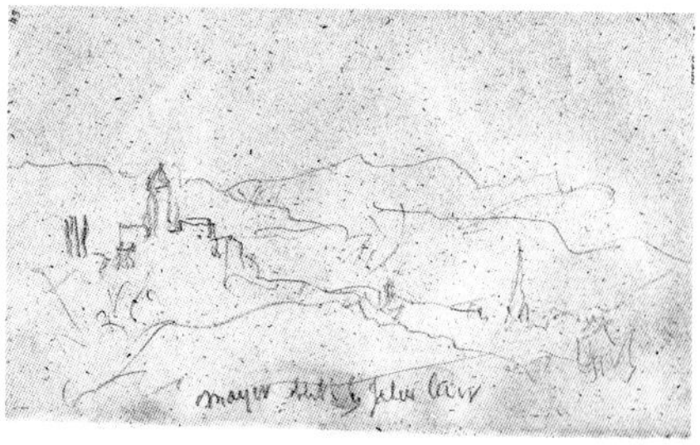

Mayen (TB CCXC 43r)

The Meuse from Liège up to Sedan

Turner's gouaches of the Meuse are here presented in a sequence taking the viewer upstream from Liège to Sedan, the direction of Turner's own tour both in 1824 and in 1839. Whereas his Mosel series includes many different towns and castles, it will at once be seen that along the Meuse and in the Ardennes he focused his attention on a comparatively small number of towns, sometimes painting as many as half-a-dozen different gouaches of the same place from a variety of viewpoints.

Three other gouache scenes in the Turner Bequest may perhaps form part of this series but their identifications are not yet regarded as certain. TB CCLIX 157 may perhaps depict the castle of Chokier; TB CCLIX 165 could be an impressionistic view of Verdun; TB CCLIX 243 may be a second view of Mézières.

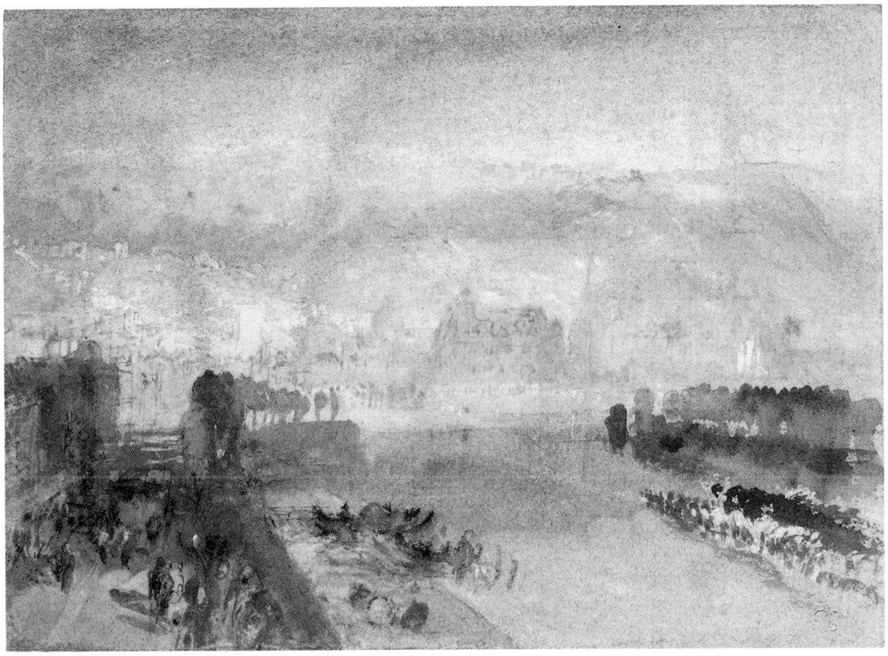

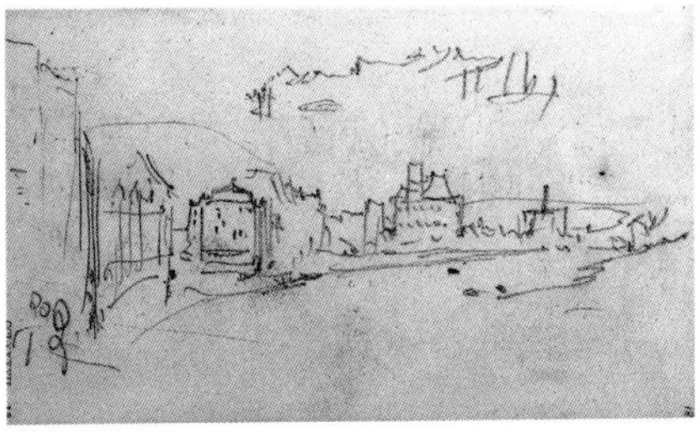

Liège (TB CCLXXXVII 18r)

84 Liège from the Pont des Arches* *c.*1839

Gouache, pen and ink, and watercolour on blue paper
141 × 191 ($5\frac{9}{16} \times 7\frac{1}{2}$)
TB CCLIX 99
D24664
EXH & LIT: National Gallery Exhibited Drawings no.123; Finberg (1909), p.794 (as 'Town on river', *c.*1826–33); International Exhibitions Foundation (1977–8), no.34 (as 'A Town on the Bend of a River', ?*c.*1826, with the suggestion that it shows Liège)

This view of Liège brings together a number of ingredients found in various Turner sketches in a fanciful but nonetheless pleasing fashion. The large house at the centre – with its steeply pitched roof, tall chimney on the left and close array of windows – is an embellished version of the Maison Curtius of *c.*1600 which also occupies the centre of his sketch on TB CCLXXXVII 18r. To its right can be seen the edge of the hill occupied by the citadel which slopes gently away exactly as it does in many of his sketches in the same book (ff.13r, 15v, 16v). Among the spreading houses on the left one can distinguish a square tower and a low dome which may perhaps have been intended to recall the Tour St Denis and St Andrew's church. The quay downstream of the Pont des Arches would certainly have been a very busy place in Turner's day, with both people and boats continually on the move; the wooded area shown on the right is part of the Outremeuse, the long island in the Meuse which lies at the heart of Liège.

85 Distant View of Liège with Factories *c.*1839

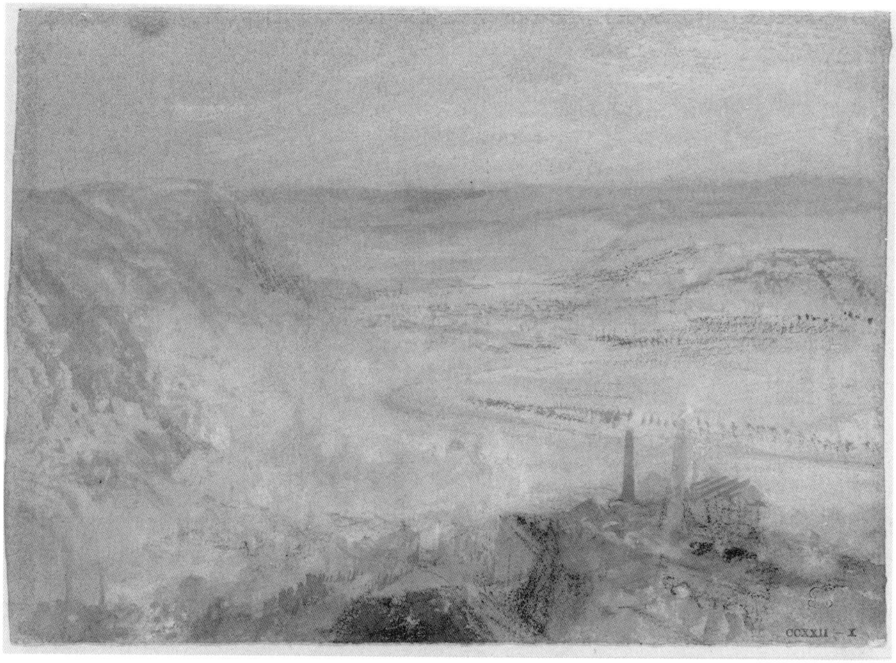

Gouache and watercolour on blue paper
137 × 190 ($5\frac{3}{8} \times 7\frac{1}{2}$)
TB CCXXII X
D20283
EXH & LIT: National Gallery 6th Loan Collection, 1896–1931, no.27; Finberg (1909), p.691 (as 'Bird's-eye view of valley, river, and town', *c.*1826); Luxembourg (1984), no.23 (as 'Vue de Luxembourg (?): la vallée de l'Alzette, Eich, Weimerskirch, Dommeldange (?)', *c.*1834(?))

By Turner's day Liège was already a thriving industrial centre with numerous ironworks and manufactories, the most celebrated being those established by the Cockerill family of Lancashire. William Cockerill (1759–1832) settled in Liège in 1807 and opened factories making spinning and weaving machinery for use at Verviers, the centre of Belgium's cloth industry. In 1817 his son John (1790–1840) created at Seraing on the south-western edge of Liège the largest iron foundry and machine factory on the Continent. The building in Turner's gouache is probably not this factory itself, however, but another establishment nearby.

This composition is based on the quick pencil sketches on TB CCLXXXVII 16v and 17r. Since these show merely the bare bones of the scene, the whole of the vast painted prospect, with its innumerable touches of colour, must have been based on memory.

Huy from the Liège Road *c.*1839

Gouache, pen and ink, and watercolour on blue paper
140 × 194 ($5\frac{1}{2} \times 7\frac{5}{8}$)
PROV: Thomas Griffith; Charles Stokes, 1850; by descent to Hannah Cooper; from whom bought by John Ruskin, 10 February 1858 for fifty guineas; by whom presented to the University of Cambridge, 1861 (under the terms of this gift the work may not be loaned for exhibition elsewhere); Fitzwilliam Museum, Cambridge
W 1024
EXH & LIT: Thornbury (1862), vol.2, p. 396 and (1877), p.593 (as 'On the Meuse'); Armstrong (1902), p.258;

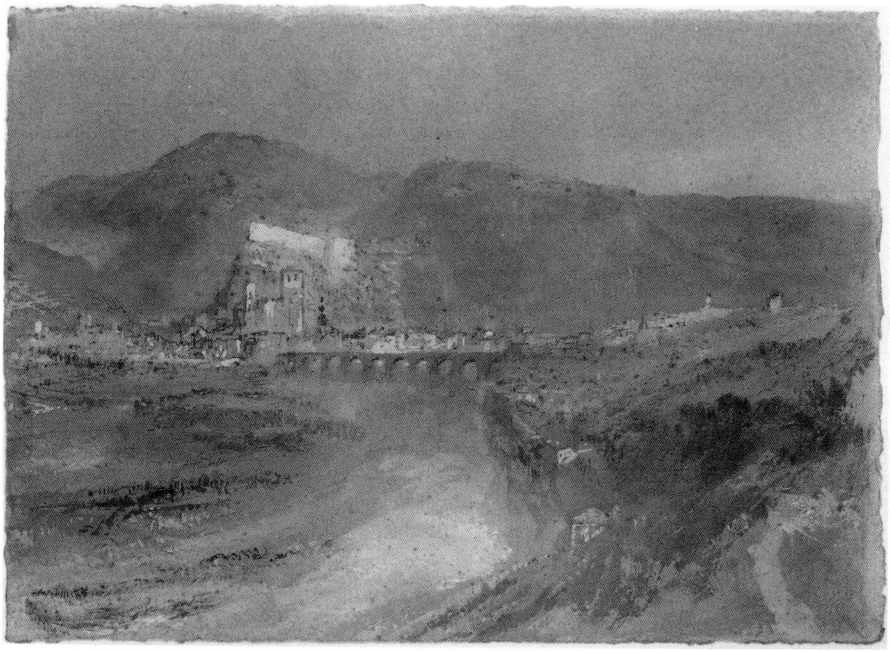

'Huy from the Liège Road' (W 1024)

Ruskin (1903–12), vol.XIII, pp.557 (no.80 or 81, 'On the Meuse'), 558 ('Real first-rate'), 601; Finberg (1909), p.671; exhibited at the Fitzwilliam Museum, 1959; Herrmann (1970), p.696; Cormack (1975), p.57 (where dated '*c*.1827–34'); Wilton (1979), p.168, pl.183 (as *c*.1825–34)

In 1839 Turner approached Huy by road from Liège, making several pencil sketches of the town and its citadel seen above the Meuse which here sweeps round in one of its most magnificent curves (one on a loose sheet of blue paper, TB CCXXIV 20, and three in his sketchbook, TB CCLXXXVII 48v, 49r, 49v). His gouache is closest to those drawn furthest away from Huy, especially that on f.49v which shows both the ample foreground vegetation (annotated 'Vines') and the grassy islands in the river which play such a conspicuous and delightful part in the gouache. However, it is not identical to this and may well be painted on top of yet another pencil sketch. It includes many architectural features not clearly visible from such a distance but found again and again in Turner's many sketches of Huy and essential ingredients in a town portrait such as this.

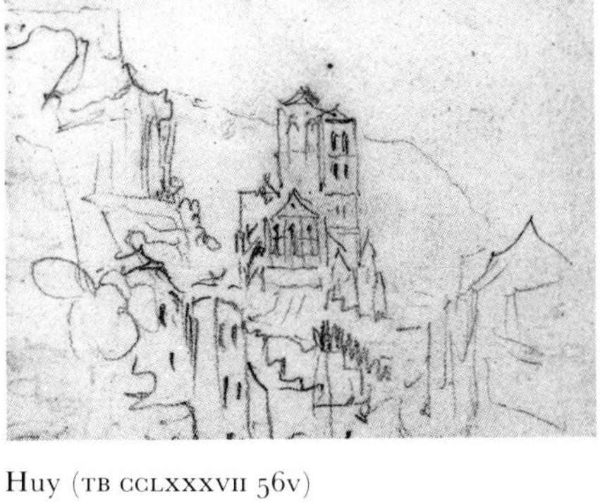

Huy (TB CCLXXXVII 56v)

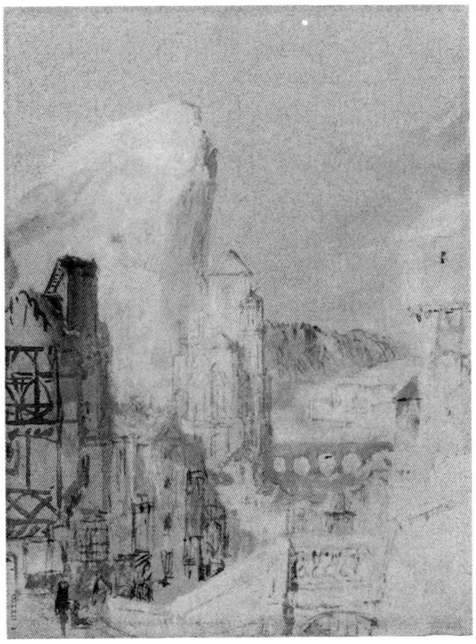

86 Notre-Dame, Huy *c*.1839

Gouache, pen and ink, and watercolour on blue paper
188 × 139 ($7\frac{3}{8} \times 5\frac{1}{2}$)
TB CCXXII I
D20268
EXH & LIT: National Gallery 5th Loan Collection, 1896–1931, no.22; Finberg (1909), p.691 (as 'Town (Rhine or Moselle?) with lofty crag', *c*.1826)

Although much of the detail in this gouache sprang from Turner's fancy, it is very close to a small pencil sketch showing the apse and towers of the collegiate church of Notre-Dame at Huy (1311–1536), constructed hard up against the precipitous cliffs that are a dramatic feature of so many parts of the Meuse. This sketch (on TB CCLXXXVII 56v) was drawn from the Place St-Denis, on the way up to La Sarte, a high viewpoint to the south-east of Huy which Turner used for the sketches leading to two other gouaches in this series, TB CCXX N and CCXX S (cat.nos.87 and 88). Such excursions away from the banks of the Meuse and the Mosel were a special characteristic of his second tour of these two rivers, distinguishing it sharply from his earlier tour on which he had kept much more closely to the rivers themselves. From the Place St-Denis it is impossible to see up the Meuse and must have been so even in Turner's day, but this has not deterred him from showing both the river and Huy's famous bridge in his composition.

The most fanciful aspect of this gouache – one of only four in the series to emphasise the abrupt contours of the terrain by using a vertical format – is the complete absence of the fort of Huy from the cliff above the church. It is perhaps worth remembering that, although these cliffs have nearly always been dominated by some sort of fortification since at least the eleventh century, they were not occupied in this way for an entire century not so very far removed from the time of Turner's visits, i.e. between the demolition of the old fort following the Treaty of La Barrière (1715) and the rebuilding of the fort by the English and the Dutch between 1818 and 1824. Perhaps, with the advent of real peace in Belgium in 1839, Turner deliberately portrayed Huy as a picturesque old town, free from external threats and once more enjoying an era of tranquillity, just as he undoubtedly did in two of his gouaches of Namur (see cat.nos.93 and 94).

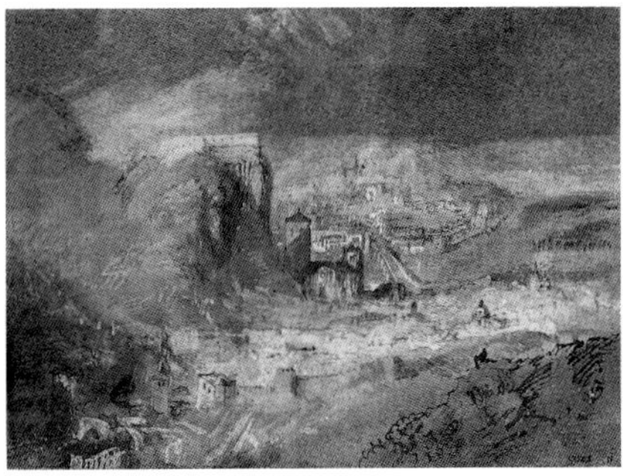

87 Huy from the South-east* *c*.1839

Gouache, pen and ink, and watercolour on blue paper
136 × 184 ($5\frac{3}{8} \times 7\frac{1}{4}$)
TB CCXX N
D20221
EXH & LIT: National Gallery Exhibited Drawings no.39b; Ruskin (1903–12), vol.XIII, p.587; Finberg (1909), p.686 (as *c*.1826); Brussels (1971), no.28; Luxembourg (1984), no.27 (as *c*.1834)

Both this gouache and the following (TB CCXX S; cat.no.88) show Huy from outside the town walls to the south-east where the plateau of La Sarte afforded Turner a superb view, nowadays unfortu-

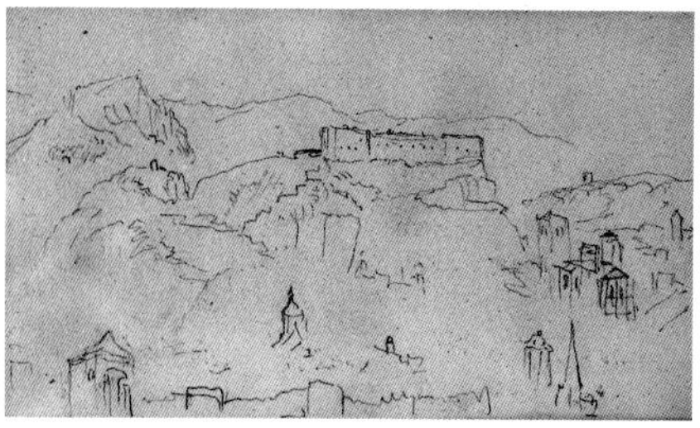

Huy (TB CCLXXXVII 50v)

nately obscured by trees. The gouache is closely based on Turner's pencil sketch on TB CCLXXXVII 50v, but he has enlivened the town walls at lower left by the addition of a few buildings included in a sketch from slightly further away in the same general direction (f.53v).

The palette of this drawing has several elements characteristic of Turner's Belgian gouaches as a whole such as the yellow and orange, together with the sugary pink found in 'Kobern' in the Mosel series (cat.no.78) and several of the Luxembourg scenes. Its expressive scarlet pen work has parallels both elsewhere in the Meuse set and in those of the Mosel. All these crosscurrents indicate that Turner worked on the scenes in small groups after he had returned home, rather than individually at the places depicted.

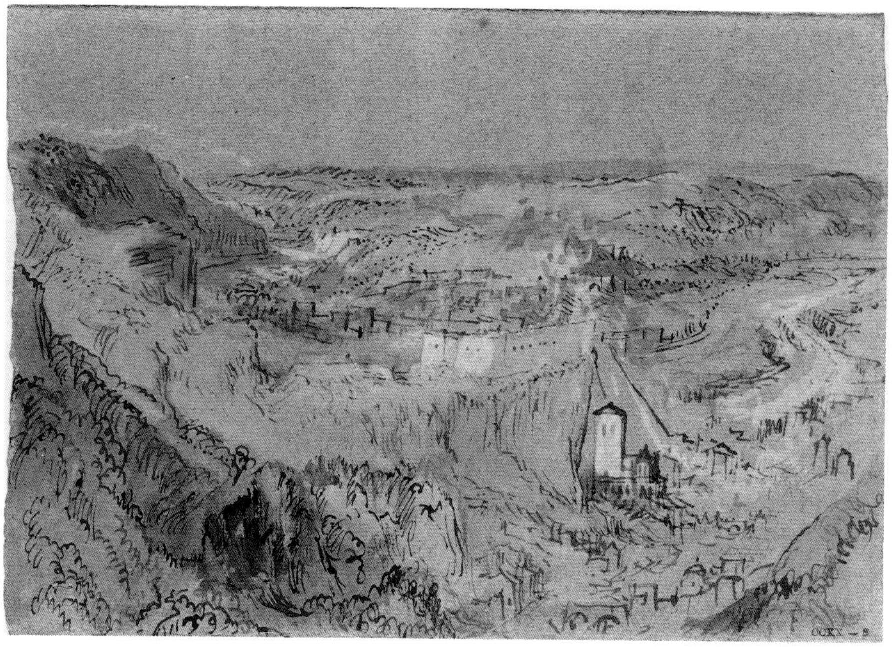

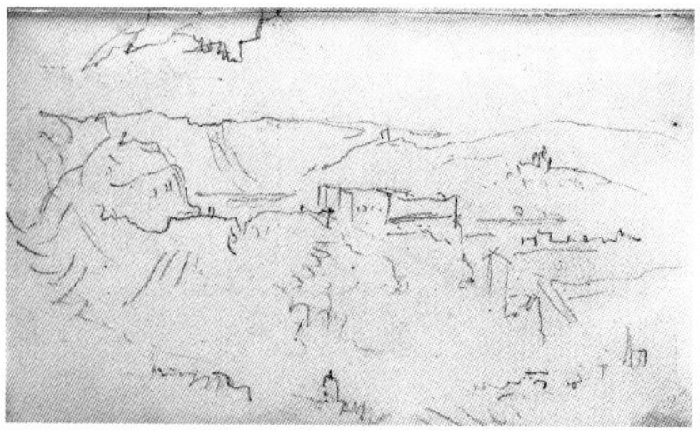

Huy (TB CCLXXXVII 8v)

88 Huy from the South-east: Bird's-eye View *c.*1839

Gouache, pen and ink, and watercolour on blue paper
139 × 191 ($5\frac{1}{2} \times 7\frac{1}{2}$)
TB CCXX S
D20226
EXH & LIT: National Gallery Exhibited Drawings no.617b; Finberg (1909), p.687 (as *c.*1826); Luxembourg (1984), no.26 (as *c.*1834)

Turner's viewpoint here is even higher than that used for TB CCXX N (cat.no.87) – so much so that the mighty fort overlooking Huy now appears well below the horizon line, almost at the centre of the gouache. To the right of the fort the parallel lines of the bridge over the Meuse can clearly be seen, as too can the vast curve of the river as it flows north-east towards Liège. The gouache is broadly based on his rough pencil sketch on TB CCLXXXVII 8v, virtually all the architectural details which have been added from memory being of a very schematic nature.

The swiftly executed pen work found here is a characteristic feature of many of Turner's Belgian and Luxembourg gouaches but is much less prevalent in those of the Mosel. Here it animates the entire scene, bringing the broad areas of colour sharply into focus as credible ingredients in a naturalistic scene.

89 Huy from the West *c.*1839

Gouache and watercolour on blue paper
138 × 187 ($5\frac{7}{16} \times 7\frac{3}{8}$)
TB CCXX O
D20222
EXH & LIT: National Gallery Exhibited Drawings no.444d; Finberg (1909), p.686 (as *c.*1826); Brussels (1971), no.29; Texas (1982), no.37; Luxembourg (1984), no.28 (where wrongly associated with TB CCXVI 41v, as *c.*1834)

Both this gouache and TB CCXXIII C (cat.no.90) show Huy from the west, as seen by the traveller rounding the curve of the Meuse beneath Mont Picard and looking downstream to the widest facade of the fort – that turned towards France – and the sturdy west tower of the church. In this view, which is similar to the pencil sketch on TB CCLXXXVII 51v, Turner's viewpoint is neither the river itself nor the river bank but a path up on the hillside, the contours of which he has freely remoulded in order to give greater prominence to the distant town. In its handling and palette this is closer to some of Turner's Mosel gouaches than to his other depictions of Huy, and it has a much more ethereal character.

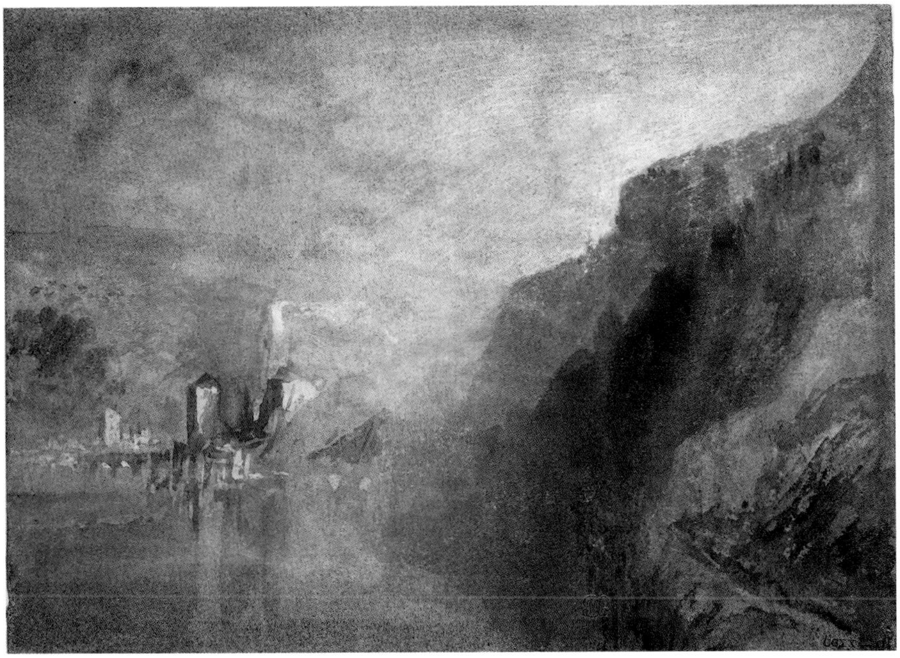

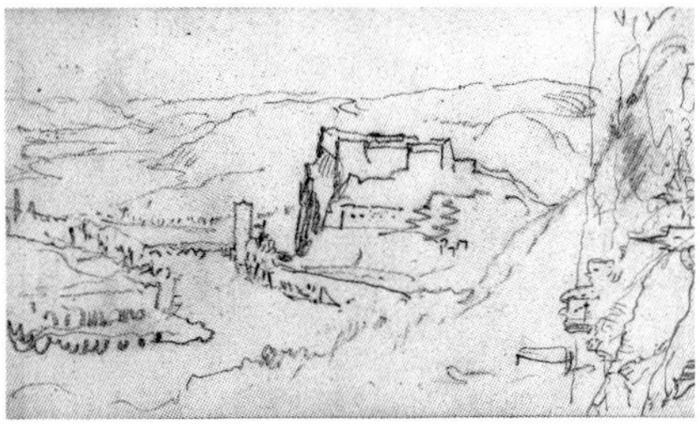

Huy (TB CCLXXXVII 51V)

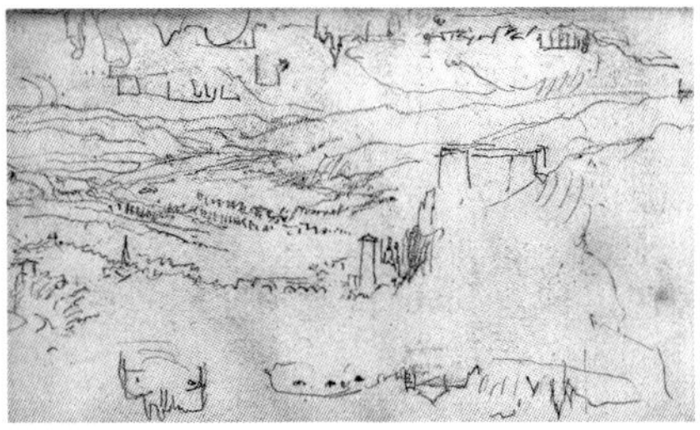

Huy (TB CCLXXXVII 52V)

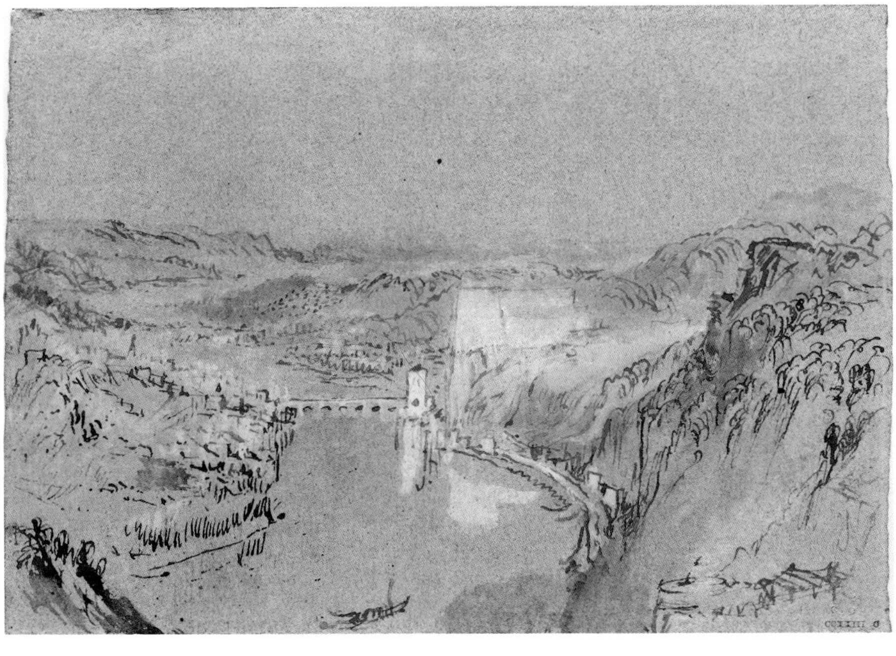

90 Huy from the West: Bird's-eye View *c.*1839

Gouache, pen and ink, and watercolour on blue paper
140 × 195 ($5\frac{1}{2}$ × $7\frac{11}{16}$)
TB CCXXIII C
D20288
EXH & LIT: Finberg (1909), p.692 (as 'Namur(?)', *c.*1826); Luxembourg (1984), no.29 (as *c.*1834)

This gouache shows a similar view to TB CCXX O (cat.no.89), albeit painted in a very different style. However, its viewpoint is further away from Huy and much higher on the hillside, close to that used for the pencil sketch on TB CCLXXXVII 52V. Although the surface of Turner's scene is enlivened by a great deal of very dynamic pen drawing (which assumes as many different styles and angles as his handwriting – compare fig.12 on p.21), the work as a whole has a limpid tranquillity thanks to the narrow range of its colours, applied in the thinnest of washes.

91 **Rocks on the Meuse at Marche-les-Dames** *c.*1839

Gouache and watercolour on blue paper
137 × 189 ($5\frac{3}{8} \times 7\frac{7}{16}$)
TB CCXXII C
D20262
EXH & LIT: National Gallery 2nd Loan Collection, 1869–1931, no.116b; Finberg (1909), p.690 (as 'Scene on Moselle', *c.*1826)

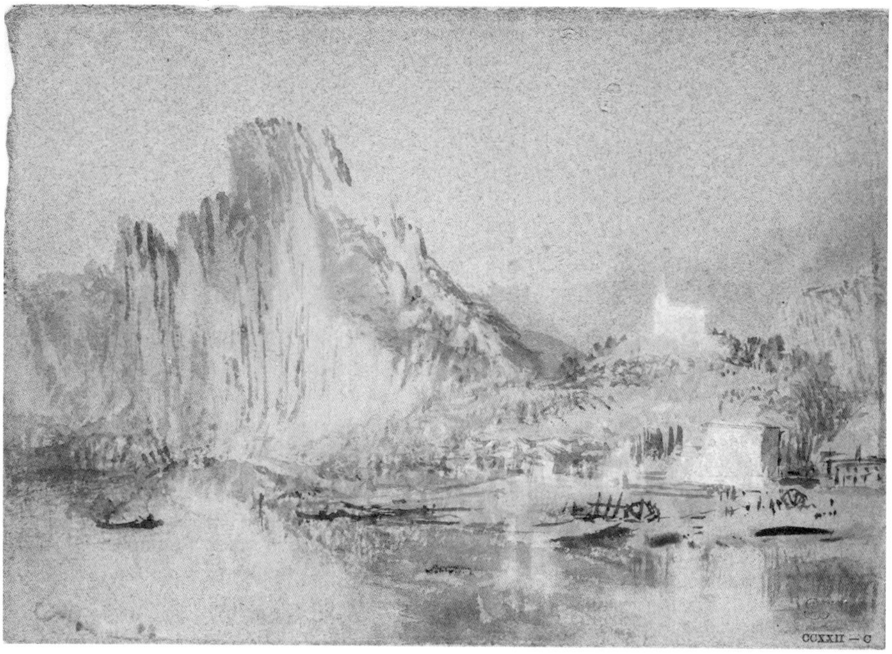

There can be few villages which have had such a chequered history as Marche-les-Dames, situated some five miles downstream from Namur. According to Baedeker, its romantic name derives from the foundation of an abbey in 1101, in an adjacent side-valley, 'by 139 noble ladies, the widows of Crusaders who had accompanied Godfrey de Bouillon to the Holy Land'. Today the area closest to the Meuse is occupied by a commando training camp and is largely inaccessible, but all the ingredients of Turner's gouache (based on the pencil sketch on TB CCLXXXVII 46v–47r) may nevertheless be identified, partly through the help of nineteenth-century prints and photographs. The imposing house on the river bank was the château of the Prince d'Arenberg. It was built in the early nineteenth century by Jean-Joseph Jaumenne, the great ironmaster of the Napoleonic empire, and it was destroyed by Belgian troops in 1914 for strategic reasons. The tiny church on the adjacent mound is today totally obscured by a grove of trees, while the jagged and precipitous cliffs which encircle the site attract the attention of scores of rockclimbers.

Whereas many of the Belgian scenes are notable for their bold pen and ink work, whether in a bright or sombre colour, in this drawing Turner has used gouache, lightly applied with a brush, to show both the characteristic fissures in the oolitic cliffs and all the details of both buildings and the riverside. The resulting crisscross effect is unusual in Turner's gouaches but the pinkness of his rocks here is similar to that in other scenes on both the Meuse (cat.no.92) and the Mosel (cat.no.49).

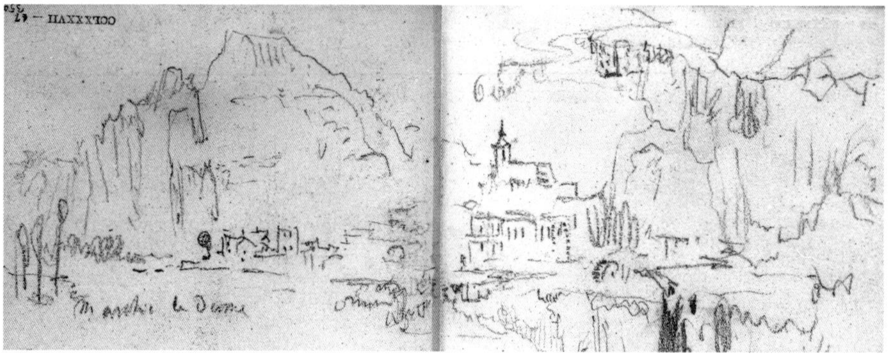

Marche-les-Dames (TB CCLXXXVII 46v–47r)

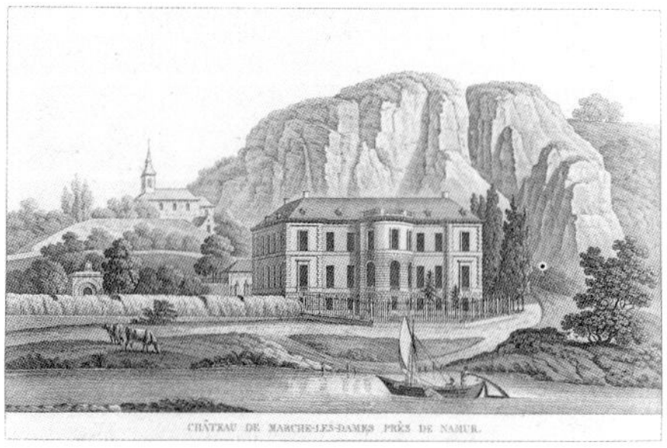

P.J. Goetchebuer, 'Château de Marche-les-Dames près de Namur', engraving from *Choix de monuments, édifices et maisons les plus remarquables du royaume des Pays Bas*, Ghent, 1827

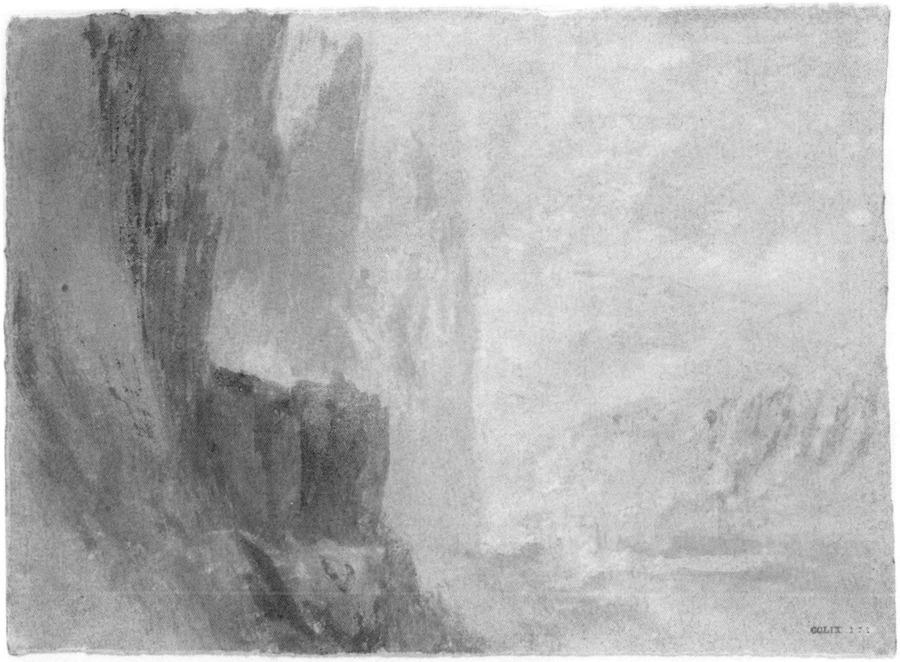

92 **Rocks on the Meuse** *c.*1839

Gouache and watercolour on blue paper
140 × 190 ($5\frac{1}{2} \times 7\frac{1}{2}$)
TB CCLIX 171
D24736
EXH & LIT: National Gallery Exhibited Drawings no.431a; Finberg (1909), p.799 (as 'Chalk rocks on the Meuse', *c.*1826–33)

It is impossible to say precisely where on the Meuse these rocks are situated, unless one postulates that they include the Roche à Bayard south of Dinant, an identification which is not wholly satisfactory (see cat.nos.99, 100). What is certain, though, is that Turner's gouache is a colouristic feast with innumerable touches of warm and neutral hues juxtaposed to provide a convincing depiction of the rich red cliffs that delight visitors to the Meuse. The perpendicular markings shown by Turner are a special feature of these limestone rocks and were also recorded by other visiting artists of his generation such as George Arnald.

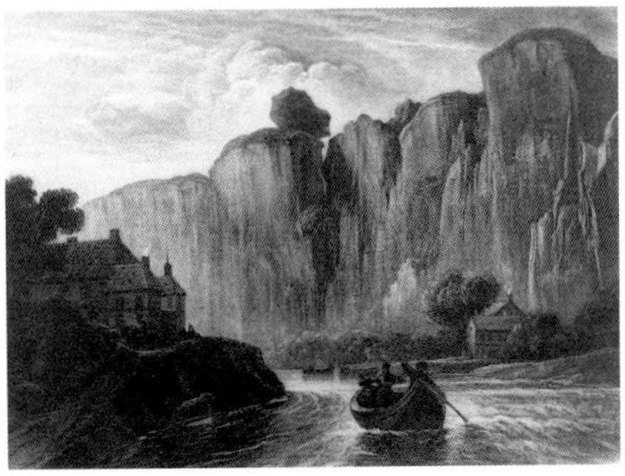

George Arnald, 'Left Bank, Meuse', mezzotint from *Picturesque Scenery on the River Meuse*, 1835

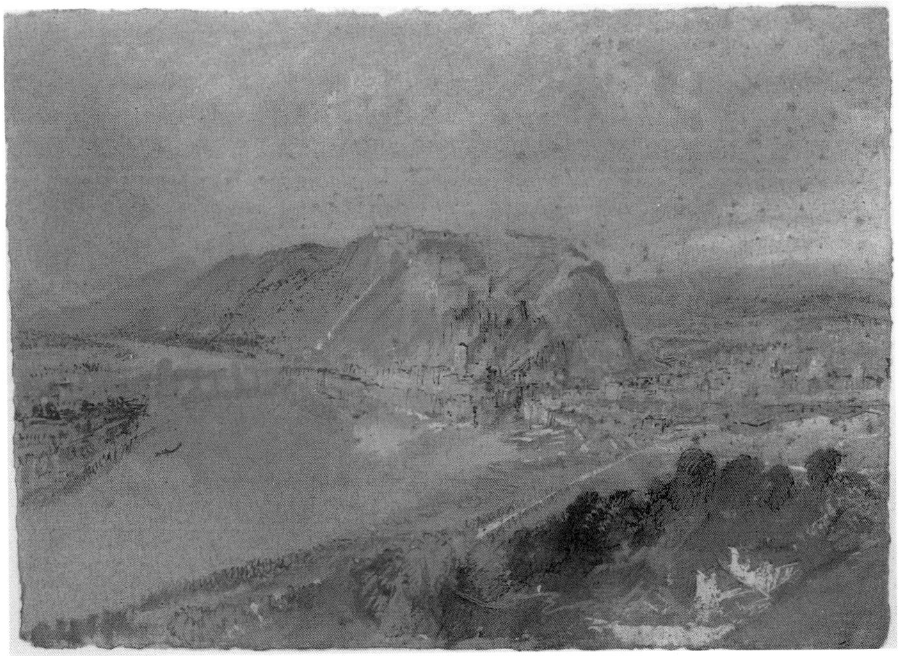

'Namur from the Liège Road' (W 1025)

Namur from the Liège Road *c.*1839

Gouache, pen and ink, and watercolour on blue paper
140 × 190 ($5\frac{1}{2} \times 7\frac{1}{2}$)
PROV: Thomas Griffith; Charles Stokes, 1850; by descent to Hannah Cooper; from whom bought by John Ruskin, 10 February 1858 for fifty guineas; by whom presented to the University of Cambridge, 1861 (under the terms of this gift the work may not be loaned for exhibition elsewhere); Fitzwilliam Museum,

University of Cambridge
W 1025
EXH & LIT: Thornbury (1862), vol.2, p.396 and (1877), p.593; Armstrong (1902), p.267; Ruskin (1903–12), vol.XIII, pp.558 ('Very fine'), 603; Finberg (1909), pp.685, 693; exhibited at the Fitzwilliam Museum 1959; Herrmann (1970), p.696; Cormack (1975), pp. 55–6 (where dated 'c.1827–34')

Of Turner's three gouaches of Namur this provides the most distant view and thus highlights the essentials of its topographical importance. The town lies at the confluence of the Meuse, seen on the left, and the very much smaller Sambre, distinguishable here only by the four tiny semicircles indicating its bridge. A long line of steep hills terminates abruptly above the confluence, providing the perfect site for a fortress. In the early 1790s Namur succumbed to French troops after three sieges and became the capital of the Department of Sambre et Meuse. After Napoleon's defeat the old fort was demolished and the years between 1816 and 1825 saw the construction of the gigantic replacement seen here, which was to be demolished in the second half of the nineteenth century.

The viewpoint of Turner's gouache is close to that used for his pencil sketch on blue paper TB CCXXIV 19 and for two of those in the *Spa, Dinant and Namur* sketchbook (TB CCLXXXVII 45r, 45v). It may well be painted over another pencil sketch also drawn on the spot.

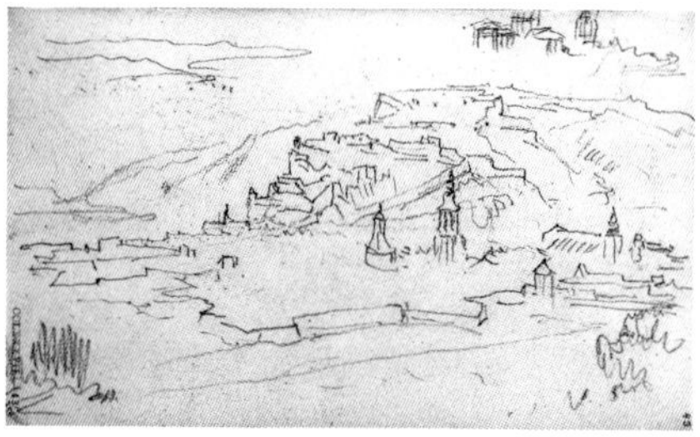

Namur (TB CCLXXXVII 43r)

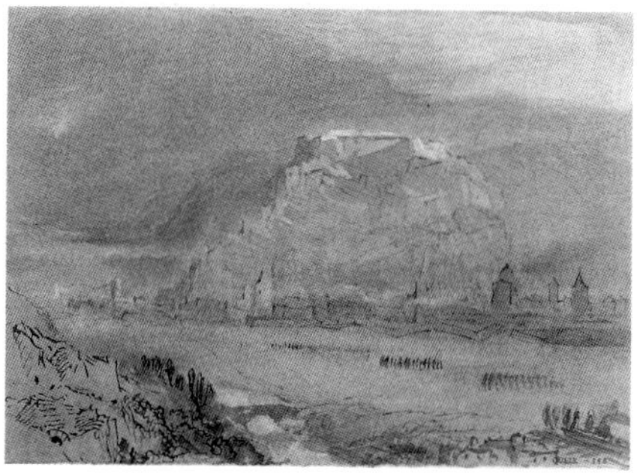

93 Namur from the Fields* *c.*1839

Gouache, pen and ink, and watercolour on blue paper
141 × 192 ($5\frac{9}{16} \times 7\frac{9}{16}$)
TB CCLIX 146
D24711
EXH & LIT: National Gallery Exhibited Drawings no.384; Finberg (1909), p.797 (as *c.*1826–33); Brussels (1971), no.63; International Exhibitions Foundation (1977–8), no.42 (as 'Namur, with the Fortress Seen from Across the River', *c.*1834); Madrid (1983), no.62; Luxembourg (1984), no.31 (where wrongly associated with TB CCXVII 12v, 13r, as *c.*1834)

The domes and towers of Namur, girdled by walls and crowned by its vast new citadel, were a sight that appealed to numerous artists and travellers of the nineteenth century when they viewed the city across the fields coming from Liège. From here, neither the Meuse nor the Sambre is visible: the Sambre curves its way between the city and the fort, while the Meuse sweeps towards it out of sight on the left. Turner's drawing is based on his pencil sketch on TB CCLXXXVII 43r (a similar view, from a slightly different angle, occurs on f.44v). Its execution is much broader than that of W 1025 and its colouring more muted, the twilight lavender used for the distant city being reminiscent of that in cat.no.47, depicting Trier.

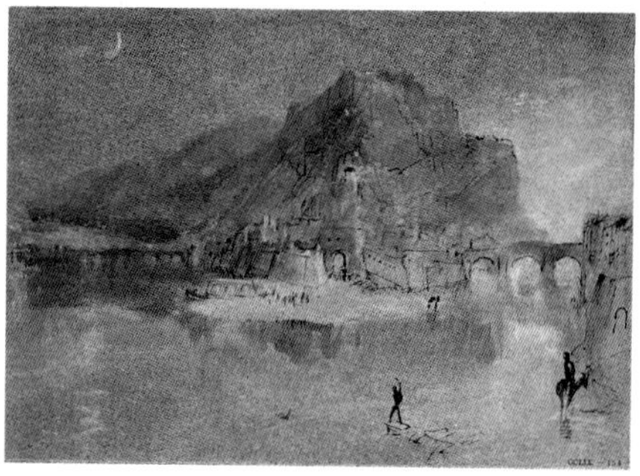

94 The Confluence at Namur: Moonlight* *c.*1839

Gouache, pen and ink, and watercolour on blue paper
142 × 191 ($5\frac{9}{16} \times 7\frac{1}{2}$)
TB CCLIX 151
D24716
EXH & LIT: National Gallery Exhibited Drawings no.389; Finberg (1909), p.798 (as *c.*1826–33); Brussels (1971), no.64; International Exhibitions Foundation (1977–8), no.43 (as 'Namur: The Fortress by Moonlight', *c.*1834); Wilton (1982), no.66 (as *c.*1834); Madrid (1983), no.63; Luxembourg (1984), no.30 (where wrongly associated with TB CCXVII 14, as *c.*1834)

In this highly evocative drawing Turner's viewpoint is similar to that of the tiny dark figure in his foreground, ankle deep in the cool waters of the Meuse on a warm night under a new moon. Above him, the mighty fortress of Namur on its rocky spur guards the confluence of the broad Meuse with its long, many-arched bridge and the Sambre, much magnified here, with its huddle of ancient houses. At this historic spot – besieged, sacked and rebuilt countless times over the centuries – all is now, for a moment at least, completely at peace.

All the ingredients in Turner's scene can be found, in two instalments, in his pencil sketch on TB CCLXXXVII 41r. It seems very likely, however, that a swift pencil sketch, with the same material properly arranged, underlies the painted image. A beautiful feature of this work is the disposition of the light with the soft shadows of the left-hand side providing a perfect foil to the gleaming radiance of the right. Many of the Meuse and Mosel scenes incorporate similar contrasts, since if one river bank was shown in bright sunlight the opposite bank would necessarily have been in shadow. To use such a compositional device for a confluence of rivers – and to put the smaller river under the limelight, as Turner does here – was a stroke of genius.

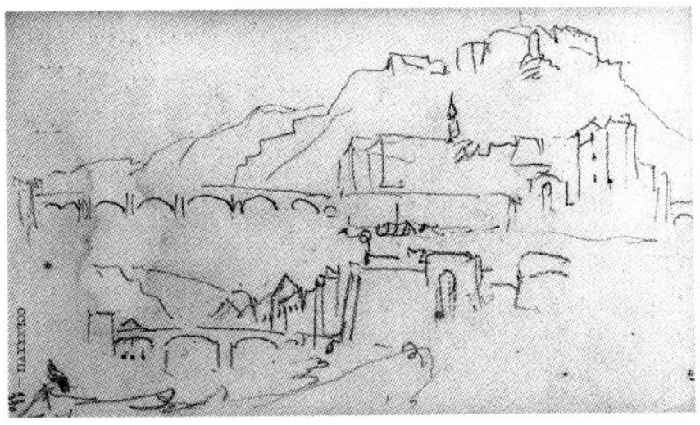

Namur (TB CCLXXXVII 41r)

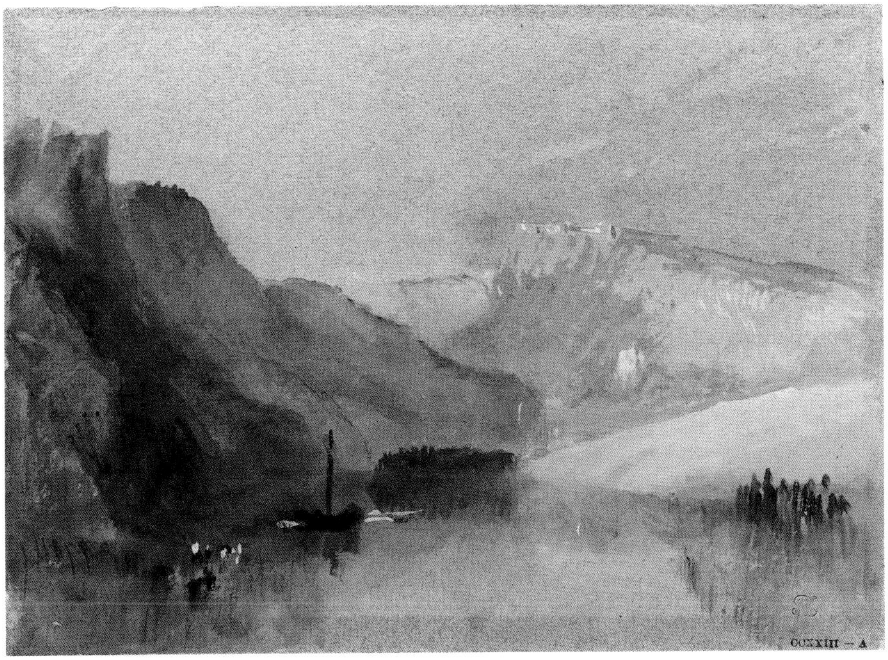

95 **Cliffs and Cornfields by the Meuse with Poilvache in the Distance** *c.*1839

Gouache and watercolour on blue paper
141 × 188 ($5\frac{9}{16} \times 7\frac{3}{8}$)
Watermarked: . . . & s/. . .8
TB CCXXIII A
D20286
EXH & LIT: National Gallery 6th Loan Collection, 1896–1931, no.7; Finberg (1909), p.692 (as 'River scene with mountains', *c.*1826)

On the twenty-mile stretch between Namur and Dinant the Meuse becomes increasingly like the Middle Rhine, with the river curving its way past frowning rocky cliffs, steep wooded hills, picturesque towns and the remains of several lofty medieval castles. In cat.no.95 Turner uses many of the same radiant colours as in one of his gouaches of Dinant (TB CCXX U; cat.no.96) and it is very close to a pencil sketch on TB CCLXXXVII 63r, adjoining several others depicting that town and its surroundings from the north which are themselves closely related to cat.no.96. All these sketches were drawn along a single short stretch of road, within a few minutes of each other, on what was clearly an evening of exceptional beauty. The foreground of cat.no.95 is dominated by a sweep of dazzling yellow paint representing the field of 'Corn in Light' noted on Turner's little sketch, while the distant hill is crowned by the walls and towers of the ruined fortress of Poilvache, destroyed in 1554, which commands the Meuse just to the north of Dinant. The contrast between the two banks of the river at this point is especially striking: 'the road runs beneath a wall of naked rock on the left bank of the Meuse; while, on the opposite side, the valley and heights . . . are cultivated as far as the eye can reach.'[1]

1 D. Costello, *A Tour through the Valley of the Meuse*, 1845, p.186.

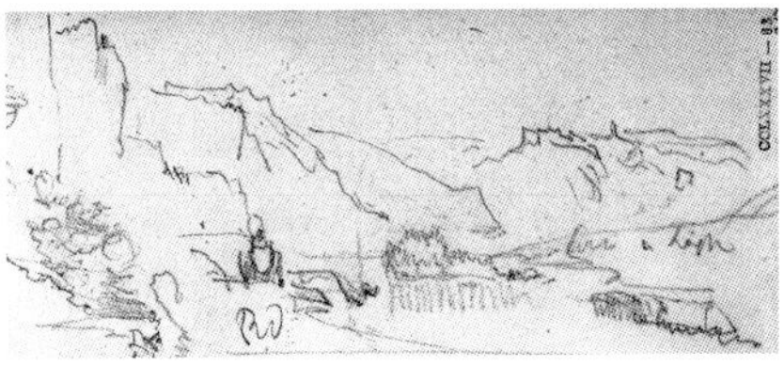

The Meuse between Poilvache and Dinant (TB CCLXXXVII 63r)

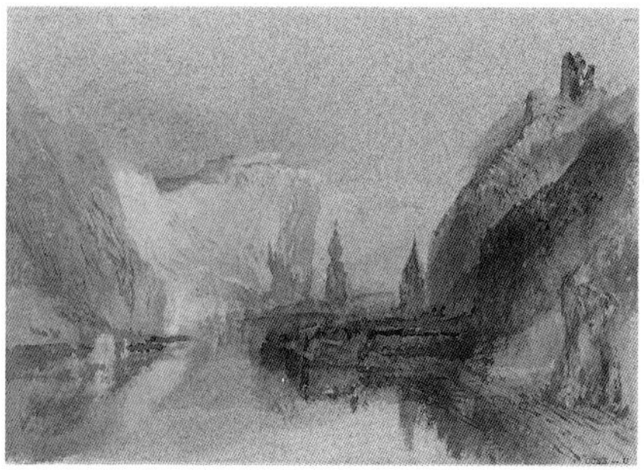

96 Dinant, Bouvignes and Crèvecoeur: Sunset* *c.*1839

Gouache and watercolour on blue paper
136 × 188 ($5\frac{3}{8} \times 7\frac{3}{8}$)
TB CCXX U
D20228
EXH & LIT: National Gallery Exhibited Drawings no.184; Ruskin (1903–12), vol.XIII, p.386 ('a mighty one'); Finberg (1909), p.687 (as *c.*1826); Wilkinson (1975), p.82; Texas (1982), no.39; Wilton (1982), no.67 (as *c.*1826); Luxembourg (1984), no.32 (as *c.*1834)

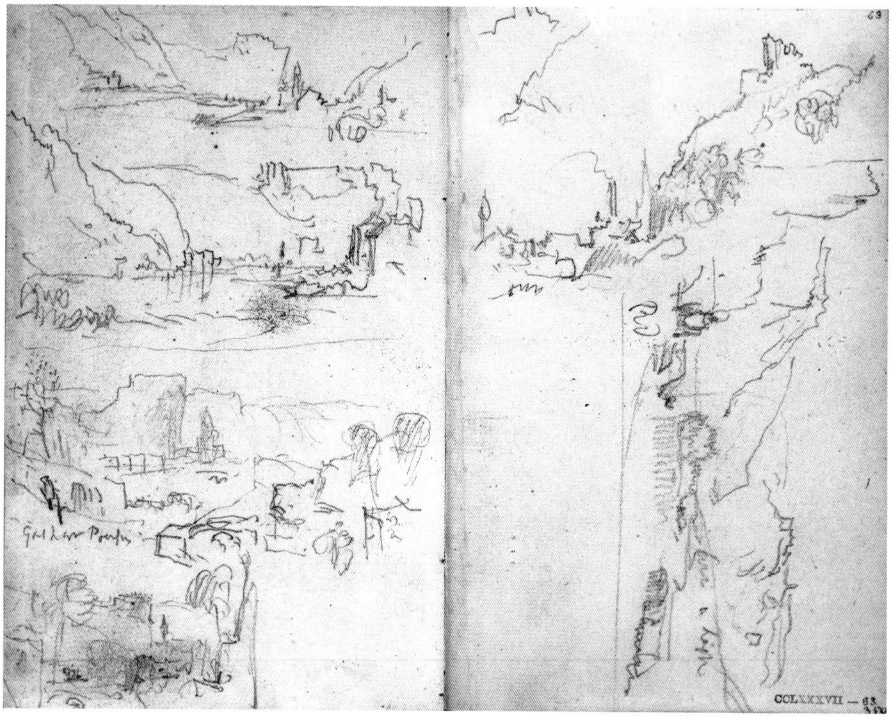

Dinant and Bouvignes (TB CCLXXXVII 62v–63r)

In this drawing Turner captures in brilliant colours the shimmering effects of light and shade which he had recorded in several strongly hatched but tiny pencil sketches on TB CCLXXXVII 62v–63r and may well have recorded also in a schematic pencil outline on this very sheet of blue paper. The newly built citadel of Dinant and the bare limestone rocks of the east bank contrast dramatically with the wooded hillside and darker brooding shapes of the older buildings opposite – the church of Bouvignes, Dinant's ancient enemy, and the ruins of Crèvecoeur – while both banks are mirrored with equal beauty in the still waters of the Meuse.

A view very similar to this was drawn by Thomas Allom and engraved for Thomas Roscoe's *Belgium Picturesque & Romantic* of 1841. Since it appeared there only in black and white, it was accompanied by a long description which may usefully be quoted here:

> The approach from the point in which the artist took the accompanying view, is striking and picturesque; and when the evening sun gilds the spire of Notre Dame, and the salient parts of the fortress and surrounding hills, it appears illuminated with a golden flood . . . the splendid ruins of an antique tower, erected on the summit of a vast rock, as early as 1321, . . . bears the singular name of Crèvecoeur, or heart-break . . . From its walls three lovely sisters are stated to have beheld their respective lords fall in battle, defending the castle from its invaders; and when on the point of falling into the enemy's hands, choosing death rather than dishonour, they threw themselves from the loftiest battlements . . . The ruins of the castle are still a conspicuous object, and with the character of the surrounding scenery, the wooded and jagged rocks, the bright expanding river, the town and fortress of Dinant resting upon the hills seen beyond . . . form a *coup d'oeil* of extreme beauty. . . The effect of the sun-light upon the spires and towers; the rich hues reflected in the waters, the deep blue, and green tinged sky, threw a halo of warm and brilliant colors over the spot as we saw it, than which nothing could be more attractive to a painter's eye. It is perhaps of all the most picturesque and romantic that is to be seen along the banks of the Meuse.
>
> (pp.263–4)

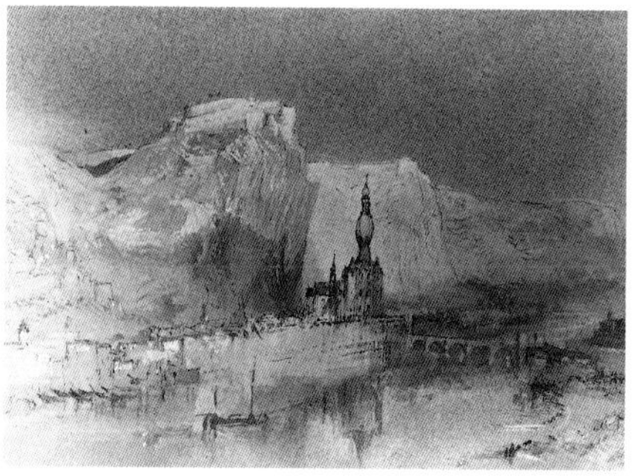

97 Dinant from the North-west* *c.*1839

Gouache, pen and ink, and watercolour on blue paper
133 × 190 ($5\frac{1}{4} \times 7\frac{1}{2}$)
PROV: Thomas Griffith; Charles Stokes, 1850; by descent to Hannah Cooper from whom bought by John Ruskin; Arthur Severn; Agnew, from whom purchased by the Trustees of the John Wigham Richardson Bequest to the Walker Mechanics' Institute, 1925 and placed on permanent loan to the Laing Art Gallery, Newcastle upon Tyne
Laing Art Gallery, Newcastle upon Tyne (Tyne and Wear Museums Service)

W 1026
EXH & LIT: Thornbury (1862), vol.2, p.396; Thornbury (1877), p.593; exhibited at the Fine Art Society, 1878 (see the Ruskin references below); Armstrong (1902), p.249 (as '1830–5'); Ruskin (1903–12), vol.XIII, pp.450 (no.53), 463, 557 (no.79), 599; Herrmann (1970), p.696; Wilton (1979), where the provenance begins '?John Ruskin' and it is wrongly associated with TB CCXCII 37; Paris (1983), no.175 (as 'vers 1825–1834')

Turner's viewpoint is high up on the opposite side of the Meuse from Dinant and his gouache is very closely based on the pencil sketch on TB CCLXXXVII 62r. The gouache was no.53 in the 1878 exhibition of Turner drawings owned by Ruskin, whose comments in the catalogue ran: 'It will be seen . . . how absolutely determined Turner's execution was, leaving the grey or warm tinted paper entirely untouched for part of his ground colour. This Dinant is a study of the highest quality, the rock drawing under the fort insuperable' (p.450). According to Ruskin's note under no.77 in the same exhibition (pp.462–3 and n.), he had bought his 'Dinant' from Hannah Cooper, so its early history must have been identical to that of his 'Huy' and his 'Namur' (W 1024 and W 1025), i.e. it passed via Turner's agent Thomas Griffith to Charles Stokes, thence by descent to his niece Hannah Cooper, and so to Ruskin. The sale of all these exceptionally fine drawings through Griffith is particularly interesting in the context of the present exhibition, since it must have occurred during the same decade as his dealings with Turner over the sample studies and commissions for Swiss subjects and one drawing of Coblenz (see under cat.nos.135–6).

A view by Thomas Allom very similar to this work was engraved in Roscoe's *Belgium Picturesque & Romantic* of 1841. This may just be a coincidence and due to the artistic fashions of the moment, but the presence of three scenes in that book so close to three of Turner's (see also cat.nos.96 and 107) suggests direct contact between the two artists.

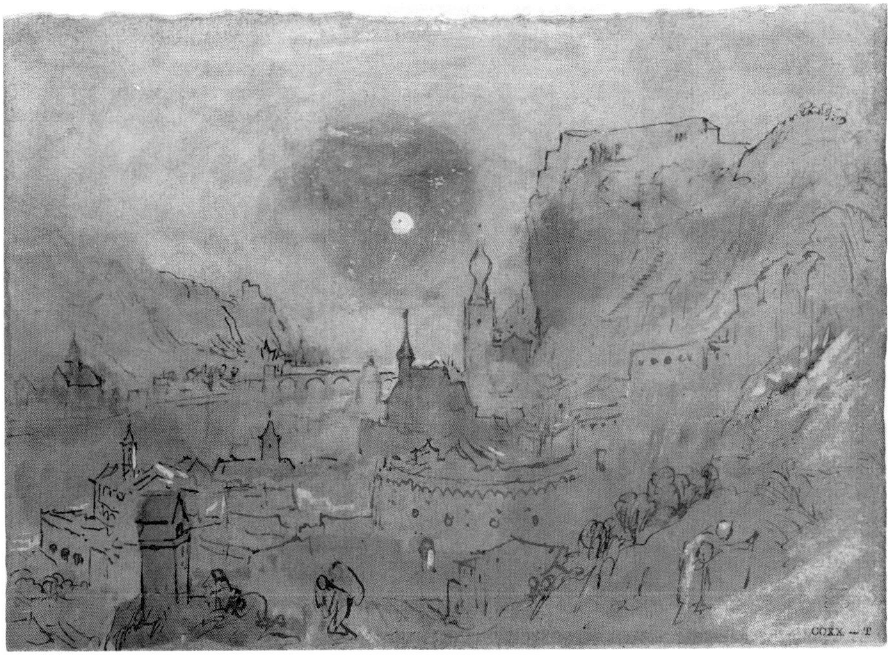

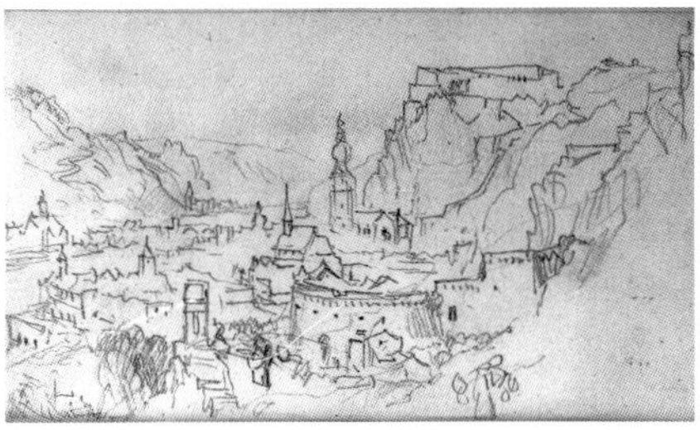

Dinant (TB CCLXXXVII 27v)

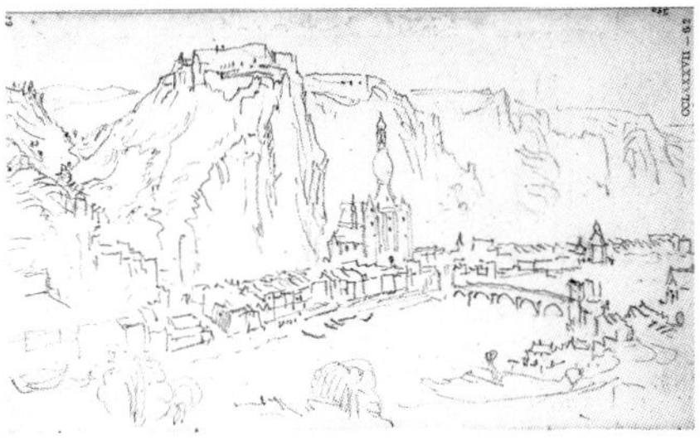

Dinant (TB CCLXXXVII 62r)

98 Dinant from the South-east: Evening *c.*1839

Gouache, pen and ink, and watercolour on blue paper
139 × 191 ($5\frac{1}{2} \times 7\frac{1}{2}$)
TB CCXX T
D20227
EXH & LIT: National Gallery Exhibited Drawings no.617c; Finberg (1909), p.687 (as *c.*1826); Luxembourg (1984), no.33 (as *c.*1834)

Turner's drawing, which is very closely based on the pencil sketch on TB CCLXXXVII 27v, shows Dinant from the steep hillside outside the town walls. The citadel and church of Notre-Dame are silhouetted sharply against the sky and, as evening spreads its calm over the Meuse, peasants trudge homewards with heavy burdens or pause reverently at a wayside shrine.

The experimental mixed media technique of this work gives it an unusual appearance, leaving the viewer in some doubt as to whether this is a twilight scene or a moonlit one. Its similarity to cat.no.99 may, however, be an indication that it is the latter.

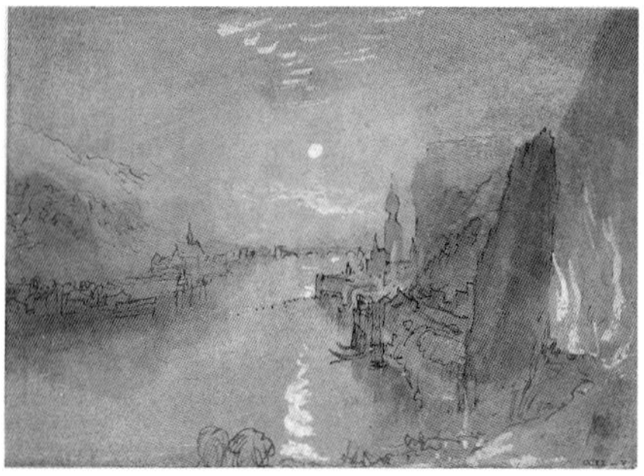

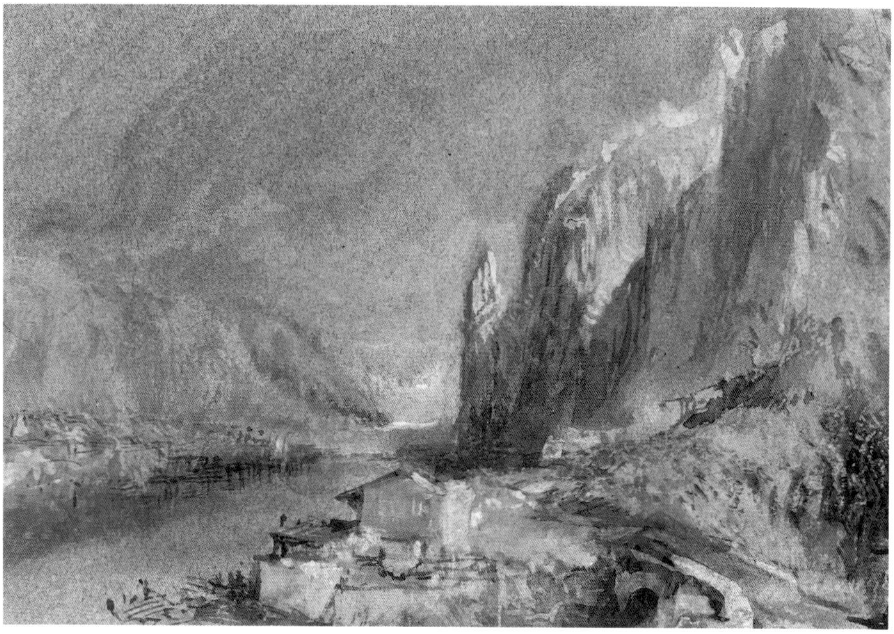

99 Dinant from the Roche à Bayard: Moonlight* *c.*1839

Gouache, pen and ink, and watercolour on blue paper
138 × 188 ($5\frac{7}{16} \times 7\frac{3}{8}$)
TB CCXX V
D20229
EXH & LIT: National Gallery Exhibited Drawings no.185; Ruskin (1903–12), vol.XIII, p.386 ('Bronzed sunset. Firm and good'); Finberg (1909), p.687 (as *c.*1826); Texas (1982), no.40; Wilton (1982), no.68 (as *c.*1826); Luxembourg (1984), no.34 (where wrongly associated with TB CCXVI 56v, as *c.*1834)

Many of the ingredients in this gouache are the same as those in TB CCXX T (cat.no.98), but Turner's viewpoint is now on the river bank and is further upstream, next to the gigantic rock known as the 'Roche à Bayard'. This detached pinnacle is named after the fabulous horse given by Charlemagne to the legendary 'Quatre Fils Aymon'. So great was his strength that he splintered the rock from the cliff with a flick of his hoof as he leaped over the Meuse, bearing all four brothers on his back.

The Roche à Bayard appears in many of Turner's pencil sketches of 1839 (TB CCLXXXVII 1r, 64r, 65v, inside back cover), none of which corresponds with this scene. It was probably sketched in pencil on this very sheet to which watercolour and gouache were added later. Although it has long been regarded as a sunset scene, it has a dense and ghostly quality unusual in Turner's sunsets and is in fact far more likely to be a moonlit scene, painted under the influence of that by Clarkson Stanfield from a similar viewpoint (see fig.37 on p.48). Turner's narrow and rather muddy colour range and heavy impasto lighting are both entirely explicable as counterparts to those found in Thomas Shotter Boys's lithograph of this scene published in Stanfield's *Sketches on the Moselle, the Rhine, & the Meuse* in 1838.

100 The Roche à Bayard *c.*1839

Gouache, pen and ink, and watercolour on blue paper
127 × 184 ($5 \times 7\frac{1}{4}$)
PROV: . . .; J.E. Taylor; his sale, Christie's, 5 July 1912 (92); bought Blaker; Gwendoline E. Davies
National Museum of Wales, Cardiff (2957)
W 1027
EXH & LIT: Armstrong (1902), p.249 (as 1830–5)

The limestone rocks which line many parts of the Meuse inspired some of Turner's most powerful gouaches, notable for their colourful and dynamic contrasts of light and shade and their extremely expressive pen drawing. The Roche à Bayard is one of the most notable rock formations on the Meuse: monolithic in form, it rises very close to the river bank and reaches around 180 feet in height. A narrow road was cut behind it at the end of the seventeenth century to allow for the progress of Louis XIV's army. Neither this passageway nor Dinant itself can be seen in Turner's gouache where all the attention is focused on the magnificent rocks themselves and the cluster of humble cottages in the foreground.

Although Turner's sketchbooks contain several pencil sketches of the Roche à Bayard, none corresponds with this scene. It may be painted over a pencil outline made on the spot, but it could almost equally well be based on Turner's general knowledge and memory of the cliffs along the Meuse. In its rendering of the rock contours and in the way in which light and shade play on vertical, horizontal and diagonal fissures in the limestone it is remarkably true to nature.

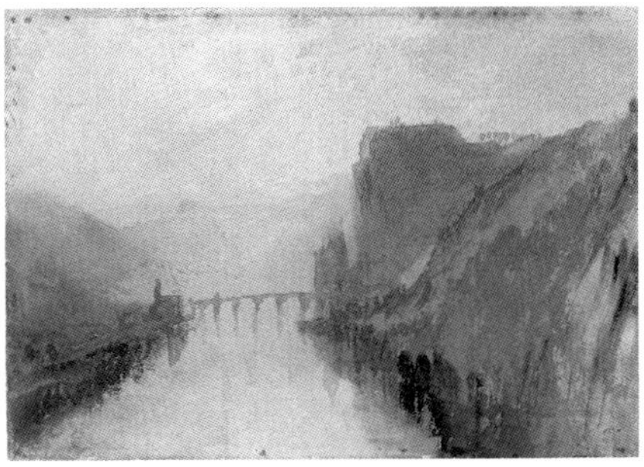

101 Dinant from the South *c.*1839

Gouache and watercolour on blue paper
139 × 192 ($5\frac{1}{2} \times 7\frac{9}{16}$)
TB CCLIX 159
D24724
EXH & LIT: National Gallery Exhibited Drawings, no.427c; Finberg (1909), p.798 (as 'On the Meuse(?)', *c.*1826–33); Athens (1981), no.41 (as 'A bridge over a river under a high cliff' *c.*1826–8, with the suggestion that it shows Huy); Paris (1983), no.174 (as 'Sur la Meuse: Dinant?', 1826?)

This very impressionistic drawing is not based on any single pencil sketch but it undoubtedly shows the view down the Meuse to the bridge and citadel at Dinant. These occur time and time again in Turner's pencil sketches and form a very striking composition quite different from that found at any other fortress town on the Meuse.

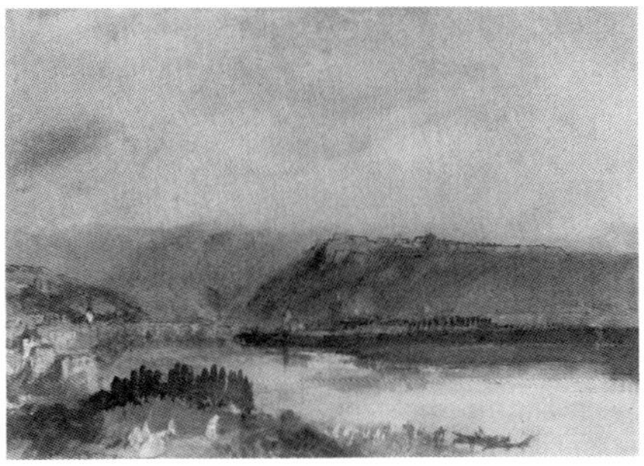

102 Givet from the North* *c.*1839

Gouache and watercolour on blue paper
134 × 187 ($5\frac{1}{4} \times 7\frac{3}{8}$)
PROV: . . .; Myles Birket Foster by 1863; his sale, Christie's, 28 April 1894 (44) (as 'On the Moselle'); Worsley for £42; Philip J. Worsley; Dr Thomas Besterman; his sale, Christie's, 14 December 1971 (102, as 'Ehrenbreitstein'); Agnew
Private Collection
Not in Wilton
EXH & LIT: Album of Photographs of the Birket Foster Collection of Turner Watercolours, no.61; Yardley (1988), p.44 and ill.7 (as 'Ehrenbreitstein', *c.*1834)

This gouache is recognisable in a watercolour drawn by Myles Birket Foster showing his own drawing-room at 'The Hill', Witley, Surrey, signed and dated 1863 (reproduced in Yardley, 1988, as ill.1). In the sale catalogue of his collection in 1894 it was described as 'On the Moselle', but more recently it has been described as 'Ehrenbreitstein'. However, the river seen here is not the Mosel but the Meuse with Givet, a small French frontier town about fourteen miles south of Dinant. Turner's gouache shows the view looking upriver with all the principal features of the town clearly distinguishable. From left to right he depicts the Tour Grégoire, the spire of Notre-Dame, the stone bridge over the Meuse, the church of St-Hilaire and, finally, the flat mass of Fort Charlemont spread out on its cliff guarding the town and the crossing-point. Many artists have depicted Givet thus – including Turner himself in a very fine pencil sketch of 1824 – and it is easy to appreciate the reason. From here the strategic importance of Givet is readily apparent as is, too, the picturesque contrast formed as the Meuse valley changes abruptly from being narrow and hemmed in by steep cliffs to one that is much wider and is fringed with luxuriant vegetation.

The ingredients of Turner's gouache can all be seen again and again in his quick pencil sketches in the sketchbook used here in 1839 (TB CCLXXXVIII 2v–11r). Several of these show the same contrasts as in the gouache between very dark trees and their lighter surroundings, while that on f.9v was drawn from a similar viewpoint. In Turner's scene it is the nearer, eastern part of Givet, with its brighter colours and shining white church, that attracts the eye but it was Givet's other church – St-Hilaire – that was soon to be the more famous of the two. This was not through its own intrinsic merits but thanks to the scorn heaped upon its tower by Victor Hugo in *Le Rhin* (1842), Letter v:

> The good architect has taken the square cap of a priest or lawyer; on this square cap he has built an upside-down salad-bowl; on the back of this salad-bowl, used as a platform, he has placed a sugar-basin; on the sugar-basin a bottle; on the bottle a sun fitted into its neck by its lowest vertical ray; and, finally, on the sun a cock spitted on to its highest vertical ray. Assuming that he took a day to produce each of these six ideas, he must have rested on the seventh day.

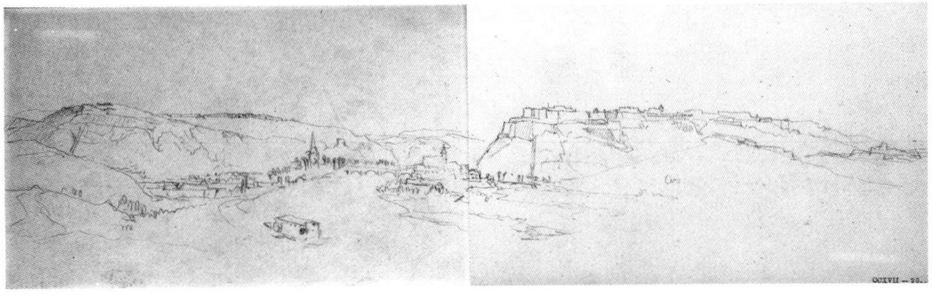

Givet, 1824 (TB CCXVII 19v–20r)

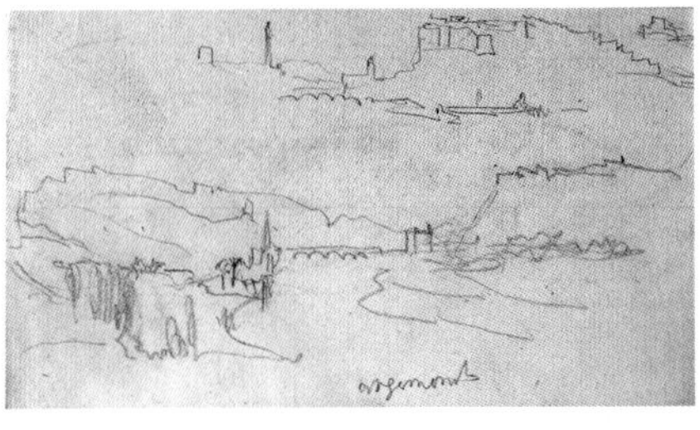

Givet, 1839 (TB CCLXXXVIII 9v)

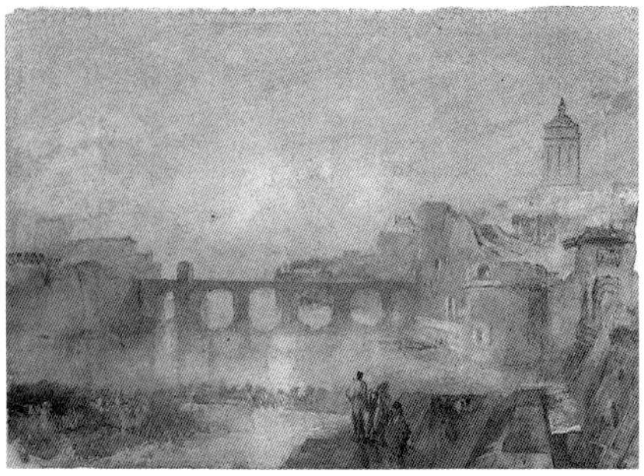

103 Mézières, with the Pont de Pierre and Church of Notre-Dame* *c.*1839

Gouache and watercolour on blue paper
139 × 193 ($5\frac{1}{2} \times 7\frac{9}{16}$)
TB CCLIX 166
D24731
EXH & LIT: National Gallery Exhibited Drawings no.429d; Finberg (1909), p.799 (as 'Town, with bridge', *c.*1826–33); International Exhibitions Foundation (1977–8), no.41 (as 'A Town by a River with Bridge and Classical Monument', *c.*1830); Paris (1983), no.177 (as 'Ville au bord d'une rivière, avec pont et monument classique', *c.*1830–4)

The subject matter of this superb drawing – so long unidentified – is the Pont de Pierre and Notre-Dame d'Espérance, Mézières, as seen from the south-east. The composition of the drawing is that of Turner's pencil sketch on TB CCLXXXVIII 13r which includes all its important features, but its detailed depiction of the church tower derives from his numerous other sketches of it from many different angles (ff.14r, 15r, 15v, 17r, 18r, 19v). The domed top storey shown by Turner was replaced by a tall tapering spire in the late 1850s, but fortunately its previous appearance is recorded in two of the earliest known photographs of Mézières, believed to date from 1855 (reproduced in F. Guérin and H. Hardy, *Charleville-Mézières à la Belle Epoque*, vol.2, Verdun, 1982, pls.1–2).

Nowadays Mézières forms part of the larger complex of Charleville-Mézières, which spreads across two huge whiplash curves of the Meuse, but in Turner's day the two were still separate towns. He made several quick sketches of the spires of Charleville in 1824 but paid no attention to it in 1839 when he was clearly fascinated by the numerous and complex fortifications of Mézières and its imposing sixteenth-century Gothic church crowned by a classical tower completed in 1610. The sight of such monumental buildings inspired him to paint one of his grandest gouaches of all, reminiscent of his own history paintings of a much earlier period such as 'The Decline of the Carthaginian Empire' of 1817 (B&J 135; Clore Gallery).

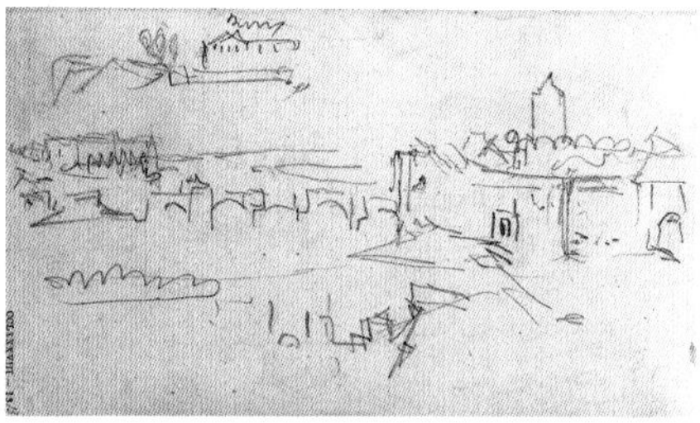

Mézières (TB CCLXXXVIII 13r)

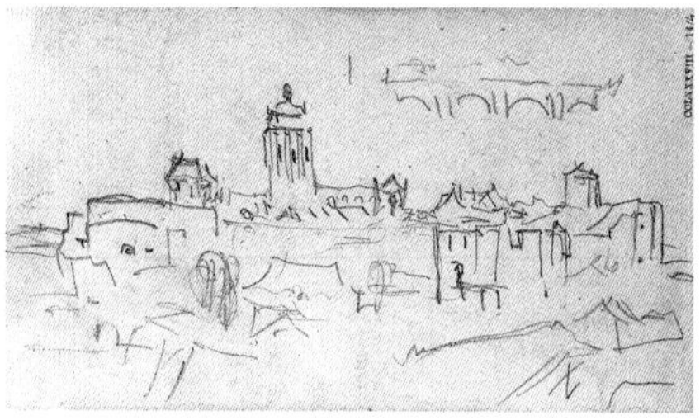

Mézières (TB CCLXXXVIII 14r)

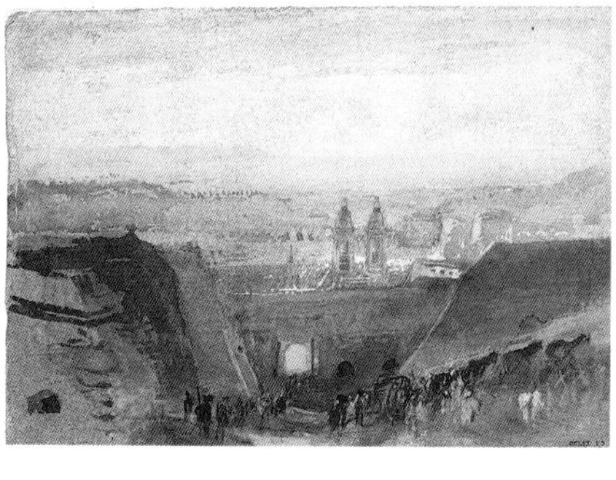

104 Sedan from the South-east* *c.*1839

Gouache and watercolour on blue paper
141 × 191 ($5\frac{9}{16} \times 7\frac{1}{2}$)
TB CCLIX 13
D24578
EXH & LIT: Oxford Loan Collection 206-138; Finberg (1909), p.790 (as 'Entrance gate between bastions', *c.*1826–33); Paris (1981), no.96 (with the suggestion that it depicts Sedan and a reference to Turner's first Meuse–Mosel tour); Athens (1981), no.50 (as 'Entrance gate of a town between bastions', *c.*1830)

In the middle distance of this work Turner shows the two principal buildings of Sedan, the seventeenth-century church of St Charles with its two black, domed towers and the colossal fortified castle dating from the Renaissance. His viewpoint is to the south-east, just outside the Porte de Bouillon, where he made a small and very schematic pencil sketch of this composition (TB CCLXXXVIII 18v, top). The depiction of the massive fortifications around Sedan is close to that found in another sketch of the town drawn from a different viewpoint (f.21v). The military activities of the foreground have been added to provide the scene not only with an appropriate human element but also with the requisite sense of scale.

This majestic, landlocked scene provides the greatest possible contrast to the pyrotechnics on the river at Mézières (cat.no.103); together they form a superb conclusion to Turner's views of the Meuse.

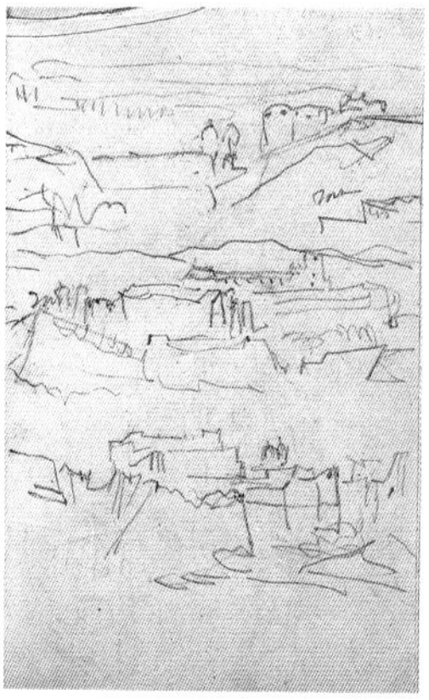

Sedan (TB CCLXXXVIII 18v)

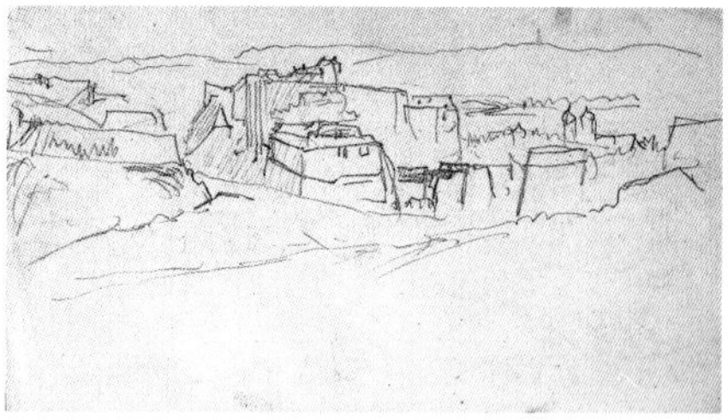

Sedan (TB CCLXXXVIII 21v)

Other Belgian Subjects

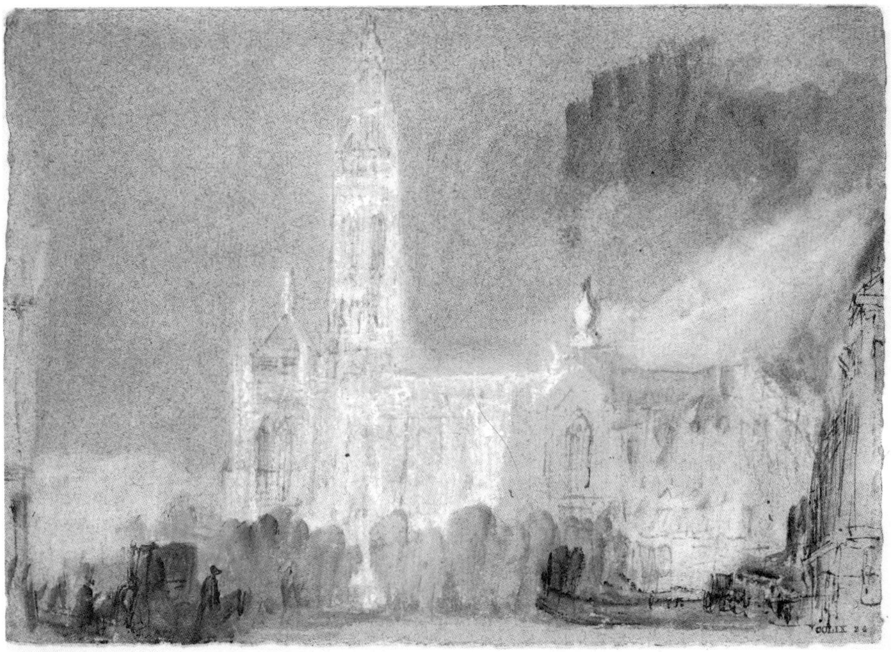

105 Antwerp Cathedral from the Place Verte *c.*1839

Gouache, pen and ink, and watercolour on blue paper
139 × 189 ($5\frac{1}{2} \times 7\frac{7}{16}$)
TB CCLIX 24
D24589
EXH & LIT: Finberg (1909), p.791 (as *c.*1826–33); Brussels (1971), no.48 (as *c.*1826–33)

Turner's gouaches of Brussels, Louvain, Franchimont and Spa (cat.nos.106–19) were all inspired by sights he had enjoyed in the first few days of his 1839 tour, before he began his intensive study of the Meuse and the Mosel. He did not visit Antwerp in 1839 but the style of this work is very similar to that of those showing Brussels and Louvain, a fact which points to the gouaches having been executed in Turner's studio on the basis of both memories and sketches rather than in the course of a tour.

A striking feature of this scene – which has no parallel in the Brussels and Louvain views – is the bright green tree in the centre. It is hard to resist making the suggestion that this is a deliberate pun on the name of the square depicted – comparable to that on the 'Orange Merchant' in his oil painting of 1819 (cat.no.13).

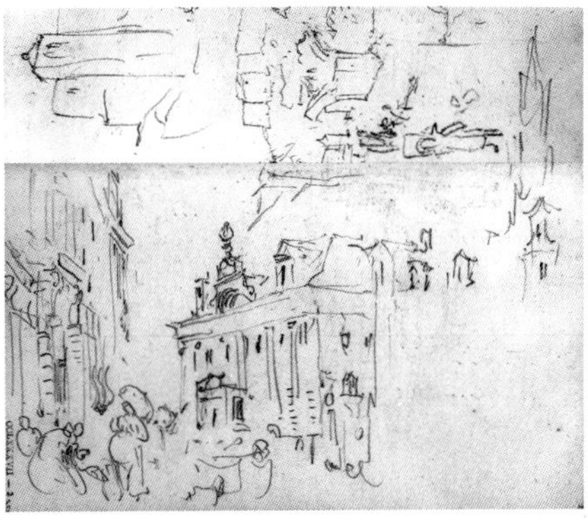

Brussels (TB CCLXXXVII IV–2r)

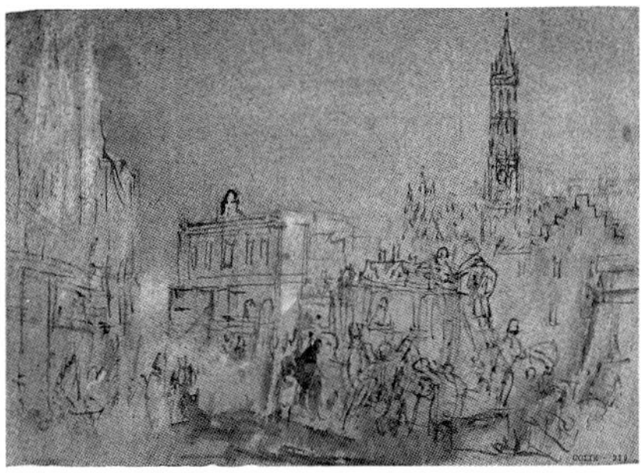

106 Brussels: the Diligence* *c.*1839

Gouache, pen and ink, and watercolour on blue paper
140 × 195 ($5\frac{1}{2} \times 7\frac{11}{16}$)
TB CCLIX 219
D24784
EXH & LIT: National Gallery Exhibited Drawings, no.721; Finberg (1909), p.802 (as 'A French diligence', *c.*1826–33)

This lively scene is based on a rough pencil sketch evidently made while Turner was waiting in Brussels for the diligence that would take him to Louvain at the very start of his 1839 tour (TB CCLXXXVII IV–2r). It can at once be seen that he has modified the architecture of each of the buildings shown, but he has kept some of their essential characteristics and the composition as a whole has remained the same. Such a procedure can be found again and again in Turner's mature work and is entirely explicable: it was the ensemble that pleased him as an architectural grouping rather than the minute details of any one individual building.

A notable feature about Turner's pencil sketch is that the buildings on the left and in the centre are carefully represented, while the celebrated town hall of Brussels is given only very summary treatment and the lower right-hand corner of the page is empty. It may be that Turner himself chose to act thus, wishing to concentrate on unfamiliar buildings rather than one he had already sketched in 1817 (see fig.15 on p.25); or perhaps he was called upon to climb into the diligence before his sketch was finished. However this may be, his memory gave him sufficient information to show the many ornate tiers of the immensely tall Gothic town hall in a thoroughly convincing, if somewhat impressionistic, manner.

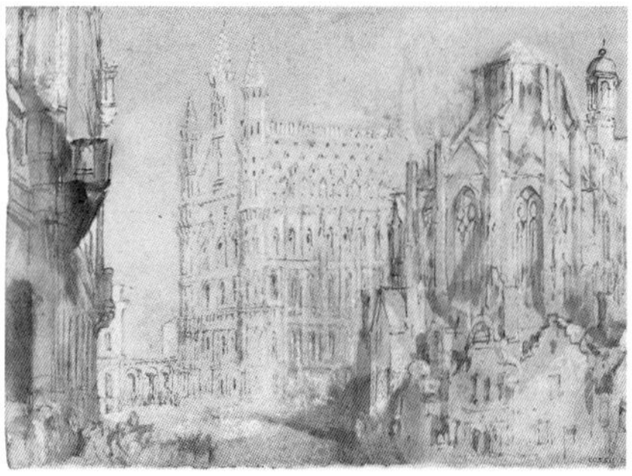

107 The Town Hall, Louvain, and the Choir of St Peter's Church* *c.*1839

Gouache, pen and ink, and watercolour on blue paper
140 × 188 ($5\frac{1}{2} \times 7\frac{3}{8}$)
TB CCXXII D
D20263
EXH & LIT: National Gallery 5th Loan Collection, 1896–1931, no.15; Finberg (1909), p.690 (as *c.*1826); Wilkinson (1975), p.87

Like many other artists who have visited Louvain, Turner was clearly delighted by its two most famous fifteenth-century Gothic buildings and immediately started sketching them in compositions that brought out their characteristic features. Here (and in the pencil sketch on TB CCLXXXVII 2v on which this gouache is based) he depicted its tiny but superbly ornate town hall, one of the gems of Belgian architecture, at the centre. On the right is the lofty choir of St Peter's church, supported by massive flying buttresses and surrounded by side chapels. The same two buildings are seen again, from a different angle, in cat.no.108.

Few of Turner's contemporaries saw Louvain town hall without remarking that it was more like a large jewelled casket than a small building. Turner conveys much the same idea here, partly through his deliberate contrast between bright and sombre colours, partly through his composition: the town hall is glimpsed between much larger structures which extend far beyond the picture space. An engraving of a very similar scene to this, drawn by Thomas Allom, was published in *Belgium Picturesque & Romantic* in 1841 with the comment that this view 'offers one of the finest *coup d'oeils* that is perhaps to be seen of the elaborate Gothic style – the most perfect and intact that is to be met with in Belgium' (p.286).

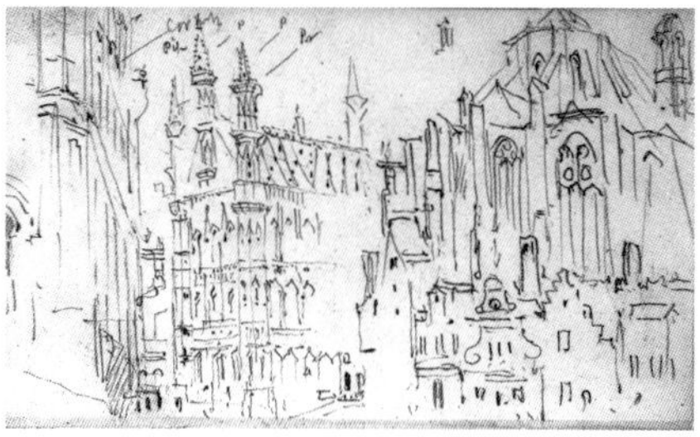

Louvain (TB CCLXXXVII 2V)

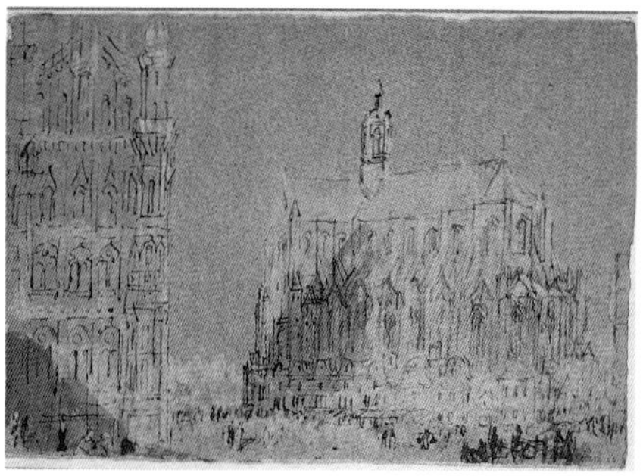

108 St Peter's Church, Louvain, from the East Side of the Town Hall* *c.*1839

Gouache, pen and ink, and watercolour on blue paper
140 × 195 ($5\frac{1}{2} \times 7\frac{11}{16}$)
TB CCLIX 25
D24590
EXH & LIT: [Cook] (1905), p.48 (as 'Cologne Cathedral'); Finberg (1909), p.791 (as *c.*1826–33); Brussels (1971), no.49 (as *c.*1826–33)

As in cat.no.107, Turner here shows Louvain town hall as an ornate jewel of a building and its principal church as a much more sombre one. Among the devices which contribute to this general effect are the strongly cast shadows of grey wash and the articulation of the architecture with fine lines – warmly coloured for the golden town hall, black for the grey church.

This scene (based on the pencil sketch on TB CCLXXXVII 3v) can still be admired today. The only real changes are that St Peter's church now boasts a tall twentieth-century spire over its crossing and the picturesque old houses surrounding its choir (and seen in depictions of the church by several of Turner's contemporaries such as Thomas Allom and W.H. Bartlett) have now been stripped away, leaving the east end of the church in its original form.

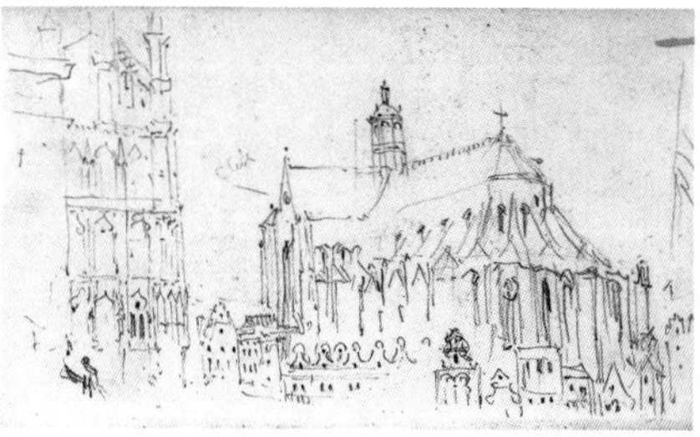

Louvain (TB CCLXXXVII 3V)

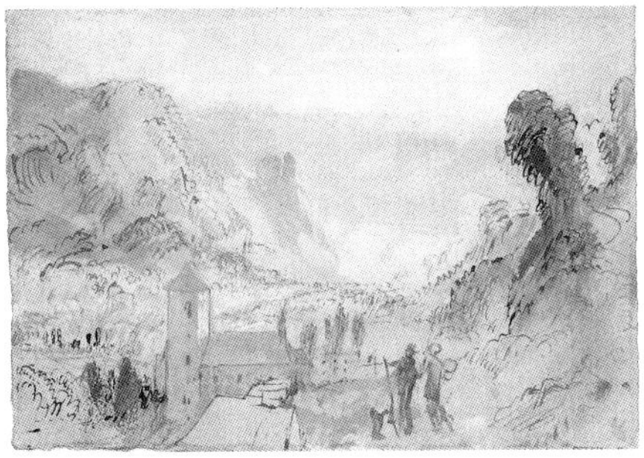

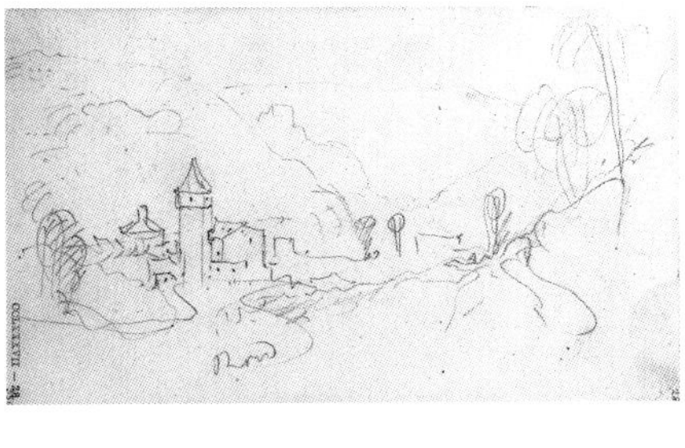

Franchimont from Theux (TB CCLXXXVII 28r)

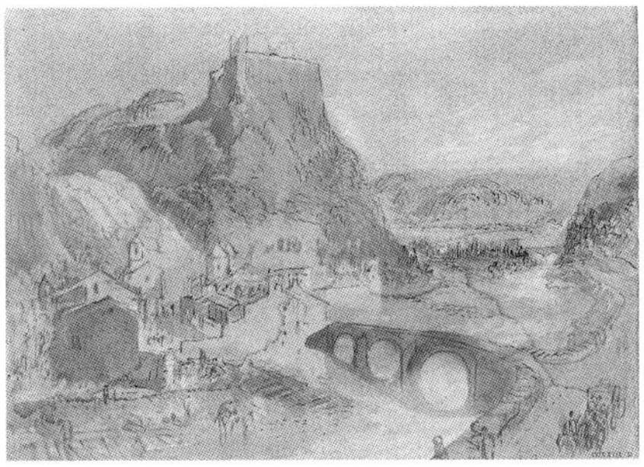

109 Franchimont with the Church of SS. Hermes and Alexander, Theux* *c.*1839

Gouache, pen and ink, and watercolour on blue paper
141 × 192 ($5\frac{9}{16} \times 7\frac{9}{16}$)
TB CCXXII U
D20280
EXH & LIT: National Gallery 6th Loan Collection, 1896–1931, no.48; Finberg (1909), p.691 (as 'River scene, with town and castle', *c.*1826); Wilkinson (1975), p.84 (untitled); Luxembourg (1984), no.57 (as 'Vue de la Meuse (?)', *c.*1834)

Before travelling up the Meuse in 1839, Turner made an excursion from Liège to Spa which took him past the ruined medieval castle of Franchimont. Apart from the addition of two wayfarers and a delightful dog, this gouache corresponds very closely to two pencil sketches on TB CCLXXXVII 27r and 28r, both taken from the Liège–Spa road (inscribed 'Road' on f.28r), very soon after Franchimont came into sight. The eleventh to twelfth century church at Theux is a very striking and unusual building (it is the only three-aisled basilica with flat ceilings of equal height to be found between the Loire and the Rhine, and one of only two churches in Belgium to have its tower on its north side). Turner has modified the arrangement of its parts in his gouache but its essential character remains unaltered.

Turner's five gouaches of Franchimont have some stylistic and colouristic elements in common but each has its own special mood. Here he suggests a pearly dawn with the castle just catching the first rosy light of the morning.

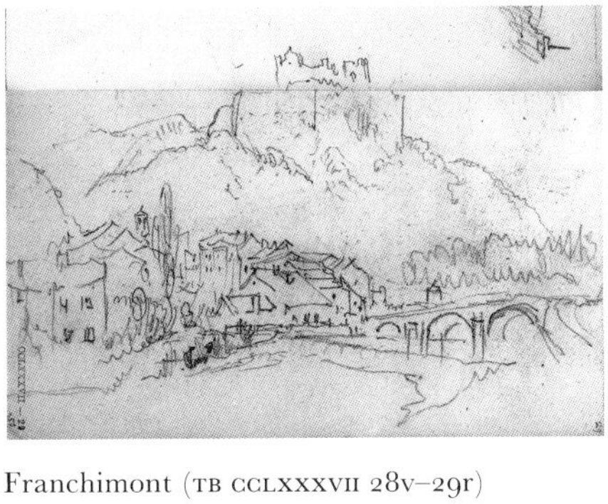

Franchimont (TB CCLXXXVII 28v–29r)

110 Franchimont and the Bridge over the Hoëgne at Marché de Theux* *c.*1839

Gouache, pen and ink, and watercolour on blue paper
144 × 193 ($5\frac{11}{16} \times 7\frac{9}{16}$)
TB CCXXIII D
D20289
EXH & LIT: Finberg (1909), p.692 (as 'Namur(?)' *c.*1826); Luxembourg (1984), no.25 (as 'Vue de Marteau près de Spa (?)', *c.*1834)

The ascent to Franchimont commences at the little village of Marché de Theux and Turner's gouache shows an ensemble of great appeal to visitors throughout the nineteenth century. In 1815 Southey – who seems to have been unaware of its identity – remarked upon 'a castle on the left, appearing like a square of brickwork without any loopholes. It shows well, with a brook and bridge and village in the foreground, and we had seen it at a considerable distance' (1903, p.140). An engraving of exactly the same view as Turner's appeared in the 1830s (see fig.40 on p.51) and a very similar view was published in 1878 in *La Belgique Illustrée* (vol.2, p.377). Turner's drawing is close to the pencil sketch on TB CCLXXXVII 28v–29r while the same general view was also recorded on three loose sheets of blue paper, TB CCXXIV 22, 23, 87. On f.30r of his sketchbook he drew a similar sketch from a higher viewpoint; this excluded the main bridge but shows the tiny bridge seen in the distance in the gouache.

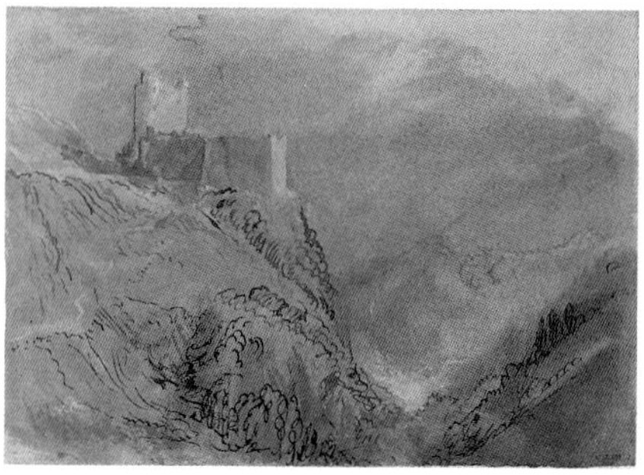

111 Franchimont and the Valley of the Hoëgne* *c.*1839

Gouache, pen and ink, and watercolour on blue paper
137 × 190 ($5\frac{3}{8} \times 7\frac{1}{2}$)
TB CCXXII J
D20269
EXH & LIT: National Gallery 5th Loan Collection, 1896–1931, no.5 (as 'Brantôme, France'); Finberg (1909), p.690 (as 'Castle, with mountain background (?on Moselle)', *c.*1826); Wilkinson (1975), p.84 (untitled)

Turner's composition is based on two very similar pencil sketches on TB CCLXXXVII 31r and 31v. The sketch on f.31r provided the general composition of the castle perched on its hill above the valley, but the compact and sturdy shape of the castle in the gouache is taken from f.31v. The sketches were drawn as Turner crossed the Hoëgne at Marché de Theux and walked up the hillside to look at the castle at close quarters; by f.32v he was recording the three heraldic shields carved on its entrance portal.

Among Turner's five gouaches of Franchimont, TB CCXXII J is the one which best captures the aspect of the ancient ruin which appealed to the Romantic imagination of the early nineteenth century. Since he had recently been engaged in illustrating the works of Sir Walter Scott (see cat.nos.26–8), he was probably familiar with the passage in the introduction to the sixth canto of *Marmion* (*Poetical Works*, vol.VII, p.301) in which Scott retells the story of the ancient treasure of Franchimont guarded by the devil, which he had learned from his friend Richard Heber:

Did'st e'er, dear Heber, pass along
Beneath the towers of Franchémont,
Which, like an eagle's nest in air,
Hang o'er the stream and hamlet fair?
Deep in their vaults, the peasants say,
A mighty treasure buried lay,
Amass'd through rapine and through
  wrong
By the last Lord of Franchémont.

The burnt autumnal colouring, the energetic depiction of the stormy windswept hillside, the dark and misty distance – all these fill the gouache with a sense of high drama without equal in Turner's gouaches of Belgium and Germany.

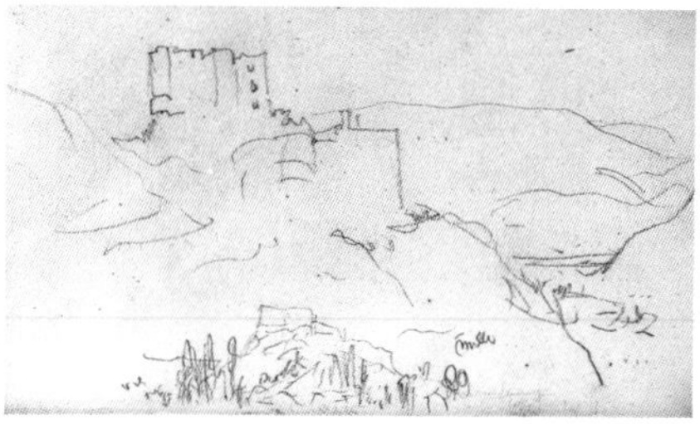

Franchimont (TB CCLXXXVII 31v)

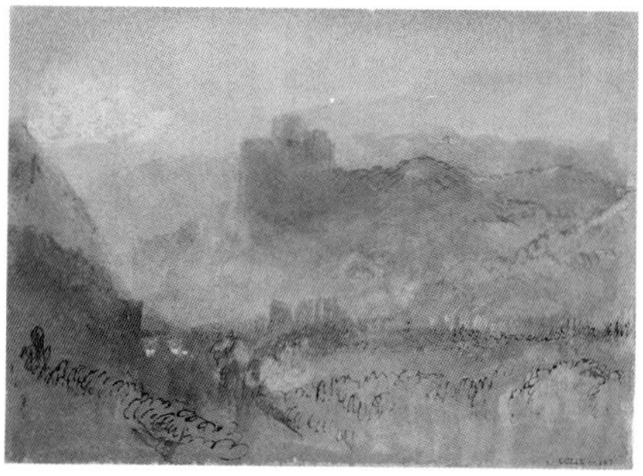

112 Franchimont from the South* *c.*1839

Gouache, pen and ink, and watercolour on blue paper
140 × 191 ($5\frac{1}{2} \times 7\frac{1}{2}$)
TB CCLIX 167
D24732
EXH & LIT: National Gallery Exhibited Drawings no.430a; Finberg (1909), p.799 (as 'Tancarville(?)', *c.*1826–33)

In this gouache (based on the pencil sketch on TB CCLXXXVII 33r) Turner is looking back at Franchimont as he travels on southwards to Spa. His execution is still as dynamic as that in cat.no.111, but a much lighter mood prevails. Particularly refreshing notes are provided by the crisp black line drawing against areas of clear green in the foreground and the flourishes of red against the warmer colours in the distance. Here, and in cat.no.113, one may sense Turner's real enjoyment of the rolling countryside between Liège and Spa that reminded Southey so strongly of Monmouthshire: 'heights covered with brushwood, and streams of clear water – much that is soothing and picturesque' (1903, p.140).

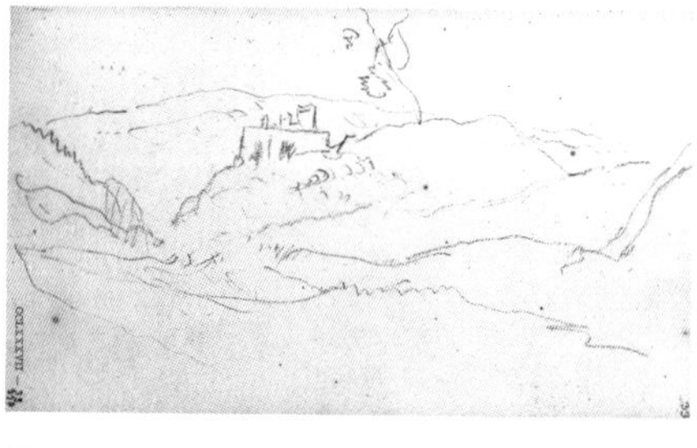

Franchimont (TB CCLXXXVII 33r)

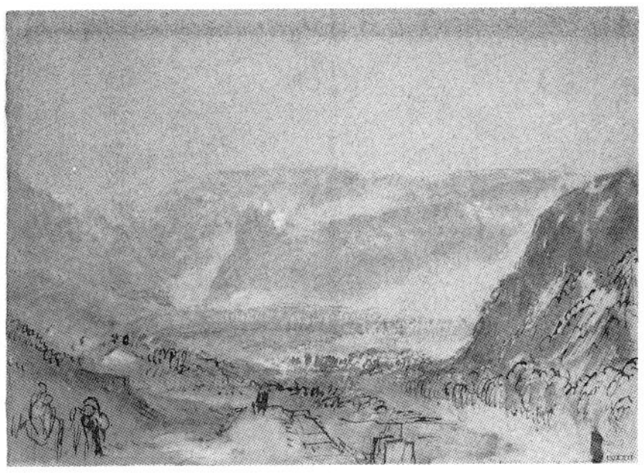

113 Franchimont from the South: Distant View *c.*1839

Gouache, pen and ink, and watercolour on blue paper
139 × 189 ($5\frac{1}{2} \times 7\frac{7}{16}$)
TB CCXXII G
D20266
EXH & LIT: National Gallery 5th Loan Collection, 1896–1931, no.27; Finberg (1909), p.690 (as 'Valley enclosed by mountains', *c.*1826)

This drawing shows Turner's last view of Franchimont from the Liège–Spa road. It is based on the pencil sketch on TB CCLXXXVII 32v, inscribed 'Road', on the left, and with colour notes on the hills on the right, which was drawn slightly later on the road than that on which TB CCLIX 167 (cat.no.112) was based.

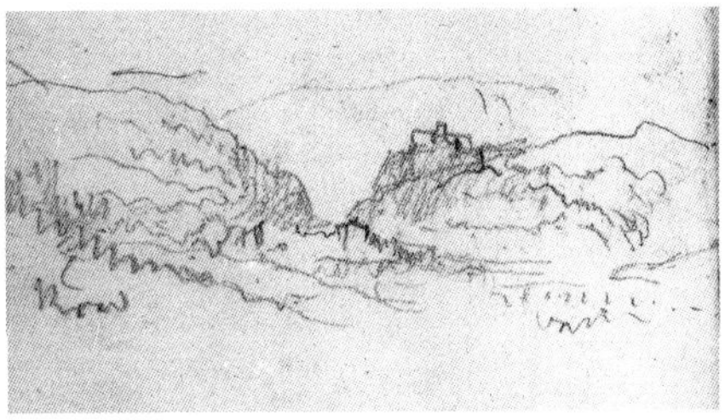

Franchimont (TB CCLXXXVII 32v)

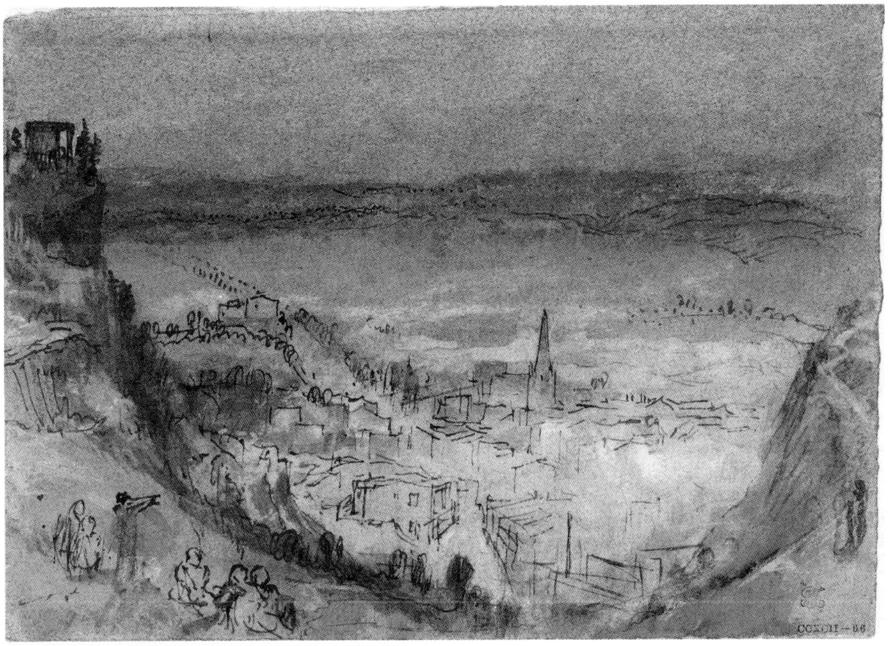

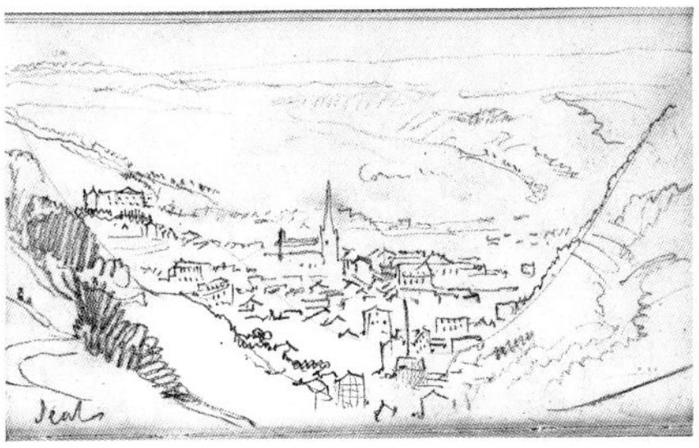

Spa (TB CCLXXXVII 24v)

114 Spa from the Liège Road *c.*1839

Gouache, pen and ink, and watercolour on blue paper
140 × 190 ($5\frac{1}{2} \times 7\frac{1}{2}$)
TB CCXCII 66
D29017
EXH & LIT: Finberg (1909), p.942 (as 'View of Spa(?)', *c.*1834); London (1974) (p.115 under cat.no.370)

The town of Spa, situated in a dip in the Belgian Ardennes some twenty miles south-east of Liège, is the oldest watering-place in Europe, but it has been very popular also for its social attractions and the natural beauty of its situation. In 1815 Southey described it as 'a little quiet place, in that respect resembling Tunbridge Wells', though 'before the Revolution . . . it was, perhaps, the most fashionable place of resort in Europe' (1903, pp.141, 143). By the date of Turner's visit, the town was well on its way to recovery from the fire, deforestation, floods and military encampments mentioned by Southey and it enjoyed a new lease of life in the years that followed. In this gouache, based on the pencil sketch on TB CCLXXXVII 24v, Turner shows one of the glimpses of Spa seen by travellers as they wind their way down from the hills that encircle it.

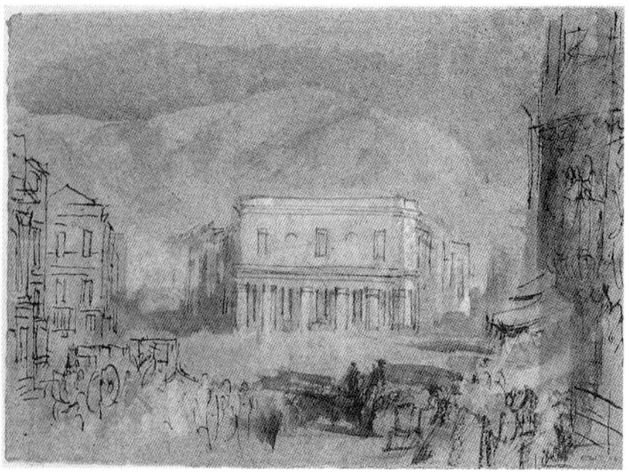

115 The 'Pouhon Pierre Le Grand' at Spa* *c.*1839

Gouache, pen and ink, and watercolour on blue paper
141 × 191 ($5\frac{9}{16} \times 7\frac{1}{2}$)
TB CCLIX 45
D24610
EXH & LIT: Finberg (1909), p.792 (as 'A market place', *c.*1826–33)

Tsar Peter the Great visited Spa to take the waters in 1717 with considerable success. The classical building named in his honour ('pouhon' = 'puits', well) was erected over the main mineral spring in the centre of the town between 1815 and 1820, as a centenary tribute; it was later destroyed to make way for an even grander building, still standing today, which was constructed in 1879–80.

The pencil sketch on which Turner's gouache is based – TB CCLXXXVII 35r – shows clearly the five bays of the building above its peristyle of Tuscan columns, and it also records the inscription on its entablature, 'A LA MEMOIRE DE PIERRE LE GRAND' (see also fig.38 on p.49). It does not include either the diligence or the canopied building on the right of the gouache. However, nineteenth-century prints show that in Turner's day this corner was occupied by a hotel, so that the scene depicted in TB CCLIX 45, with travellers arriving and departing in the square, would undoubtedly have been a sight which he himself had witnessed.

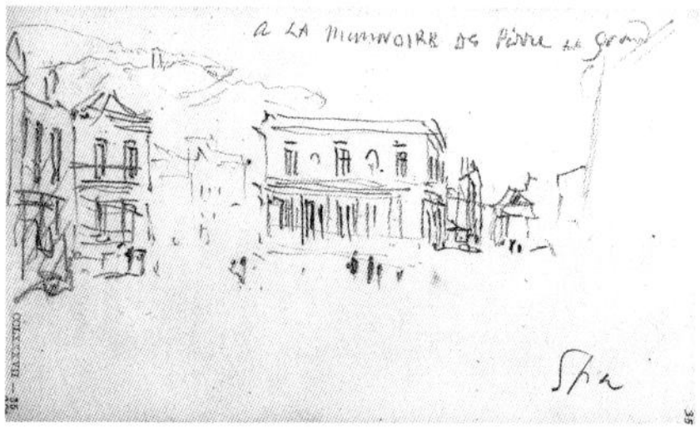

Spa (TB CCLXXXVII 35r)

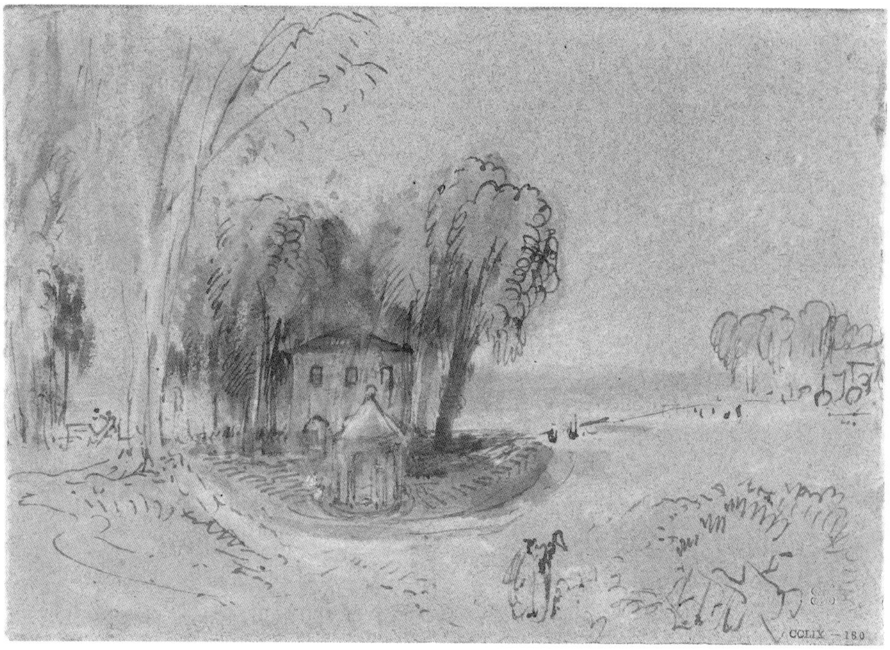

116 The Géronstère Mineral Spring at Spa *c.*1839

Gouache, pen and ink, and watercolour on blue paper
142 × 190 ($5\frac{9}{16} \times 7\frac{1}{2}$)
TB CCLIX 180
D24745
EXH & LIT: National Gallery Exhibited Drawings no.433b; Finberg (1909), p.799 (as 'Turn on a French road', *c.*1826–33)

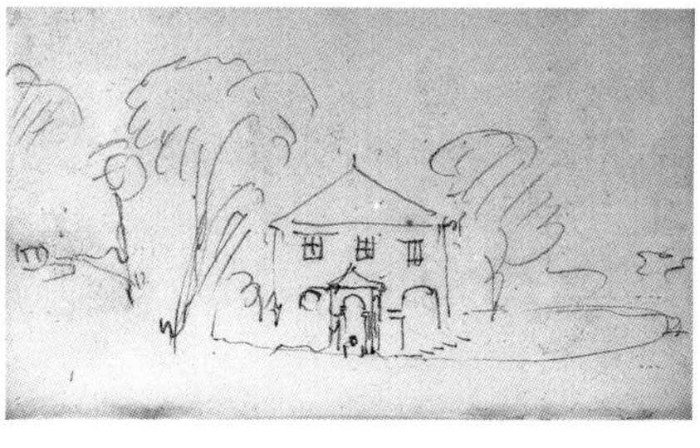

Spa (TB CCLXXXVII 19v)

Turner made several sketches of the Géronstère mineral spring in its beautiful wooded setting in the hills about two miles south of Spa (TB CCLXXXVII 18v, 19v, 20r, 20v). Both his gouache and the sketch on which it is based (f.19v) show the buildings at the spring from above and from directly in front, thus emphasising their unity and the way in which they nestle in a hollow in the woods. Other artists (e.g. Théodore Fourmois in 1839) preferred to show the complex at an oblique angle, providing a more dynamic image and also recording the fact that the cottage and the roofed aedicule over the spring were linked by an arcade in which visitors could sit and rest.

Turner must have worked on all his gouaches of Spa at the same time, since they share a similar technique and a common basic palette in which white, yellow, grey and a blue similar to that of

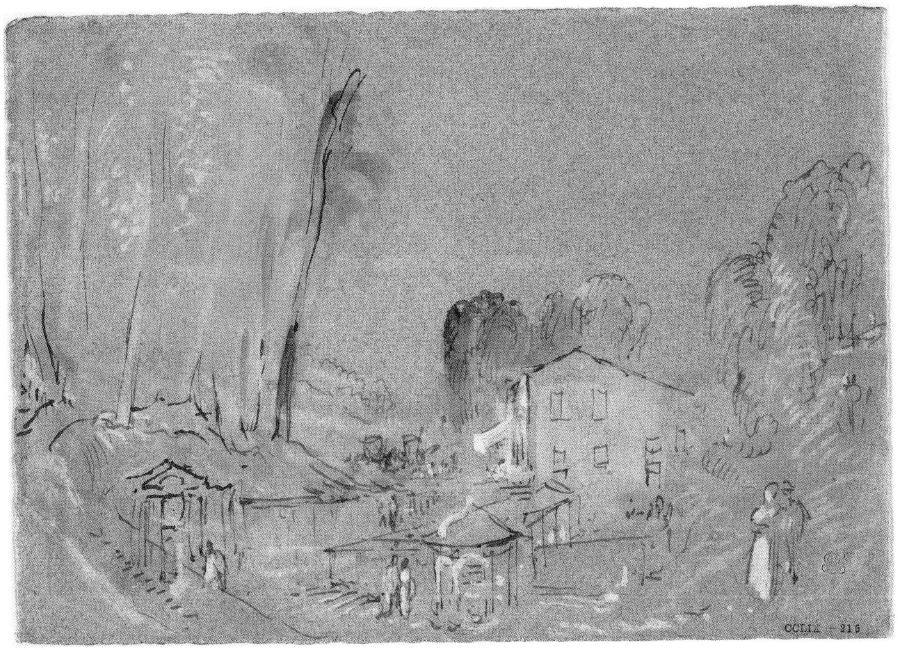

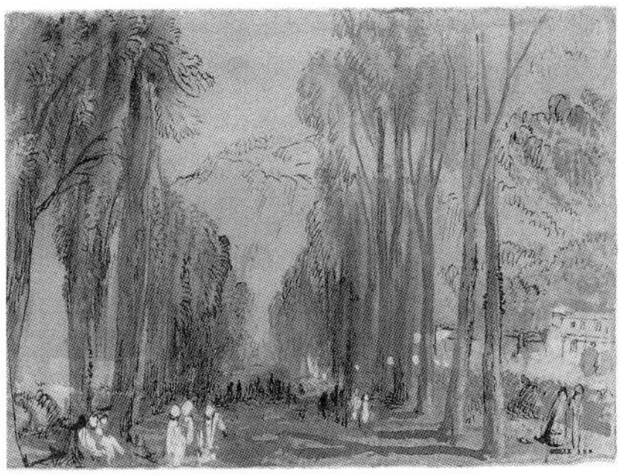

the paper are little more than colour renderings of light and shade. Cat.no.116 is the least developed of the series. In the others, a bolder rendering of shadows and one or more stronger colours – bright blue, warm orange, pink or brown – introduce a note of poetic charm into the scenes which culminate in the magical depictions of the 'Promenade de Sept Heures' (cat.nos.118–19).

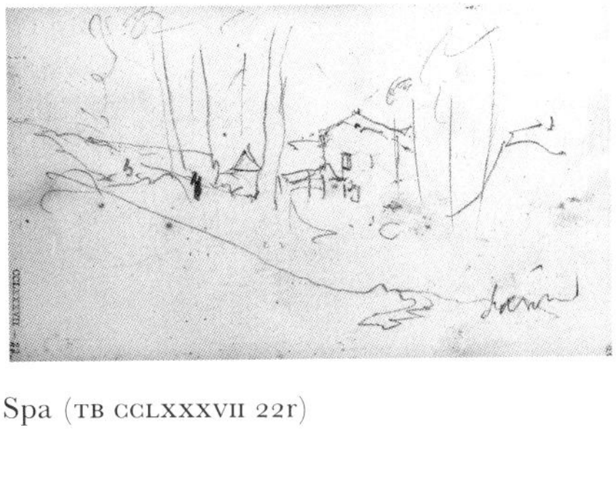

Spa (TB CCLXXXVII 22r)

117 The Groesbeck and Sauvenière Mineral Springs at Spa *c*.1839

Gouache, pen and ink, and watercolour on blue paper
140 × 190 ($5\frac{1}{2} \times 7\frac{1}{2}$)
TB CCLIX 215
D24780
EXH & LIT: National Gallery Exhibited Drawings no.709; Finberg (1909), p.802 (as 'Honfleur', *c*.1826–33)

The Groesbeck and Sauvenière springs are situated in the woods some two miles east of Spa, where the visitor finds a substantial three-storeyed house linked to the Sauvenière spring by an arcade similar to that at the Géronstère. A few yards away a pedimented stone aedicule shelters the Groesbeck spring. Southey recorded that 'both are strong chalybeaters, tho' one is stronger than the other, and in the strongest you see bubbles rise' (1903, p.141). Turner's gouache is based on his pencil sketch on TB CCLXXXVII 22r, on the verso of which he sketched the ensemble of the two springs from the opposite direction.

118 The 'Promenade de Sept-Heures' at Spa* *c*.1839

Gouache, pen and ink, and watercolour on blue paper
140 × 189 ($5\frac{1}{2} \times 7\frac{7}{16}$)
TB CCLIX 188
D24753
EXH & LIT: National Gallery Exhibited Drawings no.435b; Finberg (1909), p.800 (as 'Avenue of poplars', *c*.1826–33)

In the mid-eighteenth century the aristocratic and wealthy visitors to Spa were accustomed to lounge and divert themselves after supper in a meadow adjacent to the Place Royale, which soon acquired the name 'Parc de Sept-Heures'. By the mid-nineteenth century the avenue of elms planted here in the 1750s provided luxuriant shade for afternoon and evening strolls, while a nearby band supplied musical entertainment for the fashionable throng.

Turner's gouache is based on his pencil sketch on TB CCLXXXVII 35v to which he has added figures and a more elaborate house. In the sketch his trees are no more than scribbles, but in the gouache the avenue has both elegance and an almost architectural grandeur. His brown washes nicely convey the idea of an enclosed space which is at the same time both warm and shaded.

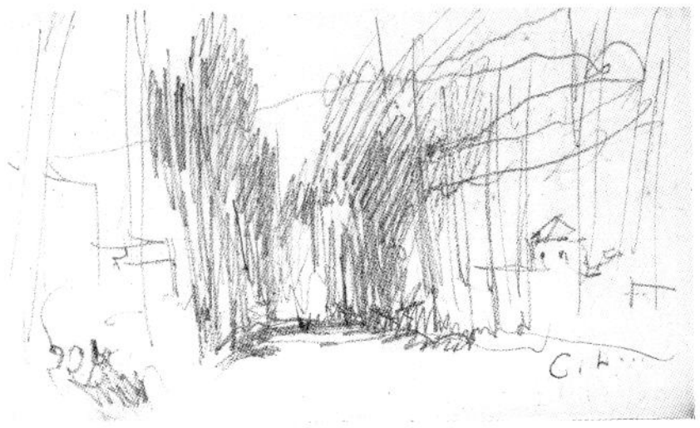

Spa (TB CCLXXXVII 35v)

119 The Place Royale, Spa, from the Entrance to the 'Promenade de Sept-Heures'* *c.*1839

Gouache, pen and ink, and watercolour on blue paper
140 × 189 ($5\frac{1}{2} \times 7\frac{7}{16}$)
TB CCLIX 223
D24788
EXH & LIT: National Gallery Exhibited Drawings no.755; Finberg (1909), p.802 (as 'Honfleur', *c.*1826–33); Wilkinson (1975), p.94 (as 'Honfleur')

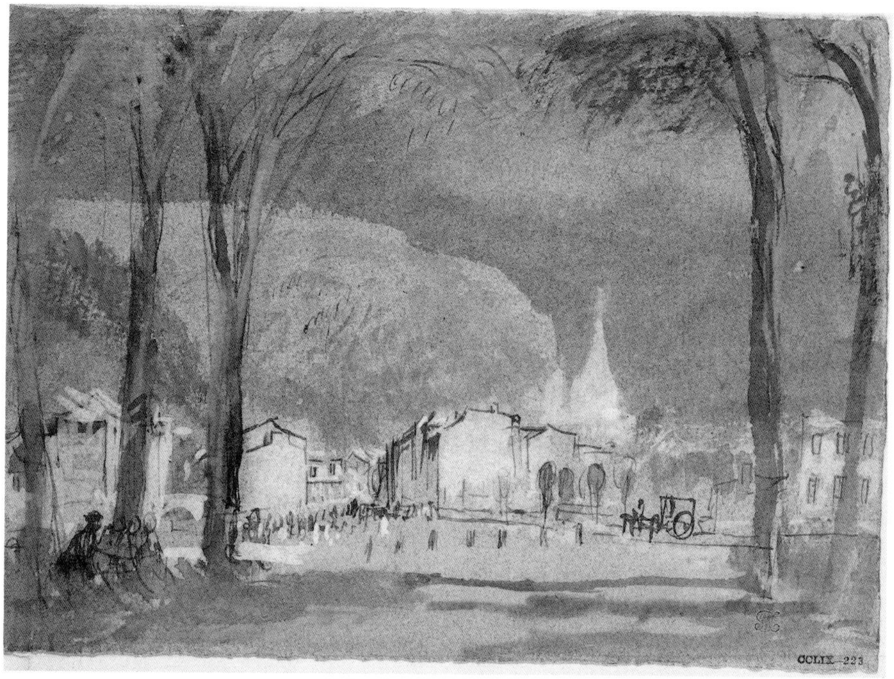

The pencil sketch on which this gouache is based (TB CCLXXXVII 36r) was almost certainly drawn from the identical spot as that on f.35v, so that TB CCLIX 188 and CCLIX 223 (cat.nos.118 and 119) depict the view looking in both directions along the 'Promenade de Sept-Heures'. Beyond the Place Royale Turner shows the spire of the old parish church of Spa dedicated to St Rémacle. This was demolished in 1883 and replaced by the present building in 1885.

Although the gouaches of Spa do not possess the spectacular colour range of some of those depicting the Meuse and the Mosel, this avenue of trees catching the evening sunlight has an extraordinary beauty of its own, making it one of the most enchanting of Turner's Belgian scenes.

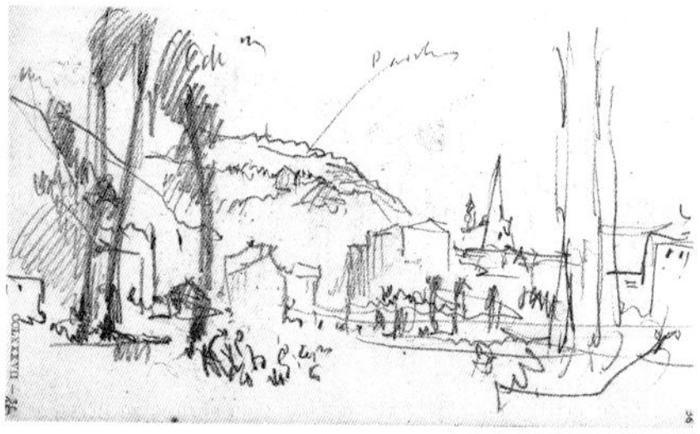

Spa (TB CCLXXXVII 36r)

Luxembourg

Turner's gouaches are here presented in a topographical sequence similar to that in the *Turner in Luxembourg* catalogue (1984), to which the present work is much indebted. It begins to the west of Luxembourg and then proceeds down the valleys of the Pétrusse and the Alzette, i.e. anti-clockwise round the St-Esprit citadel and the Rocher du Bock, with a short detour up the Alzette valley. A number of works previously listed elsewhere as views of Luxembourg by Turner are here excluded; some of these definitely show places elsewhere in Europe (e.g. W 1019, 1021); one features elsewhere in this catalogue under its proper identification (TB CCXXII X; cat.no.85); some, known only from listings in nineteenth-century sale catalogues, with no description or illustration, have been held over while research into them continues.

The present list of twenty works includes four which did not feature in the 1984 catalogue mentioned above, most notably the very fine 'Luxembourg from the South' (cat.no.122), now presented to the public for the first time. It is quite possible that still further depictions of Luxembourg by Turner also exist, unrecorded and unsighted since their execution.

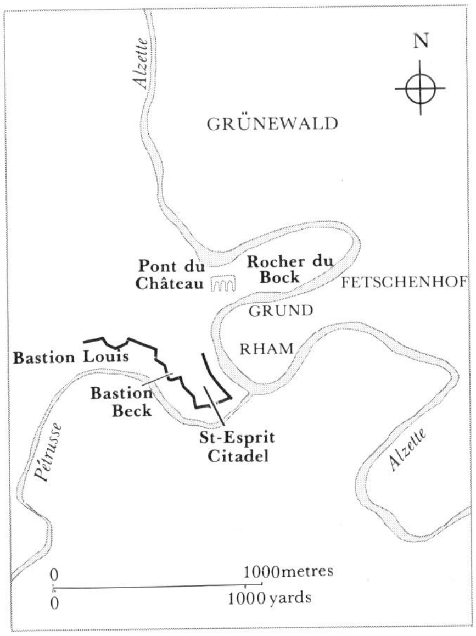

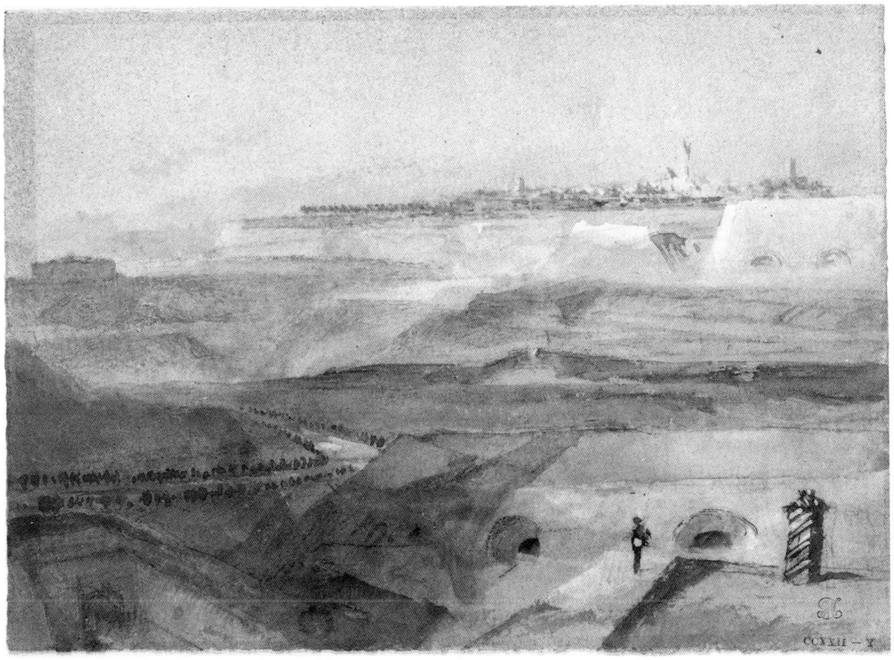

'Distant View of Luxembourg from the Bourbon Plateau' (TB CCXXII Y)

Distant View of Luxembourg from the Bourbon Plateau *c.*1839

Gouache and watercolour on blue paper
137 × 188 ($5\frac{3}{8} \times 7\frac{3}{8}$)
TB CCXXII Y
D20284
EXH & LIT: National Gallery 6th Loan Collection, 1896–1931, no.4; Finberg (1909), p.691 (as 'Fort and earthworks', *c.*1826); Wilkinson (1975), p.87 (untitled, 1826?); Clifford (1977) (unpag., as 1834); Luxembourg (1984), no.1 (as *c.*1834)

This distant view of Luxembourg from the west gives a good idea of the extensive fortifications constructed a considerable distance beyond the town itself, perched on its rocky cliff above the rivers Pétrusse and Alzette. The silhouette of Luxembourg was recorded by Turner in a rough pencil sketch (TB CCLXXXVIII 34r), but the foreground of his gouache seems to be the product of his memories of the countless fortifications seen throughout his 1839 tour.

120 Luxembourg from the Bourbon Plateau *c.*1839

Gouache, pen and ink, and watercolour on blue paper
141 × 188 ($5\frac{9}{16} \times 7\frac{3}{8}$)
TB CCXXII E
D20264
EXH & LIT: National Gallery 5th Loan Collection, 1896–1931, no.10; Finberg (1909), p.690 (as 'Fortified town (? Luxembourg)', *c.*1826); Clifford (1977) (n.p., as 1834); Luxembourg (1984), no.2 (as *c.*1834)

Turner's viewpoint here is much closer to Luxembourg than it was in TB CCXXII Y, so that the contours of the citadel of St-Esprit and the fortified Rham plateau to the right are now both clearly distinguishable. As with TB CCXXII Y, Turner's foreground is based on a fusion of memory and imagination.

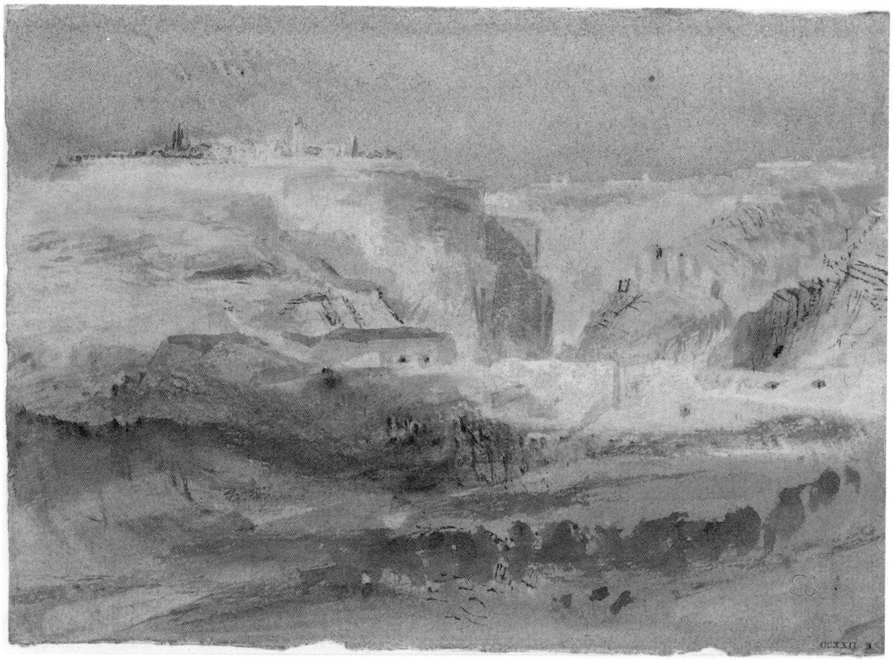

121 The Citadel of St-Esprit, Luxembourg* *c.*1839

Gouache and watercolour on blue paper
140 × 194 ($5\frac{1}{2} \times 7\frac{5}{8}$)
TB CCXXI O
D20248
EXH & LIT: National Gallery Exhibited Drawings no.190; Holme (ed.) (1903), ill.98; Ruskin (1903–12), vol.XIII, p.386; Finberg (1909), p.689 (as 'Luxembourg (?)', *c.*1826); Exhibition held in Luxembourg for the State Visit of H.M. King Baudouin of Belgium (1959); *Cahiers Luxembourgeois* (1964); Brussels (1971), no.36; Wilkinson (1975), p.86 (as 1826?); Programme of the State Visit of H.M. Queen Elizabeth II to Brussels (1976); Clifford (1977) (unpag., as 1834); Annual Report of the Crédit Européen, Luxembourg (1978), pp.16–17; Wilton (1982), no.70 (as *c.*1834); Luxembourg (1984), no.3 (as *c.*1834)

In this gouache it is easy to appreciate the colossal height and near-impregnability of Luxembourg, frequently referred to in Turner's day as the strongest fortress in Europe. Turner's view is from the south-east (on today's Boulevard d'Avranches) and depicts the first close-up view of the town on its rock seen by the traveller coming – as he himself did – from Metz and Thionville. The gouache is based on the main pencil sketch on TB CCLXXXVIII 33v and shows the citadel of St-Esprit rising perpendicularly from the valley of the Pétrusse – swathed in blue mist – and, on the extreme right, that of the Alzette. Two further bastions – Beck and Louis – can be seen to the left, while the skyline is broken only by the tower of the seventeenth-century Jesuit church, elevated to the status of cathedral in 1870. The mastery of scale here exhibited by Turner led Ruskin to describe this work as 'Probably the grandest drawing of this date', an opinion which it is hard to dispute.

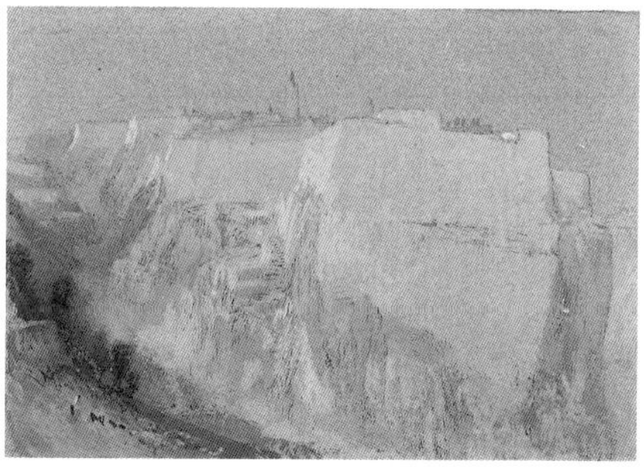

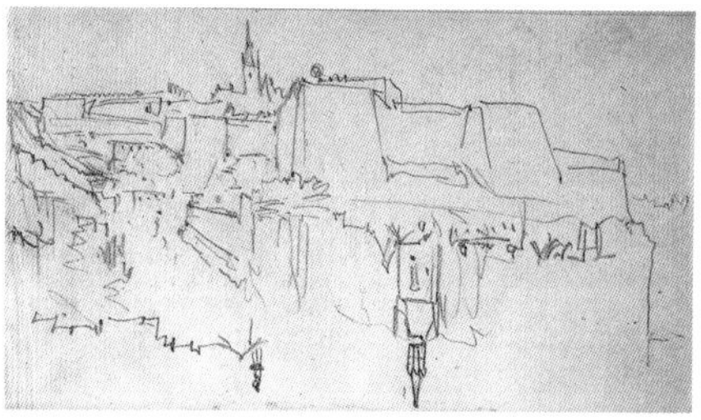

Luxembourg (TB CCLXXXVIII 33v)

Luxembourg from the South *c.*1839

Gouache and watercolour on blue paper
135 × 190 ($5\frac{5}{16} \times 7\frac{1}{2}$)
PROV: . . .; Henry Vaughan; J.L. Roget; S.R. Roget; sale of a descendant, Sotheby's, London, 12 March 1987 (64); Sotheby's, London, 16 November 1989 (90); private collection
Not in Wilton

This gouache is equally notable for its wonderfully subtle – indeed, near-visionary – twilight colouring and for its idealised and all-embracing view of Luxembourg. The St-Esprit citadel, the Pont du Château, the Grünewald, the Grund and the Rham have all been brought together by Turner in a perfectly composed scene that no visitor to Luxembourg can ever have seen, but many must have dreamed of.

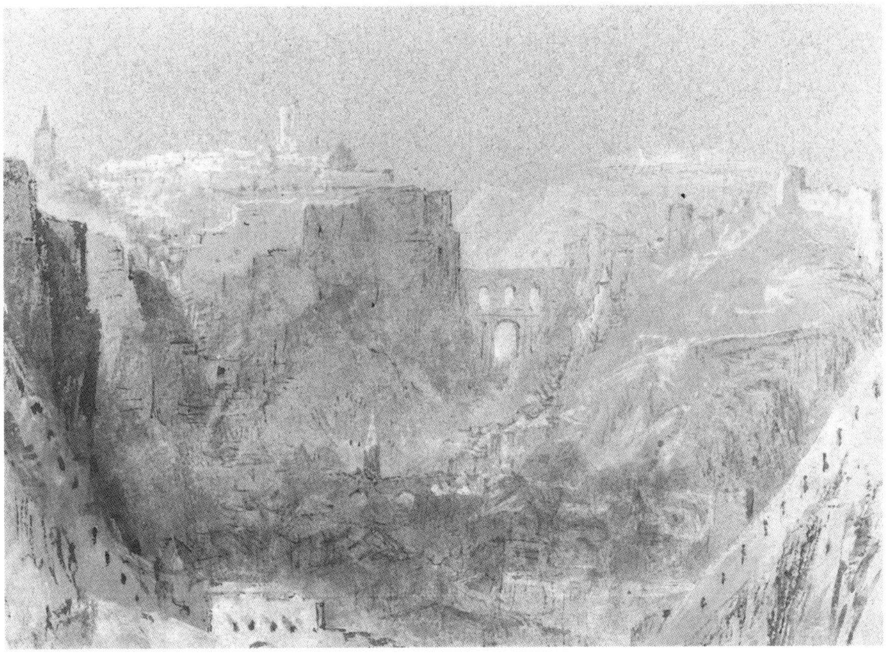

'Luxembourg from the South' (not in Wilton)

122 Luxembourg from the South* *c.*1839

Gouache, pen and ink, and watercolour on blue paper
133 × 187 ($5\frac{1}{4} \times 7\frac{3}{8}$)
PROV: . . .; by descent to present owner
Private Collection
Not in Wilton

This magnificent but previously unrecorded work is similar to that in Dublin (W 1010) and is particularly notable for its delicate blending of warm colours: peaceful yellow, soft pink and gentle orange. The viewpoint is further away from the Pont du Château than in that work or in the drawing sold at Sotheby's in 1989 to which it is also comparable.

Like several of Turner's other gouaches of Luxembourg, this is a somewhat idealised view of the grandest fortress town in all Europe: he treats the soaring fortified cliffs as though they were Alpine summits with villages nestling at their feet, and the Pont du Château is transformed into a 'devil's bridge' perched across an Alpine chasm. Nevertheless, nearly all its principal features are to be found in the pencil sketches on TB CCLXXXVIII 32v–33r which record both the masses in the middle distance and much of the foreground detail.

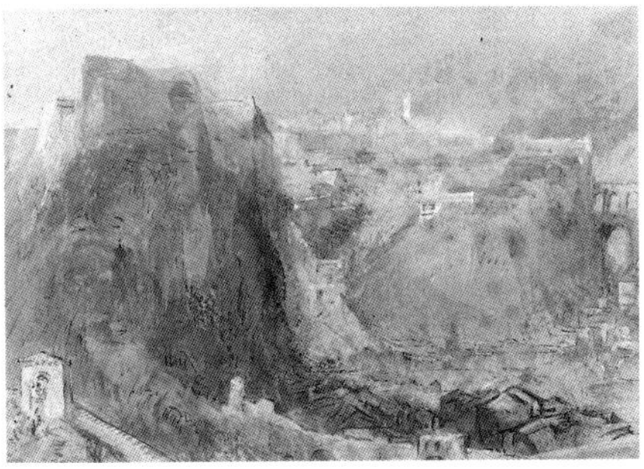

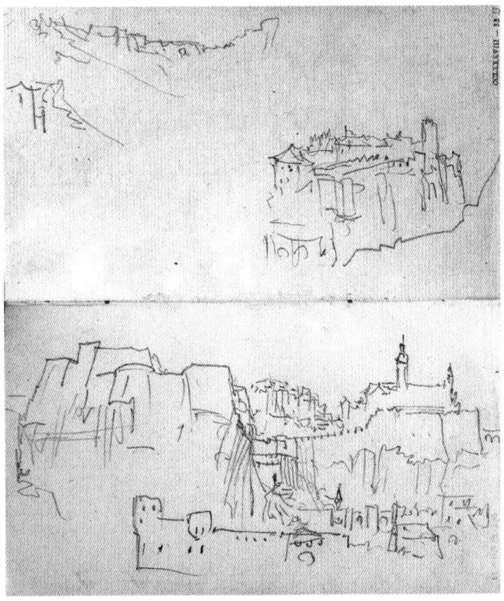

Luxembourg (TB CCLXXXVIII 32v–33r)

View up the Alzette Valley, Luxembourg, with the Fortifications of the Rham Plateau *c.*1839

Gouache, pen and ink, and watercolour on blue paper
138 × 192 ($5\frac{7}{16} \times 7\frac{9}{16}$)
TB CCXXII K
D20270
EXH & LIT: National Gallery 5th Loan Collection, 1896–1931, no.49 (as 'Fortified Defile, Italy (?)'); Finberg (1909), p.690 (as 'Town in valley, with fortifications on hills above', *c.*1826); Clifford (1977) (unpag., as 1834); Luxembourg (1984), no.5 (as *c.*1834)

Although the Rham plateau features frequently in Turner's gouaches of Luxembourg, this seems to be the only one showing it from the west, looking eastwards along the Alzette valley past the Porte de Thionville. Virtually all the ingredients of the scene appear in the pencil sketch on TB CCLXXXVIII 34r where a notable feature is the heavy hatching on the cliff face above the valley, rendered with equal emphasis in the gouache itself.

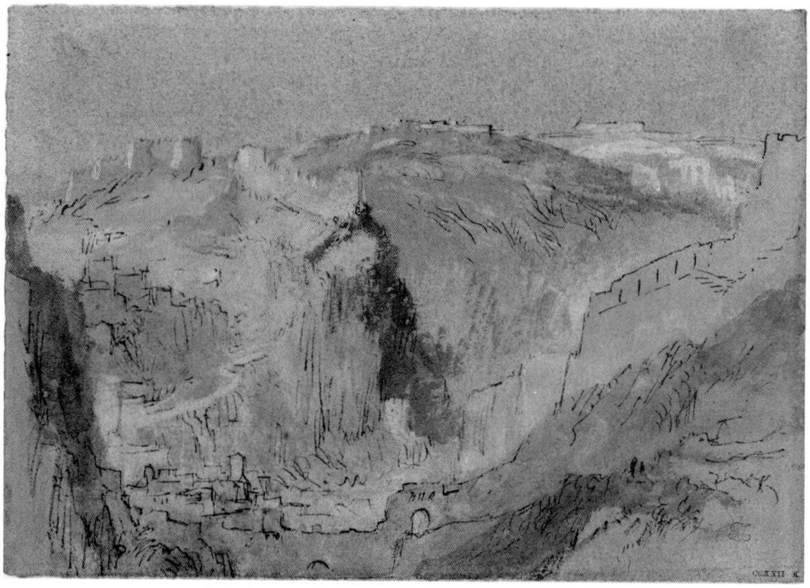

'View up the Alzette Valley, Luxembourg, with the Fortifications of the Rham Plateau' (TB CCXXII K)

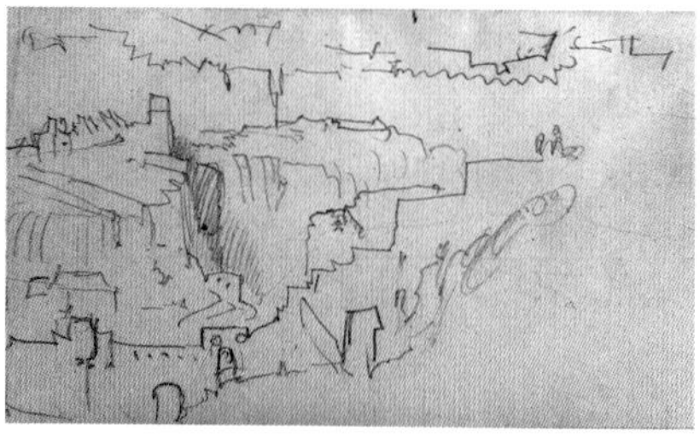

Luxembourg (TB CCLXXXVIII 34r)

Luxembourg from the Alzette Valley *c.*1839

Gouache, pen and ink, and watercolour on blue paper
138 × 187 ($5\frac{7}{16} \times 7\frac{3}{8}$)
TB CCXXII M
D20272
EXH & LIT: National Gallery 5th Loan Collection, 1896–1931, no.48; Finberg (1909), p.691 (as 'Ehrenbreitstein', *c.*1826); Clifford (1977) (unpag., as 1834); Luxembourg (1984), no.6 (as *c.*1834)

Turner's viewpoint is here south-east of the Rham plateau, with the rest of Luxembourg visible high above and beyond its towers. In its general portrayal of this part of the Alzette valley and the distant town, the gouache is close to Turner's pencil sketch of the same scene (TB CCLXXXVIII 56v), but he has dramatically compressed the towers of the Rham just as he did in another gouache in the series (cat.no.120).

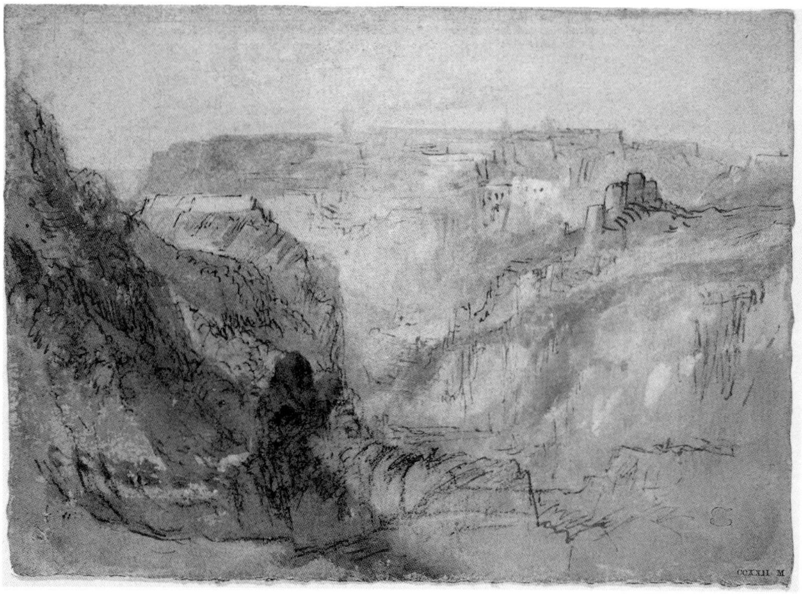

'Luxembourg from the Alzette Valley' (TB CCXXII M)

123 The Rham Plateau, Luxembourg, from the Alzette Valley *c.*1839

Gouache, pen and ink, and watercolour on blue paper
140 × 193 ($5\frac{1}{2} \times 7\frac{5}{8}$)
TB CCLIX 177
D24742
EXH & LIT: National Gallery Exhibited Drawings, no.432c; Finberg (1909), p.799 (as 'The Great Fortress', *c.*1826–33); Luxembourg (1984), no.7 (as *c.*1834)

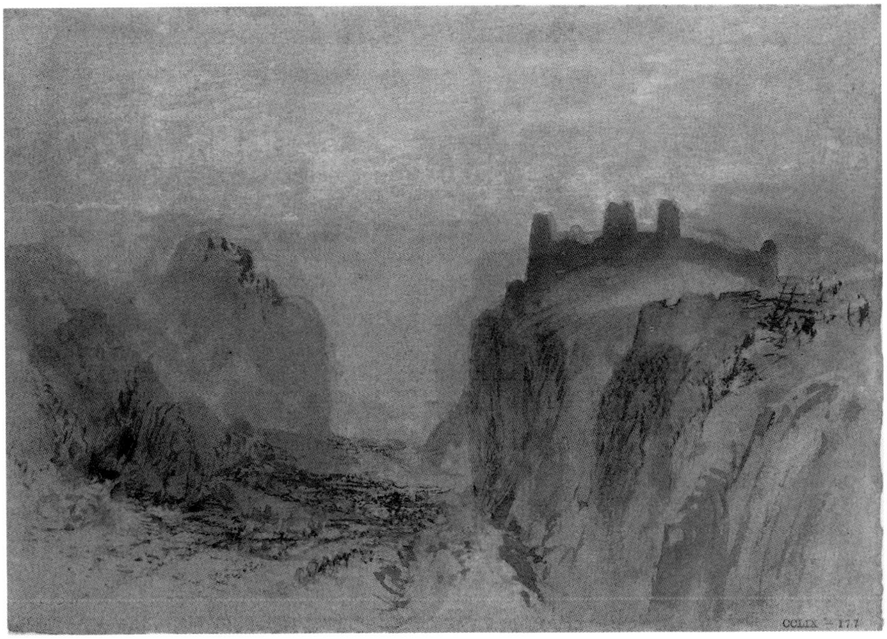

Turner's most distant view of the Rham from the east is a wonderfully stark evocation both of the fortifications themselves and of the grassy river valley which they dominate. The artist achieved this by a careful adaptation of his scene from the pencil sketch on TB CCLXXXVIII 56v: he blocked out the central vista of Luxembourg and left only its flanking wings of rocky precipices and brooding light and shade.

This gouache shares its predominant colour – a warm brown suggestive of sunbaked ancient brickwork – with another, equally dominated by fortifications (cat.no.104, showing Sedan).

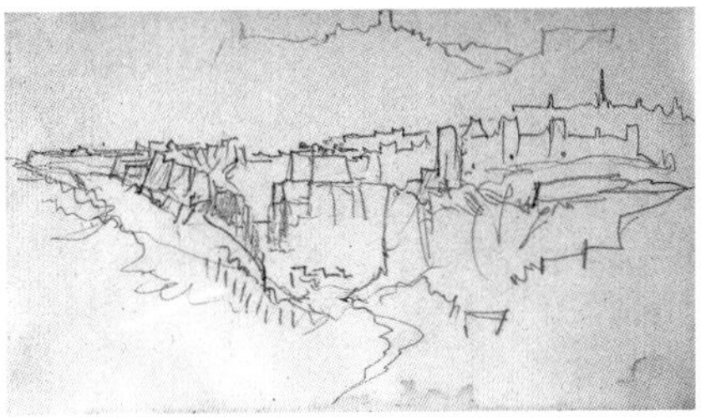

Luxembourg (TB CCLXXXVIII 56v)

The Pont du Château, Luxembourg *c.*1839

Gouache, pen and ink, and watercolour on blue paper
139 × 191 ($5\frac{1}{2} \times 7\frac{1}{2}$)
PROV: . . .; Henry Vaughan Bequest 1900; National Gallery of Ireland, Dublin (2429)
W 1010
EXH & LIT: Armstrong (1902), p.278 (as 'Sisteron, Basses Alpes (?)', 1830–5); Luxembourg (1984), no.13 (as *c.*1834); B. Dawson, *Turner in the National Gallery of Ireland* (1988), pp.88–9 (as *c.*1830).

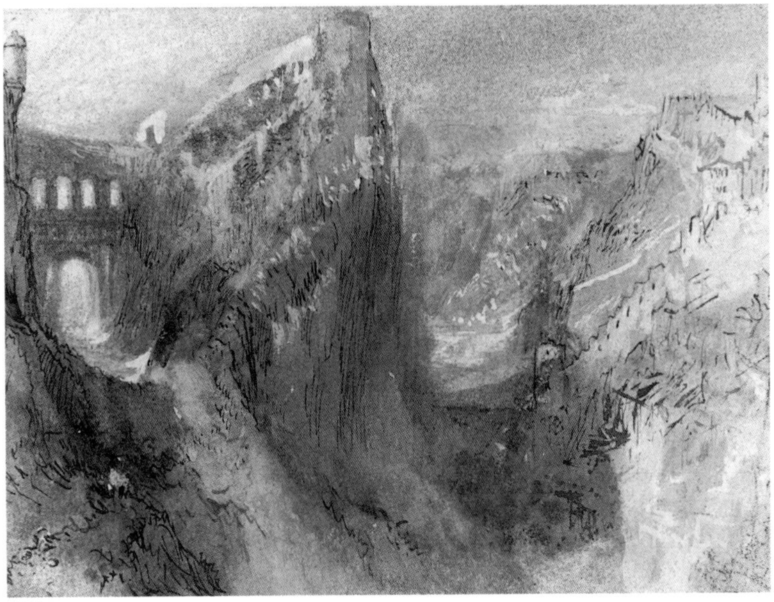

'The Pont du Château, Luxembourg' (W 1010)

This magnificent work – which cannot be seen outside Dublin – is one of the highlights of Turner's work inspired by Luxembourg. Comparison with the pencil sketches on which it is based (see under cat.no.43) shows Turner at his most masterful and ingenious in compressing or extending his subject matter, elaborating or eliminating it entirely to suit his own personal vision of this fortified rock created by man from the raw materials of nature.

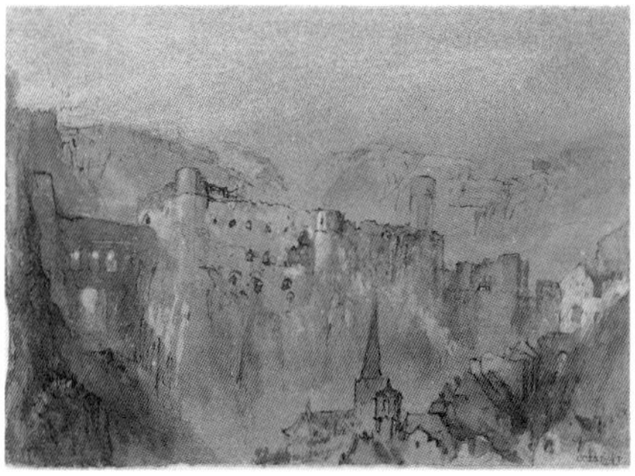

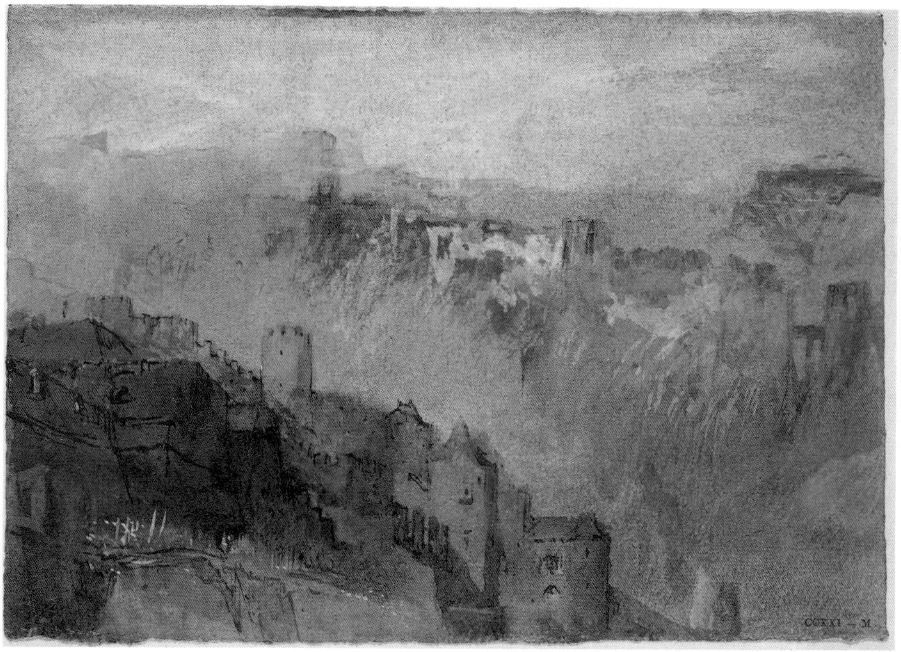

124 The Pont du Château and the Bock, Luxembourg* *c.*1839

Gouache, pen and ink, and watercolour on blue paper
140 × 190 ($5\frac{1}{2} \times 7\frac{1}{2}$)
TB CCXXI P
D20249
EXH & LIT: National Gallery Exhibited Drawings, no.191; Ruskin (1903–12), vol.XIII, p.386 ('Too blue and red, but noble'); Finberg (1909), p.689 (as 'Luxembourg (?)', *c.*1826); Tockert, *Luxembourg vu par les auteurs anglais et americains* (Touring Club Luxembourg, 1938), p.22; M. Noppeney, *Luxembourg autrefois* (1958), vol.III, p.5; Hemmer and Schroeder, *Aspects du Luxembourg* (1958); Exhibition held in Luxembourg for the State Visit of H.M. King Baudouin of Belgium (1959); *Cahiers Luxembourgeois* (1964); Brussels (1971), no.34; Wilton (1982), no.71 (as *c.*1834); Texas (1982), no.50; Luxembourg (1984), no.12 (as *c.*1834)

The left-hand part of this gouache shows the Pont du Château which links the main fortified rock of Luxembourg (unseen but suggested by the vertical mass on the extreme left) with the Rocher du Bock (centre) which bears the Bock, or castle, and its own set of fortifications. The valley of the Alzette which encircles the latter is here suggested by vaporous blue haze, while in the right foreground Turner shows some of the buildings of the suburb of the Grund – St John's church and the Porte de Trèves.

Several different pencil sketches in TB CCLXXXVIII contributed to this complex scene. Most of the main ingredients feature in those on ff.32v (lower sketch), 33r and 60v (right hand half), both drawn down in the Alzette valley. However, Turner's viewpoint in the gouache is much higher than any of these, since he now looks down on to the Alzette and the Grund and over the top of the Bock to the northern fortifications of Luxembourg on the Grünewald; this view was sketched from a similarly high position but slightly further to the east on f.59v.

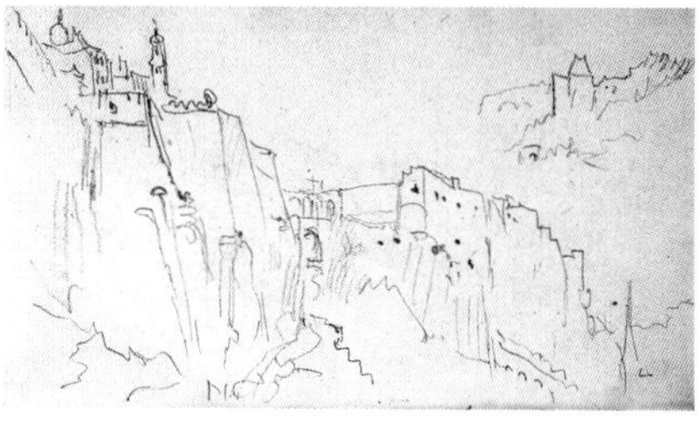

Luxembourg (TB CCLXXXVIII 60v)

125 The Bock and the Rham, Luxembourg, above the Alzette Valley *c.*1839

Gouache, pen and ink, and watercolour on blue paper
142 × 191 ($5\frac{9}{16} \times 7\frac{1}{2}$)
TB CCXXI M
D20246
EXH & LIT: National Gallery Exhibited Drawings no.188; Ruskin (1903–12), vol.XIII, p.386 ('Highest quality'); Finberg (1909), p.689 (as 'Luxembourg?', *c.*1826); *Cahiers Luxembourgeois* (1954); Exhibition held in Luxembourg for the State Visit of H.M. King Baudouin of Belgium (1959); Brussels (1971), no.27; Programme of the State Visit of H.M. Queen Elizabeth II to Brussels (1976); Clifford (1977) (unpag., as 1834); Annual Report of the Crédit Européen (1978), p.12; Wilton (1982), no.69 (as *c.*1834); Texas (1982), no.47; Luxembourg (1984), no.11 (as *c.*1834)

As in cat.no.124, Turner here spreads the fortified Rocher du Bock across the centre of his drawing, with the Grünewald above it in the right-hand distance. The foreground is occupied by the Rham, now presenting an entirely different face from those seen in TB CCXXII E, CCXXII K, CCXXII M and CCLIX 177 (cat.nos.120, 123). The scene derives largely from

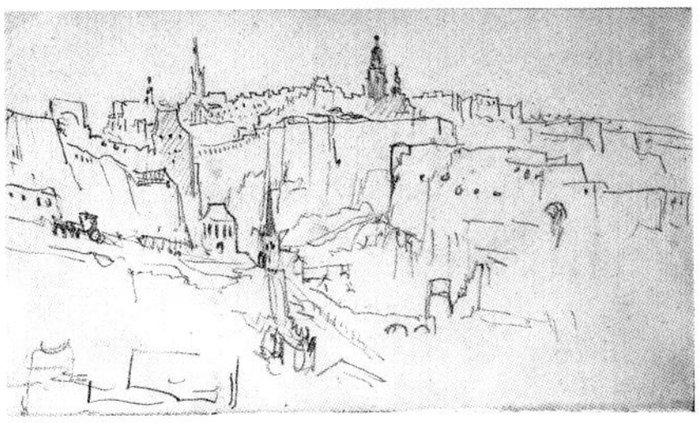

Luxembourg (TB CCLXXXVIII 58v)

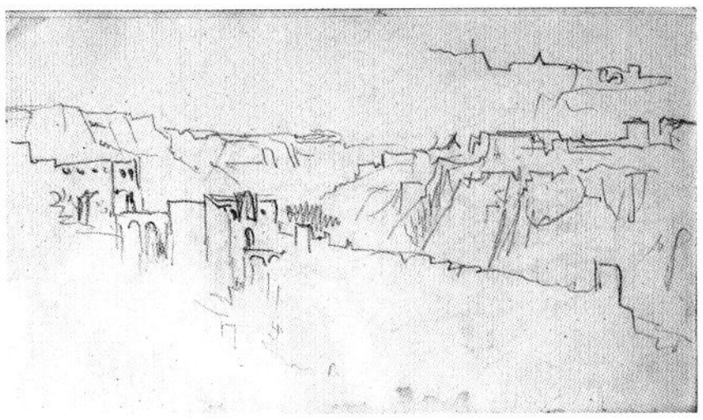

Luxembourg (TB CCLXXXVIII 57v)

Turner's pencil sketches on TB CCLXXXVIII 58v and 57v which, taken together, form a ninety degree panoramic sweep of the view to the west and the north from a high viewpoint east of the Porte de Trèves. However, much has been omitted and much added from the storehouse of Turner's imagination – most notably the army of spear-carrying soldiers on the left.

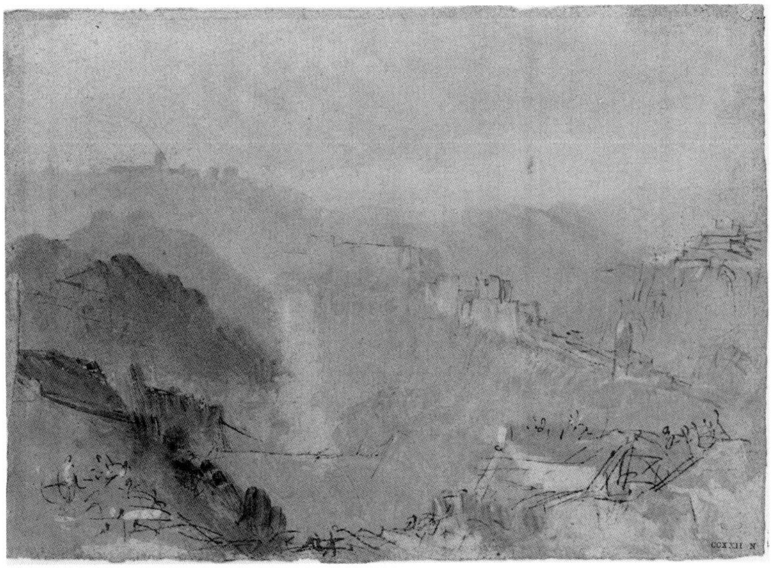

'The Bock, Luxembourg' (TB CCXXII N)

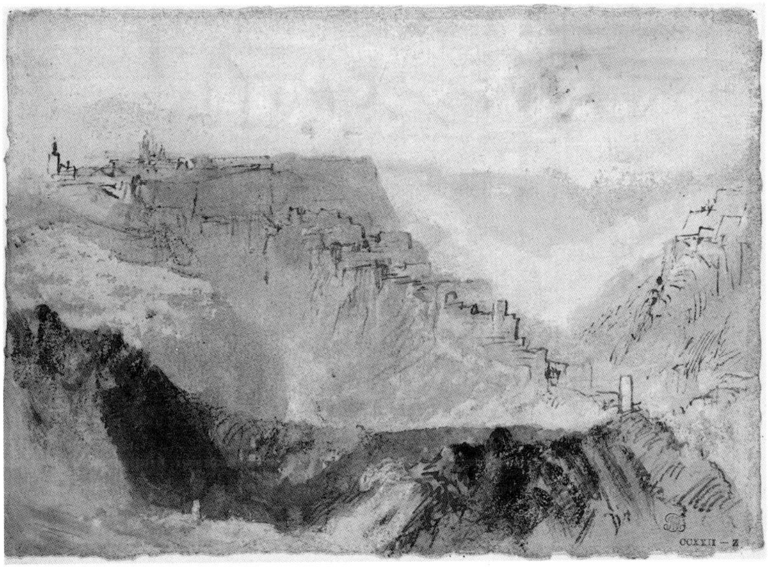

'The Bock, Luxembourg' (TB CCXXII Z)

The Bock, Luxembourg *c.*1839

Gouache, pen and ink, and watercolour on blue paper
139 × 189 ($5\frac{1}{2} \times 7\frac{7}{16}$)
TB CCXXII N
D20273
EXH & LIT: National Gallery 5th Loan Collection, 1896–1931, no.46 (as 'Italian town, with distant waterfall (Tivoli?)'); Finberg (1909), p.691 (as 'Town on hills', *c.*1826); Clifford (1977) (unpag., as 1834); Annual Report of the Crédit Européen (1978); Luxembourg (1984), no.8 (as *c.*1834)

The Bock, Luxembourg *c.*1839

Gouache, pen and ink, and watercolour on blue paper
137 × 188 ($5\frac{3}{8} \times 7\frac{3}{8}$)
TB CCXXII Z
D20285
EXH & LIT: National Gallery 6th Loan Collection, 1896–1931, no.5 (as 'Sion, Switzerland'); Finberg (1909), p.691 (as 'Town on hill', *c.*1826); Clifford (1977) (unpag., as 1834); Luxembourg (1984), no.9 (as *c.*1834)

Both these works concentrate on Luxembourg's third great fortified rock, the Bock, showing it from a high viewpoint to the east, so that its entire length is seen, running diagonally across the page. It appears more or less thus – amongst many other features – in several of Turner's pencil sketches (TB CCLXXXVIII 57r, 57v, 58r, 59v, 60r), but his purpose in both these two gouaches has been experimental: masses are simplified, and a variety of colours are used – many of them non-representational but highly evocative.

Luxembourg from the Fetschenhof *c.*1839

Gouache, pen and ink, and watercolour on blue paper
140 × 190 ($5\frac{1}{2}$ × $7\frac{1}{2}$)
PROV: John Ruskin; sold 5 June 1880 to George Allen; B.B. Macgeorge; George Goyder; Musée de l'Etat, Luxembourg (1983–183)
W 1020
EXH & LIT: Macgeorge sale catalogue, Glasgow (1958), p.12; London (1974), no.374; Luxembourg, presentation at the Grand-Ducal Palace, 24 January 1984; *Télécran* 28 January 1984, pp.24–5; Hemecht (1984), no.1; Luxembourg (1984), no.10 (as *c.*1834)

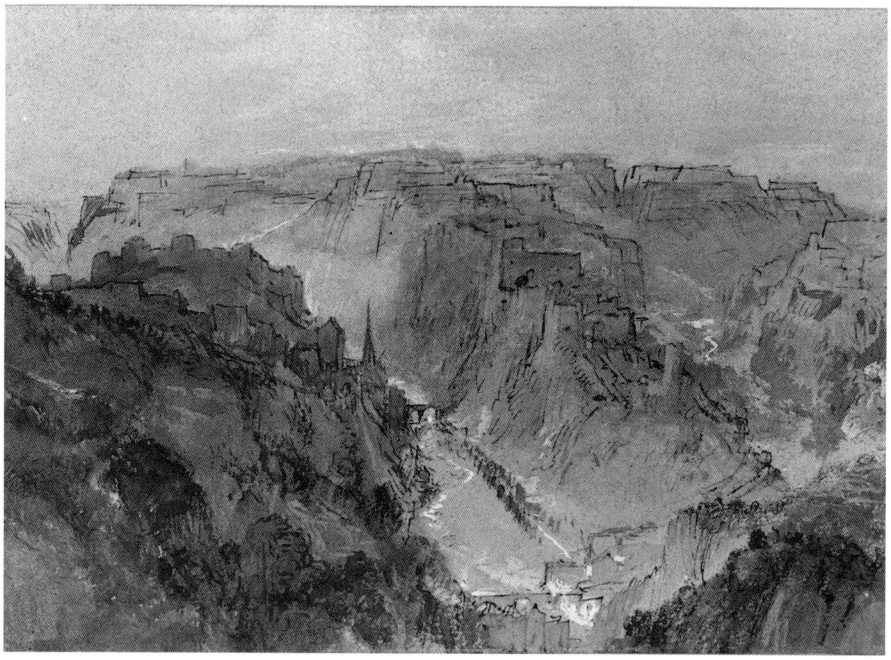

'Luxembourg from the Fetschenhof' (W 1020)

This view – which may be usefully compared to the pencil sketch on TB CCLXXXVIII 57r has elements in common with TB CCXXII N and CCXXII Z, notably its subject and viewpoint and also its palette and the handling of both gouache and ink. It is, however, a far more comprehensive view from further away and higher up, so that the Rham and Grünewald are visible as well as the Bock. It is also infinitely more subtle in its atmospheric effects and rendering of scale and distance. The vaporous light palette, enlivened by rapid outlines in ink, is typical of many of Turner's Belgian and Luxembourg scenes and it is indeed a gem among those of Luxembourg.

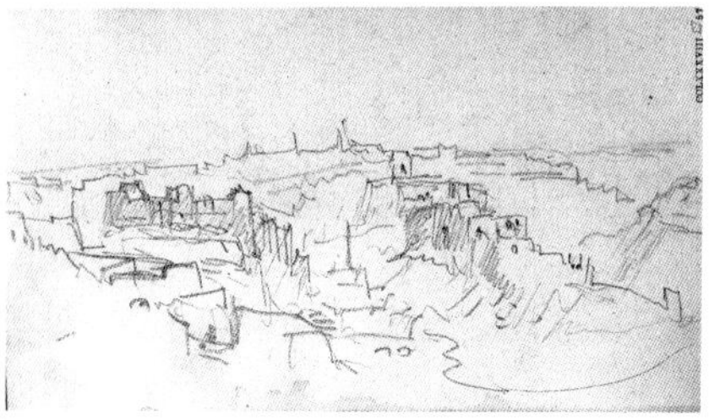

Luxembourg (TB CCLXXXVIII 57r)

Luxembourg from the East *c.*1839

Gouache, pen and ink, and watercolour on blue paper
140 × 190 ($5\frac{1}{2}$ × $7\frac{1}{2}$)
PROV: . . .; Christie's, 30 November 1901 (41); Agnew; E.B. Moser; Shrewsbury School
Not in Wilton
EXH & LIT: Agnew's Autumn Exhibition of English Watercolours, Manchester, November 1902; *Turner Studies*, vol.3, no.1, 1983, p.63; Yardley (1988), p.45, n.5

This work uses the same strong diagonal structure as is found in several other Turner gouaches of Luxembourg, its dark rendering of the wall-girdled hillside on the left being especially comparable to that in TB CCXXI M (cat.no.125). However, Turner is here looking back at Luxembourg from much further along the Alzette valley beyond the Porte de Trèves. His gouache shows a similar view to that sketched in pencil on TB CCLXXXVIII 60r. Many of the same buildings and hills are shown as in W 1020, but from a much lower viewpoint.

126 **The Rham Plateau and the Bock, Luxembourg, from the North-east*** *c.*1839

Gouache, pen and ink, and watercolour on blue paper
142 × 190 ($5\frac{9}{16}$ × $7\frac{1}{2}$)
Watermarked: B,E . . ./18 . . .
TB CCXXI L
D20245
EXH & LIT: National Gallery Exhibited Drawings no. 187; Ruskin (1903–12), vol. XIII, p.386 ('Forced, and poor'); Finberg (1909), p.689 (as 'Luxembourg (?)', *c.*1826); Exhibition held in Luxembourg for the State Visit of H.M. King Baudouin of Belgium (1959); *Cahiers Luxembourgeois* (1964); Brussels (1971), no.33; Texas (1982), no.46; Luxembourg (1984), no.18 (as *c.*1834)

The central part of this gouache is occupied by the fortified Rocher du Bock, seen from the north-east in a very foreshortened view. Its length and the complexity of its fortifications, which are so predominant in Turner's other gouaches of Luxembourg (TB CCXXI M, CCXXI P,

CCXXII N, CCXXII Z, W 1020; cat.nos. 124–5), are here largely veiled from sight, in contrast to the verdant and delightfully fresh foreground, belonging to yet another high plateau overlooking the Alzette valley and apparently unfortified.

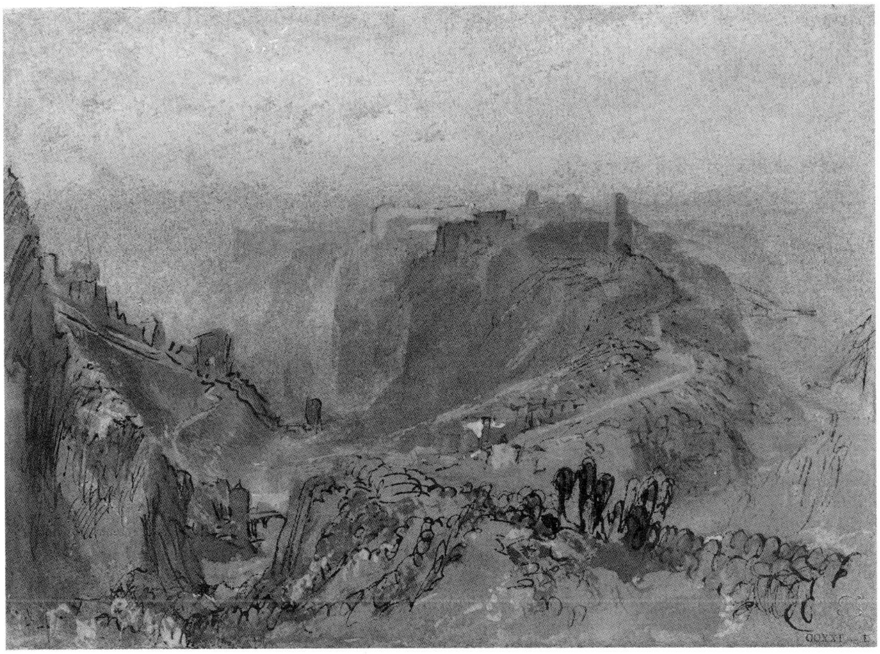

The Rham and the Bock, Luxembourg *c.*1839

Gouache, pen and ink, and watercolour on blue paper
140 × 190 ($5\frac{1}{2} \times 7\frac{1}{2}$)
TB CCXXI K
D20244
EXH & LIT: National Gallery Exhibited Drawings no.186; Ruskin (1903–12); vol.XIII, p.386 ('Splendid'); Finberg (1909), p.688 (as 'Luxembourg (?)', *c.*1826); Exhibition held in Luxembourg for the State Visit of H.M. King Baudouin of Belgium (1959); *Cahiers Luxembourgeois* (1964); Programme of the State Visit of H.M. Queen Elizabeth II to Brussels (1976); Clifford (1977) (unpag., as 1834); Luxembourg (1984), no.17 (as *c.*1834)

This gouache shows the same two fortified plateaux as TB CCXXI L (cat.no.126) from the same general direction but a much closer viewpoint. Both now seem far more precipitous, especially since the foreground is depicted in such a way as to suggest a deep chasm between the viewer and the hillside immediately opposite. Neither work seems to be based on pencil sketches in the sketchbook TB CCLXXXVIII but both combine elements which can be found there with material from Turner's memory.

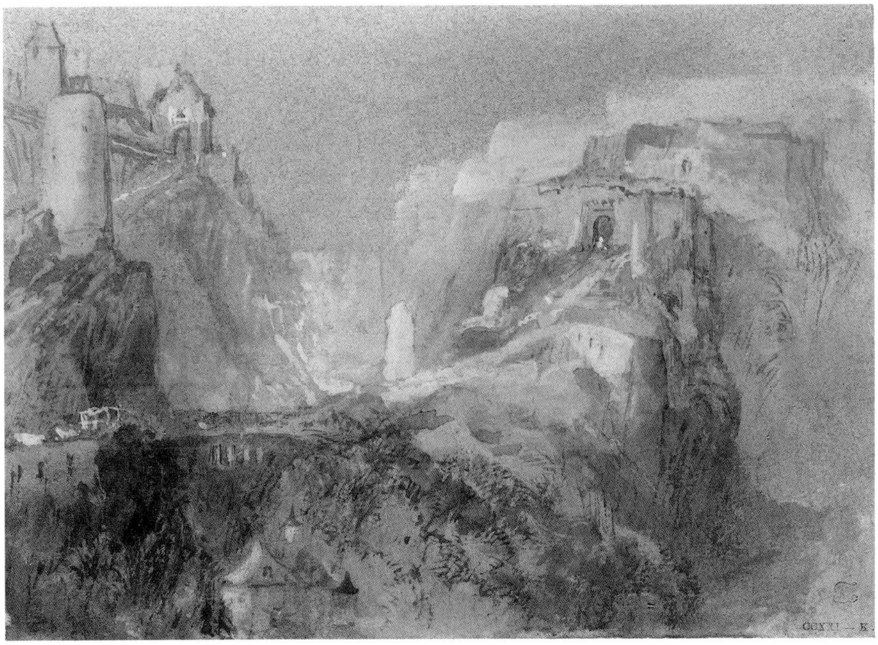

'The Rham and the Bock, Luxembourg'
(TB CCXXI K)

Luxembourg from the North *c.*1839

Gouache and watercolour on blue paper
140 × 190 ($5\frac{1}{2} \times 7\frac{1}{2}$)
PROV: . . .; Myles Birket Foster; his sale Christie's London, 28 April 1894 (39); J & W Vokins for £75 12s; Sir Donald Currie; Captain Wisley; by descent to present owner
Not in Wilton
EXH & LIT: Album of Photographs of the Birket Foster Collection of Turner Watercolours, no.62; probably the first 'Luxembourg' listed by Armstrong (1902, p.265): 'Town seen along crest of rock, deep red in evening light' (1830–5); Yardley (1988), p.41 and ill.2 (as *c.*1834)

This seems to be a very similar work to W 1022 (cat.no.127) and the work sold at Sotheby's in 1989. Turner evidently executed many visionary views of Luxembourg, seen at a distance, as well as those from close to. It is easy to imagine the attractions of both types of view.

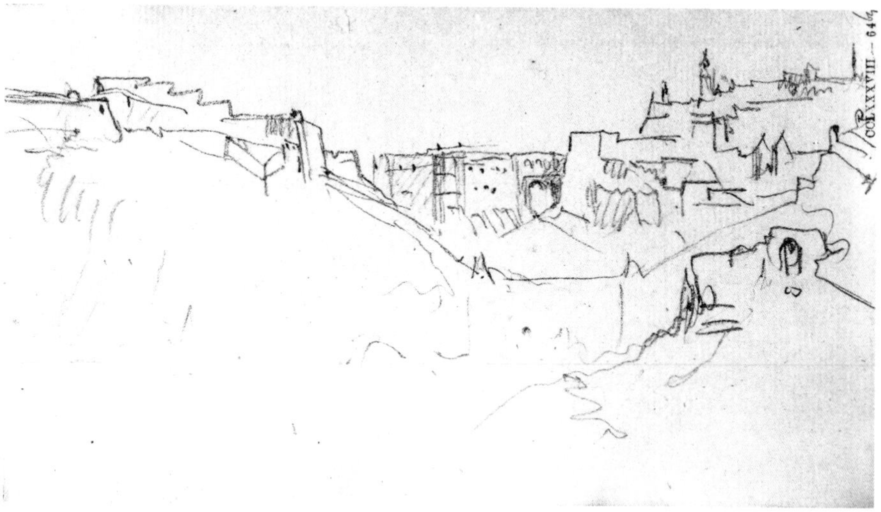

Luxembourg (TB CCLXXXVIII 64r)

127 **Luxembourg from the Alzette Valley to the North** *c.*1839

Gouache and watercolour on blue paper
140 × 187 ($5\frac{1}{2} \times 7\frac{3}{8}$)
PROV: . . .; Beresford Rimington Heaton Bequest
N05240
W 1022
EXH & LIT: Clifford (1977) (unpag., as 1834); Luxembourg (1984), no.21 (as *c.*1834)

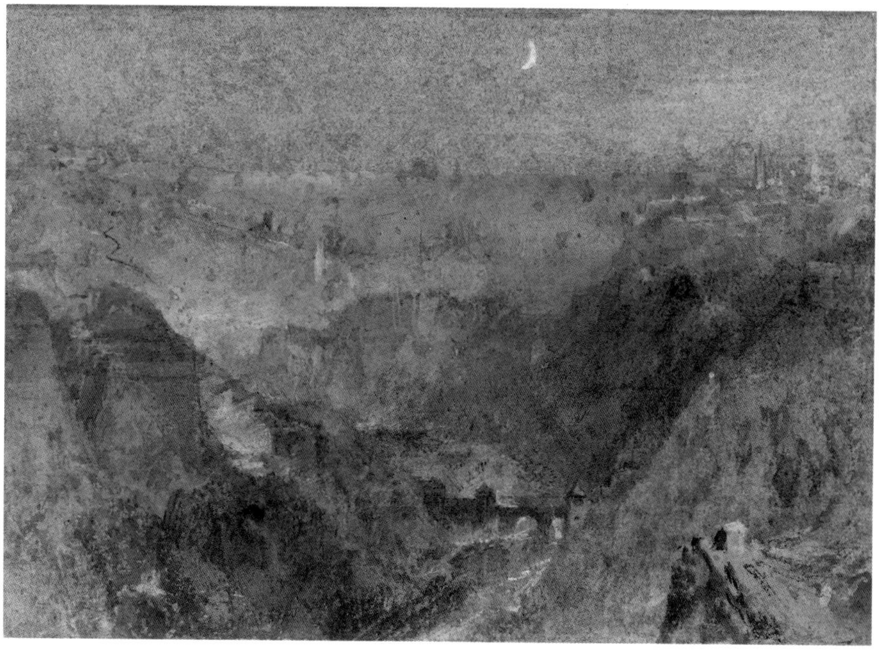

Turner made numerous sketches of Luxembourg from the northern stretch of the Alzette valley, looking back to the multifarious fortifications of the town from beyond the bridge with the towers built by Vauban (TB CCLXXXVIII 64r, 64v, 65r, 66r, 66v, 67r). Elements from several of these sketches are fused in this gouache, where the radiant colours – similar to those in TB CCXXII E, CCXXI M (cat. nos.120, 125) and CCXXII M but far more saturated – transform Luxembourg into an enchanted city bathed in glorious rosy light.

This work is one of two gouaches bequeathed to the Tate Gallery by Beresford Rimington Heaton in 1940, of which the other drawing, traditionally also known as 'Luxembourg' (W 1021), clearly depicts some other European city and is not on blue paper. It has previously been believed that W 1021 once belonged to Myles Birket Foster; however, it is evident from Edward Yardley's account of Foster's collection of Turner watercolours (1988) that this is not the case and the provenance of neither W 1021 nor W 1022 can be traced back further than Beresford Rimington Heaton.

Luxembourg from the North *c.*1839

Gouache and watercolour on blue paper
140 × 192 ($5\frac{1}{2} \times 7\frac{9}{16}$)
TB CCXXI N
D20247
EXH & LIT: National Gallery Exhibited Drawings no.189; Holme (ed.) (1903), ill.101; Ruskin (1903–12), vol.XIII, p.386 ('Supreme of the set, except [for TB CXXI O]'); Finberg (1909), p.689 (as 'Luxembourg (?)', *c.*1826); Exhibition held in Luxembourg for the State Visit of H.M. King Baudouin of Belgium (1959); *Cahiers Luxembourgeois* (1964); Clifford (1977) (unpag., as 1834); Texas (1982). no.48; Luxembourg (1984), no.22 (as 'Vue de Luxembourg (?): la vallée de Pfaffenthal depuis la ville-haute (?)', *c.*1834)

Although it has not yet proved possible – even for experts in the topography of Luxembourg – to fix the precise scene here depicted, there can be little doubt that it does depict that town. The type of fortified plateaux depicted, the characteristic turret on the left, the straggle of houses clinging to the incline on the right – all these are so typical of Luxembourg itself and Turner's depictions of it that it is hard to believe that the gouache was inspired by any other site. Although many of the details have been altered, the structure of the scene as a whole has much in common with the pencil sketch on TB CCLXXXVIII 61r.

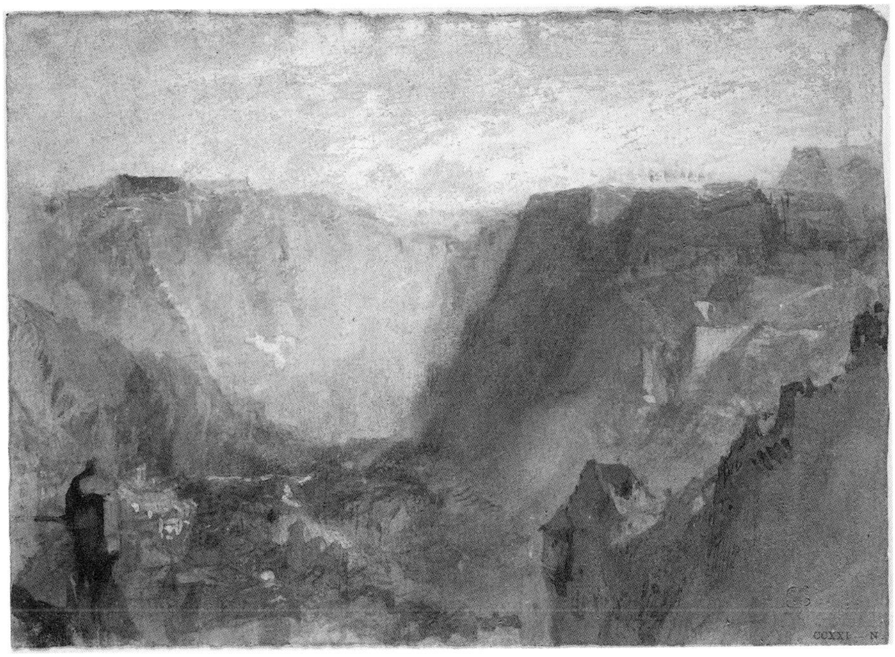

'Luxembourg from the North' (TB CCXXI N)

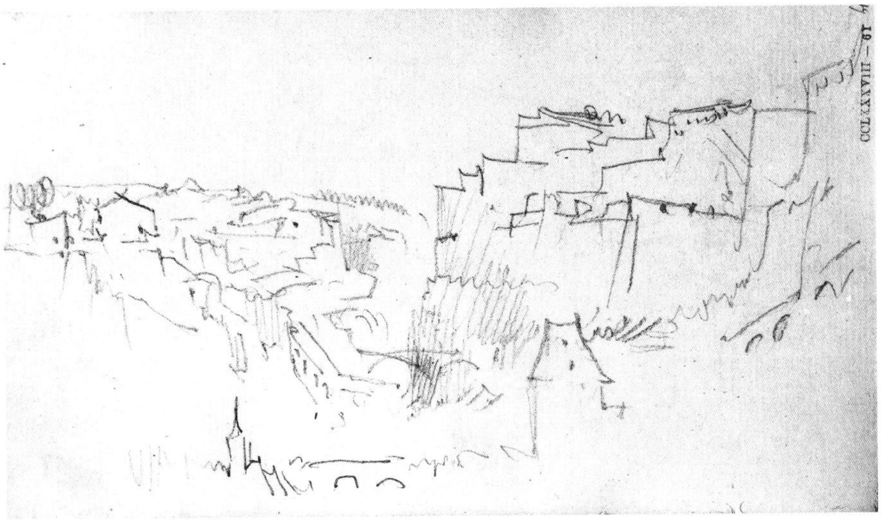

Luxembourg (TB CCLXXXVIII 61r)

The Late Ehrenbreitstein Colour Studies

Cat.nos.128–34 all show the fortress of Ehrenbreitstein from across the Rhine at Coblenz under different light and weather conditions but always in late afternoon or early evening when the multi-faceted west-facing fortress was catching the evening sun and the moon was rising. While Ehrenbreitstein appears as a vast rock which is gold, orange, yellow and red by turns, the dark pontoons of the bridge of boats are seen in a great variety of colours: turquoise, purple, crimson, brown and black. Some scenes still hold the sense of a warm afternoon, while others hint at the onset of a cool evening.

Turner's viewpoints are by no means identical: in two drawings he is just downstream of the bridge of boats (cat.nos.128, 129); in the other five he is at different spots upstream (cat.nos.130–4). However, these differences are easily explained and do not prevent the works being regarded as a series. Just like the visitors of today, nearly all nineteenth-century tourists in Coblenz sought to stay in one of the large hotels on the Rhine front which command this incomparable view and Turner must surely have stayed there too. He would have been able to choose from three: the Giant or 'Riese' which was the nearest to the landing-stage and described by Murray's *Handbook for Travellers on the Continent* of 1836 as 'moderate and respectable'; and two others which adjoined each other, the Bellevue and the Trois Suisses. All Turner's drawings show combinations of what he could actually have seen from his window or walking up and down on the quay outside. He would probably have dashed off all these studies in his hotel room, either simultaneously or in a couple of sessions. The speed of his work is shown not only in his handling of the colour washes and the expressive calligraphy of his pen work, but also in the jagged edges of his paper caused by his hasty division and subdivision of large sheets into the sizes he wanted.

Watching the light change across the surface of a great river was an activity which brought Turner particular pleasure in his later years. On the roof of his house in Cheyne Walk, Chelsea, he had a small platform, caged in by railings, specially constructed so that he could gain the widest possible view over his beloved Thames. Almost until the day he died, he would apparently rise at daybreak and, with a blanket or dressing-gown carelessly thrown over him, climb up to his viewing post to watch the colours of the sun flush into the pale morning sky.

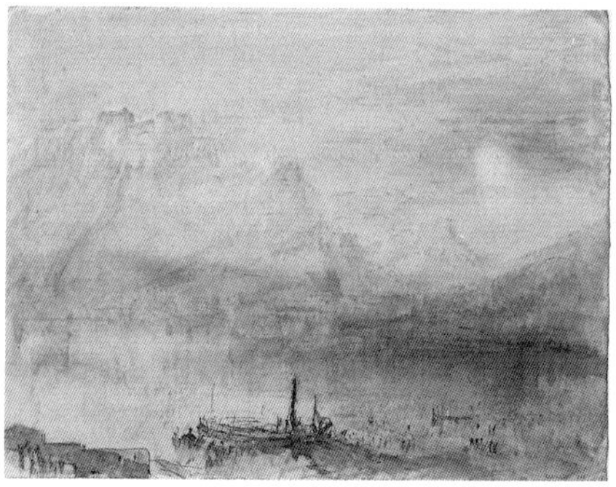

128 Ehrenbreitstein* 1841

Watercolour and pen and ink on white wove paper
237 × 300 ($9\frac{5}{16} \times 11\frac{13}{16}$)
TB CCCLXIV 346
D36206

This drawing is notable for its broad washes of warm colours contrasting with cooler passages and for its dynamic crimson pen drawing. Its viewpoint is the furthest downstream of the series, the bridge of boats being situated beyond the right-hand edge of the paper, the confluence of the Rhine and the Mosel beyond that on the left.

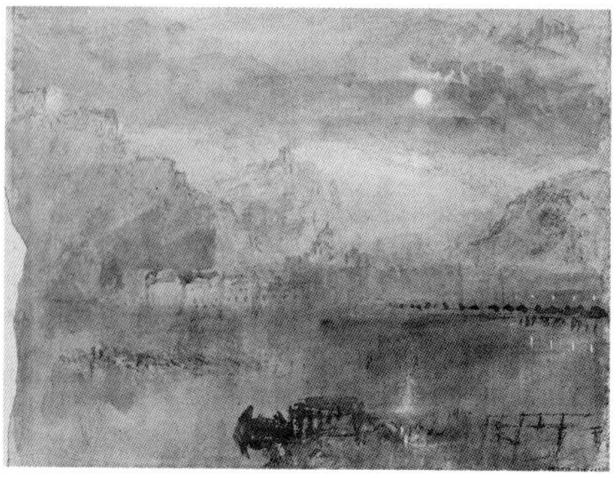

129 Ehrenbreitstein* 1841

Watercolour on white wove paper
240 × 305 ($9\frac{7}{16} \times 12$)
TB CCCLXIV 328
D36186

This drawing is one of the most magical and vivacious of the series, with its rich variety of colours including a strong turquoise for the bridge of boats and blood red on the raft and for the quay in the foreground. The moon has risen and flares have been lit along the opposite bank, producing bright reflections on the water. The composition of this work, with the domed church of the Holy Cross at its centre, is almost identical to that of one of Turner's 1839 gouache scenes (cat. no.81).

130 Ehrenbreitstein 1841

Gouache and watercolour on white wove paper
243 × 300 ($9\frac{9}{16} \times 11\frac{13}{16}$)
TB CCCLXIV 328a
D40181

The viewpoint of this work is slightly further upstream than that of cat.no.129, beyond the bridge of boats. Many of the colour washes used are the same but the predominant effect is that of pinkish purple shot with turquoise blue as in an expanse of silken fabric. Sadly this drawing has suffered grave injury over the years, particularly in the sky, and is no longer as beautiful as it must once have been.

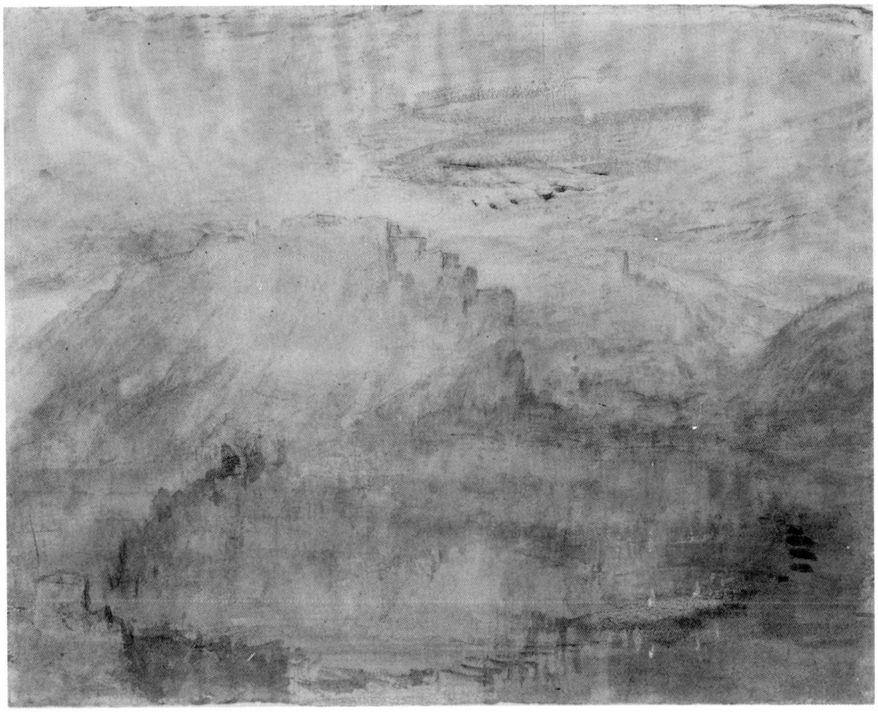

131 Ehrenbreitstein 1841

Watercolour on cream wove paper
245 × 305 ($9\frac{5}{8} \times 12$)
Watermarked: C. ANSELL/1828
TB CCCLXIV 309
D36166

As with cat.nos.130 and 132, Turner's position is just upstream of the bridge of boats. Two or three of these have been moved aside to allow the passage downstream of the raft of logs shown in the right-hand corner.

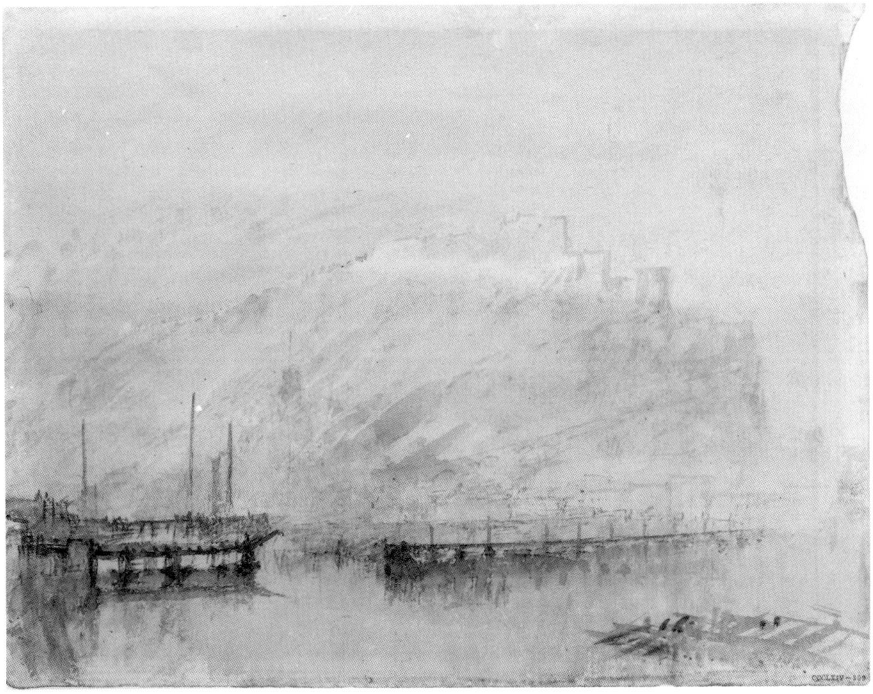

132 Ehrenbreitstein* 1841

Watercolour on white wove paper
242 × 302 ($9\frac{1}{2} \times 11\frac{7}{8}$)
Watermarked: J WHATMAN/
TURKEY MILL/1822
TB CCCLXIV 319
D36177

Although the general effect of this drawing and cat.no.131 is very different, they share some of the same foreground colours, notably the burnt orange, the turquoise green of the river and the plum-like brown used with such expressive economy for the bridge of boats. Here – as in cat.no.131 – the bridge is portrayed open and a steamer is shown on the left puffing its way upstream.

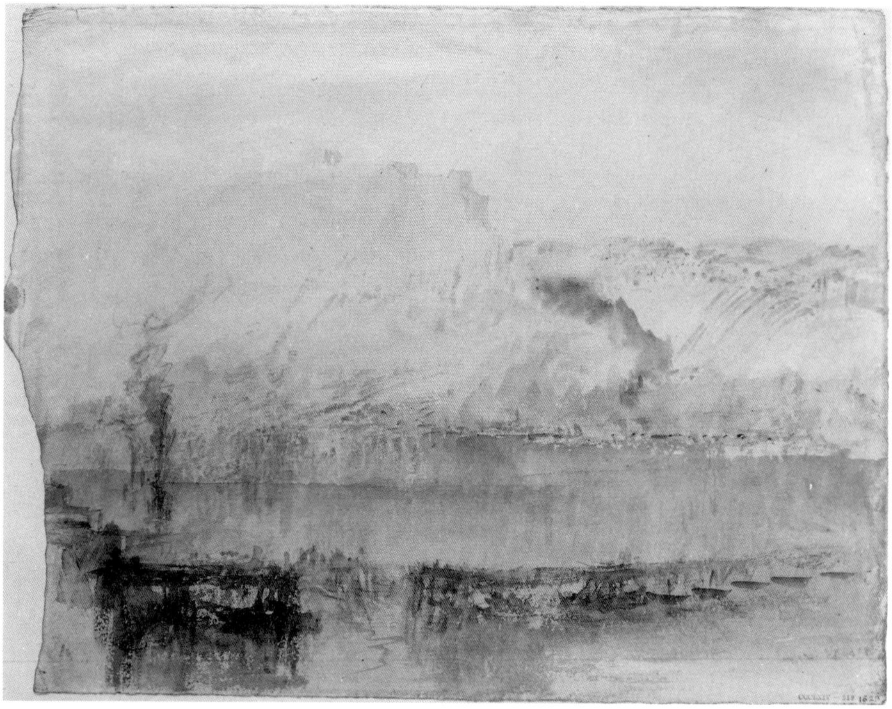

133 Ehrenbreitstein 1841

Watercolour and pen and ink on
white wove paper
250 × 315 ($9\frac{13}{16} \times 12\frac{7}{16}$)
TB CCCLXIV 285
D36138

Here Turner is well upstream of the bridge of boats which now almost appears to line the Rhine shore beneath the fiery heights of Ehrenbreitstein rather than traverse the water. On the far left can be seen the twin towers of St Castor's church, close to the confluence with the Mosel.

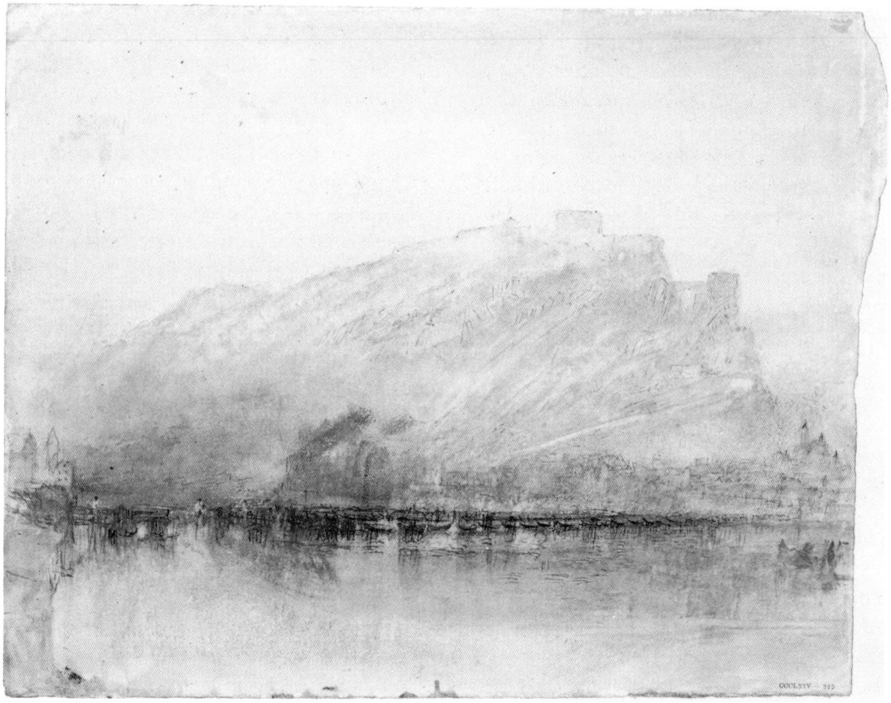

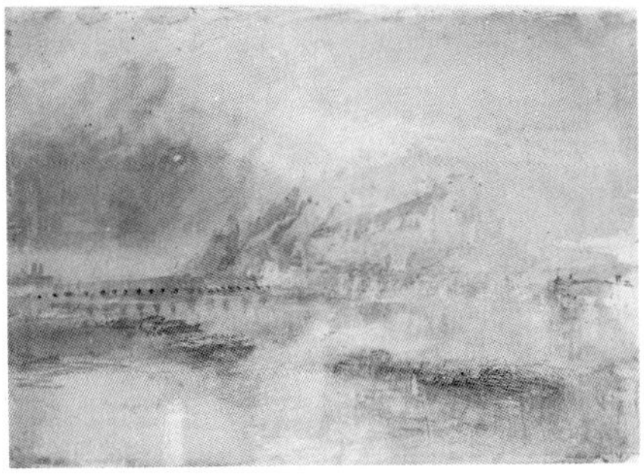

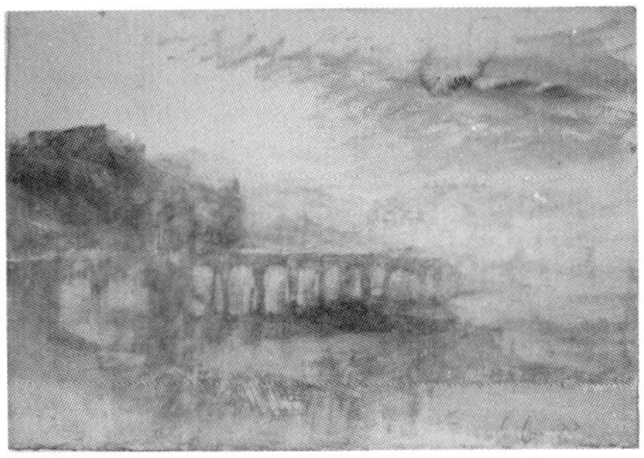

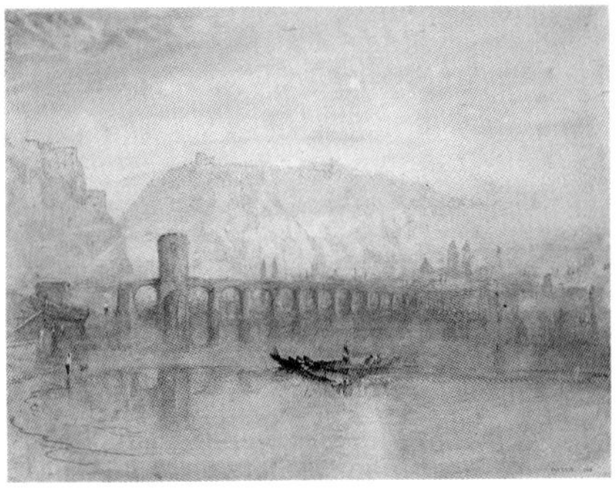

134 Ehrenbreitstein* 1841

Watercolour on white wove paper
249 × 340 ($9\frac{13}{16} \times 13\frac{3}{8}$)
Watermarked: J WHATMAN / TURKEY MILL / 1825
Inscribed in pencil, on the verso, with a poem of six lines
TB CCCLXIV 26
D35863

This drawing has hitherto been known as 'Lake, with mountains', but there is no doubt that it actually shows the Rhine, with St Castor's church, Coblenz, on the left, Ehrenbreitstein and the bridge of boats in the distance and, in the foreground, one of the gigantic rafts of timber which Turner so often included in his Rhine scenes. On this both men and their living quarters may be distinguished, scratchily rendered in the same way as the foreground of cat.no.128. In its juxtaposition of warm and cool areas of colour, this drawing is a perfect embodiment of Byron's lines in *Childe Harold's Pilgrimage*, canto IV:

> The moon is up and yet it is not night,
> The sun as yet divides the day with her.

Turner quoted or adapted these very lines to accompany the captions of two of his oil paintings at the Royal Academy at about this time (B & J 379 in 1839; B & J 412 in 1844) and many other works besides cat.no.134 show that he found this moment of the day particularly magical.

Turner's own lines on the verso of this drawing are faint and almost illegible but they must surely relate to the Rhine and Ehrenbreitstein: the words 'Bright', 'stone', 'flood' and 'pour' are all just legible.

135 The Mosel Bridge at Coblenz: Colour Study* *c.*1841–2

Gouache and watercolour on white wove paper
246 × 348 ($9\frac{11}{16} \times 13\frac{3}{4}$)
Watermarked: J WHATMAN / TURKEY MILL / 1825
Inscribed in pencil, at lower right, 'Coblenz'
TB CCCLXIV 336
D36194

This work is clearly a preparatory study for cat.no.136, with the same colours used in a much simpler and more spontaneous way. Washes of blue and pink, red, mauve, yellow and turquoise float separately and intermingled on the white paper, creating an image of great intensity and limpid beauty. The inner faces of the arches of the bridge glow with dazzling light, the blueness of the sky is suggested by the thinnest of washes interrupted by a swirl of bright wet colour, while Ehrenbreitstein appears as a dream-like cliff of pinkish red arising from a lavender-grey hill, evocatively soft yet crystal clear against its white backdrop.

136 The Mosel Bridge at Coblenz: Sample Study* *c.*1841–2

Watercolour on white wove paper
236 × 295 ($9\frac{1}{4} \times 11\frac{5}{8}$)
Watermarked: J WHATMAN / TURKEY MILL / 1822
Inscribed in pencil, on the verso, 'J. Ruskin, Junr, Esq',
TB CCCLXIV 286
D36139

This work is slightly smaller than its preparatory study (cat.no.135). Turner has used the same colours but in a far more saturated form, blending them together with a myriad tiny touches and producing a work of immense richness and subtlety. He has also made significant changes to its composition, adjusting the shapes, colours and positions of the hills and forts beyond the Rhine so that they do not divert the eye from the true subject of the work, the bridge over the Mosel. The viewer's attention is firmly directed to the foreground by the reflection of the bridge, the introduction of the very dark boat, the figures on the river bank and Turner's wonderful handling of the surface of the water with its iridescent gleam caught from the rising moon.

Although this work may appear to be a 'finished' watercolour, it is not in fact Turner's final statement on this particular theme. It is one of around twenty to thirty 'sample studies' produced in the 1840s for his agent Thomas Griffith to show to potential patrons in order to attract commissions. The first group of large watercolours, which were painted in 1842 (W 1523–33), included several of Turner's most famous late masterpieces such as 'The Blue Rigi', 'The Red Rigi' and 'Zurich'. 'Coblenz' (W 1530, based on cat.no.136) was exceptional in the group in not showing a Swiss subject. It was commissioned by Ruskin who also bought two of the others, depicting Lucerne and Lake Constance. His name was duly noted on the backs of the sample studies. W 1530 is now untraced and is known only from copies made under Ruskin's supervision by his pupils and followers, such as that by William Ward now in the Art Museum, Cincinnati.

Appendix: The Sketchbooks Used on Turner's Tours of 1817, 1824 and 1839

Explanations

The following signs are used in transcripts of inscriptions:

[Yellow]	editorial insertion
[? *Yellow*]	uncertain reading
[. . .]	missing or undeciphered letters or words
⟨*Yellow*⟩	deleted word
⟨. . .⟩	undeciphered deletion

TB CLIX *Itinerary Rhine Tour* sketchbook 1817 (see cat.no.1)

Bound in brown leather, with a pocket for a pencil and the remains of a brass clasp. On the spine is a white paper label inscribed in ink by Turner *42 Rhine*. On the back cover, also in ink, *Ostend Rhine*.

Turner's notes in ink on ff.1r–30r were taken from the publications of Hills, Campbell and Gardnor (see above, pp.21–2); their sources are given at the start of each sketchbook page, those from Gardnor here being identified by reference to the pages of the 1792 edition.

Inside front cover
Foreign phrases, including:
Vier ist myn Simmer (twice)
Where is my Chamber
Shelaltiq a Key Clef

1r (Hills, pp.4–13)
Ostend
⟨. . .⟩ to the left Laisser passer sans aucune empéchement
Inn The Hotel de la Cour Imperiale
Badly served. Charges dear. 2 francs for
Breakfast En passant Napoleons and francs need
to have. Table d'hote. $\frac{1}{2}$ *past one 2 fr* $\frac{1}{2}$
Sass the place of the Schuyts to Bruges – $\frac{1}{2}$ *a*
League Canotte freight $\frac{1}{2}$ *a franc*
Trechschuyts. Barque jagartje postillion

1v (Hills, pp.12–13)
Schippers horsemen . . best cabins a franc time
2 hours 12 miles to Bruges
Pencil sketch of hills, extending on to f.2r, illegibly inscribed

2r Financial calculations

2v A carriage

3r (Hills, pp.14–22)
Bruges
Porters for luggage with brouette. Barrow. passport
Ex. printed blanks to fill up at the Inn.
Inn. Fleur de Bled near the Grande Place
Table de Hote very early. [. . .] *dinner at 3 francs*
Saint Sauveur Hospital a few pictures one
of Phillip the good by John of Bruges The Martyr
dom of St Quinctilianus in White of Eggs, 7 acts
of Mercy by V Oost & Lucas Blundell 1545.
an Hospital near has some others

3v (Hills, pp.25–9)
Buildings the Halle nr the Grand place
the Establissement des Dames ⟨des⟩ Anglaises

4r Figures
Inscr. *ylow*

4v Buildings and trees

5r (Hills, pp.31–47)
Ghent
Schuyts come Morning at 9 a Bell gives notice from
the Town poorte or quay best cabins 5 francs 3
courses second price 3 francs common: 1 franc
dinner at one oClock. Bourdeaux Wine 2 fr $\frac{1}{2}$
per bottle
Inn. Hotel de Flandre or Duc de Wellington
both in the High Street
Buildings Church of the dominicans
St Michael. the Crucifixion by Vandyke
St Bavon or Cathedral Chaires a precher/preacher
built about 860 Maison de Ville – beaureax de
(superimposed on the above:) *verite truth*

5v *passports*
(Also six names in pencil)

6r Bridge and spires

6v Blank

7r (Hills, pp.53–68)
Brussells
35 miles from Ghent
Inns Hotel de Holland 3 oClock 3 fr de Belle Vue 4 – 4 fr.
Prince of Wales on one side of the Park the Hotel
de Angleterre – Bill Carte with prices Fourberies Cheats
Road to Louvain the best view
Buildings. The Cathedral St Gudule New Church
of Condenberg Palace of Laeken
(inserted into the above in pencil:)
[after *Brussels*] *to Liege 15 francs*
[above *Holland*] *Flanders*

7v (Hills, pp.69–81)
failles viels sabots wooden shoes chaise à timon
a cart with a Hood & 2 Horses
Waterloo lies on the road to Charleroi Jean de
Nivelles a simpleton – at the end of St Jean
the roads from Charleroi and Nivelles meet

8r (in pencil and not part of the sequence of notes in ink:)
Liege
15 francs
Sketch of boats and barrels
Inscr. *R*[ed] *W*[hite] *B*[lue] (against a flag); *Dutch casks*

8v Blank

9r (Hills, pp.106–30)

Antwerp
Inns Grand Hotel de l'Ours – Place de Meir
du Grand Labourer de l'Empereur
B[ig] *Cathedral Notre Dame Church St Jacques*
The Jesuits Church – by Rubens
Fare to Rotterdam 23 francs
Guilder or florin about 20 pence
(added in pencil:) *St Antoine Place du Vert 8*

9v Blank

10r (Hills, pp.132–51)

Amsterdam
Inn the Arms of Amsterdam corner of q Rusland
table d Hote 3 oClock 2 florins with a pint of Bourdx
Pictures. the Surgeons Theatre de Anatomie
Stad House Rembrandt Corp de Garde over the
Museum gratuity a florin

10v A bridge

11r (1) (in pencil, not part of the guidebook notes:)
With the fever of diar[rhoea] *or vomiting H*[. . .] *m*[?ixed]
in weak ⟨. . .⟩ *warm water washed off with W Gruel*
If costive a Glyster Drink 2 of water whey
or gruel to each quart a tea spoon full
of cream of tartare if lax motion No other
medicine or food until the P becomes
cooler Bleeding to be avoided
(2) Financial calculations

11v–12r Line of hills

12r (Hills, pp.156–63)

Haarlemn 9 miles from A
Schuyts from the Haarlche Poorte all hours
fare ½ a Guilder
Inn The Gekroonde Zwaan near the Leydche
Poorte
(also a separate pencil note:) *Brussels*

12v Blank

13r (Hills, pp.168–72)

The Hague
or Huys de Bosche
Inn Bosse Veerhuis op de Spui

13v (Campbell, pp.224–49)
Helvoatsluys. Sluice dam 80 feet of water
Brill to Rotterdam 12 Miles 2 ducats 4 francs
Scheedam 6 WSW Maesluice
Statue of Erasmus by Keiser Boom Quay
Dort 12 Miles Maese called the Merwe Gorcum 12 to Dort
Delft 6 miles from the Hague 9 from R
Vyverburg and Palace in the Wood Scheveling 2
Leyden 9 Miles from Hague in the Town House
a Paintg of the Judgment by Lucas de Leyde
Haerlem 10 Miles from Amsterdam

14r (Hills, pp.176–89)

Rotterdam
Boomptjee or Boom quay
Doight Boats – 8 D to a Stiver
Inn Marchal Turrene Hoff Von Berlyn
on the Spanische Kaai Mons. Cock
Spiel Houses Golve

14v (Hills, p.195n.)
Can we de Rasphuys see
Waar can ich naar de Stadthuys
Will ye me branna or ing naar de
Haagste poorte woor ses sex stivers
Geeft me de wyne en water
Wat is dat
Dat is de Groote Kerch
Ich will geeft ye
Ich bedanckye Mynheer
Wat Uure is het
Waer is de Post

15r (Hills, p.195n. and p.196)
Can ich here eten – Can I have anything to Eat

Een	*Eleve*	*Dirtigh*	*Vraght fare freight*
Twee	*Twaelf*	*Veertigh*	*Dagh en Nachte*
Dree	*Derteen*	*Vuyftigh*	*Plyer of passengers*
Vere	*Veereteen*		
Vyve	*Vuyfteen*		
Sis	*Sesteen*		
Seen	*Seventeen*		
Aucht	*Auchteen*		
Negen	*Negenteen*		
Teene	*Tweentigh*		

15v Blank

(Between ff.15 and 16 at least two pages have been torn out)

16r (in ink, from Gardnor, p.19)

Spire – on the Rhine
(in pencil, not from Gardnor)

Hidelberg – about 70
miles above Spire the most [. . .]
way to Frankfort on the Main then
by Darmstadt to Hidelburg
(also a separate pencil note:) *Antwerp The Black Bear*

16v Blank

17r (Gardnor, pp.20–3)

Manheim
Building the Jesuits Church Town House
Inn Cour Palatine – good

17v Blank

18r (Gardnor, pp.24–5)

Mentz to Manheim flat
Bridge of 40 Boats

18v Blank

19r (Gardnor, p.26)

Mentz to Bingen 21 Miles
between which there are 40 towns with
several castles – Waalluff a small town
on the Nahe at its junction with R is
Bingen

19v Blank

20r (Gardnor, pp.27–8)

Bingen lock
a castle and Abbey on the Nahe whirl-
fall . . the Island and Tower Bridge
over the Nahe built by Drusus
(also a diagram in blue ink, now smudged)

20v Blank

21r (Gardnor, p.29)
Rudesheim opposite to Bingen
Johannis-berg about the middle of the
Rhinegau
Bridge and town

21v Blank

22r (Gardnor, pp.30–6)
Baccharah or Bacchi-ara
Inn the Star le Etoile
in the way Heisbeck an ancient Gateway
Castle of Hoygesteim and two others on
the way – from the apartment at Bacc
the city of Kaub and two more Castles
and the remains of a Church Gothic
3 Miles below Baccharah is Pfalz
and a Castle on a rock in the middle of the R

22v Blank

23r (Gardnor, pp.36–40)
Oberwesel 6 Miles below B
Boat ten pence a franc Castle of Tefels
commands the town or Vessel Castle
Church of St Martin

23v (separate note in pencil:)
French language D.L. 292 Holborn
2 Gs the Month

24r (Gardnor, pp.43–57)
St Goar
a small distance below Vessel a dangerous
whirlpool a mile below where the banks are
very close Castle of Rhenfels good
Inn the Bois Verd – Schwalbak [corrected to *ch*] *water*
or sour water sold here which corrects
the sour wine. The castle of the Cat seen
from the Inn. the E Bank with
Goarhausen at the base and Patisberg

24v (Gardnor, p.61)
likewise the Mouse Castle with the
village of Welmich

25r (Gardnor, pp.64–92)
Boppart
a Tower and Nunnery
Braback by Speiz
small Inn by the water side but badly
The castle of Marxburg Rense
Ober Lahnstein
Castle of Lonack Hermitage near

25v Blank

26r (Gardnor, pp.94–100)
The Entrance of the Lahn
at Nether Lahnstein
Castle of Capelle seen from the Inn –
Ober Lahnstein at its foot Tiberius
Haverdorf E side of R
½ way between Nether Lahnstein and
Coblenz fine view of Ehrenbreitstein

26v Blank

27r (Gardnor, pp.101–4)
Coblenz
Stone Bridge over the Moselle 14 Arches
Cit[adel] *the palace*
Inn at the rivers side opposite Ehrenbreitstein
Friar's grace

27v Blank

28r (Gardnor, pp.110–16)
Andernach Roman
Castle and Walls Rafts Touffstein
Hammerstein E
Castle and town
Lintz opposite
opposite Hammerstein is Reineck
Castle. at its foot lower Reineck

28v Four sketches near the Godesburg
(2) Inscr. *opposite Drachenfels*

29r (Gardnor, pp.117–20)
a league below towards Cologne
Rowland-sheitz castle – v romantic
with Umkel or Unkel
Bonne
a watering place near here mntnd by Miller
Cologne

29v Peasants carrying burdens, studies of headdresses; gourd-shaped vessels
Inscr. *White; Men Black; Scotch Bonnet; Nun Black; Striped with a Hood; Blue; Blue; White frocks*

30r (Gardnor, pp.120–44)
Aix la Chapelle
Inn Cour des Londres
castle of Schonfort 3 miles not remarkable
Castle of Shoquier
near Liege
Hui
Namur
Sketch of lady in a bonnet
Inscr. *White Cap; Sometimes colord but most red or pink spots*

30v Nonnenwerth and Rolandseck, looking upstream from the west bank
Inscr. *Island*

31r *Brussels Hotel de Flandres do Angleterre Hotel de Belle Vue* [. . .]

Cortenberg	$1\frac{1}{2}$	
Louvain	$1\frac{1}{2}$	
Tirlemont	$2\frac{1}{4}$	
St Trond	2	
Orey	$2\frac{1}{4}$	
Liege	$2\frac{1}{4}$	*Hotel l'Aigle Noir Hotel de Flandres*
Batizza	$2\frac{1}{2}$	
Aix le Chapple	3	*Le Grand Hotel le Dragon d'Or*
Juliers	3	*Pardon tho off the Rd of*
Berchina	$2\frac{1}{2}$	*Castle* [. . .] *ouft Rheinberg*
Cologne	3	*La Ville de Prague Le Grand*

31v *$5\frac{1}{2}$ Hours* *3 posts* 15 $3\frac{1}{2}$ 15 2 $\frac{1}{2}$ 17
R $2\frac{1}{2}$ $12\frac{1}{2}$
A

32r

Bonn	3	*La Cour Imperiale*
Remagen	$2\frac{1}{2}$	
Andernach	3	
Coblentz	3	*Les Trois Suisses Le Cour de Treves*
		Left Bank of the Rhine La Lille La Poste

Boppart	$2\frac{1}{2}$	*La Poste Le Miroir*
St Goar	$1\frac{3}{4}$	*La Forest Verte Le Lys*
Bacharach	$1\frac{3}{4}$	
Bingen	$1\frac{3}{4}$	
Mayence	3	*Les Trois Couronnes Le Cour de Mayence*

32v Blank

33r

Hadersheim	2	*L Blanc Le Bonce Noir*
Franckfort	2	*L'Hotel de Angleterre La Cigne*
Darmstadt	3	*La Cour de Hesse La Poste*
Hepperheim	$3\frac{1}{2}$	*Le Soleil*
Wissheim	$2\frac{1}{2}$	
Heidelberg	2	*Le Brochet D'Or Les Trois Rois*
Wissloch	2	*Baden She Hoff*
Bruchsal	$2\frac{1}{2}$	*Le Cerf*
Darlach	2	*La Poste*
Eltlingen	1	
Rastadt	2	*La Croix Le Soleil*

33v Blank

34r

Buhl	2	
Appenweler	3	
Offenborg		*La Couronne*
Treissenheim	$1\frac{1}{2}$	
Kenzingen	3	
Emmendingen	$1\frac{1}{2}$	
Fribourg	2	*Le Negre*
Krotzingen	1	
Muhlheim	2	
Kaltenhenborge	2	
Basle	3	*Les Trois Roi La Cicogne*
	93	

Also a number of foreign words and their English equivalents, mostly in a hand other than Turner's, including *egalement; good; geschwind; Abtritt privy*; etc.

34v Blank

35r *Coblentz to Frankfort Right bank of Rhine*

Nassau	3	*Hoofd*
Nastadten	2	*Rotterdam the Swines Hoof*
Schwalbach	2	*Boars Head*
Wisbaden	2	
Hadersheim	$2\frac{1}{2}$	
Francfort	2	
	$13\frac{1}{2}$	
	5	
	65	

35v Blank

36r (1) Peasant women at work
Inscr. *women sewing* [. . .] *and Bleaching cloths*
(2) Castle
Inscr. *7 Hills*; [. . .]

36v Blank

37r Tower and buttressed wall, probably at Sinzig
Inscr. *B*[. . .]

37v The walls of Sinzig
Inscr. *Sinsig*

37v–38r View upstream from the west bank looking toward Sinzig church
Inscr. *Sinzig*

38v The town walls and gate at Sinzig
Inscr. *Sinzig*

39r Men and women carrying casks and baskets; studies of bottles, etc.
Inscr. *Red and White*; *Blue coat*; *Red collar*; *Blue*; *Mustard Pot shaped*

39v–40r Soldiers and peasants; jugs and urns
Inscr. (on f.39v) *Blue*; *Red*; *Pale Red Collar*; *Cuff*; *W*[hite] *Pantaloons*; *Shoes* [. . .] *Leather apron*; *Red*; (on f.40r) *Blue*; *Drab with red cuffs and E*[paulettes]; *Brown*; *Tin*; *Green*

40v Figures with burdens
Inscr. *R*[ed] (three times)

41r Figures with burdens
Inscr. *Green*; *Y*[ellow]

41v–42r Blank

42v Blank

43r Clouds over a river
Inscr. *B*; *B*; *Y*[ellow]; *Light*

43v–44r Stormy sky over a river
Inscr. *Yell*[ow]; *B*; *Grey*

44v Clouds

45r Blank

45v–46r Distant view of York
Inscr. *York*

46v Three figures

47r The Rhine front at Cologne with Great St Martin's church, cathedral and flying bridge

47v The Rhine front at Cologne with the flying bridge

48r The flying bridge at Cologne

48v The flying bridge arriving at Deutz with a carriage on board

49r Cologne from the Rhine with the town hall, Great St Martin's and cathedral

49v Distant view of York

50r Study for the oil painting 'The Great Dort' (B & J 137)

50v Distant view of York

51r Cloud study

51v–52r (1) Raby Castle and its park
(2) Cloud study

52v (1) Raby Castle
(2) *Savoir tout decidment*
know indubitably
(3) Fighting stags

53r Landscape with bridge and trees; also cloud and castle studies
Inscr. *W*; *Blue*; *Road*; *yellow*

53v Butting stags

54r Two deer

54v Two deer

55r Clouds

55v (1) Standing woman
(2) Landscape
Inscr. *Wall*

56r	(1) Two figures on horseback (the Raby hunt) (2) *Expedition des Kollnischen Postwagen von Vetter Paule* (not written by Turner)
56v	Raby Castle
57r	Burg Katz and St Goarshausen, looking downstream Inscr. *Katz*
57v–58r	(1) The Lorelei, looking upstream from the west bank above St Goar Inscr. *Road above S Goar* (2) A raft (superimposed)
58v	Blank
59r	The riverfront at Mainz, looking upstream to the Holzturm
59v–60r	The riverfront at Mainz, seen from the bridge of boats to Kastel, showing the cathedral and Eisenturm on f.59v and the bridge itself, mostly on f.60r (this sketch continues that on f.59r)
60v–61r	Blank
61v	Distant view of Aachen
62r	Three figures Inscr. *W*; *Straw B*; *Red*; *Red* [. . .]
62v	Hounds at Raby Castle Inscr. *Mary*; *Grafton*
63r	Hounds at Raby Castle Inscr. *Martin*
63v	(1) Hounds at Raby Castle Inscr. *Chesterfield* (2) Hilly landscape with distant tower Inscr. *Aix*
64r	Hounds at Raby Castle Inscr. *Martin*
64v	Hounds at Raby Castle Inscr. *Mary*; *Blucher*; *M*; [*?Boy*]
65r	Mounted huntsmen at Raby Castle
65v	Bridge over the river at York
66r	The Seven Hills under a stormy sky
66v–69r	Blank
69v	Figures and horse-drawn carts Inscr. *Coal*
70r	Horses and carts
70v–73r	Blank
73v	Distant town (?Aachen)
74r	Blank
74v	Figures, including footmen unloading boxes
75r	Blank
75v	Burg Stahleck and Bacharach, looking downstream from the west bank Inscr. *Backarah*
76r	Figures carrying burdens Inscr. *Backarach*
76v	The Schönburg and Oberwesel, looking downstream from the west bank Inscr. *Willows*; *Tffels* (i.e. the Schönburg; see f.23r)
77r	Two sketches of Burg Gutenfels Inscr. *Kaub*
77v	Burg Gutenfels, Kaub and the Pfalz, looking upstream from the west bank Inscr. *Kaub*; *Phalz*
78r	The Schönburg, looking downstream Inscr. *Rock*; *Teffels*
78v	The Schönburg, looking downstream Inscr. (twice) *Teffels*
79r	(1) Schloss Stolzenfels Inscr. *Capelle* (2) Schloss Stolzenfels and Kapellen
79v	The archbishops' castle at Andernach, seen from the south, just outside the town walls Inscr. *E*[. . .]
80r	The archbishops' castle at Andernach from the south with the Christuskirche behind it Inscr. *Andernack*
80v	(1) Burg Lahneck (2) Distant view of Aachen Inscr. *Aix la Ch*
81r	Female headdresses and hairstyles Inscr. *Blue*[*?Cotton*]; *R*
81v	(1) Burg Lahneck Inscr. *Lonak* (2) View with cross and tower Inscr. *Ren*
82r	View up the Rhine from the west bank towards Hammerstein and Burg Rheineck Inscr. *Rineck*; *Road*; *W*
82v	Ploughs drawn by oxen, with a peasant woman Inscr. *Or*[ange]; *Red*; *Blue striped gown*, *Red Handkerchief cloth*
83r	The Seven Hills and the Rhine
83v	Drachenfels, looking downstream from south of Oberwinter Inscr. *Drakenfels*; *Oberwinter*; *Road*
84r	Church and trees Inscr. *Henndorf*
84v–85r	The Seven Hills, looking upstream from the west bank north of Bonn Inscr. *Bonne*
85v–86r	Bonn and the Seven Hills, looking upstream from the west bank Inscr. *Seven Mountains*; *W*; *Bonne*
86v–87r	Distant view of Aachen, with ruined building in the foreground Inscr. *Aix*
87v	Archway and castle
88r	Houses by a river
88v	Figures at a well and studies of wayside crucifixes Inscr. *Red*
89r	Buildings (? at Andernach)

89v Peasant woman; casks, jugs, urn, churn, glass, etc.
Inscr. *Red or White straw*; *Metal top*; *Brass Hoops*; *Butter*; *Brass*; *Clay Blue*; *Brass*; *Glass*

90r A jug

90v Men ploughing with an ox
Inscr. *No headpiece*; *Prussian*

91r Blank

91v Figures with baskets and on horseback, and a plough

91v–92r Boats and carts
Inscr. *Hay*[. . .] *and Market Boats at Cologne*

92r (1) The Drachenfels from the road near the Godesburg (compare sketches on f.28v)
(2) Boat near a cliff

92v Figures amidst barrels, baskets and pails
Inscr. *Boy holding up a Kite*; *Red*; *Corbelle*; *Red bonnet with gold Band*; *Dark jacket and gold band*[. . .]

93r (1) Figures carrying burdens
Inscr. *Nalumettes*; *Machand a la*[. . .]
(2) Bucket
Inscr. *Brass Bu*[c]*ket with Red* [*?lining*]

93v A cart, a horse and their appurtenances
Inscr. *Red*; *Chariot*; [. . .]; *all Black and Gold Stud*

94r Peasants with burdens and a horse-drawn cart
Inscr. *4 Chevaux*

94v Harbour and lighthouse

95r Financial calculations

95v Distant view of a port, probably Ostend

96r Distant hills (continuing on to f.95v); also calculations:

Coblentz	*2*	*Naps*	
Neder	*1*		
Mayence	*1*		
St Goar	*1*		*5*
Cologne	*–2*		
Aix	*1*		
Liege	*1*		
Brussels	*2*	*1 Change 10*	

96v Two boats

97r

Bought of L–	*6fr*
H[. . .]	*4fr*
2 Pound note	*2*
Cologne	*20*
	32

97v A boat
Inscr. *Barke de So*[. . .]; *Chieggune*[. . .]*gold*; *Zoulma*

98r *Manuel pour les Voyageurs sur le Rien Aloise Schrieber*
Manuel pour les Voyageurs sur le Rien Rhine a la Holl[ande] *by Aloise Schriber or Schriede*

98v Study of sky above distant cliffs
Inscr. *B*; *Yellowish grey*; *Clouds rather red*; *grey*

99r Five studies of carriages, the last
inscr. *Anvers*

99v Study of sky above the sea, with a boat in the foreground
Inscr. *G*; *Yellow*; *G*
(a continuation of the itinerary begun on f.100r:)
R[otterdam] *12*
S *13*
S *14*
L[ondon] *15*

100r

	Sunday	*10 August left London*	
	Monday	*off Margate*	*11*
	Tuesday	*Ostend–Bruges*	*12*
	Wednesday	*Ghent*	*13*
	Thursday E[vening]	*Brussels*	*14*
	Friday	*ditto*	*15*
	Saturday	*Waterloo*	*16*
	Sunday diligence	*Liege, Aix le C*	*17*
	Monday	*Cologne*	*18*
	Tuesday – walked	*Bonne*	*19*
	Wednesday ditto	*Remagen*	*20*
	Thursday –	*Coblentz*	*21*
	Friday –	*ditto*	*22*
	Saturday –	*St Goar*	*23*
2	*Sunday –*	*ditto*	*24*
	Monday –	*Mayence*	*25*
	Tuesday –	*ditto*	*26*
	Wednesday	*St Goar –*	*27*
	Thursday	*Coblentz –*	*28*
	Friday	*Cologne –*	*29*
	Saturday	*Ditto –*	*30*
3	*Sunday diligence*	*Aix*	*31*
	Monday ditto	*Liege*	*1*
	Tuesday –	*Antwerp*	*2*
	Wednesday	*Antwerp*	*3*
	Thursday –	*Rotterdam*	*4*
	Friday	*ditto –*	*5*
	Saturday –	*Hague –*	*6*
	Am[sterdam]		*7*
	U[trecht]		*8*
	R[otterdam]		*9*
			10
			11

100v Study of sky over the sea with a boat in the foreground
Inscr. *Green*; *yellow*; *sea grey green* (and illegible words)

101r *Bankers account*
J.D. Hirstatt Cologne
Aug[t] *Tuesday 17–20*
Lost in the Walatt
a Book with Leaves
ditto Cambells Belgium
3 Shirts
1 Night ditto
a Razor
a Ferrele for Umbrella
a pair of Stockings
a Wais Coat
½ Doz of Pencils
6 Cravats
1 Large ditto
1 Box of Colors

101v Sun setting amongst clouds, seen across the sea
Inscr. *Orange*; *Reddish*; *Purple*

102r Dutch phrases and their English equivalents, including *What church do you call it*; *can I leave my mantle*; *Have you seen my baggage*

102v Coast and lighthouse
Mr W.F. Sunday
Revd R. Harrison Westoe
South [?*Shieds*]
(continued from inside back cover:)
English and Dutch phrases

Inside back cover:
Books
Pouch
Fever medicine
Bark
Pencils
Colours
followed by English and Dutch phrases

TB CLX *Waterloo and Rhine* sketchbook 1817 (see cat.no.2)

Bound in brown leather with the remains of a brass clasp and two loops for a pencil at the top of the back cover. Inscribed by Turner in ink on the back cover *Rhine*. Finberg records a label on the back inscribed *25 Rhine* but this is no longer extant.

ff.92 and 93 are currently bound into the sketchbook between ff.48 and 49 and ff.57 and 58 respectively and have therefore been catalogued here at those points. In terms of their subject matter and the course of Turner's tour, the present positions of both pages make good sense, but cannot be proved correct until the sketchbook is rebound.

1r Distant walls and towers (? a harbour)

1v (1) The Lorelei, looking downstream to Burg Katz
Inscr. *Laureligh*; *Luruley*
(2) The Lorelei, looking downstream to Burg Katz
(3) Cliffs on the Rhine near the Lorelei
(4) The Lorelei, with a moored boat

2r (1) The Lorelei, looking downstream
(2) The Lorelei, looking downstream, with a boat
(3) The southern end of Oberwesel, looking upstream
(4) Oberwesel and the Schönburg, looking upstream

2v–3r The Halles and Belfry, Bruges, from the Grand' Place
Inscr. (not by Turner) *La Halle sur la grande Place a Bruges*; (by Turner) *North door*

3v–4r The church of Notre-Dame, Bruges

4v Blank

5r The chapel of the Holy Blood, Bruges

5v The Minne-water, Bruges

6r The Minne-water, Bruges

6v Blank

7r The Minne-water, Bruges

7v The Minne-water, Bruges

8r Blank

8v–9r St Michael's church, Ghent, from the Quai au Blé, with the Quai aux Herbes on the left

9v The town hall, Brussels, from the Grand' Place

10r Blank

10v–11r Brussels from the north
Inscr. *Corn*

11v–12r St Gudule's cathedral, Brussels, from the north

12v–13r Brussels from the north with the spire of the town hall
Inscr. [. . .]; *G*; *Bruxelles*

13v Distant view of Brussels from the north
Inscr. *Brux*

14r The Palace of Laeken outside Brussels
Inscr. *Corn*; *Palace Laeken*

14v The Waterloo Gate, Brussels
Inscr. *W*; *Corn*; *Brux*; *Gate to Waterloo*

15r The Waterloo Gate, Brussels
Inscr. [?*Grass*]; [?*Stone*]; *Ditto*

15v Street in ?Antwerp
Inscr. *Coal*; *Doric*

16r Quayside houses at Antwerp and sailing vessels
Inscr. *Anvers*; *Lake*

16v The village of Waterloo from the road to Charleroi, with the domed Royal Chapel
Inscr. *Waterloo*

17r View at Antwerp with the spire of the cathedral

17v (1) The Field of Waterloo from the north
Inscr. *Farm Ho*[use]
(2) Diagram of the crossroads at Waterloo showing the positions of the farmhouses of La Haye Sainte and La Haye
Inscr. *Field of Waterloo*; *Haie Sainte*; *Field to Haie*

18r The Field of Waterloo from the north
Inscr. *Fichermont*; *Picton Fell*; *Road*

18v The Field of Waterloo

19r The Field of Waterloo from the north
Inscr. *Belle Alliance Inn*; *Haye Saint*

19v The Field of Waterloo
Inscr. *Battery of* [?*French*]

20r The Field of Waterloo
Inscr. *Corn*; *Monument*

20v La Haye Sainte, Waterloo, from the north with La Belle Alliance in the distance
Inscr. *Belle Alliance*; *Causeway*; *Haye Sainte*

21r La Haye Sainte, Waterloo, from the south and the tree where Sir Thomas Picton fell
Inscr. *ditto N*

21v (1) Diagram of the disposition of British forces at Waterloo
(2) La Haye Sainte from the south
Inscr. *4000 killed here*; *Line of Army E*[nglish]; *Orchard*; *Picton killed here*; *1500 killed here*; *Causeway down which Buonaparte advanced*

22r The Field of Waterloo and La Haye Sainte from the south (i.e. the French station)

22v (1) The Field of Waterloo and La Belle Alliance from the south

Inscr. *British Lines* (in the distance); [?*Corner*] *of Hill*; *French lines* (in the foreground); *Haye Sainte*; *Belle Alliance*
(2) The farmhouse of Hougoumont, Waterloo
Inscr. *Orchard Entrance of Hugomont*
(3) Hougoumont (continues on to f.23r)
Inscr. *Side wall of Hugomont*

23r Diagram of the disposition of British forces at Waterloo with the roads leading northwards to Brussels, Hougoumont and La Haye Sainte

23v Blank

24r Hougoumont among the trees

24v (1) Hougoumont
Inscr. *Corn*
(2) Diagram of its layout and the action there (superimposed)
Inscr. *Entrance Gate of Hugomont forced 4 times*; *Picton*; *Causeway to Belle*; *Belle*; *Haye Saint*; *Mon*; *Hollow where the great Carnage took place of the Cuirassiers by the Guards*; *British Lines*; *French Lines*; *Orchard*; *Farm*

25r Hougoumont
Inscr. *Ruins of Hugomont Gate*

25v Distant view of the front of Hougoumont among trees

26r Hougoumont
Inscr. *General View of Hugomont from the British Lines*

26v–27r Quayside scene at Bonn with shipping

27v Great St Martin's church and the Rhine Gate, Cologne, from the north
Inscr. *Piles of Wood*

28r Blank

28v–29r The Godesburg, looking south from the Bonn road
Inscr. *Corn*

29v–30r The Seven Hills, with the Drachenfels and Königswinter on the right, from across the Rhine

30v–31r The Godesburg, looking south from the Bonn road, with harvesters at work
Inscr. *Corn*

31v–32r View from the Hochkreuz, looking south towards the Drachenfels (left) and the Godesburg (right)
Inscr. *Corn*; *Road*

32v–33r View from just past the Hochkreuz, looking south towards the Drachenfels (left) and the Godesburg and Michelskapelle (right)

33v The Godesburg from Bad Godesberg, with a bridge in the foreground

34r Hills seen through trees

34v–35r The Godesburg, looking south
Inscr. *Corn*; [. . .]

35v–36r The Petersberg and Drachenfels, with Königswinter beneath, looking across the Rhine from the west bank near the landing-stage for Bad Godesberg
Inscr. *Dark Rock*; *Road*

36v–37r The Petersberg and Drachenfels, looking across the Rhine from the road on the west bank near the landing-stage for Bad Godesberg
Inscr. *Cor*[n]; *Road*; *Wasser*

37v–38r The Drachenfels, looking across the Rhine from the road on the west bank
Inscr. *W*; *Road*; *Large figure mending the Road*; *vines b*[e]*low*

38v–39r The Drachenfels (centre), looking downstream from the road on the west bank below Rolandseck, with Nonnenwerth (right); a carriage on the road and a figure seated on a wall

39v–40r The Erpeler Lei, Erpel and Linz (left) and Remagen (right), looking upstream from the road on the west bank near Oberwinter

40v–41r St Martin's chapel on the Apollinarisberg just outside Remagen, looking upstream from the road on the west bank
Inscr. *W*

41v (1) St Goar from the Forstbachtal behind Burg Katz
Inscr. *Katz*
(2) (extending across to f.42r) Church and hills (?Sinzig)
(3) View along the Mosel front at Coblenz, looking upstream from the confluence to the St Florinskirche, Alte Burg and bridge

42r (1) View along the Mosel front at Coblenz, looking downstream towards Ehrenbreitstein past the St Florinskirche towers and Alte Burg
(2) continuation of f.41v sketch (2)
(3) Ehrenbreitstein, from the confluence of the Rhine and the Mosel

42v–43r (1) (continues across f.43r)
Coblenz and Ehrenbreitstein, looking down the Rhine from the west bank from the quayside towards St Castor's church
(2) (continues across f.43r)
The Seven Hills and the Rhine
(3) View from behind Burg Katz, looking westwards
Inscr. *Katz*

43v Walls and boats

43v–44r St Martin's chapel on the Apollinarisberg outside Remagen, looking downstream from that town

44v–45r (1) Boats
(2) Hills and distant church

45v–46r ?Unkel from across the Rhine

46v (1) Houses (? near the landing-stage at Remagen)
Inscr. *5*
(2) ? Shrine and the Apollinarisberg outside Remagen
(3) Gateway
Inscr. *Remagen*

47r View from Remagen downstream towards the Apollinarisberg

47v (1) River view with distant castles
(2) Burg Rheineck, looking upstream from the west bank

48r Burg Rheineck, with Hammerstein in the distance, looking upstream from the west bank
Inscr. *W*; *G*; *R*; *B*; *Vines*, *W*; *R*; *R*; *Ryneck*

48v Three sketches, each showing Hammerstein, looking upstream from the west bank beneath or soon after Rheineck
(1) Inscr. *Road*
(2) Inscr. *V*[ines]; *Runeck*, *Wood*; *Road*
(3) This clearly shows Andernach in the distance

(now inserted between ff.48 and 49):

92v (1) Houses
Inscr. *Road*
(2) Hammerstein and Andernach, looking upstream from the west bank towards Leutesdorf, with travellers on the road
Inscr. *P*; *R*
(3) Andernach, looking downstream from the landing-stage at the Rhine Gate towards the watch tower and the crane

92r The watch tower at Andernach with the town's western walls to its right and old houses

49r (1) Andernach, looking downstream to Namedy, with the watch tower
Inscr. *Belongs to Andernach*
(2) Andernach, looking downstream from the landing-stage by the crane towards Hammerstein and Leutesdorf
(3) Leutesdorf
(4) The crane at Andernach with Hammerstein seen in the distance to its right

49v (1) Andernach, looking upstream from the road from Namedy, with the town walls, the chapel of the Annunziatenkloster, the watch tower and the four-towered Liebfrauenkirche. Also architectural details belonging to the watch tower
Inscr. *L Tower Round*
(2) Small composition study of the same scene but with the riverside crane in the foreground
(3) View from the landing-stage near the crane at Andernach, looking downstream towards Leutesdorf
Inscr. *Rock*

50r The archbishops' castle at Andernach, seen from the north together with the spires of the Annunziatenkloster and the Christuskirche
Inscr. *Virgin and Christ on her Lap with flowers Blue*; *B*

50v–51r The archbishops' castle at Andernach, seen from the south, just outside the town walls by the Coblenz Gate
Inscr. *Road*; *Linen*; *Wall*; *Road*

51v Four views of a bend in the Rhine, perhaps that at Filsen, near the Marxburg (depicted on f.52r)
(1) Inscr. [. . .]*itzen*
(3) extends across f.52r

52r (1) The Marxburg, seen from the path beneath it, with figures in the foreground
(2) (3) Two smaller versions of the same scene

52v (1) Part of the fortress of Ehrenbreitstein
(2) View up the Rhine from Ehrenbreitstein towards Pfaffendorf

53r The fortress of Ehrenbreitstein, from the south, next to the church of the Holy Cross and the Heribertturm

53v Ehrenbreitstein from the valley behind the fortress

54r Part of the fortress of Ehrenbreitstein

54v Ehrenbreitstein from the valley behind the fortress

55r The Rhine front at Coblenz, looking downstream to the confluence, with the Electoral Palace, Liebfrauenkirche, Carmelite church and St Castor's church

55v View up the Rhine to Burg Lahneck and Schloss Stolzenfels

56r The fortress and town of Ehrenbreitstein from the east Rhine bank, looking downstream, with the Dikasterialgebäude, Capuchin church, Heribertturm and church of the Holy Cross

56v View up the Rhine from Pfaffendorf, with the ruined abbey on Oberwerth, and Oberlahnstein and Schloss Stolzenfels in the distance
Inscr. *Oberwerth*

57r Burg Lahneck and the mouth of the river Lahn with St John's church, Niederlahnstein

57v (1) Schloss Stolzenfels, looking upstream
Inscr. *Capelle*
(2) ? Burg Lahneck from Schloss Stolzenfels

(now inserted between ff.57 and 58)

93r (1) The Martinsburg at Oberlahnstein with Schloss Stolzenfels on the hillside in the background
Inscr. *Children playing at a Well w*[. . .]
(2) Castle

93v (1) Boppard, looking downstream to the Franciscan church, Ritter-Schwalbach Haus, Sandtor and town walls
Inscr. *Old Wall*; *Wall*; *Boat*; *Linen drying*
(2) Burg Sterrenberg and Burg Liebenstein ('The Brothers'), looking downstream from the west bank
Inscr. *Lavenstein*

58r (1) 'The Brothers', looking downstream from the west bank
Inscr. *Liebensten*
(2) A similar sketch of 'The Brothers'
Inscr. *Belongs next to Boppart*
(3) Boppard, looking downstream to the Sandtor, town walls, spires of St Severus's church and the Burg

58v (1) and (2) 'The Brothers', from across the Rhine
(3) Burg Sterrenberg, looking upstream from the west bank soon after Boppard
(4) Boat
Inscr. *Fishing Boat St Goar*

59r (1)–(4) Small sketches of Burg Sterrenberg and Bornhofen
(5) Burg Sterrenberg and Bornhofen, looking upstream from the west bank near Bad Salzig

59v View from behind Burg Katz upstream to the Lorelei and across the Rhine gorge to the hills above St Goar

60r (1) The Rhine bend at Hirzenach, looking downstream from the west bank
(2) View looking downstream towards the Ehrenthaler Werth and Hirzenach from the west bank opposite Wellmich
(3) Burg Maus and St Martin's church, Wellmich, looking upstream from the same spot used for sketch (2)

60v (1) View looking downstream towards the Ehrenthaler Werth and Hirzenach from the west bank
(2) View looking upstream to Burg Maus and St Martin's church, Wellmich, from the same spot used for sketch (1) (these two sketches extend slightly on to f.61r which is otherwise blank)
(3) and (4) Two views of Burg Maus and Wellmich, looking upstream through the trees on the west bank

61v Bacharach and Burg Stahleck, looking upstream from the west bank to the Zehnttor

62r (1) The Pfalz, Kaub and Burg Gutenfels, looking downstream from the west bank
(2) View looking downstream from the west bank to Burg

Sooneck, Burg Stahleck, Bacharach, Lorch and Burg Nollig
Inscr. *Sonneck C*

62v–63r The apse of St Peter's church, Bacharach, and adjacent half-timbered houses
Inscr. *Cows*

63r Bacharach, looking south from the Steegertal just outside the Steegertor, with St Peter's spire and the Wernerkapelle to its right and Burg Stahleck on the hillside
Inscr. *Backara*

63v Details of buildings at Bacharach including St Peter's church, the Wernerkapelle and half-timbered houses

64r (1) Burg Fürstenberg, looking upstream from the west bank
(2) Burg Fürstenberg and the village of Rheindiebach from the waterside
Inscr. *Cows*; *Rhine*
(3)–(5) Two sketches and one small composition study of Burg Sooneck looking upstream from the west bank

64v The Wernerkapelle and the tower of St Peter's church, Bacharach, with details in a separate sketch
Inscr. *Wall*; *Door*; *Timber*

65r (1) The Bautsburg, looking upstream from the west bank to Assmannshausen and Burg Klopp
Inscr. *Wo*[od]
(2) View from near the Bautsburg, looking upstream to the Mäuseturm
(3) Cliffs near the Bautsburg, looking upstream to Assmannshausen
Inscr. *Walnut*

65v (1) The Bautsburg, looking downstream from the west bank
Inscr. *Wall*
(2) The Bautsburg, looking downstream from the west bank, from slightly further upstream than (1)
Inscr. *Wood*; *Road*

66r (1) View downstream from the west bank just above the Mäuseturm, with Burg Ehrenfels seen on the eastern hillside
(2) Tiny sketch of Rüdesheim
Inscr. *Rudesheim*

66v View up the Nahe, past the Drusus bridge, from the west bank of the Rhine
(this sketch extends slightly on to f.67r)

66v–67r (1) The Drusus bridge over the Nahe, looking down the Nahe to Bingen at its confluence with the Rhine; on the hillside, Burg Ehrenfels and Burg Klopp
(2) View from Bingen across the Rhine to Rüdesheim, the Johannisberg and the Rheingau
Inscr. *Johannisberg*; *Rhinegau*

67v (1) The Bautsburg and the Clemenskapelle, looking upstream from the west bank
(2) View upstream to Kastel and Mainz (extends onto f.68r)
(3) View down the Rhine with Biebrich Palace (extends onto f.68r)
Inscr. *Bibirah*
(4) View down the Rhine to Walluf and Eltville (extends onto f.68r)
Inscr. *Walluf*
(5) View up the Rhine to Walluf
Inscr. *Walluff*

Note: ff.67v–68r are stained with golden yellow watercolour blotches

68r (1) Burg Klopp, Bingen and the bridge over the Nahe, as seen from the Rhine
(2) View up the Rhine to Burg Ehrenfels
(3)–(7) Small composition studies of which (7) shows the bridge and abbey at Bingen
Inscr. *Bingen*
(8) View down the Rhine from just above Eltville
Inscr. *1*; *2*; *Elfelt*

68v–69r The Rhine front at Mainz, looking downstream to the cathedral and Holzturm

69r Two small sketches at top right
(1) Burg Klopp, Bingen church and the Mäuseturm, looking downstream
(2) Kastel and distant hills

69v–70r (1) The Rhine front at Mainz, showing the Augustinians' church, the cathedral, Holzturm, Eisenturm, and the churches of St Christopher and St Peter
Inscr. *Timber*; *Boat with Hay*
(2) View down the Rhine at Mainz to the Rheingau showing the bridge of boats to Kastel (this sketch continues the view shown in (1))

70r (1) Burg Heimburg and Niederheimbach from the Rhine, looking downstream
(2) Burg Nollig and Lorch from the Rhine, looking downstream
Inscr. *Lorch*

70v–71r Six sketches of the Rhine and the Rheingau from a boat on the river
Inscr. *Edrich*; *Johannisberg*; *Vines*; *Elfeldt*; *Clouds*

71v–72r (1) View downstream from mid-river to Bingen and Rüdesheim (plus enlarged sketch of Rüdesheim on the right)
Inscr. *Rudesheim*
(2) View downstream from mid-river to St Roch's chapel, Bingen and Rüdesheim
(3) View downstream from mid-river to Burg Klopp, Bingen, the Mäuseturm and Burg Ehrenfels
(4) View downstream from mid-river to the church at Bornhofen and 'The Brothers'
Inscr. *Bornhophen Church*; *Burg Liebeneck*

72v (1) ? View downstream to Burg Fürstenberg
Inscr. *Starklech Burg above Bac* (not the subject of the sketch)
(2) ? View upstream to Burg Fürstenberg
(3) Hills and buildings by the Rhine

73r (1) View downstream to the Pfalz and Burg Gutenfels
(2) View downstream to the Pfalz, Burg Gutenfels and Kaub
(3) Hills and building
Inscr. *B*[e]*low Erehn*; [. . .]

73v–74r (1) View downstream to the Schönburg, Oberwesel, the Pfalz, Kaub and Burg Gutenfels
(2) View downstream as above, but from closer to the Pfalz
(3) View upstream at the bend above Braubach, looking towards Osterspay, with travellers on the road and a rainbow
Inscr. (in the sky) *Light*; (on the rainbow) *P*; *Y*; *Red*; (in the foreground) *B*; *G*; *R*; *Water Yellow*; *Sky Grey*; *Blue extremely* [*? Vivid*]; *Ray of Light upon river* [. . .] *with Bank bright*; *Bridge*; *Wall*; *b*[e]*low Boppard*

74r (1) View upstream towards Peterspay, with figures and a boat
Inscr. *b[e]low Peterspay*
The inscription above this sketch (*Pink beneath white cap; dark body; child green with yellow border*) obviously refers to the group of tiny figures in this sketch rather than to ff.73v–74r(1) although it is located on the latter
(2) A large sketch of the Pfalz, from between the island on which it stands and the east bank
Inscr. (on its brickwork) *Red*

74v Three sketches of the Lorelei drawn travelling downstream towards it

75r (1) (2) Two sketches of the Lorelei, drawn travelling downstream towards it
Inscr. *Lurelligh*
(3) Probably a continuation of the last sketch of the Lorelei on f.74v
(4) Storm over the hills at Peterspay
Inscr. *Dinkholder Vineyard*
(5) The Marxburg and Braubach church from the Rhine
Inscr. *Road*

75v (1) The Lorelei
(2) Burg Katz and St Goarshausen, looking downstream from just below the Lorelei
(3) Two villages on the Rhine
Inscr. *Red* [*?Corner*]; *Bridge*; *Red*; [. . .]; *Wood*; *R*
(this sketch continues across f.76r)

76r (1) Hills
(2) Hills and distant church

76v 'The Brothers' and Bornhofen church, looking upstream

77r (1) Distant view of Burg Lahneck
Inscr. *Larnstein*
(2) The Marxburg and Braubach church (continues on to f.76v)
Inscr. *Marxburg*

77v (1) View up the Rhine at Coblenz from the confluence
(2) View up the Mosel at Coblenz from the confluence

77v–78r Weissenthurm, with the 'White Tower' itself and the Hoche Monument, looking across to Neuwied
Inscr. *Neuwied*; *Road*; *White*

78r (1) View up the Rhine at Coblenz from the confluence
(2) Four sketches of the superstructures used on flying bridges on the Rhine: two of them show the two boats lashed together to make one, on to which such superstructures were fixed; the fourth shows the diagonally striped poles which were a characteristic feature and are included in watercolours such as w 687 and w 1051

78v–79r Five sketches from a boat on the Rhine
(1) Distant hills
Inscr. *Keysheim*
(2) View downstream to Andernach in the far distance
Inscr. *andernach*
(3) View downstream to Weissenthurm, Andernach and Neuwied, including the flying bridge
(4) View upstream to Neuwied and Weissenthurm, including the flying bridge
Inscr. *Neuweid*; *Wisen Thurm*
(5) View downstream to Andernach and the Devil's House below Neuwied

79v Three sketches from a boat on the Rhine, drawn above and below Andernach
(1) The waterfront at Andernach with the watch tower and crane
(2) The waterfront at Andernach, looking downstream (this sketch extends across f.80r)
(3) View upstream past Hammerstein to Andernach (this sketch extends across f.80r)
Inscr. *Hammerstein*

80r View up the Rhine to Sinzig
Inscr. *Sinsig*

80v–81r Three sketches from a boat on the Rhine
(1) Burg Rheineck above the village of Brohl, looking downstream
Inscr. *Bruhl*
(2) Burg Rheineck, looking downstream
Inscr. *Rineck*
(3) Sinzig
Inscr. *Sinzig*; *R*[. . .] *R*[. . .]

81r Tower on hillside
Inscr. *opposite Sinzig*

81v Four sketches from a boat on the Rhine, looking downstream
(1) Distant hills
(2) Linz
Inscr. *Lintz*
(3) Unkel, with Drachenfels in the distance
Inscr. *Unkel*; *Next below Erpfel*
(4) Nonnenwerth and Drachenfels
Inscr. *Rowland*
(these two sketches extend across f.82r, crossing the other sketches there)

82r (1) Hills and distant castle
(2) View upstream to Burg Rheineck
Inscr. *Rineck*
(3) Hills and town (?Sinzig)

82v The Drachenfels and the convent on Nonnenwerth from a boat passing the island

83r Three sketches from a boat on the Rhine, looking downstream
(1) Rolandseck, Nonnenwerth and Drachenfels
(2) Part of the Seven Hills, with a mill
Inscr. *Mill*
(3) Rolandseck, Nonnenwerth and Drachenfels
Inscr. *Dona Verth* (i.e. Nonnenwerth)

83v Two sketches from a boat on the Rhine, looking downstream
(1) The Drachenfels
(2) The Godesburg and Bonn
Inscr. *Bonn*

84r The Seven Hills
Inscr. *G*; *Rudorf* (?Rhondorf)

84v Drachenfels from the Rhine near Bad Godesberg

84v–85r View upstream, from a boat, towards Drachenfels and Rolandseck
Inscr. *Rowland*

85r (1) Hill and church
(2) The Godesburg, looking downstream from the Rhine

85v (1) The Seven Hills, the Rhine and Rolandseck, looking upstream (a continuation of sketch (2) on f.86r)

(2) The bastion of the Alte Zoll at Bonn, with boats and horses; the Seven Hills in the distance
Inscr. *Gate*

86r (1) Bonn from the Rhine
(2) The Seven Hills

86v The landing-stage at Bonn by the Böselager Hof, with boats and the flying bridge

87r Two views of Cologne from the Rhine
Inscr. *Cologne*

87v Cologne from the Rhine, looking downstream towards the Bayenturm, cathedral, Great St Martin's and St Cunibert's

88r Cologne from the Rhine, looking downstream; Deutz, on the east bank, is sketched in the sky above
Inscr. *Two Bridges*

88v–89r Blank

89v–90r (1) (2) Cross-sections illustrating the art of fortification (not by Turner)
(3) (4) Sketches of 'The Brothers'
Inscr. *Lavenstein*
(5) Village street (?Oberwesel)
(6) Riverside view with a wayside shrine to Our Lady

90v (1)–(4) Four sketches of the buildings at Oberwesel: St Martin's church; the Schönburg and the spire of the Liebfrauenkirche; two sketches of the Schönburg
(5) Inscr. (not in Turner's writing) *Alvis Schreiber Reisebeschreybung von Basel bys Holland price 2M 45*; (by Turner) *57m cinque Fino*

91r (1) (2) Views upstream towards Oberwesel and the Schönburg
(3) View downstream to 'The Brothers', from the road along the west bank (this sketch extends on to f.90v)
Inscr. *Rock*; *Lavenstein*

91v Ground plan illustrating the art of fortification (not by Turner)

TB CLXI *Rhine* sketchbook 1817 (see cat.no.3)

Bound in brown leather, with three small loops for a pencil at the top of the front cover and the remains of a brass clasp. Inscribed by Turner in ink on the front *Rhine*. On the spine, Turner's paper label, inscribed in ink, *19 Rhine*.

This sketchbook was dismembered so that particularly fine sketches could be exhibited at Oxford and in the 5th Loan Collection, 1896–1931. The pages have not always been replaced in their correct sequence; in this list, ff.24–28 are given in what is thought to have been their original order.

1r Blank, apart from *VIATORIBUS 1809*, which must have been copied down from a Latin inscription, beginning 'to travellers', on the *route Napoléon*

1v Tiny sketch of hills and a valley

2r Peasants working outside cottages beneath Rolandseck; Drachenfels opposite

2v Small composition study, similar to sketch on f.2r

3r Rolandseck, Drachenfels and Nonnenwerth, looking downstream from the west bank

3v–4r The Rhine under Hammerstein, looking downstream from the west bank (on the right, the cottages among trees seen on the left of f.4v)
Inscr. *Hammerstein*

4v–5r The Rhine under Hammerstein, looking downstream from the west bank (slightly further upstream than the sketch on ff.3v–4r)

5v–6r Blank

6v–7r The Mosel bridge at Coblenz, with Ehrenbreitstein seen rising above its northern arches and the St Florinskirche and Liebfrauenkirche above its southern arches
Inscr. on 6v: [?*Cloud*]

7v–8r Ehrenbreitstein and the Mosel waterfront at Coblenz, from the bridge
Inscr. *Blocks of Timber*

8v–9r Ehrenbreitstein from the Rhine

9v Blank

10r Coblenz and Ehrenbreitstein, looking downstream from the west bank north of Kapellen

10v–11r Coblenz and Ehrenbreitstein, looking downstream from the west bank north of Kapellen

11v–12r Coblenz and Ehrenbreitstein, looking downstream from the west bank north of Kapellen

12v–13r Burg Lahneck, Oberlahnstein, Niederlahnstein and Schloss Stolzenfels, looking upstream from the west bank just below the junction of the Lahn and the Rhine
Inscr. *Boat coming in*; *Road*

13v–14r Burg Lahneck, Oberlahnstein, Niederlahnstein, Kapellen and Schloss Stolzenfels, looking upstream from a roadside fountain (slightly further upstream than the sketch on ff.12v–13r)

14v Blank

15r Distant view of Coblenz and Ehrenbreitstein, looking downstream from the west bank, near the fountain depicted on f.14r

15v Blank

16r Schloss Stolzenfels and Kapellen from the east bank
Inscr. *Cappelle*

16v–17r View up the Lahn with the turreted customs house and Burg Lahneck, from the landing-stage at Oberlahnstein
Inscr. (on house) *R*[ed]

17v Tiny sketch of the Marxburg with illegible inscription

17v–18r The Marxburg and Braubach, from the Lahnstein road
Inscr. *Peasants mixing manure*

18v Blank (marked '174' when f.18 was detached)

19r The Marxburg and Braubach, from the landing-stage, looking upstream

19v–20r Braubach and the Marxburg, with Schloss Stolzenfels and Oberlahnstein in the distance, looking downstream

20v–21r Filsen and Boppard, looking upstream from the west bank

(much faded, and marked '173', having been stuck down when f.21v was exhibited)

21v–22r Burg Rheinfels, looking downstream to Wellmich church and Burg Maus in the distance, from the riverside at St Goar
Inscr. *Wood Timber and Tree*

22v–23r Burg Katz, St Goarshausen, St Goar and Burg Rheinfels, looking upstream from the riverside north of Burg Rheinfels

23v–24r The Rhine gorge and Burg Rheinfels, from the Grundelbachtal

24v–26b Burg Katz and St Goarshausen from the riverside road by the landing-stage at St Goar, with a fishing boat in the foreground
Inscr. *Road*

26c–27r Burg Rheinfels and St Goar, Wellmich church and Burg Maus, St Goarshausen and Burg Katz, looking downstream from the riverside at St Goar, with a fishing boat in the foreground

27v Shipping at St Goar with Burg Rheinfels on the left, Wellmich church and Burg Maus in the distance, looking downstream from the riverside at St Goar
Inscr. *Two Boats lashed together making one*; *Children fishing*

25r St Goarshausen and Burg Katz from the riverside at St Goar
Inscr. *Ducks Diving Faster*

25v–26r Burg Katz, St Goarshausen, the Lorelei and the southern edge of St Goar, looking upstream from the riverside at St Goarshausen

26v Burg Katz, St Goarshausen, and a glimpse of the Rhine gorge and St Goar, from the Forstbachtal
Inscr. *Wood*

28r Burg Katz, St Goarshausen, and a glimpse of the Rhine gorge and St Goar, from the Forstbachtal
Inscr. (twice) *W*[ood]

28v Burg Katz, St Goarshausen and across the Rhine to St Goar, from the hillside north of Burg Katz (marked '175' when f.28 was detached)

29r View across the Rhine to St Goar and Burg Rheinfels, from the hillside close to Burg Katz. Late afternoon sun above St Goar

29v–30r The Rhine gorge with Burg Katz in the foreground and Burg Rheinfels in the distance, from the hillside behind Burg Katz

30v–31r Bacharach and Burg Stahleck, with Burg Gutenfels seen in the distance on the east bank, looking downstream from the west bank south of Bacharach

31v Burg Fürstenberg and Rheindiebach, with Bacharach and Burg Stahleck in the distance, looking downstream from the west bank south of Rheindiebach

32r Blank

32v–33r The Bautsburg (left) and Assmannshausen (right), looking downstream from the west bank, with travellers on the road
Inscr. *Wood*

33v–34r Burg Ehrenfels, the Mäuseturm, Bingen and Burg Klopp, looking upstream from the west bank north of Bingen
Inscr. [?*Vines*]; [?*Willow*]

34v–35r Burg Reichenstein and the Clemenskapelle (centre) and Assmannshausen (right), looking downstream from the west bank north of Bingen, with figures working on the left
Inscr. *Wood cutters*

35v–36r Burg Ehrenfels and the Mäuseturm (left), Rüdesheim (in the distance) and Bingen (right), looking upstream from the west bank north of Bingen

36v–37r The monument to General Hoche above Weissenthurm and view down the Rhine towards Andernach and Neuwied

37v–38r Burg Rheinfels, looking towards the Rhine gorge from the west

38v–39r Burg Rheinfels, looking towards the Rhine gorge from the west

39v–40r Burg Rheinfels, from inland

40v Blank

41r Burg Rheinfels, from inland

41v–42r St Goar, looking upstream from Burg Rheinfels. Burg Katz and St Goarshausen in the distance, and a raft on the Rhine

42v View upstream, from south of Hirzenach (much faded, and marked '232', having been stuck down when f.42r was exhibited)

43r Burg Maus and Wellmich church, looking upstream from the west bank south of Hirzenach
Inscr. (on road) *Women & Men Making Road*; (on hillside) *Conical Hills*

43v–44r Burg Maus and Wellmich church, looking upstream from the west bank at the bend south of Hirzenach
Inscr. illegibly on f.43v; (on f.44r) *Willows*; *Wood*; *W*; *Road*; *Rock*

44v The bend of the Rhine by Hirzenach, looking upstream from the west bank, with a traveller in the foreground
Inscr. *Rock*

45r ?The Rhine near Hirzenach, looking downstream from the west bank, with a traveller in the foreground
Inscr. *Hattesheim*

45v–46r The castles of the Two Brothers and the church at Bornhofen, looking upstream from the west bank between Boppard and Bad Salzig, with travellers in the foreground
Inscr. *R*; *W*; *R*; *W*; *Wood*

46v–47r View up the Rhine from the west bank at Hirzenach

47v Boppard, looking downstream from the landing place by the Burg (the hills extend on to f.48r)
Inscr. *Earth*; *Wall*; *B*; *B*; (on f.48r) [?*a Vineyard*]

48r Boppard, looking upstream from the riverside to the mole, Sandtor, Ritter-Schwalbach Haus, Capuchin church and roadside crucifix
Inscr. *St Antoni Ora Pro Nobis*

48v Schloss Stolzenfels, Niederlahnstein, Oberlahnstein and Burg Lahneck, looking downstream from the west bank
Inscr. *Lonack*

49r Braubach and the Marxburg from the west bank
Inscr. *Maxburg*

49v Schloss Stolzenfels, Niederlahnstein and Oberlahnstein, looking downstream from the west bank at Rhens with the Scharfenturm in the centre

50r Braubach and the Marxburg looking upstream from the west bank at Rhens next to the Scharfenturm and Hotel Königstuhl
Inscr. *The* [?*Steep*] *Hill here*

50v Schloss Stolzenfels and Oberlahnstein, looking downstream from the west bank at Rhens with St Joseph's gate on the left
Inscr. *Timber*; *Linen d*[?*ry*]*ing*

51r Schloss Stolzenfels, Niederlahnstein and the Martinsburg at Oberlahnstein, looking downstream from the west bank north of Rhens
Inscr. *Martinsburg a Sketch*; *Ober Lanstein*

51v–52r Schloss Stolzenfels, Niederlahnstein, Oberlahnstein, Burg Lahneck and the Martinsburg, looking downstream
Inscr. (over a point in the far distance) *Coblentz*

52v Blank

53r The choir of Cologne cathedral with adjacent houses and townsfolk
Inscr. *Heaps of Ruin of Old Windows*; *Timber*; *Brow*[n] *spotted G and Hood*; (on clothes) *P*; *B*

53v–54r Shipping at Cologne, looking upstream to the Seven Hills with Great St Martin's church and the Rhine Gate
Inscr. (on cart) *Hay*

54v Blank

55r The river front at Cologne, looking upstream with the Bayenturm, Great St Martin's, the town hall, the choir of the cathedral and St Cunibert's; in the corner: Deutz on the east bank of the Rhine

55v Blank except for inscriptions
St Cunebeare (i.e. Cunibert); [?*Wafenwerft*] (? an attempt at 'Wasserwerfer', water cannon)

56r The south tower and choir of Cologne cathedral from the south-east
Inscr. (on the entablature of the church in the centre) *LAUDE JESUS CHRISTUS*

56v Blank (marked '239' when f.56 was detached)

57r The town hall, Cologne
Inscr. (on one of the decorated panels) *Daniel*

57v The buildings of Deutz, forming a continuation of the right-hand side of the sketch on f.58r (marked '230' when f.57 was detached)

58r The river front at Cologne, looking downstream with the cathedral, town hall, Great St Martin's and St Cunibert's

58v The Bayenturm, Cologne, looking upstream to the Seven Hills

59r–60v Blank

TB CLXII *Dort* sketchbook 1817

This sketchbook does not form part of the present area of study, having only been used in Holland.

TB CCXVI *Rivers Meuse and Moselle* sketchbook 1824 (see cat.no.37)

Bound in brown leather, with the remains of one brass clasp.

Inside front cover
Sketch map of the Meuse between Verdun and Mouzon and other notes and sketches

1r Sketch map of the Meuse between Mouzon and Sedan and notes on distances:

Verdun to Sedan	*75 Miles*
Sedan to Mezieres	*26 Miles*
Mez to Charleville	*6*
Ch to Givet	*67*
Givet to Dinant	*16*
Verdun to M	*101*
V to Charleville	*106*
V to Givet	*173*
V to Dinant	*189*
Sedan to D	*114*

2½ German Miles Equal 10 English

1v Sketch map of the Meuse between Sedan and Fumay

2r Sketch map of the Meuse between Givet and Dinant; and part of a fort

2v List of places on the upper Meuse; and sketches of fortifications

3r List of places, between Frénois and Agimont

3v List of places, between Verdun and Douzy

4r List of places, between Bazeilles and Dinant

4v Sketch map of the Meuse between Dinant and Andenne; and landscape sketches

5r Sketch maps of the Meuse between Huy and Liège and Liège and Maastricht; and sketch of Sedan

5v List of places on the *Left Bank* of the Meuse (actually the east) between Dinant and Wyck

6r List of places on the *Right Bank* of the Meuse (actually the west) between Bouvignes and Maastricht

6v (The following notes on sights between Coblenz and Trier come from the 1st English edition of A. Schreiber, *The Traveller's Guide down the Rhine*, 1818, pp.173–94 and continue onto f.8r of this sketchbook. On f.6v the names *Oberwinggen* and *Alken* are underlined in red pencil.)

Treves 24 Leagues by Land
from Coblenz 49 by Moselle
Mwiss Guls Road to Ley Rock
Old Castle belongs to C^s Leyen near it
Oberwinggen Mt Town 2 Leagues
Unterwinggen from Coblentz
Cobern ancient had 2 Castles
Altenbourg Castle and Chapel
Convent ancient in the Stoperwald Forest
Gondorff *Kattenes*
Niederfell *Echenach Right*
Oberlemen
Oberfell
Alken Mt Town Castle Turant or Thorn
Loff
Brodenbach

Steinburg Castle
Hezenport
Bischofstein or Bishop Castle
on a Mountain by the Mosselle and
Rhon on the other Chapel of 3 Maries

7r (On this page *Treis* and *Zell* are underlined in red pencil)
Rhon Kern
Burgen Eltz
one League from Kern Elz & Castle
Baudouin or Baldwin, near
Pyrmont a League further Castle and
Fall of the Elz. Carden Mt *Town*
Church Castle Mon^{r} *Sontag Pictures*
Opposite to Carden Hermitage of Zilles
berg on a high Rock fine View of M
Treis M^{t} *T*
Pommern Wine Roman Camp on Mt
I L Rosenthal Convent Wild Situation
Klotten Klottenberg Castle
Kochen Anchor and Roman King
3 L baths of Bertrich
Bieltein Castle Prison Convent
Marienberg Convent on a Steep Rock
A great bend of Moselle to Zell M^{t} *T*
Merl Inn Mon^{r} *Koch*
Enkirchen St
Starkenbourg Castle Mt *Stephanberg*

7v (On this page *Erden* and *Mulheim* are underlined in red pencil)
Trarbach Ancient Thronus
Bacchi I L Castle of Grafinburg
Brass Tomb of John 4th *and the*
Kellereyhof ancient Hall
Traben flying Bridge
Risbach Old Chapel
$\frac{3}{4}$ *L from Traerbach Croff*
Erden M^{t} *T wine Moselle Convent of*
Wachern Nachtig
Zeltingen
Martinhof Farm of K^{n} *of Malta*
Wehlen Krach
Bernkastel Old Castle Mt *Town*
Chain of the Hunsdruck M^{ts}
Golden Grape and 3 Kings
Mulheim 1 L $\frac{1}{2}$ *M*^{t} *Town*
Lyser
1 L up the Muhlbach Veldentz
Castle burnt in the 30 Years War
1 L from M Dusemont 1 L West of V
Emmel
Minnlages Convent

8r (On this page *Neumagen* is underlined in red pencil)
Many bends of the Moselle
Tron
Neumagen M^{t} *T Castle near a*
curious Roman Tower with Bas reliefs
Trittenheim
Riol Reigebourg Rigodulum Castle
Erzig
Pfaltz Pfalzel A intrench
Treves Palace of the Elector C^{h} *of*
Notre Dame 1227 St *Simeon Roman 2*
Arches Entrance Black Gate C^{h} *Paulin*
Pict Roof Domo St *Peter University Gym*
Roman Piers of the Moselle Bridge
Amphitheatre 1 L from Black Gate
Wyttenbach's Hist of Treves
Igel 1 L $\frac{1}{4}$ *Roman Pyramid near*
the Ruwer River 2 L an Aquaduct
4 Convents St *Martin S*^{t} *Martha and*
Mary aux Martyrs Maximin
Red House and Fountain

8v Sketch map of the Mosel between Trier (Trèves) and Traben-Trarbach, with *Neumagen*, *Mulheim* and *Erden* underlined in red pencil
This map and those on ff.9r and 9v are derived from that in Schreiber's *Guide* (see note on f.6v)

9r Sketch map of the Mosel between the Starkenburg and Müden, with *Zell*, *Knockheim* (Cochem) and *Treiltz* (Treis) underlined in red pencil

9v Sketch map of the Mosel from Burg Bischofstein to Coblenz, with *Alken* and *Ober Winnigen* underlined in red pencil

10r Harbour scenes and three seagulls

10v Distant hills

11r Cliffs and a boat

11v Distant hills

12r Distant buildings and harbour

12v Cliffs, harbour, sailing vessels, etc.

13r On the coast

13v (1) Figure studies
Inscr. *French fishing Caps Striped*; *Red Shoes*; *jacket Blue*; *Blue*; *Large Brass Earrings*
(2) House and church
Inscr. *Calais*

14r Gateways and fortifications at Calais

14v Bridges and fortifications

15r Buildings

15v (1) Cloud study
Inscr. *Beautiful Cold Grey and Pink Clouds before sunrise*; *orange*
(2) Landscape and windmill
(3) Hills and clouds
Inscr. *One streak of light all the rest grey*

16r (1) Cloud study
Inscr. *Warm Clouds over Cold Sky*; *grey*
(2) Bridge
Inscr. *grey*; *warm yellow fresh*; *orange*
(3) Figures and boat
Inscr. *Barque*
(4) Buildings
Inscr. *Soldier fishing*

16v Various hasty sketches, including a windmill and a cart
Inscr. *Blue*; *Cart like Rubens*; *Blue smock frock*; *Sabots*; *Tan Cloth*

17r Buildings on hill

17v Landscape and cloud study
Inscr. *Blue*

18r ? Cloud study
Inscr. *Blue*

18v Sky study
Inscr. *Blue*; *Yellow*; *Grey*; *Blue*; *Blue*; *Yellow*; *Grey*

19r (1) Landscape and windmill
Inscr. *Gold Blue dark*; *Corn in Light*
(2) Windmill
Inscr. *Callcott*; [?*Douai*]
(3) Walls and gateway

19v Twin-spired church

20r Group of figures

20v View in a town with bridges

21r View in Liège, with a barge

21v Riverside view with hills

22r River view with church and boat

22v River scenery

23r River view with churches

23v Study of sky over the Meuse near Liège
Inscr. *Blue*; *Livid Red*

24r View at Liège

24v View on the Meuse near Liège
Inscr. *Blue*; *GGR only*; *Boys playing with a* [?*lamb*]; *Timber*

25r Sky study
Inscr. *Brown*; *Blue*; *V Yellow*

25v (1) Boat
(2) View on the Meuse from mid-stream

26r Meuse scene with a boat

26v House and timber
Inscr. [?*Cliney*]

27r Three views on the Meuse from mid-stream
Inscr. (twice) *Corn*

27v Houses by the Meuse
Inscr. [?*Overia*]; [?*Ouvre*]

28r Three views of Tilleur
(2) Inscr. *Tielluer*; *Water*; *Floats of Unbarked Timber Trees lasht*

28v Three Meuse views
(1) Inscr. *1*; *5*; *10*; *Green Shutters* (on house)
(3) Inscr. *Cows drinking*; *Women washing*; *Wood*; *Horses obliged to Swim*; *Ferry*

29r Boats and figures
Inscr. *Two Barges* [. . .] *the Ropes*

29v Three Meuse views from mid-stream
(1) Inscr. *Corn*
(3) Inscr. *Horses again across the E*[. . .] *River*

30r Three Meuse views from mid-stream
(2) Inscr. *12*; *13* (on bays of house)
(3) Inscr. *Sheep*; *Wood*

30v (1) Distant view of the castle of Chokier on the Meuse, looking upstream
(2) View near Chokier
Inscr. *Corn*; *Only Light*; *Boats*

31r Several overlapping views on the Meuse including three depictions of Chokier, looking upstream
Inscr. *Chateaux Chok*; *Chock*

31v Two views at Chokier, looking upstream
Inscr. *Chok*

32r Chokier from the river below

32v Two sketches of Chokier, looking downstream

33r Four views of and near Chokier
(4) Inscr. *Sail in Light*

33v Five views on the Meuse between Chokier and Flône
(1) Inscr. *Wind blowing up*; [. . .] *the Light*

34r Four views on the Meuse between Chokier and Flône

34v Five views at and near Flône

35r (1) River view near Flône
(2) (3) Two views of the abbey at Flône, looking downstream
Inscr. *Flone*

35v Three views at and near Flône
(1) Inscr. *Corn*

36r Four views just below Huy, the last showing the mansion at Neuville-sous-Huy

36v Two views just above Huy

37r (1) Cliffs on the Meuse near Huy
Inscr. *Red Ore*
(2) Huy, looking upstream

37v Huy, looking upstream

37v–38r Huy, looking upstream

38r Barge moored at the quayside at Huy, just below the bridge
Inscr. (on cargo) *Tiles*

38v Huy from the Rue de Ramparts

39r Huy from the outskirts with waterwheels and watermills

39v Four sketches of Huy from the outskirts
(1) Inscr. *With a* [. . .] *of two* [. . .]

40r (1) (2) Views in Huy near the Porte Maillet
(3) View in Huy looking towards the apse of Notre-Dame

40v Blank

41r (1) The apse of the church of Notre-Dame, Huy, and the Bethlehem Portal
(2) The Bethlehem Portal

41v Huy from the Ahin road, looking downstream

42r Huy from the Liège road, looking upstream

42v (1) Distant view of Huy, from the Liège road
Inscr. *Convent of St Martin*; *Vineyard*
(2) The Meuse near Huy
Inscr. *Red Castle*; *Goats coming from Vines*
(3) The Meuse near Huy
(4) Distant view of Huy from the Ahin road
Inscr. *Light*

43r (1) Distant view of Huy from the Liège road
Inscr. *Vines*
(2) Distant view of Huy from the Liège road
(3) The Meuse between Huy and Chokier
Inscr. *Vineyard*
(4) Chokier, looking downstream

43v (1) Chokier, looking downstream
Inscr. *Rainbow with Rain – the Pink and Green most visible*
(2) The quay at Liège by the Pont des Arches

44r The Pont des Arches, Liège, with adjacent houses

44v Several sketches of moored boats filled with figures and their wares (at Liège)
Inscr. *Women walking along the Qy*; *Horse* [. . .] *the* [. . .]

45r (1) (2) Groups of figures
(1) Inscr. *Colour* [?*Pail*]
(3) The tower of Notre-Dame, Mézières
Inscr. *Mez*
(4) (5) Slight sketches of a town, probably Mézières
Inscr. *M*

45v (1) Grand house
(2) Landscape
Inscr. *Thon*
(3) (4) Slight sketches of landscape

46r (1) Rocks at Samson
Inscr. *Samson*; *Meuse*
(2) Rocks at Samson
Inscr. *Meuse*
(3) Rocks at Samson
Inscr. *Viv*[?id] *Rock and B Wood*

46v (1) Rocks on the Meuse
Inscr. *Long bank*; *the Light and all* [. . .] *in the Meuse without a* [. . .] *or Light*
(2) The abbey of Flône
Inscr. *Flume*
(3) Distant view of a fortress
(4) Hand carts and wine bottles

47r Many distant views of Namur, mostly looking upstream to the confluence of the Meuse and the Sambre

47v Many sketches of rocks and hills along the Meuse near Namur
(1) Inscr. *Corn*
(2) Inscr. *Women white Cloth*
(3) Inscr. *Road*

48r Five sketches of the Meuse near Namur, mostly of Marche-les-Dames
(3) Inscr. *Marche les Dames*
(4) Inscr. *Children at play*

48v (1) (2) (3) Three views of rocks along the Meuse
(4) A gateway
Inscr. *Gardens*; *3 to the Sambre*

49r Three views of the citadel at Namur, as seen from the Sambre
Inscr. (in the opposite direction) *P from Profondville Rouillon Engher Bouv*

49v Several views at Namur, two looking up the Meuse to the confluence, three looking down the Meuse towards the citadel, bridge and Jambes

50r Six views on the Meuse at and near Namur
(1) Inscr. *Des Chretiens – – Soyez vous Favourable*
(2) Inscr. *Figure landing*
(3) Inscr. [?*St Mark*]
(5) Inscr. *Light*; *Vines*

50v Many sketches of rocks and hills near Namur
Inscr. *Road*; *Cattle*; *Corn*; *Cor*[n]; *Light*; *Wood*; *Profond Ville*; *Water Mill above Pro*[fondville]

51r Several views on the Meuse between Godinne and Yvoir
Inscr. *St Bruno or Pruino*; *Goudon – Maison de*; *Road*; *Roulay*; *Palace of Eau*; *Wood*; *Evrey*

51v Several views of Yvoir and the fortress of Poilvache
Inscr. *D*[. . .] *Convent*; *Road*; *Eviru*

52r Several views of Poilvache
Inscr. *Polvache*; *Hahu* (i.e. Houx, the village beneath Poilvache); *Road*; *M*[euse]; *Polvach Castle*

52v Distant views of Bouvignes and the castle of Crèvecoeur, looking up the Meuse to Dinant (seen in the last sketch)
Inscr. *Wood*; *Lighter than Maas*; *Road*; *Bouvine Chatux*

53r (1) A detail of Crèvecoeur
(2) Dinant, looking upstream
(3) Crèvecoeur and Bouvignes, looking upstream
(4) Dinant, Bouvignes and Crèvecoeur, looking upstream
(5) Dinant, Bouvignes and Crèvecoeur, looking upstream
Inscr. *Road*

53v Several overlapping sketches of Dinant looking upstream

54r Views at Dinant, looking upstream from the eastern riverbank
(2) Inscr. *Woman Washing F*

54v Three views of Bouvignes and Crèvecoeur

55r (1) Dinant, looking upstream from the eastern bank
(2) Bouvignes and Crèvecoeur, looking downstream
Inscr. *E foreground*; *B*[ouvignes]; *D*[inant]
(3) Distant view of Dinant, looking upstream

55v Views at Dinant, looking downstream from outside the town walls
(1) Inscr. *Mon*[r] *Decoux Hotel de Poste*; *House to* [?*Lodge*]
(4) Inscr. *ancient Wall of D*

56r Several sketches of the Roche à Bayard, south of Dinant; Dinant as seen from the vicinity of the Roche
(1) Inscr. *Rock Baard*; *D*[inant]
(2) Inscr. *Figures in Light*
(3) Inscr. *Blue*; *Dark*

56v Views near Dinant
(1) Inscr. *River Lesse*
(2) Inscr. *Women washing*; *River Lesse*
(3) Inscr. [. . .]
(4) Inscr. *Blue*; *Meuse*

57r Views between Dinant and Givet
(1) Inscr. *Chateaux Fete*; *B*; *Wood*; *Road*
(2) Inscr. *Road*
(3) Inscr. *Rock*; *Road*; *Din*

57v Six views of Givet and Fort Charlemont from the north

58r Six views of Givet and Fort Charlemont

58v–59r Many rough sketches of Givet and Fort Charlemont

59v Givet and Fort Charlemont

60r Givet and Fort Charlemont

60v–61r Several views of Givet and Fort Charlemont, looking downstream

61v The Meuse near Givet

62r (1) (2) The castle of Hierges
(2) Inscr. *Eauges*
(3) Vireux
Inscr. *Viraux*

62v Figures, inscr. *G*; *BG*[? *Collar*]; and several landscape studies, inscr. *Road*; one inscr. *Wood and Corn*; *Soldiers drinking at a spring*; *Piles Wood*

63r Several views of countryside and villages near Montigny, inscr. *Mont Tine* (twice); *slates* (twice)

63v	Several views of hills, the last possibly including a distant view of Fumay (inscr. *F*)
64r	Views by or near the Meuse, and at Montigny
64v	Views by or near the Meuse
65r	Views of a fortress town, one inscr. *Cuyp*
65v	Several views of a fortress town Inscr. *Yellow* (twice); (against a bridge) *23 arches*
66r	Fortifications at Mézières
66v	Several distant views of Sedan
67r	(1) Landscape Inscr. *Bla*[ck]; *W*[...] (2) Sedan (3) (4) Charleville
67v	(1) Distant view of Charleville (2)–(5) The Meuse valley above Charleville Inscr. *Wood*; *Corn*
68r	Six sketches of the Meuse valley above Charleville
68v–70v	Many sketches of the same unidentified town
71r	Landscape sketches
71v	The cathedral, Porte Chaussée and St Nicholas's church, Verdun
72r	Blank
72v	Fortifications
73r	The bishops' palace and cathedral, Verdun, from the bridge over the canalised Meuse to the south-west
73v	Verdun, with the Porte Chaussée and St Nicholas's church
74r	Three distant views of Verdun
74v	Distant view of Verdun
75r	Distant view of Verdun
75v	Two sketches of the Roman aqueduct at Ars-sur-Moselle from Ancy
76r	Three sketches of the Roman aqueduct, looking from Ancy to Ars and vice versa (1) Inscr. *3*; *5*
76v	Four sketches of the Roman aqueduct at Jouy-aux-Arches (2) Inscr. *Road*
77r	Five sketches of the Roman aqueduct at Jouy-aux-Arches
77v	Five sketches of the Roman aqueduct at Ars-sur-Moselle (4) Inscr. *Ancey*
78r	Five sketches of the Roman aqueduct at Ars-sur-Moselle (4) Inscr. *19* (against the arches)
78v	Views at and near Ancy and Ars-sur-Moselle, one inscr. *Ancey*
79r	Distant views of ?Metz from the aqueduct
79v	The Roman aqueduct at Ars-sur-Moselle Inscr. [...] *Equal to 4*
80r	(1) The Roman aqueduct (2) Landscape
80v	Views at and near Metz, variously inscr. *Fete of S*[t] *Louis* (i.e. 25 August); *Blue Li*[ght]; *chateau Fort*; *Metz*
81r	Three views of Thionville
81v	Distant town
82r	Towers, probably at Luxembourg
82v	Tower, probably at Luxembourg
83r	Luxembourg
83v	Luxembourg
84r	Luxembourg
84v	Sketches drawn from a moving carriage
85r	Sketches drawn from a moving carriage
85v	Sketches drawn from a moving carriage
86r	Sketches drawn from a moving carriage
86v	River valley
87r	Sketches from a moving carriage
87v	Valley, bridge and village
87v–88r	Several sketches of a village and bridge Inscr. *Wasserbillig*
88r	Landscape sketches
88v–89r	Views at and near Trier, including:
88v	(2) The waterfront at Trier, looking upstream past the Martinskloster
89r	(3) The junction of the Saar and Mosel near Igel Inscr. *Saar and Moles*
89v	Pallien, looking down the Mosel from the Napoleonsbrücke
90r	(1) Trier from Pallien (2) The Roman column at Igel (3)–(5) Hills near Trier
90v	Trier from the west
91r	Trier from the west, looking upstream from the hillside above Pallien
91v	Pallien from the hillside above it Inscr. *Road*
92r	Three sketches near Pallien (3) includes the Roman bridge at Trier Inscr. *Road*
92v	Several sketches of the buildings at Trier as seen from Pallien (1) Inscr. *Palli*
93r	Several sketches of the buildings of Trier, as seen from the Napoleonsbrücke (the subject of the last sketch)
93v	Trier from the hills above Pallien
94r	(1) On the Mosel near Pallien Inscr. *Loading a* [*? Cart*] (2) Trier from the river bank beneath Pallien (3) View of Pallien and Trier (4) Two figures carrying jugs Inscr. *Blue*; *Red*
94v	Several sketches of the Roman bridge at Trier and the buildings adjacent to it, looking upstream Inscr. *Warm*; *Cold*
95r	Views down the Mosel north of the bridge at Trier, with Pallien and the buildings of Trier shown in three separate sketches

95v The Imperial Baths, Trier

96r (R) The Imperial Baths, Trier
(L) Interior of the cathedral, Trier, with worshippers(?)

96v (1) (3) Ruins at Trier
(2) The cathedral, Trier

97r Trier from the south with the cathedral seen beyond the Baths
Inscr. *Road*

97v Interior of the cathedral, Trier, with worshippers
Inscr. ⟨*Notredame*⟩ *Domo*, *Gold*

98r Five sketches of the Mosel near Trier
(1) Inscr. *St Mar Martyr*

98v Eight sketches of the Mosel
(4) Inscr. *Phaltz* (i.e. Pfalzel)
(5) Inscr. *Rower* (i.e. Ruwer)
(6) (7) (8) Inscr. *1*; *2*; *3*

99r Six sketches of the Mosel
(4) Inscr. *5*
(5) Inscr. *Erang* (i.e. Ehrang); *6*
(6) Inscr. *C*[. . .]; *7*

99v Eight sketches of the Mosel between Ehrang and Issel
(1) Inscr. *8*
(2) Inscr. *9*; *W*
(3) Inscr. *10*; *E*
(4) Inscr. *11*; *W*; *Swits* (i.e. Schweich)
(5) Inscr. *WN*; *12*
(6) Inscr. *13*; *WNW*; *Red Rock*
(7) Inscr. *14*; *ES*
(8) Inscr. *Esel* (i.e. Issel); *15 W*; *Esl*

100r Seven sketches, mostly showing Schweich and Kirsch facing each other across the Mosel
(1) Inscr. *Esel* (i.e. Issel)
(2) Inscr. *White* [?*House*] (actually the Ferry Tower); *Switch*; *Kirtch*

100v Eight sketches of the Mosel between Riol and Mehring
(3) Inscr. *Riol*
(4) Inscr. *V*[ines]; *E*; *Wood*
(5) Inscr. *Merich* (i.e. Mehring)
(6) Inscr. *Riol*; *W*
(7) Inscr. *Merich*
(8) Inscr. *M*; *E*

101r Seven sketches of the Mosel between Mehring and Detzem
(1) Inscr. *ES*
(2) Inscr. *E*
(4) Inscr. *Pigs*
(5) Inscr. *ENN*; *Ilzen* (? i.e. Detzem)
(6) Inscr. *Pohl* (? i.e. Polich)
(7) Inscr. *SW*

101v Nine sketches of the Mosel between Ensch and Klüsserath
(1) Inscr. *SE*
(2) Inscr. *N*
(3) Inscr. *S*; *Erths*
(6) Inscr. *W*
(7) Inscr. *Ferry*
(9) Inscr. *Klukserhof*; *Smoke*

102r Seven sketches on the Mosel between Trittenheim and Dhron
(2) Inscr. *R* (?Rock)
(3) Inscr. *Drettenh*; *Misty*
(4) Inscr. *Neumagen*
(6) Inscr. *Tron*

102v Seven sketches on the Mosel between Dhron and Piesport
(2) Inscr. *Blue*; *Mist clearing*
(4) Inscr. *Dr*
(5) Inscr. *Pisport*
(6) Inscr. illegibly

103r Six sketches of the Mosel near Piesport, including three of the so-called Mosel Lorelei
(2) (6) Inscr. *Pisport*

103v Five sketches of the Mosel between the Mosel Lorelei and Wintrich
(3) Inscr. *Minheim*
(5) Inscr. *Wintrich*; *E*

104r Six sketches of the Mosel between Wintrich and Mülheim
(3) Kesten
(4) Inscr. *Filzen*
(5) Inscr. *Mulheim*
(6) Inscr. *Duse*[. . .] (obscured by Inventory stamp)

104v Sketches, chiefly of Bernkastel, Kues and the Landshut
(1) Inscr. *Duse*[. . .]*Lock*; *W*
(2) Inscr. *Mul*; *E*

105r (1) (2) The Landshut
(3) Half-timbered houses at Bernkastel
(4) The flying bridge at Bernkastel

105v (1) Bernkastel and the Landshut, looking upstream
(2) Bernkastel and the Landshut, looking upstream, with St Nicholas's Hospital, Kues, on the right
Inscr. *Hospital Cau*; *Cause*
(3) Bernkastel and the Landshut, looking upstream, with St Nicholas's Hospital, Kues, on the right

106r (1) Distant view of Bernkastel and the Landshut, looking upstream
(2) Zeltingen
Inscr. *Zelting*
(3) (4) Near Zeltingen

106v (1) Zeltingen
Inscr. *Ferry*
(2) Zeltingen
(3) Kloster Machern between Zeltingen and Ürzig
Inscr. *Landing Ch* [. . .], *Urtl*, *Hurtzl*
(5) (6) The Hermitage on the Michaelslei, Ürzig
Inscr. *St Michael*; *Hermitage*

107r (1) (2) Sailing boats on the Mosel between Ürzig and Kröv
(3)–(5) Wolfer Kloster above the east bank of the Mosel, looking downstream
(3) Inscr. *Wolve*

107v Five sketches of Wolfer Kloster from different viewpoints going downstream round the Gockelsberg

108r (1) (2) The Grevenburg, looking downstream from the approach to Traben
Inscr. [?*Curious*] *Effect of Smoke Cold* [?*Wind*] *and Light cloud and dawn* [?*Sun*]
(3) (4) The Grevenburg
(5) Trarbach church

108v Traben, Trarbach and the Grevenburg

109r Trarbach and the Grevenburg, looking downstream

109v Traben and the flying bridge

110r Trarbach church and the Grevenburg, as seen from the

entrance to the town by the footpath from Bernkastel
Inscr. *Trarbach*

110v (1) Half-timbered houses, probably at Trarbach
(2) Houses and gate tower, Trarbach

111r (1) (2) The river front at Trarbach with the round tower, boats and flying bridge
(3) A half-timbered butcher's shop, probably at Trarbach, with the shopkeepers at work, hanging carcasses and domestic animals in the foreground
Inscr. *Dogs and Cats*

111v (1) Inscr. *Sky*; *Traven*
(2) Inscr. *Starkenburg*
(5) Inscr. *Enterach* (i.e. Enkirch)
Rest of page: tiny views of the Starkenburg and Grevenburg

112r Tiny sketches, mostly looking upstream from near Burg to the ruined fortress of Montroyal on the hill above Traben
(2) Inscr. *Ingel* (? i.e. Enkirch)
(3) Inscr. *Marinal Hof*
(6) Inscr. *Burg*; *R*; *Hof Male*

112v (1) Inscr. *Burg*
(2) Inscr. *Bleaching Linen*; *E*[ast]; *Water Conduit and*
(6) Inscr. *Kirch* (i.e. Reilkirche); *W*[est]; *Mill*; *Riol* (i.e. Reil)
(4)–(6) The Marienburg, looking downstream
(4) Inscr. *Marienburg*

113r Five views at and near the Marienburg
(1)–(3) The Marienburg
(4) Inscr. *Breedi* (i.e. Briedel); *V*[ines]
(5) Briedel and the Marienburg, looking upstream

113v (1) Briedel and the Marienburg, looking upstream
(2) (3) Zell, looking downstream

114r (1) Boats moored at the river's edge at Zell, with men at work mending nets
(2) Zell, looking upstream
Inscr. *Zell*
(3) Kaimt
Inscr. *Kum*
(4) Merl, looking upstream
Inscr. *Merl*
(5) Zell, looking upstream
Inscr. *V*[ines]

114v Eight sketches of the Marienburg from Merl with separate sketches of the ruins and the village of Merl
(4) Inscr. *Marienburg Con*[vent]
(5) Inscr. *Marienburg*
(6) Inscr. *Merl*

115r Ten sketches made travelling downstream from the Marienburg to Kloster Stuben
(1) The Marienburg
(2) View downstream to Alf and Bullay
Inscr. *Rock*; *Aluff*; *Pouley*
(5) Inscr. *Blue*; *Red*
(6) Inscr. *Aluff*; *Pouly*
(7) Inscr. *Aldehund* (i.e. St Aldegund)
(9) Inscr. *Neef*
(10) Inscr. *Bremm*; *Stop* (i.e. Stuben)

115v (1) Inscr. *Red R*[ock]
(3) Kloster Stuben from the riverside at Bremm
(4)–(7) Kloster Stuben from different viewpoints travelling downstream
(6) Inscr. *Stuben*
(7) Inscr. *Effect of Pink Sunset*; *Stuben*

116r Four views of Kloster Stuben from different viewpoints travelling downstream
(4) Inscr. *All Cold*; *All Light*; *Stuben*; *Stuben*; *Mist*

116v (1) View upstream from Eller
Inscr. *Alf*; *Petersberg*; *Stuben*; *Eller*
(2) Ediger
Inscr. *Hedder*
(3) (4) The Leymerturm, Nehren
(3) Inscr. *Nearne*
(5) Nehren

117r Two Mosel views, with Senheim church
(2) Inscr. *Beaut* [*?Range*] *Warm Light*
(3)–(6) Burg Metternich above Beilstein

117v Ehrenbreitstein from the Rhine quay at Coblenz

118r (1) Distant view of Metz
(2) Metz cathedral, showing the Tour de la Mutte, the façade with the rose window and the eighteenth-century portal designed by Blondel
Inscr. *Metz*
(3) ? Part of Ehrenbreitstein

118v (1) The Burgverlies, Beilstein, and Burg Metternich from the Mosel
(2) St Joseph's church, Beilstein, and Burg Metternich, looking downstream

119r Beilstein and Burg Metternich, looking upstream from Ellenz

119v Three views of Beilstein, looking upstream, each drawn from slightly further downstream than the last
(1) Inscr. *Bilielstein*

120r Beilstein and Burg Metternich, looking upstream

120v Four views of Beilstein, looking upstream

121r (1) Burg Metternich in the distance
(2) The Burg at Cochem
(3)–(5) Views at Cochem
(3) The river front looking upstream
(4) The river front looking upstream, with the Peterskapelle
(5) The river front looking upstream, with the Burg and St Martin's church

121v Cochem, looking upstream

122r (1) The Burg at Cochem
Rest of page: small views of Cochem and the Burg from various directions; also Klotten and Burg Coraidelstein

122v Two views of Cochem, looking downstream, one accompanied by a separate sketch of the spire of St Martin's church

123r Two views of Cochem, looking downstream from slightly further away from the town than the sketches on f. 122v

123v Three views of Klotten and Burg Coraidelstein from level with it and looking upstream

124r (1) Klotten and Burg Coraidelstein, looking upstream
(2) The Mosel near Klotten
(3) and (4) Klotten and Burg Coraidelstein, looking upstream
(3) Inscr. *Clottenburg*
(5) Pommern, looking downstream
Inscr. *Pomeron*

(6) Klotten, seen in the distance looking upstream
Inscr. *Cloten from Pomeron*

124v Seven sketches near Treis, the last four showing Burg Treis
(1) Inscr. *Treis*
(3) Inscr. *Mending a Wall*
(4) Inscr. *Beaut and Light Grey*

125r (1) Burg Treis from the river, looking downstream
(2) Karden and Treis, looking downstream, with separate details of St Castor's church, Karden and the Zilleskapelle, Treis
(3) Burg Treis, looking upstream
(4) The Zilleskapelle and Treis, looking upstream
(4) The Zilleskapelle and Karden, looking upstream

125v (1) A canopied boat on the Mosel, looking upstream towards the Zilleskapelle, Treis, and St Castor's church, Karden
(2) St Castor's church, Karden, looking upstream
(3) Müden, looking upstream
Inscr. *Muden*
(4) Karden from Müden
Inscr. *Carden*
(5)–(7) River views and boats between Müden and Moselkern
(7) Inscr. *Mosell Karn*

126r Six sketches drawn going downstream approaching Burgen and Burg Bischofstein and the Pauluskapelle, with details of the Burg and the chapel separately inserted

126v Six sketches drawn going downstream away from Burgen and Burg Bischofstein and looking back at them
(3) Inscr. *Burgen*

127r (1) Hatzenport, looking upstream
Inscr. *Hazenport*
(2) Brodenbach, looking downstream
Inscr. *Brodenba*; *G*[. . .] *Old W*
(3) View upstream towards Hatzenport
(4) Burg Thurandt in the distance, looking downstream

127v (1) Hatzenport, looking upstream
Inscr. *Haz*
(2) Inscr. *Ferry*
(3)–(5) Löf
(4) Inscr. *Luf R*
(6) Distant view of Burg Thurandt, looking downstream

128r Five sketches of Burg Thurandt, above Alken, looking downstream

128v (1)–(3) Three sketches of Burg Thurandt and Alken, looking downstream
(4) Alken and Burg Thurandt, looking upstream
Inscr. *Wall* [?*Mending*]

129r Five sketches of Alken and Burg Thurandt

129v (1)–(3) Alken and Burg Thurandt, looking upstream
(2) Inscr. *Rock*
(4) Gondorf, looking downstream
Inscr. *Ondoff*

130r Nine sketches between Alken and Gondorf
(1) Inscr. *Oberfell*
(5) Inscr. *S*
(7) Inscr. *Oberfell*
(8) Inscr. *M*[. . .]; *Spring*; *Boy Bathing*
(9) Lehmen
Inscr. *Leemen*

130v Five sketches of the Leyen Burg at Gondorf, looking downstream
(3) Inscr. *Gondorf*
(4) Inscr. *Road*

131r (1) (2) (5) The Oberburg and St Matthias chapel, Kobern, looking downstream
(3) Inscr. *Niederfell*; *Gondorf Obg*
(4) Inscr. *Niederfell*
(6) Inscr. *Niderfell Gondorf Obg*

131v Three sketches of Kobern, with additional details

132r (1) Kobern
(2) The river front at Kobern
Inscr. *Coberen*
(3) The Niederburg at Kobern

132v (1) Dieblich and Kobern, looking upstream
Inscr. *Divelich*
(2) (3) Views upstream towards Kobern
(4) (5) Views downstream towards Winningen
(4) Inscr. *Ferry*[ing] *over a load and* [?*Cattle*]

133r Twelve sketches at and near Winningen
(5) Inscr. *Lyel* (i.e. Lay)
(9) Inscr. [?*Stones*]
(10) Inscr. *Ferry of Ober Wineging*

133v (1) Winningen and Lay, looking downstream
Inscr. *Lyus* (i.e. Lay)
(2)–(6) Views between Lay and Güls
(3) Inscr. *F*[. . .]; *2*
(4) Inscr. [?*Rock*]
(5) Inscr. *Stone* [. . .] [?*grey*]
(6) Inscr. *Cutting the Vines* [. . .]

134r Numerous views between Güls and Coblenz including distant views of Ehrenbreitstein
(1) Inscr. *Guil*
(2) Moselweiss
Inscr. *Weiss*

134v Several overlapping sketches of Ehrenbreitstein and the Mosel bridge at Coblenz
Inscr. (under its arches) *12*

135r (1) Ehrenbreitstein from the Mosel
(2) The Mosel bridge at Coblenz

135v Ehrenbreitstein

136r The Mosel front at Coblenz, looking downstream with moored boats and people at work

136v The Mosel front at Coblenz (further downstream than in f.136r), looking downstream to the spires of St Castor's church, with sailing craft

137r Moored boats at Coblenz

137v The Rhine front at Coblenz, looking downstream towards the bridge of boats, with boats and figures

138r Ehrenbreitstein from the Rhine, looking downstream

138v (1) The island of Oberwerth, with its ruined abbey, south of Coblenz
(2) (3) Coblenz and Ehrenbreitstein in the distance, looking downstream from the east Rhine bank above Oberwerth

139r Three sketches making up a composite view of Coblenz and Ehrenbreitstein, looking downstream from near Pfaffendorf

(1) Inscr. (on the inner and outer bays of the former Electoral Palace) *5; 12*
(2) Inscr. (against the boats in the bridge of boats) *26*

139v Burg Lahneck, Schloss Stolzenfels and Kapellen, looking upstream from the west bank of the Rhine

140r Distant views of Coblenz and Ehrenbreitstein, looking down the Rhine (also the Charterhouse at Coblenz)

140v Burg Lahneck, Schloss Stolzenfels and Kapellen, looking upstream from the west bank of the Rhine

141r Blank

141v Four views of Burg Lahneck and Oberlahnstein

142r (1) Burg Lahneck
(2) St John's church, Niederlahnstein

142v Quick sketches at Coblenz

143r (1) A covered boat
(2) A flying bridge
(3) Leutesdorf, looking downstream with Hammerstein in the distance
Inscr. *Hammerstein*

143v (1) Stormy sky
(2) The Rhine front at Coblenz, looking downstream
(3) The landing stage on the Rhine front at Coblenz looking upstream
Inscr. *Square Pack with Smooth Corn* [?ers]

144r (1) River view
(2) Boat with passengers
(3) Andernach, looking upstream
(4)–(6) Hammerstein and Rheineck

144v (1) Hammerstein, looking upstream
(2) Hammerstein, looking upstream with Andernach in the distance
(3) Burg Rheineck, looking downstream
Inscr. *Rinek*
(4) Burg Rheineck, looking downstream with sailing boats

145r Several sketches including one of Linz and one of Rolandseck and Drachenfels

145v The landing stage at Bonn with the Seven Hills in the background

146r The landing stage at Bonn, with figures

146v The Seven Hills

147r (1) (2) The waterfront at Cologne, looking downstream
(3) Quick sketch (? at Cologne)

From here on this sketchbook contains sketches made during the latter part of Turner's tour which took him away from the Rhineland through Belgium to the north of France (see pp.38–9 above and the timetable on f.270r).

Some of the following pages may be misplaced in the sketchbook:

258v Includes three views up the Meuse towards Namur and two sketches of the bridge between Namur and Jambes

259r Seven sketches of the Meuse and its rocks at and near Samson
(1) Inscr. *Me*[use] *at Sams*[on]
(3) Inscr. *at Samson. Going on board the Packet*
(4) Inscr. *On board the Packet boat from Samson*

259v Includes five sketches of rocks along the Meuse, probably near Namur, one inscr. *Clearing off of Rain*

260r Several sketches of rocks along the Meuse, one inscr. *Samson*; and of boats, inscr. *Liege*

260v Quayside view at Liège, looking up the Meuse to the Pont des Arches, with boats

261r Buildings and details of buildings at Liège, including the Maison Curtius
Inscr. *Cock*; *Fox*; *Stork*; *Doric*

261v Quayside view at Liège, with the Pont des Arches and boats

262r Quayside view at Liège, with the Pont des Arches and figures

263v Gabled houses (? near Brussels)

264r Walls and trees
Inscr. *Bruxelles*

264v Brussels from the north
Inscr. *Hall under repair* (against the town hall)

265r Brussels from the north

266r The Palais de la Nation, Brussels

270r Financial calculations and the following timetable:

	10 Left	*XX*	*22 Sedan*
	11 Calais		*23 Verdun*
	12 Bruxelles		*24 Metz*
	13 Liege		*25 Metz*
	14 Huy – Sam[edi]		*26 Luxemburg*
	15 Liege		*27 Treves*
17	*16 Namur*		*28 Treves*
	18 Dinant		*29 Numagen*
	19 Givet		*30 Taerback*
	20 Foumay		*31 Cochem* [. . .]*day*
	21 Mez – Sam[edi]		*1 Sept Coblentz*
			2 Sept Coblentz
			3 Cologne Sundy
			4 Liege
			5 Bruxelles
			6 Gand
			7 Ostend
			8 Dunkirk
		W	*9 Calais*
		T	*10 Abbeville*
		F	*11 Dieppe*
		S	*12 Dieppe Samedi*
			13 Abb [eville]
			14 Cal[ais]
			15

TB CCXVII *Huy and Dinant* sketchbook 1824 (see cat.no.38)

Bound in boards covered in grey-blue marbled paper, with brown leather spine and the remains of a brass clasp.

1r Liège from the south with the St Laurent barracks on the horizon

1v View down the Meuse towards Chokier

1v–2r View down the Meuse to the abbey at Flône

2v The waterfront at Huy, looking upstream to the bridge, church of Notre-Dame and citadel, with bargemen working and resting on the quay
Inscr. *Pan Tiles*

2v–3r The citadel, church and bridge at Huy, looking upstream

3v–4r The citadel, church and bridge at Huy, looking upstream to the hills beyond
Inscr. *Clothes*

4v Blank

5r (1) The western half of the bridge at Huy, looking upstream to the Maison de Batta (a continuation of the sketch on ff.3v–4r)
(2) View along the Roman bridge at Trier to the city walls and spires

5v Blank, except for tiny continuation of sketch on f.6r
Inscr. [?*Way*]

6r The citadel, church and bridge at Huy, looking upstream from the south bank of the Meuse with part of the ruined town walls

6v The bridge, church and citadel at Huy, looking downstream

7 Missing (blank substitute inserted)

8r Old houses, probably on a quay at Liège
Inscr. *Grey*; *Black*; *Red*; *G*; *Grey*

8v–9r The Pont des Arches, Liège, looking upstream towards the spire of the cathedral from the Quai de la Batte

9v–10r The citadel and Pont des Arches, Liège, from a boat on the Meuse, looking downstream, with the twin spires of St Bartholemew's church visible above the bridge
Inscr. *Y*; *Red*; *Y*; *Y*; *Gr*; *Grey*; *G*; *R*; *Yellow* (all in the sky); [?*Cap*]; [?*Wood*] (in foreground)

10v–11r The citadel and Pont des Arches, Liège, looking downstream

11v–12r View at Liège, looking towards the dome of St Andrew's church

12v–13r The confluence of the Meuse and the Sambre at Namur, looking upstream

13v Blank

14r The confluence of the Meuse and the Sambre at Namur, looking upstream, from slightly further downstream than in ff.12v–13r

14v–15r The confluence of the Meuse and the Sambre at Namur, looking upstream (from further downstream still). At top right a continuation of the sketch of the brick-built church of Notre-Dame by the Hospice d'Harscamp
Inscr. *Brick Corn*[ice] *and Windows*

15v Blank

16r The citadel, church of Notre-Dame and bridge over the Meuse at Dinant, looking downstream from the west bank

16v Blank

17r The citadel, church and bridge at Dinant, looking downstream from the west bank, from a point further upstream than in f.16r so that the town hall is included

17v (1) Dinant, looking downstream from the west bank
Inscr. *St Nil*; *Meuse*
(2) Dinant, looking downstream from the west bank
(3) Dinant, looking downstream from the east bank by the town hall
Inscr. (left) [?*Bell*]; *Niche*; (right) *Cloaths dry*[ing]; *Fair*; [?*Long*]; *R*
(4) View down the Mosel towards the Roman bridge at Trier with the city on the right and details of its spires repeated above

18r Dinant, looking downstream from the west bank opposite the town hall

18v Blank

19r Dinant, looking upstream from the west bank
Inscr. *Road*

19v–20r Givet and Fort Charlemont, looking upstream from north of the town
Inscr. *Corn*

20v Blank

21r Trier, looking down the Mosel towards the Roman bridge from the west bank

21v Blank

22r Distant view of Abbeville from next to a windmill

22v Blank

23r Windmill, with Abbeville in the distance
Inscr. *Corn*

24r–44v Blank

TB CCXVIII *Trèves and Rhine* sketchbook 1824 (see cat.no.39)

Roll sketchbook bound in brown paper. Front cover inscribed near centre in pencil by Turner, *Trèves and Rhine* (now barely visible).

Inside front cover
T (a capital T with prominent serifs, probably the start of a Roman inscription seen in Trier)

1r (Watercolour) View down the Rhine to Coblenz and Ehrenbreitstein, from the east bank

2r (Watercolour) View up the Rhine towards Schloss Stolzenfels, from a similar viewpoint to that used for f.1r
Inscr. *Fete de* [. . .]

3r The Porta Nigra, Trier, from the north (i.e. outside the gate)

4r The Porta Nigra, Trier, from the north-west (a less detailed sketch)

5r River and distant hills with a house on the left

6r River and distant hills (possibly a view on the Rhine near Coblenz?)

7r Pallien and the Napoleonsbrücke from the river bank at Trier, looking up the Mosel

7v Small sketch of two figures, probably from a classical relief seen at Trier
Inscr. *Ch–l–ch*

8r (Watercolour) Trier from Pallien, looking up the Mosel with the Roman bridge in the distance and the Napoleonsbrücke on the right

9r (Watercolour) Cloud study

10r (Watercolour) The Mosel from the hillside at Pallien, looking upstream with the Roman bridge in the distance and Trier hidden behind the trees on the left

11r Trier from Pallien, looking up the Mosel with the Roman bridge in the distance

12r View from the heights above Pallien, looking down the Mosel and down on the White House and the northern edge of Trier

13r Trier from Pallien, looking up the Mosel with the Roman bridge in the distance

14r Trier from Pallien, looking up the Mosel with the Roman bridge in the distance

15r Trier from the west, looking up the Mosel (a similar viewpoint to the earlier sketches but from lower down, nearer the riverside)
Inscr. *Red*

16r Trier, Pallien and the Napoleonsbrücke from the river bank to the north-west, looking up the Mosel

17r View down the Lahn towards its confluence with the Rhine, with Burg Lahneck in the distance

18r View down the Lahn looking towards Burg Lahneck (from further up the Lahn than f.17r)

19r Burg Lahneck and the mouth of the Lahn, with the domed customs house and the landing-stage at Oberlahnstein

20r Schloss Stolzenfels and Kapellen from the junction of the Lahn and the Rhine

21r Burg Lahneck and the mouth of the Lahn, looking up the Rhine to Oberlahnstein and Schloss Stolzenfels

22r View down the Lahn to the Rhine with the Martinsburg at Oberlahnstein, Schloss Stolzenfels and Kapellen and St John's church, Niederlahnstein

23r Distant view of Coblenz and Ehrenbreitstein, looking down the Rhine from the west bank on the road to Kapellen

TB CCXIX *Moselle* (*or Rhine*) sketchbook 1824 (see cat.no.40)

Roll sketchbook bound in soft red leather with a back flap made of fabric and the remains of a green fabric pencil holder.

The present order of pages in this book does not correspond to their numerical sequence as recorded below.

1r Blank

2r The Marienburg

3r The Marienburg

4r Kloster Stuben

5r Beilstein and Burg Metternich, looking downstream
Inscr. *Pydelstein*

6r Beilstein and Burg Metternich, looking downstream

7r View of hills
Inscr. *Prida* (? i.e. Briedel near Zell)

8r River and hills with light cloud and a new moon
Inscr. *W*[arm]; *Cold*

9r River and hills with billowing clouds
Inscr. *Wood Pile*

10r Blank

11r Kloster Stuben

12r River, hills and village

13r The banks of the Mosel

14r On the Mosel

14v Inscr. *Crash* (i.e. Graach, near Bernkastel)

15r Bernkastel and the Landshut, looking upstream

16r Bernkastel and the Landshut, with St Nicholas's Hospital, Kues, on the opposite bank, looking upstream

17r Distant view of the Landshut, looking downstream

18r The Landshut from the river beneath it

19r View downstream from the riverfront at Bernkastel with St Nicholas's Hospital, Kues, on the left

20r Bernkastel and the Landshut, looking downstream

21r Bernkastel and the Landshut, looking downstream

22r Wehlen and Zeltingen, looking downstream

23r Ürzig and the hermitage on the Michaelslei, looking upstream

24r Wolf and the Gockelsberg

25r Traben, Trarbach and the Grevenburg, looking downstream

26r The Marienburg

27r Church on the Mosel

28r River and village
Inscr. *Marten*

29r River and village
Inscr. *Hof*[. . .]

30r Traben, Trarbach, the Starkenburg and the Grevenburg, looking downstream

31r Bernkastel and the Landshut, looking upstream

31v Inscr. *Weelen*; *Zelting* (i.e. Wehlen, Zeltingen)

32r–45v Blank

TB CCLXXXVII *Spa, Dinant and Namur* sketchbook 1839 (see cat.no.42)

Bound in boards covered in brown and white marbled paper, with parchment spine. The inside front cover bears a printed stationer's label:

P.J. HEYVAERT PAUWELS
Imprimeur, Papetier,
Rue de la Madelaine a Sect. 7, N°.445,
A BRUXELLES,
Tient Magazin de BRONZES.

The pages of this sketchbook are almost certainly not in their original order.

1r (1) Group of figures
(2) Figures on a riverside road among hills
(3) Dinant, looking downstream from the quay by the town hall
Inscr. *Yellow*; *3 Effects*; *sky good Blue*; *1 the W Brown House*; *2 W Clouds*

1v Three sketches of the citadel at Huy, from the south, along the valley of the Houyoux

2r Waiting for the diligence, Brussels

2v The town hall and St Peter's church, Louvain, from the north-east corner of the market place
Inscr. *Cornice*; *Pil*[aster]; *P*; *P*; *P*[...]

3r St Peter's church, Louvain
Inscr. *B Sky*[...] *Black Walls*

3v The town hall and St Peter's church, Louvain, from the south-east corner of the market place
Inscr. *Clock*; (on f.4) [...]*de G*[...]

4r (1) Riverside scene
Inscr. *Cattle*; *Red Tufts*; *C*[...] *Yellow R*[...]
(2) (3) Two sketches of Huy, looking downstream from the hillside to the west at Ahin

4v Three distant views of Louvain

5r Distant view of Louvain

5v The church of Notre-Dame, Huy, and the bridge over the Meuse, looking downstream from the north bank

6r ? View near Louvain
Inscr. *Louvain*

6v The quay and citadel at Huy, looking upstream from the north bank above the bridge near the Maison de Batta

7r Two sketches of Louvain from Mont César

7v Houses and mill by a stream, probably on the outskirts of Huy

8r Two views near Louvain, with a railway viaduct under construction

8v Huy from the hillside to the south-east

9r (1) View up the Meuse towards Dinant (left) and Bouvignes and the castle of Crèvecoeur (right), which extends on to f.8v
Inscr. *Beauvill up* [*to*] *Dinant*
(2) Distant view of Louvain
(3) Detail of a fort

9v Distant view of Louvain

10r Distant view of Louvain

10v–11r Buildings at Louvain, including St Peter's church

11v–12r Buildings at Louvain, including St Peter's church

12v Distant view of Namur from St-Servais
Inscr. *Sambe*; *Road*

13r The citadel, Pont des Arches and St Bartholemew's church, Liège, looking downstream from the Quai sur Meuse

13v Huy and its citadel from the hillside to the north

14r St Paul's cathedral and the citadel at Liège, seen from the Quai Marcellis looking downstream to the Pont de la Boverie

14v Namur from St-Servais, with the cathedral seen above the town walls
Inscr. *Sambre*

15r Liège and its citadel

15v Liège from the Louvain road

16r (1) (2) Views at and near Liège, one with travellers in a coach
(2) Group of figures by the roadside
Inscr. *B*; *R*; *Man w Pig*

16v Two distant views of Liège from the south-west

17r View down the Meuse towards Liège from close to a factory with chimneys

17v Fashionable ladies with elaborate hairstyles and corsages

18r The Quai de Maestricht, Liège, looking downstream to the Maison Curtius from the Pont des Arches

18v The Géronstère spring, Spa

19r Two distant views of Spa

19v The Géronstère spring, Spa

20r The Géronstère spring, Spa, and female figures carrying bundles
Inscr. (on one cap) *W*

20v The Géronstère spring, Spa

21r Distant view of Spa
Inscr. *Corn*; *Spa*

21v Hills near Spa

22r The Sauvenière spring, Spa
Inscr. *Savon*

22v (1) The Sauvenière and Groesbeck springs, Spa
Inscr. *Gorsbecke*; *Geronston*; *Gerostan*
(2) The Tonnelet spring, Spa
Inscr. *Tonely*

23r Distant view of Spa
Inscr. *Wood*; *Road*

23v Villas on the outskirts of Spa
Inscr. [?*Bellevue*]

24r Spa from the hillside
Inscr. *Lake*; *Corn*

24v Spa from the hillside
Inscr. *Corn*; *Seats*

25r A promenade at Spa

25v Spa from the hillside

26r Spa from the hillside

26v Blank

27r The church of SS. Hermes and Alexander, Theux, from the Liège-Spa road, with the castle of Franchimont seen on the brow of the hill in the distance

27v Dinant, looking downstream from the hillside south of the town, with Bouvignes and the castle of Crèvecoeur seen in the distance

28r The church of SS. Hermes and Alexander, Theux, from the Liège-Spa road, with the castle of Franchimont seen in the distance
Inscr. *Road*

28v (1) Huy, looking upstream from the Liège road
(2) Huy, from the hillside to the east

28v–29r Marché de Theux, the castle of Franchimont and the bridge over the Hoëgne, from its west bank

29v Blank

30r Marché de Theux and the castle of Franchimont from the path to the castle
Inscr. *Marchey*

30v Two sketches of Franchimont
Inscr. *Franchimont*

31r Franchimont from the banks of the Hoëgne

31v Franchimont from the hillside

31v–32r Marché de Theux and Franchimont
Inscr. *Rock*; *Babbly brook*; *Mills*

32r General view of Franchimont, together with extra architectural details (top right) and the three shields carved on its entrance portal
Inscr. (against the last shield) *3 Lions*

32v (1) Houses
(2) Distant view of Franchimont from the Liège-Spa road south of the castle (extending on to f.33r)
Inscr. *Road*; *Vines*; *Corn*; *red*
(3) Reclining figure

33r Distant view of Franchimont from the Liège-Spa road south of the castle

33v Houses beneath a rocky cliff
Inscr. *Rock*

34r A town square with people at a fountain
Inscr. *Hotel de Vil*; *K*[. . .]*G*[. . .]*ds*; [. . .] *of Pay Bas*

34v Spa from the hillside

35r The 'Pouhon Pierre Le Grand', Spa
Inscr. *A LA MEMNOIRE DE Pierre Le Grand*; *Spa*

35v The 'Promenade de Sept-Heures', Spa
Inscr. *C.L*

36r The Place Royale, Spa, from the entrance to the 'Promenade de Sept-Heures'
Inscr. *Oak*; *P*[. . .]

36v (1) Two figures, one carrying a bundle
Inscr. *Wom 2 Vieu*; *D olive*; *gn* [*?ch*]; *W Lapel*; *BS*; *Savert* (i.e. Sauvenière)
(2) Old houses and bridge over a stream at Spa

37r Old houses and bridges over a stream at Spa

37v Houses at Spa, with St Rémacle's church on the left

38r (1) Roadside scene on the outskirts of Spa, with a mother and baby
(2) Group of seated figures
Inscr. *Red*; *1 Gre*; *W*; *B*[. . .]

38v Blank

39r Two views of Spa from the hillside
Inscr. *Wood*; *C Wood*

39v Spa, with St Rémacle's church
Inscr. (against architectural features) *4*; *5*; *3*; *4*

40r Figures

40v View up the Sambre at Namur, showing the bridge, the old mill (through its centre arch) and the 'rampe verte' up to the citadel

41r The confluence of the Meuse and the Sambre at Namur (the upper sketch looks up the Meuse, the lower up the Sambre)

41v View down the Meuse from Jambes towards the citadel of Namur and the Pont de Jambes

42r (1) View down the Meuse from Jambes towards the citadel at Namur and the Pont de Jambes
(2) (3) Two groups of figures with merchandise and a cart

42v (1) The citadel and Notre-Dame, Dinant, from the opposite river bank, with figures in the foreground
(2) Waulsort from the Meuse
Inscr. *Walfort*

43r Namur from the Liège road

43v Blank

44r Blank

44v (1) Namur from the Liège road
(2) The quayside next to the town hall at Dinant, looking downstream with figures loading a cart
Inscr. [*?Mason*]

45r Distant view of Namur from the Liège road

45v Distant view of Namur from the Liège road

46r Village on the banks of the Meuse

46v Three sketches of rocks on the Meuse near Namur

47r Three sketches of rocks and villages on the Meuse near Namur, the first extending on to f.46v, inscr. *Marche le Dame*

47v (1) Rocks on the Meuse above a house and bridge
(2) Huy, from the hillside to the north
(3) The church, citadel and Quai aux Charbons, Huy, from the Maison de Batta
Inscr. *1*; *2*; *3*

48r The church, citadel and bridge at Huy, looking upstream from the north bank

48v (1) Huy, looking upstream from the Liège road
(2) Huy, from the road to La Sarte

49r Huy, looking upstream from the north bank of the Meuse below the town
Inscr. *Pink*

49v (1) Distant view of Huy, looking upstream from the Liège road
Inscr. *Vines*; *St Hiln*
(2) Distant view of Huy, from the road to La Sarte
Inscr. [?*Mills*]

50r (1) Slight sketch
(2) Twilight view of Liège
(3) Distant view of Huy, looking upstream from the hillside to the north

50v Huy from the south-east (with architectural details)

51r Dinant, looking upstream from the castle of Crèvecoeur above Bouvignes

51v (1) Huy and its citadel from the hillside to the west, looking downstream
(2) The castle of Crèvecoeur and the church of Bouvignes, looking downstream from the hill opposite Dinant

52r The church, citadel and bridge at Huy, looking upstream from the quay on the north bank (then 'Quai des Recollets')

52v (1) Architectural details
(2) Huy and its citadel from the hillside to the west, looking downstream
(3) Huy from the east

53r (1) Seated women and standing soldiers
(2) Distant view of Dinant, looking upstream
Inscr. *Din*
(3) Distant view of Huy from the north

53v Distant view of Huy from the south-east
Inscr. *Meuse*

54r–56r Blank

56v (1) Distant view of Huy from the south-east
Inscr. *Road*
(2) The Roche à Bayard, south of Dinant, looking southwards up the Meuse
(3) Notre Dame, Huy, from the east
Inscr. [?*Tower*]

57r (1) The castle of Chokier, looking upstream
Inscr. *Ce Chocire*
(2) The abbey of Flône, looking downstream
Inscr. *Abbey de Thron*
(3) Church overlooking the Meuse
(4) Distant hills
Inscr. [?*Meuse*]

57v Huy from the outskirts to the east

58r View of the Meuse from the hillside

58v Namur from the heights of St-Servais

59r (1) Distant view of Namur from the heights of St-Servais
Inscr. *Sam*[bre]
(2) The Meuse from the hillside

59v (1) Dinant, looking upstream from the western river bank below the bridge
(2) Smaller version of the same view

60r Blank

60v–61r The church and citadel, Dinant, from the Grand' Place

61v Blank

62r Dinant, looking upstream from the hillside opposite

62v Four views looking upstream to Dinant and Bouvignes and the castle of Crèvecoeur (two extending on to f.63r)
(3) Inscr. *Gaspar Poussin*

63r View down the Meuse from Bouvignes to Poilvache, with a carriage on the road
Inscr. *R*[oa]*d*; *Corn in Light*

63v (1) Dinant, looking downstream from the river bank near the Roche à Bayard
(2) Dinant, looking upstream from the opposite river bank
Inscr. *Ferry Boat*; *Road*

64r (1) Dinant, looking upstream from the castle of Crèvecoeur
Inscr. *Din*
(2) The castle of Crèvecoeur and the church of Bouvignes, looking downstream from the hillside opposite Dinant
(3) Dinant, looking downstream from the Roche à Bayard
Inscr. *Din from the rock of Bayard*

64v Dinant, looking downstream from the western river bank south of the town

65r Dinant, looking downstream from just above the bridge
Inscr. *Timber*

65v Dinant, looking downstream from the river bank opposite the town hall, plus a larger detail of the spire of the church

65v–66r (inserted between the sketches on ff.65v and 66r) The church, citadel, town hall and eastern edge of the bridge at Dinant, looking downstream

66r Dinant, looking upstream from the eastern river bank below the bridge
Inscr. *Straw*; [?*Tan*]; *White*

66v Dinant, looking downstream from the west bank above the bridge
Inscr. *Dinant*

Inside back cover
(1) The Roche à Bayard, looking upstream from the Dinant road
(2) A Belgian woman
Inscr. *Yell*; *Red W Black*; *Yellow and Grey*; [?*Brussels*]

TB CCLXXXVIII *Givet, Mézières, Verdun, Metz, Luxemburg and Trèves* sketchbook 1839 (see cat.no.43)

Bound in boards covered in dark blue mottled paper, with a brown leather spine. The front cover has a vertical edging of brown leather and an inside pouch with the gussets made from pieces of vellum previously used for a music manuscript. The back cover has corners of brown leather.

Inside front cover
(1) Bridge and hills
Inscr. *Rogers de Bahar* (i.e. Roche de Bayard) and *Borass des Dou*
(2) Two figures
(3) Woman with a broom, with a repetition of her head
Inscr. *Pink*

(4) Four-arched bridge and fortifications
Inscr. [?*Mezieres*]

1r Several overlapping sketches of hills and buildings, including two of the Roche à Bayard

1v (1) The Meuse south of Dinant
(2) A thistle
(3) Three women in a boat washing

2r (1) Group of figures in front of a church
Inscr. *Ho*[. . .] *St Ronsard*; *Women mixing up Coal and Earth*
(2) Figures with a horse and cart in front of a bridge
(3) Female figure with pots, urns, jugs, etc.
Inscr. *White ware Blue*; *White Light Jacket Fan tail*; *Red Pot BA*; *Black* [?*Italy*]

2v Distant view of Givet and Fort Charlemont from the north (from the road above the village of Heer)

3r Distant view of Givet and Fort Charlemont from the north

3v The Meuse and hills near Givet

4r Givet and Fort Charlemont from the north

4v Fort Charlemont, the Tour Victoire and church of St-Hilaire, Givet, looking upstream

5r Houses by the Meuse and the Tour Grégoire, Givet

5v The Tour Victoire, Fort Charlemont and St-Hilaire, Givet, looking upstream, with boats

6r Fort Charlemont, St-Hilaire and the bridge at Givet, looking upstream

6v Buildings at ?Mézières

7r The castle of Hierges, south of Givet, seen from the road

7v Givet, looking up the Meuse to Fort Charlemont and the Tour Victoire

8r Givet, looking down the Meuse to St-Hilaire and the bridge

8v Givet, looking down the Meuse from south of Fort Charlemont

9r The east bank of the Meuse at Givet looking upstream towards Notre-Dame and the Tour Grégoire

9v Two sketches of Givet, looking up the Meuse from its northern outskirts on the east bank
Inscr. *Angemont* (i.e. the nearby castle of Agimont)

10r View upstream at Givet towards St-Hilaire and Fort Charlemont

10v The ruins of the Imperial Baths at Trier, with the tower of St Gangolf's church in the distance

11r Fort Charlemont at Givet from the south

11v–12r Four sketches of towns between Givet and Mézières
(1) Vireux
Inscr. *Vireux*; *all colours of* [?*rock*]
(2) Vireux (with the buildings on f.11v shown again in more detail on f.12r)
(3) Distant view of Fumay
Inscr. *Fumai* (next to another name struck out); *Slate Quy* (i.e. Quarry)
(4) Town

12v The Meuse valley near Mézières

13r The church of Notre-Dame d'Espérance, Mézières, and the Pont de Pierre, from the south-east

13v ?Mézières

14r Notre-Dame, Mézières, from the south-west

14v (1) Fortifications at Mézières outside the Porte de St-Julien
(2) Trier with the ruins of the Imperial Baths on the left

15r Notre-Dame, Mézières, with the Porte de St-Julien and fortifications

15v Notre-Dame, Mézières, from the north-east with fortifications including the Tour d'Ecole and the Tour Militaire and the Meuse in the distance

16r Two views of the viaduct of the 'Pré au pont' between Charleville and Mézières

16v ?Mézières

17r Notre-Dame, Mézières, from the north-east, with the Pont d'Arche on the right

17v (1) Metz with the cathedral, bridge over the Moselle and church of St Vincent
(2) ?Metz

18r Notre-Dame, Mézières, from the south-east, with the Pont de Pierre in the foreground (with two additions in the corners inscr. *2*; *3*)

18v–19r (starting at the foot of the page)
(1) Sedan from the south-east (outside the Porte de Bouillon) with the towers of St Charles's church and the fortress
Inscr. [?*Fort*]
(2) Distant view of Sedan
(3) Sedan from the north-east

19r The Roman bridge at Trier looking up the Mosel
Inscr. *7 eqal* (against the arches of the bridge)

19v Notre-Dame, Mézières, from the south-east (Rue Monge), showing the porch of the south transept and the tower, with the Porte de St-Julien in the distance

20r Blank

20v The Roman bridge at Trier looking upstream (continued both above and below, the latter sketch including buildings of the city)
Inscr. *7*[. . .] (against the arches of the bridge)

21r The Roman bridge at Trier, looking upstream

21v Sedan from the north-east, looking down on to the fortress and the towers of St Charles's church

22r ?Sedan with the viaduct of Torcy

22v Distant view of Sedan from the north-east
Inscr. *B*; *R*; *Cloth*

23r Verdun from the Meuse about a mile to its north

23v (1) View across the Meuse at Verdun showing the wooden bridge, the Porte Chaussée, the Jesuits' church and the cathedral of Notre-Dame
(2) Details of the Jesuits' church and the cathedral
Inscr. [?*Cath*]

24r Four views of Verdun, one of a pedimented doorway
Inscr. *Doric*

24v Countryside near Verdun

25r Countryside near Verdun

25v Distant view of Metz with a bridge over the Moselle, the towers of St Vincent's church, and the cathedral of St-Etienne
Inscr. *6* (by the arches of the bridge); *Fete of* [. . .]

26r Metz with a bridge, St Vincent's church and the cathedral

26v (1) Metz cathedral and fortifications
(2) Metz cathedral and bridges over the Moselle

27r (page partly torn away)
Metz cathedral and a bridge over the Moselle
Inscr. *St B*[. . .]; *Metz*

27v Towers
Inscr. illegibly

28r Distant view of Metz from a hillside cemetery to the north
Inscr. *St Pierre* [. . .] *et Roche* (L); *Vines* (R)

28v Distant view of Metz

29r Figures around a vehicle in a town square
Inscr. *Change de Logement*

29v Three distant views of Thionville
(1) Inscr. *Ferry*; [?*Baskets*]; *Moselle*
(3) Inscr. illegibly

30r Two distant views of Thionville from the Moselle
(1) Inscr. *Waiting at the Ferry*
(2) Inscr. *Nets Drying*; *Blanchuses* (i.e. Blanchisseuses)

30v Blank

31r Bridge over a river

31v Blank

32r Blank

32v (1) The citadel of St-Esprit, Luxembourg, and St Michael's church from the Rham
(2) The fortifications of the Bock, Luxembourg (a continuation of sketch 1)

33r Two sketches of the fortifications of the Bock, Luxembourg

33v (1) The citadel of St-Esprit, Luxembourg, from the south (Boulevard d'Avranches)
(2) The Jesuits' church, Luxembourg, and surrounding buildings

34r (1) Luxembourg with the outer Porte de Thionville in the foreground
(2) Luxembourg from the south
Inscr. *Lux*

34v Metz cathedral and bridge over the Moselle

35r Metz cathedral from the corner of the Place d'Armes

35v Metz cathedral from the south-west and bridge over the Moselle

36r View at Metz from the Rue de la Garde looking down the Moselle under its four bridges and (centre) at the towers of St Vincent's church

36v The market place at Thionville, looking towards the towers of St Maximin's church and the belfry of the sixteenth-century town hall
Inscr. *Cafe*

37r Two views of Thionville from the Moselle, showing the towers of St Maximin's church, the belfry and the town hall of 1695
Inscr. *Trionville*

37v–38r Two views of Roussy-le-Bourg and Roussy-le-Village (between Thionville and Luxembourg)
Inscr. *Rouelburg*; *Roussy*

38v–42r Blank

42v ? Roman ruins at Trier

43r Blank

43v Trier from Pallien looking up the Mosel to the Roman bridge

44r The ruins of the Imperial Baths, Trier

44v–45r Blank

45v Trier from the Mosel showing St Paulin's church, the Porta Nigra, the cathedral, Liebfrauenkirche, St Gangolf's church and Basilica

46r (1) Trier from the north-west, looking up the Mosel to the bridge
Inscr. *Mill*
(2) Trier from the west, looking down the Mosel towards the cliffs at Pallien

46v–47r Blank

47v–48r The west choir and towers of Trier cathedral and the adjacent Liebfrauenkirche

48v–49r Blank

49v Trier from the hillside above Pallien, looking down on to the White House and up the Mosel to the Roman bridge

50r Trier from the Mosel, near Pallien
Inscr. *Coney* [. . .]; *St W*; *Can*[. . .]; *St*[. . .]; *St Martin*

50v View down the Mosel from the Napoleonsbrücke with the church of SS. Simon and Jude, Pallien, in the foreground
Inscr. *Pallien*

51r Trier from Pallien, looking up the Mosel to the bridge in the distance

51v The northern part of Trier from the Mosel, looking upstream

52r The southern part of Trier from the Mosel, looking upstream

52v–54r Blank

54v–55r (1) Trier from across the Mosel near the White House
Inscr. *White House*
(2) The river, walls and towers of Trier with its cranes and bridge, looking up the Mosel
Inscr. *White* (near the cranes); *Treves*
(3) Trier from the Mosel with its towers, walls, cranes and bridge
Inscr. *8* (under the arches of the bridge)
(4) Ruined tower by the walls of Trier
Inscr. *Ditch*

55v–56r Blank

56v Luxembourg with Vauban's towers on the plateau of the Rham from the Alzette valley

57r The Rham and the Bock, Luxembourg, from the Fetschenhof

57v The Bock, Luxembourg, with the Grünewald in the distance

58r The Rham and the Bock, Luxembourg, from the Fetschenhof

58v The town of Luxembourg, the Rham and the Bock from outside the Porte de Trèves

59r The town of Luxembourg and the buildings of the Rham and Grund from the Porte de Trèves

59v The Bock and the Grünewald, Luxembourg, from the hillside east of the Rham

60r The Rham, Luxembourg, and the Bock from the hillside east of the Rham

60v St Michael's church, the Pont du Château and Bock, Luxembourg, looking north-eastwards along the valley of the Alzette

61r Luxembourg

61v The Bock, Luxembourg, and St John's church, from the south-west

62r The Pont du Château, Luxembourg, looking north-eastwards to the Rham

62v–63r Many overlapping sketches of Luxembourg

63v The Bock, Pont du Château and Spanish turret, Luxembourg, from the north

64r The Grünewald, Bock, Pont du Château and town of Luxembourg from the north, along the valley of the Alzette beyond the bridge with the Vauban towers

64v The Grünewald, Bock and Luxembourg town from the north, beyond the Vauban towers

65r The Grünewald, Bock and Luxembourg town from the north, beyond the Vauban towers

65v Fortifications at Luxembourg and a plan of its situation

66r View from the Grünewald of the Bock, the Rham and Luxembourg town

66v View at Luxembourg (probably further north along the Alzette valley than the sketches on ff.64v and 65r)

67r View at Luxembourg (probably further north along the Alzette valley than the sketches on ff.64v and 65r)

67v ? Final view of Luxembourg from the north

68r Two rough sketches of buildings, illegibly inscribed

68v River view with wooden bridge and distant towers
Inscr. (in the opposite direction) *at Treves* [. . .]

Inside back cover
? Rough sketch of the Bock
Inscr. at top right (not in Turner's writing) *1 fr 10* (possibly the price of the sketchbook)

TB CCLXXXIX *First Mossel and Oxford* sketchbook 1839 (see cat.no.44)

Bound in boards covered in black and white marbled paper, with maroon leather spine and corners, each embellished with narrow gold lines.

Turner's Mosel sketches were fitted into the spaces left by the larger and more careful Oxford ones that clearly predate them. The latter have, for obvious reasons, been excluded from the list below. For the sake of clarity, the sketches on each page have been numbered from the outer edge of the sketchbook inwards, regardless of the way in which they themselves happen to be facing.

2r Three tiny sketches of the Mosel, each showing a distant castle and a boat in the foreground

2v Klotten and Burg Coraidelstein
Inscr. *Mos*; *Cloth* [?*drying*]

3r (1) Cochem, looking downstream (plus a separate, larger, sketch of the Burg)
(2) Cochem, looking downstream from closer to the town than (1)
(3) Cochem, looking downstream from slightly closer to the town than (2)

3v (1) Mosel scene with distant buildings
(2) Figures and boats
Inscr. [?*Beaching*] *a Boat*
(3) Figures on board a boat laden with barrels
(4) Cochem, looking upstream
(5) Hills and church
Inscr. [?*Wisu*]

4r (1) Gondorf and Niederfell, looking downstream
Inscr. *Niderfell*
(2) View up the Rhine from the landing-stage at Coblenz, with the bridge of boats to Ehrenbreitstein

4v (1) Sailing boats with awnings; a crock and a barrel
Inscr. *Blu*[*e*]; *8 Herr*
(2) Figures in a boat with ?Klotten in the distance, looking upstream
(3) The ruined convent at Stuben, Kloster Stuben (plus a separate, larger, sketch of the ruin)

5r (1)–(4) The Marienburg and its surroundings
(5) The bridge over the Alf at Alf and Burg Arras
Inscr. *Aress*
(6) Alf, with its bridge, church and houses

5v (1) Gondorf, looking upstream
Inscr. *Gondorf*
(2) Kobern, looking downstream
(3) Kobern, looking upstream
Inscr. *Evenburg or Altenburg*
(4) Kobern, looking upstream

6r (1) Kobern, looking upstream
(2) Kobern, looking upstream, from further downstream than (1)
(3) View across the Rhine from Coblenz, showing the bridge of boats to Ehrenbreitstein
Inscr. *Belle Vue White H*[?ouse]
(4) Hills

6v–7r The fortress and town of Ehrenbreitstein from Coblenz
Inscr. [?*Shot*]

7r (these cut across part of the large sketch on ff.6v–7r)
(1) Beilstein and Burg Metternich, looking upstream from Fankel
Inscr. *Washing*
(2) Beilstein and Burg Metternich, looking upstream from slightly further downstream than (1)
Inscr. *Fangels*

8r (1) Alken and Burg Thurandt, looking downstream
Inscr. [?*By Thurent*]
(2) Alken and Burg Thurandt, looking downstream from closer to the town than (1)
(3) The Leyen Burg at Gondorf

8v (1) (2) Distant forts at Coblenz from the Mosel
(3) (4) Ehrenbreitstein from the Mosel
(5) Ehrenbreitstein, Coblenz and the Mosel bridge, looking down the Mosel
Inscr. *13* [or *B*] (by the bridge)
(6) Part of Coblenz upstream from the Mosel bridge

9r (1) Alken and Burg Thurandt, looking upstream
(2) Alken and Burg Thurandt, looking upstream from further from the town than (1)
Inscr. [. . .]; *Sky strong*; *Thuron*; *M of Etz* (i.e. the mouth of the River Eltz, some six miles upstream from here)

9v (1) Traben, Trarbach and the Grevenburg, looking downstream
(2) Trarbach and the Grevenburg, looking downstream
(3) (4) The Grevenburg, looking upstream from successive downstream viewpoints

10r Klotten and Burg Coraidelstein, looking downstream
Inscr. *Cloten*; *Moss*

10v (1) The ruined monastery at Wolf, Wolfer Kloster, in the distance and detail of its tower
Inscr. *Wolfer Clers*
(2) Wolfer Kloster
(3) The Grevenburg, looking downstream from below Wolf
(4) Traben, Trarbach and the Grevenburg, looking downstream
Inscr. *Trabach*

11r (1) The Hermitage on the Michaelslei at Ürzig, looking downstream with separate, enlarged, detail
Inscr. *Mo*
(2) Ürzig and the Hermitage on the Michaelslei, looking upstream
(3) (4) Wolfer Kloster, looking downstream

11v (1) Bernkastel and the Landshut, looking downstream
(2) Bernkastel and the Landshut, with Kues opposite, looking upstream
Inscr. *Flying Bridge*
(3) Bernkastel and the Landshut, with Kues opposite, looking upstream from a point further downstream than (2)
Inscr. *Vi*[nes]
(4) River and village
Inscr. [?*Leekstin*]

12r (1) The Landshut, looking downstream
(2) Kues and the Landshut, looking downstream from closer than (1)
(3) Kues, Bernkastel and the Landshut, looking downstream from closer than (2), plus an enlarged detail of the Landshut
(4) Riverbanks near Bernkastel and the flying bridge

12v (1) View downstream towards the Druidenstein
(2) View downstream towards Burg Bischofstein in the distance
(3) (4) Burg Bischofstein and Burgen in the distance, looking downstream (interrupted by larger sketches of the Burg and the Pauluskapelle)
(5) Burg Bischofstein and the Pauluskapelle

13r (1) Distant view of Burg Treis, looking downstream
Inscr. *Tris*
(2) Pommern
Inscr. *Pomeron*
(3) Burg Treis, looking downstream
Inscr. *Mos*; *M*
(4) Treis, looking downstream
Inscr. *Triess*
(5) Karden and Treis, looking downstream, plus an enlarged detail of St Castor's church, Karden
Inscr. *Kastors*; *St Cilia* (i.e. the Zilleskapelle at Treis)

13v (1) Burg Bischofstein and the Pauluskapelle, from below
(2) Ehrenbreitstein from the Petersberg, with the monument to General Marceau in the foreground
(3) Ehrenbreitstein from the Petersberg, with the monument to General Marceau in the foreground

14r (1) Distant hills
(2) (3) Ehrenbreitstein from the Petersberg, with the monument to General Marceau in the foreground

14v (1) The Burg at Cochem
Inscr. *Cochem*
(2) Cochem, looking upstream
(3) Clouds over a river valley
Inscr. [?*Storm*]

15r (1) (2) Boats, one with flags
(3) Cochem, looking upstream
(4) Burg Bischofstein, looking upstream
Inscr. [. . .] *R*[. . .]

15v Three sketches of Beilstein and Burg Metternich, looking upstream from viewpoints successively further from the town going downstream
(1) Inscr. *Balstin*

16r Beilstein and Burg Metternich, looking downstream, with a detail of the spire of St Joseph's church
Inscr. *Jos*

16v (1) Tower
(2) ? Ehrenbreitstein from the Petersberg
Inscr. illegibly

19r (1) Trittenheim, looking downstream towards Piesport
Inscr. *Trittenheim*; *Pesport*
(2) Neumagen, looking downstream
Inscr. *Neumagem*
(3) ?Piesport
(4) (5) Quick sketches of the Mosel, probably drawn near (1)–(3)

20v Five quick sketches of the Mosel
(2) Inscr. *Townich* (i.e. Thörnich)

23r (1) Mosel view with distant castle
Inscr. *Berncastle* (not the subject of the sketch)
(2) The ferry and ferry-tower at Schweich

27v (1) ?Kues
(2) Klotten and Burg Coraidelstein, looking upstream
Inscr. *Blow Coch* (i.e. Below Cochem)

27v–28r (in the sky above the Oxford view)
Mosel view with a church and flying bridge

28v (1) The pair of ferry-towers on the Mosel at, and opposite to, Schweich with the ferry in mid-river
(2) Distant hills
Inscr. *Castrum Mo*[...]

TB CCXC *Trèves to Cochem and Coblenz to Mayence* sketchbook 1839 (see cat.no.45)

Bound in boards covered in brown and white marbled paper, with brown leather spine and corners and two loops on the back cover to hold a pencil.

On the front cover of the sketchbook is stuck a white paper label inscribed by Turner with a list of the five sketchbooks used in 1839:
No. 1 Brussels up to Givet
2 Givet Mis Ver Metz Lux Treves
3 First Mossel and Oxford
4 Mayence Wis Coblenz and 2 Mosel to Cochem
5 Cockum to Cob. Home
Just above this label, on the book itself, Turner has also written *4* in ink, indicating that this is the fourth in the group.

Inside front cover
Two sketches of a valley and mountains
(1) Inscr. *Bridge*; *Chapel*; *Mill*
(2) Inscr. *All* [*?Light*] *Mill*

1r The fortress of Ehrenbreitstein, looking downstream from the town of Ehrenbreitstein

1v Coblenz and the fortress of Ehrenbreitstein, looking downstream from the town of Ehrenbreitstein

2r The fortress of Ehrenbreitstein, looking downstream from the town of Ehrenbreitstein, with the Heribertturm in the foreground

2v Coblenz and the Rhine – Mosel confluence, from Ehrenbreitstein

3r The Deutsches Eck and Mosel bridge, Coblenz, with the Rhine – Mosel confluence, from Ehrenbreitstein

3v The fortress of Ehrenbreitstein, looking downstream from the town of Ehrenbreitstein

4r Four sketches drawn on the way through the hills towards Cochem, with the Burg seen in the distance
Inscr. (twice) *Road*

4v (1)–(3) Three sketches drawn on the way through the hills towards Cochem, with the Burg seen in the distance
(4) The Burg at Cochem
Inscr. *Coch*

5r Cochem, looking downstream

5v Cochem, looking upstream from the river bank at Cond, showing the southern part of the town

6r (1) Cochem, from Cond, showing the northern part of the town (continuing the view on f.5v)
(2) The Burg at Cochem and its neighbouring hills

6v Cochem, looking upstream from the Endertbachtal

7r Cochem and the Winneburg, looking downstream from the Burg

7v (1) Beilstein, looking upstream from near Fankel
Inscr. *Fangl*
(2) Bruttig, looking upstream from near Ernst
Inscr. *Prudich*
(3) Ellenz
Inscr. *Erentz*; *Ellenz*
(4) Burg Metternich at Beilstein

8r Four sketches of Beilstein and Burg Metternich, from the Mosel

8v Beilstein and Burg Metternich, from the landing-stage opposite

9r Two sketches of Beilstein and Burg Metternich, looking downstream

9v (1) and (2) Beilstein and Burg Metternich, looking downstream
(1) Inscr. *Vines*
(3) Burg Metternich and riverside buildings at Beilstein
(4) ? Distant view of Trarbach
Inscr. *Trabach*

10r (1) Mesenich, looking downstream
Inscr. *Mezen*; *7 H* (i.e. Senheim or Senhals); *Ferry*
(2) Briedern, looking downstream
Inscr. *Bridon*
(3) Beilstein, looking downstream from near Briedern
Inscr. *Cattle*

10v Several sketches of Senhals, Senheim and Nehren
Inscr. *Senhaltz*; *Senhall*

11r (1) Nehren and Senheim, looking downstream
Inscr. *Naren*; *Sinh*[...]
(2) (10v–11r) The Lehmener tower, Nehren
Inscr. *Askerf*
(3) (10v–11r) Ediger

11v (1) The mouth of the Alf
Inscr. *Wood*
(2) Cliffs on the Mosel
Inscr. *St Nicolo*

12r Alf, with Burg Arras in the distance

12v (1) Alf, with Burg Arras in the distance
Inscr. *Arras*; *Alf*
(2)–(4) Kloster Stuben and its environs
Inscr. *Stuben*; [*?Capel Pope ... Martin Bor ...*]
(3) Eller
Inscr. *Eller*

13r (1) Kloster Stuben, looking downstream
(2) ?Enkirch
Inscr. *Enkirn*
(3) ?Alf

13v–14r Several sketches of Zell, Kaimt, St Aldegund, Neef and Bremm
Inscr. *K*[...]; *Aldecunt*; *Neef*; *Brem*

14v St Michael's church, Merl
Inscr. *Merel*
The rest of the page is filled with sketches of the Marienburg and its setting

15r (1) The Marienburg
Inscr. *Wood*; *Road*
(2) The Marienburg
(3) Zell
Inscr. *Zell*
(4) Continuation of sketch of the Marienburg on f.14v

15v (1) ? Distant view of the Marienburg
(2)–(4) Rough landscape sketches, one inscribed ½ *H 4 by WNW*

16r Four quick sketches, the third inscr. *Brilil* (?Briedel)

16v Many quick sketches, some of the abandoned fort of Montroyal, others inscr. *Bridel* (i.e. Briedel); *Road*

17r Many quick sketches of Montroyal and its setting
Inscr. *Montroy*

17v–18r Many small sketches of the Mosel between the Marienburg and Montroyal, one inscr. *Ponrich* (i.e. Pünderich), another *Sh*[...] *of WOW*

18v–19r Many small sketches of the Mosel between the Marienburg and Montroyal, three inscr. *Riol* (i.e. Reil), others inscr. *Rekirch* (i.e. Reilkirch); *Road*; *Burg*

19v Many small sketches of the Mosel and boats, between Trarbach and Enkirch, inscr. *Starnby* (i.e. Starkenburg); *Road*; *Cattle*; *Kevenich* (i.e. Kövenig)

20r (1) (2) Two river views
(3) A sailing boat with a canopy
Inscr. [?*after* or ? *above*] *Trabach*

20v Traben, Trarbach and the Grevenburg, looking downstream

21r Traben, Trarbach and the Grevenburg, looking downstream, with the flying bridge in the foreground

21v Several overlapping sketches of Trarbach and the Grevenburg including ones of St Nicholas's church and houses and the watch tower

22r Several sketches of Trarbach and the Grevenburg from inland, one showing the entrance into the town from the hill path from Bernkastel, inscr. *Tra*

22v Three sketches of Trarbach and the Grevenburg, looking upstream from the path from the town to the ruins
(1) Inscr. *Vines*

23r The Grevenburg and Trarbach, looking upstream from the path from the town to the ruins

23v A soldier and peasant men and women
Inscr. *B Coler*; *Red*; *Red*

24r Quick sketches of hills
Inscr. *Lutzig B* (i.e. Lützel?)

24v Hills

25r Hills

25v Trarbach, looking upstream from the path to the Grevenburg and up the hill-path to Bernkastel

25v–26r Four views near Trarbach
(2) Inscr. *Light* [...] [?*Cattle*]
(4) Traben and the Grevenburg, looking downstream from the hillside, plus a detail of the Grevenburg

26v Many views near Trarbach

27r (1) Wolfer Kloster, looking downstream
Inscr. *Cattle*; *Stones*
(2) Wolfer Kloster, looking downstream
Inscr. *Croff* (i.e. Kröv, on the left bank opposite to Wolf); *W Boat*; *Beaut Light*
(3) Wolfer Kloster, looking upstream

27v Many sketches near and of Ürzig with the Michaelslei

28r (1) Zeltingen, looking upstream
Inscr. *Cloth* [?*Bleaching*]
(2) Wehlen, looking upstream
Inscr. *Wm waiting at the Ferry*; *Rocrich* (? i.e. Rachtig)
(3) Ürzig
Inscr. *Urzig*; [?*Mill*]

28v (1) Graach, Bernkastel and the Landshut, looking upstream
(2) Graach, Bernkastel and the Landshut, looking upstream
Inscr. *Garash*
(3) Zeltingen, looking downstream
Inscr. *Zeltinten*
(4) Wehlen and Zeltingen, looking downstream
Inscr. *Welen*; *Zeltighen*

29r Bernkastel and the Landshut, looking downstream from the east bank

29v (1) Bernkastel and the Landshut, looking upstream
(2) A boat
(3) Detail of the Landshut
(4) Bernkastel from Graach

30r (1) Bernkastel and the Landshut, looking downstream from the riverside at Kues
Inscr. *Willow*; *B*
(2) ? The hospital at Kues

30v Several intermingled views of Bernkastel and the Landshut, two drawn on the hillside

31r Two views of the Landshut from the hillside

31v (1) Kues, Bernkastel and the Landshut, looking downstream from the hillside south of Bernkastel
(2) Detail of the Landshut

32 Missing and replaced with blank page

33r Three sketches, perhaps of Enkirch
(1) Inscr. *Enkirch up* [to] *Trabach*

33v Quick sketches of castles

34r Quick sketches of castles

34v Several overlapping quick sketches

35r Several overlapping quick sketches, including one of Quint

35v (1) Piesport
Inscr. *Pisport*
(2) Minheim
Inscr. *Minheim*
(3)–(4) Quick sketches of hills

36r Several overlapping sketches, including
(1) Inscr. *Keson* (?Kirsch, opposite Schweich)
(2) Village with bridge of boats (?Kirsch)
Inscr. *Napoleon passed here*

36v (1) The gateway near the Peterskapelle, Cochem
Inscr. *Cochem*
(2) Church and village (?Kirsch)

37r Several sketches near Trittenheim including
(3) Inscr. *Leiben* (? i.e. Leiwen)
(4) Inscr. *Kluserich* (i.e. Klüsserath)
(5) Inscr. *Trittenheim*

37v Several sketches including
(1) Inscr. *Piesport*

38r Several sketches including
(4) Inscr. *Numege* (i.e. Neumagen)

38v Several sketches including
(2) Inscr. *Maring* (i.e. Mehring)
(3) Inscr. *Cattle and Hay cart going over*
(4) Close-up version of church, boat, cliff in (3)

39r Three sketches including
(1) Inscr. *Light*

39v Several sketches near Trier

40r Several sketches including
(1) (2) Two sketches of the spires of Trier, seen from the Mosel, with a boat in the foreground
(3) Figures
Inscr. *Fishing*
(5) Inscr. *Effel*

40v (1) The Roman bridge at Trier
(2) The church of SS. Simon and Jude, Pallien, and the Napoleonsbrücke from Trier

41r The north face of the Porta Nigra, Trier

41v (1) Distant mountains
(2) Figures, some inscr. *W Washing*

42r (1) Inscr. *Wiellin*
(2) Inscr. [?*Tessel*]

42v Two views of Mayen dominated by the Genovevaburg
Inscr. *Mayen*

43r Mayen with the Genovevaburg and St Clement's church
Inscr. *Mayen built by Julius Caesar*

43v Mayen with the Genovevaburg, St Clement's church and Brückentor shown in enlarged detail
Inscr. *Mayen*

44r Ehrenbreitstein

44v Coblenz and Ehrenbreitstein from just south of the fort
Inscr. *Well*

45r Coblenz from Ehrenbreitstein

45v Coblenz and Ehrenbreitstein from the south

46r Coblenz and Ehrenbreitstein from the south

46v (1) Ehrenbreitstein
(2) The Rhine and distant mountains

47r Blank

47v (1) The confluence at Coblenz, looking up the Mosel from Ehrenbreitstein
(2) Ehrenbreitstein

48r The confluence from Ehrenbreitstein

48v Ehrenbreitstein from the south

49r Coblenz and Ehrenbreitstein in the distance, looking downstream from near Kapellen

49v Niederlahnstein and Burg Lahneck with the mouth of the Lahn, from the Rhine

50r (1) Schloss Stolzenfels and Kapellen, looking down the Rhine
Inscr. *Wood*
(2) St John's church, Niederlahnstein

50v Burg Lahneck and Niederlahnstein, looking upstream from the west bank

51r Niederlahnstein, Burg Lahneck, Oberlahnstein and the Martinsburg, looking downstream

51v Niederlahnstein, Burg Lahneck and Oberlahnstein, looking downstream

52r Burg Lahneck and Niederlahnstein

52v Burg Katz, St Goarshausen and St Goar, looking upstream from the northern edge of St Goar

53r Burg Rheinfels from the hillside at St Goar, looking downstream with Burg Maus in the distance
Inscr. *Masons* [?*trellis*]

53v Burg Rheinfels and St Goar, looking downstream from the riverfront at St Goar

54r (1) Burg Katz, St Goarshausen and St Goar, looking upstream
(2) The Lorelei, looking upstream
(3) St Goar and Burg Rheinfels, looking upstream

54v Burg Katz, looking downstream from the Lorelei

55r Oberwesel and the Schönburg, looking upstream towards Burg Gutenfels in the distance

55v Oberwesel and the Schönburg, looking upstream

56r Oberwesel and the Schönburg, looking upstream from inland behind the Ocksturm

56v (1) (2) Two sketches of the Rhine near Oberwesel
(3) The Ocksturm at Oberwesel

57r Several sketches of buildings at Oberwesel

57v Oberwesel and the Schönburg, looking upstream from inland

58r Oberwesel and the Schönburg, looking upstream past the Liebfrauenkirche from inland

58v The Schönburg
Inscr. *Sunneburg*

59r Oberwesel from inland

59v Oberwesel, looking downstream from the approach to the Schönburg

60r Oberwesel, looking downstream from the approach to the Schönburg

60v Mainz from the Rhine

61r Mainz from the Rhine

61v–62r The Liebfrauenkirche at Oberwesel and the Schönburg, looking upstream

62r Bacharach and Burg Stahleck, looking downstream

62v Burg Nollig and the Heimburg, looking upstream from near Bacharach

63r Sailing boats on the Rhine

63v The Kursaal, Wiesbaden, seen from across the lake in the Kurpark
Inscr. *Wis*; *26* [. . .]

64r Distant view of the Rhine from the hills above Mainz, looking downstream
Inscr. *Biberich*

64v The Sonnenburg, near Wiesbaden

65r The Sonnenburg, near Wiesbaden

65v The Sonnenburg, near Wiesbaden

66r The Sonnenburg, near Wiesbaden

66v Sketchmap inscr. *Gusbach* and *Sonnweg* and sketch of the Sonnenburg

67r Mainz, showing the cathedral from the north-east
Inscr. *Gasthaus* [. . .]

67v Mainz cathedral from the east

68r Mainz cathedral from the north-east

68v Wiesbaden from the Sonnenburg, with separate details of its cupolas and towers
Inscr. *Wi*

69r Mainz cathedral from the Gutenbergplatz, with the statue of Gutenberg by Thorvaldsen, erected in August 1837
Inscr. *Joh Gensfleish de Gutenberg*; *Fete of*

69v Mainz, looking downstream from its eastern outskirts
Inscr. *Nass* [au] [*?seat*]; *Flu*[sbad]

70r Mainz, looking downstream; the bridge of boats to Kastel continued at the top; also details of the west tower of the cathedral, and an awning over a boat or raft
Inscr. *Raft*[. . .]; *Lake bath*; *Flusbad*

70v View up the Main from Mainz
Inscr. *Main*; *Raft*

71r Mainz, looking downstream; separate sketches of the bridge of boats to Kastel, houses, boats
Inscr. *Moles*; *White Moles*; *Flusbad*

71v The Mäuseturm

72r Burg Ehrenfels, the Mäuseturm, Burg Klopp and Bingen, looking upstream from below the Binger Loch

72v Burg Rheinstein, with Burg Reichenstein and the Clemenskapelle seen beyond it, looking downstream
Inscr. *Rheinstein*
Also separate sketches of hills and buildings

73r Burg Reichenstein and the Clemenskapelle, looking downstream

73v Burg Reichenstein, looking upstream

74r Oberwesel and the Schönburg, looking upstream
Inscr. *Sonberg*

74v The Schönburg and Kaub, looking downstream

75r Burg Gutenfels, Kaub and the Pfalz looking upstream

75v Oberwesel and the Schönburg, looking downstream; larger details of the Schönburg and the Liebfrauenkirche

76r The southern end of Oberwesel from the river

76v The Schönburg and the Liebfrauenkirche at Oberwesel

77r Oberwesel and the Schönburg looking upstream

77v Salmon fishing boats with their lines out, probably near the Lorelei

78r Salmon fishing boats at the Lorelei, looking upstream
Inscr. *Lauliberg*

78v St Goar, Burg Rheinfels, St Goarshausen and Burg Katz, looking downstream

79a St Goar and Burg Rheinfels, looking downstream

79b The Lorelei, with a buoy, looking upstream

79c Burg Rheinfels

79d St Goar and Burg Rheinfels, looking upstream from the northern approach to St Goar

80r Bornhofen and Burg Sterrenberg

80v Wellmich and Burg Maus, looking upstream

81r Bornhofen, Burg Sterrenberg and Burg Liebenstein, looking downstream

81v Bornhofen, Burg Sterrenberg and Burg Liebenstein, looking upstream, with a passenger boat in the foreground
Inscr. *Umbrellas of all* [*?Colors*]

82r Bornhofen, Burg Sterrenberg and Burg Liebenstein, looking upstream

82v (1) Boppard, looking downstream
(2) Distant view of the Marxburg

83r Braubach and the Marxburg, looking downstream

83v Braubach and the Marxburg, looking downstream

84r Braubach and the Marxburg, looking upstream

84v The Marxburg, seen in the distance looking upstream, with Rhens on the right
Inscr. *Marx*; *Smoke the Light the Yellow*

85r Oberlahnstein, Burg Lahneck and the Martinsburg, looking downstream
Inscr. *Laneck*

85v Schloss Stolzenfels and Kapellen, looking downstream

86r St John's church, Niederlahnstein, the entrance to the Lahn, and Burg Lahneck

86v (1) Schloss Stolzenfels and Kapellen, looking upstream
(2) Burg Metternich at Beilstein on the Mosel, looking downstream from the hillside

87r (1) Burg Metternich at Beilstein on the Mosel, looking downstream from the hillside
Inscr. *Bidelstein*
(2) Niederlahnstein, Burg Lahneck and the junction of the Lahn and the Rhine
(3) Schloss Stolzenfels
Inscr. *Cappelle*

87v The Mosel bridge at Coblenz, looking from the Rhine towards the buildings of the Mosel waterfront and the Petersberg

88r View from the Mosel bridge at Coblenz towards Ehrenbreitstein and the spires of Coblenz

88v Three distant views of Coblenz and Ehrenbreitstein from the Mosel

89r Coblenz and Ehrenbreitstein from the Mosel

89v Several views of Coblenz and Ehrenbreitstein, the largest taken from the Petersberg
Inscr. [?*Raft*]; *25*; [?*July*]

90r (1) The Mosel waterfront at Coblenz from the bridge
(2) Peasant woman
Inscr. *Red*

90v Ehrenbreitstein, from the Mosel below the bridge

91r The Mosel waterfront at Coblenz, below the bridge, with Ehrenbreitstein beyond

91v Several rough sketches including one of Burg Metternich at Beilstein on the Mosel

Inside back cover
Rough sketch of river and fort (probably Ehrenbreitstein) with illegible notes

TB CCXCI *Cochem to Coblenz – Home* sketchbook 1839 (see cat.no.46)

Bound in boards covered in black and brown mottled paper with brown leather back and corners and three broken leather loops (two at one end, one at the other) for holding a pencil and thus closing the book. These have stained the adjacent pages at both ends of the book. On the back cover is a paper label, inscribed by Turner, *5 Cockem to Cob.*

Inside front cover
A walled harbour
Inscr. twice [?*Flushing*]

1r (1) A harbour, from the sea
(2) Harbour scene

1v A harbour from the sea

2r The spire of St Martin's church, Cochem

2v The Enderttor and Alte Thorschenke, Cochem, from the east

3r The Enderttor and Alte Thorschenke, Cochem, from the north with the Burg in the distance

3v Cond (top left) and Cochem, looking upstream
Inscr. *Cloth* [. . .]

4r The market place at Cochem

4v–5r Cochem, looking upstream

5v Cochem, looking upstream

6r Cochem, looking upstream

6v Cochem, looking upstream
Inscr. *Cun* (i.e. Cond)

7r Cochem in the distance, looking upstream

7v Klotten, with St Maximin's church and Burg Coraidelstein

8r Klotten, looking upstream

8v (1) Klotten, looking upstream
(2) Klotten and Pommern, looking upstream
Inscr. *Clotten*; *Pom*

9r (1) Distant view of Pommern, looking downstream
Inscr. *Pommern*
(2) Pommern, looking downstream
Inscr. *Pommern*
(3) Pommern, looking upstream to Klotten
Inscr. *Clot*
(4) Distant view of Pommern, looking upstream
Inscr. *Triers*

9v Treis, with the Zilleskapelle and St John the Baptist's church

10r Burg Treis from the Mosel

10v Karden, with St Castor's church and the Burghaus, looking downstream
Inscr. *Carden*

11r Treis, with the Zilleskapelle, St John the Baptist's church and Burg Treis, looking upstream

11v Karden, with St Castor's church and the Burghaus, looking upstream

12r Müden, looking upstream
Inscr. *Muden*

12v View downstream below Müden, with the Druidenstein

13r Moselkern and the bridge over the river Eltz

13v Distant view of Burg Bischofstein from Moselkern

14r Burg Bischofstein and Burgen, looking downstream
Inscr. *Bishopstein*; *Burgen*

14v Burg Bischofstein and the Pauluskapelle

15r Burg Bischofstein and the Pauluskapelle

15v Burgen and Burg Bischofstein, looking upstream

16r Hatzenport
Inscr. *Hartzenport*

16v Two boats on the Mosel, just below Hatzenport

17r Ruined building at Löf

17v Brodenbach, looking downstream

18r Alken and Burg Thurandt, looking downstream
Inscr. *Alken*

18v Alken and Burg Thurandt, looking downstream

19r Alken and Burg Thurandt, from the hillside beyond the Michaelskapelle, looking down on the Wiltberg house

19v Alken and Burg Thurandt, from an inland viewpoint

20r Alken and Burg Thurandt

20v Alken and Burg Thurandt

21r Alken and Burg Thurandt, looking downstream

21v Blank

22r Alken and Kattenes, looking upstream
Inscr. *Alken*; *Cothenesh*

22v Oberfell, looking downstream
Inscr. *Oberfeldt*

23r View down the Mosel from below Oberfell

23v View down the Mosel from below Oberfell

24r Lehmen, looking downstream
Inscr. *Laben*

24v Gondorf, looking downstream

25r Gondorf, looking downstream

25v Gondorf, looking downstream

26r The inner face of the Leyen Burg (from today's von der Leyen Platz)

26v The Leyen Burg, looking upstream

27r The Leyen Burg, looking upstream

27v Dieblich and Kobern, looking upstream
Inscr. *Diblich*

28r Dieblich and Kobern, looking upstream

28v Kobern, looking downstream from the hillside

29r Kobern, looking upstream

29v Oberwinningen from the Mosel

30r Kobern, looking downstream from the Mühlental to the Niederburg and the bell-tower

30v Lay, looking downstream
Inscr. *Light*

31r Ehrenbreitstein from the Mosel

31v Güls from the Mosel

32r Güls from the Mosel
Inscr. *Kulz*

32v Moselweiss, looking downstream
Inscr. *Moselwilz*

33r (1) Güls, looking upstream
(2) A riverside castle
Inscr. *Chateau Nass*

33v Distant forts at Coblenz, with boats in the foreground
Inscr. *G*; *G*; *R*

34r View up the Mosel to Moselweiss and Güls

34v (1) Ehrenbreitstein and the Mosel bridge at Coblenz
(2) The Mosel front at Coblenz upstream of the bridge

35r (1) (2) Forts at Coblenz
(3) Church
Inscr. *Red D*; [*?St Sebastian*]

35v Ehrenbreitstein

36r Ehrenbreitstein and Coblenz, looking up the Rhine

36v Ehrenbreitstein, looking up the Rhine
Inscr. *Raft*; *Coblen*; [*?Wood*]

37r Towers at Coblenz

37v Towers at Coblenz

38r (1) Three sketches of the monument to General Hoche at Weissenthurm
(2) Weissenthurm and Neuwied and the flying bridge, looking down the Rhine

38v Rhine passenger boat

39r Rhine barges and bargemen

39v The east end of the Mosel bridge at Coblenz, with the gate tower and the Alte Burg

40r Rhine view

40v The Drachenfels, from the Rhine

41r The Drachenfels, from the Rhine

41v Rolandseck, Nonnenwerth and Drachenfels, looking down the Rhine

42r The Godesburg, from the Rhine, looking downstream

42v Linz

43r Hill and castle

43v Rolandseck, Nonnenwerth and Drachenfels, looking down the Rhine

44r Rolandseck, Nonnenwerth and Drachenfels, looking down the Rhine

44v Rolandseck, Nonnenwerth and Drachenfels, looking down the Rhine

45r (1) Bonn
Inscr. *Bonn*
(2) The Seven Hills

45v (1) The Drachenfels
(2) The Godesburg from the Rhine

46r The Drachenfels

46v Aachen, with cathedral and town hall

Most of the remaining pages in this book are blank. The few that were used contain sketches of stormy skies, a harbour (the same as that shown on ff.1r, 1v), and an unidentified town. There are also two notes that clearly do not relate to Turner's foreign tour: one records the time of a meeting with his cousin and solicitor Henry Harpur (f.66v) while the other, a list of food and beverages, mentions ale, stout and gin which were presumably all consumed in England (f.52r).

Lenders

Numbers refer to the catalogue entries

Aberdeen City Arts Department, Art Gallery & Museums 17

Visitors of the Ashmolean Museum, Oxford 61

Trustees of the British Museum 13 (engraving), 21, 25, 31, 41 (engraving)

Bury Art Gallery and Museum 24

National Museum of Wales, Cardiff 100

Courtesy of Hildegard Fritz-Denneville Fine Arts Ltd, London 54

Laing Art Gallery, Newcastle upon Tyne (Tyne & Wear Museums Service) 97

Private Collection 4, 6, 7, 9, 11, 20, 36, 41 (oil), 52, 102, 122

Private Collection, courtesy of the Leger Galleries 30

Tate Gallery 1, 2, 3, 12, 13 (oil), 14, 15, 16, 18, 19, 22, 23, 26, 27, 28, 29, 32, 33, 34, 35, 37, 38, 39, 40, 42, 43, 44, 45, 46, 47, 48, 49, 50, 51, 53, 55, 56, 57, 58, 59, 60, 62, 63, 64, 65, 66, 67, 68, 69, 70, 71, 72, 73, 74, 75, 76, 77, 78, 79, 80, 81, 82, 83, 84, 85, 86, 87, 88, 89, 90, 91, 92, 93, 94, 95, 96, 98, 99, 101, 103, 104, 105, 106, 107, 108, 109, 110, 111, 112, 113, 114, 115, 116, 117, 118, 119, 120, 121, 123, 124, 125, 126, 127, 128, 129, 130, 131, 132, 133, 134, 135, 136

Board of Trustees of the Victoria and Albert Museum, London 10

Whitworth Art Gallery, University of Manchester 8

The Warden and Scholars of Winchester College 5

Photographic Credits

Aberdeen City Arts Department, Art Gallery & Museums
Thos. Agnew & Sons Ltd
Ashmolean Museum
British Museum
Bury Art Gallery and Museum
National Museum of Wales, Cardiff
Richard Clive Photography
Fitzwilliam Museum
Frick Collection, New York
Hildegard Fritz-Denneville Fine Arts Ltd
Indianapolis Museum of Art, Bequest of Kurt F. Pantzer, Sr
Laing Art Gallery
Leger Galleries Ltd
Musée National d'Histoire et d'Art, Musées de l'Etat, Luxembourg
National Gallery of Ireland
National Galleries of Scotland
Art Gallery of Ontario
Sotheby's
Tate Gallery Photographic Department
V & A Picture Library
John Webb
Whitworth Art Gallery
Yale Center for British Art

INDEX

For the Concordance see p. 233

Concordance

The gouaches described on pp.130–83 of this catalogue correspond to the Turner Bequest references in Finberg's *Inventory* as follows:

Inventory	Catalogue
CCXX	
N	no.87
O	no.89
P	no.76
S	no.88
T	no.98
U	no.96
V	no.99
W	no.48
Z	no.72
CCXXI	
A	no.60
D	no.69
E	no.67
F	no.62
G	no.58
K	p.181
L	no.126
M	no.125
N	p.183
O	no.121
P	no.124
T	no.64
U	no.83
Z	no.59
CCXXII	
B	no.79
C	no.91
D	no.107
E	no.120
G	no.113
H	p.147
I	no.86
J	no.111
K	p.176
L	no.78
M	p.176
N	p.179
P	no.57
R	no.51
U	no.109
X	no.85
Y	p.173
Z	p.179
CCXXIII	
A	no.95
C	no.90
D	no.110
CCLIX	
13	no.104
23	no.77
24	no.105
25	no.108
45	no.115
99	no.84
144	no.73
146	no.93
150	no.47
151	no.94
152	no.56
158	no.68
159	no.101
160	no.66
166	no.103
167	no.112
170	no.71
171	no.92
176	no.49
177	no.123
180	no.116
188	no.118
215	no.117
217	no.53
219	no.106
223	no.119
224	no.55
239	no.82
241	no.65
244	no.80
258	no.50
268	no.81
CCXCII	
39	no.63
66	no.114
70	no.74
72	no.75
78	no.70

The Friends of the Tate Gallery

Since their formation in 1958, the Friends of the Tate Gallery have helped to buy major works of art for the Tate Gallery Collection, from Stubbs to Hockney.

Members are entitled to immediate and unlimited free admission to Tate Gallery exhibitions with a guest, invitations to previews of Tate Gallery exhibitions, opportunities to visit the Gallery when closed to the public, a discount of 10 per cent in the Tate Gallery shop, special events, *Friends Events* and *Tate Preview* magazines mailed three times a year, free admission to exhibitions at Tate Gallery Liverpool, and use of the new Friends Room at the Tate Gallery which will open in November 1991.

Three categories of higher level memberships, Associate Fellow at £100, Deputy Fellow at £250, and Fellow at £500, entitle members to a range of extra benefits including guest cards, and invitations to exclusive special events.

The Friends of the Tate Gallery are supported by Tate & Lyle PLC.

PATRONS

The Patrons of British Art support British painting from the Elizabethan period through to the early twentieth century in the Tate Gallery's Collection.

The Patrons of New Art support contemporary art in the Tate Gallery's Collection. They promote a lively and informed interest in contemporary art and are associated with the Turner Prize, one of the most prestigious awards for the visual arts.

Benefits for both groups include invitations to Tate Gallery receptions, an opportunity to sit on the Patrons acquisitions committees, special events including visits to private and corporate collections and complimentary catalogues of Tate Gallery exhibitions.

Further details on the Friends and the Patrons may be obtained from:

Friends of the Tate Gallery
Tate Gallery
Millbank
London SW1P 4RG

Tel: 071-821 1313 or 071-834 2742

Tate Gallery London – Sponsorships since 1988

Academy (Art & Design Magazine)
1988, Academy Forums
Henry Ansbacher & Co. plc
1988, *Turner and the Human Figure* exhibition
AT&T
1988, *David Hockney: A Retrospective* exhibition
Barclays Bank plc
1991, *Constable* exhibition
British Gas plc
1989, Education study sheets
British Gas North Thames
1989, *Colour into Line: Turner and the Art of Engraving* exhibition
The British Land Company plc
1990, *Joseph Wright of Derby* exhibition
The British Petroleum Co
1989, *Paul Klee* exhibition
1990–93 *New Displays*
British Steel plc
1989, *William Coldstream* exhibition
Carroll, Dempsey & Thirkell
1990, *Anish Kapoor* exhibition
Channel 4 Television
1991–93, The Turner Prize
Daimler Benz
1991, *Max Ernst* exhibition
Debenham Tewson & Chinnocks
1990, Turner *Painting and Poetry* exhibition
Digital Equipment Co Ltd
1991–92, *From Turner's Studio* touring exhibition
Donaldsons
1988, *Hans Hofmann* exhibition
Drexel Burnham Lambert
1987/88, The Turner Prize
Drivers Jonas
1989, *Turner and Architecture* exhibition
Erco Lighting
1989, Sponsorship in kind
Gerald Metals Limited
1988, Education and contemporary art exhibitions programme
Global Asset Management Ltd
1988, *Late Picasso* exhibition
Hepworth & Chadwick
1988, *Turner and Natural History* exhibition
KPMG Management Consulting
1991, *Anthony Caro: Sculpture towards Architecture* exhibition
Linklaters & Paines
1989, Japanese Guide to the Turner Bequest
Lin Pac Plastics
1989, Sponsorship in kind
Olympia & York
1988, *Turner's Wilson Sketchbook* publication
1990, Frameworkers Conference
PA Consulting Group
1989, Video projector
Plessey plc
1988, Sponsorship in kind
Pro Helvetia Foundation
1988, *Agasse* exhibition
Reed International plc
1990, *On Classic Ground* exhibition
SRU Ltd
1989–94, Voluntary guide and market research
Swissair
1988, *Agasse* exhibition
Tate & Lyle PLC
1991–93, Friends relaunch marketing programme
UBS Philips & Drew
1988, *Turner at Petworth* publication
Ulster Television plc
1989, *F.E. McWilliam* exhibition
Volkswagen
1989–92, The Turner Scholarships
Westminster City Council
1989, Trees project
1989, *Tate Gallery: An Illustrated Companion*
New Displays

Turner is universally acclaimed as one of the greatest painters of sky, light and water. His mastery of all these is amply demonstrated in his many depictions of three of the great rivers of northern Europe, the Rhine, Meuse and Mosel, which exerted such an important influence on the Romantic imagination with their towering rocks, gaunt ruins and mighty citadels.

Cecilia Powell has studied Turner's most important tours of these rivers in detail and here traces his abiding fascination with their scenery. The gravity of the earliest Rhine drawings in the exhibition, painted as Europe was still recovering from the Revolutionary and Napoleonic Wars, gradually gives way to a lighter and brighter mood, culminating in the freely drawn and vaporous late colour studies of the fortress of Ehrenbreitstein presiding over the confluence of the Rhine and the Mosel.

Turner's visits to the Meuse and the Mosel inspired him to paint over a hundred delightful gouaches on blue paper which have remained largely unseen since his death. These works are here presented to the public for the first time, newly identified and dated and in the sequences which Turner himself intended. This volume provides a complete catalogue raisonné of these drawings, not all of which can be exhibited (works included are given exhibition numbers, while those not displayed are listed without numbers at the appropriate places in the topographical sequences). The series can now at last take its rightful place as yet another example of Turner's extraordinary genius.

ISBN 1-85437-079-0

9 781854 370792